D0874647

THE COMPLETE

VISUAL

BIBLE

A LAVISHLY ILLUSTRATED TOUR OF THE OLD AND NEW TESTAMENTS

THE COMPLETE

VISUAL

BIBLE

BARBOUR

STEPHEN M. MILLER

AUTHOR OF *THE COMPLETE GUIDE TO THE BIBLE*

For a helpful index
and other details on the *Complete Visual Bible*,
please visit www.completevisualbible.com

© 2011 by Stephen M. Miller

The author is represented by The Steve Laube Agency LLC, Phoenix, Arizona.

ISBN 978-1-60260-688-3

All rights reserved. No part of this publication may be reproduced or transmitted for commercial purposes, except for brief quotations in printed reviews, without written permission of the publisher.

Churches and other noncommercial interests may reproduce portions of this book without the express written permission of Barbour Publishing, provided that the text does not exceed 500 words and that the text is not material quoted from another publisher. When reproducing text from this book, include the following credit line: "From *The Complete Visual Bible,* by Stephen M. Miller, published by Barbour Publishing, Inc. Used by permission."

Unless otherwise indicated, all scripture quotations are taken from the *Holy Bible,* New Living Translation, copyright © 1996, 2004. Used by permission of Tyndale House Publishers, Inc. Wheaton, Illinois 60189, U.S.A. All rights reserved.

Scripture quotations marked HCSB have been taken from the Holman Christian Standard Bible © copyright 2000 by Holman Bible Publishers. Used by permission.

Scripture quotations marked CEV are from the Contemporary English Version, Copyright © 1991, 1992, 1995 by American Bible Society. Used by permission.

Scripture quotations marked NCV are taken from the New Century Version of the Bible, copyright © 2005 by Thomas Nelson, Inc. Used by permission.

Scripture quotations marked MSG are from *THE MESSAGE.* Copyright © by Eugene H. Peterson 1993, 1994, 1995, 1996, 2000, 2001, 2002. Used by permission of NavPress Publishing Group.

Scripture quotations marked NIrV are taken from the HOLY BIBLE, NEW INTERNATIONAL READER'S VERSION™. Copyright © 1995, 1996, 1998 by International Bible Society. Used by permission of Zondervan. All rights reserved.

Scripture quotations marked TNIV are taken from the Holy Bible, Today's New International® Version, TNIV©. Copyright 2001, 2005 by International Bible Society®. Used by permission of International Bible Society®. All rights reserved worldwide. "TNIV" and "Today's New International Version" are trademarks registered in the United States Patent and Trademark Office by International Bible Society®.

Scripture quotations marked NRSV are taken from the New Revised Standard Version Bible, copyright 1989, Division of Christian Education of the National Council of the Churches of Christ in the United States of America. Used by permission. All rights reserved.

Scripture quotations marked TLB are taken from The Living Bible © 1971. Used by permission of Tyndale House Publishers, Inc. Wheaton, Illinois 60189. All rights reserved.

Cover design: Faceout Studio, www.faceoutstudio.com

Published by Barbour Publishing, Inc., P.O. Box 719, Uhrichsville, Ohio 44683 www.barbourbooks.com

Our mission is to publish and distribute inspirational products offering exceptional value and biblical encouragement to the masses.

Printed in The United States of America.

TABLE OF CONTENTS

INTRODUCTION

AN ATHEIST complimented me today.

Perfect timing. Wonderful compliment.

I was taking a last pass through this book, polishing the writing and making sure I had all the pictures and maps ready to go to the editor. All the while I was wondering what to write in this intro, one of the last things I do before sending a book on its way.

I was in Revelation and nearly done with my polishing when the atheist's e-mail came. He's a photographer in Germany. I had e-mailed him yesterday, asking permission to publish one of his photos.

"After thinking awhile," he wrote, "I have decided that you may use it for the book you are writing on the Bible.

"To tell you frankly," he added, "I am a decided atheist and thus felt kind of strange about the intended context for the use of the photo. So I read samples of your previous books on the Internet.

"Actually, I found them written with care and sensitivity, and your approach will surely be interesting."

I stopped working.

I sat for a while and thought about what he had said.

I looked out the window of my upstairs home office. Past the lavender blooms on our redbud tree and the brownish green buds on the ash. To the homes of my neighbors.

There's one neighbor whose wife works half the nation away, but who comes home when she can.

Next door to them is another couple. The husband was recently diagnosed with lung cancer; he's younger than me.

Across the street there's a couple who brought my family some food several years ago when they heard our high school son was in the hospital, deathly sick with a virus he eventually managed to beat, barely.

On Sunday mornings when it comes time to back the car out of the driveway and go to church, those neighbors of mine stay home. Of the 10 houses I can see from my window, only one household attends worship services.

I write for the other nine. And for my atheist friends and colleagues.

So I figure you can imagine how I felt when I read today's e-mail.

Books like this take a full year of my life, researching and writing. It sometimes worries me that I'm spending all that time creating something that works only for religion insiders—as though I'm singing to the choir, when what I want to do is sing to the rest of the world.

So today, on the last day of another year's long work—a day before the start of a new year on a new book—an atheist writes to tell me he has heard my song, and it's not so bad.

I wonder. What would an atheist say if I told him that he, an unbeliever, has become the voice of God—heaven-sent to encourage a believer?

Coincidence is not a deity, he might argue.

Not always, I would agree. But sometimes.

Today, perhaps.

A WORD OF THANKS

I write this book alone, like a monk isolated in his cell.

Yet I'm not the only human bringing this book to life and putting it into your hands. There's a team at work. And I'd like to name names.

Linda Miller, my wife. She has let me work in the risky business of full-time freelance writing for more than 15 years. That makes her a sanctified gambler.

Becca Miller, my daughter. She got her Facebook friends to join the fan page my publisher asked me to start. She has more friends than most pastors have eyeballs staring at them on Sundays.

Brad Miller, my son. His online marketing company has helped market my books: sheppix.net.

Virginia Miller, my mom. I send her copies of each book I write, and she always says she loves the book. Let me tell you, it doesn't hurt.

Steve Laube, my agent. He's a bit like the Holy Spirit in a bone bag. He's my advocate, helper, counselor, and sometimes my comforter.

Paul K. Muckley, Barbour editor. God gave him the perfect quality for a soul trapped between a writer pleading for excellence and a production crew swamped with work: grace under fire.

Donna Maltese, freelance copy editor and fact checker. I requested her because her attention to detail on a previous book I wrote convinced me she's a cyborg.

Kelly Williams, Annie Tipton, Ashley Schrock, Ashley Casteel, and the rest of the in-house team at Barbour keep these big projects moving along, toward the light at the end of the tunnel.

The team at FaceoutStudio designed the pages for beauty and readability.

Shalyn Hooker, Barbour marketing manager. Without Shalyn and her team, my books would hear the sound of one hand clapping.

God bless each one of these people.

And God bless you as you read this book, and more importantly as you read his Book.

Steve
STEPHEN M. MILLER
STEPHENMILLERBOOKS.COM

OLD
TESTAMENT

// DON'T EVEN TRY THINKING OF THE BIBLE AS A BOOK. //

IT'S NOT.

It's a library of books written over a stretch
of a thousand years. Maybe more.

THE BIBLE COMES IN TWO MAIN SETS:

// OLD TESTAMENT

This is the Jewish Bible. It traces the story of the
Jewish people—from their founding father, Abraham, to their near annihilation by invaders from
what is now Iraq. Home to 39 of the Bible's 66
books, the Old Testament makes up the first two-thirds of the Bible.

// NEW TESTAMENT

This is the Christian add-on to the Jewish Bible.
It traces the story of the Christian movement—from the birth of Jesus to the spread of Christianity throughout the Roman Empire about a
century later.

HOW THE JEWS SETTLED on which books to include in their Bible, the Old Testament, is anyone's guess. Scholars speculate that the oldest stories—like those about Abraham and Moses—were passed along by word of mouth for generations. Then when David became king, as one theory goes, palace officials starting writing down the stories to document their nation's history.

Moses had apparently done some writing earlier, since God told him to write down the 10 Commandments and other Jewish laws (Exodus 34:27). Those laws appear in the first five books of the Old Testament. And this was the first section of the Bible that Jews embraced as sacred. Jesus himself described the stories in those books as "the writings of Moses" (Mark 12:26).

Later, Jews added the books of the prophets to their sacred collection. And finally the rest of their Bible—a diverse assortment of writings including sacred lyrics called Psalms, a collection of wise sayings known as Proverbs, and the sad tale of Job.

This is the Bible Jesus read—the Jewish Bible. It's also the Bible the apostle Paul was talking about when he said:

"Everything in the Scriptures is God's Word. All of it is useful for teaching and helping people and for correcting them and showing them how to live."

2 TIMOTHY 3:16 CEV

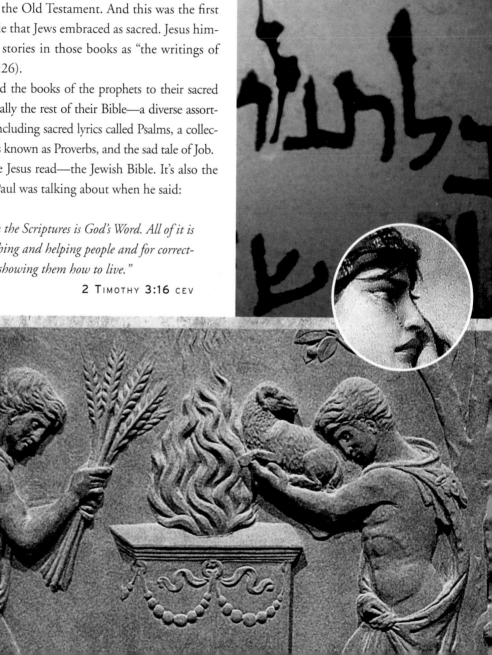

Light bursts from a fledgling solar system in an artist's depiction of photos taken by NASA's Spitzer Space Telescope. On day one of creation, God produces light and separates it from darkness.

BIG SCENE

LET THERE BE LIGHT

BIBLE HISTORY		**BEFORE 4000 BC** God creates universe		**BEFORE 2500 BC** Noah saves family and animals from flood; ark stops in Ararat mountains
WORLD HISTORY	ALL DATES APPROXIMATE	**4.5 BILLION BC** Geologists estimate birth of earth and solar system		**4500 BC** Ocean breaks through Bosporus Strait, flooding freshwater lake that becomes Black Sea 200 miles (322 km) north of Mount Ararat (see page 14 for map).

GENESIS

PARADISE POLLUTED

STORY LINE

GOD CREATES THE UNIVERSE, life on earth, and a garden paradise for the first humans, Adam and Eve.

Sadly, the couple breaks God's one and only rule. They eat fruit from a forbidden tree—which God warned would kill them. Perhaps God intended Adam and Eve to live forever. But now they're sentenced to die, after a lifetime of hard labor.

Their sin not only alienates them from God, it seems to contaminate the world—like a spiritual toxin dumped into the physical universe.

Some Bible experts say the rest of the Bible is the story of God working his plan to undo the damage—to restore his perfect creation and his relationship with humanity.

God starts with one man who trusts him completely: Abraham. From this man, God will grow a nation devoted to him. Abraham's grandson Jacob fathers a dozen sons who become the founding ancestors of Israel's 12 tribes.

By the end of Genesis, Jacob's favorite son, Joseph, has risen to the number-two position in Egypt. And when a drought strikes Canaan, in what is now Israel, Joseph invites his father's entire extended family to move to Egypt to weather out the dry spell by enjoying the lush pastures along the drought-proof Nile River.

They will overstay their welcome. Generations later the Egyptians will enslave them.

// LOCATION: The stories take place throughout the Middle East, mainly in what are now Israel and Egypt (see page 14 for map).

// TIME: Genesis starts with Creation, which some Christians say took place about 6,000 years ago. Others agree with most scientists who theorize it began countless eons ago. Genesis ends in the time of Abraham's great-grandson Joseph in about 1800 BC.

// AUTHOR: Unknown. Ancient Jewish tradition says Moses wrote this book and the four that follow.

2000 BC
Abraham almost
sacrifices his son

1900s BC
Jacob fathers 12 sons,
ancestors of Israel's 12 tribes

1800s BC
Jacob's family moves to
Egypt during drought

2500 BC *King Naram-Sin in what is now Iran declares himself a god*

1800 BC *Egypt expands crop cultivation to desert oasis town of Faiyum, south of Cairo*

Creation countdown

BEFORE THE BEGINNING, a great nothing exists.

Genesis describes it: formless, empty, dark. There is no universe.

There are just "deep waters," (Genesis 1:2). Many interpret this as a symbol of pre-creation matter, chaotically scattered. Presumably, God supplies these creation building blocks and then forms them into the universe.

He does all this in six days, which some Bible students take literally as 24-hour days. Others read it figuratively.

Under God's spoken direction, creation unfolds like a cosmic drama in six acts.

Act seven: God rests. Not that God's tired. Rest, many scholars say, is a symbolic model for humans to follow: Take a day off. Moses later cites God's day of rest as the reason for the Sabbath, the law that God's people should rest every seventh day.

Creation story, version two

GENESIS CHAPTER 2 tells a different creation story. So say many Bible experts. Others argue it's not different. It's just more detail on the earlier story.

God creates the earth. Then from the dust of the ground he forms a man and breathes into him the breath of life—the original CPR.

God plants a riverside garden in Eden. Then he plants the man there—home alone in paradise.

COLORFUL CREATION CHAOS

/ A thousand light-years from earth, a nebula in the constellation Perseus puts on a light show that NASA astrophysicists describe as "the beautiful chaos of a dense group of stars being born."

GOD'S SPIRIT HOVERS OVER THE WATER.

"Water" in other ancient creation stories refers to pre-creation chaos—as in one story from Babylon (now Iraq) written at least 200 years before Moses. At the start of that story, called *Enuma Elish*, heaven and earth are unformed. Their raw material mingles together in the "waters of chaos," personified as the goddess Tiamat. Babylon's chief god, Marduk, kills Tiamat and divides her body. With half he creates the heavens, and half the earth. Genesis says it was God, not Marduk, who turned chaos into creation.

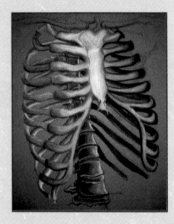

▲RIB COUNT.

Genesis says God made Eve from Adam's rib. That sparked an urban legend: Men have fewer ribs than women. Both have 12 on each side. Some folks who defend the story as literal ask: Who's to say Adam didn't have 13 pairs to begin with?

ADAM.

The name of humanity's first man reads like a play on words. He's Adam (Hebrew for "man"), made from dirt (*adama* in Hebrew).

EVE.

This is the Hebrew word for "life-giver." Adam "named his wife Eve, because she would be the mother of all who live" (Genesis 3:20).

"It is not good for the man to be alone," God says. "I will make a helper who is just right for him" (Genesis 2:18).

The next few sentences sound a little like a chauvinistic joke. Or perhaps a report of beta testing on potential helpers. Anticipating a "helper" for the man, the reader might expect God to create a woman. Instead, he creates wild animals. Then birds. Then livestock.

Sadly for women—it might seem—they come after livestock.

God, a bit like an anesthesiologist, puts Adam into a deep sleep. Then, like a surgeon, he removes a rib. But in the end, like someone out of this world, he sculpts a living, breathing woman. She's wearing nothing but a smile.

The first words out of Adam's mouth when he sees her: "At last!" (Genesis 2:23). Or, as a churchgoing gent might put it today: "Hallelujah!"

ACT ONE:
GOD CREATES LIGHT.

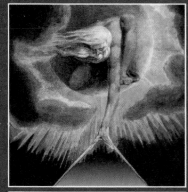

ACT TWO:
SEA AND SKY.

ACT THREE:
LAND TEEMING WITH PLANTS.

ACT FOUR:
SUN AND MOON.

ACT FIVE:
SEA LIFE AND BIRDS.

ACT SIX:
LAND ANIMALS AND CREATION'S CLIMAX: HUMANITY.

Forbidden fruit

IN THE GARDEN OF EDEN, Adam and Eve have just one rule: "You must not eat the fruit of the tree that is in the middle of the garden. Do not even touch it. If you do, you will die" (Genesis 3:3 NIrV).

But a snake throws Eve a line. And she bites. The Bible later identifies this snake as "the ancient serpent called the devil, or Satan" (Revelation 12:9).

The snake says God is lying and that if Eve eats the forbidden fruit, she'll become like God, "knowing both good and evil" (Genesis 3:5).

Eve makes a choice fit for a blond joke. Adam makes a choice fit for a jock joke. They both bite.

Suddenly, they realize they're as naked as a jaybird, plucked.

God apparently has been joining them for evening walks. This particular evening, Adam and Eve feel underdressed for the occasion. So they hide.

Something about this sin seems to change creation for the worse. It's just a guess, but some scholars speculate that God may have intended for Adam and Eve to live forever in a paradise on earth. But now, because of disobedience, death enters the world—and Adam and Eve suffer paradise lost.

God exiles them from the Garden. He condemns Eve to suffer the pain of delivering children. And he condemns Adam to struggle in his effort to grow food. In time, God warns, both will die. "You were made from dust, and to dust you will return" (Genesis 3:19).

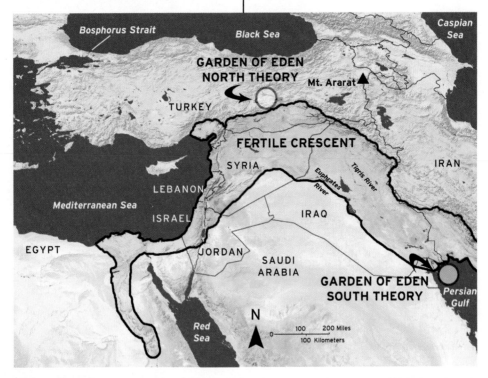

QUEST FOR EDEN / The Bible's clue of a river flowing out of Eden and branching off into four rivers has led to many theories about where Eden was. One theory puts it in the mountains of Turkey. Another puts it in the Persian Gulf, a former river valley until the ocean flooded it.

World's first murder

BIG BROTHER CAIN—humanity's first big brother—kills his little brother, Abel.

Motive: jealousy, apparently with only four people on the planet.

It isn't that Cain, son of Adam and Eve, figures his parents love Abel best.

Worse, Cain seems to think God loves Abel best—with good reason, as far as Cain's concerned.

Each brother brings God a gift from their year of hard work. Cain, a farmer, brings "some of his crops" (Genesis 4:3). Abel, a shepherd, brings "the best of the firstborn lambs from his flock" (Genesis 4:4).

God accepts Abel's gift. But not Cain's.

Why the rejection?

Some Christians guess it's because God prefers blood offerings. Yet Jewish law later allows for grain offerings, too.

Some guess it's because Abel brought the "best" of his flocks, while Cain scraped the bottom of the barrel for "some" crops.

Others say they see unidentified sin in Cain, based on God's cryptic explanation for the rejection:

> *"If you had done the right thing, you would be smiling. But you did the wrong thing, and now sin is waiting to attack you like a lion. Sin wants to destroy you, but don't let it!"*
>
> GENESIS 4:7 CEV

Cain lets it.

He murders Abel.

God forbids Cain to farm again. "You will be a homeless wanderer," God says (Genesis 4:12).

. . . .

MARK OF CAIN / The mysterious mark God put on Cain wasn't a curse. It was a blessing. Condemned to homeless wandering, Cain feared someone would kill him. So, "The LORD put a mark on Cain to warn anyone who might try to kill him" (Genesis 4:15). Some speculate the mark was black skin, but most scholars would call that a shot in the dark.

HOMELESS CAIN / Forbidden to farm anymore after polluting the ground with the blood of his brother, whom he murdered, Cain moves east of Eden. There, he raises a family and lives as a nomadic herder.

Flood zone: Earth

GOD PUTS UP WITH HUMANITY'S SIN for 1,656 years. Assuming, as many do, that the Bible's genealogy of Adam's descendants is literal (see Genesis 5).

By that time the human race has tanked. There's only one blameless man left standing: 600-year-old Noah.

In a creation do-over, God decides to give humanity a fresh start. Noah will become humanity's new founding father. God tells him, "I am about to cover the earth with a flood that will destroy every living thing that breathes" (Genesis 6:17).

Using God's design specifications, Noah builds a survival barge—a floating warehouse. It will protect him and his family. He'll also take along male-female pairs of land animals to help reboot the planet's critter life.

For 40 days water attacks the land from above and below: pummeling rain and erupting groundwater. In the end, all breathers outside the boat lie dead. Even those who scrambled to the highest mountaintops lost their footing. Earth looks like Waterworld.

Five months after the first raindrop, Noah's salvation barge grinds to a halt somewhere in the Ararat mountain range. But all on board have to wait inside for another seven months. In all, Noah and passengers stay in the boat a little more than a year. That's how long it takes the land to dry.

Afterward, God makes a promise to Noah—a contract he signs with a rainbow:

> *"I will never again destroy all living things. As long as the earth remains, there will be planting and harvest, cold and heat, summer and winter, day and night."*
> GENESIS 8:21-22

ONE-YEAR CRUISE. To survive a coming flood, Noah builds a barge big enough to hold his family, a zoo-load of animals, and enough supplies to sustain them all for the 12 months they'll stay aboard. The barge is longer than a football field and half as wide—and about half the size of cruise ships today. Length: 150 yards (137 meters). Width: 25 yards (23 meters). Height: 15 yards (14 meters).

SUPER-HUMAN LIFESPANS

BEFORE THE FLOOD

AFTER THE FLOOD

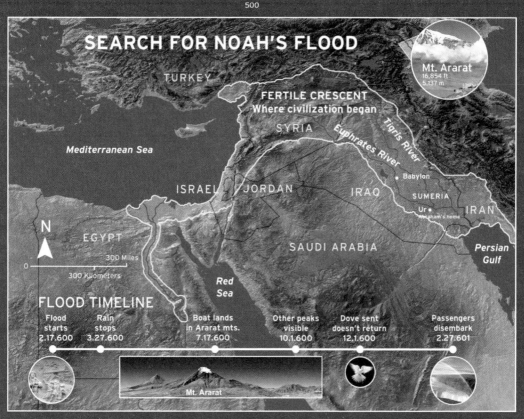

ADAM
930

METHUSELAH
969

NOAH
950

SHEM
(NOAH'S SON)
500

ABRAHAM
175

MOSES
120

DAVID
70

DID PEOPLE LIVE HUNDREDS OF YEARS?

Before the flood they did. So says a literal read of the Bible—as well as a 4,000-year-old clay prism from Sumeria (right), the world's first known civilization. The prism says the reign of eight kings spanned nearly a quarter of a million years. The average reign of a king was 30,000 years, which makes the Bible's oldest character, 969-year-old Methuselah, look like he died in the crib.

SEARCH FOR NOAH'S FLOOD

Mt. Ararat
16,854 ft
5,137 m

TURKEY

FERTILE CRESCENT
Where civilization began

SYRIA

Euphrates River

Tigris River

Mediterranean Sea

ISRAEL

JORDAN

IRAQ

Babylon

SUMERIA

Ur •
Abraham's home

IRAN

N

EGYPT

300 Miles

300 Kilometers

SAUDI ARABIA

Persian Gulf

Red Sea

FLOOD TIMELINE

Flood starts
2.17.600

Rain stops
3.27.600

Boat lands in Ararat mts.
7.17.600

Other peaks visible
10.1.600

Dove sent doesn't return
12.1.600

Passengers disembark
2.27.601

Mt. Ararat

Timeline dates are in Noah years: 2.17.600 is month two and day 17 of Noah's 600th year of life.

WAS ALL THE EARTH FLOODED? Many Christians say yes, and that today's lay of the land was shaped by this flood. Others side with most scientists who insist there's no evidence of such a flood. But there is evidence that floods wiped out cities in the Tigris and Euphrates river valleys, where civilization began with the Sumerian Empire. As far as the ancients were concerned, many scholars say, this area in the Fertile Crescent was their entire world.

Tower of Babel

ONCE UPON A TIME humans spoke just one language, according to the Bible.

Not hard to believe if we figure Genesis got it right—that the human race started with one couple, and then rebooted after the flood with only Noah's family.

From the Ararat mountains, many of Noah's descendants—if not all—migrate "to the east" and settle in "a plain in the land of Babylonia" (Genesis 11:2).

There, they get cocky.

They say, "Come, let's build a great city for ourselves with a tower that reaches into the sky. This will make us famous and keep us from being scattered all over the world" (Genesis 11:4).

They're proposing a monument to themselves. Not a lofty idea, God apparently concludes.

What God does about this, some scholars say, spins a play on words in the original language. The people plan to mix up mud for bricks. Instead, God mixes them up like the dust of the earth they are.

God confuses them by making them talk in different languages. It's the United Nations working on a construction crew without translators. Project "Stairway to Heaven" falls on its face. In time, the people scatter abroad, apparently by language groups.

That's how the Bible says the would-be tower town "came to be called Babel, because there GOD turned their language into 'babble'" (Genesis 11:9 MSG).

When Jews in Bible times spoke of Babylon, they used *babel*—as in, "Babble on."

BUILDING BLOCKS. A worker presses mud and straw into wooden molds. Straw binds the mud together, like steel reinforces concrete today. Dried only in the sun, the bricks could last a few decades exposed to weather. Fired in a kiln afterward, they can endure for centuries.

CLIMBING TO THE GODS. A temple for Babylon's chief god, Marduk, crowns the top of a ziggurat in this model on display at the Louvre in Paris. The tower dominated Babylon's cityscape. Some wonder if this kind of stair-step tower, popular throughout the ancient Middle East, is what builders of the Tower of Babel had in mind.

Abraham leaves home at 75

IT ISN'T GOD'S IDEA for Abraham to leave his hometown of Ur and move to what is now Israel. Not as the Bible tells it.

Abraham's father, Terah, comes up with the idea. But he settles his family in Haran instead, a city two-thirds of the way to Canaan.

It's only after Terah dies that God tells Abraham to pick up where Terah left off.

"Leave your native country, your relatives, and your father's family, and go to the land that I will show you. I will make you into a great nation."

GENESIS 12:1-2

Quite a promise to a 75-year-old man with no kids—and little hope of producing any. Not with his 66-year-old infertile wife.

Abraham packs it all up and moves anyhow. He takes his flocks, servants, and the family of his orphaned nephew, Lot.

Perhaps a couple of months later they reach Shechem, a highland village in the heart of what is now Israel.

There, God adds zip to his earlier promise: "I will give this land to your descendants" (Genesis 12:7).

As if Abraham had any.

Yet in response, Abraham builds a stone altar and worships God.

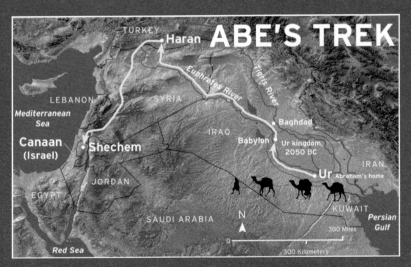

ABE'S TREK

UR. New York City of its day— rich, cultured, and the center of activity. This Euphrates River town commanded about 200 miles of riverfront property.

▲ **WHY DID ABRAHAM'S FATHER LEAVE UR?** Ancient documents found in the region report that foreign pioneers were moving in, threatening the kingdom's stability. Perhaps it was a bit like American settlers driving out the Native Americans. Terah couldn't retreat south: Persian Gulf. Or west: Syrian Desert. Or east: Elamites from what is now Iran; they were among the settlers encroaching on Ur's territory. So Terah moved north, following caravan routes along the Euphrates River.

Contract signed in blood

ABRAHAM IS CIRCUMCISED when he is 99 years old. This procedure is a stipulation in a contract he makes with God—a *covenant*, many call it.

This contract formalizes the promise God first made to Abraham almost 25 years earlier, and repeated about a decade later in a vision:

> *"Look up into the sky and count the stars if you can. That's how many descendants you will have! . . . I am the LORD who brought you out of Ur of the Chaldeans to give you this land as your possession."*
>
> GENESIS 15:5, 7

Abraham and his wife, Sarah, apparently misunderstand this promise. Sarah, at about age 75 at the time of the vision, figures she can't have a child. So she offers Abraham her servant Hagar as a surrogate mother to produce a child for the family. A son is born, Ishmael.

But this isn't the son God has in mind. So God appears to Abraham again. By this time, Abraham is 99 years old. Young Ishmael is about age 13. God says that by this time next year, Sarah will have a son. It's to the descendants of this son that God "will give the entire land of Canaan. . . . It will be their possession forever, and I will be their God" (Genesis 17:8).

God formalizes this promise, turning it into a contract. Abraham's responsibility is to obey God and to circumcise the foreskin of his penis. His descendants are to do the same, circumcising every boy on the eighth day after his birth.

A year later, Sarah gives birth to a son, Isaac. His name means "laughter." Sarah had laughed at the idea she'd get pregnant at age 89. And now she's laughing for joy.

ISHMAEL. A nomadic woman poses with her child in the camp. Sarah convinces Abraham to send Hagar and son, Ishmael, away from their camp, perhaps to ensure that Isaac would inherit all of Abraham's property rather than just a third. It was custom for the oldest son to get a double share. God okays the plan and promises to make Ishmael into a great nation, too. Many consider him the father of the Arab people. He fathered 12 sons who founded tribes scattered throughout what is now the Middle East.

Torching Sodom and Gomorrah

ABRAHAM'S FLOCKS grow so huge that Abraham has to part company with his nephew Lot. The land can't support both flocks.

Lot moves to the city of Sodom, where he can graze his flocks in the fertile Jordan River Valley. But Sodom and its twin city of Gomorrah, along with satellite villages in the valley, earn themselves a bad reputation. Think pre-Flood bad. God seems to. And he decides to purge the valley, this time with fire instead of water.

God sends two angels disguised as humans to warn Lot to get his family out of town. Pronto. As if Sodom needed to confirm its bad rep, a gang of men surrounds the house and order Lot to send out the guests, "so we can have sex with them!" (Genesis 19:5).

The angels blind the men and tell Lot to round up his relatives. He rushes out to tell the fiancés of his two daughters that God is about to destroy the city, but they think he's joking. Or perhaps enjoying some late-night wine.

By dawn, only Lot, his wife, and their daughters hit the ground running.

"Don't look back or stop anywhere in the valley," the angels warn, "or you will be swept away!" (Genesis 19:17).

Lot's wife pauses to look back, as Sodom bursts into flames. She turns into a pillar of salt.

The devastation is so widespread that Lot's daughters conclude that they and their father are the last three people on the planet. The daughters get Lot drunk enough to impregnate them, to reseed the planet. Their sons, Moab and Ben-ammi, become the founding fathers of the Moabites and the Ammonites—Arab tribes in what is now Jordan.

▲ **LOT'S WIFE SALTED.** Some wonder if Lot's wife got caught in the explosive shower of chemical spray.

▶ **LOOKING FOR SODOM.** Some speculate that Sodom is buried in the southern shallows of the Dead Sea—the result of sudden flooding after an earthquake dropped the land mass, allowing the water above to sweep over the plain. Or maybe all that's left are ruins along the southeast shoreline, such as Bab edh-Dhra.

THEORY OF NATURAL DISASTER. God may have destroyed the cities with an earthquake that tore open pockets of natural gas, some speculate. Lightning or early-morning lamp fires may have ignited the gas, propelling sulfur, salt, and other minerals high into the air. The earthquake-prone land around the southern Dead Sea—where some say the cities may have rested in a previously fertile valley—is rich in these resources.

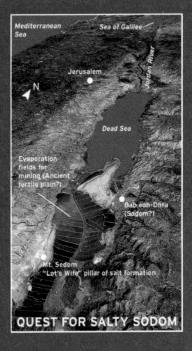

QUEST FOR SALTY SODOM

Abraham almost sacrifices his son

"TAKE YOUR SON. . .AND SACRIFICE HIM," (Genesis 22:2).

That's God talking. He's telling Abraham to kill Isaac—Abraham's only son with Sarah. The son through whom God promised to build Abraham a nation of descendants.

The news shocks Sarah to death, a Jewish legend says. She dies at age 127 (see Genesis 23:1). If the legend is true, that puts Isaac at about age 37. The Bible doesn't report his age.

Abraham and Isaac leave their home in Beersheba, in southern Israel. They travel three days north. At about 20 miles (32 km) a day—an average day's walk—that would put them in range of Jerusalem, about 50 miles (80 km) north. Jewish tradition says that's where they went.

They take firewood, fire, and a knife. When Isaac asks why they don't have a sheep to sacrifice, Abraham says God will provide one. Some scholars say that's a clue that Abraham doesn't expect God to make him go through with this.

Abraham piles up some stones, making an altar. On top, he arranges the wood. Then he ties up his son, lays him on the altar, and picks up the knife.

"Don't hurt the boy," an angel calls out. "Now I know that you truly obey God, because you were willing to offer him your only son" (Genesis 22:12 CEV).

The angel promises to bless Abraham with a large family of descendants who will:

// defeat their enemies

// take over the cities of their enemies—presumably a reference to the conquest of Canaan during Joshua's days

// and become a delight to all the nations on earth.

ABRAHAM'S AGE	KEY EVENT	GENESIS SOURCE
10	Future wife, Sarah, is born	17:17
75	Leaves home in Haran	12:4
85	Marries Hagar as secondary wife	16:3
86	Ishmael born to Hagar	16:16
99	Abram renamed "Abraham"; circumcised	17:5, 24
100	Isaac born to Sarah	21:5
137	Sarah dies	23:1
140	Finds wife for Isaac	25:20
160	Grandsons born, Esau and Jacob	25:26
175	Dies	25:7

WHY TEST ABRAHAM? The test isn't for the all-knowing God, most Bible experts agree. Some see it as a foreshadowing of the painful sacrifice God will make 2,000 years later. What Abraham was willing to do—sacrifice his only son—God actually did.

Jacob cheats his twin

ESAU AND JACOB are twins born moments apart, sons of Isaac and Rebekah. Esau arrives first. Jacob next, clutching Esau's heel.

That's not all he'd grab of Esau's.

As the first to exit the uterus, Esau earned a big perk. By custom, he'd get a double share of Isaac's inheritance—two-thirds for him, one-third for Jacob.

As a bonus for being a daddy's boy, Esau was fairly certain to get a favorable blessing from his father. It was a custom for fathers to pass on words of hope and blessing to their children.

Jacob cheats Esau out of both.

INHERITANCE. A manly man, Esau comes home famished from a day's hunt. Jacob, a stay-at-home momma's boy, is waiting with red lentil stew he cooked. He sells the stew to his brother. Menu price: "Your rights as the firstborn son" (Genesis 25:31). More hungry than smart, Esau agrees.

BLESSING. Old and growing blind, Isaac decides to bless Esau. He asks Esau to prepare him a meal of wild game, so Esau goes hunting. Rebekah convinces Jacob to steal the blessing by pretending to be Esau. Jacob brings Isaac a meat dish. And so he'll smell like Esau, Jacob wears his brother's clothes. Jacob even straps goat hide to his arms and neck, to mimic Esau's hairy body. Fooled by the fraud, Isaac blesses Jacob:

> *"May many nations become your servants. . . . May you be the master over your brothers."*
> GENESIS 27:29

When Esau gets home and finds out that the only blessing left is one that sounds more like a curse, he vows to kill Jacob. But Rebekah warns her favorite son, who flees to her relatives living in what is now Turkey. That's the last time Momma's Boy sees his momma.

OVERPRICED SOUP. Famished from a hunt, Esau agrees to trade his inheritance rights as the oldest son for a bowl of his younger brother's soup. The oldest son gets a double share of inheritance.

RED LENTIL STEW. Esau sells his birthright privileges for "some of that red stuff" (Genesis 25:30 HCSB), later identified as lentil stew (verse 34). Lentils, from the pea family, come in many colors including red, green, and brown.

BLESSING. It's more than a prayer, but less than a guarantee. It's a statement of hope, with the expectation that God will bring the words to life. Once spoken, the ancients seemed to believe, the words of blessing couldn't be taken back.

FIRST-SON PRIVILEGES. In addition to getting a double share of the family inheritance, the oldest son usually becomes leader of the clan—the extended family. It's unclear if Esau exchanged his double share for Jacob's single share, or if Jacob got everything.

Jacob's payback

RUNNING FOR HIS LIFE from the brother he cheated, Jacob flees about 700 miles (1,100 km) north, from Beersheba to Haran.

That's where his mother, Rebekah, grew up, in what is now Turkey. It's also where her brother, Laban, lives with his family—including two daughters: Leah, the oldest, and Rachel.

Jacob falls in love with Rachel, who has "a beautiful figure and a lovely face" (Genesis 29:17).

Trouble is, he needs to pay Laban a bride fee— and he left home with nothing much more than his survival instinct. So he works for Laban for seven years, as payment.

After a nighttime marriage—apparently to a heavily veiled bride—Jacob wakes up in the morning next to Leah.

Not a pleasant surprise. The Bible's vague description of Leah implies she's not easy on the eyes.

Jacob confronts Laban about the switcheroo. Laban simply says it's the custom to marry off the oldest daughter first. But he says Jacob can have Rachel in seven days if he agrees to work seven more years.

Done deal.

The women enter into what looks like a competition for who can give Jacob the most sons. Each woman even gives him her maid as an add-on surrogate mother. Together, the four women give Jacob 12 sons—forefathers of the 12 tribes of Israel.

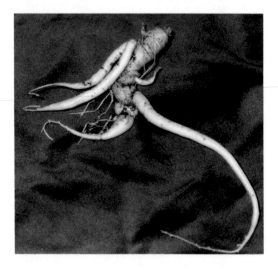

FERTILITY TREATMENT / Some believed that the root of the mandrake plant, shaped a bit like a human, works as a fertility drug. Leah had some. Rachel traded for it, offering Leah an extra night with Jacob in exchange. The trade worked, but it was Leah who got pregnant. Sperm 1. Mandrake 0.

JACOB'S LADDER / On his escape from Esau's revenge, Jacob has a dream. He sees angels going up and down on a stairway to heaven. God apparently sees something good in Jacob, which readers don't yet see. For God vows that the promise he made to Abraham will be carried out through Jacob, not Esau. Jacob will become one of Israel's forefathers.

Jacob's nervous reunion with Esau

AFTER 20 YEARS OF HARD LABOR working for his father-in-law—14 years paying for his brides and another 6 building his own flocks and herds—Jacob makes a bold decision.

He's going home.

He hopes his brother, Esau, has cooled off by now. But clearly, Jacob is terrified.

As Jacob gets ready to cross the Jordan River into Canaan, he sends messengers to Esau to announce his return and to ask for a happy reunion.

The messengers come back with frightening news: Esau is coming to meet Jacob—and he's bringing an army of 400 men.

Jacob nervously responds by dividing his caravan in half, hoping that if Esau attacks one group, the other might escape. Then Jacob sends more messengers. Wave after wave of them, each wave bearing gifts for Esau—hundreds of prime livestock: cattle, donkeys, camels, goats, and sheep.

The night before the crossing, Jacob can't sleep. He wakes his family and sends them across the Jordan River at a shallow ford. He follows later, but only after wrestling a blessing out of a mysterious man who shows up in the camp.

The next morning Esau arrives, with hugs and kisses.

Their mother has since died, but their father, Isaac, is still alive. Jacob returns to his father at what is now Hebron, a city south of Bethlehem. Esau goes home to Edom, a territory a few days away in what is now Jordan. When Isaac dies, the brothers reunite to bury him.

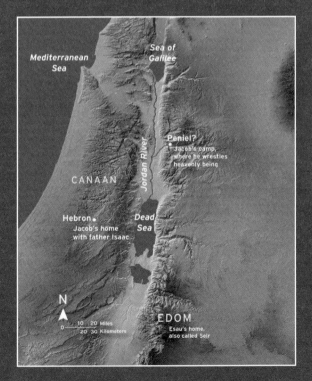

Mediterranean Sea
Sea of Galilee
Jordan River
Peniel?
Jacob's camp, where he wrestles heavenly being
CANAAN
Hebron
Jacob's home with father Isaac
Dead Sea
N
0   10   20 Miles
   20 30 Kilometers
EDOM
Esau's home, also called Seir

JACOB WRESTLES GOD? Some wonder if the wrestling match is a poetic way of saying Jacob wrestled with himself over his decision to go home. But a brief reference earlier to Jacob coming upon angels in "God's camp" (Genesis 32:2) lead many to conclude he wrestled an angel, if not God in human form. Jacob refuses to let go until the man blesses him. Jacob gets his wish—and a new name: Israel. Then Jacob names the place Peniel, meaning "face of God" (Genesis 32:30). Apparently, Jacob thought the man who blessed him was God himself.

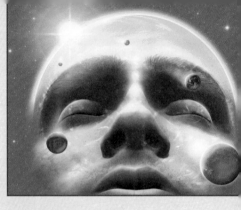

Joseph's dream becomes a nightmare

JOSEPH'S BROTHERS don't like him to begin with.

From the first day he dirties his diaper, he's daddy's pet—the favorite of Jacob's 12 sons. Joseph is, after all, the first child of Jacob's most beloved wife, Rachel.

As the special son, Joseph gets a special robe—a gift from his father that sets him apart as Daddy's Boy. While Joseph wears what amounts to a top-of-the-line designer outfit, his brothers get standard-issue shepherd wear.

Prompting added hate value, Joseph grows into a tattle-tale—a 17-year-old little brother who does what little brothers do: tell Daddy every bad thing they see their big brothers do.

But it's a pair of dreams that prod his brothers to retaliate.

In dream one, Joseph and his brothers are bundling grain stalks in the field. "Suddenly my bundle stood up, and your bundles all gathered around and bowed low before mine!" (Genesis 37:7).

In dream two, "The sun, moon, and eleven stars bowed low before me!" (Genesis 37:9).

Even his father gets ticked. "What kind of dream is that?" Jacob scolds. "Will your mother [apparently represented by the moon] and I [sun] and your brothers actually come and bow to the ground before you?" (Genesis 37:10).

Joseph's brothers get their chance to shut him up a short time later. They have taken their flocks about a three-day walk north from their home in Hebron to graze the pastures of Dothan. At first, they plan to kill him. Until slave traders happen by, headed for Egypt.

They sell little brother down the desert. They keep his tailored robe, dip it in goat's blood, rip it up like a wild animal had chewed on it, and then send it to their dad. Heartbroken, old Jacob assumes some beast ate his boy.

DREAMS.

People in many ancient cultures taught that the gods communicate to people through dreams. Jews taught that, too, of God. Prophets generally received their messages from God in dreams as well as daytime visions or trances.

. . . .

BEAUTIFUL ROBE.

Bible experts aren't sure what distinguished Joseph's "beautiful robe," as some Bible translations describe it. Some speculate the original Hebrew words refer to a robe with long sleeves or perhaps with many colors. One other person wears a robe like this: King David's daughter, Princess Tamar (see 2 Samuel 13:18).

Joseph dreams that his brother's sheaves of grain bow to his.

Joseph, from slave to master

IN A STROKE OF GOOD LUCK, Joseph gets sold to an Egyptian prison official whose wife falsely accuses him of attempted rape.

At least the story turns out looking like good luck—if not God tweaking destiny.

The official is Potiphar. He's captain of the guards protecting the Egyptian king. Potiphar notices that Joseph has a special touch: success in all he does. So he promotes Joseph to household manager.

Potiphar's wife notices Joseph is "a very handsome and well-built young man" (Genesis 39:6). And she wants him to use his special touch on her, so to speak. After he repeatedly refuses, she screams rape. She tells her husband that this

COUGAR DREAMS / It's an ancient version of a bored housewife lusting over the pool guy with great abs. But in this nearly 4,000-year-old story, the wife of a palace official in Egypt dreams of having sex with her household servant Joseph, who's "a very handsome and well-built young man" (Genesis 39:6).

CHEERS / Wine fit for a king was served in cups like this alabaster-stone chalice from King Tut's tomb, decorated with lotus blossoms. Joseph predicts that one of his fellow prisoners, the king's former wine tester, will be reinstated. As for another prisoner, the palace baker, Joseph says he's toast.

. . . .

handsome, well-built young man lustfully tried to have his way with her.

Judging by Potiphar's response, he doesn't buy it. Instead of executing Joseph, as he could have done, he simply puts him in prison. Perhaps Potiphar figures he has to do that, at least, to protect his wife's reputation.

In prison, Joseph predicts the future of two fellow prisoners—based on dreams they have. The king's top wine taster will get his job back. But the king's top baker will get himself executed. That's what happens.

Two years later, the king—known by his title of Pharaoh—has two nightmares. Seven scrawny cows devour seven fat cows. And seven withered heads of grain gobble up seven plump ones. When the king asks his advisors what this means, and no one seems to know, the reinstated wine taster suggests the king consult Joseph.

Joseph tells the king that Egypt will enjoy seven years of bumper crops, followed by seven years of drought. And he advises the king to stockpile extra supplies during the good years so they can get through the tough years ahead.

The king not only gives Joseph the job, he puts him in charge of all Egyptian officials. As the king explains, "Only I, sitting on my throne, will have a rank higher than yours" (Genesis 41:40).

Suddenly, Egypt's second-in-command is a Jew.

Joseph's family reunion

THE PREDICTED DROUGHT COMES. And so do Joseph's brothers, hoping to buy grain somewhere in the drought-resistant Nile River Valley.

Since Joseph's in charge of all the stockpiled grain, his brothers have to come and bow before him—in what looks like fulfillment of Joseph's dream perhaps 20 years earlier about their stalks of grain bowing to his.

The men don't recognize their little brother. But he recognizes them. They're all there, all 10 who sold him into slavery. The only brother missing is Benjamin—Jacob's youngest son, and Joseph's only full brother; both are sons of Rachel.

Joseph tests the men, accusing them of being spies. They insist they're brothers buying food for their family, and that their other brother, Benjamin, is with their father. Joseph slaps them in prison for three days, long enough to overhear them expressing regret for selling him into slavery.

He releases them but holds one hostage until the others return with Benjamin. Old Jacob at first refuses to let his son go. But as the drought lingers, he needs more grain from Egypt. So he sends his boys back with Benjamin.

In a second test, Joseph threatens to enslave Benjamin, to see if the brothers hate Rachel's other son. Judah, the oldest son, offers to take Benjamin's place as a slave.

Joseph bursts into tears. "I am Joseph," he cries. "Is my father still alive?" (Genesis 45:3). Jacob is. So Joseph invites his father's entire extended family—66 souls—to move to Egypt where they can weather out the drought.

MIXED-RACE EGYPTIANS. Joseph's family wasn't the only one migrating to Egypt. People of many races were drawn to the fertile land along the Nile River. Skeletal remains suggest many Egyptians were a mixture of several races: white, black, and Asian.

Pharaoh Akhenaton, based on ancient statues of him.

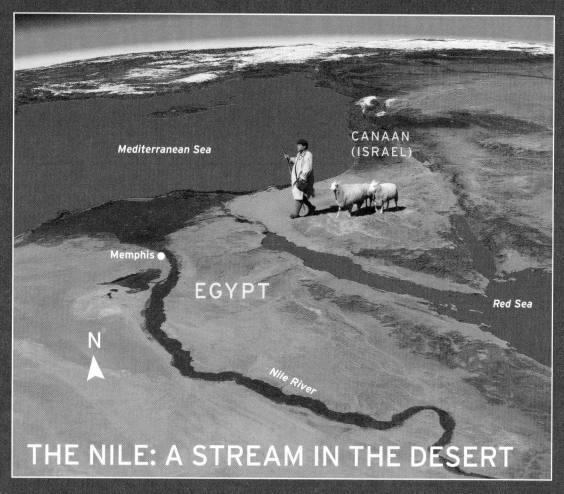

Mediterranean Sea

CANAAN (ISRAEL)

Memphis

EGYPT

Red Sea

N

Nile River

THE NILE: A STREAM IN THE DESERT

DROUGHT-RESISTANT NILE RIVER. When droughts struck the Middle East, foreigners flocked to the Nile River to graze their livestock and to plant crops. Most fields and farmland in the Middle East of Bible times relied on rainfall. But in Egypt, the land relied on the ever-flowing Nile River, which nourished a narrow strip of land as it sliced through the desert.

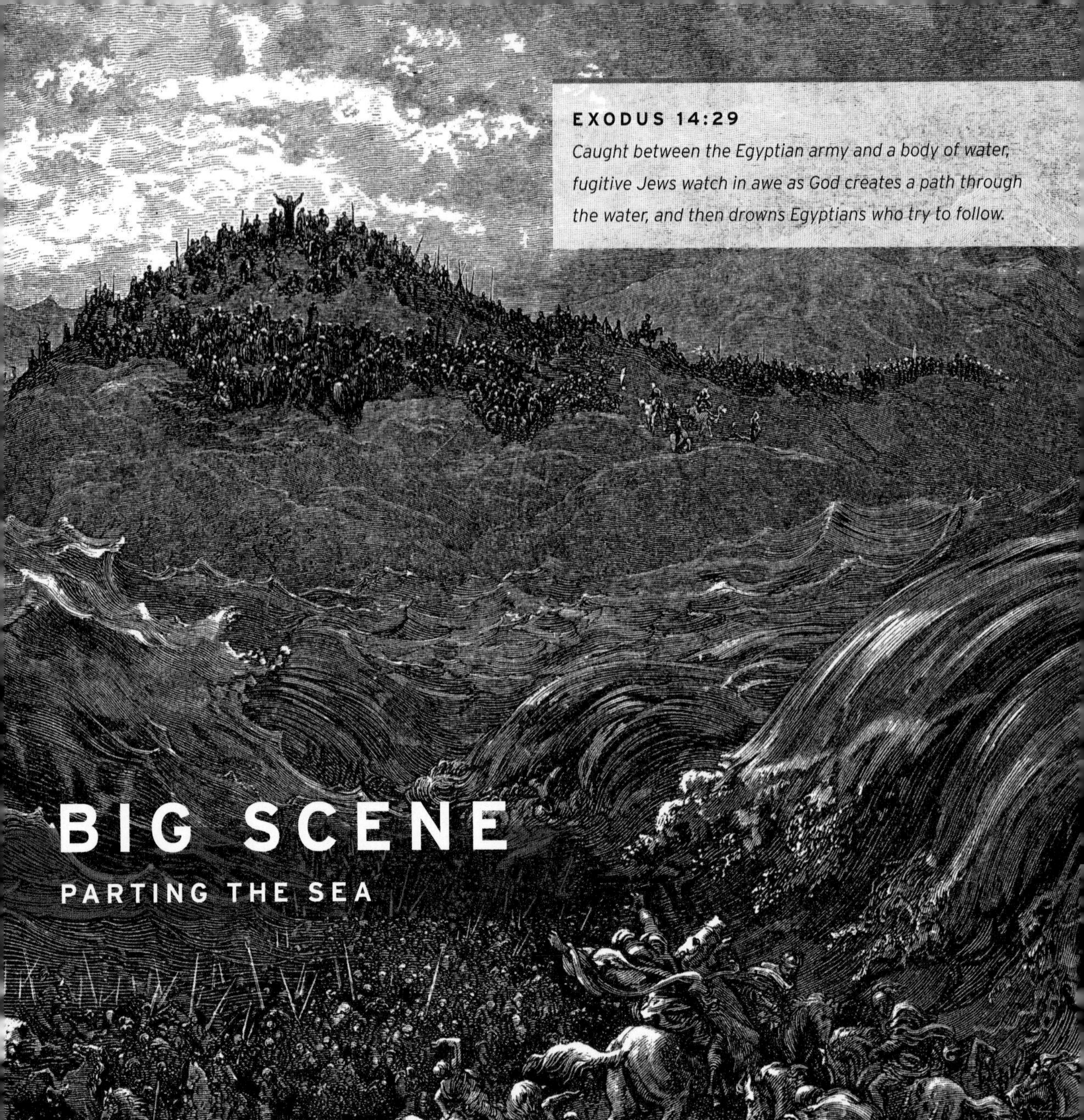

EXODUS 14:29

Caught between the Egyptian army and a body of water, fugitive Jews watch in awe as God creates a path through the water, and then drowns Egyptians who try to follow.

BIG SCENE

PARTING THE SEA

BIBLE HISTORY

ALL DATES APPROXIMATE

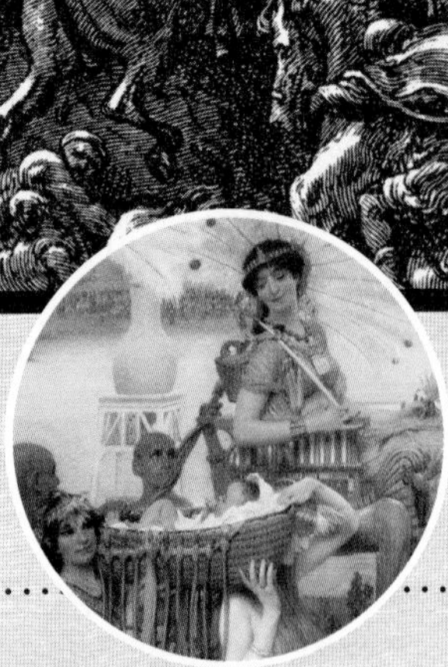

1520 BC
Moses born

WORLD HISTORY

Code of Hammurabi, first known set of laws
1700 BC

Irrigation machine for lifting water from Nile
1500 BC

EXODUS
JEWS ON THE MOVE

STORY LINE

JOSEPH'S FAMILY GUESTS from Canaan—today's Israel—overstay their welcome in Egypt.

So the Egyptians put them to work. As slaves.

The Jews had come to escape a drought. The drought ends. But the Jews stay. For 430 years. Joseph dies. So does the host king.

Egypt's new king worries that the minority Jews—a fertile crowd—have grown large enough to become a threat to national security. They might join enemies in a war against Egypt.

He orders them enslaved. Then he orders lethal population control measures: Throw their newborn sons into the croc-infested Nile River.

Baby Moses survives the river. He floats—inside a waterproof basket, and near where the princess bathes. The king's daughter finds him and raises him as a prince of Egypt.

By age 40, Moses is connecting with his people. He murders an abusive Egyptian slave driver. Then he flees the country.

Moses marries and becomes a shepherd for his father-in-law. Forty years later, God appears to him as a voice in a burning bush, convincing him to go back to Egypt and free the Jews.

Moses has to unleash 10 plagues on Egypt before the stubborn king frees his cheap labor.

The Jews escape and spend about a year camped at the foot of Mount Sinai. There, God gives Moses the 10 Commandments and hundreds of other laws that will help organize the refugees into a nation and govern their behavior.

// LOCATION: Egypt.

// TIME: Some scholars set the story in the mid-1400s BC. Others say 200 years later: 1200s BC.

// AUTHOR: Unknown. Jewish tradition says Moses wrote this book. Jesus called Exodus "the writings of Moses" (Mark 12:26). And God told Moses to write down the laws reported in the book (see Exodus 34:27).

1440 BC
Exodus to Canaan
10 Commandments

1400 BC
Moses dies; Jews invade Canaan

1290 BC
Alternate date of the Exodus

Pharaoh Thutmose III rules until 1425 BC
1479 BC

Pharaoh Rameses II rules until 1213 BC
1279 BC

Jewish guests become slaves

JEWISH GUESTS IN EGYPT enjoy more than a generation of hospitality in Goshen, "the best land of Egypt" (Genesis 47:6).

Decades later, perhaps several generations, these immigrants find themselves no longer welcome. A new king comes along and he starts to worry about their growing numbers.

> There are too many of those Israelites in our country, and they are becoming more powerful than we are. . . . If our country goes to war, they could easily fight on the side of our enemies.
>
> EXODUS 1:9–10 CEV

Hard work should slow down their sex drive, he figures. So he enslaves them as forced labor. They build entire cities, including Pithom and Rameses.

But the more they're oppressed, the faster they grow.

The king orders the midwives who deliver Jewish babies to kill the boys. But they refuse and lie about it: "The Hebrew women. . .have their babies so quickly that we cannot get there in time" (Exodus 1:19).

So the king issues an order to all Egyptians: "Throw every newborn Hebrew boy into the Nile River" (Exodus 1:22).

It's the patriotic thing to do, he figured. Like picking up trash.

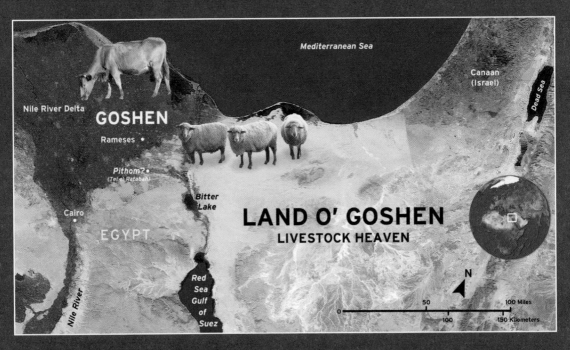

GOSHEN. Scholars speculate this territory in Egypt covered the east side of the Nile Delta. There, the river fans out into streams that irrigate the land before emptying into the Mediterranean Sea. These fields would have been a perfect fit for the Jews. Great for grazing the livestock. And closest to Canaan.

Moses, prince of Egypt

INFANT MORTALITY RATE SOARS among Jewish slaves. That's because Pharaoh has ordered all patriotic Egyptians to help thin out the immigrant infestation by killing any newborn Jewish boys they discover—pitching them into the Nile River.

Jochebed gives birth to a son. Lousy timing. Somehow, she manages to hide him for three months. But she realizes she can't keep this up. So she hatches a cunning plan.

She takes a basket made of papyrus reeds and waterproofs it with tar. She puts her baby in the basket and has his big sister, Miriam, set the basket in the Nile—where the princess bathes beside tall reeds. Technically, Jochebed complies with Pharaoh's order.

The princess finds the baby, realizes it's probably a Jewish boy, but can't resist its helpless cries.

Young Miriam walks up to the princess and asks if she'd like a Hebrew nurse for the baby.

Mother Jochebed gets the job. Even better, she gets to take the baby home—at least during those early months when babies need fed every few hours. And unlike most other mothers, she gets an extra perk: a salary.

When the boy grows older, Jochebed brings him back to the princess who adopts him as her own son. She names him Moses.

PAPYRUS.
Harvesting papyrus reeds from the Nile delta. These tall, triangle-shaped reeds also grew along the banks of the Nile River. Egyptians made paper from the spongy, fiber core—laying strips side by side in two crisscrossed layers and pressing them into sheets. From the fibers in the outer stem they made sails and mats.

MOSES, THE NAME.
It works for several reasons. It sounds like the Hebrew word for "pulled out," as in "pulled out of the river." In Egyptian, it means "son." It's also part of the name used by many Egyptian kings, including Thutmose I, who ruled about the time some say Moses was a young man.

HASTA LA VISTA, BABY /
Wiping tears from her eyes, Jochebed, mother of Moses, prepares to set her son adrift in the Nile River. She can only hope the bathing princess will take pity on him.

A burning bush that talks

DRAWN TO HIS PEOPLE, 40-year-old Moses rides out to the slave fields. When he sees an Egyptian slave driver beating one of the Jews, Moses murders the Egyptian.

Word gets back to the king, who probably knows Moses was born a Jew. The king orders Moses caught and executed.

Moses runs for his life. He heads east through the Sinai Peninsula and into the land of Midian. There, he meets a Midian priest with seven daughters. Good odds for a single guy. He marries one of the ladies: Zipporah, who gives birth to their son, Gershom.

At age 80, Moses is still working as a shepherd for the family. He takes the flock several days from home, looking for grazing pasture. He ends up at the foot of Mount Sinai. There, he notices a bush on fire—yet it's not burning up.

As he approaches, a voice calls out from inside the bush: "I am the God of your father—the God of Abraham" (Exodus 3:6).

God says he has heard the cries of his enslaved people, and he has chosen Moses to free them and lead them back to their homeland.

Moses politely declines, offering four excuses.

// He's a nobody. God promises to go with him, and God's a somebody.

// The Jews will ask for the name of the god who sent him. God says to tell them, "I AM has sent me" (Exodus 3:14).

// The Jews won't believe him. God promises to convince them with miracles.

// He gets tongue-tied. God says he made the mouth. And for added support, God sends Moses' older brother, Aaron, to help as his spokesman.

Excuses exhausted, Moses returns to Egypt.

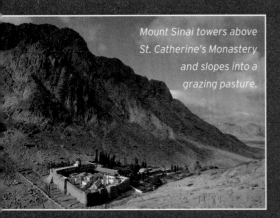

Mount Sinai towers above St. Catherine's Monastery and slopes into a grazing pasture.

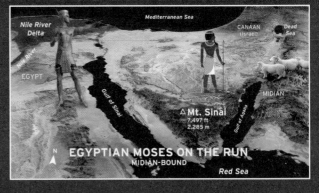

EGYPTIAN MOSES ON THE RUN
MIDIAN-BOUND

MOUNT SINAI. The Bible doesn't identify the location of "Sinai, the mountain of God," (Exodus 3:1). But a tradition going back at least to the AD 100s points to a granite mountain known in Egypt by its Arabic name: Jebel Musa, "Mountain of Moses."

MIDIAN. In Moses' time, the nation of Midian covered a small area east of the Red Sea's right rabbit ear, the Gulf of Aqaba. But there is evidence that some of the nomadic herders moved west of the Gulf and settled in the pie wedge of land called the Sinai Peninsula, where Exodus says God spoke to Moses at Mount Sinai.

"Let my people go"

TEMPORARILY. That's the implication of the request Moses and Aaron make to Pharaoh.

> *"The LORD God says, Let my people go into the desert, so they can honor me with a celebration there."*
>
> EXODUS 5:1 CEV

What Moses and his brother fail to mention is that after the festival, Pharaoh doesn't need to wait up. The Jews won't be coming back.

Leaving that out makes it seem like Moses and Aaron are afraid to tell Pharaoh the whole story— that God is taking his people home to Canaan.

As it turns out, they have good reason to think that. Pharaoh won't let the Jews leave even temporarily.

Pharaoh—who portrays himself as the son of Re, powerful sun god in this desert country—says he's never heard of this Lord of the Jews. If this Lord is so great, Pharaoh must think, why has he abandoned the Jews to slavery? It must be because Egypt's gods are stronger.

While Moses and Aaron talk with Pharaoh, it seems the Jews have stopped working and are waiting to hear good news from Moses. Pharaoh complains about their "laziness," and says all they really want is a vacation.

He figures if they have enough spare time to stand around doing nothing, they can cut their own straw for the mud bricks—without reducing their daily quota of bricks.

The Jews aren't happy. They tell Moses and Aaron, essentially, "With friends like you, who needs a slave driver?"

HIS NAME IS MUD. Stamped onto this brick of mud and straw from about 1250 BC is the seal of Rameses II. Egyptians used straw as a binding agent to hold mud together. Formed in a mold, the bricks were left to dry in the desert sun.

GOD WHO? Moses and Aaron tell the king of Egypt that God wants his people—the enslaved Jews— freed. But the king, who presents himself as a god— son of the sun god Re—says he's never heard of the Jewish god. So, request denied.

10 plagues for one king

STUBBORN doesn't seem like a word strong enough to describe Pharaoh—not given what he puts his country through, for the sake of his pride.

In fairness to him, God takes some of the blame: "I will make the king so stubborn that he won't listen to you" (Exodus 7:3 CEV). God says he wants everyone to know he's no would-be god or a wimp of a god compared to Egypt's gallery of gods. He's the real God—the one and only.

But it's unclear how much "stubborn" God has to add to a king who already says he's a god himself, son of Egypt's chief god Re, no less.

What follows sounds a little like a wrestling match. Moses gets Pharaoh in a headlock. Pharaoh says, "Uncle." Moses lets him go. And Pharaoh says, "Fake out."

An example: After frogs swarm the land in plague two, Pharaoh says, "Plead with the LORD to take the frogs away from me and my people. I will let your people go, so they can offer sacrifices to the LORD" (Exodus 8:8). Moses does. God does. Pharaoh doesn't.

And Pharaoh doesn't six times: plagues of frogs, flies, hail, locusts, darkness, and death of firstborn.

Yet it's not a wrestling match. It's a series of plagues. And not just any plagues. The selection, some scholars say, looks like a direct challenge to some of Egypt's most revered gods—including Pharaoh.

Battle of the gods?

BIBLE EXPERTS wonder why God chose these particular plagues to arm-twist Pharaoh into freeing the Jews.

Some say the plagues prove God's power over the Egyptian gallery of gods.

Others speculate the plagues may have followed a three-season cycle of natural disasters, starting with the autumn flood of the Nile and ending with the springtime harvest of contaminated crops. For a visual overview of that theory, see the chart at right.

◄ **PLAGUES ON RECORD IN EGYPT.**
Plague reports in Exodus track with descriptions in an Egyptian story written about the time some say Moses confronted Pharaoh: *The Admonitions of Ipuwer (1200 BC).*

EGYPTIAN REPORT	EXODUS REPORT
"The river is blood."	"The whole river turned to blood!" (Exodus 7:20).
"Blood is everywhere."	"There was blood everywhere throughout the land of Egypt" (7:21).
"Trees are down."	"Hail struck down everything....Even the trees were destroyed" (9:25).
"The barley crop has been destroyed."	"Flax and barley were ruined by the hail" (9:31).
"Plague is throughout the land."	"Boils had broken out on. . .all the Egyptians" (9:11).
"People who bury their brother are everywhere."	"There was not a single house where someone had not died" (12:30).

PLAGUE 1:
Nile River turns blood red
GOD OVERPOWERED:
Hapi, god of annual Nile flood
NATURAL DISASTER:
Toxic bacteria from decaying algae
washed into the river from upstream
swamplands during autumn flood season

PLAGUE 6:
Boils
GODS OVERPOWERED:
Isis and other health gods such as Ptah
NATURAL DISASTER:
Stable flies carry diseases
that produce blisters

PLAGUE 2:
Frogs
GOD OVERPOWERED:
Heqet (Heket), goddess of childbirth,
pictured with frog head
NATURAL DISASTER:
Frogs flee the poisoned water

PLAGUE 7:
Hail
GOD OVERPOWERED:
Shu, god of dry air
NATURAL DISASTER:
Harvest begins in February,
and hail can wipe out a crop

PLAGUE 3:
Flying gnats
GOD OVERPOWERED:
Thoth, god of magic, can't
help Egypt's magicians
NATURAL DISASTER:
Mosquitoes, midges, and other insects
breed in pools of receding floodwater

PLAGUE 8:
Locusts
GOD OVERPOWERED:
Min, god of fertile crops
NATURAL DISASTER:
Even with pesticides today,
locusts are still a problem

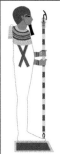

PLAGUE 4:
Flies
GOD OVERPOWERED:
Ptah (Peth, Peteh), creator god,
can't control the flies
NATURAL DISASTER:
Stable flies lay eggs in
decaying frogs, wet straw

PLAGUE 9:
Three-day darkness
GOD OVERPOWERED:
Re, sun god
NATURAL DISASTER:
A lingering, springtime sandstorm
called *Khamsin* (Arabic: "50 days"),
blowing in from Sahara Desert

PLAGUE 5:
Livestock disease
GOD OVERPOWERED:
Hathor, mother goddess,
pictured with cow ears, horns
NATURAL DISASTER:
Anthrax can be transmitted
through toxic drinking water

PLAGUE 10:
Death of firstborn
GOD OVERPOWERED:
Pharaoh, son of Re
NATURAL DISASTER:
Pampered oldest children get
extra food, from crops contaminated
with locust droppings

First Passover

NOT ONE of the first nine plagues convinces Pharaoh to release the Jews. But God assures Moses that Plague 10 will finish the job.

"At midnight tonight," God says, "I will pass through the heart of Egypt. All the firstborn sons will die in every family in Egypt" (Exodus 11:4–5).

But God promises to pass over the homes of the Jews, without harming any of them. To identify themselves as God's people, and to give them energy for their departure that very night, they're to eat a meal.

God tells them to kill a sheep or goat and smear the blood on the outside doorposts, as a sign that they're Jews. Then they're to roast the meat and eat it. There won't be time to make bread and let the dough rise. So they'll have to eat flat bread baked without yeast.

At midnight, the Jews hear screams coming from Egyptian homes. Even Pharaoh's oldest son dies.

"Get out!" Pharaoh tells Moses. "Leave my people" (Exodus 12:31). The Jews ask their Egyptian neighbors for silver and gold, as instructed by God. Egyptians comply, perhaps out of fear. Anything to get the Jews out of Egypt.

But just as Pharaoh had changed his mind after earlier plagues, he's about to do it again. Big mistake.

◄ A MEAL TO REMEMBER. Jews in Amsterdam, like many throughout the world, celebrate the springtime holiday of Passover (*Pesach* in Hebrew). The main feature is a meal rich in symbolism. Jews call this meal the *Seder* (SAY-dur), Hebrew for "order," since the ritual meal follows a scripted order of worship.

PASSOVER MENU. On the first Passover, Jews ate meat, flat bread without yeast, and bitter salad greens. Over the centuries, Jews added other menu items. Mixed nuts and fruit symbolize mortar the slaves used to build Egypt's cities. Saltwater dip represents tears of the slaves. Boiled eggs represent sacrifices Jews made once they reached Israel and built the Temple. Wine celebrates God's promises to them: "I will free you. . .rescue you. . . redeem you. . .claim you as my own people" (Exodus 6:6–7).

Crossing the sea

ON A MIDNIGHT RUN, Jews flee Rameses, the city of their enslavement. Pharaoh has just agreed to release them, and they're not waiting for the light of day. Four hundred and thirty years in Egypt, to the day, is long enough.

Besides, Pharaoh has been known to change his mind.

They rush eastward to Succoth, roughly 20 miles (about 30 kilometers) toward the barren Sinai badlands. They could turn north and take the short route home along the coast (see map page 43). Egyptian reports say Thutmose III (1479–1425 BC) and his army made the trip to Gaza, Canaan in just 10 days. It might take the Jews a month, with older folks and kids in tow.

But God doesn't want them confronting Egyptian soldiers stationed at forts along the popular coastal route. God, in a pillar of light, leads them on a not-so-scenic route into the heart of the Sinai Peninsula.

Back at the palace, it dawns on Pharaoh that he has just freed what amounts to his worker bees. He sends his entire army led by his elite chariot corps to bring them back.

When the Egyptians catch up to the slow-moving crowd of refugees, it looks like an easy

(continued next page)

"RED SEA" VS. "SEA OF REEDS." The original Hebrew language says the Jews crossed the *yam sup. Yam* is "sea," and *sup* can mean "far away" or "reeds." "Sea of reeds" suggests a lake or stream with papyrus reeds growing along the bank, such as one of the Bitter Lakes. When Jewish scholars translated their scriptures into Greek shortly before the time of Christ, they used "Red Sea." Most English Bibles prefer "Red Sea," often footnoting the alternate reading as "sea of reeds."

PARTING WHICH SEA?
GUESSING THE ROUTE

Mediterranean Sea
Suez Canal
Rameses
Succoth (Tel el Maskhuta)
Lake Timsah
Pithom? (Tel el Retabah)
Great Bitter Lake
Little Bitter Lake
EGYPT
Suez Canal
N
Gulf of Suez (RED SEA)

TRACKING MOSES. Which route Moses and the Jews took out of Rameses remains a mystery. Exodus names many landmarks that the ancients apparently knew well. But the sites are lost today. Bible experts aren't even sure which body of water God parted.

roundup. The Jews are trapped between the army and a body of water that the original Hebrew language calls the "sea of reeds."

Suddenly, the pillar of light that has been leading the Jews moves to the rear, between the Jews and the Egyptians. As night falls, Moses acts on God's command:

> *"Pick up your staff and raise your hand over the sea. Divide the water so the Israelites can walk through the middle of the sea on dry ground."*
>
> EXODUS 14:16

All night long a strong east wind blows. And in perhaps the most famous miracle of the Bible, the water opens a path—an escape route for the Jews. The Egyptian army follows, but the water crashes in on them, drowning everyone.

In the Exodus adventure story that follows, Jews will face other enemies. But not the Egyptians. That threat is dead and gone.

NAPOLEON'S NEAR-DROWNING IN THE RED SEA /
When Napoleon invaded Egypt in 1799, he rode along the Red Sea shoreline as receded water rushed back to shore. A French report says his skillful horsemanship saved him. But an Egyptian report says he tumbled off his horse and got fished out of the drink.

600,000 MEN?

Exodus puts the refugee count at "600,000 men, plus all the women and children" (Exodus 12:37). With one woman and two kids for each man, that's about 2.5 million. If they walked in rows 100 yards (91 meters) wide, the line crossing the sea could have stretched around 20 miles (32 kilometers). Many Bible students say God could have managed a group this size in the Sinai badlands. Others pitch theories like these, which reduce the numbers.

Translators used wrong word: "600 thousand" should be "600 groups" or "600 extended families"—for maybe 20,000 people or fewer.

Symbolic numbers: Hebrew numbers have letter equals, such as 1=A, 2=B, etc. A later census puts the exact number at 603,550 (see Exodus 38:26). Add Moses and you have 603,551. That's the total when you add the numbers linked to the common Hebrew phrase "sons of Israel," implying that all the Jews were there—however many there were.

WIND ON THE WATER—ONE SCIENTIFIC THEORY.

Scientists specializing in meteorology and oceanography, in two separate studies, concluded that a strong, sustained wind blowing on the narrow, northern tip of the Gulf of Suez could push back the water. This would extend the beachfront by about a mile (1.6 kilometers). People could walk on the beach, or perhaps even on a reef with water on both sides. Once the wind stops, theorists say, the water would rush back into place within 30 minutes—and up to 10 feet (3 meters) deep. Sources: *Bulletin of the Russian Academy of Sciences*, 2004; *Bulletin of the American Meteorological Society*, March 1992.

Sweet water

MORE WATER THAN THEY COULD HANDLE was the problem Jews faced at the sea of reeds. But now, three days into the desert of Shur, they can't find any water at all.

Eventually they reach the oasis of Marah, a name that means "bitter." Sure enough, the water is too bitter to drink.

Some of the people storm over to Moses and demand, "What are we going to drink?" (Exodus 15:24).

Beats Moses.

He turns to God for help.

God shows him a hunk of wood and tells him to toss it into the water. Sure enough, the wood seems to neutralize the bitterness.

WOOD IN THE WATER / Botanists say there's no known wood that could have neutralized the salty taste of the water. Yet some Bible commentators speculate that the barberry bush might have done the job. Egyptians used berries of the barberry bush to treat cuts, diarrhea, and even to ward off the plague during the Middle Ages. Other scholars wonder if the wood was more of a reminder of the parting of the sea since Moses used a staff to cue the wind.

Barberry
(Berberis vulgaris)

THIRST QUENCHER.
An oasis like this in the Sahara desert is a mouth-watering sight to a parched hiker who hasn't seen water in days. But there's bitter disappointment if the water tastes like the rusted fender of a Buick. That's what greets Exodus trekkers when they reach the oasis of Marah.

MARAH.
The location of this oasis, like many sites mentioned in this story, remains a mystery.

BITTER WATER.
Mineral-laced soil in the Sinai Peninsula—rich in salt and alkaline—leaves some of the water tasting metallic and bitter. That's a giant step down from what the Jews were used to: sweet water of the Nile. Some Sinai water holes are so bitter that even today nomadic herders avoid them.

Fire on the mountain

TWO MONTHS INTO FREEDOM, the Jews arrive at the foot of Mount Sinai. This is where it had all started—where God first contacted Moses perhaps a year earlier, speaking from a fiery bush.

Now God decides to reveal himself to all the Jews. As he explains it to Moses, "Then they will always trust you" (Exodus 19:9).

God makes quite an entrance. A thick cloud drapes the mountain peak as a trumpet blast terrifies the crowd. God arrives on the mountain in the form of a fire that churns the sky into smoke. Even the earth trembles as though quaking in fear.

"I am GOD," he says, "your God, who brought you out of the land of Egypt" (Exodus 20:2 MSG).

Then God speaks what will become known as the 10 Commandments.

> **//** *No other gods, only me.*
> **//** *No carved gods.*
> **//** *God won't put up with the irreverent use of his name.*
> **//** *Observe the Sabbath day, to keep it holy. . . . Don't do any work.*
> **//** *Honor your father and mother.*
> **//** *No murder.*
> **//** *No adultery.*
> **//** *No stealing.*
> **//** *No lies about your neighbor.*
> **//** *Don't set your heart on anything that is your neighbor's.*
> EXODUS 20:3-17 MSG

The Jews find it hard to warm up to a talking flame. At this point in their understanding of God, all they seem to get is the fear factor. So they ask Moses a big favor: "Don't let God speak directly to us, or we will die!" (Exodus 20:19).

Here on out they say they'd prefer God to talk to them through Moses. "You speak to us," they tell Moses, "and we will listen" (Exodus 20:19).

BAAL THE BULL RIDER / Canaanite weather god Baal—lightning bolts ready to fling—rides on a bull, a symbol of strength. Some wonder if this is what the Jews had in mind for the golden calf they built later, while Moses was up on Mount Sinai: It was a pedestal for God. Other scholars say it's unlikely, given God's reaction. He acted as though the Jews had already broken the first two of the 10 Commandments by making and worshipping an idol.

Ark of the Covenant replica

HOLY TERROR / God appears to the Jews in a fire on Mount Sinai. Earthquakes rumble as God himself recites the 10 Commandments. This terrifies the Jews so much that they ask Moses to serve as their intermediary—so they don't have to go through anything like this again.

. . . .

LONG ROUTE, SAFE ROUTE / Moses decides against the quick route to Canaan, along a coastal road guarded by Egyptian forts. Instead, he takes a road less traveled. Which road remains unclear. But it leads him into the Sinai badlands, to the "mountain of the LORD," and eventually to the Kadesh oasis, where the Jews spend most of their 40 years in the badlands wilderness.

10 COMMANDMENTS IN A BOX, TO GO.

Jews carried the stone slabs etched with the 10 Commandments—their most sacred object—in a chest called the Ark of the Covenant. *Covenant* means "contract." The chest measured roughly 4 feet long by 2 feet wide and high (more accurately, 115 x 69 centimeters). Resting on top was a lid crowned with a pair of golden angelic beings.

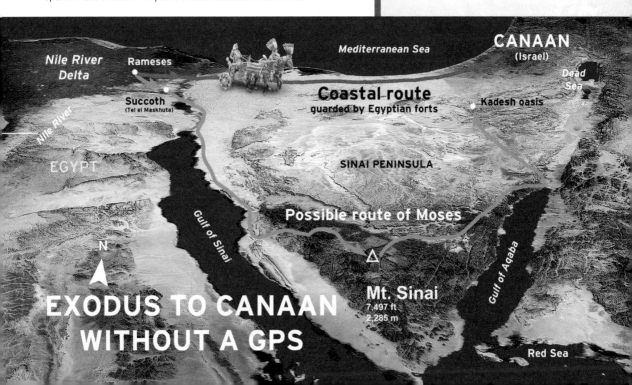

Nile River Delta

Rameses

Succoth
(Tel el Maskhuta)

EGYPT

Nile River

Mediterranean Sea

Coastal route
guarded by Egyptian forts

CANAAN
(Israel)

Dead Sea

Kadesh oasis

SINAI PENINSULA

Possible route of Moses

Gulf of Sinai

Gulf of Aqaba

N

Mt. Sinai
7,497 ft
2,285 m

Red Sea

EXODUS TO CANAAN
WITHOUT A GPS

A tent for God

GOD WANTS TO LIVE IN A TENT and travel with the Jews on the Exodus. So he tells Moses, "Have them make a sacred tent for me. I will live among them" (Exodus 25:8 NIrV).

This tent will become known as the Tabernacle, Israel's first worship center. It's a mobile version of the Jerusalem Temple that King Solomon will build in a few centuries.

It's not that God needs a place to lay his weary head. Instead, this facility is a way of making himself available to the people. And it's a reminder that they're not alone. It's at this holy place that the Jews will come to worship God, bringing their requests. They'll also bring their sacrifices to express gratitude for God's blessings or regret for sins they committed.

Jews pitch God's tent in the center of the camp. As a Jewish man approaches it, leading a sacrificial lamb, the first thing he sees is a wall of linen curtains surrounding the tent and the courtyard in front of the tent—an area 50 yards (46 meters) long and half as wide.

Inside the fabric-walled courtyard, he sees a bronze altar. It sits in front of the tent. It looks a bit like a barbecue pit, hollow in the center for wood that will burn the sacrificial meat.

The tent sits at the back end of the courtyard. The interior is shaped like a railroad boxcar, 15 yards long and 5 yards wide and high (14 by 4.5 meters). The snap-together frame is acacia wood,

GOD'S HOME ON EARTH. A tourist attraction in Israel, this life-sized replica of the Tabernacle gives Holy Land pilgrims a sense of what the first Jewish worship center looked like. But it's not made of the same material, which included gold-plated wooden beams and fine linen. Jews of the Exodus used the best materials available for the tent that represented God's presence among them.

covered with plates of gold and silver. Covering this frame are four layers of cloth and leather. The inside layer, which forms the interior roof and walls, is crafted of fine linen, decorated with angelic beings: cherubim. But only priests see these, for only priests are allowed inside. And only the high priest is allowed into the back room—the holiest room in this sacred tent of God. It contains the Ark of the Covenant, the chest that holds the 10 Commandments.

WHERE DID THE GOLD COME FROM?

Gold, silver, fine linen, and other supplies used to build the worship center came from an offering the Jews gave for the project. They got the supplies the night they left Egypt. Egyptians gave them "clothing and articles of silver and gold" (Exodus 12:35).

ACACIA / It's the most common tree in the Sinai Peninsula; it grows to about 15 to 20 feet (4–6 meters). Jews used acacia hardwood to build the framing for the tent worship center, the bronze-plated altar, and the gold-plated Ark of the Covenant.

Acacia tree in Sinai badlands

LEVITICUS 17:11

Sin is a capital offense. God allows the Jews to sacrifice animals to atone for the sins of humanity. The sacrifice is a dramatic reminder of how deadly serious sin is.

BIG SCENE

SACRIFICE

BIBLE HISTORY	**1440 BC** *Jews get laws and priesthood*	**1400 BC** *Jews reach Canaan (Israel)*	**1290 BC** *Alternate date of the Exodus*
WORLD HISTORY	*Chinese priests lead worship of ancestors, nature gods* **1400 BC**		*Sun god Aton becomes Egypt's only official god* **1350 BC**

ALL DATES APPROXIMATE

LEVITICUS

JEWISH RULE BOOK

STORY LINE

IN THE SHADOW OF MOUNT SINAI Jewish refugees organize themselves into a nation.

They divide into 12 tribes descended from Jacob's 12 sons. Each tribe camps together, circling their tents around the worship center.

Moses keeps them here for about a year, while he meets with God on Mount Sinai. There, Moses begins gathering the hundreds of laws that will govern them politically and nurture them spiritually.

Some laws deal with civil and criminal matters, such as how to punish a cattle thief.

Other laws deal with spiritual matters, such as how God expects his chosen people to behave and how to seek forgiveness when they fail.

Many of the laws are unique. But that's the point. These laws—such as resting on the Saturday Sabbath, eating only kosher food, and observing religious holidays such as Passover—will distinguish the Jews as the world's first nation devoted to God.

To guide the people in worship, God puts the tribe of Levi in charge of the worship center. From that tribe, he appoints Aaron's family as priests. Aaron becomes the first high priest. His sons serve as priestly assistants.

Levi's tribe is where Leviticus gets its name. *Leviticus* means "about the Levites." That title and some material in Leviticus suggest the book is a how-to guide for priests. But it's more. Most laws apply to all the Jews. That makes Leviticus a how-to manual for all Jews, teaching them how to live as God's people.

// LOCATION: Somewhere in the Sinai Peninsula, camped at the base of a mountain. Which mountain is uncertain.

// TIME: Some Bible experts put the story of the Jewish refugees returning home in about the 1440s BC. Others put it around 1290 BC.

// AUTHOR: Unknown. Jewish tradition says Moses wrote it.

960 BC
First Jewish Temple replaces tent worship center

Troy falls in Trojan War
1193 BC

Phoenician (Lebanese) ships dominate Mediterranean Sea
1000 BC

A human sins, an animal dies

THIS JEWISH GUIDEBOOK for how to worship God and live in peace with others starts with bad news for livestock.

Leviticus reports hundreds of laws and rituals God expects the Jews to observe. But it starts with the most important ritual of all: animal sacrifice.

With detail fit for a butcher, Leviticus explains how to slice and dice sheep, goats, bulls, and birds and burn the carcass parts on an altar.

The first sacrifice Leviticus describes is called the burnt offering. In a sense, it's a sincere apology to God for sin. The entire animal gets burned. With other offerings, the worshipper gets to keep and eat part of the animal.

God explains why animals have to die for humanity's sins.

In the eyes of a holy God, sin is a capital offense. But God says he will accept the death of animals as a substitute for humans.

> *"The life of each creature is in its blood. So I have given you the blood of animals to pay for your sin on the altar."*
>
> LEVITICUS **17:11** NIrV

Killing an animal and burning it engages a wagonload of senses:

// the sight of the animal's throat being cut
// the sound of its squeal
// the slippery touch of the blood, and
// the barbecue aroma of burning meat.

Each sense grips the soul in a graphic reminder that as far as God is concerned, sin is deadly serious.

HOLOCAUST OFFERING. That's another name for the burnt offering. *Holocaust* means "completely burned up." It's from the Greek *holocaustos*: *holo* (whole), *kaustos* (burnt). That's also why the execution of the Jews during World War II is called the Holocaust. Bodies of millions were incinerated.

· ·

WORLD'S FIRST SACRIFICE. In the beginning, sin was a capital offense. God warned Adam and Eve if they ate the forbidden fruit, "You will die" (Genesis 3:3). In time, they did—which is how some speculate death entered God's perfect creation. But before they died because of their sin, a critter died because of their sin. After sinning, they grew embarrassed about their nakedness. To hide that effect of their sin, "God made clothing from animal skins for Adam and his wife" (Genesis 3:21). It was the first time an animal died for the sins of people.

Adam and Eve in leathers

JEWISH SACRIFICES

God sets up an elaborate system of sacrifices—rituals allowing the Jews to express not only regret for their sins.

Scattered through Leviticus are sacrifices to thank God for help, to celebrate peace and prosperity, and even to seek forgiveness from neighbors. But the how-to manual for the most common sacrifices shows up in the first seven chapters.

	NAME OF SACRIFICE	WHAT'S OFFERED	WHAT HAPPENS	REASON	FIND IT IN LEVITICUS
	BURNT	Rich people: bull* Others: sheep, goat Poor: dove or pigeon	The animal is cut up and burned on the altar.	Atones for sin and ritually cleans the worshipper	1:1–17 6:8–13
	GRAIN	Baked goods, roasted kernels	Priest burns some of it and keeps the rest as salary.	Thanks God for the harvest	2:1–16 6:14–23
	PEACE	Grain or livestock (sheep, goats, cattle)	Part of the offering is burned. Part goes to the priest as salary. Worshipper eats the rest with family and guests.	Thanks God for something noteworthy, such as birth of a child	3:1–17 7:11–36
	ACCIDENTAL SIN	Priest: bull Others: goat or female sheep	Priest burns the fat and keeps the meat as salary.	Purifies a person who sinned without meaning to.	4:1–5:13 6:24–30 16:3–22
	RESTITUTION (OR GUILT)	Ram (male sheep) or value of the ram, and value of property damaged plus 20 percent	Priest burns part of ram and keeps the rest along with the fine.	Makes restitution to God or a person. To God for desecration of something sacred. To a person for some wrongdoing.	5:14–6:7 7:1–7

All sacrificial animals must be free of disease or other obvious defects. Worshippers are often instructed to lay hands on the animal, to symbolically transfer their sins to the animal (see Leviticus 16:21). Some of the blood is poured on the altar, symbolizing spiritual cleansing of sin.

Israel's first priest

THERE'S NO ORGANIZED RELIGION for the Jews— not until the Exodus refugees reach Mount Sinai. Earlier, in the days of Abraham, Isaac, and Jacob, each man of the house (or tent) served as the family priest, offering sacrifices to God.

But at Mount Sinai, everything changes. God organizes religion. He has a tent worship center built, and he puts the tribe of Levi in charge of taking care of it. As for who will lead the worship rituals, including the sacrifices, God picks a single family from the Levi tribe: Aaron (the older brother of Moses) and his descendants.

Aaron will serve as Israel's first high priest, and his sons will assist him as lower-ranking priests. This is a family dynasty that will continue for almost a thousand years. Only descendants of Aaron will serve as priests. And they will serve until Babylonians destroy Jerusalem's Temple in 586 BC.

AUTOMATIC DISQUALIFICATIONS. Aaron's descendants couldn't serve as a priest if they were married to a divorcée or prostitute. The high priest couldn't even marry a widow; she had to be a virgin. Physical defects also disqualified them, including blindness, crippled arms or legs, along with skin diseases (see Leviticus 21).

URIM AND THUMMIN (LEVITICUS 8:8). These were mysterious objects the high priest carried and used when seeking direction from God. The objects may have provided "yes" or "no" answers, a bit like the flip of a coin does. Jews taught that God controlled the outcome.

AARON'S MIRACLE ALMONDS / An almond tree blossoms. That's what happened to Aaron's staff one night. To stop questions about the right of Aaron to lead the people as high priest, Moses collected wooden staffs from each of the 12 tribal leaders. He put them in the tent worship center, by the chest called the Ark of the Covenant, which held the 10 Commandments. The next day, Aaron's staff "had sprouted, budded, blossomed, and produced ripe almonds!" (Numbers 17:8).

Kosher meat only

JUST SAY NO to buttered lobster. Observant Jews do.

But they've got God's go-ahead for crunching down on deep-fried grasshoppers and salted crickets.

In what could sound like a divine joke or a streak of anti-Semitism, God sets up a Jewish menu that takes some fine delicacies off the table and serves up insects instead.

God doesn't explain why some meat makes the menu while other meat doesn't. But he does explain why Jews can't eat a red, juicy steak—or any other meat with blood in it:

"Blood is life. That is why blood pays for your sin. So I say to the people of Israel, 'You must not eat meat that still has blood in it'" (Leviticus 17:11–12 NIrV).

(continued next page)

WHY KOSHER LAWS?

Some Bible experts speculate it might be because of health concerns. Pork, which is off the menu, is more likely to harbor dangerous parasites than other meats—especially the larvae of a worm called Trichinella. Other experts say God is focused mainly on teaching the Jews to obey him, and on creating customs that set Jews apart from other people—so the world knows these are his people.

FRESH MEAT / An osprey—also known as a sea hawk—swoops up a kosher meal. Fish with scales and fins are among the animals Jews are allowed to eat. The osprey isn't. It's on the list of forbidden birds, along with other kinds of hawks and birds of prey.

KOSHER—ALLOWED	NOT KOSHER—FORBIDDEN

TROUT

FISH WITH SCALES AND FINS:

Salmon, trout, bass, tuna, grouper, halibut

BUTTERED CRAB

FISH WITHOUT SCALES AND FINS, ALONG WITH SHELLFISH:

Catfish, dolphin, shrimp, oyster, crab

DEER (AKA BAMBI)

ANIMALS WITH SPLIT HOOVES AND THAT CHEW THE CUD*:

Cattle, sheep, goats, deer

ALL OTHER MAMMALS

Pig, rabbit, donkey, camel

DUCK

ALL BIRDS NOT ON THE "FORBIDDEN" LIST:

Chicken, turkey, duck, quail, dove

EAGLE

SCAVENGERS AND BIRDS OF PREY:

Vulture, hawk, osprey, eagle

GRASSHOPPER

INSECTS WITH WINGS AND JOINTED LEGS THAT CAN JUMP:

Locusts, crickets, grasshoppers

LADYBUG

INSECTS WITH WINGS THAT CAN'T JUMP:

Ants (chocolate-covered or plain), beetles

Cud: Food in stomach that returns to mouth for a second chewing. On purpose.

Day of forgiveness

IT'S THE HOLIEST DAY OF THE YEAR for Jews. They call this autumn day *Yom Kippur* (yahm KIP er). That's Hebrew for "Day of Atonement."

The Bible says God set up this annual holy day during the Exodus. He intended it as a way of calling his people to repentance for their sins during the past year. He wanted to purify them—to wipe the slate clean.

The Day of Atonement takes place on the tenth day of the Jewish lunar month called Tishri, putting it in September or October. Jews are to treat this like the Sabbath—no work allowed.

It's on this day that Aaron, the high priest, enters the most holy room in the tent worship center. The room where the Jews store their most sacred object: the Ark of the Covenant, the chest holding the 10 Commandments. Aaron and high priests after him sacrifice a bull to cover any inadvertent sins he and his family may have committed during the past year. And he sprinkles some of its blood on the sacred chest. He does the same with the blood of a goat, sacrificed for the people.

A second goat, famous as the scapegoat, symbolically carries away the sins of the people. Aaron lays "both of his hands on the goat's head. . . . In this way, he will transfer the people's sins to the head of the goat" (Leviticus 16:21).

AZAZEL (LEVITICUS 16:8). Is it a demon, a barren place, or a goat? Bible experts don't agree. Some say it's the wilderness where Jews drove the goat. Others say it's a name for the animal: "goat of removal," aka "scapegoat." Still others say it's the name of a demon or the devil—which could be a bit like the Jews telling their sins, symbolized by the goat, to go to hell.

▲ **FORESHADOWING JESUS.** One New Testament writer says the Day of Atonement rituals point to Jesus as both the high priest and sacrifice. "He entered the Most Holy Room by spilling his own blood. He did it once and for all time. He paid the price to set us free from sin forever" (Hebrews 9:12 NIrV).

◄ **SCAPEGOAT.** Jews chase off a goat, running it into the barren Sinai badlands on the Day of Atonement (Yom Kippur). The goat symbolizes the sins they've committed during the past year. And they want nothing more to do with their sins or the goat.

Happy holy holidays

GOD LIKES TO PARTY, it seems—in a good way.

The clue is that he sets up a calendar tagged with religious holidays. Most are intended to give the Jews an opportunity to express their happiness. As in happiness for food at harvest time. Or for God's long history of taking care of the Jewish people.

There's a cycle to the holidays.

Most come once a year, like Passover and the Jewish New Year's Day. All but the solemn Day of Atonement (Yom Kippur) are happy times of celebration with food, music, and dancing.

The Sabbath comes weekly, from sunset on Friday through sunset on Saturday. Jews rest and worship. No work. Not even cooking.

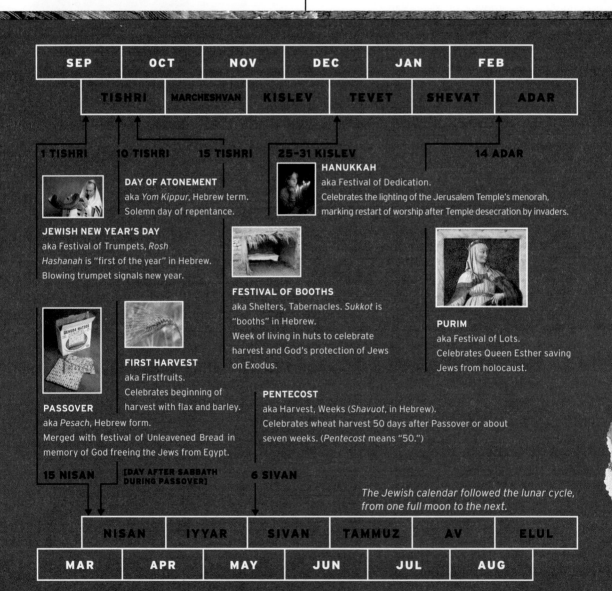

SEP	OCT	NOV	DEC	JAN	FEB

TISHRI	MARCHESHVAN	KISLEV	TEVET	SHEVAT	ADAR

1 TISHRI   **10 TISHRI**   **15 TISHRI**   **25-31 KISLEV**   **14 ADAR**

DAY OF ATONEMENT
aka *Yom Kippur*, Hebrew term. Solemn day of repentance.

HANUKKAH
aka Festival of Dedication.
Celebrates the lighting of the Jerusalem Temple's menorah, marking restart of worship after Temple desecration by invaders.

JEWISH NEW YEAR'S DAY
aka Festival of Trumpets, *Rosh Hashanah* is "first of the year" in Hebrew. Blowing trumpet signals new year.

FESTIVAL OF BOOTHS
aka Shelters, Tabernacles. *Sukkot* is "booths" in Hebrew.
Week of living in huts to celebrate harvest and God's protection of Jews on Exodus.

PURIM
aka Festival of Lots.
Celebrates Queen Esther saving Jews from holocaust.

FIRST HARVEST
aka Firstfruits.
Celebrates beginning of harvest with flax and barley.

PENTECOST
aka Harvest, Weeks (*Shavuot*, in Hebrew).
Celebrates wheat harvest 50 days after Passover or about seven weeks. (*Pentecost* means "50.")

PASSOVER
aka *Pesach*, Hebrew form.
Merged with festival of Unleavened Bread in memory of God freeing the Jews from Egypt.

15 NISAN   **[DAY AFTER SABBATH DURING PASSOVER]**   **6 SIVAN**

The Jewish calendar followed the lunar cycle, from one full moon to the next.

NISAN	IYYAR	SIVAN	TAMMUZ	AV	ELUL

MAR	APR	MAY	JUN	JUL	AUG

Contract with carrots, sticks

A DEAL THEY CAN'T REFUSE. That's what God offers the Jewish refugees. They're barely a nation. Just getting organized. They don't even have a king, except God.

Yet God promises them heaven on earth—as long as they comply with the laws he has given them.

If they don't, the consequences become hell on earth.

Sounds like a no-brainer.

OBEY GOD AND ENJOY:

// peace—no need to lock doors

// an enemy-free zone—100 Jews will chase away 10,000 enemies

// bumper crops in nonstop harvests from early spring to late fall

// lots of kids to help with the harvest

DISOBEY AND SUFFER:

// disease

// rainless skies and parched earth

// raiders stealing crops and livestock

// defeat by enemies

God further warns that if these tough consequences don't turn them back to compliance, life will get even tougher.

"I will scatter you among the nations and bring out my sword against you. Your land will become desolate, and your cities will lie in ruins. . . . You will die among the foreign nations and be devoured in the land of your enemies" (Leviticus 26:33, 38).

COLORFUL CARROTS. Researchers have bred carrots that cover most colors in the rainbow. God urges the Jews to obey his laws by promising an even wider array of carrots as a reward—including peace, prosperity, and one big harvest after another.

FAST-FORWARD TO BROKEN CONTRACT. Several centuries after Moses, in 586 BC, Jews lose their homeland—just as God said they would if they persisted in disobeying him. Babylonian invaders from what is now Iraq overran the Jewish nation and exiled the surviving citizens.

HOPE BEYOND THE CONTRACT. God promised that if the worst happened—defeat and exile—he'd still not abandon the Jews. "I will not cancel my covenant with them by wiping them out" (Leviticus 21:44).

LOTS OF GRAPES, NO WRATH. God vows there'll be grapes for the plucking in the Promised Land if Jews honor their agreement to serve him. But if they break their word, he warns, they'll experience more than sour grapes.

BIG SCENE
LAND OF PLENTY

NUMBERS 13:25–35

Camped on the border of Canaan, Moses sends scouts to find out what's ahead. Scouts bring back evidence of a fertile land. They also tell tall tales of giants and walled cities, which terrify the Jews.

BIBLE HISTORY

ALL DATES APPROXIMATE

1440 BC
Jews leave Egyptian slavery

1400 BC
Jews invade Canaan

WORLD HISTORY

Egyptian children learn to write by copying ancient Egyptian works
1400 BC

Pharaoh Akhenaton sets up one-god worship: sun god Aton
1350 BC

NUMBERS

SENTENCE: 40 YEARS IN THE BADLANDS

STORY LINE

AFTER CAMPING A YEAR AT MOUNT SINAI, the Jews, newly equipped with God's laws, are now organized into a 12-tribe nation.

They break camp and head north some 200 miles (322 km) to the Kadesh oasis near Canaan's southern border.

Moses chooses a dozen men, one from each tribe, and orders them to scout out Canaan and bring back a report about what lies ahead.

The majority report of 10 scouts accents the negative: Canaanite giants along with cities protected by huge walls. Two scouts—Joshua and Caleb—accent the positive: fertile land and God's reliable promise that it will all be theirs.

Terrified, the people refuse to invade. For such blatant lack of trust, despite the miracles they've seen God do, God sentences them to 40 years in the badlands. They have to stay in their self-imposed refugee camp until the entire generation of adults dies. Of the adults, only Moses, Joshua, and Caleb will live to see the Promised Land.

Sentence served, Generation Next fights their way through hostile nations before arriving on the east side of the Jordan River, in what is now the Arab country of Jordan. It will become the staging ground for their invasion.

// **LOCATION:** The story starts at the foot of Mount Sinai and ends in Moab, today's Jordan, with the Jews getting ready to invade their ancient homeland of Canaan.

// **TIME:** The story covers 40 years—in either the 1400s BC or the 1200s BC. Scholars debate which.

// **AUTHOR:** Unknown. Ancient Jewish tradition points to Moses. But there's at least one line he probably didn't write: "Moses was very humble—more humble than any other person on earth" (Numbers 12:3). If he wrote that, he wasn't especially humble.

1290 BC
*Alternate date
of Exodus start*

*First mention of Israel: Egyptian King Merneptah
says he invaded, wiped them out*
1210 BC

Moses, the census taker

ON THE BRINK OF LAUNCHING AN INVASION, the Jews take a census. Just a partial one. God tells Moses to count only the men fit to fight, and 20 years of age or older. He's to skip the Levites, the tribe devoted to maintaining the tent worship center.

Moses delegates the job. He turns to each tribal leader—the head of each extended family. There are actually 13 tribes of Israel, counting the Levites, not 12. Each tribe is made up of descendants from Jacob's dozen sons. But Jacob's favorite son, Joseph, who became what amounts to a prime minister in Egypt, produced two tribes. They don't bear Joseph's name. Instead, they bear the names of his two sons, Ephraim and Manasseh.

But when it comes to fighting, and when it would come time to divide Canaan among the tribes, Levi doesn't count. They don't fight. And they won't get any plug of territory. Instead, they'll live in 48 cities scattered throughout the land—so all the Jews are relatively close to a worship leader.

The census tally comes in at 603,550. This represents "all the men of Israel who were twenty years old or older and able to go to war" (Numbers 1:45).

TALLY-HO / Before pressing on to Canaan, Moses takes count of how many men he has of fighting age. Final count: 603,550.

TRIBE SIZE.
Judah has the most able-bodied soldiers and will eventually become Israel's dominant tribe.

Tribe	Soldiers
Judah	74,600
Dan	62,700
Simeon	59,300
Zebulun	57,400
Issachar	54,400
Naphtali	53,400
Reuben	46,500
Gad	45,650
Asher	41,500
Ephraim, son of Joseph	40,500
Benjamin	35,400
Manasseh, son of Joseph	32,200

603,550 SOLDIERS.
Though some scholars take this number literally, many don't. For theories about how to interpret this number, see note on page 40.

Adultery test: drink dirt

WOMEN ONLY are the subjects of a strange trial by ordeal called "the test of the bitter water."

If a man and woman are caught having an adulterous affair, both "must be put to death" (Leviticus 20:10). But what if a husband only suspects his wife is having an affair?

Jewish law allows the man to take his wife to the priest who performs the test of the bitter water. The jealous husband also brings a jealousy offering: about two quarts or liters of barley flour, which the priest burns.

The priest takes some holy water, probably from one of the worship center's basins used to wash sacrificial animals. Then he adds dirt from the worship center—holy dirt, some might call it.

There's one more ingredient: the ink of a curse. The priest writes a curse onto leather and then scrapes it into the water. This curse asks that the water not harm the woman if she is innocent; but if she is guilty, it asks that the water will swell her stomach and leave her unable to have children.

That's the punishment. Infertility. It appears the matter is left in God's hands. Some scholars speculate that this trial by ordeal, relatively harmless compared to other such trials of the day, is a way to placate a jealous husband during a time when men rule and might otherwise take violent action.

TOASTING THE JEALOUS HUSBAND / For the husband who thinks his wife had an affair, God creates an infidelity test that placates the man and spares the woman serious injury. She drinks a sanctified cocktail: holy water, sacred dirt, and a paragraph of ink scraped off a leather scroll.

▶ **HOW TO PROVE MARITAL FAITHFULNESS BY WALKING ON WATER.** Some ancient trials by ordeal were lethal. Hammurabi's law code, written several hundred years before Moses, used a trial by river. The accused jumped in the river. If they drowned, they were guilty. In similar tests popular during the Crusades, judges tied flour-grinding millstones onto the accused—like adding sinkers on a line of fish bait.

SWOLLEN BELLY. Some commentators say the infidelity test makes perfect sense when it talks about a swollen belly or infertility. If the woman is guilty, her stomach could swell in pregnancy—or she might become infertile because of a sexually transmitted disease. "Rotting thigh" is the literal translation of the curse, which some scholars interpret as infertility.

Fast food: manna and quail

ONE YEAR INTO FREEDOM, the Jews break camp at the foot of Mount Sinai and set out for the Promised Land of Canaan, now called Israel.

Three weeks into their march, many refugees are grumbling.

"Oh, for some meat!" they complain. "We remember the fish we used to eat for free in Egypt. And we had all the cucumbers, melons, leeks, onions, and garlic we wanted" (Numbers 11:4–5).

Their current diet is mostly manna, mysterious flakes that appear each morning. *Manna* is Hebrew for "What is it?" The Jews crush the flakes to flour and make flat cakes of sweet bread.

Now they want more. They want meat.

"The LORD sent a wind that brought quail from the sea and let them fall all around the camp. For miles in every direction there were quail flying about three feet [one meter] above the ground" (Numbers 11:31).

It's easy picking when a bird flies no higher than a changeup, low and inside.

Meat-famished refugees pluck birds from the air. "No one gathered less than fifty bushels" (Numbers 11:32).

That means leftovers. In the desert badlands. With no refrigeration.

"Severe plague" (Numbers 11:33) follows. The writer of Numbers says the plague expressed God's anger at the complaining people. Some Bible experts say it may also express the danger of eating spoiled meat.

FAST FOOD FLOWN IN / Springtime quail the Jews ate were probably the stubby quarter-pounders that still migrate from Africa to Europe each spring.

Weak fliers, they lumber low and slow during their marathon migration. The Bible puts their altitude at three feet (one meter), adding that a wind blew them off course—and probably exhausted them as well.

Ancient pictures show Egyptians catching them with their bare hands. That may be how the Jews plucked them from the air, too.

Quail, after the hunt

MANNA BUG / Plant-sucking mealy bugs similar to these may have produced sweet balls of manna that dried into white flakes, some scholars speculate. The largest bug here, sipping on a red plant, excretes two red balls of nectar. No, they're not eyeballs. Wrong end.

QUARTER-POUNDER TO GO / The stubby quail with a repeating name *Coturnix coturnix* weighs in at a quarter pound (113 grams) and stretches half the length of a foot-long doggy (15 cm). Migrating ancestors of this bird, many say, fed the meat-hungry Exodus crowd.

MYSTERY MEAL.

From the Bible's description of manna, botanists have speculated about what it might have been. The description from Numbers 11 and Exodus 16:

> like small coriander seeds (about the size of a pea)
> pale yellow like tree sap
> falls overnight with the dew
> picked up from the ground
> tastes sweet like honey wafers
> crushed into flour
> made into sweet-tasting flat cakes of bread

Two theories get most of the ink among Bible commentators:

Bug juice. The manna, some say, might be pea-sized sugary secretions from aphid-like insects called "manna mealy-bugs" or "tamarisk manna scale" insects (*Trabutina mannipara*). The females suck sap from Sinai tamarisk trees (*Tamarix gallica*) in May and June. Put bluntly, their sap secretions are sweet balls of bug poop. The balls dry into pale-colored flakes that encrust the stems. Traveling herders in the Sinai call the flakes "manna." They use it as gourmet sweetener.

Tree sap. Others say it may be the sweet sap from a variety of trees and bushes, including the tamarisk, the camel thorn (*Alhagi maurorum*) and the flowering ash (*Fraxinus ornus*).

FOOD POISONING.

Bacteria spoils unrefrigerated meat. Eaten, spoiled meat can produce symptoms in two to six hours: cramps, diarrhea, fever, nausea, and vomiting. Some food poisoning, such as botulism, left untreated, can kill. This may have been the plague the Jews suffered after eating the quail, say some Bible experts.

Intel report: mission impossible

FINALLY, about a year and a half after escaping Egypt, the Jewish refugees arrive at Canaan's border. They camp in the Wilderness of Paran at Kadesh oasis. The likely oasis, many say, is on Egypt's side of the border with today's Israel.

Moses sends a dozen scouts ahead into Canaan, one scout from each tribe. Their mission: gather intelligence.

CANAANITES. Are there a lot of them? Are they weak or strong?

CITIES. Protected by walls or open like camps?

LAND. Good for farms and pasture or good for nothing?

CROPS. Bring back samples.

Scouts spend 40 days venturing at least as far north as Hebron, a distance of about 75 miles (120 kilometers). They return with good news and bad news.

The land is wonderful. Plenty of crops. But the people are strong. They live in cities surrounded by thick walls. Giants walk among them.

Only two scouts recommend invasion: Joshua and Caleb. The other 10 spread so much fear that the masses revolt against Moses. Like a spent donkey, they refuse to take another step forward.

God grants them their wish. For 40 years. He sentences them to stay put until a newer, braver generation grows up.

Camped at Kadesh oasis, Moses sends spies ahead to scout Canaan.

GIANTS.
These were the descendants of Anak, a warrior hero famous for his height. Think NBA player. Maybe shorter. Burial remains suggest that most men in the region stretched anywhere from 5 feet 7 inches to 6 feet (170–183cm), taller than previously believed.

40-YEAR SENTENCE.
The entire generation of adults who refused to invade died in the desert. Only Moses, Joshua, and Caleb lived to see the Promised Land.

◄ HEALTH FOOD.
Jewish scouts bring Moses a sample of the late-summer harvest in Canaan. That's the good news—the harvest is huge. Unfortunately, so are some of the farmers. "Next to them," the scouts report, "we felt like grasshoppers" (Numbers 13:33).

Revolt of wanna-be priests

A GANG of 250 Jewish leaders follow a single man—Korah—into a revolt against Moses and Aaron.

Korah is from the same tribe as Moses and Aaron. He's a Levite. Not priests, Levites were from the extended family responsible for taking care of the tent worship center. But that's not good enough for him. He challenges the right of Moses and Aaron to lead.

His argument: "This entire community is holy and GOD is in their midst. So why do you act like you're running the whole show?" (Numbers 16:3 MSG).

"Holy" is a clue that Korah thinks he's good enough to serve as a priest, many scholars say.

Moses decides that if Korah and his insurgents want to be promoted to the priesthood, let them audition before God. After all, the Bible says it was God who chose Aaron's family as priests.

Moses tells the 250 leaders to bring metal containers of burning incense to the worship center. That's a priest's job—presenting fragrant incense offerings to the Lord.

God cracks open the ground and swallows up Korah and two other top leaders of the revolt. As for the rest of the rebels who thought it would be okay to bring fire to God, he brings fire to them.

Whether it comes as lightning or something otherworldly, it burns them to death.

Hardened frankincense tree sap

Incense burner

INCENSE. One of the sacrificial offerings God set up was the burning of fragrant incense, a function that only priests could perform. God even provided the recipe: one part each of sweet-smelling tree sap (perhaps myrrh), onycha (from Red Sea mollusks), sap from flowering galbanum plants, and frankincense sap from Boswellia trees.

GOD'S TRAPDOOR. In a part of the world scarred with quake-producing fault lines, the earth cracks open and swallows Jews who rebel against the leadership of Moses and Aaron.

There's water in the rock

GOD OVERREACTS and dooms Moses to death, vowing that the Jewish leader will never step foot in the Promised Land. So it certainly seems—at least to many readers of one famous story in the Bible.

The Jews are nearing the end of their 40-year sentence in the badlands south of Canaan. They've run out of water, just like they did at the same location in a story reported in Exodus 17. They're complaining, too, like they've done a lot throughout the trip.

In the Exodus story, God tells Moses to strike a rock, promising that water will burst out. He does, and it does. In the Numbers story, God tells Moses to simply talk to the rock, promising that water will burst out. Instead, Moses thumps the rock with his wooden staff. Twice. And he tells off the people. Perhaps worse, he seems to take credit for the miracle.

"Listen, you rebels!" he shouts. "Must we bring you water from this rock?" (Numbers 20:10).

Something Moses does or doesn't do tips God over. Without explaining what it is, God simply says, "Because you did not trust me enough to demonstrate my holiness to the people of Israel, you will not lead them into the land I am giving them!" (Numbers 20:12).

MERIBAH.

This is the name of the place where Moses produced water from rock, after the Jews complained about not having water. In Hebrew, *Meribah* means "argue." Location is uncertain. Some say it's the new name Moses gave for the oasis they had been camping at for 40 years: Kadesh. Others say it was nearby.

RERUN FROM EXODUS 17, WITH AN ALTERNATE ENDING?

The nearly identical stories of "water in the rock" are different versions of the same story, many Bible experts say. Others say it's two stories in one location, separated by decades. In Exodus, Moses hits the rock at Meribah and water comes out; no punishment mentioned.

THEORY ABOUT WHAT GOT GOD ANGRY.

Moses didn't follow God's instructions. And at this early stage when the Jews are learning the importance of obeying God, disobedience from a leader is a big deal.

ROCK WATER. Water hides in a rock crevice in the badlands of southern Israel. When Moses hit a rock with his staff, producing water, some wonder if he broke through a thin layer to expose a spring below. Desert-savvy herders sometimes find small pockets of water inside porous rocks by noticing dampness on cracks in the rock.

Snake-bit, snake-healed

COMPLAINING ABOUT GOD'S COOKING gets the Jews in big trouble. God sends poisonous snakes to bite the life out of them.

In the backstory, the Jews have left Kadesh oasis, bound for the Promised Land. For some unexplained reason, they decide to take the long route. Again. Just as they had done to get to Kadesh (see map page 43).

Now, instead of heading north into Canaan, they head east, apparently intending to enter Canaan from what is now Jordan. Perhaps Moses wants to avoid another fight in Canaan's southland; they've already fought at least three battles—and lost two (see Numbers 14:45; 21:1–3).

Moses sends ambassadors to Edom, asking for permission to pass through their land peacefully. Edom refuses. So Moses decides to detour around the nation.

That requires turning south—into the harshest part of the badlands. This is where the Jews complain about the lack of food and water. And as for God's miracle food: "We hate this horrible manna!" (Numbers 21:5).

They repent when the snakes arrive. God tells Moses to make a bronze snake, saying when snake-bit people look at it, they'll be healed.

SNAKE CROSSING

SNAKES ON A PLAIN / Refused passage through Edom, Jews turn south where they encounter an infestation of poisonous snakes.

ANCIENT REMEDY FOR SNAKEBITE. Earwax. That's the remedy reported by Pliny, first-century Roman author of a series of books called *Natural History*.

WHY A BRONZE SNAKE? The Bible doesn't say. Some scholars speculate it could have boosted the faith of the people by giving them something visible to look at.

DEVIL OF A SNAKE / The horned viper is one of a half-dozen species of poisonous snakes in Israel's badlands—along with the Egyptian cobra.

Balaam and his talking donkey

MOSES AND THE JEWS finish their long detour around Edom. They camp on the plains of Moab—in full view of nervous locals living in villages on the hills.

The king is worried. "This mob is going to clean us out—a bunch of crows picking a carcass clean" (Numbers 22:4 MSG). So he hires a crow-killer—Balaam—a famous seer living by the Euphrates River, some 400 miles (644 kilometers) away. He wants Balaam to put a curse on the Jews so the Moabite army can drive them off.

On the trip south, Balaam's donkey sees something invisible to the seer: an angel with a sword blocking their path. The irony is that God lets a dumb jackass see what a renowned seer can't.

The donkey refuses to go ahead. Balaam beats it. And the donkey asks, "What have I ever done to you that you have beat me these three times?" (Numbers 22:28 MSG). Suddenly, the seer sees the angel.

On God's orders, Balaam not only refuses to curse the Jews, he blesses them—four times—predicting their victory.

MOAB.
A nation east of the Dead Sea, in what is now the Arab country of Jordan (see map page 67). Later the homeland of Ruth, great-grandmother of one of Israel's most famous kings: David.

BALAAM'S DEATH.
Jews killed Balaam later during a battle with Midian, a nation in what is now parts of Jordan and Saudi Arabia (see Numbers 31).

ANCIENT EVIDENCE OF BALAAM.
Archaeologists found an inscription in Jordan a few miles east of the Jordan River, near where the Jews camped. Dating to roughly 850–700 BC, it says Balaam was a "seer of the gods" who received messages from them.

NOW A FEW WORDS FROM THE DONKEY /
Sure-footed donkeys were a preferred mode of travel for the well-to-do in Bible times. In one famous story, a donkey saves his master's life by refusing to take another step. Then they chat. Argue, actually.

Battles before the invasion

MOSES AND HIS PEACE-LOVING JEWS ask only to pass through the lands east of the Jordan River, in what is now the Arab country of Jordan. They even promise to stay on the main road.

But nobody seems to trust them. Amorites are the first to attack. But the Jews crush their army and take their land.

Then comes one of the giants the earlier generation of Jews had feared: King Og, ruler of 60 walled cities in Bashan, now southern Syria. Same results.

Moab is the exception. They don't want the Jews there. But failing to get the seer Balaam to curse the Jews, Moab's king orders his army to stand down. It's the Moabite women who bring down their nation. They seduce some of the Jewish men into sex rituals to entertain the local fertility god, Baal. For this, the Jews kill the offenders.

Much the same happens with Midian, farther south—for the same sin of luring Jews into idol worship. Five Midian kings form a coalition army determined to defend their land or die trying. They die trying.

Jews now control all the land along Canaan's eastern border.

▲ **SEDUCED TO DEATH.** Women of Moab seduce Jewish men into sexual fertility rites, in worship of the god Baal. For that, the people of Moab lose their lives and their land.

GIANT KING OG. He slept in an iron bed more than 13 feet long and 6 feet wide (4 meters by 2 meters).

BAAL. Canaanite god of fertility in family, fields, and flock. (See photo page 42.)

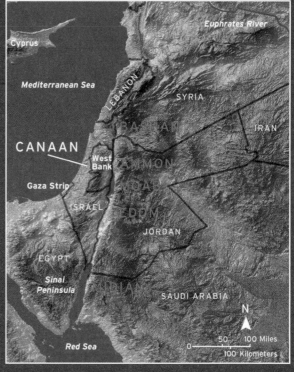

▲ **BLOODLETTING.** Attacked, the Jewish refugees defend themselves. In the process, they defeat four nations on Canaan's eastern border, along with Midian in the south. Some Jews settle there, in what are now Jordan and Syria.

DEUTERONOMY 34:1–5

Now 120 years old, Moses climbs Mount Nebo. There, he admires the vista across the Jordan River Valley in what is now Israel. Then he dies.

BIG SCENE

MOSES SEES THE PROMISED LAND

BIBLE HISTORY	**1440 BC** *Jews leave Egypt*	**1400 BC** *Moses dies*
WORLD HISTORY	*Egypt's Thutmose III defeats Hittites in Canaan* **1468 BC**	*Seaport trade thrives in Phoenician cities of Tyre and Sidon (Lebanon)* **1400 BC**

ALL DATES APPROXIMATE

DEUTERONOMY

THE LAST WORD OF MOSES: OBEY

STORY LINE

HOME IS A HALF-DAY WALK AWAY. Just across the Jordan River. Yet Canaan, today called Israel, is a strange land to the Jewish refugees.

Jews have spent most of the last five centuries in Egypt: 430 years along the Nile River—part of that as slaves—and another 40 in the badlands south of Canaan's border.

Moses freed them. Then he led them during those 40 years. Now, at age 120, he's about to die.

Deuteronomy records his last words and actions.

His last words are a history lesson. Most of the Jews were children when the Exodus out of Egypt began. Of all the adults age 20 and older who left Egypt, only Moses, Joshua, and Caleb are still breathing. So Moses tells Generation Next the stories of how God brought them out of Egypt and protected them along the way.

He reminds them, too, of the agreement their parents made with God. It's a covenant promise to obey his laws, in return for his divine protection.

In a solemn ceremony, Moses leads the nation in a ritual of renewing that covenant—to make it personal for each of them, so they know this promise is for their generation, too.

In his last act, Moses appoints his successor, a man chosen by God: Joshua. His credentials seem a perfect match for the job ahead. He's a warrior with absolute trust in God. He will need both for the final leg of the journey: the invasion of Canaan.

// LOCATION: Near Canaan's eastern border, across the Jordan River in what is now the Arab nation of Jordan.

// TIME: Bible experts debate which century: 1400s BC or 1200s BC.

// AUTHOR: Unknown. Ancient Jewish tradition says Moses wrote this book and the four before it. Much of Deuteronomy reports the speeches of Moses.

1250 BC
Alternate date for invasion of Canaan

Gold idol of Phoenicia

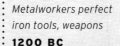
Metalworkers perfect iron tools, weapons
1200 BC

Most important beliefs

LIKE A GRANDPA telling stories to his grandchildren, 120-year-old Moses begins spinning the tale of how they all got to this point in their journey, on the eastern banks of the Jordan River.

Moses traces their steps out of Egypt, to Mount Sinai, and to the nearly 40 years they spent at Kadesh oasis—and why they had to stay there for so long. It's a tale of what happens when the Jews obey God, and what happens when they don't.

Then Moses launches into what he may consider the most important last words he has for this new generation.

"Listen carefully to these decrees and regulations that I am about to teach you. Obey them so that you may live, so you may enter and occupy the land that the LORD, the God of your ancestors, is giving you" (Deuteronomy 4:1).

The audience had grown up in Kadesh because their parents disobeyed God. That must have provided quite a motivation booster to do just as Moses said: Listen carefully.

Moses repeats the laws preserved in the books of Exodus, Leviticus, and Numbers—including the 10 Commandments. But of all the laws, none remains more revered among Jews than this one, which serves as their unofficial creed:

> *"The LORD is our God. The LORD is the one and only God. Love the LORD your God with all your heart and with all your soul. Love him with all your strength."*
> DEUTERONOMY 6:4–5 NIrV

▲ **FROM GENERATION TO GENERATION.**
A 100-year-old Jewish man gets a hug from his great-granddaughter. Moses told the Jews to memorize God's laws and pass them on: "Make sure your children learn them" (Deuteronomy 6:7 NIrV).

. . . .

***DEUTERONOMY*, THE WORD.**
It's from Greek, meaning "second law." Moses repeats the laws God gave the Jewish people, so the new generation will know them.

. . . .

▼ **GOD'S LAW IN A HEAD BOX.**
A Russian Jew, like many around the world, wears tiny scrolls of sacred Jewish laws inside phylacteries (*tefillin* in Hebrew)—leather boxes tied to his forehead and left arm. Moses told the Jews to tie the laws "to your hands and wear them on your forehead as reminders" (Deuteronomy 6:8). Many Jews, however, don't take this literally.

Worship 101

IMMIGRANTS BLEND IN as best they can when they move to a new land. At least that's the general rule. But it's not God's rule for the Jews. Not in Canaan.

"Do not fall into the trap of following their customs," Moses warns. "Do not inquire about their gods, saying, 'How do these nations worship their gods? I want to follow their example' " (Deuteronomy 12:30).

Canaanites worship idols, in temples and at outdoor shrines—often on hilltops. They offer sacrifices similar to the Jews, but some of the rituals seem disgusting. Infant sacrifice. Sex with temple prostitutes—performed as worship rituals honoring Baal, god of fertility among people, plants, and animals.

Moses says God wants the Jews to tear down all the pagan temples and shrines.

Unlike most other religions in the Middle East, Moses says the Jews will one day worship God in just one central place. In times past, they could offer sacrifices anywhere. At the moment, they worship at the tent worship center in the heart of the camp.

But sometime after they cross into Canaan, their pattern of worship will change. "You must seek the LORD your God at the place of worship he himself will choose from among all the tribes" (Deuteronomy 12:5).

HAIL TO THE CHIEF GOD / Canaanites worshipped a gallery of gods. But the top god was El, father of many gods, including his more famous son: Baal. (See picture of Baal, page 42.) This gold-covered figurine of El was excavated in the 1930s in Megiddo, a ruin in northern Israel.

▲ SEX AND WORSHIP.
Some scholars say the Canaanite sex rituals were intended to stimulate Baal to have sex. When he did, it rained. The rain, Canaanites seemed to believe, was his semen. And in this arid land during an agricultural era, lack of rain was a constant worry.

JEWISH HOLOCAUST IN REVERSE.
Moses said God ordered all Canaanites killed so they wouldn't pollute Jewish faith. Jews killed many, but not all. In time, some Jews adopted Canaanite religious practices. At least two kings sacrificed their children: Ahaz and his grandson Manasseh (see 2 Kings 16:2–3; 21:6)

JERUSALEM TEMPLE.
Jewish and Christian scholars say the worship center Moses predicted was the Temple that King Solomon built in Jerusalem several hundred years later, in the 900s BC.

Rules for the king

ISRAEL WON'T HAVE A KING for at least two centuries. Maybe more, depending on which scholars are right about when the Jews arrive in Canaan—in the 1400s BC or 1200s BC. But Moses is already warning the Jews about kings who abuse their power.

If the Jews decide they want a king—like other nations have—Moses warns that Israel's king better not be like those other kings.

Moses offers a checklist of do's and don'ts about Jewish kings.

DO:
- // let God choose the king
- // crown a Jew, not a foreigner
- // have the king write out a copy of God's laws in front of the priests
- // keep a copy of those laws and read some of them every day

DON'T:
- // let the king build a large stable of horses for himself
- // buy horses in Egypt—never go back there
- // let the king marry a lot of wives
- // let the king amass great wealth

Moses explains that these rules are intended to keep kings from thinking they're better than the people they're supposed to serve. Obeying these rules, Moses adds, "will ensure that he and his descendants will reign for many generations in Israel" (Deuteronomy 17:20).

Otherwise, don't count on it.

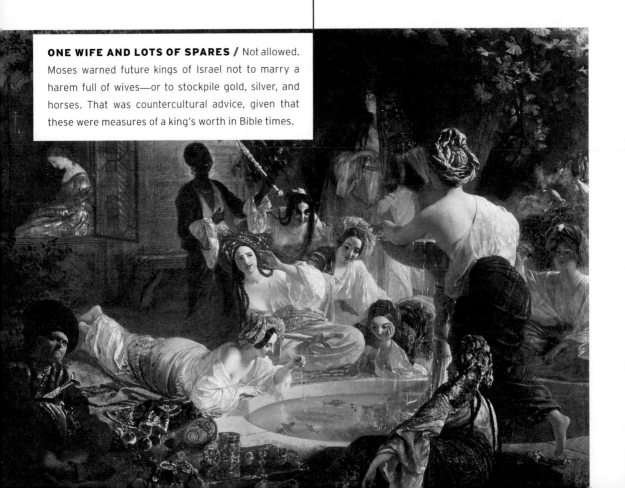

ONE WIFE AND LOTS OF SPARES / Not allowed. Moses warned future kings of Israel not to marry a harem full of wives—or to stockpile gold, silver, and horses. That was countercultural advice, given that these were measures of a king's worth in Bible times.

Perks and penalties

GOD WILL HAMMER THE JEWS if they don't honor their contract with him by obeying his laws, Moses warns. On the other hand, Moses says God will lavish them with prosperity if they do.

After carefully reviewing all the laws God gave the Jews at Mount Sinai and during the 40 years that followed—laws that appear in Exodus, Leviticus, and Numbers—Moses goes over what would amount to the fine print in contracts today: penalty clauses.

But first, he throws the spotlight on what marketers today would spotlight as well: the perks of the agreement.

If Jews obey God and keep his laws, they can expect: bumper crops at harvest, plenty of livestock, success in their ventures, big families, and protection from enemies.

If they break their promise to obey God, they can expect a gradual buildup of calamity. It'll start with crop failure, disease in herds and family, followed by raiders charging in to steal what little the Jews have left—even kidnapping wives and children.

In the end, if the Jews still don't come to their senses, "The LORD will scatter you among all the nations from one end of the earth to the other" (Deuteronomy 28:64). They will lose the Promised Land.

THE MORE THE MERRIER / Obeying God ensures happiness in Canaan, Moses promises: big families, plenty of livestock, and one whopper harvest after another.

▼ **ANCIENT TREATIES.** Rewards and punishments were common in ancient contracts in the Middle East between a ruler (suzerain) and a vassal pledged to servitude.

Jewish King Jehu bows before his overlord, King Shalmaneser III of Assyria.

PERKS OF A BIG FAMILY. Huge families are often a financial burden today. It was just the opposite in Bible times. The more children a man had, the more help he had with crops and livestock. And the more protection he had when threatened. Even as adults, children often lived near one another and worked as a family unit.

WORST-CASE SCENARIO. The prediction that God would scatter the Jews abroad was fulfilled in 586 BC, when Babylonians from what is now Iraq overran the nation, exiled the survivors, and wiped the Jewish nation off the political map. Jews were free to go home only after Persians from what is now Iran defeated Babylon 50 years later.

Moses' replacement

JOSHUA SHOULD HAVE BEEN GERSHOM. If Moses had followed the usual practice of the day, he would have put his oldest son in charge of the Jews. That's Gershom. Or perhaps his second son, Eliezar. Instead, he appointed Joshua.

The reason's simple. God chose Joshua: "Take Joshua. . .and publicly commission him to lead the people" (Numbers 27:18–19).

Moses assures the Jews that it's God who'll be doing the leading—just as he has done all along. Then Moses writes "this entire body of instruction" (Deuteronomy 31:9), presumably the laws preserved in Deuteronomy. And he gives it to the priests.

Finally, Moses climbs Mount Nebo. From there, God lets him see the Promised Land of Canaan—all the way across to the Mediterranean Sea. It's a land he'll never step foot in. But he can find joy in knowing that his people will.

He dies and is buried in a secret spot somewhere in a nearby valley. The people mourn him for a month. And through the centuries that follow, they revere him as one of a kind. "There has never again been a prophet in Israel like Moses. The LORD spoke face to face with him" (Deuteronomy 34:10 CEV).

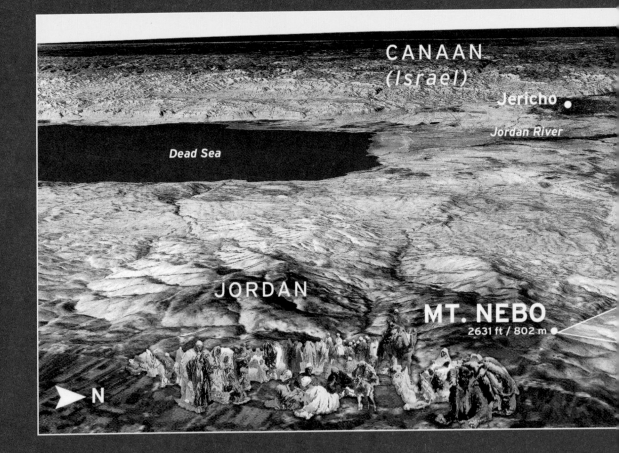

CANAAN (Israel)

Jericho

Jordan River

Dead Sea

JORDAN

MT. NEBO
2631 ft / 802 m

N

JOSHUA. A warrior from the beginning of the Exodus story, Joshua commanded the Jewish army in their first battle—against soldiers from Amalek (see Exodus 17). His expertise would come in handy during the invasion of Canaan.

BURIAL OF MOSES. Some ancient copies of Deuteronomy say God buried Moses. Others say "They" buried him, suggesting the Jews.

▲ **ONE LAST LOOK.** Standing on Mount Nebo, Moses looks across the Jordan River Valley to see the land where he will never set foot. He dies in what is now the Arab country of Jordan.

Acacia Grove

◄ **MOUNT NEBO.** Ten miles (16 kilometers) east of the Jordan River, Mount Nebo is part of the Pisgah mountain range that stretches alongside the Dead Sea and Jordan River. Locals call it by its Arabic name: *Jabal Naba* ("Mountain of Naba." *Naba* is perhaps a variation of Nebo).

Dead Sea

View from Mt. Nebo

BIG SCENE

TUMBLIN'

JOSHUA 6:20
With a shout, Jericho's double walls fall outward, some archaeologists say, creating ramps for Israelite invaders storming into the doomed border town.

J O S H U A

I N V A S I O N F O R C E

STORY LINE

TIME HAS COME for God to deliver on the promise he made to Abraham some 700 years earlier:

> *"I will give you and your family all the land you can see. It will be theirs forever!"*
> GENESIS 13:15 CEV

That land was Canaan—roughly the same area today as Israel along with Palestinian territories.

Abraham's extended family had just returned from more than 400 years in Egypt. They went there as guests to escape a drought in Canaan. But they ended up enslaved. Moses led them to freedom. Then, at age 120, he died.

That's where the book of Joshua starts.

It's up to Moses' successor, Joshua, to lead the Hebrews across the Jordan River and into Canaan. There, they begin a crusade to take back their homeland from pioneers who had settled there. The first city of many to fall is Jericho.

From there, the Jews turn south, destroying cities and coalition armies in the rugged highlands—where their lightly armed militia has the advantage over chariot forces and heavily armored infantry. Next, they do the same in the highlands up north, around the Sea of Galilee.

With the highlands conquered, Joshua orders each of the 12 tribes to mop up the resistance in their individual tribal areas.

// LOCATION: The story starts in what is now the Arab country of Jordan. Jewish invaders fight their way to what are now Israel and the West Bank (see map page 86).

// TIME: The story is set in the 1400s BC, or the 1200s BC. Scholars debate which.

// AUTHOR: Unknown. Because Joshua is the starring character and there are some scenes only he would have known about, ancient Jewish tradition says he wrote most of it.

1250 BC
*Alternate date
of invasion*

*Rameses II,
Exodus pharaoh?*
1270-1213 BC

*First known mention
of Israel, chisled in stone*
1210 BC

Spies take a business trip

IT'S TIME TO INVADE. Joshua sends two spies to scout Canaan's eastern border, but they end up in the house of Rahab, a prostitute.

Business or pleasure? The Bible doesn't say.

Rookie spies, they let it slip that they're gathering intelligence for the invasion force that left the Egyptian army drowning in the sea and that overpowered the nations east of the Jordan River.

Someone smuggles word to Jericho's king: "Israelites have come here tonight to spy out the land" (Joshua 2:2). The king sends officers to arrest the Jews.

Rahab, however, hides the men under stalks of flax drying on her roof. Then she helps them escape at night, advising them to head for the hills and lie low until the search parties come home empty-handed.

In return for this help, the spies agree to spare Rahab and her extended family in the battle to come.

. . . .

GET SMART / Two spies sent by Joshua probably cross the Jordan River at a popular ford. In Jericho they blow their cover and almost get arrested. But with help from a prostitute, they escape to the hills and hide while search parties look for them near the river. Three days later, they return to the Jewish camp at Acacia Grove.

RAHAB: PLEASURE IS HER BUSINESS.
A hooker on the job in Jericho, Rahab protects two spies Joshua sends to scout the defenses of the city. In exchange, the spies agree to spare her and her family. Rahab not only joins the Jews. She shows up in Jesus' genealogy—as the great-great-grandmother of King David.

FLAX.
The first major crop of the new year, flax was harvested in February and March. Weavers spun the stalk fibers into a variety of products, from fine linen to fishnet. Flax seeds are edible. Ground up, they work like eggs to bind ingredients together. The seeds also produce linseed oil.

. . . .

HOUSE OF PROSTITUTION.
Rahab's house may have been an inn, and a natural place for travelers to spend the night. An inn sometimes doubled as a house of prostitution. Owners provided the extra amenity for those who requested it. Even if Rahab's house was strictly for prostitution, the spies may have figured they would draw the least attention there. It's a place where strangers passing through might go—and a place locals might avoid.

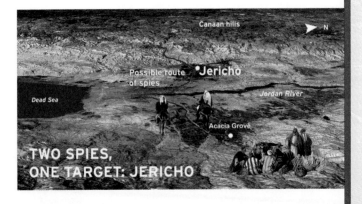

Canaan hills

N

Possible route of spies

Jericho

Dead Sea

Jordan River

Acacia Grove

TWO SPIES, ONE TARGET: JERICHO

God stops the Jordan

"THE LORD HAS GIVEN US THE WHOLE LAND," Joshua's spies report. "All the people in the land are terrified of us" (Joshua 2:24).

Joshua orders the Jews to break camp at Acacia Grove and head toward the Jordan River, about six miles (nine km) west.

It's springtime and the river has topped its banks. But God dams the Jordan upstream "at a town called Adam" (Joshua 3:16).

Once the Jews cross into Canaan, they camp "at Gilgal, just east of Jericho" (Joshua 4:19). There, Joshua builds a memorial to commemorate the crossing: a dozen stones, one for each tribe.

JORDAN RIVER STATS

> 2–10 feet (1–3 meters) deep; deeper in spring
> 30 yards (27 meters) wide on average
> 65 miles (105 km) long as a dove flies, between the Sea of Galilee and the Dead Sea
> 135 meandering miles (217 km) long as a fish swims
> Jordan River Valley averages 6 miles (10 km) wide

JORDAN RIVER: STOP

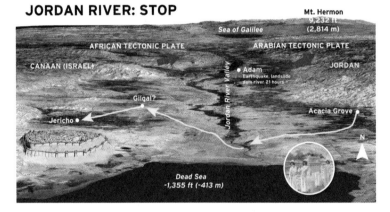

GOD LAYS OUT THE WELCOME MAT / When priests carrying the sacred chest that holds the 10 Commandments reach the Jordan River, God stops the water upstream at Adam—maybe with an earthquake, some say. Some wonder if the 150-foot cliffs near Adam crumbled into the river and stopped the flow.

MIRACLE OF TIMING? Landslides shaken loose by earthquakes have dammed the Jordan River many times—in 1927 blocking it for 21 hours at the site the Bible mentions: Adam, upriver from Jericho less than 20 miles (32 km). Other landslides blocked the Jordan in 1267, 1546, 1834, 1906, and 1956. The Jordan flows along the seam of two shifting land plates. NASA technologies such as global positioning systems suggest both plates are headed northeast at different speeds.

GILGAL. A popular contender for Gilgal is the ruin Khirbet Mefjir, less than two miles (three km) northeast of Jericho. Archaeologists have found pottery there from Joshua's era. The name of the ruin means "ring of stones."

Jericho's walls tumble

DOUBLE WALLS surround Jericho, a city built on a mound rising 70 feet (21 meters) above the valley plain. It looks impregnable.

Until the walls fall down.

God gives Joshua these instructions for capturing the city:

DAYS 1-6. March one time around Jericho each day, accompanied by seven priests continually blowing ram horns and other priests carrying the Ark of the Covenant.

DAY 7. Ditto. But this time march around the city seven times. Then have the seven priests signal a long blast with their horns—a cue for the Jewish army to join in and empty their lungs with primal screams.

The walls fall. "The Israelites charged straight into the town and captured it" (Joshua 6:20).

Jericho's only survivors are Rahab and her extended family.

WHY SOME DOUBT THE JERICHO STORY

Jericho was a 150-year-old ghost town by the time Joshua arrived, many archaeologists agree—perhaps most.

They're siding with one of their kind, Kathleen Kenyon. She excavated Jericho's ruins from 1952–1958. She dated the city's fall to about 1550 BC, long before Joshua arrived.

One of two earlier archaeological teams agreed: Ernst Sellin and Carl Watzinger (1907–1909; 1911). But another archaeologist disagreed: John Garstang (1930–1936). He dated the fall to about 1400 BC, the time some say Joshua arrived.

Date problem aside, archaeologists did uncover evidence supporting the Bible story: crumbled walls, charred remains, and jars full of springtime grain.

QUAKE AFTERSHOCK?

Some Bible students wonder if God leveled the playing field with an aftershock from an earthquake that dammed the Jordan River more than a week earlier. The Bible doesn't say how God managed either miracle.

◄ **FALL!**

Jewish warriors scream, while priests carry the sacred chest holding the 10 Commandments and blast on ram horns. It's the combo cue for Jericho's walls to collapse.

JERICHO NUMBERS

> One of world's oldest cities, founded about 9000 BC

> World's lowest city, 750 feet (229 m) below sea level

> Size: 10 acres, about 350 x 150 yards (320 x 137 m), smaller than most Walmart parking lots

> Six miles (10 km) west of Jordan River

> 15 miles (24 km) northeast of Jerusalem

▲ **JERICHO GRAIN.** Storage jars uncovered at Jericho. Grain filled some jars. That tracks with the Bible story that the Jews didn't take any supplies from the city. Invaders on the move typically snatched up the food.

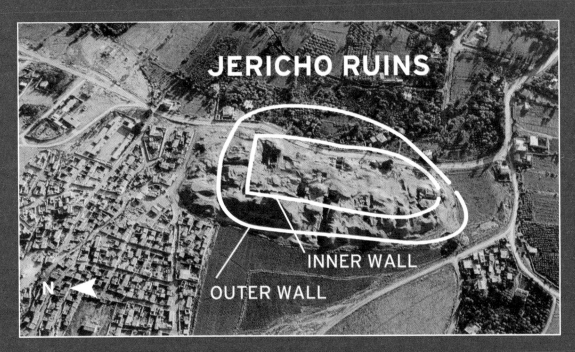

JOSHUA'S SPEED BUMP. A mound of earth is all that remains of Jericho—a city the Jews besieged for only a week before it fell. Called Tell es-Sultan, Arabic for "Hill of the Sultan," it stretches about three football fields long and it bears the scars of archaeologists armed with shovels. What they found is that the city had two main walls. The outside wall sat on top of a retaining wall that held the base of the mound in place. Evidence suggests the two walls fell outward, forming ramps that allowed invaders to storm in and burn the city.

Hills alive, with the sound of contracts

MOSES knew how to leave a message.

Make it visual. And make it big. As big as two mountains.

He told the Jews when they arrive in Canaan, they should go to Shechem and renew their contract with God, promising to obey his laws. This was where God first told their ancestor Abraham, "I will give this land to your descendants" (Genesis 12:7).

After destroying the border towns of Jericho and Ai, Joshua led his people north to Shechem, about 30 miles (48 km) north of Jericho. There, 6 of Israel's 12 tribes stand on the slopes of Mount Gerizim and recite from Deuteronomy 28 the rewards the contract says they'll get for obeying God's laws—rewards including protection and prosperity.

The other six tribes stand on Mount Ebal and recite the punishments for disobedience—including invasion and exile.

Joshua builds an altar, coats it in plaster, and writes the laws on it—perhaps a condensed version, such as the 10 Commandments. Then he reads aloud: "Every word of every command that Moses had ever given" (Joshua 8:35).

Mt. Ebal

Shechem ruins

NABLUS, WEST BANK

Mt. Gerizim

N

FIRE ON THE MOUNTAIN / Nablus, a predominately Palestinian city, has swallowed up the valley where the town of Shechem once stood. Joshua built an altar of uncut stones on Mount Ebal. Afterward, the Jewish nation stood on the slopes of both mounts Ebal and Gerizim and pledged their allegiance to God.

SHECHEM. This was a valley town along a well-traveled caravan route running east and west between Mount Gerizim and Mount Ebal. Excavations suggest it had been destroyed before the 1400s BC, when many say Joshua arrived, and was rebuilt about the same time the Jews began settling in the land.

READING THE LAW ALOUD. It's unclear what laws Joshua read to the crowd. Moses' laws are preserved in the books of Exodus, Leviticus, Numbers, and Deuteronomy. Perhaps Joshua read Deuteronomy, a summary of the laws.

Battle that stopped the sun

THERE SHOULDN'T have been a battle at all.

The Bible suggests there wouldn't have been if the Jews had consulted God before making a peace treaty with strangers who suddenly show up in their camp at Gilgal.

Introducing themselves as ambassadors, they say they come "from a distant land" (Joshua 9:6). They have the moldy bread, ragged clothes, and patched sandals to prove it.

Truth is, they come from the village of Gibeon—a day's walk west.

They have heard about the miraculous exploits of the Jewish militia. And they know the Jews aren't negotiating peace treaties with the locals—other than to help them rest in peace.

Joshua and the Jews buy the lie. They agree to an alliance "in the name of the LORD. . .but they did not consult the LORD" (Joshua 9:18, 14).

When Joshua finds out the ambassadors outmaneuvered him, he still feels obligated to honor his vow. Instead of killing the citizens of Gibeon, he puts them to work. They haul wood and water for the tent worship center, perhaps for washing and burning animal sacrifices.

Jerusalem's Canaanite king hears about the alliance. He forms an alliance of his own, with four other city kingdoms in the area: Hebron, Jarmuth, Lachish, and Eglon.

(continued next page)

FREEZING THE SUN / With his Jewish troops engaged in battle after an all-night march, Joshua issues a bizarre order: "Sun, stand still over Gibeon. Moon, stand still over the Valley of Aijalon" (Joshua 10:12 NIrV).

This coalition army attacks Gibeon. But Gibeon manages to get a messenger through to Joshua, asking the Jews to honor their treaty by rescuing the city.

Joshua leads his militia on an all-night march up into the Judean hills, and then launches a surprise attack.

Joshua asks God to stop the sun and moon, in a two-line prayer written as poetry.

Some Bible students say God literally stopped the earth's rotation—no big deal for the Creator.

Others say the prayer is poetry, and deserves the poetic license needed to drive in the direction of a metaphor: The prayer is a way of asking for God's help to finish the job.

Coalition forces scatter, running for home. Few make it. Joshua's militia catches and kills many. A deadly hailstorm finishes the job, slaughtering more enemy soldiers than the Jews did.

Joshua captures the five kings and executes them.

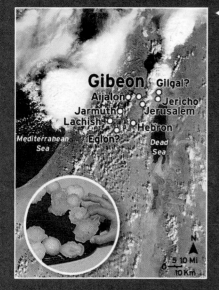

HAILSTORM REMATCH. Jagged hail the size of tennis balls pummel Israel on October 16, 1992, in the same area where the Bible says a hailstorm destroyed Joshua's enemies as they fled west from Gibeon. A NASA satellite tracked the storm as it struck the ruins of Gibeon and pounded west into the Mediterranean Sea.

DID THE SUN "STOP" OR "STOP SHINING," HIDDEN BEHIND STORM CLOUDS? The Hebrew word *damam*, often translated as "stand still," can also mean "stop" as in "stop shining." If Joshua asked God not to let the sun sap the energy from his soldiers who had marched all night, he got what he asked for. A hailstorm rolled in, blocked the sun, and killed most of the enemy as they ran for home.

URBAN LEGEND OF THE LOST DAY. Some say NASA calculations show there's a lost day in history. NASA has denied this, and insists it would be impossible to calculate such a thing.

POOL OF THE WATER SLAVES. Joshua ordered citizens of Gibeon to "carry water for the place of worship" (Joshua 9:23 CEV). This shaft chiseled through limestone bedrock 35 feet (11 meters) deep was part of an impressive water system found at Gibeon's ruins. It connects to a tunnel that feeds into a spring. Some wonder if this was "the pool of Gibeon" (2 Samuel 2:13).

Bloodbath in the hill country

"WHEREVER YOU SET FOOT," God promised Joshua, "you will be on land I have given you" (Joshua 1:3). Joshua chooses to set his foot mainly on Israel's hills. There, his lightly armed militia can outmaneuver armored enemy soldiers and their chariots.

After defeating the combined armies of five kings that had attacked the city of Gibeon, Israel's new ally, Joshua turns his troops south. There, the Jews capture and destroy half a dozen major towns—each ruled by a king. Joshua's troops also overrun neighboring villages and destroy reinforcements sent from kings in other regional towns, such as Gezer.

Southland crushed, Joshua returns to his camp at Gilgal. But King Jabin at Hazor, dominant city of the northland, forms his own huge coalition army. There's no telling how many armies Jabin mustered. The Bible lists more than a dozen cities,

(continued next page)

TESTING THEIR METAL / In highland battles, Joshua's lightly armed militia easily outmaneuvers the heavily armed Canaanites and their chariots.

CHARIOTS. Early war chariots like those of Egyptians allowed a driver and an archer to stand side by side. Rawhide lashes held the frame together. Bronze pins kept the wooden wheels from flying off the wooden axle.

regions, and races, including Hazor's neighboring towns of Madon, Achshaph, and Shimron.

For the army's staging area, Jabin selects Merom. It's famous for its ample supply of spring water, which a massive army would need. Fortunately for Joshua, it seems to have been located in the hills a few miles north of the Sea of Galilee, and near forests from which Joshua could have launched a surprise attack.

"Do not be afraid," God tells Joshua. "By this time tomorrow I will hand all of them over to Israel as dead men" (Joshua 11:6).

Jews cripple the enemy horses, burn the chariots, and then run down the fleeing soldiers and kill them so they don't live to fight another day.

HAZOR. Archaeologists say Hazor was probably Canaan's largest city kingdom at the time—roughly 200 acres, about the size of 150 football fields. Joshua burned Hazor, one of few he torched. Evidence suggests the city was burned in the 1400s BC. The lack of burned Canaanite cities during the conquest has led some scholars to speculate that many battles reported in Joshua never took place.

MEROM. Site of Joshua's battle on the northern front, perhaps the ruin today called Tell el-Khureibeh, about nine miles (14km) west of Hazor.

Putting Israel on the map

IF JOSHUA MAKES A MISTAKE, it's in figuring that the hardest job is over and all that's left is to mop up the Canaanite stragglers.

Joshua divides the land among the 12 tribes and tells each tribe to finish the job of conquering its own territory. (See map on page 97.)

It doesn't quite work out that way. Many will learn to get along with their Canaanite neighbors.

The tribe of Dan gets assigned the southern coast near the Gaza Strip. Unfortunately, that's where Philistine invaders are settling. They're fierce warriors. Dan will end up heading for the hills, settling near Mount Hermon.

Israel's tribes take their names from the sons of Jacob. Descendants of one son, Levi, get no territory. These Levites serve as priests and worship assistants, maintaining the worship center. Others live in 48 Levite cities scattered among the tribes, so all Jews have worship leaders nearby. Six of those cities become justice centers called "cities of refuge." People charged with crimes can flee to these cities for a trial rather than face the blood vengeance of a victim's family and friends.

. . . .

PROMISED LAND BOUNDARIES / Bible descriptions vary. Sometimes the southern border is reported as the Red Sea (see Exodus 23:31). Sometimes it's the Negev badlands. God told Joshua the land stretched "from the Negev wilderness in the south to the Lebanon mountains in the north, from the Euphrates River in the east to the Mediterranean Sea in the west" (Joshua 1:4). Solomon's kingdom stretched that far. But in Joshua's day, the Jews controlled less than even modern Israel, which is about the size of New Jersey.

Jacob's favorite son, Joseph, also misses out on tribal land named after him. But his two sons, Ephraim and Manasseh, each get a tribe of their own. Manasseh works both sides of the Jordan River.

Together, these tribes take the name God gave their forefather Jacob: "From now on you will be called Israel" (Genesis 32:28).

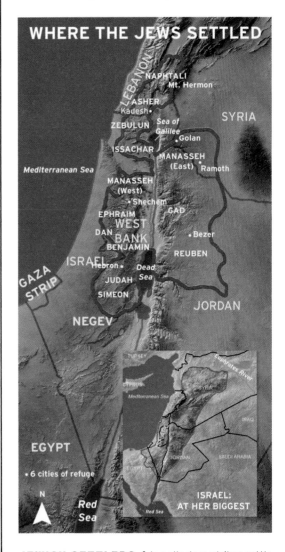

JEWISH SETTLERS / Israel's dozen tribes settle mainly in the hills of what is now Israel, along with parts of Jordan and Syria. In time, the Jews pushed their boundaries out. They grew largest during King Solomon's reign, 200–400 years later—controlling land all the way to the Euphrates River.

BIG SCENE
HAIRCUT

JUDGES 16:19

When Samson's Philistine girlfriend, Delilah, finds out that the source of his strength lies in a vow not to cut his hair, she arranges a haircut—and reaps a hefty reward.

BIBLE HISTORY

ALL DATES APPROXIMATE

1375 BC
Joshua dies (1200 BC alternate date)

WORLD HISTORY

Paved roads in some Middle Eastern cities
1200 BC

JUDGES

HEROES ON CALL

STORY LINE

JOSHUA'S JEWS CALL IT QUITS, refusing to finish what they started: the conquest of Canaan.

Joshua thought he had wrapped up the big stuff, destroying enemy armies. But he should have sweat the small stuff. It's the small stuff that does them in.

The Jews are supposed to mop up Canaan, driving out the last of the locals. It's so the Jews don't pick up pagan Canaanite customs and religious practices—like worshipping idols.

Instead, the Jews learn to live alongside Canaanites, as neighbors. And they start picking up some bad habits. When they see Canaanites having more success at growing crops, some Jews seem to conclude it's because of the Canaanite gods. As though it has nothing to do with the fact that Canaanite families have been farming for centuries, while Jews have been making bricks in Egypt.

What follows is a cycle of reruns, a bit like the movie *Groundhog Day*.

Jews break their agreement to obey God's laws. God imposes the consequences written into the agreement—usually oppression by foreign nations. The Jews repent and ask God for help. God sends a hero (known as a judge) to defeat the oppressors.

Then it's back to the same ol' same ol'. At least a dozen times. By the book's end, anarchy reigns and the Jews are killing each other in their first civil war.

// LOCATION: Most stories take place in what are now Israel and Jordan.

// TIME: The stories take place after Joshua dies in about 1375 BC or around 1200 BC (scholars debate which), but before Saul becomes Israel's first king in about 1065 BC.

// AUTHOR: Unknown. Some guess the prophet Samuel. Others guess someone compiled the stories that had been passed down by word of mouth from generation to generation.

1150 BC
Gideon and 300 drive off 135,000 invaders

One of first-known zoos started by Chinese empress
1150 BC

1075 BC
Delilah helps Philistines capture Samson

Most Chinese prophets are women
1000 BC

Less than conquerors

GENERATION TWO, as it turns out, isn't much more devoted to God than Generation One—the feeble-faith followers of Moses.

Generation One gets sentenced to 40 years in the badlands for being bad. They refused to invade Canaan, fearing the giants and walled cities. Though Generation Two, led by Joshua, invades, swarms over city walls, and destroys enemy armies, they settle into comfort zones instead of finishing the job.

Canaanites remain in the land. So do their pagan temples and hilltop shrines.

By the time Generation Three comes along, the Jews "did not acknowledge the LORD or remember the mighty things he had done for Israel" (Judges 2:10).

They might as well have been Canaanites.

They even worship Canaanite gods, especially Baal and Ashtoreth.

That's when God invokes the penalty clause in the agreement he has with Israel. Cue the foreign raiders to sweep into Israel and take whatever they want.

Arab raiders harass Jewish settlers.

PENALTY CLAUSE.
Moses warned that if the Jews disobeyed God, the Lord would let their enemies oppress them. Invaders would steal their crops, and foreigners living among them would grow stronger and exploit them.

BAAL AND ASHTORETH.
Canaan's divine fertility couple. They were a god and a goddess Canaanites said controlled the size of a person's family, the amount of harvest, and the number of livestock. Some ancient Middle Eastern records, including some in Egypt, call Ashtoreth by the name Ishtar.

◄ **FERTILITY GOD.**
Worshipped as a god of fertility in Bible times, this marble figurine still enjoys a pedestal—in a Dallas museum. Jews began worshipping idols like this after settling in Canaan. The Bible says that's why God unleashed raiders on them.

Madam General

THREE JUDGES DEEP into Jewish history, Deborah comes along. She's a prophetess as well as a judge in the legal sense; she settles disputes. But she's about to start a war.

The Jews have already suffered through a trio of sin-salvation cycles. They'd sin and then call on God to save them. God sent a savior each time: Othniel, then Ehud, and finally Shamgar.

Now, the Jews are 20 years into a fourth cycle of sinning. That's how long the northland Jews have been oppressed by King Jabin of the Canaanite city of Hazor, north of the Sea of Galilee. His army includes 900 iron chariots. As far as infantry is concerned, that's the ancient equivalent of tanks. Foot soldiers hate to see them coming.

Again, the Jews call on God's help. God tells Deborah to have Barak, the Jewish general, recruit 10,000 men from the northern tribes of Naphtali and Zebulun. He's to stage them on high ground, along the slopes of Mount Tabor above the wide Valley of Jezreel.

Barak refuses. He won't go into battle unless Deborah goes with him.

Fine, she says, "But understand that with an attitude like that, there'll be no glory in it for you" (Judges 4:9 MSG).

A sudden rainstorm turns the valley stream into a flood, washing away some enemy chariots and trapping the rest in mud. Suddenly charioteers become infantrymen—on the run. Jews charge down the hill and into the valley. They win the day and, in time, kill the enemy king. Deborah's generation enjoys peace for 40 years.

IF I HAD A HAMMER / With a tent peg and a hammer, a herder's wife named Jael kills the Canaanite commander of a chariot corps that attacked the Jews. The unlucky commander is Sisera. On the run from a lost battle, he makes the mistake of taking a nap in Jael's tent. Apparently a Jewish sympathizer, or a terribly inhospitable host, she drives the tent peg through his temple.

OPERATION: MUDDY WHEELS

CHARIOTS VS. INFANTRY / King Jabin of Hazor throws the bulk of his armored division at the Jews: 900 iron-plated chariots. The battlefield fear factor is comparable to modern infantry facing tanks. A deluge levels the playing field—and muddies it up. Charioteers become foot soldiers, running for their lives.

···

JUDGE, THE WORD ODDLY USED / We call the dozen heroes in this book "judges." But most weren't like Deborah, who actually settled disputes. In Hebrew, the word meant "tribal leader."

Gideon's 300

CENTURIES BEFORE 300 SPARTANS took on Xerxes and his Persian hordes, estimated by various ancient sources at anywhere from 80,000 to 2 million invaders—300 Jews take on 135,000 Arab invaders.

Unlike the Spartans, the Jews win. So says the Bible.

For seven years, camel-riding raiders from Midian in what is now Saudi Arabia swarm into Israel's most fertile farming area: Galilee, in northern Israel. They invade at harvest time, stealing crops and livestock—dooming many Jews to starvation.

Jews finally call on God for help. He sends an angel to tell Gideon to muster an army. Some 32,000 rally around him—four-to-one odds against the Jews. But God has Gideon whittle down his army to a strike force of only 300—producing terrible odds of 450 to one.

With an ancient version of smoke-and-mirrors trickery, Gideon's men eliminate the camel advantage. They surround the enemy camp at night. Then they blow ram horns, smash jars, light torches, and scream.

Quite a wake-up call for the raiders.

In the pitch black of night, they're so confused they start killing each other. Some survive to run for their lives. But Gideon calls on his full army to join the chase and run them down. Gideon brings back the heads of the Midian commanders.

In gratitude, Jews offer to make Gideon king. But he insists they already have one: the Lord.

AND THEY'RE OFF / Camels sprint across a Middle Eastern field, in a friendly race. But in Gideon's day, Arab raiders harassing the Jews stormed in on camels, which can sprint up to 40 miles (64 km) an hour. Quite the element of surprise.

THIRST-QUENCHER / Author Stephen M. Miller scoops water from "Gideon's Spring." It may have been at this spring-fed stream, which widens into a creek, that Gideon reduced the size of his army from 10,000 to 300. He selected only men who drank by scooping water rather than by putting their face into the water. After the author's drink, he noticed fellow tourists upstream, sitting with their feet in the water.

◄ GIDEON'S BATTLEGROUND. In a nighttime attack, Gideon's strike force surprises and routs foreign raiders. The raiders had set up camp in Israel's most fertile farmland—the Jezreel Valley—hoping to steal the harvest.

MIDIANITES. Traders from Midian (along the northwest border of Jordan and Saudi Arabia) started the ball rolling that got the Jews enslaved in Egypt. They bought Joseph from his brothers and sold him there as a slave. Joseph rose to power in Egypt and invited his family to move down during a drought. In time, Egyptians enslaved the Jews. Moses led them to freedom.

CAMELS. Gideon's story is the first in history of people using camels in battle. Camels can cruise at 25 miles (40 km) an hour for an entire hour—double the speed of an Olympic marathon runner.

WHY ONLY 300 SOLDIERS? God wanted the Jews to know he's the one who saved them. "I do not want Israel to brag that their own strength has saved them" (Judges 7:2 NIrV).

Samson's weakness

FAMOUS FOR HIS MANLY STRENGTH, Samson dies because of his weakness for women. And they're not the kind of ladies he'd bring home to Mother.

His entire life story spins around three unsavory Philistine women and the misery they cause: his bride, a prostitute, and Delilah.

He's a miracle baby, born to a previously infertile woman. An angel announces that Samson is to live as a Nazirite, observing monklike vows that include not cutting his hair.

Anything but a monk, Samson is driven by lust and revenge.

When his bride betrays him by telling the wedding guests the answer to a riddle he bet them they couldn't solve, Samson kills the guests and storms off. Calmed down, he returns to get his bride. But she married the best man.

SAMSON PAST HIS PRIME / Enslaved and blinded by the Philistines, Samson is forced to do an animal's job: pushing a millstone that grinds grain into flour.

Angry at all Philistines now, he ties torches to 300 foxes and turns them loose to burn fields, vineyards, and orchards. Philistines retaliate by killing his bride and her father and by invading Jewish land.

At the Jews' request, Samson turns himself in. Then he turns on the Philistines, killing 1,000 with the jawbone of a donkey.

Philistines later lay a trap for him while he's with a prostitute in Gaza. They figure he'll be weak after a night of sex. Wrong. Before they can do anything, he tears the massive city gate off the wall. They watch in shock as he carries it away. He discards it some 40 miles (64 km) later, near Hebron.

Samson later falls for Delilah, who lives in the Valley of Sorek just a few miles from his home in Zorah. Philistine leaders offer her silver equal to thousands of dollars if she'll find the secret of his strength.

One haircut later, Samson is captured, blinded, and enslaved.

Philistines bring him into a temple to celebrate their victory. But his hair has grown back. Standing between two support pillars, he pushes them down. The roof collapses, killing him and more Philistines than he had killed during his entire life.

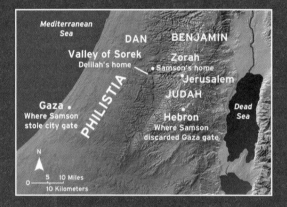

Harvesting olives into nets by shaking tree and beating branches.

▲ **PHILISTINES.** They were probably the Sea People thought to have migrated into the area from islands around Greece. They settled on Israel's coast about the same time Joshua and the Jews arrived. They dominated the Jews with their secret weapon: the knowledge of how to make iron weapons that could slice through bronze weapons the Jews used.

NAZIRITE VOW. It's a vow of devotion to God, often for just a short time—a bit like giving up something for Lent. Nazirites refused to drink wine, eat grape products, cut their hair, or come into contact with the dead. Samson, it seems, broke all these vows.

▲ **FIRE DAMAGE.** When Samson burned some fields, infuriating the Philistines, the damage could have lasted for decades. Some crops, like wheat, would suffer just one season's loss. But replanted vineyards took three to five years to produce good crops—and olive orchards took 40 years or more.

PHILISTINE TEMPLE. In 1971, archaeologists found a Philistine temple that matches the description of the one Samson demolished. Located near Tel Aviv, at a ruin called Tel Qasila, the temple included a roof supported by a massive crossbeam that rested on two cedar pillars.

Priest for hire

ISRAEL SINKS LOWER. So low that one priest sets up a shrine of idols—apparently thinking it's okay with God.

The sad story starts with a man named Micah stealing from his mother. He takes 28 pounds of silver (12.5 kilograms). His mother puts a curse on the unknown thief. So Micah confesses and returns the loot. Forgiving and grateful, Micah's mother uses five pounds (2.2 kilograms) of the silver to make an idol.

When a Levite happens by, looking for a place to live, Micah hires him to become the family priest—in charge of their shrine of idols.

Then along comes a 600-man war party from the neighboring tribe of Dan, heading north to capture land at the foothills of Mount Hermon. Micah lives in Ephraim, tribal territory just north of Dan's assigned region. Dan's tribe has decided to move north apparently because they can't drive out the Philistines.

The war party steals Micah's idols. And they convince the priest to go with them, arguing, "Isn't it better to be a priest for an entire tribe and clan of Israel than for the household of just one man?" (Judges 18:19).

GALLERY OF THE GODS / Worshipped as gods, stone figurines like these may have been on display at a Jewish shrine in Israel. Worse, the shrine was run by a Levite, a Jewish worship leader.

VALUE OF SILVER. Micah stole 1,100 silver shekels (about 28 pounds, or 12.5 kilograms). One ancient transaction shows this would have bought more than 70 bulls. On today's market, when silver sells for about $10 a troy ounce, the value of the stolen silver is about $3,360.

LEVITES. Men from the tribe of Levi, who served as worship leaders. They had no assigned tribal territory in Israel, but lived in 48 Levitical cities scattered among the tribes. Oddly, this Levite lived in Bethlehem, not one of the 48 cities.

Gang rape and payback

CHOPPED MEAT starts Israel's first civil war. The meat is a woman, cut into 12 pieces—one hunk for each of Israel's 12 tribes.

Before her husband butchers her, the two of them are headed home from Bethlehem to the tribal land of Ephraim. In a choice bad enough to inspire a horror movie, they decide to spend the night in Gibeah, a Jewish town in their neighboring tribe of Benjamin. A gang spots them as strangers and decides to gang-rape the man.

Less than chivalrous, the man pushes his wife outside. Men rape her all night long. Less than sensitive, when the husband steps outside the next morning and sees his wife lying there, he tells her to get up so they can go home—as though she's well rested.

She's dead.

He cuts her up and sends her body parts to the tribal leaders, calling for justice. Livid, they muster an army and attack the unrepentant tribe of Benjamin, nearly exterminating it. Only 600 men of Benjamin survive—without women or children. Afterward, Israel's tribal leaders are sorry they took the payback that far.

To make amends, they agree to give each survivor a woman, so Benjamin's tribe will live on.

Their extreme solution: wipe out a Jewish village that didn't fight in the war—Jabesh in Gilead—but save their virgins. That nets 400 women. For the last 200, they allow the men of Benjamin to raid a Jewish festival at the worship center in Shiloh, snatching unmarried women who are dancing.

The writer ends this dismal story with what sounds like a plea for a king who can end the anarchy: "In those days Israel had no king; all the people did whatever seemed right in their own eyes" (Judges 21:25).

LEFTY / Benjamin's army included 700 left-handed slingers "who could sling a rock at a target the size of a hair and hit it every time" (Judges 20:16 CEV).

ISRAEL'S 12 TRIBES

▲ **BENJAMIN BULLS-EYE.** In a Jew-on-Jew holocaust of revenge, 11 tribes united against the lone tribe of Benjamin converge on Gibeah in the center of Israel. They almost completely wipe out the tribe of Benjamin.

CONCUBINE. The man's wife was a concubine, which is a lesser, secondary wife. Concubines were often from a poor family. Sometimes they were slaves captured in a battle.

BODY COUNT. Israel's coalition army of 400,000 decimated Benjamin's army of about 26,000, leaving only 600 survivors. Israel lost more than 40,000 men during its three attacks on Gibeah.

BIG SCENE

WHERE YOU GO, I'LL GO

RUTH 1:16

*Widowed Naomi tells her two widowed daughters-in-law
to go back to their fathers. But Ruth refuses to leave the
old woman by herself, and goes with her to Israel.*

**BIBLE
HISTORY**

ALL DATES APPROXIMATE

1250 BC
*Jews invade Canaan
(1400 BC alternate date)*

**WORLD
HISTORY**

1213 BC *Rameses II dies;
many scholars consider him
the Exodus pharaoh*

1210 BC *Egyptian King
Merneptah says he invaded
Israel and wiped out the Jews*

R U T H

ARAB MOTHER OF THE GREATEST JEWISH KINGS

STORY LINE

TO ESCAPE A DROUGHT, a Jewish couple moves from Bethlehem to a small Arab country on the opposite side of the Dead Sea: Moab, in what is now Jordan. Their two sons marry women from Moab. But within 10 years, all three men are dead.

In this man-run culture, widowed women without male relatives are destitute. In the eyes of the law, they're minors—unable to own property. Their main options: remarry, beg, or become prostitutes.

Old Naomi tells her daughters-in-law to go back to their families and try to find other husbands. As for her, she'll go back to Bethlehem and hope some distant relative will take her in.

Ruth refuses to leave Naomi. Both return to Bethlehem. With other poor folks, Ruth picks leftover grain in a harvested field. The farmer, Boaz, is impressed with Ruth's devotion to Naomi. And as it turns out, he's related to Naomi's husband—which makes him related, by marriage, to Ruth.

Jewish law encourages men to marry their widowed relatives—an ancient form of social security, though a bit more social than today's system. Ruth proposes. Boaz accepts. And the two have a notable son: He'll grow up to become the grandfather of King David. Naomi lives with them and takes care of her grandbaby.

// LOCATION: Ruth's story starts in Moab and ends in Bethlehem.

// TIME: The story is set in the time of the judges, perhaps in the 1100s BC.

// AUTHOR: The writer is unknown. Too bad, since many consider this story one of the finest examples of writing in the Bible. Jewish tradition says the prophet Samuel wrote it.

1150
Ruth marries Boaz

1065 BC
Saul becomes Israel's first king

1180 BC *Rameses III drives back an invasion of seafaring people*

1175 BC *Seafaring Philistines invade Canaan's coastland, creating Philistia*

Home to Bethlehem

TRYING TO SAVE THEIR FAMILY from a drought, a Jewish couple in Israel makes a radical decision. They leave the homeland God selected for the Jews and move to an Arab country.

Elimelech and Naomi take their two sons to Moab, a fertile plateau above the eastern banks of the Dead Sea. Their sons, Mahlon and Kilion, marry Moabite women: Orpah and Ruth. But within 10 years, all three women are widowed.

Since women typically aren't allowed to conduct business or own property, Naomi decides to go back to her hometown of Bethlehem. She hopes one of her relatives will take her in. She urges Orpah and Ruth to go back to their fathers and try to find new husbands.

Orpah reluctantly leaves, crying. But Naomi refuses. In perhaps the most moving words of the story, Ruth says, "Wherever you go, I will go; wherever you live, I will live. Your people will be my people, and your God will be my God" (Ruth 1:16).

Bethlehem's citizens happily welcome the two.

THE PLIGHT OF WIDOWS. Women in the ancient Middle East were usually under the care of a man. First their father. Then their husband. And finally as widows, their sons. Young widows without any of these could only hope a relative would take pity on her and marry her. Older widows, like Naomi, depended on the charity of family and friends.

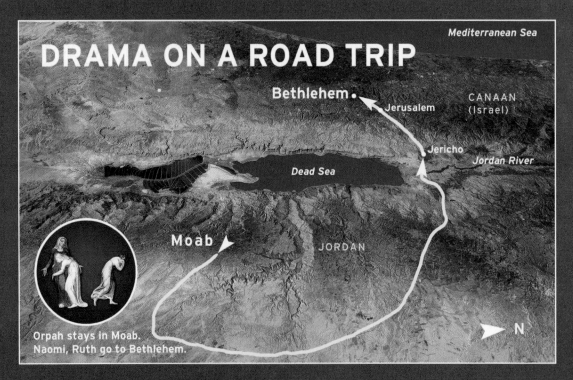

DRAMA ON A ROAD TRIP

Mediterranean Sea

Bethlehem.
Jerusalem

CANAAN
(Israel)

Jericho
Jordan River

Dead Sea

Moab

JORDAN

N

Orpah stays in Moab.
Naomi, Ruth go to Bethlehem.

▲ **LONG WALK HOME.** Widowed, Naomi and Ruth make the long trek from Moab to Naomi's hometown of Bethlehem. Huge canyons north of Moab force the women on a wide roundabout. The trip of more than 100 miles (160 km) could have taken them a week or more, depending on Naomi's stamina.

HILLS OF MOAB.
A view from Israel across the Dead Sea. Fertile pastures lie on the far side of the ridge.

....

MOAB.
People in this Arab nation were distant relatives of the Jews. They descended from Abraham's nephew, Lot.

....

NAOMI'S NEW NAME: MARA.
Naomi asks the people of Bethlehem to call her Mara. Naomi means "pleasant," Mara "bitter." "I went away full, but the LORD has brought me home empty" (Ruth 1:21).

▲

HOME IS A CAVE.
Bethlehem widow outside her cave home. The shawl she's wearing—tattered but clean—is the best she has. She swapped it from her everyday shawl for the photo.

ARAB AT LARGE / Most Bedouin traveling herders, like this young woman in Israel, are Arab. So was Ruth, the mother of Israel's most revered dynasty of kings. Ruth became the great-grandmother of King David.

Ruth proposes

UNDER A BLANKET seems like an odd place to propose marriage.

The scene gets even weirder. In this man-run world, it's Ruth doing the proposing. The startled listener—who doesn't have a clue what's coming—is an older man, Boaz.

He's rich.

The two had met just a few weeks earlier, at the beginning of the barley harvest. Jewish law allows poor folks to follow harvesters and pick the left-over crops. Ruth had asked permission to do that in the fields of Boaz.

Some would call it a lucky break. Boaz had heard of Ruth, and he admired her incredible devotion to Naomi. So he not only approved, he told his workers to leave extra for her. He also invited Ruth to eat with the harvest workers, and to stay throughout the barley harvest and the wheat harvest that followed.

Naomi is ecstatic. She knows Boaz is a close relative, and by Jewish law a contender for marrying Ruth. So she tells Ruth to take a bath, pour on the perfume, and dress in her best clothes.

Boaz and some of his workers are sleeping outside to guard the grain. So Naomi tells Ruth to wait until Boaz is asleep—then crawl under the covers with him, lying at his feet. "He will tell you what to do" (Ruth 3:4).

And it probably won't be to rub his feet.

He wakes. She proposes. And the old man says, "The LORD bless you" (Ruth 3:10).

GOT IT COVERED / A Paris groom covers his bride with his prayer shawl (Hebrew: *tallit*). It's a symbol of his vow to protect her. Ruth proposed marriage by asking Boaz to do that for her: "Spread your cover over me, because you are a relative who is supposed to take care of me" (Ruth 3:9 NCV).

GRAIN HARVEST. Farmers in the Bethlehem area begin harvesting barley by early May and wheat by early June.

ANCIENT SOCIAL SECURITY FOR WIDOWS. When a man dies, Jewish law calls for his brother to marry the widow (see Deuteronomy 25:5). Any son born to them inherits her first husband's property, keeping the land in the family. Boaz wasn't the brother, but the second-closest male relative. He had to clear his marriage to Ruth with the closest relative, who refused to marry Ruth.

It's a boy

NEGOTIATING MARRIAGE, Boaz shows some savvy. He tells the number-one contender for Ruth—her closest male relative—that someone in the family needs to buy Naomi's land from her.

Number One is happy to add the land to his estate.

Then Boaz drops the bomb. The land comes with baggage: Ruth.

Deal-breaker.

Boaz gets the land and the lady. The lady and Boaz have a son together, which means Naomi finally has a grandchild.

"Naomi took the baby and held him in her arms, cuddling him, cooing over him, waiting on him hand and foot" (Ruth 4:16 MSG).

The couple names their son Obed. He will grow up to become the father of Jesse. And Jesse will grow up to become the father of King David.

▶ **ARAB MOMMY /** Arab Ruth and Jewish Boaz have a son. They call him Obed. Years later, King David would call him Grandpa.

◀ **MARRIAGE AGREEMENT SEALED BY A SANDAL.** When Ruth's closest male relative offered Naomi's land and Ruth's hand in marriage to Boaz, he also offered his sandal. This custom that sounds like it was invented by a cobbler validated the deal—much like a handshake or a signature does today.

THE MORAL OF THE STORY. Some scholars say Ruth's story isn't just history. It's an appeal from history to refute Ezra's preaching 600 years later that Jews shouldn't marry foreigners. "The holy race has become polluted by these mixed marriages" (Ezra 9:2). As it turns out, the most revered dynasty of Jewish kings came from an Arab.

BIG SCENE
THE BIGGER THEY COME

1 SAMUEL 17:48-49

Armed with only a slingshot, teenage David drops the Philistine's champion warrior, a giant named Goliath who's armed with state-of-art, newly invented iron weaponry.

BIBLE HISTORY

ALL DATES APPROXIMATE

1100 BC
Young Samuel raised by priest Eli

1065 BC
Saul anointed as Israel's first king

WORLD HISTORY

1,2 SAMUEL

FIRST KING: A DONKEY HERDER

STORY LINE

A DONKEY HERDER REPLACES GOD as Israel's king.

For several generations, Jews in Israel don't bother with a king. Elders run the dozen tribes. God runs the country. When the people call on God for help, he sends leaders to rally the tribes. But now the Jews ask for a king, "like all the other nations have" (1 Samuel 8:5).

The prophet Samuel appoints God's choice: Saul, a content donkey herder who doesn't want the job. But with a little convincing, he takes it anyhow.

He turns out to be a fine warrior, but he gets greedy. He keeps livestock as spoils of war though God had ordered him to destroy everything the enemies owned.

Later, he grows insanely jealous of a shepherd boy named David who's hailed as a national hero. Young David killed a Philistine champion warrior in mortal combat: the giant Goliath. Saul wants David dead, and seems to think of little else. Perhaps that's one reason the Philistine army is able to outmaneuver him on the battlefield. Saul loses the battle, his life, and the lives of most of his sons.

The tribes soon rally around their national hero and appoint David as king.

He, too, is a fine warrior. He secures Israel's borders. He's also a man of God—but flawed. Especially in family matters. He has an affair. He doesn't punish his son who rapes his own half-sister (they have different mothers). And that so angers the woman's full brother, Absalom, that he murders the rapist and leads a coup against his father.

// LOCATION: Most stories take place in what is now Israel (see map page 119).

// TIME: During the 1000s BC.

// AUTHOR: Unknown. The two books were originally one, but were later divided to fit on standard-size scrolls.

1011 BC
David becomes Israel's second king

City of Damascus founded
1050 BC

Alpha

Hebrew alphabet starts to develop
1010 BC

Chinese invent icehouse refrigeration
1000 BC

Infertile

HANNAH WANTS A BABY. But she can't seem to get pregnant. Her husband's second wife, a baby dispenser, constantly ridicules Hannah to tears.

Hannah's husband, however, shows his infertile wife nothing but compassion. He gives her the most tender cuts of meat—and tender words: "You have me—isn't that better than having ten sons?" (1 Samuel 1:8).

Not by a long shot.

It would be like Henry Ford with no assembly line.

During one of the family's trips to the worship center at Shiloh, Hannah sobs a prayer. She vows that if God gives her a son, she'll give that son back to him, to serve in the worship center.

Eli the priest sees her babbling and he thinks she's been chugging the wine. So he confronts her. When he hears that she's pouring out her soul to God, he blesses her and asks the Lord to grant her request.

It's like Eli threw a switch. Suddenly, Hannah is happy. She can eat again. She can get pregnant, too. Samuel is born. Once her Samuel is weaned off of breast milk, Hannah honors her vow. She takes him to the worship center, where Eli will raise him.

LEAVING HOME

SHILOH WORSHIP CENTER / Before Solomon built the Jerusalem Temple, Jews set up their tent worship center at Shiloh.

. . . .

A DAY AWAY / Samuel is born in Ramah. But as soon as he's weaned from milk his mom fulfills her promise to God by taking him to the worship center at Shiloh. There, less than a day's walk away—about 15 miles (24 km)—the high priest will raise him.

TEARS OF LOSS / A Middle Eastern woman weeps over lives lost on a national day of mourning. Hannah of ancient Israel wept for lives never born. She was infertile. Even relatives treated her as cursed of God.

Bad news for a good boy

BAD-BOY PRIESTS, the sons of High Priest Eli, sleep with the female help at the worship center. And they help themselves to prime cuts of sacrificial meat they have no right to—meat that belongs to the worshipper or to God.

Eli asks his boys to behave, but that's all he does. Talk.

God sends Eli a double-barreled message. A prophet fires the first barrel. The second comes from young Samuel—working as a priest apprentice at the worship center.

The prophet warns that because Eli let his sons get away with dragging worship through the mud, the family name would become mud. Eli's family dynasty will end with his sons. Worse, "all the members of your family will die before their time. None will reach old age" (1 Samuel 2:31).

Young Samuel gets a similar message one night while he's sleeping in the worship center. God calls him by name and then breaks the bad news: "I am going to carry out all my threats against Eli and his family. . .because his sons are blaspheming God and he hasn't disciplined them" (1 Samuel 3:12–13).

Samuel tells Eli the next morning. Eli replies, "Let him do what he thinks best" (1 Samuel 3:18).

YOU CALLED? / Twice, Samuel reports to High Priest Eli when the boy hears his name called while he's trying to fall asleep. After the second time, Eli says if it happens again Samuel should say, "Speak, LORD, your servant is listening" (1 Samuel 3:9).

◀ FRESH MEAT FOR PRIESTS. Some of the sacrificial meat went to priests, as part of their salary. Depending on which sacrifice was offered, they could get the breast and right thigh (see Leviticus 7:31–32). Or they might get the shoulder, the two jowls (cheeks), or the stomach (see Deuteronomy 18:3)—considered a delicacy by some. Eli's sons, however, took whatever they wanted—including fat reserved for God, which should have been burned on the altar.

Cow jowls, reserved for priests

PRIESTS COMMITTING ADULTERY. Eli was old and nearly blind when his sons committed adultery. At least one son was married: Phinehas (see 1 Samuel 4:19). And given the importance of family in ancient times, Hophni was probably married, too. Yet they had sex with women who worked at the worship center. Adultery was a death-penalty offense for anyone, priests included. God warned that both priests will "die on the same day" (1 Samuel 2:34).

Lost: Three priests, sacred Ark

IN A SINGLE DAY, Israel loses perhaps every symbol of God's holiness they hold dear.

All three of their priests die. Philistines steal the Ark of the Covenant, Israel's most sacred relic, kept in the holiest part of the worship center. And the Shiloh worship center itself is likely destroyed.

It's the result of a war lost to the Philistines. The Philistines live on Israel's southern coast and are apparently expanding their turf farther inland and north.

Jews lose the first battle. But they figure they can win the next if they bring the Ark of the Covenant to the battlefront—figuring it has special power.

They figure wrong. Eli's sons die in the battle along with 30,000 Jewish soldiers. When 98-year-old Eli gets the news later that day, he falls backward out of his chair. The fall breaks his neck, killing him.

Philistines treat the Ark as a war trophy. They put it on display in a temple—at the foot of a statue of Dagon, their top god. Mysteriously, Dagon's statue crumbles. And wherever Philistines take the Ark, a plague breaks out, producing sores. In time, Philistines decide to send the Ark back.

ISRAEL'S ARK OF THE COVENANT ON 7-MONTH PHILISTINE TOUR

BATTLE OF EBENEZER. Jews lose a war with the Philistines. They also lose their high priest and both of his sons, all dead. Philistines capture the Ark of the Covenant and send it on tour as a war trophy that's proof their god is stronger than Israel's. Cue the plague—possibly bubonic.

◄ **THE ARK OF THE COVENANT IN WAR.** During battles fought on the Exodus out of Egypt and at Jericho, the gold-covered chest containing the 10 Commandments was front and center—at God's command. But in this battle, God plays no role in the planning.

▲ **PLAGUE IN A BOX.** Bubonic plague may have been the disease that produced sores on the Philistines as they carried Israel's sacred Ark from town to town. Rats spread the bubonic plague. The Bible offers a clue that this was bubonic plague. Philistines returned the chest with telltale gifts: "five gold tumors and five gold rats, just like those that have ravaged your land" (1 Samuel 6:4).

Saul, from donkey herder to king

ISRAEL'S FIRST KING seems to prefer donkeys to people.

Saul, the son of a donkey herder, doesn't want the job of king. And Samuel, the nation's spiritual leader and chief judge, doesn't want Saul for a king, either.

But Samuel is getting old. And the people apparently fear what life will be like when Samuel's two crooked sons start running the country. They both take bribes.

The Jews ask Samuel for a king—like other nations have. Samuel feels offended. But God consoles him: "It is me they are rejecting, not you. They don't want me to be their king any longer" (1 Samuel 8:7).

God selects Saul. But when Samuel takes Saul to town to present him to the tribal leaders, Saul disappears. He hides. God points him out: "He is hiding behind the baggage" (1 Samuel 10:22 CEV). And perhaps with the critters that carry the baggage: donkeys—which would get him back into his comfort zone.

SAMUEL'S WARNING.
Samuel warns the Jews that a king will draft young men for the military and women for palace labor. He'll confiscate the best property for himself and take a tenth of the crops. "You will be his slaves," Samuel says (1 Samuel 8:17).

SAUL.
"Saul was the most handsome man in Israel—head and shoulders taller than anyone else in the land" (1 Samuel 9:2). A member of the tribe of Benjamin, he grew up in the village of Gibeah, a few miles north of Jerusalem. He was 32 years old when he became king, and he reigned 42 years (see 1 Samuel 13:1). He and his wife, Ahinoam, had five sons and two daughters. He also had two sons by his concubine, a secondary wife of less stature.

DONKEY MAN / Donkeys near a seaside resort in Wales wait for tourists interested in a bumpy ride. Saul raised donkeys for his father—until the prophet Samuel tapped him to become Israel's first king. As it turns out, Saul trades one bumpy ride for another.

David, teenage king in waiting

FOR A DONKEY HERDER, Saul turns out to be a fine warrior. He unites the tribes for battle, and he takes on enemies from all four directions. "Wherever he turned, he was victorious" (1 Samuel 14:47).

But in one battle against the Philistines, he oversteps his authority. Saul has waited a week to launch his attack. He's waiting for Samuel to come and offer a sacrifice on behalf of the army, so the battle can start. Tired of waiting, Saul offers the sacrifice himself—a ritual reserved for priests. For breaking this Jewish law, Samuel tells Saul, the king's dynasty will be one and out. None of Saul's sons will inherit the throne.

God sends Samuel to Bethlehem to anoint Israel's future king—one of Jesse's eight sons. Samuel is impressed by one son in particular, apparently handsome and tall. But God tells Samuel, "He isn't the one I've chosen. People judge others by what they look like, but I judge people by what is in their hearts" (1 Samuel 16:7 CEV).

God picks David, Jesse's youngest. Even Jesse hadn't considered David worth the meeting with Samuel, since Jesse put him on sheep patrol so the older boys could greet Samuel and share a meal with him. But the prophet tells Jesse to bring him in.

"He's the one!" God tells Samuel. "Pour the olive oil on his head" (1 Samuel 16:12 CEV).

GOD'S ANOINTED / Samuel, prophet and spiritual leader of Israel, pours olive oil on young David. It's a ritual anointing him God's choice as the king who will someday replace Saul.

ANOINTING WITH OIL.
In a blistering hot and dry climate, olive oil—often scented—was a cooling and welcome balm, whether poured on the head, feet, or hands. People sometimes welcomed guests with the oil. But Jews also used it as a ritual to identify servants known as "God's anointed." This could refer to a priest or a king.

ROCK-SOLID PROOF OF DAVID.
Some scholars argued that David was just a myth, like King Arthur, since there was no ancient proof he ever existed. Proof turned up in Israel in 1993, and it dates to about 100 years after David. It's a stone engraved with the words "House of David," an ancient way of referring to David's dynasty.

DAVID.
Israel's most famous king grew up as a shepherd in Bethlehem. A gifted musician, he was sometimes called on to soothe the troubled King Saul by playing the harp—music therapy, it's called today. But David is most famous as the teenager who killed a heavily armed giant, Goliath, with only a slingshot—a heroic act that eventually propelled him to Israel's throne. David's dynasty continued 400 years, until Babylonian invaders wiped the Jewish nation off the political map in 586 BC.

Goliath meets a giant-killer

IN A BORDER WAR, turf-protecting Philistines from the coastal flatlands form a battle line on one side of the Valley of Elah.

Across the valley stands the Jewish militia—hill people led by King Saul. At stake is the land where the Mediterranean coast merges into the hills of Judea, just a few miles east of some major Philistine cities.

The two armies have been eyeballing each other for over a month, wondering who will make the first move. Each day, a Philistine champion warrior named Goliath steps forward. He offers to settle the war by mortal combat. He will fight any Jew, winner take all.

He is nearly 7 feet (two meters) tall according to the oldest copies of the story—almost 10 feet (3 meters) tall according to other copies. The iron tip of his spear alone weighs as much as a 15-pound (7-kilogram) bowling ball.

Silence meets his challenge.

King Saul offers a reward for any Jew who kills Goliath: his princess daughter in marriage and no taxes for life. The offer doesn't produce a peep among the ranks. Who would marry or tax a corpse?

Jewish shepherd boy David, probably still a teenager, arrives with a care package for his older brothers: roasted grain and fresh bread.

He hears Goliath's challenge, takes it as an insult against God, and volunteers to become God's instrument for silencing the warrior.

"Don't be ridiculous!" Saul replies (1 Samuel 17:33).

David insists, arguing that God has helped him kill lions and bears threatening his sheep, and that God would help him kill this beastly Philistine, too.

(continued next page)

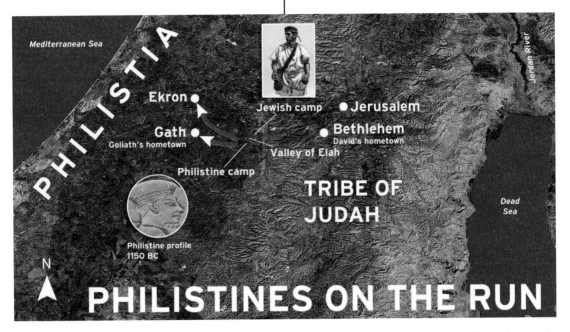

Mediterranean Sea

PHILISTIA

Jordan River

Ekron

Jewish camp • Jerusalem

Gath • Bethlehem
Goliath's hometown David's hometown

Valley of Elah

Philistine camp

TRIBE OF
JUDAH

Dead
Sea

Philistine profile
1150 BC

N

PHILISTINES ON THE RUN

PHILISTINE RETREAT / Once David stunned the Philistine army by killing its best warrior, the soldiers ran to their closest walled cities: Gath about 7 miles (11 km) west and Ekron about 10 miles (16 km) northwest.

As David walks into the Valley of Elah and crosses the stream, he picks up five smooth stones, loading one into his slingshot.

Goliath is insulted. Moments later, he's dead.

The Philistine army is supposed to surrender. Instead, they run back to the protection of their walled cities at Gath and Ekron—with the suddenly brave Jewish militia charging after them.

MORTAL COMBAT / With a slingshot and plenty of chutzpah, young David drops Goliath—a giant of a man. Goliath is the champion of Philistine warriors, armed with state-of-the art iron weaponry. But the Stone Age wins.

◄ **SLINGSHOT WEAPONS.** It wasn't a forked slingshot David used, with rubber bands. He used two strips of leather with a wide pad in the middle, which held a rock. David held the two ends of leather, loaded a rock into the patch, and then swirled the sling above his head in a tight circle. When he released one strip of the leather, momentum could have driven the rock at about 100 yards (meters) a second. The force was so lethal that warriors used slingshots as low-budget artillery.

◄ **CASKET FOR GOLIATH.** Philistines buried their dead in ceramic caskets like this one (left) from Goliath's century, found in Israel.

GOLIATH ARMED AND DANGEROUS. Armor: bronze helmet, bronze coat of mail weighing 125 pounds (57 kilograms), and bronze leg armor. Weapons: shield carried by armor bearer, bronze javelin, likely an iron sword, spear "thick as a weaver's beam" (1 Samuel 17:7)—two inches (5 centimeters) or more, with an iron spearhead.

▶ **ANCIENT NOTE.** "Goliath." That's the word some scholars agree is scratched onto this broken piece of pottery found in Goliath's hometown. It dates to about the 900s BC, perhaps just a few decades after shepherd boy David defeated him in mortal combat.

David drives father-in-law insane

IT WASN'T DAVID'S FAULT. All he did was kill a giant—the heavily armed champion of the Philistine army.

With a shepherd's slingshot.

Suddenly, everyone and his brother are singing David's praises.

Saul gripes, "Next they'll be making him their king!" (1 Samuel 18:8).

In time, Saul appoints David commander of more than 1,000 soldiers. Then Saul sends him off to fight, probably hoping he'll come back dead. But David enjoys one victory after another.

Saul owes David a princess wife. It's the reward Saul promised for anyone who killed Goliath. But Saul tacks on another task. He wants David to bring him the foreskins of 100 Philistines, or die trying. Preferably the latter.

David delivers 200. His prize is Saul's daughter, Michal.

Saul urges his oldest son, Jonathan, to assassinate David. But the brothers-in-law are best buddies, and Jonathan talks his dad out of the idea.

Eventually, Saul can't take it anymore. He orders his soldiers to go to David's house and kill him. Michal gets word of it and warns David, who escapes.

Now he's a fugitive. Saul marries Michal off to another man.

MUSIC THERAPY / Depressed, Saul often listens to the soothing hum of David's harp. Twice, however, he grabs a spear and heaves it at David—whose reflexes are apparently better than Saul's aim.

CELEBRATE THE HERO / After David kills Goliath, the Jews "sang and danced for joy with tambourines and cymbals." It's the song that drives King Saul bonkers. "Saul has killed his thousands, and David his ten thousands!" (1 Samuel 18:6-7).

David's ragtag militia

ON THE RUN, David slowly gathers a following.

First his brothers and other relatives. Then strangers, "men who were in trouble or in debt or who were just discontented" (1 Samuel 22:2).

Before long, he has a militia of 400 men, which later grows to 600.

Saul remains obsessed with killing David. He even orders the execution of 85 priests he wrongly accused of siding with David; the families are slaughtered, too.

Instead of focusing on the real threat to Israel, the Philistines, Saul spends his energy and assets on a manhunt.

David is a master of the dodge. He and his men hide among the Philistines, sometimes even working for them as mercenaries hired to kill Jews—but secretly killing Philistines instead. Double agent.

Once, Saul and 3,000 soldiers corner them at the En-gedi oasis beside the Dead Sea. But David eludes them by hiding in one of the caves.

Rotten luck, Saul picks that cave to relieve himself.

David's men want to kill him while he's doing his not-so-regal business. Instead, David sneaks over to Saul and silently cuts off part of his robe—the point being, he could have cut off something else. When Saul leaves and reaches some distance, David calls out to the king and raises the robe piece to show he has no desire to hurt the king.

Saul sobs, "You are a better man than I am" (1 Samuel 24:17). He leaves. But his humility proves temporary, and he goes back to his manhunt.

DAVID'S OASIS HIDEOUT

WHY DAVID FLED TO GOLIATH'S HOMETOWN. Gath wasn't just the largest Philistine city, it was the hometown of their champion warrior—Goliath—whom David killed years earlier. A fugitive in Israel, he had to go somewhere. The king of Gath recognized David as a great warrior and eventually hired him as a mercenary, putting him in charge of his bodyguards.

SPRING WATER IN THE BADLANDS. David and his militia hide in En-gedi oasis, showered by this spring-fed waterfall.

Saul kills himself

MORTALLY WOUNDED IN BATTLE with the Philistines, King Saul falls on his own sword rather than face capture and inevitable torture.

Philistines had mustered an army and staged it for battle at Shunem, in the vast and fertile Jezreel Valley of Israel's northland.

Saul counters by gathering his own army on the slopes of Mount Gilboa, overlooking the valley.

But when he sees the size of the Philistine army, his jaw drops.

The prophet Samuel had died, and Saul doesn't trust anyone else to give him advice from God. So he slips behind enemy lines to consult a medium. He asks her to contact Samuel from the dead.

A fraud, the medium screams in horror when Samuel actually shows up.

"Tomorrow the LORD will let the Philistines defeat Israel's army," Samuel says. "Then you and your sons will join me down here in the world of the dead" (1 Samuel 28:19 CEV).

Jonathan and two of his brothers die in the battle.

Philistines nail Saul's headless body to the city wall at Beth-shan. Jews retrieve the body, burn it, and bury the bones by a tree.

BAD NEWS FROM BEYOND / Samuel's ghost, conjured up by a medium, warns Saul that by day's end he'll be dead, too.

NO MEDIUMS ALLOWED. By Jewish law, trying to contact the dead was a sure way to reach them—by joining them. It was a capital offense (see Leviticus 20:27).

MOUNT GILBOA. Like the Mount of Olives, Gilboa is actually a ridge of hills with several peaks. It's one of two ridges in the eastern Jezreel Valley. The other is the Hill of Moreh. In preparation for battle with the Philistines, Saul staged his army at Gilboa. The Philistines gathered at Shunem beside the Hill of Moreh.

David, new king of Israel

DAVID KILLS THE MESSENGER who delivers the tragic news that King Saul and three of his sons have died in the battle Israel lost to the Philistines.

The man made the mistake of saying he put the wounded king out of his misery. Saul committed suicide. The man lied probably because he thought David would reward him. But David, anointed by Samuel years earlier to become Israel's future king, isn't fond of people killing "the LORD's anointed one" (2 Samuel 1:16).

David also executes two men who assassinate Saul's surviving son, King Ishbosheth. For the same reason.

With Ishbosheth dead, tribal leaders rally around David. In Hebron, near his Bethlehem hometown, David becomes king of Israel. He's 30 years old, and he'll reign 40 years—seven and a half of them from his capital in Hebron.

PALACE INTRIGUE.
The two-year reign of Saul's son, Ishbosheth, might have stretched longer had he not accused his general, Abner, of sleeping with one of Saul's wives. The royal harem belonged to Ishbosheth. Abner—who didn't deny the charge—switched his loyalty to David and prepared a coup. But David's general, Joab, murdered Abner before he could carry out the coup. Joab's motive was revenge; Abner had killed Joab's brother in battle. Ishbosheth, suddenly without his general, became paralyzed with fear. Two of his soldiers assassinated him.

AMALEKITES.
Persistent enemies of Israel whom David defeated, these nomads lived in what is now southern Israel. They attacked the Jews during their Exodus out of Egyptian slavery. They were also among the raiders Gideon drove off. Saul fought them, too. And Samuel got mad at him for not exterminating them.

David, king of Israel by age 30

Israel's new capital: Jerusalem

WHY DAVID PICKS JERUSALEM is anyone's guess. But a popular theory is one that real-estate agents understand: location.

His Hebron capital in the tribe of Judah made it look like David favored his own tribe of Judah over the others. Jerusalem—then called Jebus—remained an unconquered city in no-man's-land, on the border assigned to the tribes of Judah and Benjamin. There, the capital would favor no tribe. Also, Jerusalem crowned a steep ridge, making the city hard to attack and easy to defend.

That's why the Jebusites inside taunt David and his soldiers: "You might as well go home! Even the blind and the lame could keep you out" (2 Samuel 5:6 MSG).

David recognizes the challenge. So he offers an incentive to his men. "Whoever is first to attack the Jebusites will become the commander of my armies!" (1 Chronicles 11:6).

He also gives some advice. "Whoever attacks them should strike by going into the city through the water tunnel" (2 Samuel 5:8).

Joab, his sister's son, wins the race. Jebus gets a new name, City of David.

RIDGE RUNNER / Jerusalem grew up on a ridge above the Kidron Valley, right.

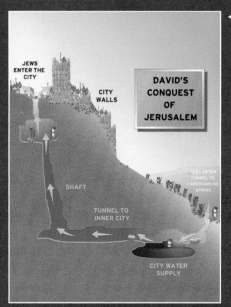

JERUSALEM'S WATER TUNNEL. Many Bible experts speculate that the "water tunnel" David talked about was a 52-foot (16 meters) vertical shaft rediscovered in 1867. The shaft inside the city plunged to an underground pool fed by Gihon Spring. The spring lay in a cave at the bottom of the ridge, outside the city walls. Scholars speculate that people inside the city drew water from the pool, like they would from a well.

RERUNS. Many stories in the books of 1, 2 Samuel and 1, 2 Kings are repeated in 1, 2 Chronicles.

JEBUS/CITY OF DAVID/JERUSALEM. This one city that went by many names, including Zion, is one of the oldest continually occupied cities in the world. It was 2,500 years old by the time David arrived.

The Ark comes to Jerusalem

DAVID ISN'T SATISFIED with a political Jerusalem. He wants it to become the spiritual capital of Israel, too.

So he goes after the nation's most sacred object, the gold-covered chest containing the 10 Commandments: the Ark of the Covenant.

It has been in storage at the neighboring village of Kiriath Jearim ever since Philistines destroyed the worship center at Shiloh more than 100 years earlier.

David's first attempt to bring the Ark to Jerusalem is tragic, perhaps because he doesn't follow God's protocol for transporting it. Priests are supposed to carry it. Instead, they put the Ark on an oxcart. And when an ox stumbles and one man grabs the chest to stabilize it, he dies instantly. David tries again three months later. He gets it right this time.

It's a day to celebrate. David leads the procession, stopping to offer sacrifices, and then resuming the trip, dancing and jumping for joy—to the cheers of the crowd and the blaring blast of ram horns—an ancient version of air horns.

BEDROCK IN THE MOSQUE. Jerusalem's most famous landmark is called the Dome of the Rock because of the huge rock inside. Many say this is the bedrock threshing floor David bought as a platform for the altar he built, and for the temple that his son Solomon later built.

DANCING DAVID / Israel's most sacred object, the chest containing the 10 Commandments, arrives at Jerusalem in a joyful procession. David strips off his royal robes and celebrates with dancing—to the embarrassment of one of his wives, Michal. "How the king of Israel has distinguished himself today," she says, "going around half-naked" (2 Samuel 6:20 TNIV).

David goes to war

WHAT SAUL ONLY DREAMED, David accomplishes. He not only secures the borders of Israel, he pushes them out. Way out. Deep into what are now Syria and Jordan. And even into Egypt's Sinai Peninsula.

David also manhandles the bullies on the Middle Eastern block: the Philistines. The closely guarded secret weapon they had brought with them when they migrated from Mediterranean islands—the knowledge of how to forge iron—proves no match for David. "The LORD made David victorious wherever he went" (2 Samuel 8:14).

And David gets around.

His hit list of conquered towns and nations includes:

// Gath, the largest Philistine town

// Damascus in Aram (Syria), occupying the city with several garrisons

// Amalek in Israel's southern badlands, and

// in modern-day Jordan, the nations of Ammon, Edom, and Moab, killing two out of every three Moabites.

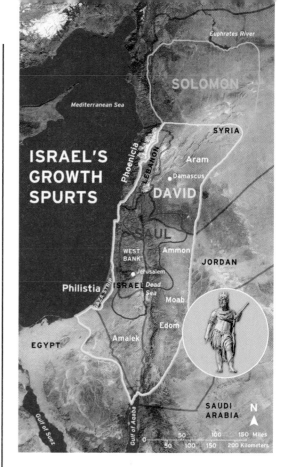

THREE KINGS, THREE KINGDOMS / Israel's first three kings grow the Jewish nation. Enemies confine Saul's kingdom mainly to the hill country. David dominates his enemies and secures his borders. Solomon kicks it up a notch, controlling the largest Jewish kingdom that has ever existed—more than double the size of modern Israel.

▶ **FASHION STATEMENT.** Beards were popular and practical in David's time—and are still fashionable throughout the Middle East. Among some groups, then as now, it was considered shameful for men not to grow a beard.

A CUT AND A SHAVE. David got insulted into conquering Ammon. He sent ambassadors there to express sorrow for their king's death. But the dead king's son, who had become the new king, thought they came to scout the nation for an invasion. So he shaved off one side of their beards and cut off their robes at the waist, sending them home half-bearded and half-naked.

David and the bathing beauty

WHEN DAVID HAS SEX with Bathsheba—the wife of a soldier who's off fighting in a war for king and country—David already has a harem of at least seven wives.

But Bathsheba, naked and dripping wet, proves irresistible.

David has just awakened from his afternoon nap and is getting some air on the flat-topped palace roof. There she is below, perhaps in the walled courtyard of her home. She's taking a bath. It's a purification ritual for spiritual cleansing required of Jewish women one week after the menstrual flow stops.

The timing of the ritual means that when Bathsheba is done with her bath, she's not only fresh and fragrant—she's fertile.

EYE OF THE BEHOLDER / It's not as though Bathsheba was putting on a show for King David by bathing outside, while he watched from his palace roof. She may have been in the walled courtyard of her home below, or inside her house with the windows open to ventilate the afternoon heat. But wherever she was, David had the angle.

David sends for her. She ends up pregnant.

Her husband, Uriah, one of David's elite commandos called The Thirty, is fighting about 60 miles (95 km) away. He's laying siege to a town near what is now Jordan's capital of Amman.

David sends for him, pretending he wants a war briefing. What he really wants is Uriah to sleep with Bathsheba, so he'll think the kid is his.

But Uriah doesn't even go home to see his wife. He sleeps at the palace entrance. When David asks him why he did that, Uriah says, "My master's men are camping in the open fields. How could I go home to wine and dine and sleep with my wife?" (2 Samuel 11:11).

David tries again, going so far as to get Uriah drunk. Doesn't work.

So David sends the soldier back to war—with a sealed message that seals Uriah's fate. Addressing the commander, David writes: "Station Uriah on the front lines where the battle is fiercest. Then pull back so that he will be killed" (2 Samuel 11:15).

Uriah dies, with several comrades.

David marries Bathsheba. Sadly, the baby boy dies.

◀ ROOFTOP PATIOS. People used their flat-toppped roofs like we use our patios, porches, and decks. It's a place to cool off, get some fresh air, and do light chores such as sewing or drying fish and grain.

Village of Capernaum by Sea of Galilee

WHY DAVID SAYS HE'S SORRY

Nathan, the palace prophet, confronts David indirectly at first, appealing to his sense of justice.

Nathan spins a parable like it's a news story. He says a rich man with huge flocks stole a poor man's only lamb—a pet. Then he killed it, cooked it, and ate it.

Livid, David says this evil man deserves to die. David demands to know who he is.

"You are that man!" (2 Samuel 12:7).

Immediately David sees the parallel. He confesses, and God forgives him.

BATHSHEBA'S SEQUEL SON. David's successor will be Solomon, a son he has with Bathsheba. Solomon certainly wasn't first in line for the crown. David had at least 9 sons before Solomon came along, possibly 16. But Solomon became the preferred choice of both David and the prophet Nathan.

Crown prince and sister rapist

INCEST IS FORBIDDEN under Jewish law. Yet David's oldest son, Amnon, the crown prince who's expected to inherit Israel's throne, falls in lust with his half sister, Tamar.

They both have the same father, David, but different mothers.

Amnon sets a sex trap. He pretends he's sick and he calls for his sister to make him some food. When she tries to serve it to him, he serves himself. He rapes her.

Afterward, in disgust, he barks out orders to his servants: "Throw this woman out, and lock the door behind her!" (2 Samuel 13:17).

No longer a virgin, Tamar tears her robe that only princess virgins customarily wear. She moves out of the palace and moves in with her full brother Absalom.

When David hears about it, he gets angry. But not angry enough to do anything.

Absalom, however, takes it personally. He sees it as an attack not only on his sister, but on his family honor. It's as though Amnon is sending a message to little brother Absalom: I can do whatever I want, and you can't stop me.

Absalom stops him.

He invites Amnon to a sheep-shearing feast two years after the rape. He gets big brother drunk. And he orders his men to murder him. Absalom then flees to his grandfather—his mother's dad— the king of Geshur in what is now Syria.

RAPED AND TRASHED / Calling it love, David's oldest son rapes his half sister. But in the afterglow he calls it hate and runs her off. If custom prevailed, she was treated as damaged goods for the rest of her life. There's no hint in the Bible that she ever married.

JEWISH LAW ABOUT INCEST. It was forbidden, even among half siblings: "Do not have sexual relations with your sister or half sister" (Leviticus 18:9).

TAMAR PROPOSES MARRIAGE. Though sex is forbidden, Tamar tried to talk Amnon out of the rape: "Just speak to the king about it, and he will let you marry me" (2 Samuel 13:13). Perhaps she thought David would bend the rules for his number-one son. In fact, David did just that by refusing to punish Amnon for the rape.

MARRIED TO YOUR RAPIST. Raped women were considered damaged goods that no man would want. Both Jewish law and Middle Eastern custom required the rapist to marry the woman "because he violated her, and he may never divorce her" (Deuteronomy 22:29).

Dethroning Dad

AFRAID TO GO HOME after murdering his brother, Absalom remains on a self-imposed exile for three years—though he's now the crown prince, next in line for the throne.

David's general, Joab, sees how much the king misses his son. So he talks David into inviting Absalom back. David agrees, but stubbornly waits two years to meet with him and reconcile.

By that time, Absalom is fed up. He's not going to wait for his dad to die so he can inherit the throne. He decides to take it by force.

First, he develops a marketing plan. He sells himself to the people by going to the city gate where daily trials are held. There, he commiserates with the people, saying he wishes the king would give them justice. And when people begin to bow to him, he stops them and gives them a hug.

After four years of this, he travels to neighboring Hebron and declares himself the new king. Absalom has developed enough of a following that David flees Jerusalem. But he leaves behind a palace advisor to fake loyalty to Absalom and give him bad advice.

Absalom accepts this advisor's bogus advice to build a massive army before going after David. This works to the advantage of David, a seasoned warrior. It gives him time to round up his loyal, experienced soldiers.

Absalom dies in the battle, despite David's orders that no one harm him.

ABSALOM, HANDSOME AND HAIRY.
"Absalom was praised as the most handsome man in all Israel. He was flawless from head to foot. He cut his hair only once a year, and then only because it was so heavy. When he weighed it out, it came to five pounds [2.3 kilograms]!" (2 Samuel 14:25–26). Sadly, his hair is the death of him. Absalom flees a losing battle against his father's army when branches of an oak tree hook him by the hair and yank him off his mule. David has ordered his soldiers not to harm his rebel son. But when David's general, Joab, sees Absalom dangling from the tree like a bull's-eye, it's too tempting. Absalom gets three daggers to the heart.

HEBRON, CITY OF KINGS.
A day's walk south of Jerusalem, about 20 miles (30 km), Hebron is where Absalom declares himself king of Israel. It's the biggest city of Judah, in his tribal region. And it's the city that first crowned David king several decades earlier.

▶ **LOOKING FOR JUSTICE /** A Palestinian and a Jew walk past each other in front of Damascus Gate, an entrance into Old Jerusalem. In Bible times, people wanting justice brought their case to elders stationed at the city gate. That's where Absalom began planting seeds of discontent about his father's reign, promising justice when he became king.

BIG SCENE

JEWS BUILD THEIR FIRST TEMPLE

1 KINGS 6:1

King Solomon orders work to begin on the first permanent Jewish worship center, a temple in Jerusalem. It will endure for 400 years.

BIBLE HISTORY	**960 BC** *Solomon builds first Jewish temple*	**930 BC** *Jewish nation splits: Judah (south), Israel (north)*
WORLD HISTORY	*Middle East farmers start using animal waste as fertilizer* **1000 BC**	*Pharaoh Shoshenq I (Shishak) invades both Jewish nations* **928 BC**

ALL DATES APPROXIMATE

1,2 KINGS

HOW TO KILL ISRAEL IN 400 YEARS

STORY LINE

THE RISE AND FALL OF ISRAEL. That's the story of Israel's kings during 400 years of reigning over the Jews, for better or worse. Mostly worse.

Only half a dozen of the nearly four dozen Jewish rulers get good reviews.

King David grows old and dies. But he leaves Israel in great shape, with wars behind and borders secured. This frees his son and successor, King Solomon, to lead the nation into its one and only golden age of peace and prosperity.

Famed for his wisdom, Solomon goes out like a fool. He lets his foreign wives lure him into worshipping idols. For this, God promises to take most of the country away from his family. The very next king, Solomon's son, treats the masses so callously that only his own tribe of Judah remains loyal to him. The northern tribes secede.

Suddenly, there are two Jewish nations: Judah in the south, Israel in the north.

As centuries pass, each nation moves further from God—with occasional spiritual hiccups in Judah, when a God-loving king shows up.

God sends prophets to warn of the consequences of sin. But few listen.

Assyrian invaders from what is now northern Iraq conquer the northern Jewish nation of Israel in 722 BC, deporting the survivors. Babylonian invaders also from Iraq conquer Judah in 586 BC, deporting the survivors.

By the story's end, there is no longer a Jewish nation on the world map. Jewish refugees are scattered throughout the Middle East.

// LOCATION: Israel.

// TIME: The stories begin in the last years of King David's reign, in the mid-900s BC and end with the collapse of the Jewish nation about 400 years later, in 586 BC.

// AUTHOR: Unknown. First and Second Kings were originally one book.

850 BC
*Elijah defeats
prophets of Baal*

722 BC
*Assyrians conquer
Israel*

586 BC
*Babylonians
conquer Judah*

*Egyptian holds Jewish prisoners,
928 BC art from Egyptian temple*

*Babylonians
conquer Assyrians*
612 BC

*Buddha seeks
enlightenment*
528 BC

Solomon, the surprise king

OLD AND DYING, King David seems confused about who's supposed to replace him as Israel's next king.

It actually sounds like the prophet Nathan and one of David's many wives hatch a plot to exploit the king's foggy memory—and make Solomon king, though Solomon is way down the line of contenders. David had at least nine sons before Solomon.

The logical choice is Adonijah, David's oldest surviving son. He throws a pre-coronation party while David lies dying. Most of the royal family and Israel's top leaders are partying with the crown prince.

But Nathan—perhaps guided by God—prefers Solomon.

Nathan tells Solomon's mother, Bathsheba, to "remind" David that he promised the kingdom to her son. While she's doing that, Nathan arrives and backs her up—adding that people at Adonijah's party are already saying, "Long live King Adonijah!" (1 Kings 1:25).

David calls Zadok the priest and has him anoint Solomon king.

Party over.

Shocked, Adonijah accepts the decision at first. But he later asks permission to marry one of King David's widows. Solomon sees this as a political maneuver: The oldest son would marry the former king's wife and later claim he's the rightful king.

Solomon has his big brother executed.

BATHSHEBA.
Solomon's mother is the same Bathsheba who had an affair with David. Bathsheba's first child with David died.

KILLING OFF THE COMPETITION.
Transfer of power in ancient times was often bloody, with many contenders leveraging for control. Some contenders played it safe by killing off all possible competition, including family members who expressed no desire to reign. One Jewish grandmother executed her grandkids so she could run the nation uncontested as queen: Athaliah (see 2 Kings 11:1).

SETTLING SCORES.
David's last words weren't so regal. He asked Solomon to assassinate two people. First: General Joab, for killing innocent people such as an allied general named Abner. Joab also killed David's son, Absalom. Second: a man who once cursed him. "You are a wise man," David told Solomon, "and you will know how to arrange a bloody death for him" (1 Kings 2:9).

JUMPING THE GUN /
David's oldest son, Adonijah, presumes he'll be the next king of Israel. He even throws a "Dad is almost dead" party. Little does he know he'll be joining his father soon.

Solomon: I have a dream

ASK FOR WHATEVER YOU WANT. That's God's offer to the newly crowned King Solomon.

The king has just visited one of the Jewish places of prayer. It's on a hilltop in Gibeon, near Jerusalem. There, Solomon sacrifices 1,000 animals.

God's generous offer comes that night, while Solomon's dreaming.

Solomon's reply: "Please make me wise and teach me the difference between right and wrong. Then I will know how to rule your people" (1 Kings 3:9 CEV).

If this exchange had taken place on Facebook, God may have hit the "Like" button, since he certainly likes Solomon's answer. God is pleased that Solomon's top request—his top priority—is wisdom. It's not wealth, a long life, or power over enemies.

God gives Solomon the works: the wisdom he asks for, along with the wealth, health, and power he didn't bother to mention.

And to prove Solomon gets his top request, the storyteller showcases Solomon's wisdom in settling a tough court case.

Two prostitutes with newborn sons are rooming together. While sleeping, one woman accidentally rolls over on her son and suffocates him. She switches him for her roommate's son. This case of the switcheroo reaches Solomon, who offers to slice the boy in two.

Fake Mom is okay with it. Genuine Mom is horrified. She pleads with Solomon to give the boy to the other woman instead.

Mystery solved. Boy returned to rightful mother. Case closed.

SPLIT DECISION / Two women each claim a baby boy belongs to them. King Solomon flushes out the fake mother by offering to cut the boy in two. Fake Mom says it sounds fair to her.

SACRIFICES AT GIBEON? Jews were supposed to offer sacrifices to God in only one place—a site determined by God (see Deuteronomy 12:14). They were not to worship on scattered hilltops, as pagans did. Yet Solomon started his reign by allowing Jews to worship God at various revered sites. In time, though, he builds the Jerusalem Temple—which God approves as the one place he'll accept sacrifices.

PROVERB WRITER. The Bible says Solomon wrote "3,000 proverbs" (1 Kings 4:32), which are wise sayings—a bit like we'd expect to read on a preacher-approved fortune cookie. The Bible also credits him with writing, or at least inspiring, many of the wise sayings and song lyrics in the Bible books of Proverbs, Ecclesiastes, and a love song called the Song of Songs or the Song of Solomon.

Israel's prefab temple

"No noise from hammers and chisels and other iron tools."

1 KINGS 6:7 MSG

GOD'S HOME ON EARTH gets an upgrade.

He has been living among his people in a sacred tent since the Exodus—for "480 years" (1 Kings 6:1). But now, God has agreed to let Solomon build Israel's first permanent worship center: the Jerusalem Temple.

Out of respect for the holy site, where the massive altar has been in operation for decades, Solomon issues an order that would have stunned any builder:

Solomon wanted the stones sized at the quarry and fitted together on site, like a giant Lego building.

Nearly 200,000 men—all drafted—work seven years to complete the sanctuary. It's a building that stretches 30 yards long, 10 yards wide, and 15 yards high (27 x 9 x 14 meters). About the size of a four-story building. (See painting next page, bottom right.)

SOLOMON'S REORGANIZATION
12 districts instead of tribes

GOOD-BYE 12 TRIBES / Solomon replaces the 12 tribes run by family elders with 12 districts run by governors he appoints—and who report to him. Some districts track with tribal boundaries. Some don't.

Solomon doesn't actually retire the tribes. He just doesn't invite them into his government.

He orders each district to provide all the food the palace needs for a month. Twelve districts. Twelve months.

Egypt's leader during this same century, Pharaoh Shoshenq I (945–925 BC, called Shishak in the Bible), does the same thing to collect supplies for one of his temples. He divides the region that the temple served, Herakleopolis, into 12 districts.

Solomon's own tribe—Judah—seems exempt. Cities inside Judah's territory don't show up in the list of districts. King's prerogative.

Inside are three rooms:

- **ENTRANCE ROOM**
- **MAIN SANCTUARY**, the largest room, cedar paneled. Priests come in every day to burn incense, light gold lampstands. Each Sabbath, they set out 12 loaves of bread representing the 12 tribes of Israel.
- **INNER SANCTUARY**, a 10-yard (9-meter) cube where Jews keep their holiest relic, the gold-covered chest containing the 10 Commandments. Only the high priest can enter this room, and only once a year: *Yom Kippur* (Day of Atonement), a national day of repentance.

GENTLEMEN IN THE QUARRY. At the turn of the 1900s, several men inspect limestone quarries under Jerusalem. Solomon's stonecutters may have chiseled some of their Temple blocks from this ancient quarry. Visitors to Jerusalem in Bible times described the limestone temple as dazzlingly white, like a flash of sunlight.

GOD'S HOUSE, SOLOMON'S PALACE. Though it took 7 years to build the Temple, it took 13 to build Solomon's palace (see 1 Kings 6:38–7:1).

▼ WHEN "BUILDER'S GRADE" MEANT TOP-QUALITY. Finest wood available—rot-resisting cedar from Lebanon—frames the Jerusalem Temple that Solomon builds. High-grade limestone blocks form the walls. Solomon commissions a foreign master in metalwork to create the bronze pillars by the sanctuary entrance, along with the huge basins that hold water for washing sacrificial animals.

Cedar of Lebanon

DIRT-CHEAP LUMBER / Solomon got his top-grade cedar and cypress lumber from King Hiram of Tyre, in what is now Lebanon. As payment for the timber, Solomon gave Hiram 20 towns in Galilee, near Lebanon's border. When Hiram came to inspect his new property, he had one word for it: "worthless" (1 Kings 9:13).

Sheba, the shopping queen

A TRIP TO THE SHOPPING MALL might be a fair way to explain why the queen of Sheba travels some 1,500 miles (2,400 km) from the opposite end of the Red Sea to visit King Solomon.

The writer hints that curiosity drives her: "When the queen of Sheba heard about the fame of Solomon and his relationship to the LORD, she came to test Solomon with hard questions" (1 Kings 10:1 TNIV). Solomon passes the test.

Sheba, however, brings more than questions. She brings a massive caravan—camels loaded with rare spices, jewels, and 9,000 pounds (4,000 kilograms) of gold.

These might be lavish gifts. But the context of the story suggests they're trade goods—same as cash—for an outing at what amounts to the King of Israel Shopping Mall.

Clues:

// "King Solomon gave the queen of Sheba whatever she asked for, besides all the customary gifts he had so generously given" (1 Kings 10:13).

// After telling the Sheba story, the writer jumps to a report of Solomon's annual revenue from traders. As though report and story are linked.

▲ **SOLOMON'S INTERNATIONAL ASSETS.** Solomon makes a bundle in trade because he controls Israel, the only popular land bridge between Africa and Arabia in the south and nations to the north. His annual take includes 25 tons (23 metric tons) of gold. He also operates a fleet of trading ships sailing the Red Sea and the Mediterranean. They return every three years, tight-packed with riches including gold, silver, and exotic animals.

SHEBA'S TRADE WITH JEWS, ON THE RECORD. A newly discovered bronze inscription reports that the kingdom of Sabaea, possibly a reference to Sheba, sent a trade expedition to the "towns of Judah." The text is written in South Arabian script and dated to about 300 years after Solomon and the Queen of Sheba.

Solomon, the marrying kind

PEACE AND QUIET is what King Solomon wants. So he marries 1,000 women.

Worse, 700 are high maintenance—each a princess used to constant attention.

Doesn't seem wise.

Not given earlier Bible stories about tension and rivalries in families with more than one wife. Jacob's two wives competed for his affection by running a baby-making race. Some in David's dysfunctional family raped and killed each other.

The peace Solomon has in mind is along his borders, with neighboring kingdoms. It's customary in his day to sign a peace treaty and then marry one of the daughters from the allied king's harem of wives.

Solomon's wives wear him out, spiritually speaking. By law, Jews aren't supposed to marry idol worshippers "because they will turn your hearts to their gods" (1 Kings 11:2). That's just what happens to Solomon.

After a promising start as a wise young ruler, he ends up an old man worshipping the idols of his foreign wives. At least three idols—Ashtoreth, Chemosh, and Molech—and probably many more.

For this, God vows to take away most of the kingdom from Solomon's family—though not the whole kingdom, out of respect for David.

DINNER FOR FOUR / A Turkish man and his wives share a meal at the turn of the 1900s. In Bible times, rich men sometimes married more than one woman. King Solomon, described as the richest man of his day, married 1,000. He lived to regret it.

◄ MOLECH. Bull-headed god associated with child sacrifice. Some theorize the idol was made of iron, with a fire built underneath it. When the iron turned red hot, the child was placed in its hands, while the people chanted and beat drums to drown out the child's screams. Two Jewish kings sacrificed a son to Molech: Ahaz and Manasseh (see 2 Kings 16:2–3, 21:6; 23:10).

ASHTORETH. Also known as Astarte, wife of Canaan's lead god Baal, she was worshipped in various ways throughout the ancient Middle East. People of Lebanon associated her with the evening star, Venus, and worshipped her as the goddess of war and sex. Babylonians worshipped her as Ishtar, Greeks as Aphrodite, and Romans as Venus.

CHEMOSH. Top god of Moabites, in what is now Jordan, Chemosh is honored in the famous Moabite Stone (discovered in 1868) as the god who helped Moab drive off the Jews.

WHY SEAL A PEACE TREATY WITH A MARRIAGE? Kings signing a peace treaty were less likely to break the deal if one of their daughters was married to the other king.

Israel: One nation becomes two

JEWS ARE FED UP WITH TAXES. And with getting drafted for Solomon's never-ending building projects: the Temple, palaces, city walls throughout the country—all of which require constant repair.

With Solomon dead and gone, and his son Rehoboam on the throne, many Jewish leaders figure it's a great time to ask the new king to lighten up.

Rehoboam takes their request to his advisors. Older counselors suggest he grant the request. But young mavericks tell him to show the people who's boss.

The king picks door number two, promising to work and tax them like never before.

In return, the northern half of Israel shows him the door. All 10 northern tribes secede from the union. And they do it with poetry. They know their grandparents had rallied around David with a chant:

> *"We're on your side, O David,*
> *We're committed, O son of Jesse."*
> 1 CHRONICLES **12:18** MSG

But now the new generation sings a new song:

> *"Get lost, David!*
> *We've had it with you, son of Jesse!"*
> 1 KINGS **12:16** MSG

The northern tribes crown Jeroboam king—probably because many years earlier a prophet had predicted he'd get the job.

Furious at the revolt, Rehoboam musters an army of 180,000, once again planning to show Israel who's boss. As it turns out, God's boss. A prophet convinces Rehoboam to stand down and accept God's judgment.

SPLIT NATION

3 WORSHIP CENTERS:
2 BULLS, 1 TEMPLE

DRAFTED FOR CIVIL SERVICE.
Just as many countries in wartime will draft young men for the army, Solomon drafted workers for his building projects. They worked in shifts, each tribe taking a project for a period.

LURE OF THE BULL.
Religion isn't the reason King Jeroboam of Israel puts gold calf idols at Bethel and Dan. It's politics. He's afraid if northern Jews head south to worship at Jerusalem's Temple in Judah, they'll eventually want to reunite with David's family of kings. He'd be out of a job, and missing a head.

Elijah in the battle of the gods

JEZEBEL, QUEEN OF ISRAEL, IS NO JEW. Raised a princess in what is now Lebanon, she hates Jewish religion and culture. Worse, married to Israel's King Ahab, she's in a position to do something about it.

She decides to retire the Jewish religion. Her strategy: permanently retire the Jewish religious leaders. She orders God's prophets assassinated. Scores run to the caves where they hide for years.

Next, she grants palace privileges to her own prophets—850 of them devoted to the Canaanite gods of Baal and Asherah. She even feeds them.

God orders one of his prophets, Elijah, to challenge Jezebel's prophets to a supernatural duel—850 prophets against one. Each side would sacrifice a bull and then call down fire from heaven.

"The god who answers by setting fire to the wood," Elijah says, "is the true God!" (1 Kings 18:24). Jezebel's prophets agree. No wonder. Baal, Canaan's rain god, shows up in ancient art holding lightning bolts (see photo page 42).

This battle of the gods takes place somewhere on the Mount Carmel ridge. But Baal does nothing, though his prophets pray all day, even cutting themselves. Yet after Elijah's short prayer, God drops a fireball so intense that it disintegrates even the altar stones.

Then on Elijah's command, Jews in the audience grab the pagan priests and execute them.

► **COUNT 'EM.** There are only four good kings in four centuries. From the time Israel split into two nations, about 930 BC, until Babylonians wipe the Jews off the political map in 586 BC, only four kings get a godly thumbs-up. They're all in the southland Jewish nation of Judah—home to the only God-approved worship center: the Jerusalem Temple.

ISRAEL'S KINGS
Jeroboam I, 22 years
Nadab, 2 years
Baasha, 24 years
Elah, 2 years
Zimri, 7 days
Omri, 12 years
Ahab, 22 years
Ahaziah, 2 years
Joram, 12 years
Jehu, 28 years
Jehoahaz, 17 years
Jehoash, 16 years
Jeroboam II, 41 years
Zechariah, 6 months
Shallum, 1 month
Menahem, 10 years
Pekahiah, 2 years
Pekah, 20 years
Hoshea, 9 years

*Assyrians destroy
Samaria, 722 BC*

JUDAH'S KINGS
(Good kings in black)
Rehoboam, 17 years
Abijam, 3 years
Asa, 41 years
Jehoshaphat, 25 years
Jehoram, 8 years
Ahaziah, 1 year
Athaliah (queen), 6 years
Joash, 40 years
Amaziah, 29 years
Azariah (Uzziah), 52 years
Jotham, 16 years
Ahaz, 16 years
Hezekiah, 29 years
Manasseh, 55 years
Amon, 2 years
Josiah, 31 years
Jehoahaz, 3 months
Jehoiakim, 11 years
Jehoiachin, 3 months
Zedekiah, 11 years

*Babylonians destroy
Jerusalem, 586 BC*

**4 GOOD KINGS
IN 4 CENTURIES**

Chariots of fire

SOUNDING MORE LIKE A TORNADO than a chariot of fire, "a strong wind took Elijah up into heaven" (2 Kings 2:11 CEV). Most Bible translations call it a whirlwind.

But celestial chariots are there, too.

Elijah and his apprentice, prophet-in-training Elisha, have crossed the Jordan River into what is now the Arab country of Jordan. Both know it's the end of the road for Elijah. So does a group of 50 prophets who cross their path along the way. Somehow, God has communicated that to all of them.

When they reach the Jordan River, Elijah rolls up his cloak and dips it into the water. The river stops, and they cross into what is now Jordan.

Elisha asks a favor. He wants to become Elijah's successor, and he wants to inherit "a double share" (2 Kings 2:9) of Elijah's spirit—perhaps spiritual power. The double share was what a father's oldest son inherits—twice as much of the estate as any younger son.

Elijah leaves the matter with God. He says if God lets Elisha see him leave the planet, the answer is yes.

A chariot of fire swoops down from the sky, separating the two men. A whirlwind carries Elijah away, leaving only his cloak. Elisha screams, "Israel's cavalry and chariots have taken my master away!" (2 Kings 2:12 CEV).

Returning home, Elisha discovers God has granted his request for miracle-working power. When he reaches the Jordan River, he rolls up Elijah's cloak, dips it into the water, and the river stops flowing.

ELIJAH'S HIGHWAY TO HEAVEN / Celestial chariots of fire swoop down to earth, apparently stirring up a whirlwind that carries off the prophet Elijah. Left behind is Elisha, who becomes his successor.

A tornado sweeps away roofing tiles and snaps electrical lines in a northern Israel village in 2006.

TORNADOES IN ISRAEL. Tornadoes are rare in the Middle Eastern areas in and around Israel, one every few years. Most occur along the Mediterranean coast.

CHARIOTS OF FIRE OR CLOUDS OF LIGHTNING? In the Bible, storm clouds sometimes represent God's chariot. Ezekiel once described God arriving on four-wheeled chariot that looked like "a huge cloud that flashed with lightning and shone with brilliant light" (Ezekiel 1:4).

Kiss Jezebel good-bye

KING AHAB IS DEAD. A stray arrow pierces the seam in his armor during a battle with Arameans near what is now Jordan's border with Syria. His son, Joram, carries the family dynasty into a third generation—after grandfather, Omri, father, Ahab, and older brother, Ahaziah, who died from injuries in a fall.

The prophet Elisha says God has had enough of this evil family. Elisha commissions a young prophet to go to Israel's eastern border, the town of Ramoth-gilead in what is now north Jordan. There, the prophet anoints the commander of the outpost, Jehu, as Israel's new king.

Jehu blows it off as religious babble—until his men hear the news and start celebrating with shouts of "Jehu is king!" (2 Kings 9:13).

With that, Jehu jumps in his chariot and is off to the coup.

King Joram, wounded in a recent battle, is recovering at the royal getaway palace in the hills of Jezreel. Queen Mother Jezebel is tending him. And King Ahaziah of Judah has come up to visit.

A Jezreel lookout recognizes Jehu coming in a cloud of dust: "It must be Jehu. . .he's driving like a madman" (2 Kings 9:20).

Both kings—perhaps fearing news of invasion along the border—ride out to meet him. Jehu and his men shoot and kill them both. Then Jehu secures his position as king by killing all possible heirs to the throne—all of Ahab's 70 sons, born to wives in the royal harem.

COUP
Race to kill Jezebel

Ramoth-gilead
Chariot commander Jehu launches coup with Elisha's blessing

Jezreel
Queen Mother Jezebel at summer palace about to become dog food

MILITARY COUP.
Stationed on Israel's eastern front at Ramoth-gilead, Jehu gets the prophet Elisha's blessing to overthrow Ahab's family dynasty. He charges 40 miles (64 km) to Jezreel, where he kills the king, Jezebel, and all of Ahab's sons.

JEHU TAKES A BOW.
Israel's king Jehu bows before the superpower ruler of the Middle East, King Shalmaneser III of the Assyrian Empire, headquartered in what is now Iraq. Assyrian artists sculpted the stone monument during Jehu's reign, in about 825 BC.

MAKEUP TO MEET HER MAKER /
Queen Mother Jezebel gets the news that her son, King Joram, has just been assassinated and that the leader of the coup is coming for her. She reaches for her makeup. Planning to die pretty and proud, she ends up splattered on the pavement where dogs pick her apart—leaving only her skull, hands, and feet.

HEADS IN A BASKET, TO GO.
Jehu ordered leaders at Israel's capital in Samaria, about 20 miles (32 km) south of Jezreel, to send him the heads of all 70 of Ahab's sons. The heads arrived in baskets. Jehu piled the heads by the city entrance. Then he killed all the rest of Ahab's relatives in Jezreel and Samaria, all the important officials, all the family friends, and the pagan priests.

Israel disappears

THIRST FOR FREEDOM KILLS ISRAEL.
They take a stand against the ancient version of a bully who steals a kid's lunch money, and they lose—not only their money, but their lives.

The bully is Assyria, a muscle-flexing, money-sucking empire extorting the entire Middle East. Assyrians work out of their home region in what is now northern Iraq. They vacuum wealth by invading neighboring nations and forcing them to pay heavy annual taxes.

Israel's last king, Hoshea, decides to stop the payments.

Assyria's king, Shalmaneser, responds with an invasion force that overruns Israel and surrounds the walled capital of Samaria. Over a stretch of three years, the Assyrians manage to starve the Jews into surrender.

In 722 BC, after about 200 years as an independent nation, Israel ceases to exist, though the southern Jewish nation of Judah survives. Assyria exiles many Jewish survivors to refugee colonies scattered throughout the empire, in what are now Iraq and Iran.

Assyrians send in pioneers to resettle Israel. Some marry Jewish stragglers, producing a race known in Jesus' day as Samaritans. A people not popular among blue-blood Jews.

ASSYRIAN TERROR TACTICS / An Assyrian soldier dismembers a live captive. Another victim hangs impaled on a stake, while disembodied heads of the dead decorate the macabre scene. Assyrians used terror as a tactic. Cultivating a bad-boy reputation, they figured, would terrify surrounding nations to give in to Assyrian demands—such as high taxes. To a great extent, they figured right.

◄ ASSYRIAN EMPIRE. The world's first mega-empire, based in Iraq, rose to power about the same time the northern nation of Israel was born—around 930 BC. Assyria survived for three centuries, one century longer than Israel. Assyrians built a reputation as terrorists who bullied and brutalized weaker nations throughout the Middle East. Coalition forces of Babylon and Medes from southern Iraq and Iran defeated Assyria in 612 BC.

SAMARITANS. They're descendants of Jews who married Assyrian pioneers. Full-blooded Jews later grew to hate Samaritans, treating them as half-breeds and spiritual heretics. The Samaritan Bible is short—just the first five books in the Bible. Jews say it's an edited version—and it substitutes Jerusalem as the God-approved worship center with Mount Gerizim. Today, about 700 Samaritans live in two communities near Mount Gerizim.

Assyrians hightail it home

FOR A GODLY KING—perhaps the most righteous in Jewish history—Hezekiah makes a whopper of a political blunder.

Assyria is breaking in a rookie king: Sennacherib (704–681 BC). Hezekiah of Judah decides this is a great time to join forces with the up-and-coming Babylonians and several other nations, to launch a rebellion against Assyria.

Sennacherib, a quick learner, beats the rebels to the punch. He knocks out the Babylonians first, and then overpowers the others. He saves Judah for last, destroying one walled city after another—46 by his count, according to one of his surviving records. Then he surrounds Jerusalem.

Hezekiah pays Sennacherib's ransom of a ton of gold and 11 tons of silver. But to do it Hezekiah has to empty the palace and Temple treasuries—and strip gold panels from the Temple doors.

Still, Sennacherib refuses to leave. He bad-mouths God, saying the Jews can't depend on him.

The prophet Isaiah assures Hezekiah otherwise.

By the next morning, the Assyrians lucky enough to wake up find 185,000 of their comrades dead, as though they died in their sleep. Sennacherib orders them to break camp and head home to Nineveh.

HEZEKIAH'S SECRET WATER TUNNEL.
Holy Land Tourist Freddia Gray wades through a 2,700-year-old tunnel beneath Jerusalem. Hezekiah had it built to funnel spring water into Jerusalem, to help withstand a long siege.

THE EMPIRE STRIKES BACK / When Assyria's new king, Sennacherib, gets word of a multinational revolt against the empire—with Judah among the rebels—he takes advantage of his swift intel. He launches a preemptive strike before the rebels have a chance to get organized.

DID RATS KILL THE ASSYRIANS?
Scholars speculate the rat-transmitted bubonic plague killed the Assyrians. Greek historian Herodotus said as much. Writing about Sennacherib's campaign 250 years later, he said a rat infestation killed many soldiers and ate holes in their leather gear.

Hezekiah, make out your will

"YOU'RE A GONER." That's the bad news King Hezekiah gets as he lies sick in bed. It comes as a message from God, delivered by the prophet Isaiah.

As Isaiah leaves the palace, Hezekiah begins to cry and pray. "LORD, please remember that I have always obeyed you. I have given myself completely to you and have done what you said was right" (2 Kings 20:3 NCV).

That's all it takes. Somehow, this prayer changes God's plan for him. Isaiah isn't even out of the palace before God turns him around, headed back to Hezekiah with a new message:

"I have heard your prayer and seen your tears. . . . I will add fifteen years to your life" (2 Kings 20:5–6).

As proof, God sends a sign. At Hezekiah's request, God moves the shadow on the palace sundial backward 10 steps.

• •

ONE PRAYER WORTH 15 YEARS / King Hezekiah gets an extra 15 years to settle his affairs—thanks to a prayer. On his sickbed, he gets word he won't recover and that he should make out his will. Instead, he prays. God grants him 15 more years.

Shadow clock

SUNDIALS IN BIBLE TIMES. Stair-step shadow clocks are one of the earliest known sundials, used to tell time. Egyptians invented them around 1500 BC, about the time many say Moses lived. Six steps faced east and six faced west. The number of steps the shadows covered indicated the approximate time of day. Lunchtime: no steps.

• •

DID GOD CHANGE HIS MIND? Why would an all-knowing God change his mind, some wonder—as though God didn't know how Hezekiah would react. Others tackle this question by arguing that it wasn't God who changed. Somehow, the prayer changed Hezekiah. So God's plans for Hezekiah had to change, too.

• •

HEZEKIAH ON THE RECORD. Taylor Prism is one of several reports from Sennacherib's day that mentions King Hezekiah. Sennacherib brags about destroying 46 Jewish cities. But he stops short of including Jerusalem. "As for Hezekiah," the 2,700-year-old report reads, "I made him a prisoner in Jerusalem. . .like a bird in a cage."

A Jewish king's human sacrifice

NOT JUST ANY HUMAN. His own son. And not just any death. Burned alive, scholars say.

Actually, two Jewish kings are on record as sacrificing their sons to idols.

Ahaz is the first. Oddly, one of his sons who survives is Hezekiah, the man one Bible writer calls the most righteous king of all.

Tragically, on Israel's timeline of kings, Hezekiah finds himself sandwiched between two of the worst. For just as his father sacrificed one of his sons to the idol Molech, Hezekiah's more famous son, Manasseh, does the same.

Manasseh is a mere 12 years old when he succeeds his father as king. He rules for 55 years—the longest of any Jewish kings. That's an embarrassment to Jews in ancient times because he was also considered the most vile king of all. Many found it hard to reconcile why God would reward him with such a long reign.

FLAMMABLE / Traditional Arab headdress, *keffiyeh* (kuh-FEE-uh), crowns a Middle Eastern boy. Sons were prized above daughters in Bible times. They were also considered top-of-the-line sacrifices for select Middle Eastern gods such as Molech. At least two Jewish kings sacrificed their sons in fire to Molech—perhaps burning them alive.

MANASSEH'S EVIL. Besides sacrificing his son in a fire, King Manasseh set up idols in the Jerusalem Temple. He practiced sorcery and consulted the dead through mediums and psychics—all of which were death-penalty offenses under Jewish law. Jewish tradition says he also ordered the prophet Isaiah cut in half with a wooden saw.

MANASSEH'S REPENTANCE. Late in life, Manasseh is said to have had a change of heart. He repented and "finally realized that the LORD alone is God!" (2 Chronicles 33:13). Some Jewish and Christian scholars aren't so sure. They wonder if the writer of Chronicles, which is an upbeat version of Jewish history, added this note—presuming it was true because of how long God allowed Manasseh to reign.

Hammering the Holy City

SLOW LEARNERS when it comes to dealing with international bully empires, the Jews lose just about everything important to them. Their freedom. Their homeland. Their holiest city. Stone by stone, Jerusalem gets dismantled. Leveled.

With that, the last surviving Jewish nation dies. All that's left of Judah are ruins—and Jewish refugees, exiled and scattered throughout the Middle East.

Many folks consider it the worst event in Jewish history, with the possible exception of the World War II holocaust slaughter of six million Jews.

Judah's fall begins with a hunger for independence—the same thing that killed the northern Jewish nation of Israel a little over a century earlier, in 722 BC.

The big difference is the superpower. Babylonians have replaced the Assyrians, after destroying Assyria's capital of Nineveh in 612 BC and finishing off their army at the Battle of Carchemish in 605 BC.

Babylon's king, Nebuchadnezzar, makes three hostile visits to Judah:

// 604 BC. He orders King Jehoiakim to pay heavy taxes to the new empire—which the king does for three years, before stopping.

// 597 BC. He comes to collect the back taxes. And as punitive damages, he takes: all treasures from the Temple and the palace, the royal family of King Jehoiachin (son and successor of Jehoiakim), the families of all the officials, and thousands of the country's best soldiers and skilled workers. He leaves only the poorest people, with a new puppet king, Mattaniah, whom he renames Zedekiah.

JERUSALEM'S LAST STAND / Jewish defenders of Judah's capital hold out against a Babylonian siege for two and a half years. But once the invaders break through the walls, all is lost.

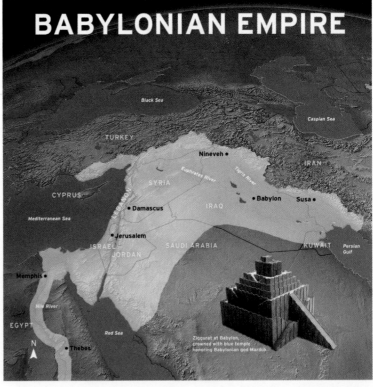

BABYLONIAN EMPIRE

Black Sea

Caspian Sea

TURKEY

Nineveh

IRAN

Euphrates River

Tigris River

SYRIA

CYPRUS

Babylon   Susa

Damascus

IRAQ

Mediterranean Sea

Jerusalem

ISRAEL
JORDAN

SAUDI ARABIA

KUWAIT   Persian Gulf

Memphis

Nile River

EGYPT

Red Sea

N

Thebes

Ziggurat at Babylon, crowned with blue temple honoring Babylonian god Marduk

// January 15, 588 BC. He arrives to crush a Jewish uprising. His army surrounds Jerusalem for two and a half years before breaking through the walls on July 18, 586 BC.

Lamentations, the saddest book in the Bible, offers an eyewitness report of the horrifying effects of Babylon's siege. It tells of Jewish mothers cooking their own babies as food, and of the dismantling of Jerusalem and the deportation of most Jewish survivors.

King Zedekiah and his army abandon the city, making a run for it. Babylonians overtake Zedekiah on the Jericho plains, a day's ride away. They make him watch as they slaughter his sons. Then they gouge out his eyes, chain him, and lead him captive to Babylon.

Babylon's main entrance, at Ishtar Gate

NEBUCHADNEZZAR / King of the Babylonian Empire during its most prosperous decades (605–562 BC). He's famous for building the Hanging Gardens of Babylon, one of the Seven Wonders of the Ancient World. He also tried to incinerate three of the prophet Daniel's friends in a furnace—Shadrach, Meshach, and Abednego. It was punishment for not bowing to an idol he made. They survived, and "didn't even smell of smoke!" (Daniel 3:27)

JERUSALEM SURROUNDED

Built on a ridge, Jerusalem was a tough city to attack. (See picture, page 117.) Babylonians—like Assyrians before them and Romans after them—chose to surround Jerusalem and chip away at the city's defenses during a siege. For two and a half years.

Babylon's strategies included:

Blockade. Cut the Jews off from all outside supplies.

Tunnels. Dig tunnels under the city walls. Collapse the tunnels until part of the wall collapsed, too.

Roman-built ramp to Masada hilltop fortress

Ramps. Build dirt ramps up the side of the city walls, under the cover of shields and perhaps hostages.

Assyrian ram and tower

Battering rams, siege towers. Target the city's weakest points, such as wooden gateway entrances. Portable towers on wheels can raise attacking archers to same level as city defenders on the wall.

Catapults. Pummel the walls with boulders. Spray the defenders with sharp objects. Infect the enemy with disease by firing human and animal corpses into the city.

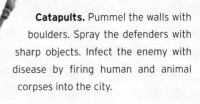

Roman catapult replica

2 CHRONICLES 36:23

After the Jews spend about 50 years exiled in what is now Iraq, Persian Emperor Cyrus, from what is now Iran, frees them to go home and rebuild their nation.

BIG SCENE
PERSIANS FREE THE JEWS

BIBLE HISTORY		960 BC	930 BC

BIBLE HISTORY

960 BC
Solomon builds first Jewish temple

930 BC
Jewish nation splits: Judah (south), Israel (north)

WORLD HISTORY

Pharaoh Shoshenq I invades both Jewish nations
928 BC

ALL DATES APPROXIMATE

1,2 CHRONICLES

THE BRIGHT SIDE OF ANNIHILATION

STORY LINE

A SUGARCOATED RERUN of Israel's history. That's what 1, 2 Chronicles sounds like to some people—a Jewish spin doctor's take on the stories of 1, 2 Samuel and 1, 2 Kings.

It starts off boring, many charge: eight numbing chapters of genealogy that take us clear back to Adam. Some 2,000 names. Then another boring list of names: Jews returning from exile in Babylon.

But that's the clue to understanding 1, 2 Chronicles, originally written as a single book but separated later to fit on uniform-sized scrolls. The exile is over. Jews have come home—at least some of them.

But to what? Clearly they broke their agreement with God by worshipping idols. That's what their spiritual leaders said cost them their country.

Now they're asking themselves tough questions.

Are we still God's people? Is the Promised Land still our land?

Yes. That's the answer the writer gives them. He uses this upbeat history to make his point.

The Jewish family tree shows that God has had a plan for Jews from the very beginning. The upbeat history shows how God has taken care of them throughout the centuries.

Now they're home. And that's proof that God kept his promise. Moses said God would give them a second chance: "He may send you to the ends of the earth, but he will gather you and bring you back" (Deuteronomy 30:4 NCV).

This is the story of a clean slate and a fresh start.

// LOCATION: Most stories are set in Israel, followed by exile in Babylon, in what is now Iraq.

// TIME: First and Second Chronicles span about 500 years, from Israel's first king in the 1000s BC until the Jews return from Babylonian exile in the 500s BC.

// AUTHOR: Unknown. Ancient Jewish tradition says Ezra wrote it, a priest who helped rebuild the nation after its 50-year exile in Babylon.

722 BC
Assyrians conquer Israel

586 BC
Babylonians conquer Judah, exile Jews

538 BC
Persian King Cyrus frees Jews to go home

Babylonians conquer Assyrians
612 BC

Persians conquer Babylonians
539 BC

David, kingdom builder

PULLING NO PUNCHES, the writer starts his story by laying blame.

"The people of Judah were taken to Babylonia as prisoners because they sinned against the LORD" (1 Chronicles 9:1 CEV).

And that's all he has to say about that.

He jumps right into good news, the happy list of Jews returning from the exile. Then he turns to Jewish national history, skimming over the not-so-great story of Israel's first king, Saul—a melancholy man who reportedly reigned about 42 years, but who nets only 24 verses.

King David, on the other hand, gets the puff treatment—nearly one chapter for every verse Saul manages: 19.

The writer skips many of David's downers—like his affair with Bathsheba and a coup led by his own son Absalom.

Instead, David captures Jerusalem. He turns the ridge-top city into his political capital. Then he turns it into Israel's spiritual center. He does this by setting up a sacrificial altar and by bringing to town the most sacred Jewish object: the Ark of the Covenant, a chest containing the 10 Commandments.

From there, he marches out to battle—for the first time in Israel's history the Jews enjoy secured borders. The first hostile neighbor David defeats is the one that manhandled them during the time of the Judges and King Saul: the Philistines.

ISRAEL'S FAVORITE KING. For securing Israel's borders and preparing the nation for what becomes a golden age of prosperity, King David becomes the measure of an ideal king. A thousand years later, during Rome's occupation of Israel, Jews will find themselves wishing for a leader like him—a messiah.

◄ **PHILISTINES, WHY SO TOUGH?** They had two big advantages over the Jews before David came along: (1) Iron. They guarded the secret to forging this tough metal that could slice through Israel's bronze weapons. (2) Teamwork. They fought as a nation, while the Jews remained a loosely knit coalition of tribes.

DAVID'S ELITE FIGHTING FORCES
/ Like the army with its Rangers and the navy with its Seals, David had two elite fighting forces of champion warriors: The Three and The Thirty. Most famous was Jashobeam, leader of The Three. In one battle, he reportedly killed 300 men with his spear (see 1 Chronicles 11:11).

David's census spawns a plague

IT SEEMS HARMLESS ENOUGH. Even wise. David wants to take a census. Not of everyone. Just of men in Israel able to fight in a war if necessary.

Yet something about that census is wrong. When David orders General Joab to count the able-bodied men, Joab asks, "Why do you want to do this, my master? You will make Israel guilty of sin" (1 Chronicles 21:3 NCV).

What's sinful about the census is anyone's guess. The Bible doesn't say.

David stubbornly demands that Joab carry out the order. Joab's tally: 1,100,000 fighters, with nearly half of them—470,000—coming from David's tribe of Judah alone.

God confronts David, who admits his sin. David gets to choose his punishment:

// three years of drought or

// three months of enemy attacks or

// three days of plague.

David chooses the plague, and 70,000 people die.

At God's instruction, David stops the plague by buying a Jerusalem farmer's bedrock threshing floor. There, David builds an altar and offers a sacrifice. This becomes the place Jews will bring their sacrifices to God. Later, David's son Solomon will build a huge altar there, in the courtyard of Israel's first Temple.

HOW TO STOP A PLAGUE / Turkish farmers separate wheat kernels from the stems by snapping the heads off the stalks and driving a flat sled over the heads to loosen the kernels—it's called threshing. To stop a plague in Israel, King David bought a Jerusalem farmer's bedrock threshing floor, built an altar on it, and offered a sacrifice. His son Solomon later built the Temple on the site.

WHAT WAS SINFUL ABOUT THE CENSUS? One of the most popular guesses among Bible experts is that the census credited David's skill at raising an army instead of giving God credit for the battlefield victories. The fighting was over; Israel's warriors had already secured the borders. Another guess is that David didn't collect the census tax required for the worship center: "Then a plague will not come on them when you count them" (Exodus 30:12 NIrV).

WHAT'S THE POINT? This tells the story of how Jews ended up with the site that became the Jerusalem Temple. Their king went here seeking forgiveness, just as Jews would do for centuries to come.

THE NUMBERS DON'T ADD UP. The same story in 2 Samuel 24 says the tally was 800,000 men in the tribes that later became Israel and 500,000 in Judah. That's 1,300,000, compared to 200,000 less in Chronicles, just 1,100,000. The Chronicles writer admitted that the tally from his source was incomplete, missing the tribes of Levi and Benjamin (see 1 Chronicles 21:6). So the actual number was uncertain.

Prepping for the Temple

WITH BLOOD ON HIS HANDS, David isn't allowed to build God's holy Temple.

God says he doesn't want the sacred Temple built by a man of war. Instead, he says David's son Solomon, a man of peace, will build it.

David does the next best thing.

First, he stockpiles many of the supplies his son will need. He collects roughly 4,000 tons of gold and 40,000 tons of silver for furnishings and decorations. He puts stonecutters to work sizing blocks of white, native limestone. And he imports rot-resistant cedar from the forests of Lebanon.

Second, he organizes what appear to be 24 rotating ministry teams, drawing from a stable of 38,000 Levites, the tribe responsible for leading Israel's worship. Each team will serve at the Temple for two weeks a year, following the lunar calendar of 48 weeks a year. David even writes job descriptions for everyone from the priests to musicians and security guards.

AGE RESTRICTIONS FOR TEMPLE MINISTERS.
There was a 20-year window of service for Israel's worship leaders. They had to fall between the ages of 30 and 50 (see Numbers 4).

TEMPLE MINISTERS.
Not all Levites are eligible to work as priests; only descendants of Aaron. Others serve in different roles: maintenance workers, guards, musicians, administrators, judges, and assistants who help priests with sacrificial rituals.

▼**STONE MASON BC /** A worker at a tourist site in Israel shows visitors how stonecutters in Bible times prepared blocks of native limestone used to construct the Jerusalem Temple.

Egypt invades divided Israel

IT'S PAYBACK TIME. The Egyptian army has come to Israel to collect.

Israel's homeland of Canaan used to fall under the broad shadow of Egypt's empire. But King David had secured Israel's borders. Solomon then launched Israel into a golden age of peace and prosperity.

But it all changes when Solomon dies. His son threatens higher taxes, and the nation splits in two: Israel in the north and Judah in the south.

Egypt's King Shoshenq I (945–925 BC; known in the Bible as Shishak) sees Israel's faded glory as his chance to shine—and to reestablish Egypt's sprawling empire.

The Bible and his surviving records both report that he invaded Judah and Israel, plundering the cities. Having already reunited Egypt's divided kingdoms, he turns to the Jewish homeland. "He came with 1,200 chariots, 60,000 horses, and a countless army of foot soldiers" (2 Chronicles 12:3).

Egyptian forces overrun both Jewish nations, ransacking even the Jerusalem Temple.

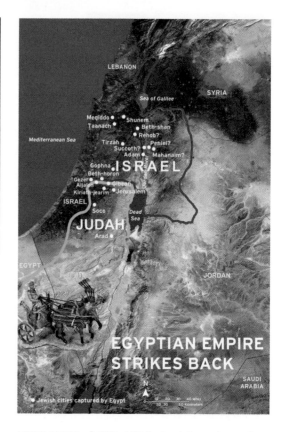

INVASION / With 1,200 chariots and countless infantry, Egypt invades the Jewish homeland and plunders more than a dozen cities in both Jewish nations, north and south.

▲ TAKE THAT. An Egyptian warrior clubs two Jewish captives, in a memorial to Pharaoh Shoshenq's victory over the Jews in 928 BC.

EXCUSE FOR AN INVASION. Hieroglyphics in the Temple of Amun in Karnak, Egypt, celebrate the victory of Pharaoh Shoshenq I over the Jews. They also claim the Jews provoked him with "attacks on the Egyptian frontier settlements." The king may have considered Solomon's fortresses in what is now Israel's southland as a threat.

ATTACKING A FORMER GUEST. Israel's king, Jeroboam, had good reason to hope Shoshenq would limit his invasion to Judah, leaving the northland Jewish nation of Israel untouched. Shoshenq had granted Jeroboam sanctuary in Egypt after a prophet told King Solomon that Jeroboam would one day rule half the kingdom. Solomon ordered Jeroboam killed. Jeroboam fled to Egypt and stayed there until Solomon died.

Hezekiah leads Jews back to God

HEZEKIAH IS LUCKY to have survived his father. One of his brothers didn't. Hezekiah's father—Ahaz, king of Judah—sacrificed one of his sons to an idol, probably Molech, a god famous for requiring infant sacrifices.

Ahaz had no use for God. He even shut down the Jerusalem Temple, the only place Jews were allowed to offer sacrifices to God. He might as well have hung a sign on the door: OUT OF BUSINESS. Certainly the priests and Temple workers were out of work.

God responded the way he said he would, as stipulated in his contract with the Jews (see Deuteronomy 28:49). He sent invaders from Syria and the northland Jewish nation of Israel. These raiders pillaged the nation and took hundreds of thousands of people, for sale as slaves.

But godless as Ahaz was, his son Hezekiah is God-loving.

Hezekiah recognizes that Judah's misery is because the Jews have abandoned God. So when he becomes king, at age 25, he reopens the Temple, calls back the priests, and reinstates the sacrificial system along with sacred festivals such as Passover.

....

AHAZ / Eleventh king of Judah (742–727 BC), he's remembered as one of the worst rulers in Jewish history. He not only led the nation away from God and into idol worship and human sacrifices, he made horrible decisions on the political front. His nation was invaded and pillaged by several enemies, including the Assyrians. When he died, his people refused to bury him with the other kings in Jerusalem's royal tombs.

HOLY SMOKE / Judah's priests prepare animal sacrifices for burning on the Jerusalem Temple's huge altar, left. Worship rituals like this ended when idol-worshipping Jewish kings closed the Temple for decades. Hezekiah reopened the Temple and restored the rituals.

Revival encore, too little too late

JUDAH'S LAST GOOD KING, Josiah, isn't good enough to save the nation. But he's good enough to delay the inevitable.

Josiah follows two horribly evil kings: (1) His grandfather Manasseh, who burned one of his sons as a pagan sacrifice, and (2) his father, Amon, who also worshipped idols.

It takes Josiah a few years to find his way to God. That's because he's only eight years old when he becomes king. And he's got two generations of paganism to overcome. But by age 16, he's found his spiritual way home. By age 20, he's confident enough that he orders his officers to destroy the pagan shrines scattered throughout the country. And by age 26, he's at work renovating the run-down Temple.

In the process, a priest finds a long-lost scroll that explains how Jews are supposed to worship God, along with the list of blessings for obedience and the list of curses for disobedience. The worst curse warns that God will bring an end to the Jewish nation, and drive the Jews out of their homeland. Many Bible experts say the lost scroll sounds like the book of Deuteronomy, which summarizes Jewish laws. Or it may be the set of writings Jews call the Torah (law)—Genesis, Exodus, Leviticus, Numbers, and Deuteronomy.

When Josiah hears what's in the scroll, he rips his robe. It's a customary way of expressing despair.

He asks a prophetess, Huldah, if the curses will come to pass. Quoting God, Huldah says, "I will not send the promised disaster until after you have died and been buried in peace. You yourself will not see the disaster I am going to bring on this city and its people" (2 Chronicles 34:28).

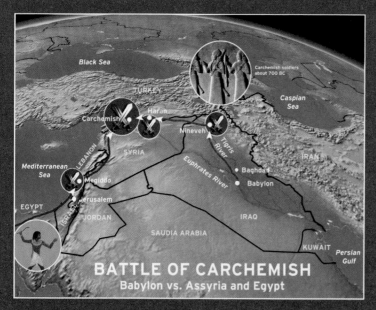

BATTLE OF CARCHEMISH
Babylon vs. Assyria and Egypt

SUPERPOWERS AT WAR. Josiah is a bit player in this monumental battle that propels Babylon to the top of the heap in the Middle East. Babylon's army overruns Assyria's capital at Nineveh, pushing them back to Haran and finally Carchemish. Egypt marches north to reinforce Assyria, defeating Josiah's Jewish army as they attempt to stop them at Megiddo. Josiah died needlessly in that battle, many scholars say, trying to defend the very empire that would destroy his nation two decades later. As it turns out, Babylon didn't need his help to overpower the Assyrians and the Egyptians.

Jerusalem dies, to rise again

FOUR EVIL KINGS follow Josiah as Judah's ruler. That's how the Bible describes them. Each one "did what was evil in the sight of the LORD" (2 Chronicles 36:5).

One by one they make a string of dumb decisions that will destroy their country and turn Jerusalem into a rock heap of a ghost town.

King Zedekiah, Judah's last king, ignores the advice of the prophet Jeremiah, who recommends accepting the dominance of Babylon as God's punishment for Judah's sins. Instead, Zedekiah rebels by declaring independence and refusing to pay the taxes Babylon demands.

Babylon has already invaded and punished Judah twice, in 604 BC and 597 BC.

The third time, in 586 BC, is anything but a charm. King Nebuchadnezzar leads his army in destroying Judah's fortified cities, including the capital city, Jerusalem. After plundering the nation's wealth, "his army burned the Temple of God, tore down the walls of Jerusalem, burned all the palaces, and completely destroyed everything of value. The few who survived were taken as exiles to Babylon, and they became servants to the king and his sons until the kingdom of Persia came to power" (2 Chronicles 36:19–20).

That's roughly 50 years later—after a generation without a Jewish nation on the planet.

◀ JERUSALEM UP IN SMOKE. Babylonians burn Jerusalem and take most of the survivors captive into what becomes a 50-year exile. With that, the Jewish nation disappears from the world map.

FIFTY YEARS OF CAPTIVITY, OR 70? Jeremiah warned the Jews they would live as captives of Babylon for 70 years (see Jeremiah 25:12). That round number is exactly the length of time the Jews lived without their Temple; it was destroyed in 586 BC and rebuilt and dedicated in 516 BC. The round number is also close to the 66 years between Babylon's first invasion of Judah in 604 BC—when they kidnapped some top Jewish citizens—and the year Persia freed the Jews in 538 BC. The captivity lasted only 48 years, however, for Jews taken captive when Jerusalem fell in 586 BC.

EZRA 3:10–13

Amid Jerusalem's ruins, Jews will begin to lay a foundation for their new Temple.

BIG SCENE
REBUILDING THE TEMPLE

BIBLE HISTORY

ALL DATES APPROXIMATE

586 BC
Jerusalem destroyed,
Jews exiled

538 BC
Persia frees
Jews to go home

WORLD HISTORY

Babylon surrenders
to Cyrus of Persia
539 BC

EZRA

EXODUS, PART DEUX

STORY LINE

AFTER 50 YEARS OF EXILE a thousand-mile (1,600 km) walk from Jerusalem, Jews are free to go home and rebuild their Temple and their nation.

Babylonians in what is now Iraq had over-run the Jewish nation, destroying the cities and exiling the citizens. But a ruler named Cyrus of Persia, in what is now Iran, overpowers the Babylonian Empire. In one of his first acts, he frees the Jews. A clay cylinder from his century confirms that he freed all Babylon's political prisoners and sent them home to rebuild their nations with his blessing.

After a generation abroad, many Jews decide to stay in the only home they've known. Others long for their native homeland and return in one of many waves of refugees.

The first wave back builds a new Temple. It's to replace the Temple that Solomon built, which the Babylonians destroyed.

Ezra, however, isn't among the first Jews back. He isn't even born yet. He returns almost a century later. He's highly motivated to go because in Babylon, he's a Jewish priest without a Temple.

Back in Israel, he begins teaching the Jews the laws of Moses—laws that most had forgotten, or never knew existed.

// LOCATION: Cyrus frees the Jews who have been exiled and scattered throughout what are now Iraq and Iran. They return to Israel (see map page 155).

// TIME: The story covers about 80 years, from the time Cyrus frees the Jews in about 538 BC until Ezra arrives in 458 BC.

// AUTHOR: Unknown. Ancient Jewish tradition says Ezra wrote it.

516 BC
New Temple completed

Persians begin ruling Egypt for a century
525 BC

458 BC
Ezra arrives in Jerusalem

Greeks build the Temple of Zeus in Olympia, Greece
460 BC

Iran puts Israel back on the map

IRANIANS RESTORE ISRAEL about half a century after the Iraqis destroyed it.

That's if we use modern map equivalents. Iraq is the land of Babylon, the empire that leveled Jerusalem and exiled the Jews. Iran is the land of Persia, the empire that overpowered Babylon and freed Babylon's political prisoners.

Oddly, a prophet named Isaiah who lived 200 years earlier not only predicted Israel's return from exile, he named the emancipator. "Cyrus. . .will command, 'Rebuild Jerusalem'; he will say, 'Restore the Temple' " (Isaiah 44:28).

That's just what the book of Ezra says happens. Ezra reports Cyrus making this announcement to the Jews:

> *"The LORD, the God of heaven, has given me all the kingdoms of the earth. He has appointed me to build him a Temple at Jerusalem, which is in Judah. Any of you who are his people may go to Jerusalem in Judah to rebuild this Temple of the LORD."*
>
> EZRA 1:2–3

NAME-DROPPING CYRUS 200 YEARS EARLY.

Many Bible experts say Isaiah's mention of Cyrus two centuries before Cyrus appears on the scene adds evidence that the book of Isaiah was written over several centuries, by two or more writers. Others insist Isaiah wrote the entire book during his lifetime, and that his mention of Cyrus is a prophecy, not history passed off as prophecy.

. . . .

CYRUS THE GREAT (ABOUT 590–530 BC).

Cyrus II was the first king of the sprawling Persian Empire. Historians in ancient times, such as Greek writer Xenophon, portrayed him as a tolerant ruler who respected the customs and religions of the many nations he ruled.

FOUR MONTHS TO HOME
Jews return from exile in Iraq

WALKING BACK TO ISRAEL. When the Iranian-based Persian Empire crushes the Iraqi-based Babylonian Empire, the Persian king frees Babylon's political prisoners—including the Jews. Ezra leads one group of Jews home.

WRITTEN IN STONE. The Cyrus Cylinder, as many call it, confirms the Bible's report that Cyrus freed political prisoners to return to their homeland and rebuild their temples. The cylinder, which dates to 536 BC, includes a prayer from Cyrus. He asks "all the gods I settled in their sacred centers" to intercede on his behalf so he might live a long life.

Old-time religion

WORSHIP IS OUT OF THE QUESTION for Jews in exile. At least traditional Jewish worship, with sacrifices. God has approved only one place for Jews to offer sacrifices: the Jerusalem Temple. But Jerusalem lies in ruins, destroyed by Babylonian invaders in 586 BC.

When freed Jews return home in 538 BC, they give top priority to rebuilding the Temple. They start by rebuilding the altar on its former site. This allows them to offer sacrifices right away, and to begin celebrating their annual religious festivals.

Next, they take a collection to buy supplies and to hire construction workers for the Temple. The returned refugees come up with half a ton of gold and three tons of silver. Not much compared to the approximately 4,000 tons of gold and 40,000 tons of silver King David stockpiled for the first Temple.

Jews begin construction in the spring of 536 BC. When they lay the foundation, young Jews celebrate. Older Jews, however, cry. Perhaps they realize they'll get what they're paying for, and that this new Temple will be a shack compared to Solomon's majestic worship center.

Local non-Jews who settled in the land during the exile convince Persia's new king to order a halt to the work. These locals apparently fear they'll lose their land if the Jews rise to power again. So they remind the king that the Jews have a long history of rebellion.

Work finally resumes a decade later, when Jews convince the next Persian king that Cyrus ordered them to build the Temple. This king, Darius, confirms this in the records and notices that Cyrus ordered the Temple built with empire funds. So he orders his governors to use tax money for the project. It's completed by 516 BC.

▶ **SACRED WORDS.** During their exile a thousand miles (1,600 km) from the Jerusalem Temple ruins, Jews worship by gathering to read their Bible—which Christians call the Old Testament. It was during this exile, many scholars say, that Jews came up with the idea of worshipping in synagogues.

70 YEARS WITHOUT A TEMPLE

WHEN	WHAT	WHERE
586 BC	Babylon destroys Solomon's Temple	2 Kings 25:8–9
538 BC	Jews return from exile, rebuild altar	Ezra 3:1–2
536 BC	Jews start building second Temple	Ezra 3:8
530 BC	Non-Jewish locals get the project halted	Ezra 4:21
520 BC	Building resumes	Ezra 4:24
515 BC	Temple completed and dedicated	Ezra 6:15–16

Ezra condemns mixed marriages

NOT THAT GOD APPROVES, but the book of Ezra closes with a harsh order. Some 113 Jewish men have married non-Jewish women. They get the order to divorce the ladies—and to abandon them and their children.

The order comes from Ezra, a priest who arrives in Jerusalem in 458 BC, about 80 years after the first wave of returning Jews. Though a latecomer, he still carries prestige as a worship leader.

Several Jews bring a complaint to him: "The holy race has become polluted by. . .mixed marriages" (Ezra 9:2).

Some Jews have married non-Jewish women. Jewish law, strictly interpreted, forbids that. Besides, marriages like this led to the exile— and might lead to an encore exile, some fear. It was King Solomon's foreign wives who lured him into idolatry. This idolatry, which persisted in Israel for centuries, became the people's main sin—the reason God punished them with exile.

Acting on the suggestion of a mysterious leader named Shecaniah, Ezra orders all Jewish men who married non-Jewish women to "send away all these women and their children" (Ezra 10:3 TNIV).

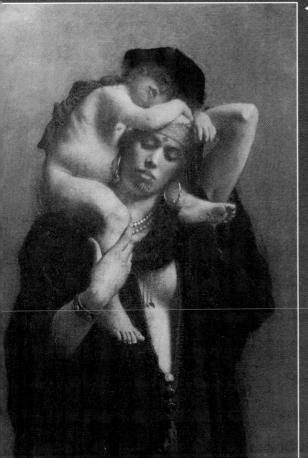

NON-KOSHER MARRIAGE. An Egyptian peasant woman and her child. Ezra forbids Jewish men from marrying non-Jews. Worse, he makes his order retroactive. Men with non-Jewish wives must divorce them and send them away—with their children.

ULTERIOR MOTIVE. Some Bible experts wonder if Shecaniah had a hidden motive for suggesting Jewish men divorce non-Jewish women. A man with his father's name, Jehiel, is on the list of guilty; he married a non-Jewish woman (Ezra 10:25–26). If Jehiel had children by more than one wife, and Shecaniah was his son by a Jewish woman, Shecaniah would get a bigger share of inheritance if his mixed-blood brothers were driven off.

COUNTERPOINT TO EZRA. Some scholars say the book of Ruth reads like a counterpoint to Ezra's story. Ruth, a non-Jew, came from what is now Jordan. Yet she became the ancestor of Israel's greatest dynasty of kings. She was the great-grandmother of King David.

NEHEMIAH 6:15

Threatened by hostile non-Jews who oppose the rebuilding of Jerusalem, Jewish construction teams rebuild the city walls in just 52 days—shocking everyone with their speed.

BIG SCENE
JERUSALEM'S MIRACLE WALL

BIBLE
HISTORY

ALL DATES APPROXIMATE

586 BC
Jerusalem destroyed,
Jews exiled

538 BC
Persia frees Jews

WORLD
HISTORY

Babylon builds famous
Ishtar Gate entrance
575 BC

NEHEMIAH

REBUILDING JERUSALEM FROM THE GROUND UP

STORY LINE

JERUSALEM'S CITY WALLS lay in a heap. That's a shocker. Jews have been living there for almost a century, since returning from exile.

News of Jerusalem's wrecked walls reach Nehemiah, a Jewish wine taster for Persia's king, Artaxerxes.

Nehemiah can't believe his fellow Jews are content to let the walls lie. Depressed, he stops eating. Artaxerxes takes notice, asks what's up, and gives Nehemiah a leave of absence to oversee the rebuilding of Jerusalem's walls.

Nehemiah even manages to sweet-talk the king into a military escort along with a letter ordering the manager of a regional forest—perhaps the cedars of Lebanon—to supply the necessary wood.

Non-Jewish settlers in Israel oppose the project. They don't want the Jews to turn Israel back into a Jewish homeland, leaving non-Jews high, dry, and landless. So they plot to assassinate Nehemiah during a proposed meeting.

Nehemiah says he's too busy for a meeting. He organizes the Jews into construction crews that fast-track the job, finishing in less than two months.

Even Nehemiah's enemies consider that feat a miracle.

// LOCATION: The story starts in Susa, capital of the Persian Empire in what is now Iran. It ends in Jerusalem, more than a thousand-mile (1,600 km) walk west, following the caravan routes along the rivers (see map page 155).

// TIME: The story takes place in the mid-400s BC, more than a century after Jews returned from exile in what is now Iraq.

// AUTHOR: Unknown. Ancient Jewish tradition says Ezra wrote it.

---

516 BC
Jews rebuild Temple from ruins

458 BC
Ezra arrives in Jerusalem

445 BC
Nehemiah arrives and rebuilds Jerusalem walls

Greeks write constitution
508 BC

447 BC
Greeks begin building Parthenon Temple of Athena

Persian king grants a Jewish wish

NEHEMIAH IS DEPRESSED. It's springtime, and he has been in a funk since fall. That's when his brother arrived from Jerusalem with disturbing news that the city walls lie in ruins.

The writer doesn't say if the Jews who returned from exile nearly a century earlier never bothered to fix the walls that the Babylonians busted, or if the Jews fixed them but someone else attacked and tore them down again.

Nehemiah is the king's wine steward. King Artaxerxes eventually notices that Nehemiah's sad, and he asks about it. Why it takes the king four to six months to notice is anyone's guess. Perhaps he just returned from a winter getaway.

"How can I help you?" Artaxerxes asks. That's a question Nehemiah is ready for.

He asks for:

// a leave of absence to rebuild the walls

// letters ordering regional governors to grant him safe passage

// free timber—perhaps rot-resistant cedar from Lebanon.

The king grants every request, and gives him a military escort as well.

GENEROUS KING / When palace wine steward Nehemiah asks Persian King Artaxerxes for a leave of absence to rebuild Jerusalem's city walls, the king not only grants the request, he gives Nehemiah a military escort.

ARTAXERXES I. King of Persia from 465–425 BC, he was a descendant of Persia's first king, Cyrus the Great. Like Cyrus, he practiced tolerance toward the Jews. But, like his father, Xerxes I (485–465 BC), he tried to slow the Greek rise to power. Xerxes is famous for defeating several thousand Greeks and 300 Spartans led by King Leonidas at the Battle of Thermopylae—a story that inspired the blockbuster movie *300*.

▲ **MORE THAN A WINE STEWARD.** Servants deliver a drink to their master in this stone sculpture from the 600s BC. That's Nehemiah's job, chief wine steward. But given the huge favor the king granted him, Nehemiah seemed much more than a goblet-toting waiter who made sure no one spiked the king's wine with poison. Stewards generally saw the king every day. Some became trusted advisors. Assyrian King Sennacherib promoted his steward to "chief of administration" (Tobit 1:22).

Rebuilding Jerusalem's walls

AN EVENING DONKEY RIDE around Jerusalem's broken walls gives Nehemiah a sense of the work ahead of him.

City leaders back the project once they hear of the Persian king's support. And Jews from all over the region arrive to help. Arabs and other non-Jewish settlers in the region, however, hate the idea; it signals the rebirth of Israel.

Sanballat leads that opposition. First, he ridicules the project. Then he plans a preemptive strike to stop the work. When Nehemiah hears about it, he turns half of his construction workers into armed guards.

Perhaps the threat of attack creates a sense of urgency. Whatever spurs the Jews, they finish the job in a mere 52 days. This terrifies their enemies because they realize, as the Jewish writer put it, "this work had been done with the help of our God" (Nehemiah 6:16).

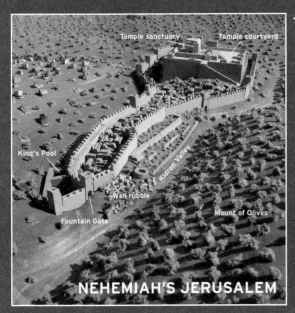

Temple sanctuary
Temple courtyard
King's Pool
Kidron Valley
Wall rubble
Fountain Gate
Mount of Olives

NEHEMIAH'S JERUSALEM

◄ **ARCHAEOLOGICAL EVIDENCE OF NEHEMIAH'S REPAIR.** Nehemiah said when he approached the Fountain Gate near the King's Pool, "my donkey couldn't get through the rubble" (Nehemiah 2:14). Archaeologists say there's evidence of especially heavy damage there, at the low end of the ridge on which Jerusalem rested.

FAST-TRACK CONSTRUCTION. Threatened with an attack aimed at stopping reconstruction of Jerusalem's city walls, Nehemiah splits his construction crews. Half pull guard duty. The other half handle the construction.

A PATCH JOB? A first-century Jewish historian named Josephus said it took the workers two years and four months to repair the walls—not 52 days. Some scholars wonder if the 52-day project was just a temporary fix, to provide security for the more permanent repair.

Jerusalem city walls

ESTHER 7

Queen Esther drops the bombshell. At a meal with her husband and Haman, she reveals that Haman's planned genocide targets her and her fellow Jews—that's news to Haman.

BIG SCENE

SURPRISE FOR HAMAN

BIBLE HISTORY

ALL DATES APPROXIMATE

516 BC
*Jews rebuild
Jerusalem Temple*

*300 Spartans
fight to the death*

WORLD HISTORY

*King Xerxes begins
21-year rule*
486 BC

ESTHER

JEWISH QUEEN OF IRAN

STORY LINE

INSULTED BY A JEW who refuses to bow to him, a top Persian official named Haman concocts a plan to wipe out all Jews in the empire and confiscate their property. King Xerxes signs off on it, apparently without bothering to ask which race Haman intends to annihilate.

As genocide goes, it's a fine plan—except that the queen is a Jew. Haman's handlers don't turn up that intel. Queen Esther is keeping her heritage under wraps for some unexplained reason—hiding it from even her husband. The only person who seems to know she's a Jew is the cousin who raised her: Mordecai. He also happens to be the culprit who refuses to bow when Haman walks by.

When Mordecai hears of Haman's planned holocaust, he convinces Esther to take a stand for the Jewish people. Though visits to King Xerxes are by invitation only—and anyone who shows up uninvited can be executed, queens included—Esther puts her life on the line.

Esther tells the king that Haman's plot would end in her death and the death of all her people.

The king kills Haman instead, and fills the job vacancy with Mordecai.

// LOCATION: Susa, capital of the Persian Empire. It's now Shush, Iran. (See map of Persian Empire page 249; of Susa page 155.)

// TIME: The story is set about 30 years before Ezra arrives in Jerusalem. King Xerxes (Ahasuerus in the Bible) reigned 21 years, from 486–465 BC.

// AUTHOR: Unknown. Writing style is similar to stories in Ezra and Nehemiah.

473 BC
Esther stops holocaust
of Jews

458 BC
Ezra arrives
in Jerusalem

Xerxes defeats 300 Spartans,
Greeks at Battle of Thermopylae
480 BC

Xerxes murdered
by uncle
465 BC

30-year truce between
Sparta and Athens
445 BC

Demoting the queen

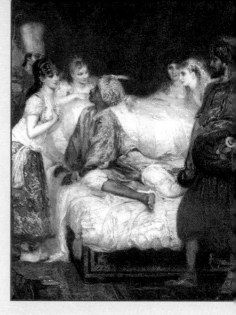

A LITTLE DRUNK at the end of a weeklong, guys-only party, Persian King Xerxes decides to show off his gorgeous wife, Queen Vashti. So he sends seven eunuchs to get her.

Vashti is his top-of-the-line model—the only wife in his harem recognized as the queen.

But she's throwing a party of her own for some ladies, perhaps wives of the men at the king's testosterone bash. For some unstated reason, Vashti refuses the king's invitation. She will not excuse herself from the ladies so she can stand like a trophy wife in front of a bunch of men, many of whom are probably too drunk to tell a beauty from a beast.

News of Vashti's refusal seems to sober up the king. It's a man's world, and Xerxes consults his advisers about the manly way to deal with this insubordination.

"Women everywhere will begin to despise their husbands when they learn that Queen Vashti has refused to appear before the king," one adviser says. Their advice: "Order that Queen Vashti be forever banished from the presence of King Xerxes. . .the king should choose another queen more worthy than she" (Esther 1:17, 19).

Xerxes agrees.

That leads to the next question. How should a man's man choose a wife?

A beauty contest.

EUNUCHS AS HAREM GUARDS.

Men who guarded a king's harem of wives were often castrated—testicles removed. Castration typically reduces the sex drive, sometimes eliminating it. Castrated men can sometimes achieve an erection, but they are sterile.

XERXES I.

King of Persia (reigned 486–465 BC). His Hebrew name shows up in many Bible translations as Ahasuerus. He's the villain in the blockbuster movie *300*. The story is inspired by Xerxes' massive invasion of Greece, where he overran 300 Spartans at the Battle of Thermopylae. Greeks defeated him later, setting the stage for the fall of Persia and the rise of Alexander the Great and his Greek Empire.

▶ **PAMPERED VIRGIN /** Esther, like other beauty contestants hoping to become the next queen of Persia, spends a year getting pampered with beauty treatments.

WOMEN IN THEIR PLACE / Strikingly easy on the eyes, this woman lives in Iran, home of the ancient Persian Empire and at least two beautiful queens: Vashti and her replacement, Esther. Vashti refused the king's request to make an appearance at his gentlemen's party, so he could put her good looks on display as a trophy wife. For daring to refuse her husband's wishes, Vashti becomes a permanent no-show. The king banishes her from his presence, apparently confining her to the harem.

Beauty queen, Persian queen

XERXES MISSES HIS TROPHY WIFE, Queen Vashti. His advisers suggest an empire-wide beauty contest, as a way of finding a replacement—a new and improved queen.

From India to Egypt, virgin beauties are brought to the royal harem at Susa in what is now Shush, Iran. All those considered worthy will live in the harem as one of the king's many wives. But only one—the lady who most pleases the king—will become queen.

Each virgin will spend the night with the king, if he likes what he sees. But first they spend a year getting beauty treatments. They're massaged and marinated in scented oils, moisturizing cream, and expensive perfume—until they're fragrant to the bone.

Among the contestants is Esther, an orphaned Jew raised by her cousin Mordecai. She gains a big advantage over the other contestants. The eunuch in charge of the harem takes a liking to her. He orders a special menu for her and assigns seven women from the palace to take care of her. He also tells her how to pleasure the king. Esther does as she's told.

Delighted at Esther's performance, Xerxes not only crowns her queen, he declares a holiday. Then he throws a huge banquet in her honor and gives expensive gifts to everyone who comes.

He's one happy king.

The plan: Kill all Jews

ONE JEW FAILS TO BOW as Persia's prime minister walks by. So the offended official—a man named Haman—decides to kill all Jews.

The unbowed Jew is Mordecai, Esther's cousin who raised her. Why he refuses to bow is anyone's guess. Perhaps it's the same reason Haman overreacts. Their races have been relentless enemies for centuries. Haman's ancestors are the Amalekites from what is now Jordan and Saudi Arabia.

Haman tells the king he'd like to wipe out "a certain race of people" who "refuse to obey the laws of the king" (Esther 3:8). Afterward, Haman promises to donate 375 tons of silver to the royal treasury, apparently from money he plans to confiscate from dead Jews. It's a kill now, pay later proposal, which the king accepts—apparently without bothering to ask what race Haman is targeting.

Haman sets the date for the ethnic cleansing: March 7, 473 BC.

He has the order for his Final Solution translated into every language of the empire. Then he sends couriers to deliver the news.

Though the king can execute anyone coming to him without an invitation—queen included—Esther decides to intercede for her people. She's reluctant at first, but Mordecai convinces her by warning that she'll die in the holocaust, too. Besides, he adds, "Perhaps you were made queen for just such a time as this" (Esther 4:14).

MORDECAI. Older cousin of Esther, he adopts her and raises her after her parents die. He seems to work in the palace, for he overhears a plot to assassinate the king. As a reward for reporting it, the king orders Haman to parade Mordecai through town on the king's own horse, and to shout praise for Mordecai. It's a funny scene since Haman hates Mordecai and is already plotting to hang him during the upcoming Jewish holocaust.

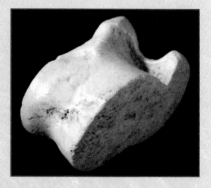

Greek knucklebone from about 300 BC, used a bit like dice.

▲ **CASTING LOTS TO FIND A GOOD DAY TO KILL JEWS.** Haman threw lots to determine the best day to kill the Jews. "Lots" may have been like dice, stones, sticks, or some other tool for supposedly getting a yes-no answer from the gods—depending on how the lots land when tossed.

◄ **HOME OF THE NEAR-HOLOCAUST.** Persian king and queen look out over their capital city of Susa. It was here, in what is now Shush, Iran, that one official planned the annihilation of all Jews in the empire—from India to Egypt. But the queen had a surprise for him.

Esther asks king hubby for help

ESTHER'S AFRAID that she's dead if she does and dead if she doesn't. If she doesn't ask King Xerxes to stop the annihilation of the Jews, she might join the pile of corpses. But if she approaches the king uninvited, he has the option of executing her. It's Persian law.

He welcomes her.

Surprisingly, Esther doesn't mention the problem. Instead, she invites Xerxes and Haman to a banquet. And then to a second meal. Perhaps she wants to control the setting of the tense discussion, and the first meal doesn't feel like the right time.

Haman, ecstatic about his invitations to private meals with the king and queen, hosts an impromptu party of his own to brag to his friends.

At the second meal, Esther drops the bomb. She says that she and her people are targeted for extermination. "That evil Haman is the one out to get us!" (Esther 7:6 CEV).

Neither Xerxes nor Haman had any idea Esther was Jewish. Xerxes leaves the room to think. Haman stays to beg Esther for his life. Haman apparently gets too close because when the king returns he says, "Now you're even trying to rape my queen here in my own palace!" (Esther 7:8 CEV).

Xerxes orders Haman hanged on the tall platform Haman had built to execute Mordecai. Mordecai gets Haman's job.

Haman's empire-wide attack on the Jews goes off as planned, since the king can't reverse his own order. But he helps the Jews defend themselves.

◄ A CHARACTER. Mask vendors love the Jewish holiday of Purim. Jews dress up in costumes—everything from Queen Esther to Bozo the Clown. The most fun-filled Jewish holiday on the calendar, Purim marks the day Queen Esther helped spare Jews from an empire-wide holocaust.

PURIM, THE JEWISH PARTY FESTIVAL. Jews celebrate their holocaust missed with a festival that has the feel of a Mardi Gras. Children dress up in costumes of characters in the story. Parents pass out gifts. And when they read the story, they make noise to drown out Haman's name whenever the storyteller speaks it. The festival is called Purim (POOR um). That comes from the Persian word for "lots" (*pur*). Haman used lots to determine which day would be best to kill the Jews.

WHERE'S GOD? The writer never mentions God. That's why some Jews argued that the story doesn't belong in the Bible. Others say God is implied when Mordecai says that if Esther doesn't help her fellow Jews, "help...will come from another place" (Esther 4:14 NIrV).

JOB 38:2

God shuts up everyone with a question: "Why do you talk so much when you know so little?" (CEV). *Then he points out how little they know.*

BIG SCENE

GOD SPEAKS

BIBLE HISTORY

ALL DATES APPROXIMATE

2100 BC
*Abraham leaves
Ur in today's Iraq*

WORLD HISTORY

J O B

NOT SO PATIENT AFTER ALL

GOD MAKES A DEAL WITH SATAN. At least it sounds like Satan, although he's addressing God in heaven as if he's an angel. The Hebrew word is *satan*, though the English translation is more vague: "accuser."

Given what this mysterious accuser does to Job, he's one devil of an angel.

He convinces God to let him test Job. God has bragged that Job is a good man. But Satan argues it's because God blessed Job with lots of kids, a wealth of herds, and wonderful health.

With God's approval, Satan takes it all away. A windstorm blows down the house, crushing Job's 10 kids. Raiders and a fire take Job's herds and kill his servants. Boils erupt all over Job's body.

Job, depressed and confused, sits in a pile of ashes, scratching himself.

Friends come. Not a good thing. They say Job must have done something terrible to tick God off this much.

Job says he hasn't done anything wrong—and they're lousy comforters.

Less than patient, Job accuses God of putting him through this misery for no apparent reason.

Eventually, God speaks. But he stops short of explaining himself. Instead, he tells Job to trust him. Then he restores Job's health and wealth and gives him 10 more children.

// LOCATION: Uz, a region that scholars haven't yet been able to identify, though one persistent guess is ancient Edom, along the Israeli-Jordan border (see map page 172).

// TIME: Perhaps about 2000 BC, Abraham's era. Clues: The writer mentions Sabeans, who live then; the father serves as the family priest; wealth is measured by the size of the herds.

// AUTHOR: Unknown.

2000 BC
Job loses his herds, children, health

1900s BC
Jacob fathers 12 sons, ancestors of Israel's 12 tribes

2000 BC *Invaders overrun Abraham's former homeland of Ur*

1950 BC *Egyptian army invades Canaan (now Israel)*

1900 BC *Cuneiform condensed from 2,000 characters to about 600*

God lets Satan torture Job

IT SOUNDS HARSH. And it's not the answer most people want to hear when they ask why God allows good people to suffer. But in Job's story, God agrees to let some kind of a spirit-being—perhaps the devil himself—run Job through a gauntlet.

It all starts with a meeting in heaven. A being called the Accuser (*Satan* in Hebrew) says he has been patrolling the earth.

"What do you think of my servant Job?" God asks. "No one on earth is like him—he is a truly good person, who respects me and refuses to do evil" (Job 1:8 CEV).

"Why shouldn't he respect you?" Satan replies. "You make him successful in whatever he does. . . . Try taking away everything he owns, and he will curse you to your face" (Job 1:9–11 CEV).

God agrees to let Satan put Job to the test.

SATAN.
Bible experts debate if the writer of Job intended readers to think of the Accuser as the devil. The Hebrew word *satan* simply means "accuser." In one case it refers to the work of a good angel: the Angel of God sent to intercept a pagan seer named Balaam (Numbers 22:22). There, some Bibles translate *satan* as "block" or "stop."

IS JOB'S STORY FACT OR FICTION?
Scholars who respect the Bible argue both sides of this debate. Some say it's a story that really happened, and that the details in the story track with life about the time of Abraham, Isaac, and Jacob. Others, however, call it a spiritual folktale. They compare it to a parable, saying it's intended to teach a spiritual truth. In this case, one truth is that we should trust God, rather than try to figure him out. Another: Sin isn't the cause of all the bad things that happen to us.

◀ **JOB'S ACCUSER.**
A mysterious spirit-being accuses Job of serving God for what he gets out of it: rich. Turn up the heat, the accuser says, and Job's faith will evaporate. The Hebrew word describing the accuser is *satan*. But Bible experts debate whether it's the devil, an angelic scout patrolling the earth, or perhaps a character in a fictional, parable-like story.

Job's assets take a dive

FLOCKS, FAMILY, AND HEALTH are three of the greatest assets a nomadic herder like Job can have. He loses them all.

In a single day:

// Sabean raiders steal his 700 teams of oxen and 500 donkeys, then kill the farmhands

// fire from the sky starts a blaze that burns up his 7,000 sheep and shepherds

// Chaldean raiders steal his 3,000 camels and kill the camel drivers, and

// a windstorm collapses the house, crushing to death all 10 of his children.

Job rips his clothes in grief. But he stops short of turning on God. "The LORD gave me what I had, and the LORD has taken it away. Praise the name of the LORD!" (Job 1:21).

Job's just trying to save his own skin, Satan tells God.

"Reach out and take away his health," Satan adds, "and he will surely curse you to your face!" (Job 2:5).

With God's go-ahead, Satan covers Job from head to toe with boils.

But the worst is yet to come: friends.

(continued next page)

CAMEL-LESS / In one of a long string of disasters, Job loses his herd of 3,000 camels. Raiders steal them and kill his herders.

SITTING IN ASHES. It's unclear why Job retreated to an ash heap "to show my repentance" (Job 42:6). Perhaps he thought of himself as trash—useless as burned-up wood.

BROKEN PIECES OF CLAY POTTERY / People in ancient times recycled broken pottery, known as potsherds. They used them like we use scrap paper, to write notes. Job apparently used them like we use backscratchers, to scratch his itching skin. But some scholars say he may have used them to cut himself to express his anger.

SABEANS AND CHALDEANS. If Job lives in Edom on what is now the border of Israel and Jordan, as many scholars speculate, he gets attacked from two directions: north and south. Sabeans come from the south, perhaps Africa or perhaps what many consider the Queen of Sheba's kingdom in the Arabian Peninsula nation of Yemen. Chaldeans come from what is now Iraq.

When friends should shut up

A WEEK OF SILENCE is the best gift three of Job's friends give him: Eliphaz, Bildad, and Zophar. They mourn silently with him "for they saw that his suffering was too great for words" (Job 2:13).

It's Job who breaks the silence with a speech. One line sums up what's on his mind: "Why wasn't I born dead?" (Job 3:11).

A debate follows. It takes up most of this long book. A fourth visitor joins the argument, which spins around what on earth Job did to deserve all this torment. That's the point his friends make. Their premise is that God's in charge of life and that he wouldn't let bad things like this happen unless Job had sinned.

A sampling of their accusations:

ELIPHAZ: "You are nothing but a windbag. . . . Your sins are telling your mouth what to say" (Job 15:2, 5).

BILDAD: "Sinners are dragged from the safety of their tents to die a gruesome death. . . . They are gone. . .into a world of darkness, without any children to carry on their name" (Job 18:14, 17–19 CEV).

ZOPHAR: "You can be sure of this, you haven't gotten half of what you deserve" (Job 11:6 MSG).

ELIHU: "Job, you deserve the maximum penalty" (Job 34:36).

◄ NOT WHAT YOU'D CALL COMFORTERS. Three of Job's friends arrive and sit silently for a week, sharing his misery. Then they open their mouths. Suddenly, misery hates company.

LINKING SIN TO SICKNESS. Many Jews in Bible times linked sickness to sin. Even in Jesus' day, when the disciples saw a man born blind they asked Jesus, "Was it because of his own sins or his parents' sins?" (John 9:2). Neither, Jesus said. "This happened so the power of God could be seen in him" (John 9:3). Jesus healed him. Some scholars say the writer of Job's story intended to show that we shouldn't assume a link between sin and tragedy.

Job pleads not guilty

"STOP ASSUMING MY GUILT," Job argues, "I have done no wrong" (Job 6:29).

Job's story reads like a debate. Four against one.

Friend number one, Eliphaz, makes his case against Job and for God. Then Job offers a rebuttal. Next comes friend number two, Bildad, and Job's rebuttal; friend three, Zophar, and Job's rebuttal.

This goes on for three rounds, with each friend getting a chance to take several potshots at ailing Job. Latecomer Elihu then arrives with more potshots.

Job comes to think of each man as more fiend than friend. He says so:

> "What miserable comforters you are! Won't you ever stop blowing hot air?"
>
> JOB 16:2-3

Not all that patient, even when it comes to God, Job points a finger at heaven and demands an explanation:

> "You, God, are the reason I am insulted and spit on. . . . I complain to you, my God. Don't just condemn me! Point out my sin."
>
> JOB 17:6; 10:1-2 CEV

In time—once the windbags have puffed themselves windless—God arrives in a whirlwind. He'll have a few words for everyone.

QUACKS / Job is fed up with his friends' inaccurate diagnosis of sin. He rejects their recommended course of treatment: confession. Instead, he gives them what for: "You're not doctors who came to treat me. You're quacks who came to irritate me with unintelligible duck sounds. Shut up and let me suffer in peace" (Job 13:4-5 AUTHOR'S PARAPHRASE).

IRAQI JOB

Some of Job's complaints sound like those of a man in a Babylonian story written about 4,000 years ago—Job's era, some scholars guess.

The story is "A Man and His God," from Sumer, the world's first known civilization, located in what is now Iraq.

BIBLE JOB	IRAQI JOB
COMPLAINING TO GOD: "Why wasn't I born dead?" (Job 3:11).	**COMPLAINING TO A DEITY:** "Let my mother who gave birth spend her life crying for me."
COMPLAINING TO GOD: "I cry out, 'Help!' but no one answers me" (Job 19:7).	**COMPLAINING TO A DEITY:** "How long will you ignore me?"
APOLOGIZING TO GOD: "I take back everything I said" (Job 42:6).	**APOLOGIZING TO DEITY:** "I have set my sights on you as on the rising sun."

The difference?

Bible Job thanks God before help comes—that's faith. Iraqi Job thanks his god after help comes—that's gratitude.

God: "You talk too much"

GOD ARRIVES 38 CHAPTERS into this long-winded debate—after the third round. The first words out of his holy mouth:

> *"Why do you talk so much when you know so little?"*
>
> JOB 38:2 CEV

Job has been asking God to explain himself—as though God doesn't know what he's doing. Questions such as, "What do you gain by oppressing me?" (Job 10:3).

God responds with a barrage of questions of his own—three chapters of them.

// "Where were you when I created the earth? Tell me, since you know so much!" (Job 38:4 MSG).

// "Is it your wisdom that makes the hawk soar?" (Job 39:26).

// "Can you shout in thunder the way I can? Go ahead, show your stuff" (Job 40:10 MSG).

Job apologizes. "I take back everything I said, and I sit in dust and ashes to show my repentance" (Job 42:6).

God never bothers to explain why he put Job through all this. He simply implies that Job should trust him. But God does restore Job's health, wealth, and family—doubling his herds and giving him 10 more children.

As for the know-it-all, holier-than-Job friends, God tells them that his servant Job will pray for them. In return, they have to pay Job. Some might call that twisting the dagger. But for fans of Job, it's a happy ending.

LIGHT ON THE SUBJECT / Job's ignorance is the subject. God spotlights it with a litany of questions Job can't possibly answer. Questions like, "Where does light come from?" (Job 38:19).

◀ **CONSTELLATION OF PLEIADES.** Nine of the brightest stars are named for the Seven Sisters of Greek mythology: Sterope, Merope, Electra, Maia, Taygete, Celaeno, and Alcyone, along with their parents, Atlas and Pleione.

PLEIADES, ORION, THE GREAT BEAR. God asks Job if he can control the movement of the stars, naming these three constellations (see Job 38:31–32). Scholars used to teach that Greeks named them. But the current theory credits Phoenicia (now Lebanon) and sets the date to before the birth of Israel. Constellation names show up on ancient Babylonian records as early as 1300 BC, but may predate even those records.

BIG SCENE
DEATH VALLEY

PSALM 23:4

"Even when I walk through the darkest valley, I will not be afraid, for you are close beside me."

PSALMS

SONGS SUNG BLUE TO GOD

STORY LINE

FORGET THE STORY LINE. There isn't any. This is a collection of songs. It's the closest thing Jews in ancient times had to a hymnbook.

A lot of the lyrics shower God with thanks and praise—like worship songs do today. That's why Jews call the book *Tehillim* (tuh-hee-LEEM). It's Hebrew for "praises."

But most psalms wouldn't qualify for a smiley face. Many are songs sung blue. The writer is upset—sometimes at God.

Some songs are tough to imagine singing in a worship service.

> Long enough, GOD—
> you've ignored me long enough.
> I've looked at the back of your head
> long enough. Long enough
> I've carried this ton of trouble,
> lived with a stomach full of pain.
>
> PSALM 13:1–2 MSG

This downer of a song ends on an upbeat note: "I'm singing at the top of my lungs, I'm so full of answered prayers" (Psalm 13:6 MSG).

Still, it feels odd to sing complaints to God. Yet that's apparently a key message behind this collection of songs. God wants to hear from us. Whether we're happy, mad, worried, or hopeful. He can handle the full range of human emotions—from rants to raves. When it comes to us, his door is always open.

// LOCATION: Most psalms are set in Israel.

// TIME: The songs span about a thousand years, from the time of Moses as early as the 1400s BC to the time of the Jewish exile in Babylon (Iraq) in the 500s BC.

// AUTHOR: Like a church hymnbook, Psalms is a collection of song lyrics by various writers. David is credited with either writing or inspiring 73 of the 150 psalms. Other psalms are linked to Solomon, Moses, Korah, and Asaph.

458 BC
Jews back from exile sing to God (see Ezra 3:11)

800 BC *Musicians accompany the reading of Homer's* Iliad *and* Odyssey

378 BC *Plato says some music has a bad effect on listeners, making it bad for Greece*

Songs sung blue

NEARLY HALF THE PSALMS qualify as downers. They're complaints, pleas for help, and expressions of disappointment or grief.

They're perhaps much like our prayers, if we set them to music.

Yet even most of these complaints, like many prayers today, tend to wrap up with a vote of confidence in God.

Take Psalm 42: "Why have you forgotten me? Why must I wander around in grief?" A few lines later the writer concludes: "Why am I discouraged? Why is my heart so sad? I will put my hope in God!" (verses 9, 11).

It might seem irrational to end this way after starting a song with words like:

// "Please, GOD, no more yelling, no more trips to the woodshed. Treat me nice for a change" (Psalm 6:1–2 MSG).

// "God, God. . .my God! Why did you dump me miles from nowhere?" (Psalm 22:1 MSG).

// "My life is full of troubles" (Psalm 88:3)

But in each case the songwriter seems to have a history with God—and apparently feels that given God's track record, the Lord deserves the benefit of the doubt.

A LYRE FOR THE LADIES / A Greek musician plays the lyre, King David's instrument of choice.

GETTING JIGGY IN POMPEII. Street musicians play instruments mentioned in Psalms: tambourine, cymbals, and flute. The mosaic is from Pompeii, Italy, a Roman town buried in ash during the eruption of Mount Vesuvius in AD 79.

SOUNDS OF MUSIC. No one on the planet seems to know what the music of Psalms sounded like.

Musical notes existed. The oldest music discovered so far dates to Abraham's time and place—about 4,000 years ago in what is now Iraq. But no one has deciphered the ancient code of notes.

The oldest surviving note system comes from Gregorian monks about 1,000 years ago: the Gregorian chant.

If the music of Psalms was as rich and diverse as the lyrics, the sounds may have ranged from the droning moans of ram horns to the soothing strum of harps to the excited chatter of cymbals.

NO RHYME, JUST REASON. Psalm lyrics are poems. Hebrew poetry doesn't rhyme. Instead of repeating sounds, it repeats ideas. Line one will say something, and line two may repeat that idea, contrast it, or expand on it. Line one: "Put me on trial, LORD, and cross-examine me." Line two, in this case, repeats the first: "Test my motives and my heart" (Psalm 26:2).

Singing the praises of God

IN THIS GO-TO BOOK for how to praise God, perhaps the most quoted psalm of all compares God to a dependable, loving shepherd.

"You let me rest in fields of green grass. You lead me to streams of peaceful water" (Psalm 23:2 CEV).

The "peaceful water" or "still water," as some Bibles translate it, seems to refer to abundant water. As the old saying goes, "still water runs deep." So the point is that God gives us everything we need, just as a shepherd provides food and water for the sheep.

Because of this song's expression of absolute trust in God in the worst of situations, it's often read to the dying and to the loved ones left behind.

"I may walk through valleys as dark as death, but I won't be afraid. You are with me, and your shepherd's rod makes me feel safe" (Psalm 23:4 CEV).

(continued next page)

SHEPHERD TOOLS.
A long staff gently nudged sheep away from dangerous paths. A short, heavy club, sometimes embedded with sharp metal, beat off wild animals. A slingshot could drive away wild animals from a distance.

HOW MANY PRAISE SONGS ARE THERE?
Psalms are tough to classify because many fit into more than one category. But most scholars agree that psalms of praise rank a close second after psalms asking for help. By some counts, each of these two categories has about 70 songs, with some crossover songs working both labels.

◀ **GOOD SHEPHERD.**
A Palestinian shepherd and son look after their flock in the springtime hills north of Jericho (see this shepherd's portrait page 180). The most famous psalm in the Bible compares God to a shepherd who lovingly cares for his sheep.

Portrait of a Shepherd

PSALMS: TOP 10 PRAISE HITS

1. "The LORD is my shepherd; I have all that I need" (Psalm 23:1).

2. "I look to the hills! Where will I find help? It will come from the LORD, who created the heavens and the earth" (Psalm 121:1–2 CEV).

3. "He lifted me out of the pit of despair, out of the mud and the mire. He set my feet on solid ground and steadied me as I walked along" (Psalm 40:2).

4. "As the deer longs for streams of water, so I long for you, O God" (Psalm 42:1).

5. "The heavens proclaim the glory of God. The skies display his craftsmanship" (Psalm 19:1).

6. "You are my mighty rock, my fortress, my protector, the rock where I am safe, my shield, my powerful weapon, and my place of shelter" (Psalm 18:2 CEV).

7. "Give thanks to the LORD because he is good. His love continues forever" (Psalm 136:1 NCV)

8. "Open your mouth and taste, open your eyes and see—how good GOD is. Blessed are you who run to him" (Psalm 34:8 MSG).

9. "What can I give back to GOD for the blessings he's poured out on me? I'll lift high the cup of salvation—a toast to GOD!" (Psalm 116:12-13 MSG).

10. "LORD our Lord, your name is the most wonderful name in all the earth!" (Psalm 8:9 NCV).

God works the complaint desk

IF EACH PSALM STOOD IN LINES like customers at a service counter, the longest line would be the saddest line.

There are plenty of happy psalms. But there are more sad songs: complaints, laments, cries for help, and frantic pleas for forgiveness.

SOME PLEAS SOUND HEARTFELT:

// "How much longer, LORD, will you forget about me? Will it be forever? How long will you hide? How long must I be confused and miserable all day?" (Psalm 13:1–2 CEV).

// "My God, why have you deserted me? Why are you so far away? Won't you listen to my groans and come to my rescue? I cry out day and night, but you don't answer" (Psalm 22:1–2 CEV).

SOME SOUND A LITTLE WACKED:

// "Rescue me, my God! Slap all my enemies in the face!" (Psalm 3:7).

Many of the songs express raw human emotion—some emotions not so saintly, like revenge. But that's the point of these psalms, Bible experts say. They show us that God can take whatever we dish out. Including delusional accusations, pent-up anger, and screams for justice.

Yet at rant's end, most songwriters calm down. As one worked-up poet put it in his complaint's finale, "I trust in your unfailing love" (Psalm 13:5).

ROCK WITH A VIEW / A lone man casts a gaze across the Jordan River Valley. Lyrics in some of the psalms sound like they're spilling out of an abandoned soul. Yet by song's end, most writers express their trust in God to help them. Many wish he'd help sooner rather than later.

Road trip, the musical

LONG TRIPS and music are a matched set. Perhaps they have been since the first barefooted traveler discovered the hum. Psalms preserves more than a dozen road songs. Jews sing them whenever they're traveling—especially when they're headed to Jerusalem.

And they go to Jerusalem a lot. It's the only place in Israel they're allowed to offer sacrifices to God, at the Jerusalem Temple.

Jews call these psalms "songs of ascent." As in songs to sing while climbing the hills to Jerusalem. Whenever Jews said they were going to Jerusalem, they said they were going "up" to Jerusalem—even if they lived in Galilee and were heading south, down to Jerusalem. No matter which direction they come from, they have to climb hills. Jerusalem sits on the crest of ridge just west of the Mount of Olives ridge, across the narrow Kidron Valley.

That's why several of the road songs talk about mountains. Others talk about protection along the way, from robbers and wild animals.

WHY WORSHIP ONLY IN JERUSALEM?

Many people worshipped idols on hilltops, conducting their own private worship. Jerusalem provided a controlled setting. Priests and other worship leaders educated in the laws of God were able to steer the Jews away from warped ideas about God. It worked sometimes. Other times, not so much.

LYRICS FOR THE LONG HAUL

I look up to the mountains—
*   does my help come from there?*
My help comes from the LORD,
*   who made heaven and earth!*

PSALM 121:1–2

Just as Jerusalem is protected
*   by mountains on every side,*
the LORD protects his people
*   by holding them in his arms*
*   now and forever.*

PSALM 125:2 CEV

◄ WALKING TUNES.

Some psalms were travel tunes, appropriate for trips to Jerusalem or for life's journey in general: "Show me the right path, O LORD; point out the road for me to follow" (Psalm 25:4).

Songs about the king

SONGS ABOUT THE PRESIDENT or other political leaders today don't usually produce the kind of lyrics we'd expect to hear in a church—though maybe in a bar.

Jews in Bible times seem to think of their king not as a political leader, but as God's chosen leader. That's where the king's title comes from: Anointed One. *Messiah* in the Hebrew language. *Christ* in Greek.

As far as many Jews are concerned, God's their true king. The current resident of the palace is just his representative. So the Jews not only pray for the king, they sing songs praising him. They also sing some of their prayers for the king.

Psalms has a dozen songs that Bible experts call royal psalms: 2, 18, 20, 21, 45, 61, 72, 89, 101, 110, 132, 144. A sampling:

"Yes, our protection comes from the LORD, and he, the Holy One of Israel, has given us our king" (Psalm 89:18).

"Please help the king to be honest and fair just like you, our God" (Psalm 72:1 CEV).

"Add many years to the life of the king! . . . May he reign under God's protection forever" (Psalm 61:6–7).

SONGS OF DAVID / Almost half of the 150 psalms are attributed to David—73. But that doesn't mean he wrote them. The byline phrasing is vague. *Of David* can mean "by David," "about David," or "inspired by David." David may have written many, though. Bible stories describe him as a musician who played the harp. He also wrote a moving lament for the funeral of Saul and Jonathan (see 2 Samuel 1:17–27).

BIG SCENE
THE RIGHT STUFF

PROVERBS 22:6
"Teach your children right from wrong, and when they are grown they will still do right" (CEV).

BIBLE HISTORY

ALL DATES APPROXIMATE

970 BC
Solomon becomes king of Israel

930 BC
Solomon dies

WORLD HISTORY

1100 BC
A sage, Amenemope, writes Egyptian proverbs

PROVERBS

WISE GUYS WITH SNAPPY ONE-LINERS

STORY LINE

IMAGINE JEWISH FORTUNE COOKIES—
each stuffed with a snappy one-liner. That's
what the book of Proverbs sounds like to some
folks.

It's as though someone hijacked a truckload of
kosher fortune cookies, cracked open the cookies,
and copied the wise sayings into a book.

Don't look for a plot in Proverbs, or a story, or
a character—at least not a hero or villain with an
honest-to-goodness name.

Heroes and villains in Proverbs are more general
than specific. Bad guys include loose women, lazy
men, and kids dumb as a bag of lug nuts (Proverbs
21:9; 26:14; 15:20). Good guys include business-
savvy wives, appreciative husbands, and friends
who don't ask us to cosign their loans (Proverbs
31:24, 31; 6:1–5).

This is a practical book written by grand-
fatherly graduates from the school of hard knocks:
old men offering their best advice to young men.

Much of the sage advice crosses the age and gen-
der boundaries.

Which is one reason Proverbs has become one
of the most quoted books in the Bible. It has wide
appeal. Besides that, it's not abstract religious philosophy. It's religion going toe-to-toe with the real
world.

// LOCATION: Israel.

// TIME: During Solomon's reign, from about
970–930 BC.

// AUTHOR: Most are attributed to King Solomon, and some to a group of wise men.

700 BC
*Hezekiah orders collection of Solomon's
proverbs (see Proverbs 25:1)*

800 BC *Homer, father of Greek
literature, writes the Iliad (fall of Troy)
and the Odyssey (travels of Ulysses)*

600 BC *Female poet
Sappho of Lesbos writes
sensual poetry*

Don't go looking for trouble

PROVERBS' HEADLINER, the advice getting first mention and top billing, is the same advice parents still beat into their kids. Sometimes literally.

> *If bad companions tempt you, don't go along with them. If they say—"Let's go out and raise some hell" . . . . don't listen to them for a minute.*
>
> PROVERBS 1:10–11, 15 MSG

Good-for-nothing "friends" like that, the sage warns, are dumb enough to think they're setting traps for other people—people they think they'll rob and kill. Instead, they're setting traps for themselves.

"They gang up to murder someone, but they are the victims. The wealth you get from crime robs you of your life" (Proverbs 1:18–19 CEV).

BE GOOD BOYS / Pick your friends carefully, the wise men of Israel tell their young students. "There are 'friends' who destroy each other, but a real friend sticks closer than a brother" (Proverbs 18:24).

MAKING TIME FOR GRAND-DAUGHTER. Pausing at a wedding celebration, an elderly leader among Hasidic Jews pauses to give his granddaughter a hug. As a Proverbs sage once put it, "Grandchildren are the crowning glory of the aged" (Proverbs 17:6).

THE OLD MAN'S ADVICE FOR KIDS

Sages of Proverbs offer the following advice, targeted just to youngsters.

> **Show good sense:** "Children with good sense make their parents happy, but foolish children are hateful to them" (Proverbs 15:20 CEV).

> **Don't mistreat Ma and Pa:** "Children who mistreat their father or chase away their mother are an embarrassment and a public disgrace" (Proverbs 19:26).

> **Pick good friends:** "Young people who obey the law are wise; those with wild friends bring shame to their parents" (Proverbs 28:7).

> **Learn from your dad:** "My children, listen when your father corrects you. Pay attention and learn good judgment" (Proverbs 4:1).

Count on God

"TRUST IN THE LORD with all your heart; do not depend on your own understanding" (Proverbs 3:5).

That sounds like advice from someone who either read the book of Job or who lived a similar tough story—a story that smells like a stinky mixture of rotten luck, bad karma, and fertilizer hitting the fan.

The sage seems to realize it's natural to want to know why God seems content to let us suffer—just as Job wanted God to explain himself. Or maybe we're feeling blessed, and we think we've figured out why: God's rewarding us for something good we did.

"Don't assume that you know it all," the sage warns (Proverbs 3:7 MSG).

Instead, "Run to God! Run from evil!" (Proverbs 3:7 MSG). And while you're running life's journey, "Listen for GOD's voice in everything you do, everywhere you go; he's the one who will keep you on track" (Proverbs 3:6 MSG).

TAKING GOD TO THE WALL / A Jew brings his prayer to God at the most sacred Jewish site on earth: Jerusalem's Western Wall (Wailing Wall). The stones once served as a retaining wall that held up the hilltop where the Jewish Temple stood. Jews and Christians alike write their prayer requests on paper and stuff them in the cracks between the stones.

WHAT NOT TO TRUST

// Idols. "Do not put your trust in idols" (Leviticus 19:4).

// Mediums. "I will also turn against those who commit spiritual prostitution by putting their trust in mediums or in those who consult the spirits of the dead" (Leviticus 20:6).

// Military power. "I do not count on my sword to save me" (Psalm 44:6).

// Cash. "Those who trust in their riches will fall, but the righteous will thrive like a green leaf" (Proverbs 11:28 TNIV).

ROI: RETURN ON INVESTMENT IN GOD

// Peace. "You will keep in perfect peace all who trust in you" (Isaiah 26:3).

// Inner strength. "Those who trust in the LORD will find new strength. They will soar high on wings like eagles. They will run and not grow weary. They will walk and not faint" (Isaiah 40:31).

The sex talk

IF YOU'RE GOING TO HAVE SEX, have it with your wife. Not with some other guy's wife.

That advice, apparently, is important for young men in Bible times. The clue: Old sages repeat it over and over—as though this particular bit of wisdom is a nail they have to hammer into thickheaded young men who, when it comes to sex, tend to think with an organ somewhat smaller than their brain.

Writing as though they know what they're talking about, the sages raise red flags like these:

TWO QUESTIONS

"Why would you trade enduring intimacies for cheap thrills with a whore? For dalliance with a promiscuous stranger?"

PROVERBS 5:20 MSG

"If you build a fire in your pants, what makes you think you won't get burned?"

PROVERBS 6:27 AUTHOR'S PARAPHRASE

TWO WARNINGS

"The lips of a seductive woman are oh so sweet. . . . But it won't be long before she's gravel in your mouth, a pain in your gut, a wound in your heart. She's dancing down the primrose path to Death; she's headed straight for Hell and taking you with her."

PROVERBS 5:3–5 MSG

"Adultery is a brainless act, soul-destroying, self-destructive; expect a bloody nose, a black eye, and a reputation ruined for good."

PROVERBS 6:32–33 MSG

DON'T EVEN THINK ABOUT IT. Lebanese actress Joelle Behlock catches the eye of Syrian actor Raheed Assaf, in a scene from the miniseries *The Last Cavalier*. Sex advice from sages quoted in Proverbs follows one of the principles that elderly Job recommended: "I made a solemn pact with myself never to undress a girl with my eyes" (Job 31:1 MSG).

HOW WOMEN SET A SEX TRAP One sage tells a graphic tale of how a married woman set a sex trap for a man.

The predator's how-to, reported in Proverbs 7:

> Pick a time when your husband is out of town on a long trip.
> Drape your bed in the finest sheets, scented.
> Dress for testosterone; accentuate the protuberances.
> Take a stroll at dusk, as night begins to thicken.
> Target a man with the common sense of a gopher hole.
> Greet him like your long-lost lover: touchy, feely, huggy, kissy.
> Invite him home for sex like he wouldn't believe.
> Lead him gently, like a jackass to the glue factory.

Bad-mouthing laziness

LAZY IS CRAZY. That's the message scattered throughout the entire book of Proverbs, like billboards posted along the highway of life.

More than a dozen billboards, spotlighting messages from bad-mouthing laziness in chapter 6 to praising the hard work of a wife in chapter 31.

A sampling:

BEYOND THE POWER NAP. "As a door swings back and forth on its hinges, so the lazy person turns over in bed" (Proverbs 26:14).

YOU SNOOZE, YOU LOSE. "A nap here, a nap there, a day off here, a day off there, sit back, take it easy—do you know what comes next? Just this: You can look forward to a dirt-poor life, poverty your permanent houseguest!" (Proverbs 6:10–11 MSG)

DOWNSIDE OF "GET RICH QUICK." "Wealth from get-rich-quick schemes quickly disappears; wealth from hard work grows over time" (Proverbs 13:11).

UPSIDE OF HARD WORK. "Work hard, and you will be a leader; be lazy, and you will end up a slave" (Proverbs 12:24 CEV).

THE HEADACHE OF HAVING A LAZY EMPLOYEE. "Having a lazy person on the job is like a mouth full of vinegar or smoke in your eyes" (Proverbs 10:26 CEV).

RIPE / A Palestinian farmer fills his hands with freshly harvested olives.

▲ ANTS R US. "Take a lesson from the ants, you lazybones. . . . They labor hard all summer, gathering food for the winter" (Proverbs 6:6, 8).

WORK ETHICS: A LESSON FROM THE CRITTER WORLD. For lessons about life, rabbis in the ancient Middle East—like the sages of Proverbs—sometimes pointed to the animal kingdom.

Warning: Don't mistreat your servants: "If you hit the donkey, it will kick" (Tanchuma, Pekudei 4).

Warning: Bad parents produce worse children. "What does a beetle produce? More beetles, only worse" (Canticles Rabbah).

Warning: Don't hang around an angry woman: "If a dog barks at you, it's safe to enter. If a bitch barks at you, leave" (Talumud Eruvin 86a).

ARE ALL THE BIBLE PROVERBS TRUE ALL THE TIME? No, most scholars agree. Many are general observations that the sages pass along to young men. Example: "Hard workers get rich" (Proverbs 10:4). Try to sell that to a coal miner.

Honesty is the best policy

HONESTY SCORES HIGH with the wise elders of Proverbs—right up there with hard work.

Lies and deceit might punch up profits for the short haul, but sages warn that in the long haul it's a killer—because God hates it.

// "God can't stomach liars; he loves the company of those who keep their word" (Proverbs 12:22 MSG).

// "The LORD detests the use of dishonest scales. . .[and] people with crooked hearts" (Proverbs 11:1, 20).

On the flip side, these same proverbs report, God "delights in accurate weights. . .[and] in those with integrity."

Over the long haul, building a reputation for honesty pays off—at least that's a principle the sages say they've seen throughout their lives. "Truth lasts" (Proverbs 12:19 MSG). But "the deviousness of crooks brings them to ruin" (Proverbs 11:3 MSG).

As far as the sages are concerned, it's "better to be poor and honest than a rich person no one can trust" (Proverbs 19:1 MSG).

SAY "CHEESE," THEN WEIGH IT.
A shop owner at a Jewish grocery store in Los Angeles beams as he prepares to weigh a block of cheese. Elders writing advice in Proverbs urge merchants to keep their business practices aboveboard. No fingers on the scales.

. . . .

SAMPLER OF PROVERBS TOPICS
Anger: "Fools vent their anger, but the wise quietly hold it back" (Proverbs 29:11)

Arguing: "The start of a quarrel is like a leak in a dam, so stop it before it bursts" (Proverbs 17:14 MSG).

Flattery: "People appreciate honest criticism far more than flattery" (Proverbs 28:23).

Marriage: "A man's greatest treasure is his wife—she is a gift from the LORD" (Proverbs 18:22 CEV). Unless she's a poor excuse of a human being, in which case she's a disease—like bone cancer (see Proverbs 12:4).

Revenge: "If people who did you wrong are hungry, take them out to lunch. If they're thirsty, have a drink with them. Your gracious spirit will shock them to their senses and they'll be ashamed of how they treated you" (Proverbs 25:21–22 AUTHOR'S PARAPHRASE).

GOD HATES DISHONEST SCALES / Proverbs says so. Some merchants hollowed out their counterweights, so customers weren't getting as much as they paid for.

Careful what you say

SHUT YOUR MOUTH. That's the default setting that the sages of Proverbs recommend to their students—at least when the young men aren't sure what to say.

Silence is partly for self-preservation: "Watch your tongue and keep your mouth shut, and you will stay out of trouble" (Proverbs 21:23).

But words can hurt others, too. Or help them. Like potent drugs—words can go either way:

// "Words kill, words give life; they're either poison or fruit—you choose" (Proverbs 18:21 MSG).

// "The words of the wicked are like a murderous ambush, but the words of the godly save lives" (Proverbs 12:6).

// "With their words, the godless destroy their friends" (Proverbs 11:9).

IT CAN GET UGLY / "The speech of a good person clears the air; the words of the wicked pollute it" (Proverbs 10:32 MSG).

◀ SWEET AS HONEY. "Kind words are like honey—sweet to the soul and healthy for the body" (Proverbs 16:24).

DEALING WITH THE GOSSIPS IN OUR LIVES. "Gossips can't keep secrets, so never confide in blabbermouths" (Proverbs 20:19 MSG).

HOW TO HANDLE VERBAL BULLIES. "Kick out the troublemakers and things will quiet down; you need a break from bickering and griping!" (Proverbs 22:10 MSG).

MATED TO A NAG. "Better to camp out by yourself in the back seat of a Buick than live in a 50-room mansion with a nag" (Proverbs 25:24 AUTHOR'S PARAPHRASE).

THE COMEBACK. "Don't make a fool of yourself by answering a fool" (Proverbs 26:4 CEV).

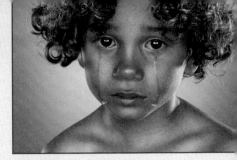

Raising kids 101

TREAT THEM LIKE SHEEP. That seems to sum up the dozen-plus proverbs about how to raise kids.

LIKE A GOOD SHEPHERD, POINT THEM IN THE RIGHT DIRECTION.

"Start children off on the way they should go, and even when they are old they will not turn from it."

PROVERBS 22:6 TNIV

LET THEM KNOW WHEN THEY'RE VEERING OFF ONTO A DANGEROUS PATH, AND NUDGE THEM BACK TO SAFETY.

"Correct your children while there is still hope; do not let them destroy themselves."

PROVERBS 19:18 NCV

SHOULD PARENTS SPANK THEIR KIDS?

Christians don't agree. Nor do Bible translators.

Some Bible translations suggest the sages of Proverbs encouraged spanking disobedient children.

> "A spanking won't kill them. A good spanking, in fact, might save them from something worse than death" (Proverbs 23:13–14 MSG).

> "Those who spare the rod hate their children" (Proverbs 13:24 TNIV).

Most Bible translations, however, focus only on the importance of disciplining children—not on the method.

As for hitting kids with a *rod*—a shepherd's tool in Bible times—shepherds say they use a rod not to wallop sheep, but to gently nudge them out of harm's way, back to safety.

◀ **KOSHER NAP.**
A Jerusalem student catches a few z's in a Yeshiva, a school for the study of sacred Jewish writings. Proverbs urges parents to point their kids in the right direction—a phrase that many scholars say means right behavior, conduct that would please God.

Don't be greedy, help the needy

IT'S MORE THAN A SUGGESTION. It's a warning and a promise rolled into one. To most folks, the warning makes perfect sense. But the promise sounds like something a preacher would say when ushers are passing the offering plates.

THE WARNING:

> *"If you won't help the poor, don't expect to be heard when you cry out for help."*
>
> PROVERBS **21:13** CEV

THE PROMISE:

> *"Give freely and become more wealthy. . . . Whoever gives to the poor will lack nothing."*
>
> PROVERBS **11:24; 28:27**

Most scholars agree that neither the warning nor the promise is a spiritual law of nature. Instead, both are general observations from a lifetime of living.

REWARDED.
A man on a park bench plants one on his beloved. He might not know it, but he's following the last sentence of advice in Proverbs—advice about how a man should treat his wife: "praise her in public" (Proverbs 31:31 CEV).

WHO GETS THE LAST WORD?
A woman's advice closes the book of Proverbs.

That's shocking. Proverbs was a book by men for men—old men giving advice to young men. And it was written in an era when men were men and everyone else was pitifully less.

The elders said as much, sometimes comparing women to a constant drip or bone cancer (Proverbs 12:4; 19:13).

Yet this collection of proverbs swimming in testosterone gives an otherwise unknown man named King Lemuel the final say—and he passes on wisdom he credits to his mother.

What follows is one of the Bible's most beautiful tributes to hardworking wives, which King Lemuel describes as "more precious than rubies" (Proverbs 31:10).

HELP WANTED /
Hand extended, a woman begs for help at the entrance to a public building. Beggars in Bible times did the same, sitting in areas of heavy traffic, such as near the city gate, worship centers, or busy shops.

BIG SCENE
SEASONS OF LIFE

ECCLESIASTES 3:1–2, 4–5, 8
*"Everything on earth has its own time and its own season.
There is a time for birth and death, planting and reaping
. . .crying and laughing. . .embracing and parting. . .war
and peace"* (CEV).

American soldier in Pakistan (see page 197).

American soldier in Pakistan (see page 197).

**BIBLE
HISTORY**

ALL DATES APPROXIMATE

**WORLD
HISTORY**

*Babylon worships Marduk
as main god*
1125 BC

ECCLESIASTES

SMARTEST MAN VS. TOUGHEST QUESTION

STORY LINE

WHY ON EARTH ARE WE HERE? That's what the smartest man who ever lived wants to know—King Solomon, "wiser than anyone who has ever lived or ever will live" (1 Kings 3:12 CEV).

Ecclesiastes reports an epic battle. Humanity's smartest person takes on life's toughest question.

Spoiler alert. Solomon can't figure it out.

And he seems really bummed about it: "Nothing makes sense! Everything is nonsense" (Ecclesiastes 1:2 CEV).

He says humans don't make any lasting difference. We're born. We live. We die. But the sun rises the next day, the wind blows, and the river flows—as though we never made any difference to them.

His conclusion: Enjoy life and treat it as a gift from God.

"Take care of yourself, have a good time, and make the most of whatever job you have for as long as God gives you life" (Ecclesiastes 5:18 MSG).

// LOCATION: Israel.

// TIME: 900s BC, if Solomon wrote it.

// AUTHOR: "Teacher." A code name that strongly hints at King Solomon: "These are the words of the Teacher, King David's son, who ruled in Jerusalem" (Ecclesiastes 1:1). If we called this book by an English name, it might be "The Teaching." But Bible translators stick with the Greek *ekklesiastes*, meaning "the one of the assembly."

1011 BC
David becomes Israel's second king, after Saul

970 BC
Solomon becomes king of Israel

930 BC
Solomon dies

Native Americans create burial mounds
1000 BC

Mexico's Olmec people develop writing, perhaps a first in Western world
900 BC

Life: What's the point?

LIFE IS THE MOVIE *GROUNDHOG DAY*—one recycled day after another.

"Everything that happens has happened before," Solomon complains. "Nothing is new" (Ecclesiastes 1:9 CEV).

He thinks about what he has done with his life: enjoying the pleasures of many wives, building massive wealth, and earning a rep as the wisest guy on the planet.

But what's the point of any of it, he wonders, when the rich and the poor, the wise and the dumb end up the same way: dead in the dirt.

Ditto for good people and bad people.

"I've seen it all in my brief and pointless life," he writes. "Here a good person cut down in the middle of doing good, there a bad person living a long life of sheer evil. So don't knock yourself out being good. . . . But don't press your luck by being bad, either" (Ecclesiastes 7:15–17 MSG).

Not quite what we'd expect to hear from a preacher. But this writer calls himself the Teacher. And he's just getting started.

JACKS ARE WILD. / So are monks from time to time. Relatively speaking. Some scholars argue that Solomon wasn't preaching against being good and godly. He was arguing against overdoing it—against holier-than-thou control freaks who stress themselves to death in the process.

HERE TODAY. A horseback rider scouts the plateau of buttes in Colorado's Monument Valley. Geologists say millennia of uplift and erosion carved these buttes out of 50-million-year-old sandstone. The writer of Ecclesiastes, pondering the meaning of life, complains that humans come and go like a wisp of wind quickly forgotten.

Time for war, time for peace

A FOLK SONG ABOUT PEACE "Turn, Turn, Turn," written by Pete Seeger in 1954, sets music to a paraphrase of Ecclesiastes 3.

> *To everything (turn, turn, turn)*
> *There is a season (turn, turn, turn)*
> *And a time for every purpose under heaven.*

Like Solomon, the folksinger recites the flip-side seasons of life, which are as opposite as summer and winter. There's a time to be born and a time to die. In between, there are times to: kill/heal; cry/laugh; hug/push away; find/lose; tear/mend; love/hate.

The difference between the seasons of weather and the seasons of life is that with the weather, we know which season is coming next. With life, we don't have a clue. We'd love to know: "God has given them a desire to know the future" (Ecclesiastes 3:11 NCV). But only God knows what lies ahead.

The best we can do, Solomon says, is to trust God through each season, believing, "He does everything just right and on time" (Ecclesiastes 3:11 NCV).

A TIME TO HEAL / A young Pakistani earthquake survivor gets a drink of water from US Army Sergeant Kornelia Rachwal during an airlift in October 2005. The quake in the Kashmir region killed more than 73,000.

SEASONS OF LIFE

In a poem, Solomon lists seven seasons of life—each season described in two lines. There's a reason for that.

The second line repeats the idea in the first, either by saying it another way, contrasting it, or expanding it. That's Hebrew poetry: no rhyme, but plenty of reason.

The number seven is probably no coincidence, either. Because God rested on Day Seven after creation, that number came to symbolize completion.

"Seven" may be Solomon's way of saying God has planned all the major seasons of human life. What we do during each season, however, is up to us.

Birth/plant
or
Death/harvest

Kill/tear down
or
Heal/rebuild

Cry/mourn
or
Laugh/rejoice

Hug/gather things up
or
Push off/throw away

Find/keep
or
Lose/discard

Tear apart/silent treatment
or
Repair/talk things out

Love/peace
or
Hate/war

Get rich, lose sleep

THE RICHEST KING ON EARTH doesn't have much good to say about wealth.

What's odd—and could seem hypocritical—is that he seems to stop short of giving his money away. He complains about it, but keeps it.

That actually seems to support his claim: "Those who love money will never have enough" (Ecclesiastes 5:10). So they won't give it back.

Yet he complains about:

SLEEPLESS NIGHTS. While workaday grunts drop weary into bed, "rich people worry about their wealth and cannot sleep" (Ecclesiastes 5:12 NCV).

BAD INVESTMENTS. Risky investments "turn sour, and everything is lost" (Ecclesiastes 5:14).

OUR KIDS INHERIT THE MONEY. We can't take it with us. So we leave this world the way we came in: "empty-handed" (Ecclesiastes 5:15).

That said, Solomon insists it's a good idea to treat wealth as a gift from God—and to enjoy it.

It's not quite the advice Jesus would give a rich young ruler a thousand years later: "Sell all your possessions and give the money to the poor, and you will have treasure in heaven. Then come, follow me" (Luke 18:22).

HOLY LAP OF LUXURY / A servant delivers a drink to a guest in the lavishly appointed home of Jerusalem's high priest. Many Jews considered wealth a blessing from God—and poverty a curse. The story of Job and the teachings of Jesus, some Bible experts argue, seem to refute that theory.

Love God, love life

HISTORY'S WISEST MAN, as the Bible describes King Solomon, ends up stumped by humanity's toughest question. He can't figure out why humans are alive—or what difference we make.

Every lead he follows takes him to a dead end.

Leads such as the pursuit of pleasure—as though having a good time is the purpose of life. Other dead ends: hard work, wealth, political power, wisdom. After exploring all of these he reaches a depressing conclusion: "Everything is meaningless. . .completely meaningless" (Ecclesiastes 12:8).

At least from humanity's limited point of view.

But he presumes there's a God point of view, too. "People cannot see the whole scope of God's work from beginning to end" (Ecclesiastes 3:11).

Though Solomon says he can't figure out the meaning of life, he wraps up his report with this advice: Enjoy life and obey God, the giver of life. "Do what he tells you" (Ecclesiastes 12:13 MSG).

Bacchus, god of the good time

A WASTE OF TIME

Nothing but dead ends. That's all Solomon finds in:

> **Pleasure:** "I had everything a man could desire!" (Ecclesiastes 2:8), yet it didn't satisfy him.

> **Hard work and wealth:** "[When I die] I must leave to others everything I have earned" (Ecclesiastes 2:18).

> **Political power:** Crowds rally around a new king, "but then another generation grows up and rejects him" (Ecclesiastes 4:16).

> **Wisdom:** "I set out to be wise, but it was beyond me. . . . Does anyone ever find it?" (Ecclesiastes 7:23-24 MSG).

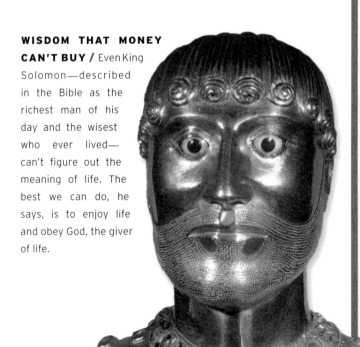

WISDOM THAT MONEY CAN'T BUY / Even King Solomon—described in the Bible as the richest man of his day and the wisest who ever lived—can't figure out the meaning of life. The best we can do, he says, is to enjoy life and obey God, the giver of life.

BIG SCENE
HONEYMOON LOVIN'

SONG OF SONGS 7:8
Comparing his lover to a slender palm tree, the man says, "I'm going to climb that palm tree! I'm going to caress its fruit! Oh yes! Your breasts will be clusters of sweet fruit to me" (MSG).

BIBLE HISTORY

ALL DATES APPROXIMATE

970 BC
Solomon becomes king of Israel

960 BC
Jerusalem Temple is built

WORLD HISTORY

Professional musicians play at weddings in Israel
1000 BC

SONG OF SONGS

THE LANGUAGE OF LOVEY-DOVEY

STORY LINE

THERE'S PLENTY OF EROTIC SEX in this poem. No God, though. He's a no-show.

That's a problem.

People who revere scripture—Jews and Christians alike—have wondered what a sexually explicit song about two people in love is doing in the Holy Bible.

Whipping out unapologetically sensual words, a woman expresses her desire to make love with a man. The man outdoes "Ditto," vowing to climb his lady like a date tree and fill his hands and mouth with the fruit of her breasts.

Whoa, Nellie.

That certainly can't mean what it sounds like it means. At least that's what Bible-loving scholars concluded for most of 3,000 years since Solomon's day.

Instead, they agreed, this book that sounds like the love letters of two youngsters juiced up on hormones is a metaphor. Jews presented it as a symbol of God's love for Israel. Christians said it symbolized Christ's love for the church.

Only in the 1800s did scholars begin to accept it as a song about a man and a woman expressing their deepest feelings of love in both words and sexual intimacy—God-approved sex.

// LOCATION: Israel. Mentioned sites: Jerusalem, Mount Carmel, Sharon Plain, Mount Hermon.

// TIME: During Solomon's rule, from about 970–930 BC.

// AUTHOR: The original Hebrew language calls this a song "of Solomon," which could mean it was by him, about him, or perhaps for him—as a song performed at one of his weddings.

930 BC
Solomon dies,
leaving 1,000 widows

Greek stories of the Trojan War are
told with music accompaniment
900 BC

Love talk

GLOWING RED WITH EMBARRASSMENT would probably describe just about anyone who wrote love letters as intimate as the Song of Solomon, and then saw them show up in print.

This is one gal and guy who know how to talk the talk, stoking passion from a dry spark to a sweaty inferno.

SHE: "Kiss me—full on the mouth!" (1:2 MSG).

HE: "Your lips are jewel red. . . . Your breasts are like fawns. . . . The kisses of your lips are honey, my love. . . . You're a secret garden. . .a whole orchard of succulent fruits" (4:3, 5, 11–13 MSG).

SHE: "Let my lover enter his garden! Yes, let him eat the fine, ripe fruits" (4:16 MSG).

HE: "Your full breasts are like sweet clusters of dates. I say, 'I'm going to climb that palm tree! I'm going to caress its fruit!' Oh yes! Your breasts will be clusters of sweet fruit to me" (7:7–8 MSG).

Clearly, these two are working up to something—and it's not a metaphor. So say most scholars today.

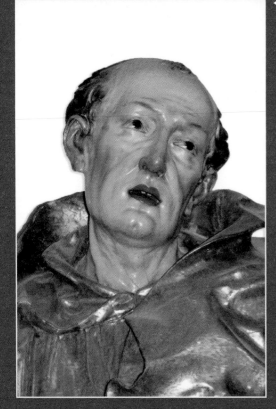

St. Bernard of Clairvaux

◄ **CELIBATE IN LOVE WITH THE LOVE SONG.** St. Bernard of Clairvaux—who took a no-sex vow—wrote 86 sermons based on the Song's first three chapters alone—two sermons per verse. He nixed the literal meaning, promoting the symbolic. For example, Bernard said that the man's promise to make the lady "earrings of gold" (Song of Songs 1:11) means "Heavenly goldsmiths. . . will fashion glorious tokens of the truth and insert them in the soul's inward ears."

CODED GOD TALK? At least as early as the AD 200s, Jewish scholars began teaching that the conversation in this Song reflects what God and Israel said to each other at either the crossing of the Red Sea, the giving of the 10 Commandments at Mount Sinai, or the dedication of the holy tent worship center during the Exodus.

BAR SONG. Ancient Jewish writings complain that non-Jews sang parts of this song in bars and at pagan parties (source: Babylonian Talmud, Sanhedrin 101a).

SONG FOR A WEDDING? Some scholars speculate that a musician may have written this song for a performance at one of King Solomon's thousand weddings.

Love feast

FOOD ON TABLE is not what this love feast is about—it's about flesh on flesh. Sex.

This is what the love talk has been working up to, love expressed in the most intimate physical way.

There is a literal banquet, perhaps: "He escorts me to the banquet hall" (Song of Songs 2:4). But even if it's literal and not a poetic way of talking about the bedroom, the meal comes across as foreplay. Surrounded by an orchard of fruit, the lady says, "All I want is to. . .taste and savor his delicious love." As for the man, the lady reports, "His eyes feasted on me!" (Song of Songs 2:3–4 MSG).

"I am my lover's, and he claims me as his own," she says (Song of Songs 7:10).

The lady then suggests the two of them slip away to a vineyard: "And there I'll give myself to you. . . . Love-apples drench us with fragrance. . . . Fruits fresh and preserved that I've kept and saved just for you, my love" (Song of Songs 7:12–13 MSG).

Most Bible experts today agree that she's probably not talking about fruit as we know it or jam preserves in a pickle jar.

(continued next page)

YOUNG LOVE / A Jewish bride and groom smile in delight as they look at one another. The young couple in the Song of Songs took a hard look at one another, too, and they liked what they saw.

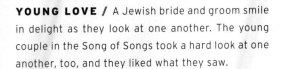

Myrrh

Mandrake roots

MYRRH.
Expensive perfume made from the red-dish sap of Commiphora bushes, imported from Arabia and Africa (far left).

LOVE-APPLES. The literal word is *mandrake*, a root that many people in ancient times considered an aphrodi-siac (left) (see Song of Songs 7:13).

DESCRIBING ONE HANDSOME MAN
Skin: "healthy and tan"
Head: "like the finest gold"
Hair: "wavy and black like a raven"
Eyes: "set like jewels"
Lips: "flowing with myrrh"
Hands: "like gold hinges"
Legs: "like large marble posts"
Mouth: "sweet to kiss"

SONG OF SONGS 5:10–16 NCV

DESCRIBING ONE LOOKER OF A LADY
Thighs: "works of art, each one a jewel"
Navel: "a wine glass filled to overflowing"
Body: "tall and slender"
Breasts: "full". . .[and soft as] "twins of a deer"
Neck: "like ivory"
Eyes: "sparkle like the pools of Heshbon"
Head: "held high like Mount Carmel"
Hair: "so lovely it holds a king prisoner"
Lips: "more delicious than. . .the finest wine"

SONG OF SONGS 7:1–5, 7, 9 CEV

WEDDING BANQUET / Singing, dancing, and a table of delights greet a bride and groom as they celebrate their wedding.

Love for the long haul

"TILL DEATH US DO PART" isn't enough for this lady in Solomon's Song of Songs.

She expects that the love she and her man have for each other will outlast their bodies.

"The passion of love bursting into flame is more powerful than death, stronger than the grave" (Song of Songs 8:6 CEV).

Torrents of rain can't quench the fire, the young lady says. Floods can't drown it. Yet this death-defying force is free. It can't be bought or sold.

The lady gives her love freely. But she wants something in return: commitment.

"Hang my locket around your neck, wear my ring on your finger" (Song of Songs 8:6 MSG).

RING AROUND THE BRIDE AND GROOM / Bulls-eye of attention, a Jewish bride and groom find themselves in the middle of a ring of dancing men. In the Song of Songs, a young lady asks a young man to consider her a seal over his heart. When it comes to romance, no one else gets in.

Seal and its imprint in soft clay

LOCKETS, RINGS, SEALS. Bible translators use different word pictures to help readers understand what the lady was asking the man to do to express his commitment to her. Wearing a wedding ring today says "we're taken." Historians say wedding rings started in Egypt more than 4,000 years ago, with the ring shape—a never-ending line—symbolizing eternal love.

The more literal Hebrew word in this passage is "seal." Made of stone or hard clay, it could press an image or words onto a soft clay plug that sealed a letter with a design that identified the sender. Like a wedding ring, the seal in the song may symbolize ownership—that the lady belongs to the gentleman; they are husband and wife.

ISAIAH 53

Isaiah predicts that an innocent man, interpreted by New Testament writers as Jesus, will die for the sins of others: "the LORD gave him the punishment we deserved" (53:6 CEV).

BIG SCENE

ISRAEL'S FUTURE "SUFFERING SERVANT"

BIBLE HISTORY	ALL DATES APPROXIMATE	765 BC *Birth of Isaiah*		740 BC *Isaiah's ministry begins*
WORLD HISTORY			*Founding of Rome* **753 BC**	

ISAIAH

ERASING ISRAEL

STORY LINE

NOT JUST BAD NEWS, the prophet Isaiah delivers the worst news in ancient Jewish history:

God is going to wipe their nation off the world map.

Isaiah's ministry begins with a dramatic vision. He finds himself in God's throne room when God asks for a volunteer to deliver his messages to the Jewish people.

"Here I am," Isaiah says. "Send me" (Isaiah 6:8).

God warns that the hard-hearted Jewish people won't listen. They've abandoned the Lord for other gods, and the time is coming when he will abandon them to their enemies, in accordance with the agreement both sides made in the time of Moses (see Deuteronomy 28:64).

Isaiah lives to see the northern Jewish nation of Israel fall. Assyrians from what is now Iraq invade, deport Jewish survivors, and give the land to their own settlers.

Like all other prophets in the Bible, Isaiah doesn't stop with bad news. He ends with hope.

God will give the Jews a fresh start, Isaiah predicts. And God will send a Messiah from King David's family to start a kingdom more wonderful than the Jews could imagine.

// LOCATION: Isaiah lived in Jerusalem. His prophecies involve his own Jewish nation of Judah, along with the northern Jewish nation of Israel, and other nations throughout the Middle East.

// TIME: The first 39 chapters are set in the 700s BC, when Isaiah lived. Chapters 40–55 describe the Jewish exile in what is now Iraq (then Babylon) during the 500s BC. Chapters 56–66 describe the return from exile in the 400s–500s BC.

// AUTHOR: Isaiah, though many scholars say he probably wrote only the first 39 chapters, which are set in his time.

722 BC
Assyrians conquer Israel

701 BC
Assyria conquers most of Judah; Jerusalem survives

700 BC
Isaiah's ministry ends

Wolf feeds twins Romulus and Remus who found Rome

Assyrians destroy Babylon, divert Euphrates River to flood city
689 BC

Isaiah's visit to heaven

ISAIAH SEES GOD in a vision of some kind—perhaps a dream or a trancelike state.

The year is 740 BC. King Uzziah has just died. Within five years Judah will crown one of its most godless kings: Ahaz. He will sacrifice one of his own sons to an idol.

In Isaiah's vision, God is sitting on a throne in a building that seems to resemble the Jerusalem Temple. He's surrounded by angelic beings called seraphim. They chant, "Holy, holy, holy is the LORD" (Isaiah 6:3).

Isaiah, however, is not holy. "I am doomed" (Isaiah 6:5), he says. He believes a sinful person can't survive in the presence of God. But just as Jewish priests go through purification rituals before entering the Temple, Isaiah is purified.

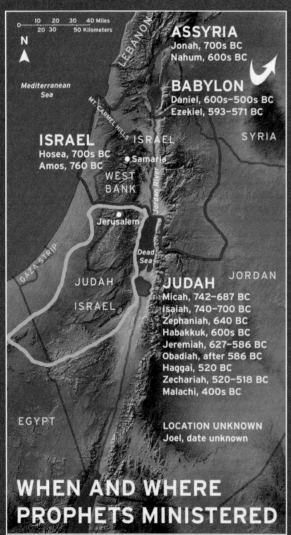

WHEN AND WHERE PROPHETS MINISTERED

◄ **WHAT'S A PROPHET?** Unlike priests, who took the requests of the Jewish people to God, prophets delivered God's messages to the people. But unlike preachers today, prophets didn't get their information secondhand, through the Bible or some other source. They got it directly from God, usually in dreams or trancelike visions, and sometimes from angelic beings.

VISIONS. Bible writers often used *vision* as just another word for *dream*, calling dreams "visions of the night." But sometimes, a vision seems to refer to a daytime trance or perhaps even an out-of-body experience, as Paul once mentioned (see 2 Corinthians 12:2–4). The prophet Elisha, seeking God's direction, asked for someone to play a harp, which seemed to lull him into a trance. "While the harp was being played, the power of the LORD came upon Elisha" (2 Kings 3:15).

SERAPHIM. One of at least two different kinds of angels (the other is cherubim). Only Isaiah mentioned seraphim. He said they stand with God and have six wings: "With two wings they covered their faces, with two they covered their feet, and with two they flew" (Isaiah 6:2).

Not just to stand before God, but to serve as a prophet and deliver his messages to the Jewish people. An angel places a burning coal on Isaiah's lips and declares, "Your sins are forgiven" (Isaiah 6:7).

Apparently addressing everyone in the throne room, God asks who will deliver his messages to the Jewish people. When Isaiah volunteers, God warns that the Jews won't listen.

But that's not the worst news.

The worst news comes when Isaiah asks how long the Jews will refuse to listen.

"Until the cities of Israel are destroyed and no one is living in them" (Isaiah 6:11 NIrV).

▼ **HOW TO PURIFY A PROPHET /** An angel takes a burning coal from a censer and touches it to Isaiah's lips in what appears to be a painless, symbolic act. Purified, Isaiah can now speak God's words to the Jewish people.

A sign from God: Immanuel is born

A JEW-ON-JEW WAR produces what is perhaps the Bible's most famous prophecy about Jesus—penned 700 years before his birth in Bethlehem.

Assyria's empire is pushing west, out of what is now Iraq, heading toward the Jewish homeland. The northern Jewish nation of Israel joins forces with Syria to protect their borders. When King Ahaz of Judah refuses to join this anti-Assyria coalition, Israel and Syria decide to attack Judah and install a new, more cooperative king.

Ahaz considers asking Assyria for help.

Isaiah advises against it. He says the attack will never happen. As proof, he offers a sign from God: "The virgin will conceive a child! She will give birth to a son and will call him Immanuel (which means 'God is with us')" (Isaiah 7:14). By the time this mystery child is eating solid food and understands the difference between right and wrong, Isaiah promises, Israel and Syria will be deserted.

Ahaz isn't convinced. He turns to Assyria for help anyway. It obliges by defeating Israel and Syria. But it also turns Judah into a nation that serves Assyria and supports the empire with high taxes.

VIRGIN #2 / An angel tells the Virgin Mary she will have a son. Seven hundred years earlier, Isaiah predicted that God would send a sign—a virgin would give birth to a son. Though Isaiah's prediction referred to a woman in his day, New Testament writers linked the prophecy to Mary as well. Isaiah's Hebrew word for "virgin" could mean "young woman." But the Greek word used in Mary's story means "virgin."

ISAIAH'S PROPHECIES ABOUT JESUS

Bible experts have a nickname for the book of Isaiah. They call it the Fifth Gospel, putting it in the same ballpark as the four New Testament books that track the life of Jesus: Matthew, Mark, Luke, and John.

The reason: Some of Isaiah's prophecies about Jesus seem dead-on—more like the report of an eyewitness than vague prophecies 700 years ahead of time. Gospel writers saw the connections to Jesus and quoted Isaiah some 50 times, pointing to passages such as these:

Peace child. "A child is born to us. . . . And he will be called: Wonderful Counselor, Mighty God, Everlasting Father, Prince of Peace. His government and its peace will never end" (Isaiah 9:6–7).

Homeland Galilee. "There will be a time in the future when Galilee of the Gentiles. . .will be filled with glory" (Isaiah 9:1).

Healer. "When he comes, he will open the eyes of the blind and unplug the ears of the deaf" (Isaiah 35:5).

Buried in rich tomb. "He was buried like a criminal; he was put in a rich man's grave" (Isaiah 53:9).

Watching Israel die

NOTHING BUT BAD KINGS for 200 years dooms the northern Jewish nation of Israel.

Isaiah not only predicts the end of his northern neighbors, he lives to see it—about halfway through his 40-year ministry.

Israel had gotten off to a pagan start. Their first king, Jeroboam, set up two shrines with golden calves. He created these pagan worship centers so his northern Jews didn't have to worship in the southern Jewish nation's capital of Jerusalem.

Later kings followed Jeroboam's lead. Queen Jezebel even tried killing off all God's prophets. Most prophets who survived seem more interested in keeping their skin than in delivering God's message.

"Those who guide the people of Israel are leading them down the wrong path," Isaiah warns. "The Lord will bring the strong and powerful king of Assyria against Samaria [capital of Israel] . . . . It will be like a wind that destroys everything" (Isaiah 9:16; 28:2 NIrV).

Not listening, Israel's leaders decide to join forces with Syria. Their goal: stop Assyria's rush to rule the entire Middle East. Both nations die trying.

Most of Israel falls in about 733 BC, leaving only the city of Samaria and the surrounding region for the puppet king to rule. He rebels later, and in 722 BC, Samaria falls, too.

Israel is gone, with most of its survivors deported—never to be heard from again. They're remembered as the Lost Tribes of Israel.

GOOD-BYE ISRAEL, HELLO IRAQ / Assyrian soldiers escort deportees into exile in 733 BC. This stone art once hung on the palace wall of Assyrian King Ashurbanipal in what is now Iraq. Assyrians kept exiled families together, allowing them to rebuild their lives abroad.

SHRINKING ISRAEL
Land Assyria captured from Israel 733 BC

◄ DISAPPEARING COUNTRY. Jews of Israel lost most of their territory when Assyrians invaded in 733 BC. They lost the rest a decade later, when Assyrians overran Samaria and deported most of the survivors.

DEPORTATION. Assyrians were the first on record to deport the citizens of conquered nations. It's a practice their conquerors, the Babylonians, would adopt and use against Judah. The motive is uncertain. Guesses: (1) Deportation dismantled the political and social structure of rebel nations, putting them out of business. (2) It scattered the citizens abroad to rural areas, so they couldn't reunite in large enough numbers to organize and then resurrect their nation.

JUDAH DOOMED, TOO. Isaiah predicted that sinful Israel wouldn't fall alone. Judah would fall, too—Jerusalem included. He said invaders would turn Jerusalem into a ghost town (see Isaiah 1:8).

Payback for Assyria and Babylon

IT'S PROBABLY NOT MUCH COMFORT to any of the Jews who actually believe Isaiah's predictions that Israel and Judah will fall to invaders—and it doesn't seem there are many who do believe him. But Isaiah vows that God will destroy the invaders, too.

Assyria, which will take out the northern Jewish nation of Israel in 722 BC, thinks it's something special, Isaiah says. But it's just a tool of God's anger: "I use it as a club" (Isaiah 10:5). God will do the same with Babylon, using it first to club the Assyrians and later the Jews of Judah in 586 BC.

But when God is done with his clubs, he's going to pitch them in the trash.

ASSYRIA. "When you are done destroying, you will be destroyed" (Isaiah 33:1).

Babylonians will crush them at the Battle of Carchemish in 605 BC.

BABYLON. Isaiah predicts Babylon's fall a century before its rise. "Look, I will stir up the Medes against Babylon. . . . Babylon, the most glorious of kingdoms, the flower of Chaldean pride, will be devastated like Sodom and Gomorrah" (Isaiah 13:17, 19).

A coalition force of Medes from what is now northern Iran and Persians from southern Iraq will overpower Babylon in 539 BC, producing the next Middle Eastern superpower: the Persian Empire.

▲ **LOST GLORY.** Guardians of a gate into Nimrud, one of Assyria's capitals, stand as museum relics representing a great empire of the ancient Middle East. Assyria, in its prime, controlled countries from what is now Iran to Egypt.

▶ **KINGDOMS WILL FALL.**
God dooms enemies of the Jews closer to home, too. In time, every nation Isaiah warned fell to invaders in the centuries that followed—some to multiple invaders: Assyrians, Babylonians, Persians, Greeks, and Romans (see chart on next page).

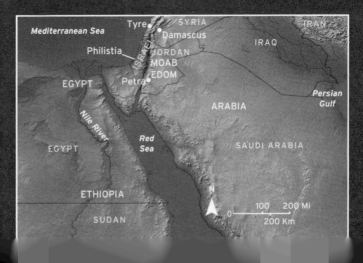

ARABIA. *Nomadic warriors of the Saudi Arabian peninsula.*
"In one year all the glory of the country of Kedar will be gone" (Isaiah 21:16 NCV). Assyrians started attacking Arabs around 732 BC.

DAMASCUS. *Capital of Syria, sometimes a Jewish ally, but often an enemy.*
"The city of Damascus will be destroyed; only ruins will remain" (Isaiah 17:1 NCV).

EDOM. *Long-term hatred between Edom and Jews began after Edom refused to let Moses and the Exodus Jews cross their land in peace. They plundered Jerusalem after Babylon destroyed it.*
"Judgment on Edom will never end. . . . The land will lie deserted from generation to generation. No one will live there anymore" (Isaiah 34:10).

EGYPT. *Often an ally, but sometimes a devastating conqueror.*
"Just to speak the name of Israel will terrorize them" (Isaiah 19:17).

ETHIOPIA. *In Bible times, this was what is now southern Egypt and Sudan.*
"Their dead bodies will be left for the birds of the mountains to eat" (Isaiah 18:6–7 NIrV).

MOAB. *Fought many wars with the Jews. The Moabite Stone reports Moab's successful war of independence from the Jews.*
"Within three years. . .the glory of Moab will be ended" (Isaiah 16:14). Perhaps a reference to Assyria's invasion about 715 BC.

PHILISTIA. *Coastal homeland of giant warrior Goliath, and modern-day Palestinians, perhaps the most persistent enemy of the Jews.*
"Melt with fear, you Philistines! A powerful army comes like smoke from the north" (Isaiah 14:31). Possibly a reference to Assyria's invasion.

TYRE. *Seaport city of Lebanon.*
"For seventy years, the length of a king's life, Tyre will be forgotten" (Isaiah 23:15). Possibly the stretch of Assyrian control of the region, from about 701–630 BC.

A better day's a-comin'

THE END OF THE JEWISH NATION isn't the end of Israel's story.

Isaiah—like all the Bible prophets who predict the destruction of the Jewish homeland—promises a fresh start. Israel will rise again.

"Though I have destroyed you in my anger," Isaiah quotes God, "I will now have mercy on you" (Isaiah 60:10).

Israel's resurrection starts with something Isaiah describes as a shoot from the dead stump of a tree. He gives the tree stump a name: Jesse, the father of King David. It's his poetic way of saying that from David's descendants God will send a righteous ruler. For a change, "The poor and the needy will be treated with fairness and with justice" (Isaiah 11:4 CEV).

Peace will come. Isaiah describes it with what sounds like a metaphor, but which some take literally: "In that day the wolf and the lamb will live together. . . . And a little child will lead them" (Isaiah 11:6).

Good times won't be limited to just the Jews, Isaiah says. Everyone will be welcome in the coming kingdom ruled by God's law of compassion and justice:

> *"Is anyone thirsty? Come and drink. . . . It's all free!"*
>
> ISAIAH **55:1**

> *"So turn to me and be helped—saved!—everyone, whoever and wherever you are. I am GOD, the only God there is, the one and only."*
>
> ISAIAH **45:22** MSG

HAS THE MESSIAH COME?

Christians tend to see Jesus as the mysterious ruler Isaiah talks about—a "righteous king" (Isaiah 32:1). But many Jews say Jesus couldn't possibly have been the Messiah because the world is anything but peaceful. Christians argue that the peace Jesus brought was spiritual, not political.

PROPHECY AS POETRY.

Most Bible prophecy is written as poetry, a genre rich in symbolism. That's why many Bible translations print the lines in poetic form. That's also why many scholars are slow to take some of the messages literally, preferring to grant the prophets some poetic license. (For tips on how to interpret Hebrew poetry, see page 178.)

PREDICTING CYRUS 200 YEARS AHEAD OF TIME.

One reason some scholars doubt Isaiah wrote the entire book is because he seems to name the Persian king who frees the Jews from their Iraqi (Babylonian) exile. "I will raise up Cyrus to fulfill my righteous purpose. . . . He will restore my city and free my captive people" (Isaiah 45:13). Prophecies aren't usually this specific. Yet many people of faith say God could have given Isaiah this insight.

◀ OUT OF THE ASHES.

Today, Jerusalem is home to about 800,000 people. Isaiah correctly predicted the city's fall. Babylonians leveled the city in 586 BC. But Isaiah also predicted the city's rebirth: "Rise from the dust, O Jerusalem. Sit in a place of honor" (Isaiah 52:2).

The end is here

THE LAST JEWISH NATION DIES—killed by two empires.

First, Assyrians from what is now northern Iraq take out most of Judah's walled cities in 701 BC (see Isaiah 36). Forty-six cities fall, says a report from Assyrian King Sennacherib.

It happens near the end of Isaiah's watch, and he reports it in chapter 36. The Assyrians are responding to King Hezekiah's poor decision to team up with several neighboring nations trying to win their independence from the Assyrian Empire. Assyria crushes the revolt. Only a miracle spares Jerusalem, sending the Assyrians running for their lives from what sounds like a plague (see page 137).

The death blow comes more than a century later, as Isaiah seemed to predict in several prophecies. Babylonians conquer Assyria and control much of the Middle East. Then they invade Judah after the Jews try again to win their independence by withholding taxes to the empire.

> *"Your country lies in ruins, and your towns are burned."*
>
> ISAIAH 1:7

> *"Your leaders ran away, but they were captured."*
>
> ISAIAH 22:3 CEV

Babylonians lay siege to Jerusalem for a year and a half, breaking through the walls in the summer of 586 BC. Jewish King Zedekiah and his army run for their lives. But Babylonians capture the king a day's ride away. Then the invaders burn Jerusalem and dismantle the buildings and walls.

Frantic note from Lachish, under attack

LACHISH: A FALLEN CITY ON THE RECORD

/ One of the Jewish cities to fall was Lachish. As Babylonians swept through Judah, a Lachish defender wrote his commander a desperate note found in the city's charred guardhouse. It reads, in part: "May God grant that you, my lord, will hear news of peace. Even now. Even now" (AUTHOR'S PARAPHRASE).

INVASION. Assyrians invade Judah and overrun 46 Jewish cities by their count, which survives in ancient Assyrian records.

The suffering savior

ISAIAH'S MYSTERY MAN who is tortured and executed—saving others in the process—is Jesus. That's what Christians have been saying since Jesus' own century.

Whoever this mystery man is, Isaiah introduces him like he's the same justice-seeking ruler who brings peace to the planet. The peacemaker grows up like "a shoot" (Isaiah 11:1). The man of suffering grows up "like a tender green shoot" (Isaiah 53:2).

Many of Isaiah's descriptions match the story of Jesus—some in remarkable ways. (See "Finding Jesus in Isaiah," next page.)

THE JEWISH VIEW OF WHO THIS MYSTERY MAN IS.

Most Jews say they don't see Jesus in Isaiah's description of a "suffering servant." Some say they see the Jewish nation, suffering through the Babylonian exile. Others say Isaiah was talking about an innocent minority of Jews who suffered because of decisions made by their sinful leaders—decisions supported by a sinful majority.

....

▼ JESUS ON TRIAL.

"He was condemned to death without a fair trial" (Isaiah 53:8 cev). This is one of many of Isaiah's predictions about an unidentified man of suffering, which seems to track with the story of Jesus' execution. At least that's how most Christians read the prophecy. Most Jews, however, beg to differ.

DESPISED.

"He was despised and rejected" (v. 3).

Jewish leaders hate him and plot his execution (see Matthew 26:3–4).

LED TO SLAUGHTER.

"Like a lamb to the slaughter" (v. 7).

Arrested and led to a secret trial (see Matthew 26:57).

SILENT.

"As a sheep is silent before the shearers, he did not open his mouth" (v. 7).

Jesus doesn't defend himself (see Matthew 27:14).

SINLESS.

"He had done no wrong" (v. 9).

Even Pilate knows Jesus isn't guilty of the charge against him: rebellion against Rome (see Matthew 27:18).

WHIPPED.

"Whipped so we could be healed" (v. 5).

Roman Governor Pilate orders him beaten (see Matthew 27:26).

PIERCED.

"Pierced for our rebellion. . . . He was beaten so we could be whole" (v. 5).

He's nailed to the cross (see Matthew 27:35).

CRIMINAL.

Treated *"like a criminal" (v. 9).*

He's crucified— the form of execution reserved for the worst offenders (see Matthew 27:31).

RICH BURIAL.

"Put in a rich man's grave" (v. 9).

He's buried in the tomb of a rich man: Joseph of Arimathea (see Matthew 27:57–60).

SIN OFFERING.

"His life is made an offering for sin" (v. 10).

New Testament writers portray him as the last sacrifice for sin— once and for all (see Hebrews 10:12). The Jewish sacrificial system ends about 40 years later when Rome destroys the Temple.

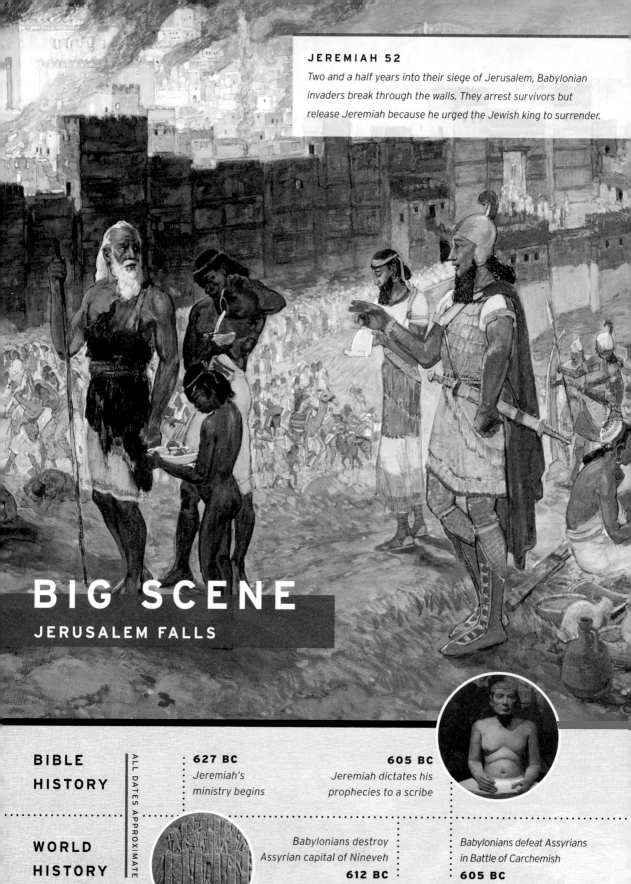

JEREMIAH 52

Two and a half years into their siege of Jerusalem, Babylonian invaders break through the walls. They arrest survivors but release Jeremiah because he urged the Jewish king to surrender.

BIG SCENE
JERUSALEM FALLS

BIBLE HISTORY

ALL DATES APPROXIMATE

627 BC
Jeremiah's ministry begins

605 BC
Jeremiah dictates his prophecies to a scribe

WORLD HISTORY

Babylonians destroy Assyrian capital of Nineveh
612 BC

Babylonians defeat Assyrians in Battle of Carchemish
605 BC

JEREMIAH

WATCHING ISRAEL DIE

STORY LINE

WORSE THAN DELIVERING BAD NEWS—that God is going to erase the Jewish nation from the world map—the prophet Jeremiah has to live it.

Like thousands of other Jews trapped inside the sacred city of Jerusalem, surrounded for two and a half years by Babylonian invaders, Jeremiah lives to see the city set on fire and then dismantled.

About 40 years earlier, when Jeremiah was still just a boy, God had called him to become a prophet who would warn the Jews that this day was coming—unless they stopped sinning.

Jeremiah spends those decades doing his best to turn the Jews back to God. He delivers God's warnings in speeches. He has them written on scrolls that are read to worshippers. He even acts out several warnings, to dramatize the consequences of Judah's sin.

But most people seem to think he's crazy. He even gets arrested as a traitor for recommending the Jews surrender.

That recommendation will earn a reward from the invaders. When Jerusalem falls, he gets to keep his freedom and stay in the area with other Jews who escape exile to what is now Iraq.

His freedom is short-lived. Other Jews assassinate a Babylonian official left to rule them. And then they flee to Egypt—forcing Jeremiah to go with them. He is never heard from again.

// LOCATION: Judah, the southern Jewish nation. With the northern Jewish nation of Israel gone, wiped out by Assyrian invaders, Judah eventually expands to assume control of the region.

// TIME: Jeremiah ministered about 40 years, from 627–586 BC.

// AUTHOR: Jeremiah dictated the prophecies to a scribe named Baruch (see Jeremiah 36:4).

588 BC
*Babylonian soldiers
surround Jerusalem*

586 BC
*Babylonians destroy
Jerusalem, exile Jews*

*Persians conquer Babylonians
and free the Jews*
538 BC

The kid prophet

"I AM ONLY A BOY" (Jeremiah 1:6 NRSV). That's Jeremiah talking to God, trying to get out of a job.

The job is to serve as a prophet in Judah, the only surviving Jewish nation. Assyrians had conquered the northern Jewish nation of Israel a century earlier, in 722 BC, exiling most of the survivors.

"Don't say, 'I'm only a boy,' " God tells Jeremiah. Prophecy is the reason Jeremiah's on the planet, God explains, perhaps in a dream or a daytime vision. "Before I shaped you in the womb. . .I had holy plans for you: A prophet to the nations" (Jeremiah 1:7, 5 MSG).

It's a thankless job in Judah, a nation with generations of expertise in breaking God's laws. No one wants to hear the messages Jeremiah will deliver. Messages of tragic consequences: "Disaster will come from the north and strike all the people who live in this country" (Jeremiah 1:14 NCV).

Jonah

OTHER PROPHETS WHO DIDN'T WANT THE JOB / Moses offered several excuses: He was a nobody, the Jews wouldn't believe him, and he wasn't a good speaker (see Exodus 3). Jonah didn't bother arguing. Assigned to go to Nineveh in what is now northern Iraq, Jonah booked passage on a ship headed in the opposite direction (see Jonah 1).

LITTLE MAN WALKING TALL. A 13-year-old Jewish boy gets a happy lift at his Bar Mitzveh, a coming-of-age celebration. Responsibility for observing Jewish laws and traditions now shifts from his parents to himself. Jeremiah may have been no older than this when God assigned him the job of prophet.

God's case against the Jews

LIKE A LAWYER making an opening statement, Jeremiah levels charges against the defendant: the entire nation of Judah.

Jeremiah charges the Jews with two major offenses against God.

SPIRITUAL ADULTERY (abandoning God for idols). "Off you went, visiting every sex-and-religion shrine on the way. . . . I [God] satisfied their deepest needs, and then they went off with the 'sacred' whores, left me for orgies in sex shrines!" (Jeremiah 2:20; 5:7 MSG).

BREACH OF CONTRACT (breaking the laws of Moses, an agreement their ancestors made with God). "Keep the Sabbath day sacred! I gave this command to your ancestors, but they were stubborn and refused to obey or to be corrected" (Jeremiah 17:22–23 CEV). Ditto for the current generation.

Worshipping only God and honoring the Sabbath as a day of rest and worship are 2 of the 10 Commandments. These 10 most basic laws of the Jewish religion, the laws on which all others are based, are intended for the benefit of God's people. When the Jews break these laws, they hurt themselves— and they invite the terrible consequences written into their ancient agreement with God (see Deuteronomy 28:15–68).

STONE-COLD MOMMA.
Female figurine, perhaps fertility goddess Astarte, found in the Gaza Strip and dating to roughly 1000 BC. Jeremiah ridiculed people who worshipped idols: "To an idol chiseled from a block of stone they say, 'You are my mother'" (Jeremiah 2:27).

JEREMIAH BAD-MOUTHS IDOLS.
Jeremiah not only condemns people who worship idols, he implies they're dumber than the block of wood they worship: "They chop down a tree, carve the wood into an idol, cover it with silver and gold, and then nail it down so it won't fall over. An idol is no better than a scarecrow. It can't speak, and it has to be carried, because it can't walk. Why worship an idol that can't help or harm you?" (Jeremiah 10:3–5 CEV).

CALL TO WORSHIP /
A temple priestess waits to worship. The Jews may have engaged in sex rituals with priestesses devoted to fertility gods such as Baal and Asherah.

SEX SHRINES.
Adultery was a perfect symbol of Judah's sin, scholars say. When the Jews worshipped idols instead of God, it was a bit like cheating on a spouse. Both sins involve breaking an exclusive contract. Some pagan worship rituals seemed to involve literal adultery—having sex with temple prostitutes. Some apparently believed that when Canaan's fertility god Baal watched worshippers having sex, it sexually stimulated him, causing him to release his semen: rain, which fertilized the dry land.

Refuting religious hogwash

THERE'S A RELIGIOUS REASON most Jews ignore Jeremiah's warning that Jerusalem is doomed.

Jerusalem is God's hometown, at least on earth: "He lives in Jerusalem" (Ezra 7:15 NIrV). The Temple is God's home, his "dwelling" (Deuteronomy 14:23 TNIV). The Ark of the Covenant—the chest holding the 10 Commandments in the Temple's holiest room—is "God's footstool" (1 Chronicles 28:2).

As far as most Jews are concerned, there's no way on earth God would let anyone destroy his hometown or chase him out of his own house.

In the Court of Common Sense, Jews would offer nearly 400 years of history as evidence for the defense. That's how long Solomon's Temple has stood inside the Jewish city that has never been destroyed. Beat up, certainly. But never destroyed.

Assyrians tried taking Jerusalem a century earlier, overrunning every other Jewish city they targeted except Jerusalem. God sent them running for their lives, unleashing what sounds like a plague (see 2 Chronicles 32:21).

Jeremiah, however, reminds the Jews that God has the option of relocating if the neighborhood goes sour.

Quoting God, Jeremiah says, "Don't be fooled into thinking that you will never suffer because the Temple is here. It's a lie! Do you really think you can steal, murder, commit adultery, lie, and burn incense to Baal and all those other new gods of yours, and then come here and stand before me in my Temple and chant, 'We are safe!'—only to go right back to all those evils again?" (Jeremiah 7:8–10).

▶ **MUD JAIL.** Accused of treason, Jeremiah is arrested and lowered into a muddy cistern. His crime was that he warned the Jerusalem citizens that everyone who stays in the city "will die from war, famine, or disease, but those who surrender to the Babylonians will live" (Jeremiah 38:2). The king later orders him released.

CRITICIZING GOD. Jeremiah asked God some tough questions that seem critical of the Lord. Questions such as why bad people prosper, and why Jeremiah was born only to live a life delivering terrible news to people who didn't believe him (see Jeremiah 12:1; 20:18). God never seemed to answer, yet Jeremiah gave him the benefit of the doubt, and continued to serve him.

God stops listening to prayer

JEWS REACH THE POINT OF NO RETURN.
They know they're in big trouble, but they don't
have a prayer. Literally.

> *The LORD said to me, "Do not pray for
> these people anymore. When they fast, I
> will pay no attention. When they present
> their burnt offerings and grain offerings
> to me, I will not accept them. Instead,
> I will devour them with war, famine,
> and disease."*
>
> JEREMIAH 14:11–12

It's not that God is refusing to forgive them.
They're refusing to change their evil behavior.

What sparks this pitiful scene is a drought, perhaps shortly before the Babylonian invasion. And
it's sucking the life out of the land. The Jews conclude God is punishing them for their sin. They
figure if they go through the motions of their religion, God will come to their rescue.

They're wrong. After some 400 years of breaking their ancient agreement with God to obey
his laws, they're about to witness God invoke the
penalty clause:

> *The LORD will make the sky overhead
> seem like a bronze roof that keeps out the
> rain, and the ground under your feet will
> become as hard as iron. Your crops will be
> scorched. . . . The LORD will let you be
> defeated by your enemies, and you will
> scatter in all directions.*
>
> DEUTERONOMY 28:23, 25 CEV

WHEN THE RIVER RUNS DRY / Shepherds in
Mongolia drive their herd to a well when the nearby river
dries up, the result of decreasing rain and diversions for
crop irrigation upstream. In Jeremiah's day, Jews pray
for water. But God says he won't listen anymore.

◄ **DROUGHTS IN ISRAEL.** Tourists are dwarfed inside the massive
water-storage cistern at the ancient Masada fortress in Israel. Water
is often in short supply in this dry part of the world. Average annual
rainfall in Jerusalem runs about 22 inches (56 cm), similar to Abilene,
in central Texas. Israel experiences occasional droughts on top of that.
The drought of 2008—the worst in 10 years—forced Israel to stop
pumping water from its major source, the shrinking Sea of Galilee.

CRACKED CISTERN. Jeremiah says God compared the faith-
less Jewish people to a cracked cistern that can't hold water: "They
have abandoned me—the fountain of living water. And they have
dug for themselves cracked cisterns that can hold no water at all!"
(Jeremiah 2:13).

Clay in God's hands

JEWS NEED A POTTERY LESSON, God decides. It's not that they make lousy pottery. It's that they live lousy lives. The pottery lesson is a metaphor—a living parable.

God tells Jeremiah to go to the house of a potter and watch the parable in action.

There, Jeremiah sees the potter produce a pot he doesn't like. It has some kind of flaw. Probably misshapen. So he smashes it into a ball and starts over.

It's the do-over God wants Jeremiah to see. God explains the point:

"People of Israel, I can do with you just as this potter does. . . . The clay is in the potter's hand. And you are in my hand, people of Israel."

JEREMIAH **18:6** NIrV

The smashing of the Jewish nation isn't inevitable. Sincere repentance can stop the fist of God. If the nation "renounces its evil ways," God says, "I will not destroy it as I had planned" (Jeremiah 18:8).

Repentance, however, won't happen. God predicts what the Jews will say to Jeremiah's warning: "Don't waste your breath. We will continue to live as we want to, stubbornly following our own evil desires" (Jeremiah 18:12).

PROPHECY THEATER

Jeremiah acted out some of his prophecies, as did Isaiah and Ezekiel. This drama helped drive home the points God wanted to make.

The visuals were easy to remember—especially after the fall of Jerusalem, when Jewish survivors experienced some of the very punishments Jeremiah had acted out. A sampling:

JEREMIAH'S ACTED-OUT PROPHECIES		GOD'S POINT
	Buy a clay jar and break it in front of Judah's leaders.	"I will shatter Judah and Jerusalem just like this jar that is broken beyond repair" (Jeremiah 19:11 CEV).
	Wear a wooden yoke around his neck.	"You must submit to Babylon's king and serve him; put your neck under Babylon's yoke!" (Jeremiah 27:8).
	Buy land during the Babylonian siege.	"In the future my people will once again buy houses and fields for grain and vineyards in the land of Israel" (Jeremiah 32:15 NCV).

A 70-year sentence

TIME'S UP. The Jews are about to begin serving a 70-year sentence God imposes on them.

> *"I will gather together all the armies of the north under King Nebuchadnezzar of Babylon. . . . I will bring them all against this land and its people. . . . This entire land will become a desolate wasteland. Israel and her neighboring lands will serve the king of Babylon for seventy years."*
>
> JEREMIAH **25:9, 11**

According to the math of some Bible experts, 70 years begins with this very prophecy, in 605 BC, "the fourth year of Jehoiakim's reign over Judah" (Jeremiah 25:1).

This is the year that King Nebuchadnezzar of Babylon crushes the last remnant of the Assyrian army, at the Battle of Carchemish. And it's the year Nebuchadnezzar pays a visit to Jerusalem to announce that he's now the boss of the Middle East. He takes many Jewish leaders home with him, against their will, which effectively makes his point.

A second exile will follow in 597 BC, when Nebuchadnezzar crushes a Jewish revolt. The big exile will come in 586 BC, with the fall of Jerusalem.

Seventy years end after Persians defeat the Babylonians and free the Jews, who begin returning home in 538 BC. That's actually about 67 years. But "70" might symbolize a generation—a round number representing the average human lifespan (see Psalm 90:10).

Seal of Baruch the scribe

EVIDENCE OF JEREMIAH'S ASSISTANT?

The scribe who copied Jeremiah's prophecies onto a scroll was "Baruch son of Neriah" (Jeremiah 32:12). Scribes sealed private letters with a glob of wax or clay pressed with an imprint of their name or an identifying mark. Among 250 ancient clay seals found in Israel in 1975, one reads like it may have belonged to Baruch, perhaps using the longer, formal names of himself and his father. It reads: "Belonging to Berekyahu son of Neriyahu the scribe." Many scholars say it's a forgery; others disagree.

BABYLONIAN BOSS / Nebuchadnezzar gazes over his capital city of Babylon, nestled along the banks of the Euphrates River. Some scholars say that the year he crushes the army of the Assyrian Empire, 605 BC, marks the beginning of the 70-year sentence God imposes on the Jews.

Jerusalem destroyed

BABYLON'S KING HAS HAD IT UP TO HERE with the Jews. Back in 605 BC, after crushing the Assyrians, King Nebuchadnezzar ordered the Jews and other Middle Eastern nations to pay taxes to his empire. The Jews complied, but for only a few years.

So in 597 BC, Nebuchadnezzar came to collect. He took back with him the king and most of Jerusalem's nobles. It wasn't but a few more years, though, and the Jews rebelled again.

This time, Nebuchadnezzar plots a final solution for the Jewish problem: Wipe the nation off the map.

He arrives at Jerusalem with his army on January 15, 588 BC, surrounding the city.

If Babylonians follow the typical strategy of siege warfare, they cut down trees and build weaponry: battering rams, catapults to heave boulders at the walls and into the city, along with rolling towers that lift archers to the same level as defenders on Jerusalem's walls.

Underground, Babylonian "sappers" dig tunnels under the wall. Then they yank the support beams, collapsing the tunnels in hopes that this section of the wall collapses, too.

Babylonians break through the walls on July 18, 586 BC—two and a half years into the siege.

Jewish King Zedekiah and his army realize they don't have chance. Under cover of night, they make a break for it, racing toward the Jericho

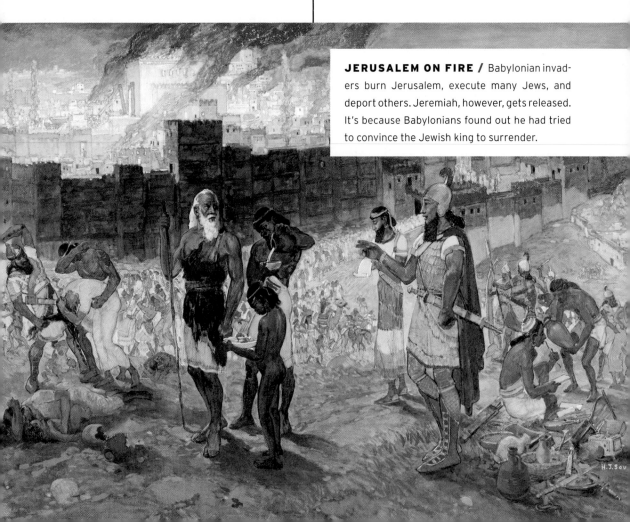

JERUSALEM ON FIRE / Babylonian invaders burn Jerusalem, execute many Jews, and deport others. Jeremiah, however, gets released. It's because Babylonians found out he had tried to convince the Jewish king to surrender.

plain by the Jordan River. That's where Babylonian soldiers catch the king.

They take him, his sons, and Jerusalem's nobles to Nebuchadnezzar, camped at Riblah, in what is now Syria. The last sight King Zedekiah sees is the slaughter of his sons and nobles. Afterward, Babylonians gouge out his eyes, chain him, and lead him away to exile in Babylon.

Babylonians burn Jerusalem, including the Temple. Limestone buildings crumble in the heat. As for the city walls, Babylonian soldiers tear them down.

Most survivors are taken to Babylon in exile, 832 of them (see Jeremiah 52:29). Only the poorest stay behind, to tend the vineyards and fields so Nebuchadnezzar can continue to collect taxes from the produce. Left in charge is a Babylonian-approved Jewish governor, Gedaliah. Jeremiah is allowed to stay, too, since he had urged the Jews to surrender.

Some Jews left behind, however, want revenge. They murder Governor Gedaliah and the Babylonian occupying force. Then they flee to Egypt, rather than face Babylon's inevitable retaliation.

Jeremiah warns against it: "Every last one of you who is determined to go to Egypt and make it your home will either be killed, starve, or get sick and die. No survivors, not one!" (Jeremiah 42:17 MSG).

The Jews go anyhow, taking Jeremiah with them against his will. He is never heard from again.

▶ **KING ON THE RUN.** When Babylonians break through Jerusalem's wall, Jewish King Zedekiah runs for his life to the Jericho plains. Babylonians run him down and take him to their king, Nebuchadnezzar, camped 200 miles (322 km) north at Riblah, on what is now Syria's side of the border with Lebanon.

SIEGE WARFARE. For background on the Babylonian siege of Jerusalem, see "Jerusalem surrounded," page 141.

HOPE. That's Jeremiah's last word for the Jews. One day, the exile will end and Babylon will fall. "The people of Israel will return home together with the people of Judah. They will come weeping and seeking the LORD their God" (Jeremiah 50:4).

Babylonian army
marches to Jerusalem.

Euphrates
River

Mediterranean
Sea

Riblah

Damascus

Sea of Galilee

Jordan River

Jerusalem Jericho

Dead
Sea

N

Jewish king abandons
Jerusalem, flees to Jericho
where invaders catch him.

BIG SCENE
STARVING MOTHERS EAT CHILDREN

LAMENTATIONS 4:10

Jews trapped inside Jerusalem during the Babylonian army's two-and-a-half-year siege resort to cannibalism. Mothers eat their own children.

BIBLE HISTORY		605 BC	597 BC
	ALL DATES APPROXIMATE	Babylon orders Judah to submit and pay taxes	Babylon attacks Jerusalem, tears down walls
WORLD HISTORY		Babylon defeats Assyria, Egypt **605 BC**	

LAMENTATIONS

THE NIGHT THE LIGHTS WENT OUT IN JERUSALEM

STORY LINE

NOT JUST THE SADDEST BOOK in the Bible, Lamentations is perhaps one of the saddest songs ever sung blue.

It *is* a song. And it's written as though Jews would sing it to commemorate one of the most tragic moments in their long history: the death of their nation.

The musician writes like an eyewitness to the fall of Jerusalem. Graphic details suggest he experiences the fear, deprivation, and starvation inside the Jewish capital city while Babylonians lay siege to it for two and a half years.

The songwriter then watches helplessly as these invaders burn Jerusalem, dismantle the city walls, and exile most of the survivors to Babylon, in what is now Iraq.

Shrouded in grief, he pens this ballad about a Jewish people who now have no king, no country, no Temple for worshipping God.

He weeps until his eyes burn red. And he prays for God to restore his nation.

// LOCATION: Jerusalem.

// TIME: The writer describes Babylon's siege of Jerusalem that began January 15, 588 BC, followed by the city's fall on July 18, 586 BC. The writer doesn't mention the Jewish return from exile in 538 BC. So scholars guess the book was written sometime during that 50-year window.

// AUTHOR: Unidentified. Jewish tradition credits the prophet Jeremiah. He wrote another book in this genre: "The Book of Laments" (2 Chronicles 35:25).

586 BC
*Babylon destroys
Jerusalem, exiles Jews*

538 BC
*Persia frees Jews
to return home*

Jerusalem's slow death

TRAPPED INSIDE JERUSALEM—the Jewish capital city surrounded by Babylonian invaders—a poet describes the misery he sees.

// **STARVING CHILDREN.** "Little children and tiny babies are fainting and dying in the streets. . . . Even the jackals feed their young, but not my people" (Lamentations 2:11; 4:3).

// **EMACIATED NOBLES.** "No one recognizes them in the streets. Their skin sticks to their bones; it is as dry and hard as wood" (Lamentations 4:8).

// **CANNIBAL MOTHERS.** "Tenderhearted women have cooked their own children. They have eaten them to survive the siege" (Lamentations 4:10).

As for the poet, he says he's on a mission. He's going to contact God who has "shut out my prayers" and "blocked my way with a high stone wall" (Lamentations 3:8–9).

His strategy: "I'll sob until the Lord looks down from heaven. I'll cry until he notices my tears" (Lamentations 3:50 NIrV).

SUFFERING FROM A TO Z. With one exception, every chapter in Lamentations has 22 verses—one for every letter in the Hebrew alphabet. Chapter 3 has three sets of 22, for 66 verses. Every verse starts with a different letter, working through the entire alphabet. It's as though the writer is saying the Jews have suffered everything from A to Z, many times over.

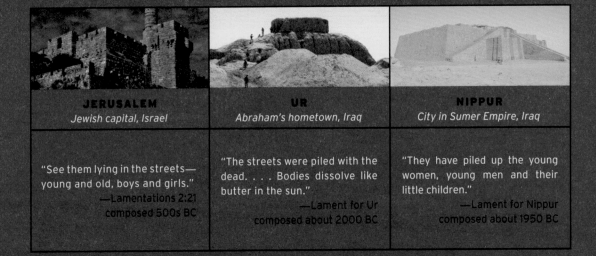

SAD SONGS FOR DEAD CITIES. Jerusalem wasn't the only defeated city that people sang about in ancient times. From the looks of the lyrics, writers were comparing notes. Or maybe they just reported what soldiers routinely did in many cities.

JERUSALEM *Jewish capital, Israel*	UR *Abraham's hometown, Iraq*	NIPPUR *City in Sumer Empire, Iraq*
"See them lying in the streets—young and old, boys and girls." —Lamentations 2:21 composed 500s BC	"The streets were piled with the dead. . . . Bodies dissolve like butter in the sun." —Lament for Ur composed about 2000 BC	"They have piled up the young women, young men and their little children." —Lament for Nippur composed about 1950 BC

Trusting God despite the facts

ABANDONED BY GOD to invaders, this poet writes the strangest words. It's a lyrical version of positive thinking: positive singing.

It's as though the writer thinks an upbeat song can create a new and improved reality for the beat-up Jews.

Surrounded by corpses piled high and Jerusalem brought low, the songwriter sings:

> *Great is his faithfulness;*
> *his mercies begin afresh each morning.*
>
> LAMENTATIONS **3:23**

God doesn't enjoy punishing his people, the poet writes, though he says they deserve it. The poet pleads with his fellow Jewish survivors to admit their sins and ask for God's forgiveness. Then he pleads with God: "Restore us, O LORD, and bring us back to you again! Give us back the joys we once had!" (Lamentations 5:21).

GOD'S OVERKILL.

The poet asked tough questions—implying that he thinks God may have carried the punishment too far:

> "Think it over. Have you ever treated anyone like this? Should women eat their own babies?"
> "Should priests and prophets be murdered in the Master's own Sanctuary?"
> "Boys and old men lie in the gutters of the streets. . . . You killed them in cold blood, cut them down without mercy."
>
> LAMENTATIONS 2:20–21 MSG

FINALE.

Hoping for the best—that God will restore the Jewish nation—the poet ends his song fearing the worst: "Do you despise us so much that you don't want us?" (Lamentations 5:22 CEV).

A POET'S HOPE / Funeral portrait of a Middle Eastern man from Bible times. One Jewish poet who details the grisly deaths of his fellow Jews in Jerusalem—preserving their memories in the song of Lamentations—clings to his hope that God will restore the Jewish nation.

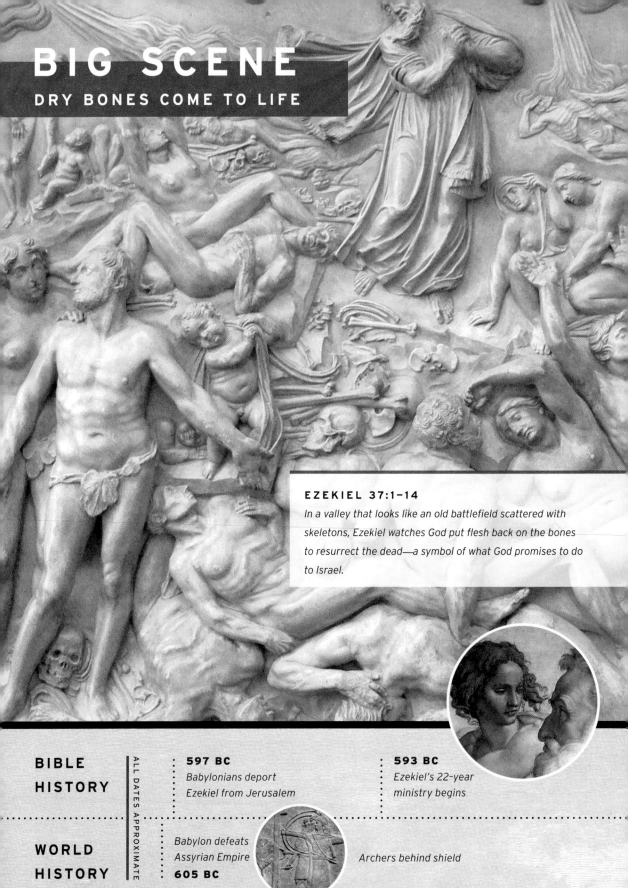

BIG SCENE
DRY BONES COME TO LIFE

EZEKIEL 37:1–14

In a valley that looks like an old battlefield scattered with skeletons, Ezekiel watches God put flesh back on the bones to resurrect the dead—a symbol of what God promises to do to Israel.

BIBLE HISTORY

ALL DATES APPROXIMATE

597 BC
Babylonians deport Ezekiel from Jerusalem

593 BC
Ezekiel's 22-year ministry begins

WORLD HISTORY

Babylon defeats Assyrian Empire
605 BC

Archers behind shield

EZEKIEL

NIGHT TERRORS: VISIONS OF ISRAEL'S FUTURE

STORY LINE

HE SHOULD BE A PRIEST. But Ezekiel never gets the chance.

He's among 3,023 Jews—the cream of society's crop—deported by Babylonian invaders in 597 BC (see Jeremiah 52:28). Ezekiel is 25 years old at the time. That's five years before he's old enough to work in the Temple, according to the Law of Moses. Priests serve from ages 30–50 (see Numbers 4:3). And only at the Jerusalem Temple. It's the only place Jews can offer sacrifices.

But when Ezekiel hits that 30-year mark, exiled to Babylon in what is in Iraq, God opens up another ministry for him: a prophet for his fellow Jewish exiles.

There, Ezekiel sees bizarre visions and terrifying images. They point to the warning he's to deliver: God is about to send the Babylonians to destroy Judah, the only surviving Jewish nation. Most survivors will get deported.

That's exactly what happens about seven years into Ezekiel's 22-year ministry.

For the last two-thirds of his ministry, he preaches hope. He promises that God will send the Jews home to rebuild their Temple and their nation. Apparently, he doesn't live long enough to see that for himself—into his mid-80s. His ministry seems to end about 30 years before Persians overpower Babylon and free the Jews.

// LOCATION: In Babylon, a city in what is now Iraq, about 100 miles (160 km) south of Baghdad. Ezekiel's first vision takes place near an ancient irrigation canal called Kebar.

// TIME: Babylonians take 25-year-old Ezekiel captive from Jerusalem to Babylon in 597 BC, about a decade before they destroy Jerusalem in 586 BC. Ezekiel ministers for 22 years, from 593–571 BC.

// AUTHOR: "Ezekiel son of Buzi, a priest" (Ezekiel 1:3).

586 BC
Babylonians destroy
Jerusalem, deport more Jews

571 BC
Ezekiel's ministry ends

Babylon
surrenders to Persia
539 BC

Ezekiel's bizarre visions

MINDING HIS OWN BUSINESS in exile, south of Baghdad, Ezekiel suddenly finds himself transported into what could sound like a Stephen King horror novel. Some readers speculate he encountered a UFO and alien beings because he describes humanoid creatures and a flying object with wheels inside wheels, reminiscent of gyroscopes.

Bible experts, however, say Ezekiel experienced a vision rich in imagery that's tailored for a Jewish priest. He sees what appears to be God's throne transported on a chariot, escorted by angelic beings. This is a symbol of the Jews' most sacred object, many say—the Ark of the Covenant, kept in the Jerusalem Temple. This gold-covered chest that held the 10 Commandments, described as the Lord's "chariot," was topped with angelic beings called "cherubim" (1 Chronicles 28:18).

A voice, presumably God's, calls Ezekiel "son of man" (Ezekiel 3:1) and assigns him the job of prophet. The voice orders Ezekiel to eat a scroll filled with words—apparently to symbolize that the words Ezekiel will speak as a prophet are God's words.

"When I ate it," Ezekiel says, "it tasted as sweet as honey" (Ezekiel 3:3).

SCARY ANGELS. Ezekiel sees God in a vision, accompanied by cherubim: four-headed, four-winged angelic beings covered in eyeballs.

MARK AND HIS EAGLE. Four evangelists credited with writing the Gospels—Matthew, Mark, Luke, and John—are linked to creatures Ezekiel saw in the four faces of the cherubim. Early Christian scholars say the evangelists did what the cherubim did: carry God's message into the world.

BABYLONIAN EMPIRE

Black Sea

Caspian Sea

TURKEY

Nineveh •

IRAN

Euphrates River

Tigris River

SYRIA

CYPRUS

• Babylon

Susa •

• Damascus

IRAQ

LEBANON

Mediterranean Sea

• Jerusalem

ISRAEL
JORDAN

SAUDI ARABIA

KUWAIT

Persian
Gulf

Memphis •

Nile River

EGYPT

Red Sea

Thebes •

N

Ziggurat at Babylon,
crowned with blue temple
honoring Babylonian god Marduk

"SON OF MAN." This phrase God used to describe Ezekiel means "human," as though God was putting Ezekiel in his place: a mortal standing before deity. Jesus often used this title to describe himself, perhaps because it worked on two levels—human and divine. It described him as a human. But it also seemed to connect him to a vision Daniel had of a celestial being: "someone like a son of man coming with the clouds of heaven. . . . His kingdom will never be destroyed" (Daniel 7:13–14).

HEAVEN'S CREATURES. Ezekiel described four glowing creatures he calls cherubim (Ezekiel 10:20): human form, human hands, hoofed feet. Each creature had four wings and four faces: human, lion, ox, eagle.

EATING GOD'S WORDS. Jeremiah also described God's words as a tasty delight. "I ate them—swallowed them whole. What a feast!" (Jeremiah 15:16 MSG).

Ezekiel's close shave

A TRIM AND A SHAVE becomes a message of horrifying doom for the Jewish nation.

God tells Ezekiel to shave his head and beard, and then divide the hair into three equal piles.

// **BURN ONE PILE OF HAIR ON A BRICK.** The brick should have a picture of Jerusalem sketched on it. Burning the hair on the picture represents that a third of the Jews trapped inside Jerusalem during Babylon's siege will die of disease and starvation.

// **CHOP THE SECOND PILE WITH A SWORD.** Chop them beside the brick, to symbolize that Babylonians will execute a third of the Jews outside the city walls.

// **SCATTER THE THIRD PILE TO THE WIND.** This shows that Babylonians will deport the survivors.

Perhaps more than any other prophet, Ezekiel has a flair for the dramatic. When it's time to condemn the people for worshipping idols on mountaintop shrines, he addresses the mountains on behalf of God. "I will kill your people in front of your idols" (Ezekiel 6:4).

And the idols—blocks of wood and stone—won't be able to do a thing about it.

PROPHET IN HEAVEN
/ Visions transport Ezekiel to heaven, where he gets instructions on how to warn the Jews about their coming disaster.

EZEKIEL BEHAVING ODDLY
Ezekiel acted out many of his prophecies. The chart, right, shows three samples from chapter 4. There are more in chapters 5, 6, 12, 21, 24, 36, and 37.

Baking flat bread

VISUAL AID	THE POINT
WAR MODEL. On a brick, draw a picture of Jerusalem. Lay it down and surround it with a dirt wall ramps and sticks.	This is a model of a coming siege. Babylonians will build ramps up the wall and crash in the gates with battering rams.
SIDE-SLEEPING. Sleep on left side 390 nights, then on right side 40 nights.	Each night is a year of sin—390 for the north Jewish nation of Israel and 40 for Judah.
DUNG-FIRED BREAD. Ration eight ounces (228 grams) of grain per day for bread cooked over animal dung.	Food and fuel will become scarce in Jerusalem during Babylon's two-and-a-half-year siege of the city.

God abandons the Jews

IN A HAIRLIFT OF AN AIRLIFT, Ezekiel has a vision of a celestial hand grabbing him by the hair and transporting him about a thousand miles (1,600 km)—from Iraq to the Jerusalem Temple.

There, Ezekiel sees the Jewish people worshipping idols and gods of nature.

In one scene, a woman weeps for the god Tammuz in a Babylonian ritual marking the autumn "death" of this god of agriculture.

In another scene, a group of men turn their backs on the sanctuary to face east, toward the Mount of Olives, so they can bow to the rising sun.

Even at God's own home on earth, the Jews have abandoned him. So he abandons them.

Ezekiel sees a "cloud of glory. . .the glory of the LORD" (Ezekiel 10:4). The cloud is inside the Temple and its courtyards. Suddenly the cloud rises, leaves the Temple, and soars away escorted by winged cherubim.

God has left the building. And the city. And the nation.

Ezekiel marks the date in a way that scholars say they can cross-reference with known dates in Babylonian history: September 17, 592 BC. In four years, Babylonian invaders will surround Jerusalem. The Jews can't imagine that God would allow anyone to destroy his holy city and the Temple, which Jews consider God's home on earth.

But what Ezekiel is trying to tell them is that God doesn't live there anymore. The Jews have driven him away.

PILLAR OF CLOUD. Crops on fire produce an effect similar to what the Bible says guided Jews during the Exodus: a pillar of cloud by day and a pillar of fire by night (see Exodus 13:21). But in the Bible story, the pillar traveled—as it does in Ezekiel's vision. This cloud represented God's presence among his people.

BEFORE SUNRISE. Jews beat the daybreak to worship on their holiest day of the year, Yom Kippur (Day of Atonement), a national day of repentance. They gather at their holiest site on earth, the Western Wall—near where the ancient Jewish Temple once stood. Ezekiel, in a vision, said he saw Jews worship the sunrise here—and then he saw God leave the Temple.

God levels charges against the Jews

WORTHLESS SLAG—scum that floats to the top and gets scraped off when metal is melted in a refiner's crucible. That's God's description of the Jewish people.

God levels that charge one breath before he threatens to turn up the heat: "I will bring you to my crucible in Jerusalem" (Ezekiel 22:19).

Ezekiel explains why the Jews are about to suffer: They've committed a long string of crimes.

// **IDOLATRY.** "You. . .have worshiped idols."

// **CORRUPTION.** "Leaders use their power to murder."

// **DISRESPECT.** "None of you honor your parents."

// **EXPLOITATION.** "You cheat foreigners, orphans, and widows."

// **DESECRATION.** "You show no respect for my sacred places."

// **SACRILEGE.** "You. . .treat the Sabbath just like any other day."

// **ADULTERY.** "Men have sex with. . .someone else's wife."

// **MURDER-FOR-HIRE.** "You accept money to murder someone."

// **LOAN-SHARKING.** "Your own people charge high interest when making a loan."

// **HERESY.** "Priests of Israel ignore my Law!"

// **BLASPHEMY.** "Prophets in Israel cover up these sins by giving false visions."

// **ABANDONMENT.** "You have forgotten me, the LORD God."

EZEKIEL **22:3, 6-8, 10-12, 26, 28** CEV

For these sins and more, God vows to punish the Jews. "They will know that I am furious. I, the LORD, have spoken" (Ezekiel 22:31 CEV).

LAYING DOWN THE LAW / An elder Jew leads young adults in a study of the Torah, the Jewish laws contained in the first five books of the Bible. Ezekiel condemns the Jews of his day for ignoring these ancient laws of Moses.

BUSTING THE 10 COMMANDMENTS. Most of the charges God leveled against the Jews stem from Jews breaking the 10 Commandments—the foundational laws on which all other Jewish laws are based (Exodus 20; see page 42).

NO TEARS FOR EZEKIEL'S DEAD WIFE. When Ezekiel's wife dies, God tells him not to cry or mourn her in any other way (see Ezekiel 24). God wants this stoic response to send a message to the Jews: When Babylon destroys their nation and takes them captive, the Jews won't be able to observe their mourning customs. They'll be marching into exile.

God dooms Judah's neighbors

ARAB NATIONS surrounding Judah face their own judgment day—kingdoms in what are today known as Lebanon, Jordan, Palestinian territories, and Egypt.

Ezekiel gives special attention to Egypt (four chapters) and to the wealthy Phoenician port city of Tyre, Lebanon (three chapters).

Tyre's island fortress

BARE TYRE.

When Alexander the Great attacked Tyre, locals retreated to an island fortress just offshore. Alexander scraped Tyre bare, using stones from the city walls and buildings to lay a causeway to the island, where he overran the fortress. Many Bible experts say this fulfills Ezekiel's prophecy.

DOOMED KINGDOMS	CHARGE	SENTENCE
Ammon, in modern north Jordan	Cheered Judah's defeat	Nomads will conquer them (Ezekiel 25:1–7)
Moab, central Jordan	Said Judah is nothing special	Nomads will conquer them (Ezekiel 25:8–11)
Edom, south Jordan	Butchered Jewish refugees	Swords will turn it into a wasteland (Ezekiel 25:12–14; 35)
Philistia, Palestinian Gaza Strip	Took revenge on conquered Jews	Utter destruction (Ezekiel 25:15–17)
Tyre, Lebanon port city	Cheered Judah's defeat	The city will be scraped to bedrock (Ezekiel 26–28:19)
Sidon, Lebanon port city	Treated Jews with contempt	A plague will slaughter them (Ezekiel 28:20–24).
Egypt	Refused to defend Jewish allies	Invaders will leave them dead and unburied (Ezekiel 29–32)

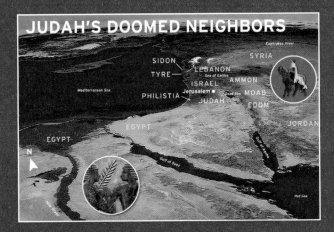

JUDAH'S DOOMED NEIGHBORS

CRYING TIME IS COMING. Ezekiel predicts a tragic future for Arab nations surrounding the Jewish homeland. In apparent fulfillment, most are overrun first by Babylonians, then Persians, and later Greeks.

Israel, back from the dead

JERUSALEM HAS FALLEN. Babylon's army captured it on July 18, 586 BC. But it takes nearly six months for a Jerusalem survivor to deliver the news to Ezekiel in what is now Iraq. News arrives there on January 8.

Before Ezekiel begins predicting that Israel will rise from the dead, he predicts more slaughter. He warns that those few Jews who escaped and are now living among the ruins will die, too. In fact, Jeremiah reports yet another Babylonian invasion five years after Jerusalem fell. In 581, Babylon deports another 745 Jews (see Jeremiah 52:30).

So ends the bad news.

Good news starts with a Good Shepherd: God. "I will search for my lost ones who strayed away, and I will bring them safely home again" (Ezekiel 34:16).

Good news continues in a vision Ezekiel sees of a valley littered with bones. Suddenly, a massive rattling thunders through the valley. Bones are snapping back together. Flesh erupts and spreads over the skeletons. On command, wind breathes life into the corpses—divine CPR. Resuscitated, they stand—a great army.

"These bones represent the people of Israel," God says. "O my people, I will open your graves of exile and cause you to rise again. Then I will bring you back to the land of Israel" (Ezekiel 37:11–12).

THEM DRY BONES.
In a vision symbolizing Israel's future resurrection as a nation, Ezekiel sees a valley full of dry bones reanimate and rise.

TEL AVIV'S LINK TO EZEKIEL.
Israel's most cosmopolitan city takes its name from the first community of Jews to hear Ezekiel's message. They lived in the Babylonian town of Tel-abib (Ezekiel 3:15), a name Israelis changed slightly to fit their Hebrew language. The name "Tel Aviv" symbolizes the rebirth of Israel, which Ezekiel predicted.

God comes home to Jerusalem

THIRTEEN UNLUCKY YEARS after Babylonians level the Jerusalem Temple, Jews exiled with Ezekiel catch a break. Ezekiel experiences a vision on April 28, 573 BC. He gets word that God intends to rebuild the Temple—and to move back in.

From a mountaintop view, Ezekiel watches as a celestial being takes a tape measure to the new Temple, reporting the size of each room, wall, and courtyard. Ezekiel also sees "the glory of the God of Israel" (Ezekiel 43:2) returning, and filling the temple.

RIVER OF HEALING / Israel's Dead Sea lies 1300 feet (396 meters) below sea level—making it the drainage tank for the region. Its water is about eight times as salty as the ocean. Fish unlucky enough to end up here don't last long. Ezekiel says one day this sea will thrive with life. A freshwater river will cut through the desert, irrigate land, and dilute the sea enough for fish to survive.

PLANNING THE TEMPLE / Solomon plans to build the first Jewish Temple. Babylonians destroy it about 400 years later. But Ezekiel promises a new one's coming.

BIG SCENE
CATS IN THE DEN

DANIEL 6

Daniel survives the night in a den of hungry lions. Political rivals orchestrated it by manipulating the king, who retaliated by feeding them to the lions.

BIBLE HISTORY

ALL DATES APPROXIMATE

605 BC
Daniel deported to Babylon, serves king

WORLD HISTORY

Draco of Athens writes the first Greek laws
620 BC

Phoenicians take three years to sail around Africa
600 BC

DANIEL

DREAM LOVER, LION TAMER

STORY LINE

A NOBLE IN JERUSALEM, Daniel finds himself deported in 605 BC to Babylon, in what is now Iraq. It's part of the strategy for Babylon's new king, Nebuchadnezzar, to show his neighbor nations who's boss of the Middle East.

Nebuchadnezzar takes many of Jerusalem's top citizens back with him. Daniel ends up working in the Babylonian palace as a royal advisor—a job he continues under new management when Persians from what is now Iran conquer Babylon.

Daniel has two specialties that endear him to kings: interpreting the meaning of dreams and predicting the future.

Yet he's most famous for surviving a night in a lions' den. Political rivals set him up. They write a law that makes it illegal for him to do what they know he'll do: pray to God.

Stories like this take up the first six chapters of Daniel. Then the book shifts to Daniel's bizarre visions about the future. Some Bible students say these visions—some of which even Daniel couldn't understand—point to the end of human history. Others say they describe with remarkable accuracy many events leading up to the time of Jesus.

// LOCATION: Most of Daniel's story takes place in what are now Iraq (then called Babylon) and Iran (Persia). Babylonians deported him from Jerusalem.

// TIME: Daniel's 60-year story begins around 600 BC. But details in some of his prophecies are incredibly on-target with events centuries later—leaving many scholars speculating that someone wrote or edited them in the mid-100s BC.

// AUTHOR: Unknown. The stories are told in the third person—not as Daniel reporting them. But the prophecies are in his voice.

586 BC
Babylon destroys Jerusalem, deports more Jews

538 BC
Persians free Jews to go home, Daniel stays to serve king

Cyrus the Great defeats Medes (northern Iran), controls growing empire
553 BC

Vegetarian Jews

NON-KOSHER FOOD IS A PROBLEM for Daniel and three of his friends, all Jews tapped to serve King Nebuchadnezzar as royal advisors.

The king wants them educated for three years in the language and writings of Babylon. And he wants them well fed, from his own kitchen.

Observant Jews like Daniel and his friends, however, follow the ancient food laws of Moses. (For an illustrated list of kosher and non-kosher food, see pages 51–52).

The royal chief of staff says he's afraid the king might execute him if the four Jews start looking gaunt. So Daniel suggests an experiment.

"Test us for ten days on a diet of vegetables and water. . . . See how we look compared to the other young men who are eating the king's food" (Daniel 1:12–13).

The result? Daniel and buddies look "healthier and better nourished" (Daniel 1:15) than the others.

ON THE MENU / Keeping it kosher at Jerusalem Restaurant in Myrtle Beach, owners Nina and Yossi (Joseph) Elmalih dish up a meal, alongside nieces Hanni Logasy and Hanni Zohar. The prophet Daniel, exiled in Babylon, refused to eat meat. He wanted to keep his diet kosher, and he feared the pagans might serve him up some non-kosher meat.

NON-KOSHER GRAPES. Wine is kosher. But Daniel may have feared the Babylonian wine was made from young vines. Jewish law permitted Jews to use only fruit of plants at least five years old (see Leviticus 19:25).

QUALIFICATIONS FOR SERVING AS PALACE ADVISOR. Nebuchadnezzar said he wanted only the cream of the Jewish crop serving as his advisors in the palace: "Israelites from the royal family and nobility—young men who were healthy and handsome, intelligent and well-educated, good prospects for leadership positions in the government" (Daniel 1:3–4 MSG).

Nebuchadnezzar's bizarre dream

SOUNDING LIKE A ROYAL FRUITCAKE, King Nebuchadnezzar demands his advisors do the impossible. He not only wants them to explain the meaning of a nightmare he had, he wants them to confirm they know what they're talking about by first telling him what he dreamed.

He refuses their pleas to tell them the dream.

No king on earth has ever asked such a thing, the advisors reply. And no human could do what the king is asking.

Furious, Nebuchadnezzar orders all the royal sages rounded up and executed—Daniel included.

Daniel, who wasn't in the palace at the time, convinces the arresting officer to take him to the king. There, Daniel says God had revealed to him both the dream and its meaning.

The king saw a statue with a gold head, silver chest and arms, bronze belly and thighs, iron legs, with feet of mixed iron and clay. The statue crumbled to dust and blew away.

Daniel said the different material represents four different kingdoms, with Babylon as the golden head and increasingly inferior kingdoms coming afterward.

Relieved, Nebuchadnezzar declared God "the greatest of gods" (Daniel 2:47) and he appointed Daniel head over all his wise men.

(continued next page)

DREAMS AS LETTERS FROM GOD. Jews in ancient times, like Babylonians and Persians, taught that dreams usually mean something. One Jew from Babylon wrote in the Talmud, an ancient Jewish collection of history and commentary: "A dream not interpreted is like a letter not read" (Berakhot 55a).

DREAM GUIDEBOOK. Jews, like Babylonians and Persians, produced guidebooks for dream interpretation. Examples: If you dream of drinking milk, it means you'll get sick but recover. If you dream of seeing demons, you'll make a lot of money.

IDOL DREAMS. In a dream, King Nebuchadnezzar sees a statue made from four kinds of material. Each material, Daniel says, represents a different kingdom coming after Babylon's golden age, which is represented by the idol's golden head. Scholars can only offer theories about which kingdoms the other three parts represent.

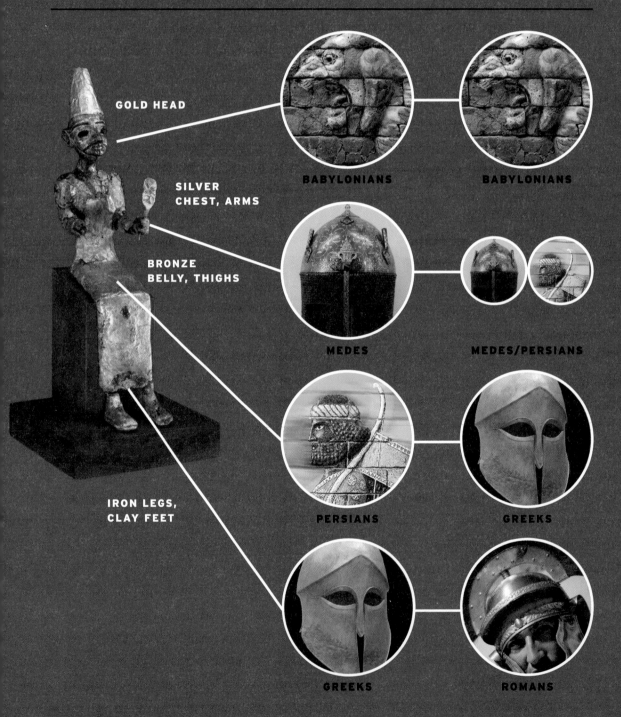

WHAT THE IDOL MEANS	THEORY 1	THEORY 2

GOLD HEAD

BABYLONIANS — BABYLONIANS

SILVER CHEST, ARMS

BRONZE BELLY, THIGHS

MEDES — MEDES/PERSIANS

PERSIANS — GREEKS

IRON LEGS, CLAY FEET

GREEKS — ROMANS

Fireproof Jews

TAKING NO FOR AN ANSWER is not on the to-do list for Babylon King Nebuchadnezzar. So when he builds a golden statue 90 feet (27 meters) high and orders everyone to bow to it, he expects everyone to bow to it.

Or face execution by burning in a furnace.

Daniel is apparently somewhere else, but his three Jewish colleagues are there: fellow deportees Shadrach, Meshach, and Abednego. They refuse to bow in worship of anyone but God.

The king erupts. "His face became distorted with rage" (Daniel 3:19).

He orders the furnace superheated and the men thrown in. The heat is so intense that it kills the executioners. But it doesn't harm the three Jews. And the king sees a fourth man standing with them—someone who "looks like a god" (Daniel 3:25).

Nebuchadnezzar calls the three back outside. They don't even smell like smoke.

The king promotes all three and orders that no one speak a word against their God.

KILN TEMPERATURES / Inside this 400-year-old kiln, fresh clay pots are set on shelves to bake in a fire built on the floor. Babylonians fired bricks in similar kilns that reached temperatures over 1800 degrees F (982 C). That's the top end of cremation chamber temps today: 1400–1800 degrees F (760–982 C). One ancient kiln found in Nippur, 50 miles (80 km) south of Babylon, was shaped like a railroad tunnel, much like the kiln shown here.

◀ **FIERY FURNACE.** Daniel's three friends get pitched into a furnace, perhaps a kiln, for refusing to bow to the king's new idol—a huge statue, possibly of himself. The fire's so hot that it kills the soldiers pushing them in. But the Jews don't burn. When the king looks inside, he sees four men—as though they've grown an extra Jew.

NEBUCHADNEZZAR'S STATUE. A Babylonian record from the king's time warns people not to desecrate "my statue as king. . .erected for posterity." Some scholars speculate that his inspiration for the statue may have been the dream he had (see Daniel 2), in which the golden head represented his Babylonian Empire.

Nebuchadnezzar goes crazy

ANOTHER BIZARRE DREAM sends King Nebuchadnezzar on the hunt for an explanation.

He dreams about a huge tree in the middle of the earth, stretching into the sky. Loaded with fruit, this tree feeds the world. A voice from heaven orders, "Cut down the tree. . . . But leave the stump and the roots in the ground" (Daniel 4:14–15).

When the king tells Daniel about the dream and asks for an explanation, Daniel takes a few moments to compose himself.

"I wish the events foreshadowed in this dream would happen to your enemies, my lord, and not to you!" Daniel says (Daniel 4:19).

The tree represents the king. He will temporarily lose his ability to rule—and even to reason. "You will be driven from human society, and you will live in the fields with the wild animals. You will eat grass like a cow" (Daniel 4:25).

Daniel pleads with the king to stop sinning and to treat the poor with mercy, a request apparently ignored.

A year later, insanity strikes the king. He remains sick for at least several months.

When he finally comes to his senses, he worships God, calling him "the King of heaven" (Daniel 4:37).

CRAZY STARTS HERE / King Nebuchadnezzar admires his city—and takes full credit for its glory. Suddenly, a voice from heaven says his reign has just ended. Within the hour, he starts acting like an animal. He withdraws from society to live outdoors.

HOW LONG DID THE INSANITY LAST?

The only hint offered in the Bible is that it lasts "seven periods of time" (Daniel 4:32) and that his fingernails and toenails grew as long as bird claws and his hair as long as eagle feathers. *Seven* symbolizes completion—as in "as long as God considers appropriate." Fingernails grow about one and a half inches (four cm) a year, and start to look clawlike at about an inch (2.5 cm).

"WORLD TREE" DREAMS.
A visitor to Sequoia National Park in California is dwarfed by the world's largest tree on record. General Sherman stands 275 feet (84 meters) with 52,500 cubic feet (1,487 cubic meters) of timber. Ancient writings report dreams about a massive tree that shades the world. Trees like that were often interpreted to represent an empire.

Handwriting on Babylon's wall

A KNEE-KNOCKER of a ghostly poltergeist— or so it seems—crashes the party of Babylon's last king, Belshazzar.

The king has thrown this party for 1,000 nobles, breaking out the sacred gold and silver cups that Nebuchadnezzar had looted from the Jerusalem Temple about 50 years earlier.

"Suddenly, they saw the fingers of a human hand writing on the plaster wall of the king's palace" (Daniel 5:5).

The king's face drains to pale, his knees start clanging, his legs give out under him.

He can read the handwriting on the wall. It's in Aramaic, Babylon's language. But he can't make sense of the four words. Neither can anyone else at the party:

"Numbered. Numbered. Weighed. Divided."

The king's mother remembers Daniel. He comes and offers a bleak interpretation that paraphrases into something like this:

"God has your number—and your number's up. You've been weighed, and you're a lightweight. Your kingdom has already been divided among the Medes and the Persians."

Belshazzar dies that night.

PERSIAN EMPIRE

WHO CONQUERED BABYLON: MEDES OR PERSIANS? / Scholars are divided over how to explain Daniel's report that Darius the Mede captured Babylon. Medes were from north Iran, Persians from south Iran—before they united. Cyrus was the king of Persia at the time. Darius may have been his general, some scholars say. A Babylonian record credits a Persian general with capturing Babylon. Others say "Darius" could have been a Babylonian name Cyrus adopted.

◀ GOD'S GRAFFITI. A disembodied hand interrupts the party of Babylon's last king, writing out a cryptic warning: The empire is about to fall.

HOW BABYLON FELL. Stories differ. Cyrus the Great, leader of the Persians who overthrew the Babylonian Empire, says in the Cyrus Cylinder (see photo page 154) that citizens of Babylon opened the gates and greeted him as a liberator. Greek historian Herodotus, writing about a century later, said Persians diverted the Euphrates River that flowed into the city, allowing his army to march in on the emptied riverbed.

KING BELSHAZZAR. Babylon's last king was the son of King Nabonidus. Father and son ruled together at the time Babylon fell. Both claimed to be descendants of Nebuchadnezzar, Babylon's most famous ruler. But most scholars say that's unlikely.

Cats

DANIEL BECOMES A BULL'S-EYE, targeted by political rivals who want his job as top administrator in the Persian Empire—new superpower of the Middle East.

Lower-level officials search for dirt on Daniel. They can't find any. So they hatch a plot to manipulate the king into approving a law they know Daniel will break.

Appealing to the king's abundant ego, they sponsor a law ordering everyone to pray to no one but the king for a month. Lawbreakers will get fed to the lions.

King Darius agrees and signs the irrevocable law. Darius soon regrets it when the sponsors report that Daniel is praying three times a day to God.

The king searches for a loophole in the law. Finding none, he's forced to arrest Daniel and send him to the lions. Sponsors of the irrevocable law insist.

Darius endures a sleepless night, refusing entertainment or food. In the morning he rushes to the lions' den and calls out for Daniel, who replies: "My God sent his angel to shut the lions' mouths" (Daniel 6:22).

Darius, furious at being manipulated, orders the sponsors of the law and their entire families thrown to the lions—which tear them apart.

....

DANIEL PRAYS FACING JERUSALEM / By facing west toward Jerusalem, Daniel may have been acting on King Solomon's prayer of dedication for the Temple. Solomon prayed that if the Jews sin and are exiled, they would face the Temple and pray (see 1 Kings 8:46–50).

FRAMING DANIEL / Prayer gets Daniel arrested and thrown into the lions' den. For what? Ambitious, rival administrators plotting to get him out of the way talk the king into passing a prayer law. They know Daniel prays every day to God. So the law they sponsor makes it illegal for an entire month to pray to anyone but the king.

Daniel's beastly nightmare

DREAM MASTER DANIEL, the go-to sage for interpreting strange dreams, has a bizarre dream of his own. The shocker is that he doesn't have a clue what the dream means.

He sees four beasts:

// winged lion

// bear

// winged leopard

// a "terrifying" creature that crushes its victims, which many scholars speculate is an elephant.

A celestial being has to explain that they represent four kingdoms—as did Nebuchadnezzar's dream about an idol crafted of four kinds

(continued next page)

MEANING OF THE BEASTS

The celestial being says only that the four beasts represent four kingdoms—but doesn't say which kingdoms. Bible experts offer their own theories. One set:

BEAST	KINGDOM IT REPRESENTS	THE LINK
 Winged lion	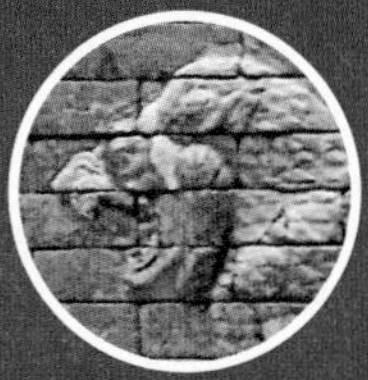 Babylon	Popular symbol of Babylon; many images survive
 Bear eating three ribs	 Persia	Ribs represent Persia's victims, perhaps Babylon, Lydia, Egypt
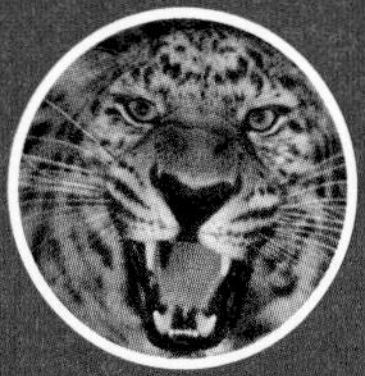 Winged leopard with four heads	 Greece	Alexander the Great swiftly conquered the Middle East, which was divided among four generals after he died
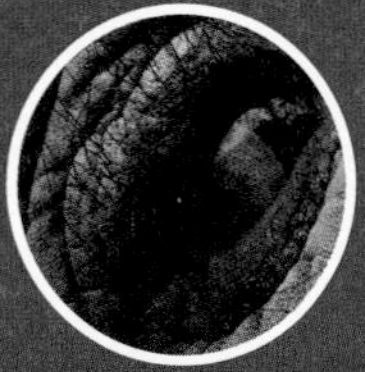 Terrifying beast with 10 horns	 Rome	Horns symbolize 10 Roman emperors from Julius Caesar to Domitian (there were 12, but two reigned just a few months)

of material (see page 246). In fact, many scholars say the four creatures represent the same four kingdoms.

Daniel had said earlier that the golden head of Nebuchadnezzar's idol represented the Babylon Empire. Daniel's dream of the winged lion seems to represent the same, many say, because the winged lion was a popular symbol of Babylon. More than 100 of these mythical creatures decorated the Processional Way, along the main entrance into the capital city.

Figuring out the other three kingdoms, though, takes more of a stretch.

GREEK EMPIRE DIVIDED

OTHER GREEK KINGDOMS
ITALY ANTIGONID KINGDOMS
GREECE
UKRAINE
ROMANIA
BULGARIA
TURKEY
CYPRUS
SYRIA
IRAQ
Black Sea
Euphrates River
Tigris River
Mediterranean Sea
JORDAN
KUWAIT
PTOLEMY EMPIRE
EGYPT
LIBYA
Nile River
Red Sea
SAUDI ARABIA
RUSSIA
GEORGIA
ARMENIA
Caspian Sea
MEDES
Babylon ● Susa ●
IRAN
SELEUCID EMPIRE
PERSIANS
KAZAKHSTAN
Aral Sea
UZBEKISTAN
TURKMENISTAN
AFGHANISTAN
PAKISTAN
CHINA
INDIA
Persian Gulf
UAE
OMAN
Arabian Sea

DANIEL'S VISION: RAM, GOAT.

Angel Gabriel interpreted a second critter dream Daniel had. Gabriel names the kingdoms these animals represent—but with such historical accuracy 200 years after Daniel that many scholars say Daniel didn't write it; someone wrote it after the events happened, and then passed it off as prophecy.

For example, the writer correctly predicts the rise and fall of the Greek Empire: "The two-horned ram represents the kings of Media and Persia. The shaggy male goat represents the king of Greece, and the large horn between his eyes represents the first king of the Greek Empire. The four prominent horns that replaced the one large horn show that the Greek Empire will break into four kingdoms, but none as great as the first" (Daniel 8:20–22).

Others Bible experts contend Daniel reported his own visions, which were prophecies.

TANK. Elephants were the battlefield tanks of Bible times—terrifying ground troops and rolling over them. This may have been the unidentified "terrifying" beast in Daniel's vision, some scholars speculate. Syrian King Antiochus IV Epiphanes, who ruled the Seleucid Empire (175–164 BC) and controlled what is now Israel, once crushed a Jewish revolt by reinforcing his army with a company of 32 elephants and their Indian drivers.

Daniel's vision of the end

IT'S THE END OF SOMETHING. Daniel gets the word from the angel Gabriel. But the end of what? That's the mystery Bible experts continue to debate.

Daniel reads Jeremiah's prophecy that Jerusalem will lie desolate for 70 years. This so upsets him that he goes into mourning. He stops eating and he prays for God to forgive the Jews and show them mercy by restoring Jerusalem.

Gabriel comes, apparently to assure Daniel that the Jewish suffering will end after "a period of seventy sets of seven" (Daniel 9:24). That cryptic timeline is the problem.

One popular theory for solving the problem is to take the number figuratively. "Seven" symbolizes completion, since God rested on day seven after Creation. Seventy times seven is the ultimate in completion. Jews will suffer the full measure of God's punishment.

Other theories start with the presumption that the numbers refer to years: 70 x 7 = 490 years. Some take those numbers literally, or as ballpark numbers, or figuratively (see theories below).

QUESTION	IT'S ABOUT THE GREEKS	IT'S ABOUT JESUS	IT'S ABOUT END TIMES
What's the starting point for the 70 sets of seven years (490 years)?	Jeremiah's prophecy about the 70 years of Jewish exile (Jeremiah 25:11; 605 BC).	Persian King Artaxerxes ordering Jews to stop rebuilding Jerusalem (457 BC).	Persian King Artaxerxes granting his Jewish officer Nehemiah permission to go to Jerusalem and rebuild the city walls (445 BC).
When do the 490 years end?	When Jews drove out the Syrians and rededicated the Temple that invaders desecrated (164 BC).	When the first Christian martyr died, Stephen (AD 33).	When Jesus comes back after a time of Tribulation on earth.
Who is the Anointed One? (Daniel 9:26)	Persian King Cyrus, who frees the exiled Jews to go home and rebuild their nation (539 BC).	Jesus Christ beginning his ministry (AD 29).	Jesus Christ beginning his ministry (AD 29).
Who desecrates the Temple? (Daniel 9:27)	King Antiochus converted the Temple of God into a temple for Zeus (167 BC).	Roman general Titus destroyed the Temple, which has never been rebuilt (AD 70).	Antichrist will order everyone to worship him (Revelation 13:15).
What's one big complaint about this theory?	The prophecies are fake. Many advocates say Daniel didn't write the prophecies, but that someone else wrote them centuries later, passing history off as prophecy.	Arbitrary dates. Critics say folks supporting this theory have no solid evidence to support either the dates or the people they have associated with this prophecy.	There's no end-time focus. The prophecy focuses on Jews, Jerusalem, and the Temple in ancient times, not on the whole world in end times (Daniel 9:24).

BIG SCENE

PROPHET MARRIES A HOOKER

BIBLE HISTORY

ALL DATES APPROXIMATE

775 BC
Jonah convinces Nineveh Assyrians to repent

WORLD HISTORY

Solar eclipse reported in Nineveh
763 BC

Massive earthquake rocks Hosea's home region
760 BC

HOSEA
MY WIFE THE HOOKER

STORY LINE

A HOOKER AND A PROPHET. It's a match made in heaven. God orders the prophet Hosea to marry Gomer, a prostitute.

It's one giant *crank it up a notch* from the acted-out prophecies God asks other prophets to do—like asking Jeremiah to skip parties, to warn the Jews that God is about to put an end to their happy times (see Jeremiah 16:8–9).

God tells Hosea to marry the prostitute to show the Jews how they have treated him. Gomer will commit adultery and get pregnant by other men. Likewise, the Jews have committed spiritual adultery against God.

It's not all bad news, though. When Gomer eventually runs off and seems to get herself enslaved, God orders Hosea to buy her back. That's the good news: In this living parable, God shows that he's willing to forgive the Jews and "love them lavishly" (Hosea 14:4 MSG).

// TIME: Hosea ministers from about 750–722 BC.

// AUTHOR: The book says this is the message God gave Hosea. But it doesn't say if Hosea is the writer or just the source for another writer.

// LOCATION: Northern Jewish nation of Israel. ▶

LEBANON
Mediterranean Sea
Sea of Galilee
SYRIA
MT. CARMEL HILLS
Samaria
ISRAEL
Jordan River
Jerusalem
Dead Sea
JUDAH
JORDAN
N
ISRAEL
EGYPT
0   10   20   30   40 Miles
    20   30   50 Kilometers

750 BC
Hosea begins ministry

722 BC
Assyrians conquer Israel, exile citizens

Rome's forum

Rome is founded
753 BC

Hosea's dysfunctional family

A ROCKY MARRIAGE is what God has in mind for his prophet Hosea.

"Find a whore and marry her," God tells him. "Here's why: This whole country has become a whorehouse, unfaithful to me, GOD" (Hosea 1:2 MSG).

Hosea marries Gomer. She gives birth to three children—not one of whom is identified as his.

That's the point. God says he wants Hosea to marry a prostitute "so that some of her children will be conceived in prostitution" (Hosea 1:2). God wants the Jews to see flesh-and-blood examples of what they've done to him by worshipping idols, which is nothing less than spiritual adultery.

God names the three children—tough names to saddle on a kid. Each name is symbolic.

JEZREEL, A SON. In the Valley of Jezreel—a popular ancient battleground—God is going to punish the Jews for the murders King Jehu committed at the city of Jezreel. This is perhaps a reference to Jehu's over-the-top vicious coup in which he slaughtered the family and friends of Ahab and Jezebel.

LO-RUHAMAH, A DAUGHTER. Her name means "'Not loved'—for I will no longer show love to the people of Israel" (Hosea 1:6).

LO-AMMI, A SON. His name means "'Not my people'—for Israel is not my people, and I am not their God" (Hosea 1:9).

BEDOUIN BABY.
A herder's wife poses with her child. Hosea's wife, a former prostitute, gives birth to two sons and a daughter. The Bible doesn't say Hosea is the father of any of them—and it strongly hints otherwise.

RELIGIOUS LEADERS COULDN'T BELIEVE GOD WOULD ASK SUCH A THING.
Many rabbis and church leaders alike taught that Hosea's story didn't really happen. Rabbis Ibn Ezra and Radak, from the AD 1100s, said the story was just the report of a vision or a dream. Others suggest it may have been a parable—a fictional story with a spiritual message.

MINOR PROPHETS.
Hosea is the first of a dozen books called "Minor Prophets." It's not that they're less important. They're shorter. Sixty-seven chapters combined. That's just one more than Isaiah's 66 chapters. Hosea comes first because it's the longest. It's also first on the timeline—at the start of 300 years covering the Minor Prophets, stretching from the 700s–400s BC. (For a map showing where the prophets ministered, see page 208).

Runaway wife

GOMER RUNS OFF. The writer doesn't say why or where. Perhaps she ends up working as a sex slave.

That could explain why Hosea has to pay to get her back—he's under God's order to bring her home. There, Hosea tells her to give up her prostitution. For a time, she can't even have sex with her husband.

This, too, is an acted-out message for the Jews. The point is that Israel will go without a king for a time, and without a nation. But when the people devote themselves again to God, they will get back everything they've lost.

"The people of Israel will again live under my protection" (Hosea 14:7 NCV).

FOR SALE / After running away from Hosea, Gomer seems to end up enslaved. Hosea buys her back, on God's order.

◀ PRICE OF A PROSTITUTE. To buy back his wife, Hosea paid roughly the value of a slave. His currency: six ounces (171 grams) of silver, five bushels (182 liters) of barley, and an undisclosed amount of wine, perhaps a few filled wineskins (Hosea 3:2). The nearly half pound of silver would be worth about $60 on today's market when it sells for $10 a troy ounce.

WHAT GOD WANTS FROM THE JEWS. "I want you to show love, not offer sacrifices" (Hosea 6:6). Rituals don't impress God if they're mindless. The ritual should be an expression of genuine love, like a wedding ceremony. A wedding means nothing much if the two aren't committed to each another.

WHAT HAPPENED TO HOSEA? Nothing is known of Hosea, son of Beeri, or his family outside this book. Clues inside the book suggest he ministered in the area of Samaria, the capital of the northern Jewish nation of Israel—during the final years of that nation. He may have been a victim of Assyria's destruction of Samaria in 722 BC.

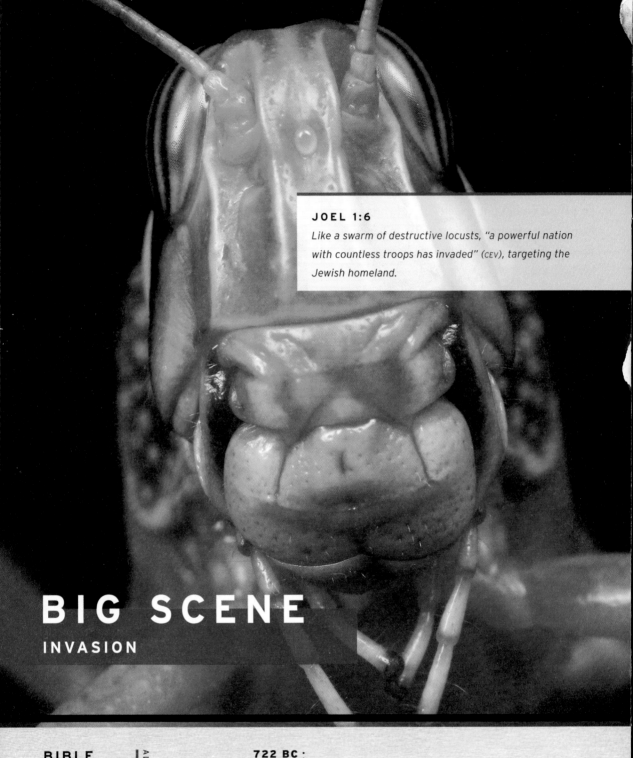

JOEL 1:6

Like a swarm of destructive locusts, "a powerful nation with countless troops has invaded" (CEV), targeting the Jewish homeland.

BIG SCENE
INVASION

BIBLE HISTORY		**722 BC**
		Assyrians conquer Israel, destroy capital: Samaria

ALL DATES APPROXIMATE

WORLD HISTORY	*First record of winners at Olympic Games* **776 BC**	

Boxing

JOEL

DAY OF THE LOCUST

LOCUSTS SWARM INTO ISRAEL and devastate the land.

They devour grain in the fields, strip the grapevines, and gobble up the fruit—even killing trees by chewing off the leaves, twigs, and bark.

Without shade, streams evaporate in the hot sun, the ground bakes to near ceramic, and drought rules the kingdom.

Joel seems to use this natural disaster—one that's all too common in the ancient Middle East—to warn of an even worse disaster: a swarm of soldiers.

The arrival of a desert locust, which stretches about two inches (5 cm) long, is bad enough when it brings enough company to darken the sky. Joel warns his readers that the next wave of locusts will ride in on war horses.

"They make the earth tremble and the heavens shake" (Joel 2:10 CEV).

Joel calls it Judgment Day for the Jews—punishment for centuries of sin.

He says there's only one escape. Quoting God, Joel says, "It isn't too late. . . . Return to me with all your heart" (Joel 2:12 CEV).

// LOCATION: The book doesn't say where Joel lived or whom his message targeted. He mentions both Jewish nations, Israel in the north and Judah in the south (see map page 261).

// TIME: Unknown. Guesses span 500 years, from around 800 BC to 300 BC.

// AUTHOR: Joel, son of Pethuel. The Bible says nothing more about him.

586 BC
*Babylonians conquer
Judah, destroy Jerusalem*

538 BC
*Cyrus of Persia
frees the Jews*

445 BC
*Jews rebuild
Jerusalem's walls*

*Greeks start
building Parthenon*
447 BC

Barbarians at the gate

"**SOUND THE ALARM,**" Joel writes. "The day of the LORD is upon us. . . . Nothing like it has been seen before or will ever be seen again" (Joel 2:1–2).

Invaders are coming to the Jewish homeland. Like locusts, a vast army will:

- // swarm over the city
- // run along the walls
- // enter the houses
- // destroy the crops and empty the barns.

This is just one more attempt by God to warn the Jews that they're headed for disaster if they don't stop sinning.

Yet even if they refuse to stop, Joel says God will show mercy. The Jews will suffer the consequences of their sins. But in time, God will bring them home.

God vows, too, that one day "I will pour out my Spirit upon all people" (Joel 2:28). Centuries later, the apostle Peter will declare that prediction fulfilled. The Spirit arrives after the resurrected Jesus returns to heaven. God sends the Holy Spirit to live inside Christ's followers and to guide them (see Acts 2:16).

INVASION FORCE. Invaders will storm into the Jewish homeland, Joel warns, like a swarm of locusts—only bigger and more destructive.

MODERN INFESTATIONS. Even with pesticides targeting them, locusts still plague Middle Eastern and African farmers. A swarm in November 2004 wiped out a third of the crops in North African nations.

DAY OF THE LORD. In Israel's early history, the Day of the Lord was a good thing. It was God stepping into Jewish history to protect them and to drive off the bad guys. Joel warns that this is about to change. Now, the Jews are the bad guys. On the Day of the Lord, God is coming after them.

HOW TO KILL A LOCUST / In Bible times, the most effective technique was to plow the ground to break up the egg pods. Female locusts bury their egg pods in the ground near where they fed. Joel's prophecy targets both the northern Jewish nation of Israel and the southern Jewish nation of Judah (map at left).

Locust egg pod buried in the sand

Locusts are migratory grasshoppers with wings.

DESERT LOCUST (*SCHISTOCERCA GREGARIA*). Born in the African and Arabian deserts, where predators are few, locust fields can grow into massive swarms of about 100 million hungry locusts per square mile (1.6 km). Locusts bury their egg pods in the ground (top right), each pod packing 80–150 eggs. Locusts can lay eggs about every couple of weeks during their short lifetime of a few months. Up to 1,000 egg pods have been found under a square yard (meter) of soil.

BIG SCENE

LET'S SEE SOME JUSTICE

AMOS 5:23–24

God is sick of watching Jews go through the motions of worship, with sacrifices and music. "Away with the noise. . . . Let justice roll on like a river" (*TNIV*).

BIBLE HISTORY	ALL DATES APPROXIMATE	**793 BC** *Jeroboam II becomes king of Israel*		**760 BC** *Approximate start of Amos's ministry*
WORLD HISTORY		*Women barred from first recorded Olympic Games* **776 BC**		*Earthquake rattles region (see Amos 1:1). Evidence found in damaged walls of Hazor* **760 BC**

A M O S

FAT COWS MILK THE POOR

CIVIL RIGHTS LEADERS come to this fig farmer, Amos, for the Bible's most damning quotes about how rich and powerful people exploit the poor. Quotes like this:

> *"They walk on poor people as if they were dirt, and they refuse to be fair."*
>
> AMOS 2:7 NCV

To deliver a message like this, God doesn't choose a prophet with uppity status and palace privileges. He picks someone who knows what it means to struggle for a living. Amos says, "I'm not a professional prophet, and I was never trained to be one. I'm just a shepherd, and I take care of sycamore-fig trees" (Amos 7:14).

Humble though Amos may be, he unloads bold messages—warning Israel's fat cats to stop:

// bribing judges

// mixing grain with filler chaff to punch up their profit margin, and

// selling the poor into slavery to recoup debts as tiny as the price of a pair of sandals.

The country's top religious leader—rather than support him—orders him to go back where he came from.

// TIME: During the reign of Judah's King Uzziah (about 792–742 BC).

// AUTHOR: These are "The words of Amos" (Amos 1:1 NRSV).

// LOCATION: Amos lives in the village of Tekoa in the southern Jewish nation of Judah. But he takes his message to Samaria, capital of the northern Jewish nation of Israel, and to Israel's worship center in Bethel (see map page 264).

722 BC
Assyrians conquer Israel, destroy Samaria

Celts live in central Europe before migrating to England
700 BC

586 BC
Babylon destroys Jerusalem, exiles Jews

Spartan women train in athletic events to become strong mothers
600 BC

A farmer turns prophet

FIG FARMER AND SHEPHERD, Amos lives in the obscure village of Tekoa, about a half day's walk south of Jerusalem. There, he has visions—messages from God—that he feels compelled to take on the road.

Though he lives in the southern Jewish nation of Judah, he crosses the border into Israel and goes to the capital city of Samaria.

There, he delivers warnings about God's coming punishment for both Jewish nations, as well as several neighboring nations in what are now Syria, Jordan, Lebanon, and the Palestinian's Gaza Strip. But it's the northern Jewish nation of Israel—just a few decades from annihilation—that gets the brunt of his condemnation.

Amos's main complaints:

// exploitation of the poor (see 2:6–7)
// sexual immorality (see 2:7)
// corruption (see 3:10; 8:5)
// injustice in the courts (see 5:7, 12)
// greed and self-indulgence (see 6:1–6)
// worship of idols (see 7:9).

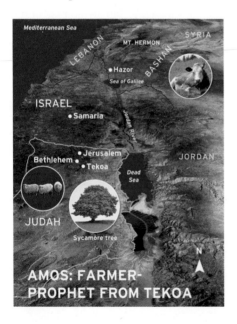

AMOS: FARMER-PROPHET FROM TEKOA

FIG: THE POOR MAN'S FOOD.
The sycamore fig (*ficus sycomorus*) won't ripen unless someone punctures it, exposing the inside to air. Growing to about an inch (2–3 cm) long, these figs were so widely available throughout the Mediterranean world that people called them "the poor man's food."

MARTIN LUTHER KING JR. AND AMOS.
Rev. King drew from Amos for his sermon "Let Justice Roll Down." Sermon excerpt: "'Let justice roll down like waters in a mighty stream,' said the prophet Amos. He was not seeking consensus but the cleansing action of revolutionary change."

Keeping the prophecies visual

BUILDING GOD'S CASE against the Jews, Amos prefers graphic word pictures. He has no intention of boring his listeners with abstract generalizations—or of giving them wiggle room to read between the lines so they can justify their sins.

ISRAEL IS A CROOKED WALL. Amos sees God taking a plumb line to a wall (see Amos 7:7). Every builder knows what you have to do if the wall you're building starts to lean. Tear it down and start over.

FAT COWS ARE HEADED TO THE SLAUGHTER. "You cows of Bashan on the Mountain of Samaria. You take things from the poor and crush people who are in need. . . . The time will come when you will be taken away by hooks" (Amos 4:1–2 NCV).

SELLING DIRT WITH GRAIN. "You say to yourselves. . . . 'Our wheat is ready, and we want to sell it now. We can't wait to cheat and charge high prices for the grain we sell. We will use dishonest scales and mix dust in the grain' " (Amos 8:5–6 CEV).

COWS OF BASHAN.
Bashan was a rich pasture northeast of the Sea of Galilee in the Golan Heights. It was famous for its plump and pampered cattle—food of the rich. The poor rarely ate meat. When Amos called the wives of rich men in Samaria "cows of Bashan" (Amos 4:1 NCV), it was a warning. The butcher's coming.

NOSE HOOKS.
Amos says the "cows of Bashan" will be dragged away "by hooks" (Amos 4:1–2 NCV) like fishermen hauling a string of fish. Assyrians capture Samaria in 722 BC. Art from Assyria and other ancient countries shows some captives with ropes attached to hooks in their noses.

AMOS'S LAST WORD.
Like other prophets, Amos ends upbeat. Though Israel will fall, God "will rebuild David's fallen kingdom" (Amos 9:11 CEV).

PLUMB LINE / A weighted string held next to a wall shows if the wall is straight. A straight wall measures the same distance from the line, from top to bottom.

BIG SCENE
WAR CRIMES

OBADIAH 14
Jews on the run from Babylonian invaders flee to the neighboring nation of Edom, where some are murdered and others are captured and turned over to the Babylonians.

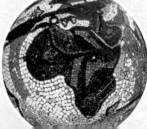

BIBLE HISTORY

ALL DATES APPROXIMATE

586 BC
Babylon conquers Judah, destroys Jerusalem, deports Jews

WORLD HISTORY

Greek philosopher Anaximander says the world comes from substance called the "unlimited"
575 BC

OBADIAH

HOW NOT TO TREAT WAR REFUGEES

STORY LINE

FROM WHAT IS NOW IRAQ, Babylonians invade the Jewish homeland. They conquer the cities and level the capital of Jerusalem.

Many Jews run for their lives as war refugees. Some flee to Edom, a cousin nation descended from Isaac's oldest son, Esau.

A far cry short of kissing cousins, the people of Edom don't welcome the Jews. Instead, they:

// murder many Jewish refugees

// arrest others and turn them over to the invaders

// loot the Jewish homeland, taking whatever the Babylonians don't want.

Quoting God, Obadiah warns them:

> *"You thought you were so great, perched high among the rocks, king of the mountain, Thinking to yourself, 'Nobody can get to me! Nobody can touch me!' Think again. . . . I'll bring you down to earth."*
>
> OBADIAH 3–4 MSG

Babylonians breach their mountain fortress 33 years later. Their main fortress city, Petra, is now a ghost town visited by archaeologists and tourists.

// TIME: Obadiah may have delivered this message during the 33-year stretch between the time Babylon conquered Judah in 586 BC and when Babylon conquered Edom in 553 BC.

// AUTHOR: Obadiah. Because his name means "servant of God" and there's no mention of his father, some scholars guess Obadiah wasn't the writer's real name, but just a description.

// LOCATION: Obadiah targets Edom, now part of Jordan, south of the Dead Sea.

Narrow passage leading into rock city of Petra, Edom

538 BC
Persians free Jews to go home

Babylon conquers Edom
553 BC

BIG SCENE
FISH BAIT

JONAH 1:17
Sailors throw overboard the runaway prophet Jonah. It's to calm the storm God whipped up to punish him. A large fish swallows Jonah and spits him out on shore three days later.

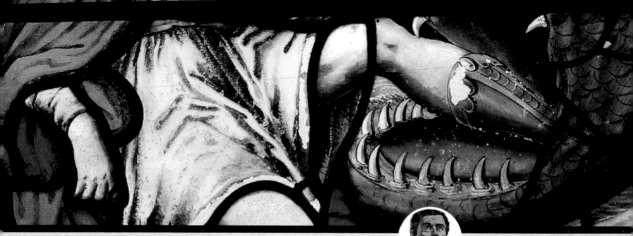

BIBLE HISTORY		793 BC	775 BC
	ALL DATES APPROXIMATE	Jeroboam II begins 40-year reign over Israel	Jonah ministers in Israel

WORLD HISTORY		Homer, father of Greek literature, writes the Iliad (fall of Troy) and the Odyssey (travels of Ulysses)
		800 BC Ulysses resists the sirens

JONAH

FISH CATCHES MAN, THROWS HIM BACK

STORY LINE

IN A WHOPPER OF A FISH STORY, a large fish catches a man and throws him back.

The man is Jonah, a prophet on the run from God. He's running because God gives him a suicidal Mission Impossible, or so it seems. Jonah lives in Israel. But God orders him to walk roughly a thousand meandering miles (about 1,600 km) into the heart of the Assyrian Empire. There, he's to threaten Assyria's capital city, Nineveh, with destruction.

Assyria is a vicious empire that brags about torturing its enemies—even hanging torture pictures on the palace walls.

This mission may have been a bit like sending a rabbi to Berlin during World War II to warn Adolf Hitler that his Nazi Party was almost over.

Nineveh lies northeast of Israel. Jonah flees in the opposite direction, southwest. He boards a ship bound for Tarshish, somewhere in the Mediterranean world, perhaps as far away as the other end of the sea: Spain.

God splashes up a storm that threatens to sink the ship. Jonah admits to the sailors that the storm is his fault. As a last resort, the sailors throw him overboard. The storm calms. A fish swallows him and spits him ashore three days later. He walks to Nineveh and delivers the warning that in 40 days the city will be destroyed.

The Assyrians repent. So instead of destroying them, God forgives them.

Jonah pouts, embarrassed that his prophecy turned out wrong.

End of story.

// TIME: During the reign of Israel's King Jeroboam II (about 793–753 BC).

// AUTHOR: Jonah son of Amittai, or possibly someone telling his story for him.

// LOCATION: Jonah lives in the north Jewish nation of Israel, but ends up in Nineveh, a city near Mosul in northern Iraq.

722 BC
Assyria conquers Israel, deports Jews

Nineveh important center of trade, literature
700 BC

Babylonians conquer Assyria
612 BC

Jonah's cruise

GOD PITS A SOLITARY JEW against an empire. Not just any empire. Assyria—the first superpower to control the Middle East. Assyria dominates the region through brute force and terror tactics, leaving small nations afraid to buck for independence.

God tells Jonah to go to Assyria's capital city, Nineveh, and announce that the city will fall in 40 days.

Jonah doesn't argue with God, which would have put him in the company of prophets such as Moses and Jeremiah. Passive-aggressive, he gets on a ship and sails off in the opposite direction—as though the God of Israel is stuck in Israel (see map on page 272).

God sends a typhoonlike storm that nearly sinks the ship. Sailors use lots to figure out which person upset the gods. The lots point to Jonah, who confesses and ends up in the sea—a sacrifice to his God.

"The LORD had arranged for a great fish to swallow Jonah. And Jonah was inside the fish for three days and three nights" (Jonah 1:17).

Inside the fish Jonah prays—oddly—thanking God for saving him "from the jaws of death!" (Jonah 2:6). Apparently he's a positive thinker. The fish vomits him up onto a beach, like a bad meal.

Stone panel from Nineveh palace, about 700 BC

WHALE?

It was a big fish, according to the writer. In a typhoon, Jonah may not have seen the fish—or recognized it if he had. Jews were landlubber shepherds and farmers, more sea-fearers than seafarers.

OVERBOARD.

Joseph Pulitzer's *New York World* newspaper printed a story in 1896, claiming that a British whaler named James Bartley spent a day and a half in a sperm whale before his crew on the *Star of the East* caught the whale and saved him. But Bartley's name wasn't on the crew roster, and the wife of the ship's captain later said Bartley never sailed with her husband. It was only Bartley's story that went overboard.

TRUE STORY OR PARABLE?

Some Bible experts say the story happened just as the Bible reports. Others say the story reads more like a parable. It's short. It's captivating. And it ends abruptly with a thunderbolt of a surprise, which leaves the reader thinking.

◄ TERROR TACTIC: SKINNED ALIVE.

Art surviving from the Assyrian palace in Nineveh shows soldiers skinning captives.

SPLASH / To quell a storm, sailors throw Jonah into the sea where a huge fish of some kind swallows him.

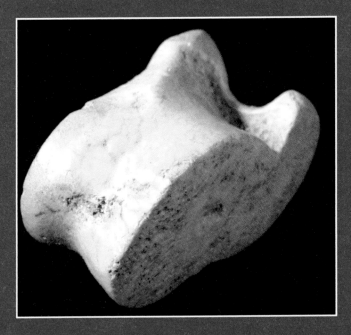

Greek knucklebone from about 300 BC, used a bit like dice.

CASTING LOTS. Sailors threw lots to determine which person on board had angered the gods and caused the storm. "Lots" may have been like dice, stones, or knucklebones (left)—some kind of tool for supposedly getting a yes-no answer. As in a coin toss: "Heads, you win. Tails, you lose." Jonah lost.

Jonah against the empire

WET AND BROKE, Jonah gets a rerun of a message from God.

"Get up and go to the great city of Nineveh, and deliver the message I have given you" (Jonah 3:2).

Perhaps Jonah goes home first, to pack supplies for the nearly thousand-mile (1,600 km) trip. Eventually, perhaps months later, he ends up in the Assyrian capital where he dutifully delivers the bad news: In 40 days, Nineveh will be destroyed.

Instead of ignoring him, like the Jews usually did with their many prophets, the people of Nineveh take him seriously. The king goes into mourning and orders everyone in the city to fast and pray to Jonah's God. He also orders them to stop all violence. Apparently, they comply out of fear for their lives.

Just as God promised to do for the Jews if they repented and changed their ways, he forgives the Assyrians and calls off the doom.

Solar eclipse

TROUBLE IN ASSYRIA / In the mid-700s, the Assyrians were facing tough times. Persistent droughts. Revolts. Defeat on the battlefield. They may have considered the solar eclipse of 763 BC a bad omen.

JONAH'S SCENIC CRUISE TO NINEVEH

WESTWARD BOUND. Ordered to Nineveh, Jonah boards a ship headed to Tarshish, which many scholars speculate is Tartessus, Spain—at the other end of the Mediterranean world.

Pouting prophet

ANYTHING BUT HAPPY about helping save a city of 120,000 souls, Jonah is ticked—which doesn't seem at all missionary minded.

"GOD! I knew it," he complains, in what sounds more like a curse than a prayer. "I knew you were sheer grace and mercy. . . . If you won't kill them, kill me! I'm better off dead!" (Jonah 4:2–3 MSG).

Jonah feels discredited—a prophet whose prophecy failed.

He walks outside the walled city and sits—long enough for a plant to grow and shade him. Jonah's happy about the shade, but ticked again when God sends a worm that kills the plant.

"It's okay for you to feel sorry for the dead plant, which you wanted me to spare," God says, "but it's not okay for me to feel sorry for 120,000 human beings, and spare them?" (Jonah 4:9, 11 AUTHOR'S PARAPHRASE).

Jonah's story ends with that stunning question.

A PROPHET DISCREDITED. Angry at God for forgiving the Assyrians instead of killing them like he predicted God would do, Jonah parks himself outside the city and sulks.

IRAQIS TEACH JEWS A LESSON. Jews read Jonah's story on the most solemn day on their calendar: Yom Kippur, the Day of Atonement—a national day of repentance. The story reminds them to follow the example of the Assyrians by asking God to forgive them of their sins.

AND THE POINT IS? Scholars offer educated guesses about the point of the story:

> God isn't just the God of the Jews; he cares about everyone.

> God's sense of justice is balanced by his sense of mercy.

> God has power over all of his creation: wind and waves, fish and fishermen, prophets and pagans.

◄ **NINEVEH.** Now a ruin mostly buried under a mound of dirt, Nineveh was the oldest and most populated city in the Assyrian Empire. Its walls ran about 7.5 miles (12 km) long and in some places were 148 feet (45 meters) high. This onetime capital of the Assyrian Empire lies along the east bank of the Tigris, across the river from Mosul, Iraq.

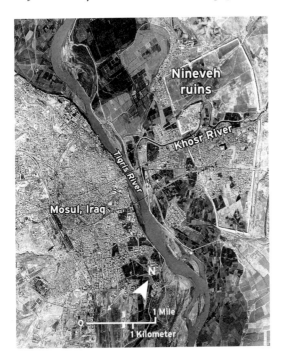

Walls of Nineveh, visible in aerial photo

MICAH 5:2

Out of Bethlehem, a ruler of Israel will come—"whose family goes back to ancient times" (CEV). Many Jews later said Micah was talking about the Messiah (see Matthew 2:4–6).

BIG SCENE
A SAVIOR FROM BETHLEHEM

BIBLE HISTORY	742 BC	722 BC	686 BC
	Micah begins his ministry	Assyrians conquer Israel, exile Jews	Micah's ministry ends

ALL DATES APPROXIMATE

WORLD HISTORY		Shalmaneser V becomes king of Assyria; he'll conquer Israel
		727 BC

MICAH

O LITTLE TOWN OF BETHLEHEM

STORY LINE

SMALL-TOWN PROPHET Micah is most famous for predicting a small-town Messiah.

Israel's future leader, Micah says, will come from the tiny village of Bethlehem—the birthplace of Jesus 700 years later.

But for Micah, this prophecy is just a fleeting reference to the good life that's coming after God punishes the Jews.

Micah preaches doom to both Jewish nations, north and south—indicting the rich and the poor.

// Rich get richer through extortion and violence.

// Judges sell their judgment for bribes.

// Prophets predict and priests teach whatever the people will pay to hear.

// Poor folks take their complaints to idols instead of God.

For these sins, Micah warns, both Jewish nations will fall. But in time, Micah adds, God will restore Jewish sovereignty, offering the Jews a fresh start and a hopeful future.

// **TIME:** Micah's ministry spans about 65 years and three kings of Judah—Jotham, Ahaz, and Hezekiah—from roughly 742–686 BC.

// **AUTHOR:** Micah of Moresheth, or someone telling his story for him. Many guess the latter because the writer talks about Babylon exiling the Jews a century before Babylon replaces Assyria as the Middle Eastern superpower.

// **LOCATION:** Micah comes from Moresheth, a village in the southern Jewish nation of Judah, a day's walk southwest of Jerusalem—about 20 miles (32 km).

Wedge-shaped cuneiform writing

King Ashurbanipal creates first systematic library
650 BC

586 BC
Babylonians conquer Judah, destroy Jerusalem

Confucius born
551 BC

Crying time

"SHAVE YOUR HEADS. . . . Bald as a goose egg," Micah tells the Jews (Micah 1:16 MSG). He's talking about an ancient ritual for extreme mourning. The Jews are about to have good reason to mourn to the max.

Micah is delivering this bad news to people in both Jewish nations: Israel and Judah. God is going to send conquerors to destroy both nations. Israel's capital of Samaria and Judah's capital of Jerusalem "will be plowed" (Micah 1:6; 3:12).

Among God's many charges, and his sentence for each offense:

"When you want a piece of land, you find a way to seize it" (Micah 2:2). For this, God will take your land.

"You have evicted women from their pleasant homes" (Micah 2:9). God will take your homes from you.

"Merchants. . .use dishonest scales" (Micah 6:11). God will take every coin you ever cheated away from an honest customer.

DOOM AND HOPE—THE TAG TEAM. Micah's prophecy reads a bit like a three-round wrestling match—with the bad guy and the good guy each taking turns getting in some shots.

// Round one: bad news (1:1–2:11); good news (2:12–13).

// Round two: bad news (3); good news (4:1–5:15).

// Round three: bad news (6:1–7:7); good news (7:8–20).

EXILE 1940s. Many Jews lucky enough to have survived the Holocaust lost their faith in God. They couldn't understand why God would allow Nazis to murder six million of them—a question that lingers for perhaps most people of faith. In Bible times, the exile and slaughter had the opposite effect. The generation of Jews after the exile saw firsthand that the prophets' warnings came true. So these Jews seemed more committed than ever to observing Jewish traditions. They didn't want to make the same mistakes their ancestors had made—and suffer the same consequences.

◄ **JEWISH REFUGEES.** Jews forced out of their homes by Nazi Germans during World War II wait to board a train. For most, it's a one-way ticket off the planet. Micah warns Jews of his day that they will be driven from their homeland, but that in time God will bring them back.

A great day's coming

A GHOST TOWN turned into a farm isn't God's last word for Jerusalem.

In the years ahead, God will allow the Jews to return from exile and rebuild their nation. Jerusalem will become "the most important place on earth. . . . And people from all over the world will stream there to worship" (Micah 4:1).

Leading the nation will be a ruler from the tiny village of Bethlehem. When he is born, Micah says, everything for Israel will change for the better. "He will be the source of peace" (Micah 5:5).

The peace ahead will last. Nations around the world "will hammer their swords into plow blades. . . . Nations will no longer raise swords against other nations; they will not train for war anymore" (Micah 4:3 NCV).

Dome of the Rock, Jerusalem

JERUSALEM: SACRED CITY FOR JEWS, CHRISTIANS, MUSLIMS.

Jews revere Jerusalem because it was their ancient capital and the center of worship at the Temple. Christians revere the city because it's where the Bible says Jesus taught, died, and rose again. Muslims worship at the Dome of the Rock (where many say the Jewish Temple once stood) because they teach that Muhammad ascended to heaven from the rock inside the domed shrine.

Hilltop village of Bethlehem, about 1900

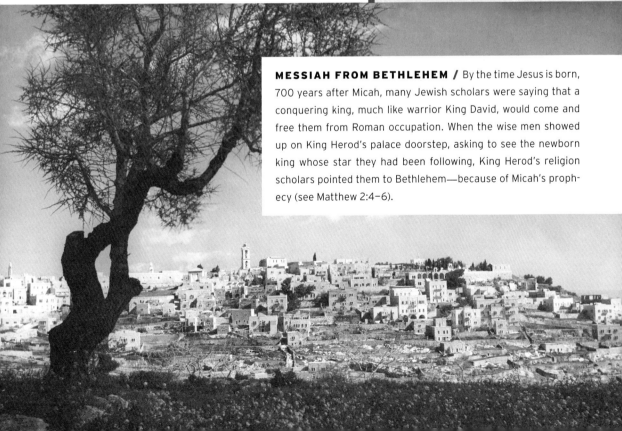

MESSIAH FROM BETHLEHEM / By the time Jesus is born, 700 years after Micah, many Jewish scholars were saying that a conquering king, much like warrior King David, would come and free them from Roman occupation. When the wise men showed up on King Herod's palace doorstep, asking to see the newborn king whose star they had been following, King Herod's religion scholars pointed them to Bethlehem—because of Micah's prophecy (see Matthew 2:4–6).

BIG SCENE

GIRLIE MEN EXPOSED

NAHUM 3:5

Feared as international terrorists who torture their enemies, Assyrian soldiers are girlie men to God who vows, "I will lift your skirts and show all the earth your nakedness."

BIBLE HISTORY

ALL DATES APPROXIMATE

775 BC
Jonah convinces Nineveh to repent

722 BC
Assyrians conquer Israel

WORLD HISTORY

Taylor Prism, an Assyrian report of war with Judah

701 BC
Assyrians destroy 46 cities of Judah

NAHUM

THE DISAPPEARING IRAQI EMPIRE

STORY LINE

ASSYRIAN BULLIES are about to meet their match—and their Maker.

Nahum delivers the same message Jonah had delivered about a century earlier: Nineveh—capital and oldest city of the Assyrian Empire—is about to be destroyed.

One difference: Jonah delivered his message in person to the Assyrians, but it seems Nahum stays home and delivers his message mainly to his fellow Jews. Here, it's a message of consolation and a promise of justice. Brutal Assyrians have already dismantled the northern Jewish nation of Israel. Also, by the empire's own count in surviving records, their armies have destroyed 46 cities in the southern Jewish nation of Judah.

God's message to Assyria: "You will have no more children to carry on your name. I will destroy all the idols in the temples of your gods. I am preparing a grave for you" (Nahum 1:14).

Nahum may well have lived to see his prophecy fulfilled.

// TIME: Clues in the book suggest Nahum experiences this vision sometime during a 50-year span: after the 663 BC fall of Egypt's capital in Thebes, which Nahum mentions, but before the 612 BC fall of Assyria's capital in Nineveh, which Nahum predicts.

// AUTHOR: Nahum, or a writer reporting Nahum's visions.

// LOCATION: Nahum lives in Elkosh, a site that remains a mystery. He targets Nineveh, capital of the Assyrian Empire. The ruins lie near the northern Iraqi town of Mosul (see maps pages 273, 281).

Ruins near Thebes, Egypt

650 BC
*Nahum warns of
Nineveh's fall*

*Assyrians destroy
Thebes, capital of Egypt*
663 BC

*Babylonians
destroy Nineveh*
612 BC

The empire strikes out

ASSYRIANS WEREN'T ALL BAD, historians say. Though the world's first international empire brutally dominated the Middle East, Assyria also opened the door to more international trade and advances in art and science. They maintained a library with a massive collection of literature—22,000 clay tablets covering history, medicine, and astronomy.

But there's a dark side to this empire, too. "Where can anyone be found who has not suffered from your continual cruelty?" God asks (Nahum 3:19).

For the horrors they've inflicted on nations, God passes sentence on them:

"YOUR ENEMY IS COMING TO CRUSH YOU" (Nahum 2:1). A coalition army of Babylonians from what is now southern Iraq, Medes in Iran, and Scythians from the Ukraine and Russia attacks Nineveh in 612 BC.

"THE RIVER GATES HAVE BEEN TORN OPEN!" (Nahum 2:6). A flood washes away part of the wall, allowing invaders inside. So says a surviving Babylonian report, the Babylonian Chronicle.

"FIRE WILL DEVOUR YOU" (Nahum 3:15). Charred ruins show the city burned.

"NEVER AGAIN WILL YOU PLUNDER CONQUERED NATIONS" (Nahum 2:13). Once known as a lions' den (Nahum 2:11) because of its ferocious reputation, Nineveh is now a grassy mound of ruins called Tell Kuyunjik, "mound of many sheep."

NINEVEH BEFORE THE FALL. Once the crown jewel and capital of the Assyrian Empire, Nineveh falls to Babylonian invaders. Never rebuilt, it now lies as a ruin near Mosul in northern Iraq.

Black Sea
Caspian Sea
TURKEY
Nineveh
CYPRUS
Euphrates River
SYRIA
Tigris River
LEBANON
IRAN
Mediterranean Sea
Damascus
Babylon
Susa
ISRAEL Jerusalem
Syrian Desert
IRAQ
JORDAN
Memphis
KUWAIT
SAUDI ARABIA
Persian Gulf
EGYPT
Nile River
Red Sea
Thebes

ASSYRIAN EMPIRE

"YOU ARE DESPICABLE!" (NAHUM 1:14).

For evidence of the Assyrian Empire's brutality, see page 136.

ASSYRIA'S PROTECTION RACKET.

Assyrians, like other ancient empires that will follow them, are in the protection racket. They promise to protect the nations in their realm, but at a high price: freedom for one, crippling taxes for another. When any nation under their control takes a stab at independence by refusing to pay the taxes due, it risks annihilation.

That's what happened to the northern Jewish nation of Israel in 722 BC. It nearly happened to the southern Jewish nation of Judah a couple of decades later, in 701 BC. Jerusalem is the only major city to survive the invasion force—and only by the miracle of something that sounds like a plague, killing thousands in Assyria's army and forcing them to retreat for home (see "Assyrians hightail it home," page 137).

HABAKKUK 3:17–18

Invaders are coming to wipe out the Jewish nation. Habakkuk promises that no matter what they do—even if they wipe out everything—he will still trust in God.

BIG SCENE

FAITH WHEN LIFE FALLS TO PIECES

**BIBLE
HISTORY**

ALL DATES APPROXIMATE

722 BC
*Assyria conquers northern
Jewish nation of Israel*

**WORLD
HISTORY**

HABAKKUK

GIVING GOD WHAT FOR

HARD TO PLEASE. Many would say that's a fair description of the prophet Habakkuk (huh-BACK-uck). He's not happy with God.

First he criticizes God for doing nothing while the Jews sin by trashing the country with violence, injustice, and perversion:

> *"How long, O LORD, must I call for help? But you do not listen!"*
>
> HABAKKUK 1:2

Then when God does something—vowing to send Babylonian invaders to punish the Jews—Habakkuk criticizes him for doing too much.

> *"You can't be serious!"*
>
> HABAKKUK 1:13 MSG

Yet, complaining isn't Habakkuk's claim to fame. Bible students remember him most, perhaps, because of his last words—a poem of trust in God no matter what happens. In all the Bible there's probably no statement of faith that's more heart-wrenching, especially for those who know the story of what happened when the Babylonians came to Jerusalem.

// TIME: Uncertain. Most scholars guess it's during the quarter century after 612 BC, the year Babylonians destroy Assyria's capital of Nineveh, but before 586 BC, when Babylonians destroy Jerusalem.

// AUTHOR: Habakkuk or someone reporting the messages he received in visions.

// LOCATION: The threat comes from the Babylonian Empire, with its capital in Babylon. Habakkuk lives in the southern Jewish nation of Judah, in what is now southern Israel (see map page 264).

---

612 BC
Habakkuk ministers as a prophet in Judah

586 BC
Babylon conquers southern Jewish nation of Judah, destroys Jerusalem, exiles survivors

Babylonians destroy Assyrian capital
612 BC

Pythagoras and student

Math whiz Pythagoras is born
580 BC

Having words with God

IN A VISION, Habakkuk sees himself arguing with God—complaining about sin gone wild in Judah.

"I see destruction and violence. . . . There is no justice in the courts. The wicked far outnumber the righteous" (Habakkuk 1:3–4).

God breaks his silence. He says he's raising up a new superpower: the Babylonian Empire. "They will march across the world and conquer other lands" (Habakkuk 1:6), Judah included.

Habakkuk knows the Babylonians. They're as brutal and pagan as the Assyrians ever were. So he asks the obvious question. He wants to know why on earth God would let "the wicked swallow up people who are better than they are" (Habakkuk 1:13 NCV).

God doesn't generally answer "why" questions. Except to say, trust me—which is what he tells Habakkuk:

"Those who are right with God will live by faith."

HABAKKUK 2:4 NCV

God promises that in time, the Babylonians will get what they deserve.

WHERE PROTESTANTS GOT THEIR START.
Roman Catholic priest Martin Luther broke away from the church and started the Protestant movement. He did this after reading an idea the apostle Paul borrowed from Habakkuk and wrote about in Romans 1:17—that we're not saved by obeying church rules and doing what the pope says. We're saved by having faith in God.

DISSING IDOLS.
God mocks the Babylonians for trusting in idols. "What good is an idol carved by man? . . . How foolish to trust in your own creation—a god that can't even talk!" (Habakkuk 2:18).

◄ **CONQUERORS ARE COMING.**
In a vision, Habakkuk learns that God will punish the Jewish nation by sending an invasion force to conquer it. Habakkuk objects, saying he knows the Jews are bad, but the pagan invaders are even worse.

Extreme faith

KNEES KNOCKING, Habakkuk shakes in terror at what he believes is coming.

He knows what invaders do. They take everything they want. They destroy everything else. Crops. Cities. People. Entire nations can die.

So what does Habakkuk do?

He sings.

His last words are a song, sung as a prayer. He's not singing the blues, either.

Somewhere, somehow, his fear turns to faith. So he sings the song of a brave soul who knows he may soon die. Yet even if it kills him, Habakkuk decides to trust in the One for whom he has lived. Because in the end, Habakkuk seems to believe, God will win—and so will God's people.

> *Even though the fig trees are all destroyed, and there is neither blossom left nor fruit, and though the olive crops all fail, and the fields lie barren; even if the flocks die in the fields and the cattle barns are empty, yet I will rejoice in the Lord; I will be happy in the God of my salvation.*
>
> HABAKKUK **3:17–18** TLB

MOUNTAIN CLIMBING / A stag pauses on a mountain meadow. Facing a mountain range of trouble, Habakkuk says, "The Lord God is my Strength, and he will give me the speed of a deer and bring me safely over the mountains" (Habakkuk 3:19 TLB).

ZEPHANIAH 1:2–3

"'I will sweep away everything from the face of the earth,'
says the LORD. "I will sweep away people and animals alike. . .
The birds of the sky and the fish in the sea."

BIG SCENE

ARMAGEDDON

BIBLE HISTORY	ALL DATES APPROXIMATE	**722 BC** Assyrians destroy northern Jewish nation of Israel	**640 BC** Earliest start date of Zephaniah's ministry	
WORLD HISTORY			Nineveh falls to Babylon **612 BC**	Greeks use science instead of gods to explain unusual phenomena **600 BC**

ZEPHANIAH
LOSING THE HUMAN RACE

STORY LINE

IT'S THE END OF THE WORLD—or a whopper of an exaggeration. Bible students can't agree which one best describes the prophecy of Zephaniah.

"I will wipe out the entire human race," Zephaniah says, quoting a message from God (Zephaniah 1:3 CEV).

Seems clear enough. We're toast.

The wrench in the gears of that theory comes at the end of Zephaniah's short prophecy:

> *Celebrate and shout with all your heart!*
> ZEPHANIAH 3:14 CEV

That's not the kind of thing you say to a corpse.

Apparently pointing to some distant future, Zephaniah adds that God's punishment of the Jews is over. God is bringing them home, presumably from the half-century exile they'll experience beginning in 586 BC.

For this reason, many scholars say Zephaniah is doing what his colleagues have been doing for decades—warning Jews in Judah that their days are numbered. The difference is that he uses exaggeration to give the Jews a sense of what it will feel like when life as they know it in the Promised Land comes to a sudden end.

// TIME: Sometime during the reign of King Josiah (640–609 BC).

// AUTHOR: The writer or source of material is "Zephaniah son of Cushi, the son of Gedaliah, the son of Amariah, the son of Hezekiah" (Zephaniah 1:1 TNIV). He's the only prophet who traces his family tree back four generations, perhaps to show he's a great-great-grandson of former King Hezekiah.

// LOCATION: Southern Jewish nation of Judah. The northern nation of Israel is gone, conquered by Assyrians.

Volcanic Eruption

586 BC
Babylonians conquer Judah, exile Jews

Ishtar Gate entrance to Babylon

538 BC
Cyrus of Persia frees the Jews to go home

Babylon builds the famous Ishtar Gate
575 BC

Milon of Greece wins his first of six Olympic wrestling titles
540 BC

Creation rewind

IT'S NOT JUST THE END OF HUMANITY on Zephaniah's radar scope. It's the end of all life on earth. As if that's not clear enough, Zephaniah lists the targets on God's hit list in the exact opposite order God created them.

God created fish first, and then birds, animals, and humans (see Genesis 1:20–27). But now he's going to purge the planet of humans first, followed by the animals, birds, and fish—rewinding Creation.

As complete as creation is now, teeming with life, that's how complete the destruction will be.

Many Bible scholars say Zephaniah isn't talking about a divinely orchestrated planet killer of an event, such as a meteor strike or suicide by nuclear warfare. Many say he's using a favorite Jewish teaching technique: hyperbole—exaggeration for emphasis. Jesus later used "the end is near" lingo to describe the horrors of Rome's coming siege and destruction of Jerusalem (see Matthew 24).

Other scholars say Zephaniah was offering two prophecies in one:

// a prophecy about God's judgment on Judah
// a prophecy about God's future, end-time judgment on humanity.

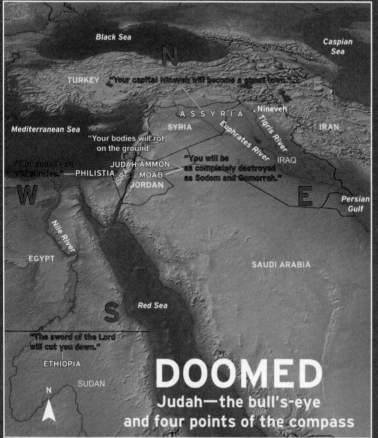

DOOMED
Judah—the bull's-eye and four points of the compass

◀ **TARGETS.** Zephaniah predicts doom for Judah and for neighboring nations in all four directions—perhaps a symbol of worldwide destruction, some say. Others say regional only.

DID ZEPHANIAH SPARK A REVIVAL? Zephaniah prophesied during the reign of Josiah. Several years into Josiah's reign, the king launched a religious reform, which included repairing the badly neglected Temple in Jerusalem.

ONE PROPHECY FOR TWO TIMELINES? Some Bible prophecies seem to describe more than one event at a time. Isaiah said God would send a sign: A virgin would give birth to a son named Immanuel. To see how that prediction worked in Isaiah's time as well as the time of Jesus 700 years later, see page 210.

Judgment Day plus one

NOT EVERYONE DIES AFTER ALL. Dooms-day is over. God has unleashed his fiery fury on the planet. But since some people survive, Bible experts are left wondering what Doomsday Zeph-aniah was talking about.

Was it the fiery fall of Judah in 586 BC? Or some future Apocalypse? Maybe it's both.

But at some point, after the doom, God prom-ises to turn his Creation around. What the prophet Zephaniah describes sounds like heaven on earth. God's "people will not do wrong. They won't lie. . . .

Content with who they are and where they are, unanxious, they'll live at peace" (Zephaniah 3:13 MSG).

At the very least, Zephaniah is talking about life in the Jewish homeland after the exile, many scholars say: "I will bring together. . .my former exiles" (Zephaniah 3:19).

But perhaps he's alluding to something far beyond that, others say—to a happy time and place described also in the last book of the Bible:

"Tears gone, crying gone, pain gone. . . .
Look! I'm making everything new."
REVELATION **21:4–5** MSG

Tower of Babel

ONE LANGUAGE FOR ALL?
God promises to give everyone "a language undistorted. . .words to address GOD" (Zephaniah 3:9 MSG). Some say this points to a reversal of the confusion God produced at the Tower of Babel, when he made people start talking in different lan-guages (see Genesis 11:1–9). Others say it's a metaphor, and it means people everywhere will worship God.

War trophy. Captured during the Six-Day War, a Syrian tank sits on display at Yad la-Shiryon Museum, Israel.

A GOOD DAY TO BE A JEW. Jews will become the butt of jokes after Babylon levels Jerusalem and exiles the survivors (see Zephaniah 2:8). But Zephaniah promises that in the future, all of that will change. Jerusalem will rise again. And with God's help, Jews will win "victory after victory" (Zephaniah 3:17 CEV). Though this could sound like a description of Jewish wars against Arab nations in the 1900s, it could also describe the war of independence they won against Greek rulers in 165 BC. Or it might simply point to God as their protector, scholars add.

HAGGAI 1:6

It's almost September, when the last crops of the season are harvested. The harvest has been terrible: "You harvest less than you plant" (CEV).

BIG SCENE
CROP FAILURE

BIBLE HISTORY	**530 BC** *Persian king orders Jews to stop rebuilding Jerusalem*	**520 BC** *Haggai tells Jews to finish the Temple*
WORLD HISTORY		*Darius begins his 35-year reign over Persia (centered in Iran)* **522 BC**

ALL DATES APPROXIMATE

HAGGAI

GOD HOMELESS

STORY LINE

GOD GETS A BUM DEAL FROM THE JEWS, the prophet Haggai complains.

God has brought the Jews home from their 50-year exile in Babylon, in what is now Iraq. They live in luxurious homes they've built. But God's house—the Jerusalem Temple—is still just a pile of rocks.

Babylonian invaders tore it down in 586 BC when they destroyed the rest of Jerusalem.

Jews started to rebuild the Temple almost as soon as they returned. But non-Jews living in the region convinced the Persian king that the Jews had a history of rebelling. So the king ordered them to stop rebuilding Jerusalem—Temple included.

But now a new king reigns—one who, perhaps, will allow the rebuilding to start back up.

The motivator for restarting the Temple project is the terrible harvest of 520 BC.

"I have called a drought" (Haggai 1:11), the prophet says, quoting God. And it won't end until the Jews rebuild God's house.

It's August 29 when Haggai delivers that message. Three weeks later, on September 21, at the end of a busted harvest, the Jews are busy rebuilding the Temple.

// TIME: August 29–December 18, 520 BC. Haggai delivers his prophecies during this time. The dates are this specific because several dates in Haggai can be cross-checked with surviving Persian records.

// AUTHOR: Haggai, or someone reporting his prophecies.

// LOCATION: Jerusalem (see map on page 292).

516 BC
Temple is completed on March 12

Jerusalem Temple

Chinese farmers add iron to front of wooden plows
500 BC

Get busy, get a blessing

THERE'S A BIG DIFFERENCE between Jews before their exile into Babylon and after the exile. Afterward, Jews seem more inclined to believe what prophets tell them.

Haggai, after the exile, tells them that their lousy harvest is God's attempt to get their attention and to prod them to rebuild the Jerusalem Temple.

They apparently start gathering wood and other supplies right away. By mid-October, the second Jewish Temple is already taking shape. It must look like a depressing downgrade compared to the first Temple because Haggai tells the Jews not to worry about it—or about their next harvest. God's going to take care of both.

TEMPLE. "The future glory of this Temple will be greater than its past" (Haggai 2:9).

HARVEST. "I am giving you a promise now while the seed is still in the barn. You have not yet harvested your grain, and your grapevines, fig trees, pomegranates. . . . But from this day onward I will bless you" (Haggai 2:19).

Temple sanctuary

Western Wall

Mediterranean Sea

LEBANON

Mt. Hermon

SYRIA

Sea of Galilee

Samaria

Jordan River

ISRAEL

Jerusalem

Bethlehem

JORDAN

Dead Sea

N

DID THE GLORY OF THE SECOND TEMPLE EXCEED THE GLORY OF THE FIRST? The Temple certainly lasted longer. Solomon's Temple lasted about 400 years. The second Temple lasted more than 500 years—nearly 600 if we count King Herod's Temple expansion.

ZERUBBABEL. Persians appointed him governor of the first wave of Jews returning from exile to their homeland. Zerubbabel (zur-ROO-bah-buhl) was a descendant of King David. Haggai said God chose Zerubbabel: "He will rule in my name" (Haggai 2:23 CEV).

TAG-TEAM PROPHETS. Zechariah and Haggai lived and ministered in the same time and place: Jerusalem after the Jewish exile. Together, they convinced the Jews to finish rebuilding the Temple.

▼ **TEMPLE UPGRADE.** In 20 BC, King Herod begins a massive, 44-year makeover of the second Jewish Temple—so extensive that many consider it the third Jewish Temple. He starts by bringing in fill dirt to double the size of the hilltop to about 525 x 330 yards (480 x 302 meters). That allows him to build a sprawling courtyard outside the sanctuary. Haggai had predicted the Temple would see better days. All that remains of it today is the Western Wall, where Jews gather to pray.

Mount of Olives

ZECHARIAH 9:9

Crowds in Jerusalem cheer when their king comes to town, "humble, riding on a donkey." New Testament writers say Jesus fulfilled this prediction on Palm Sunday.

BIG SCENE

KING ON A DONKEY

BIBLE HISTORY	**538 BC** Jews return from exile in Babylon (Iraq)	**536 BC** Jews start rebuilding Temple, but stop

ALL DATES APPROXIMATE

WORLD HISTORY	*King Darius begins reign of Persia* **522 BC**

ZECHARIAH

HAPPY NEWS FOR JEWS

STORY LINE

THE EXILE IS OVER—has been for 18 years. Waves of Jewish refugees have arrived home.

But starting over is a struggle.

// Babylonian invaders left the Jewish homeland in ruins.

// Fifty years of neglect has hurt the farms, vineyards, and orchards.

// Foreigners have settled in. And they don't want anyone turning the territory back into a Jewish homeland.

Zechariah arrives with good news, at least for the Jews. Not-so-good news for everyone else.

Zechariah in a series of visions discovers God is determined to rebuild the Temple, Jerusalem, and the Jewish nation.

"Israel will again overflow with prosperity, and the LORD will again comfort Zion [the hill on which the Temple sat] and choose Jerusalem as his own" (Zechariah 1:17).

That's a switch.

For 200 years, Jews have heard almost nothing but doom from their prophets. Zechariah's prediction comes as a refreshing change of pace.

// TIME: Zechariah's prophecies span at least two years—520–518 BC—near the start of King Darius's reign of Persia (522–486 BC).

// AUTHOR: Zechariah, or someone reporting his prophecies.

// LOCATION: Jerusalem (see map on page 292).

520 BC
Zechariah backs up Haggai, convincing Jews to finish building the Temple

515 BC
Jews finish the Temple

Cockfighting tournament near Kabul, Afghanistan

Persia introduces Greeks to cockfighting
500 BC

One night, eight visions

GOD GIVES THE JEWS A MORALE BOOSTER as they struggle to rebuild their nation. They need it. Back from exile in Babylon, they've just experienced a devastating drought that destroyed their harvest. Zechariah's prophet colleague, Haggai, has convinced them that the drought is because they haven't rebuilt God's Temple. So by September 520 BC, they're busy resuming work on it.

The morale booster comes five months into the project: February 15, 519 BC. That's about the time of the first harvest: flax (February/March) followed by barley (March–May). Zechariah sees a series of eight visions—each intended to assure the Jews that God is watching over them. Angels tell Zechariah what each vision means.

1. AN ARMY OF ANGELS ON HORSEBACK (see Zechariah 1:7–17). They're apparently peacekeepers God sent to patrol the earth.

2. FOUR ANIMAL HORNS AND FOUR BLACKSMITHS (see Zechariah 1:18–21). The horns represent nations that deported the Jews. The blacksmiths have come to pound the horns to dust.

3. MAN WITH TAPE MEASURE, HEADED TO JERUSALEM (see Zechariah 2:1–5). Jerusalem will become a crowded city.

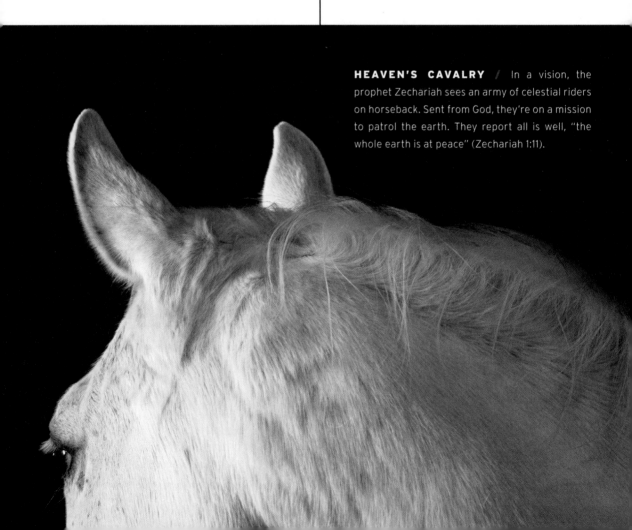

HEAVEN'S CAVALRY / In a vision, the prophet Zechariah sees an army of celestial riders on horseback. Sent from God, they're on a mission to patrol the earth. They report all is well, "the whole earth is at peace" (Zechariah 1:11).

4. **ISRAEL'S HIGH PRIEST GETS NEW ROBES TO REPLACE FILTHY ONES** (see Zechariah 3:1–10). Priests will again serve in the Temple.

Golden menorah

5. **MENORAH** (see Zechariah 4:1–14). This lampstand with seven flames lighting up the darkness represents God watching out for the Jews.

6. **FLYING SCROLL** (see Zechariah 5:1–4). A bit like an automated process server, the scroll delivers bad news to people who did something wrong.

7. **WOMAN IN A BASKET, TO GO** (see Zechariah 5:5–11). She's carried to Babylon where she'll be worshipped. She's a symbol of Babylon's evil.

8. **FOUR CHARIOTS** (see Zechariah 6:1–8). Spirit beings drive them—divine cops, patrolling the earth.

JERUSALEM'S GROWTH. Jerusalem resident Shimon Z'evi is one of some 800,000 people living in Greater Jerusalem, on about 30,000 acres (48 square miles; 125 square kilometers). That's way up from the estimated 2,000 who lived there on 15 acres when King David turned it into his capital. Zechariah said God would grow Jerusalem into a crowded city.

Good deeds trump religious rituals

JEWS LIKE TRADITION more than God does. Zechariah says so, in a roundabout way.

This news flash comes in answer to a question raised by Jews from Bethel, a village about a half-day's walk north of Jerusalem.

"Should we continue to mourn and fast each summer on the anniversary of the Temple's destruction, as we have done for so many years?" (Zechariah 7:3).

It's December 518 BC when they ask this. That's more than two years into the five-year Temple rebuilding project started in September 520 BC. Jews had been mourning the Temple since Babylonians demolished it almost 70 years earlier.

Zechariah takes the question to God, who offers a shocking reply. He says the Jews don't observe their holy days to honor him. They do it for themselves; they enjoy it.

God tells them to start thinking of others:

"See that justice is done and be kind and merciful to one another! Don't mistreat widows or orphans or foreigners or anyone who is poor, and stop making plans to hurt each other."

ZECHARIAH **7:9-10** CEV

TRADITION OF CHARITY / On Hanukkah, the Festival of Lights, many Jews give their children money (Hebrew: *gelt*). It's not for the children to use on themselves, but to give away—to help them develop the habit of brightening the lives of others in need.

PALESTINIANS IN NEED / A Palestinian family in the Gaza Strip huddles around a gas-fired light and cooker provided by a British charity. The family lost their home during an intense, three-week exchange of shelling between Palestinians and Israelis in 2009. Some 2,500 years earlier, the prophet Zechariah urged his fellow Jews to focus more on helping the helpless.

Good times ahead

LET THE GOOD TIMES ROLL—and the heads of people who mistreat Jews. Zechariah says those days are coming.

And he says it in a style that feels like the end-time writings of Revelation. It's hard to tell if he's talking about the immediate future, the distant future, or both.

Sometimes it actually sounds like he's talking about the past. For instance, he tells people to watch for the day when nations attack Jerusalem, deport half the Jews, and abandon the rest "among the ruins of the city" (Zechariah 14:2). That's a fair description of what the Babylonians did in 586 BC. Romans, too, in AD 70. But some say it could point to a future attack as well.

Zechariah promises, though, that God will send a plague on all the nations that attacked the Jews.

As for the Jewish nation—and especially Jerusalem—God will bless it and make it a source of blessing for others. It will become the place people from other countries go "to ask the LORD to bless us" (Zechariah 8:21).

PREDICTIONS OF JESUS. New Testament writers see Jesus in several of Zechariah's prophecies.

> **Jesus rides a donkey into Jerusalem** (see Matthew 21:5, 9). "Shout for joy, people of Jerusalem! Your king is coming to you.... He is gentle and riding on a donkey" (Zechariah 9:9 NCV).

> **Judas sells Jesus out for 30 pieces of silver** (see Matthew 26:15). "They handed me my wages, a measly thirty pieces of silver" (Zechariah 11:12 CEV).

> **Judas throws the money at the Temple priests.** They use it to buy a potter's field for a cemetery (see Matthew 26:15; 27:7). "I took the thirty pieces of silver and threw them to the potter in the Temple of the Lord" (Zechariah 11:13 NCV).

> **Jesus' disciples scatter when he's arrested and executed** (see Matthew 26:31). "Kill the shepherd, and the sheep will scatter" (Zechariah 13:7 NCV).

CAN I GET AN "AMEN." / Drenched in baptismal water, a Christian rejoices at being able to follow in the footsteps of Jesus, getting baptized in the Jordan River. Zechariah said it would happen. While much of Israel lay in ruins, he predicted a day when people from many nations would come to Israel as "a source of blessing" (Zechariah 8:13).

MALACHI 1:8

Instead of bringing the best of their livestock as sacrifices at the Temple—as Jewish law requires—many Jews bring the worst: the crippled and diseased.

BIG SCENE
STIFFING GOD

BIBLE HISTORY		586 BC	538 BC

BIBLE
HISTORY

ALL DATES APPROXIMATE

586 BC
Babylonians conquer Judah, exile Jews

538 BC
Persians free Jews to go home

WORLD
HISTORY

Instead of speaking Hebrew, most Jews of Israel speak Aramaic, which they learned in Babylonian exile
535 BC

Xerxes

MALACHI

REHAB JEWS SUFFERING A RELAPSE

STORY LINE

JEWS ARE AT IT AGAIN. Sinning—and thinking they can get away with it.

A century after God let Babylonian invaders conquer the Jewish nation and deport the survivors to what is now Iraq, Malachi has to remind the Jews that God punishes sin.

They're home again, returned from exile and rebuilding their nation.

They're not worshipping idols anymore—the main sin that got them booted out of the Promised Land. But they're breaking other important laws, such as shortchanging God on the 10 percent tithe of their income due to the Temple, and shortchanging the helpless by exploiting society's most vulnerable souls: widows, orphans, and immigrants.

For sinners such as these, Malachi warns, Judgment Day is coming.

It'll be a hot time, "like a red-hot furnace with flames that burn up proud and sinful people, as though they were straw" (Malachi 4:1 CEV).

// TIME: Clues in the writing point to the 400s BC.

// AUTHOR: Malachi, which might be a title instead of a personal name. *Malachi* means "my messenger."

// LOCATION: Israel, perhaps when it's still a Persian province called Judah. It's probably just a plug of turf, scholars guess. Perhaps only about 20 by 30 miles (32 by 48 km), centered around Jerusalem.

515 BC
*Jews finish rebuilding
Jerusalem Temple*

460 BC
*Approximate time of
Malachi's ministry*

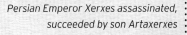

*Persian Emperor Xerxes assassinated,
succeeded by son Artaxerxes*
465 BC

*Socrates
teaches Plato*
407 BC

The Jewish tradition of sinning

JEWS LOVE TRADITION. Even in the ancient times of Malachi, some 2,400 years ago, they are already famous for their patterned lifestyle. Resting every Sabbath. Circumcising newborn boys on the eighth day after their birth. Observing each religious holiday, such as Passover.

The prophet Malachi says they have another tradition: sin.

Even the death of the Jewish nation and the exile of Jewish survivors into Babylon—God's punishment for centuries of sin—hasn't broken the nasty pattern, or changed Jewish behavior much at all.

Malachi levels God's charges against descendants of the exile:

// **THEY SKIP THE TITHE,** a tenth of their income. It pays the priests and maintains the Temple.

// **THEY SACRIFICE DEFECTIVE ANIMALS.** Jewish law says sacrificial animals shouldn't have any defects.

// **PRIESTS MAKE UP THEIR OWN RULES.** Instead of teaching God's laws, they teach lies.

// **MARRIED MEN SLEEP AROUND,** though God created each man to become one with his wife.

// **THEY EXPLOIT THE POOR,** including some of the most helpless people in society: widows, orphans, immigrants, employees, and people seeking justice in court.

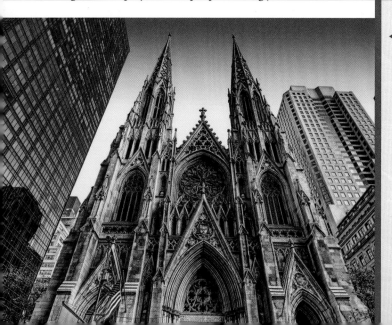

CHRISTIANS STARTED TITHING IN THE EARLY 1800s.
The first Christians didn't tithe, many historians say, because they considered tithing Jewish. Christians gave offerings.

Christian governments throughout the centuries often funded churches with tax money. That ended in the United States in 1833, when political leaders rescinded church-funding tax laws.

Ministers started looking for a new way to fund their churches and the growing missionary movement. Many latched on to the Jewish tradition of tithing. They began preaching that Christians should bring 10 percent of their income to God's "storehouse" (Malachi 3:10), which they interpreted as the local church instead of the Jewish Temple.

ANIMAL REJECTS.
Defects that disqualify an animal for use in sacrifice: blind, crippled, injured, oozing sore, skin sore, scabs, one leg short, damaged testicles, castrated (see Leviticus 22:22–24).

◄ **ST. PATRICK'S CATHEDRAL.**
New York City's most famous church was built in the mid-1800s, when Christians in the United States first started hearing sermons about tithing. With church taxes recently abolished by the government, preachers borrowed the fund-raising technique from a tradition the Jews had practiced for thousands of years.

Elijah's comeback

BEFORE JUDGMENT DAY Malachi says God will send back Elijah, a prophet who left the planet 400 years earlier. A chariot of fire escorted Elijah into the heavens.

But Malachi says Elijah is coming back on a preaching mission to "lead children and parents to love each other more" (Malachi 4:6 CEV).

Afterward, God will come in judgment.

The arrogant and wicked will burn like straw.

But for those who respect God, "the Sun of Righteousness will rise with healing in his wings. And you will go free, leaping with joy like calves let out to pasture" (Malachi 4:2).

THE LIVING DEAD / Elijah and Moses appear with Jesus, who is transfigured into a glowing, celestial-like appearance—to the astonishment of his disciples (see Mark 9:4–6). Malachi said Elijah would return before the Lord came, a prophecy literally fulfilled in this event called the Transfiguration. Yet Jesus insisted that John the Baptist further fulfilled that prediction: "He is Elijah, the one the prophets said would come" (Matthew 11:14).

◄ **SUN RISE.** A winged sun takes flight in Assyrian art from the 700s BC. Some Bible experts say that when Malachi wrote "the Sun of Righteousness will rise with healing in his wings," Jews would have thought of this common Middle Eastern symbol. But others say the Jews probably thought of God himself suddenly appearing, since Jewish scripture sometimes compares God to the sun: "God is like the sun that gives us light" (Psalm 84:11 NIrV).

THE MESSIAH'S ADVANCE MAN. Since ancient times, many Jews have taught that Elijah will become the advance man for the Messiah, a God-sent King who will restore Israel's glory and rule the nation. Isaiah described a mysterious messenger who seems to fit Malachi's description of the comeback prophet, Elijah: This messenger will tell the people, "Prepare the way for the LORD. . . . Then the glory of the LORD will appear" (Isaiah 40:3, 5 NIrV).

ELIJAH CUP. Jews often pour an extra cup of wine at the Passover meal to honor Elijah, who according to tradition will return to announce the coming of the Messiah.

SUN OF RIGHTEOUSNESS. "Sun" may convey the sense of a new day dawning. "Righteousness" suggests it will be a day when people will live godly lives. Some Christians see Jesus in this phrase, as the source of that glad new day.

NEW
TESTAMENT

**JEWS WERE READY FOR GOD TO DO
SOMETHING NEW BY THE TIME JESUS ARRIVED.**

GOD SAID HE WOULD.

"A new day is coming . . . . I will make a new covenant with the people of Israel. . . . It will not be like the covenant I made with their people long ago. . . . They broke my covenant. . . . I will put my law in their minds. I will write it on their hearts."

JEREMIAH 31:31–33, NIrV

THIS IS WHERE THE NEW TESTAMENT GETS ITS NEW.

A TESTAMENT IS GOD'S agreement, or covenant, with the Jews. But the Jews broke their agreement. They trashed even the most basic laws God gave them: the 10 Commandments. So God vowed to put his most important laws inside them. He'd bypass their thick heads and go straight for the heart.

New Testament writers say Jesus did just that, and then some. He did this by offering the Holy Spirit as a guide to anyone who seeks God—not just to the Jews. "The Friend is the Spirit of truth . . .and he will be in you. . . . He will teach you" (John 14:17, 26 NIrV).

Sad news for many tradition-minded Jews, this closed the book on their old-time religion.

No more animal sacrifices needed; Jesus became the last sacrifice. No more hundreds of laws to follow; the Holy Spirit would guide them so they'd know right from wrong.

As one New Testament writer put it, "When God speaks of a 'new' covenant, it means he has made the first one obsolete. It is now out of date and will soon disappear" (Hebrews 8:13). In fact, the entire Jewish sacrificial system disappeared about 40 years after Jesus' crucifixion. That's when Romans leveled the Jerusalem Temple—which has never been rebuilt.

Four writers penned the story of Jesus, each from a different perspective. They gave us the Gospels of Matthew, Mark, Luke, and John.

Paul, Peter, and other church leaders wrote letters to churches throughout the Roman Empire. Some of these letters got copied and passed around from one church to another, where Christians read them out loud in worship services.

By the end of the first century, preachers were already quoting some of these writings as sacred. In AD 397, church leaders met in a council and declared all 27 books now in the New Testament as inspired by God. They did this because they said the books were:

// written by apostles who knew Jesus, or by their close associates

// widely recognized in local churches as messages from God

// in line with traditional Christian teaching.

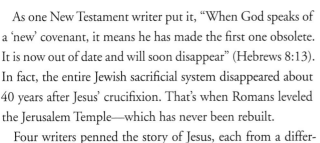

MATTHEW 28:10

"Don't be afraid!" Jesus tells women who come to his tomb on Sunday morning, expecting to find him still dead.

BIG SCENE

JESUS RISES FROM THE DEAD

BIBLE HISTORY

ALL DATES APPROXIMATE

6 BC
Birth of Jesus
(estimates range from 7–4 BC)

AD 30
John baptizes Jesus
(AD 28 alternate date)

WORLD HISTORY

King Herod the Great dies
4 BC

Pontius Pilate begins 10 years as Judean governor
AD 26

MATTHEW

THE CASE FOR JESUS AS MESSIAH

STORY LINE

A VIRGIN named Mary gives birth to a son through the power of the Holy Spirit.

"You are to name him Jesus," an angel tells Mary's fiancé, Joseph. But the child's destiny is that people will "call him Immanuel, which means 'God is with us' " (Matthew 1:21, 23).

The writer—Matthew, according to early Church leaders—says the virgin birth and the nickname Immanuel fulfill a prophecy of Isaiah from 700 years earlier. This is just one of about 60 prophecies Matthew says Jesus fulfilled, proving that Jesus is the Messiah, the savior the Jews have been waiting for.

The salvation Jesus brings, however, comes as a surprise to everyone. It's such a surprise that Matthew feels compelled to build a case for Jesus—presenting him as the real Messiah.

Jews are expecting a warrior king from David's family to free them from Roman occupiers and to restore the glory of Israel. But Jesus comes as a pacifist rabbi from David's family to free all people from the damage caused by sin.

Matthew makes his case not only by citing fulfilled prophecies, but by reporting the miracles and the insightful teachings of Jesus.

Jewish leaders, however, see Jesus as a heretic, a false messiah, and a threat to the Jewish nation. Fearing he might spark a doomed revolt against Rome, they accuse him of insurrection and they convince the Roman governor, Pilate, to crucify him.

Jesus doesn't stay dead.

// TIME: Lifetime of Jesus, from about 6 BC–AD 33, give or take a few years.

// AUTHOR: Unknown. Church leaders as early as the AD 100s said it was written by Jesus' disciple Matthew, a former tax collector.

// LOCATION: Israel. Most of Jesus' ministry takes place in northern Israel.

AD 33
Death, resurrection of Jesus
(AD 30 alternate date)

Jews drive out
Roman occupiers
AD 66

Romans crush
Jewish revolt
AD 70

Jesus' dysfunctional family

SHADY LADIES drop like rotten apples when we shake the family tree of Jesus.

// **TAMAR**, a childless widow who disguised herself as a hooker so her father-in-law would get her pregnant (see Genesis 38).

// **RAHAB**, a Jericho prostitute who helped Jewish spies during the conquest of what is now Israel (see Joshua 2).

// **RUTH**, an Arab from what is now Jordan, who started the dynasty of Israel's kings by giving birth to King David's grandfather (see Ruth 4).

// **BATHSHEBA**, wife of a soldier named Uriah, who had an affair with David (see 2 Samuel 11).

It's a wonder Matthew starts the story of Jesus with a genealogy—but even more so that he includes the likes of these women, leaving out revered matriarchs of the Jewish faith: Sarah, Rebekah, Rachel, and Leah.

Genealogies, however, are legal documents. Jews keep them as accurate as possible because family lineage determines important matters: land inheritance, the priesthood (Aaron's descendants), the king (David's descendants.)

Why Matthew included shady ladies is a mystery. One of many guesses: It shows God can work his wonders through the most unlikely people—including a young virgin.

THE MOST JEWISH GOSPEL. Matthew is the perfect first of four Gospel reports of Jesus' ministry, many say, because it's the most Jewish—making it the ideal bridge from the Jewish Bible, which Christians call the Old Testament. Matthew points out about 60 prophecies Jesus fulfilled (Mark comes in second, with about 30). Matthew also uses common Jewish phrases such as "kingdom of heaven" instead of "kingdom of God." And he compares Jesus to Moses: Both returned from Egypt, suffered in the desert, and presented laws from a mountain—Moses on Sinai, Jesus in the Sermon on the Mount.

CLASHING WITH LUKE'S GENEALOGY. Matthew's genealogy goes back to Abraham, founder of the Jewish faith. Luke's genealogy goes all the way back to Adam—perhaps a non-Jewish writer's way of saying Jesus is the Savior of everyone, not just the Jews. Yet the names don't match. Some Bible experts speculate that while Matthew traces the family tree through Joseph, Jesus' legal father, Luke traces it through Mary.

VIRGIN MARY. Matthew says Mary was a virgin when she conceived Jesus, through the power of the Holy Spirit. He said it was to fulfill a prophecy by Isaiah: "The virgin will conceive a child!" (Matthew 1:23, quoting Isaiah 7:14). In Hebrew, the language of Isaiah, the word can mean "virgin" or "young woman." Bible experts say the woman Isaiah had in mind could have been his own wife or perhaps a wife of the king. New Testament writers, however, applied a second meaning to this prophecy. They use a Greek word that can mean only "virgin." They point to Mary as that woman and to her son Jesus as the child (see Matthew 1:23).

GRANDPA IS MY DADDY / Widowed Tamar pretends she's a prostitute so her father-in-law, Judah, will get her pregnant—hopefully with a son who will take care of her in her old age. She delivers twin sons. Tamar is just one of several shady ladies dangling from Jesus' family tree.

"I'm pregnant"

QUITE THE GENTLEMAN, Joseph decides to take the high road when he finds out his fiancée, Mary, is pregnant by someone else.

But take the road, he will.

Mary may have been three or four months pregnant by the time Joseph finds out. After the angel Gabriel told her she would have a baby, Mary went to visit her relative Elizabeth in what is now southern Israel, staying "about three months" (Luke 1:56).

By Jewish law, Joseph could confiscate the dowry Mary brought to the future wedding and then report her to the village elders, insisting that she be stoned to death. Instead, he plans to divorce her quietly, to avoid humiliating her.

But before he can do anything, an angel appears to him in a vivid dream.

"Do not be afraid to take Mary home as your wife," the angel says, "because what is conceived in her is from the Holy Spirit. She will give birth to a son, and you are to give him the name Jesus, because he will save his people from their sins" (Matthew 1:20–21 TNIV).

Joseph takes Mary home as his wife but doesn't have sex with her until after she gives birth—or ever, some say.

CASH AND CARRY. A young woman in what is now Israel, at the turn of the 1900s, wears part of her dowry as coins in a headdress. If her husband divorces her, she gets to keep her dowry or its equivalent—unless she commits adultery. Then the dowry goes to her ex.

JESUS. That's the Greek version of the Hebrew name *Yeshua*—Joshua in our English adaptation of the Hebrew. It means "the Lord saves." The name works as the title of a mission statement since, as the angel put it, Jesus "will save his people."

DIVORCING A FIANCÉE. Engagement was binding among the Jews, to the extent that a couple wanting to break off the engagement had to get a divorce.

SAMPLE DIVORCE AGREEMENT. Divorced women needed a letter of divorce from their ex in order to remarry. Here's one from AD 72, found at Masada in Israel:

"I [husband] divorce and release of my own free will today you, [wife], who had been my wife before this time. You are free on your part to go and become the wife of any Jewish man you wish. This is for you a writ of release and a bill of divorce. . . . At any time that you ask me I will replace this document for you."

DREAM ANGEL Sleeping off the shocking news that his fiancée, Mary, is pregnant by someone else, Joseph encounters an angel in his dream. The surprises keep coming.

Wise men, dumb question

FOR WISE MEN, they ask a dangerously dumb question. One that could have gotten them killed.

"Where is the newborn king of the Jews? We saw his star as it rose, and we have come to worship him" (Matthew 2:2).

The current king of the Jews, Herod the Great, doesn't need to hear that question. He's paranoid enough as is. He has already assassinated half a dozen close family members—including his wife and two sons; he thinks they're plotting coups. He'll execute another son later, while he lies dying.

(continued next page)

WISE ARABS / From the shores of Tripoli, camel riders strike a pose during a festival in celebration of Libyan culture. In Bible times, star-savvy sages from a country east of Israel—possibly Iran—noticed an odd event in the sky. Whatever it was, it pointed them to the Jewish homeland where they expected to find a newborn boy who would grow up to become king of the Jews.

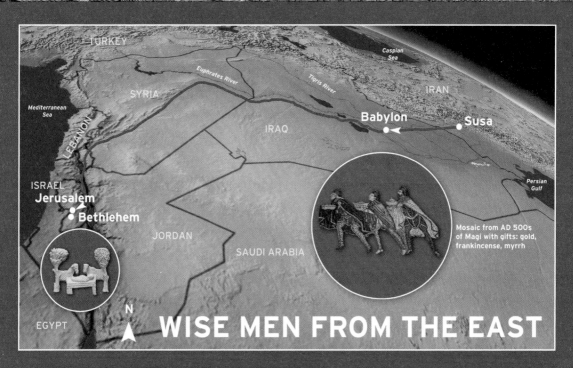

Mosaic from AD 500s of Magi with gifts: gold, frankincense, myrrh

WISE MEN FROM THE EAST

ON THE TRAIL OF THE WISE MEN. Magi may have come from Susa in what is now Iran or from Babylon, Iraq. Both were centers of astrology in ancient times. If they came from there, they probably followed one of the main caravan routes alongside the Euphrates River. It may have taken them a year or more to organize a caravan and then make the trip of roughly a thousand miles (1,600 km).

Herod responds to the question by checking with his Bible experts. He asks them where the promised Messiah will be born. They tell him that the prophet Micah predicted Bethlehem (see Micah 5:2). So Herod advises the strangers to go there, six miles (10 km) south. He asks if they find the child to report back so he can worship him, too.

The sages find Mary, Joseph, and Jesus and give them expensive gifts: gold, frankincense, and myrrh. But they don't report back to Herod. God warns them in a dream to bypass Jerusalem on their return home.

Furious, Herod orders the execution of all boys in Bethlehem under the age of two—perhaps a clue that the wise men first spotted the sign two years earlier.

Jesus escapes the slaughter because God warns Joseph in a dream to take the family to Egypt. They stay there until Herod dies.

STAR OF BETHLEHEM, A THEORY. It wasn't a star that led the wise men to Bethlehem, according to one theory. It was an unusual alignment of Jupiter and Saturn beside the Pisces constellation.

// Jupiter represented kings.
// Saturn represented Jews who worship on the day named after the god Saturn: Saturday.
// Pisces, meaning "fish," represented the land beside the Mediterranean Sea, including the Jewish homeland.

Perhaps knowing the Jews were expecting a Messiah king any moment, the sages concluded this was the moment.

Looking South of Jerusalem toward Bethlehem, 7 BC

HEROD THE GREAT (RULED 37–4 BC).

The King of the Jews was an Arab. Herod's father, Antipater, ruled Idumea, in what is now southern Israel. Decades before Herod, Jews forced Idumeans to convert to the Jewish faith or die. When Romans invaded, they appointed Antipater governor of the Jewish homeland. He assigned his son Herod to rule Galilee. Ruthless, Herod quickly pacified the region. Rome took notice and after Antipater was assassinated, they made Herod king. He's famous for expanding the Jewish Temple into the largest worship center the Jews ever had. But most Jews considered him anything but their king—more of an outsider teamed up with the Roman occupiers.

GOLD, FRANKINCENSE, MYRRH.

Ideal gifts for the wise men to bring, they were expensive enough for royalty yet easy to carry. The gold may have been in coins, jewelry, or utensils such as bowls. Frankincense and myrrh came in the form of fragrant, dried sap. People could burn it as incense or blend it into oil to make perfume. Mary and Joseph may have used these as currency to pay for their trip to Egypt.

MAGI.

Another name for the wise men, it's the plural of *magus*, meaning "magician." The first-known reference to magi, about 600 years before Christ, puts them in Persia. That's modern-day Iran. Later, their neighbors in what is now Iraq adapted the word to describe advisors who served the king as experts in astrology, fortune-telling, and magical incantations.

John baptizes Jesus

WAS JESUS A SINNER? That's the obvious question that comes to mind when we read about John baptizing Jesus.

"I baptize with water those who repent of their sins," John tells his audience (Matthew 3:11).

Then along comes Jesus. Ready to launch his short ministry, Jesus asks John to baptize him.

"I am the one who needs to be baptized by you," John answers (Matthew 3:14).

But Jesus says, "It should be done, for we must carry out all that God requires" (Matthew 3:15).

So John baptizes him.

Bible experts are left to guess what Jesus meant by "all that God requires." Some speculate that Jesus needed to link John to the prophecies of Malachi and Isaiah—about a messenger who would prepare the way for the Lord in the wilderness (see Malachi 3:1; Isaiah 40:3).

God was pleased. For as Jesus came out of the water, "he saw the Spirit of God descending like a dove and settling on him. And a voice from heaven said, 'This is my dearly loved Son, who brings me great joy' " (Matthew 3:16–17).

Jesus was no sinner, according to one New Testament writer who's presumed to be Jesus' most influential disciple, Peter: "He never sinned" (1 Peter 2:22).

INTO THE WATER / John baptizes Jesus in the Jordan River, in a ritual Christians have been following ever since. The question is, why did Jesus need John's baptism for the forgiveness of sins?

◀**JOHN THE BAPTIST.** Instead of following his father into the lucrative job of Temple priest, John became a hermitlike prophet. John, a relative of Jesus, told people to repent and be baptized as a symbol of their cleansing. He was beheaded shortly after baptizing Jesus (see "His Head on a Platter," page 347).

BAPTISM. Many cultures in the ancient Middle East baptized people for ritual cleansing. Sumerians in Abraham's homeland of Iraq used water to ritually purify worshipers. Jews took ritual baths to remove spiritual contamination, such as from touching a corpse. John baptized people who wanted to live their lives by saying no to sin and yes to God.

Satan tempts Jesus

OUT OF THE WATER after his baptism in the Jordan River, Jesus heads west—into the badlands of the Judean desert.

Why? Mark's report of the story says the Spirit compelled him (see Mark 1:12). Matthew simply says Jesus went "to be tempted there by the devil" (Matthew 4:1).

Jesus fasts 40 days, Matthew says. And during that stretch of time the devil tempts him three times, offering three enticing rewards.

FOOD. For a hungry man, this is the perfect temptation. "Tell these stones to become loaves of bread," Satan says (Matthew 4:3). Quoting Deuteronomy 8:3, Jesus replies, "People do not live by bread alone, but by every word that comes from the mouth of God."

EGO. Next, Satan takes Jesus to the highest point in the Temple, perhaps to the wall surrounding the courtyard. He tells Jesus to prove he's God's Son by jumping, since angels will catch him. Jesus quotes Deuteronomy 6:16: "You must not test the LORD your God."

POWER. Finally, Satan offers Jesus all the kingdoms of the world if Jesus will worship him. Jesus quotes Deuteronomy 6:13, "You must worship the LORD your God and serve only him."

Satan gives up, and angels come and take care of Jesus.

Israeli tour guide Ben Shiff takes in the sprawling Judean desert.

LINKS TO THE EXODUS.

Some scholars say the story links to God's test of the Jews in the desert during their exodus out of Egypt. They say it shows that though the Jews failed the test and had to spend 40 years in the desert because of it, Jesus passed. Links:

> **Water to desert.** Jews crossed the water in or near the Red Sea and went to the Sinai badlands. Jesus went from the Jordan River to the Judean badlands.

> **Forty days in the mountains.** Moses spent 40 days on Mount Sinai. Jesus spent 40 days in the hills of Judea.

> **Hunger.** Moses told the Jews that God let them go hungry "to teach you that people do not live by bread alone" (Deuteronomy 8:3)—the very passage Jesus quoted Satan.

FORTY DAYS OF FASTING?

Some Bible experts say it may not have been 40 literal days, but a way of saying a long stretch of time—a bit like the saying "a month of Sundays."

STAYING GOOD IN THE BADLANDS / After his baptism in the Jordan River, Jesus retreats to the nearby Judean badlands for a time of solitude before he launches his public ministry. There, Satan tries to lure him away from his mission.

Jesus' unlikely disciples

JESUS DRAWS A CROWD wherever he goes. Or so it seems from the Bible's report of his ministry.

The attraction:

// **HIS TEACHINGS.** Often illustrated with stories like the parable of the prodigal son—his messages sound simple yet profound; they make sense and hit home.

// **HIS MIRACLES.** There doesn't seem to be a disease he can't heal.

Men interested in studying religion often become disciples of a rabbi, a little like college students today selecting a graduate program based on a particular prof. Disciples usually pick the rabbi. But Jesus picked his disciples. Though he probably could have picked the cream of the crop, he seemed to dive for the bottom of the barrel.

Not one brainiac. All are working men. At least four fishermen—two sets of brothers: Peter and Andrew; James and John. One tax man: Matthew, presumed to have written this Gospel. And possibly one freedom fighter insurgent: Simon the Zealot.

Years later, perhaps two or three, members of the Jewish high council in Jerusalem "could see that they were ordinary men with no special training in the Scriptures" (Acts 4:13).

Yet Jesus would entrust his ministry to the likes of these common folks.

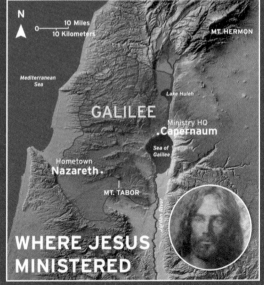

◄ **WHY GALILEE?** Jesus taught mainly in Galilee, in what is now northern Israel. Probably for many reasons. Among them, it was his home region. Also, one prophecy hinted the Messiah would come from Galilee: "There will be a time in the future when Galilee...will be filled with glory....For those who live in a land of deep darkness, a light will shine" (Isaiah 9:1–2).

ADVICE FOR WOULD-BE DISCIPLES. One respected rabbi in ancient times offered this advice to men who wanted to become rabbis: "Find a teacher and lose your ignorance" (Abot 1:16).

JESUS' DOZEN DISCIPLES. "Simon (also called Peter) and his brother Andrew; James son of Zebedee, and his brother John; Philip and Bartholomew; Thomas and Matthew, the tax collector; James son of Alphaeus, and Thaddaeus; Simon the Zealot and Judas Iscariot, who turned against Jesus" (Matthew 10:2–4 NCV).

◄ **THE DOZEN.** Jesus surrounds himself with 12 hand-picked disciples from the ranks of the unimpressive, including several fishermen and one tax man.

Jesus' most famous sermon

THE SERMON ON THE MOUNT is what Matthew calls it. Luke calls it the Sermon on the Plain.

Many who have walked the rolling hills in the area where Jesus taught, along the north shore of the Sea of Galilee, understand why both descriptions work. Hillsides slope gently into fields. Crowds following Jesus may have filled both, starting near him in the field with others behind them, sitting on the hill that rose like a natural amphitheater.

Jesus starts his sermon with a list of Beatitudes such as "Blessed are those who suffer for doing what is right" (Matthew 5:10 NIrV). His sermon is both radical and concise, a combo that many scholars say the people would have had a hard time absorbing in one sermon. So the scholars say Matthew is probably reporting highlights from many sermons.

One sermon or highlights of many, these three chapters capture some of Jesus' most important teachings:

HOW TO TREAT OTHERS. "Do to others whatever you would like them to do to you" (Matthew 7:12). It's the Golden Rule.

ENEMIES. "Love your enemies! Pray for those who persecute you!" (Matthew 5:44).

REVENGE. "No more tit-for-tat stuff" (Matthew 5:42 MSG).

ARGUMENTS. "Don't lose a minute. Make the first move; make things right" (Matthew 5:25 MSG).

ASSETS. "Don't hoard treasure down here . . . . Stockpile treasure in heaven" (Matthew 6:19 MSG).

CHARITY. "When you do good deeds, don't try to show off" (Matthew 6:1 CEV).

WORRY. "Can all your worries add a single moment to your life?" (Matthew 6:27).

MUSIC ON THE MOUNT / Pilgrims seated amphitheater-style sing on the hillside where an old tradition says Jesus preached the Sermon on the Mount. Christians built a church at the bottom of this hill about a thousand years ago. Today the Chapel of the Beatitudes, built in 1937, marks the revered site, resting like a crown jewel at the top of the hill (see photos on next page).

CHAPEL OF THE BEATITUDES / Resting on the crest of a hill about a mile (1.6 km) west of Jesus' ministry headquarters in Capernaum, the Chapel of the Beatitudes marks the area where an old tradition says Jesus preached the Sermon on the Mount. A Spanish pilgrim visiting the Holy Land in the AD 380s, Lady Egeria, mentioned the site in her letters. Below the chapel, along the shoreline, is the four-mile-long (6 km) Plain of Gennesaret.

Chapel view of the Sea of Galilee

Chapel

BE PERFECT. God is perfect, Jesus said, "so you must be perfect" (Matthew 5:48 NCV). Most Bible experts say Jesus wasn't asking us to do the impossible. He was giving us a goal to pursue, like a hiker headed to a mountain who keeps his eyes on where he's going. We're God's people, and we should act like it.

RABBI. There was no degree program to become a rabbi. People simply recognized a person with extraordinary understanding of the Jewish laws as a rabbi.

Doctor Jesus

HEALING SICK PEOPLE is what made Jesus famous—launching his ministry and drawing the crowds. As far as the four Gospel writers tell it, he never met a disease he couldn't cure.

Ailments he cured included:

// demon possession
// blindness
// leprosy
// fever
// paralysis
// lameness
// speech problems
// deafness
// shriveled hand
// excessive menstrual bleeding
// swollen arms, legs
// dismembered ear.

Once, he healed an entire village—Capernaum, his ministry headquarters: "The people brought those who were sick to Jesus. Putting his hands on each sick person, he healed every one of them" (Luke 4:40 NCV).

PHYSICIAN AT WORK / A doctor bandages the arm of a boy. A science writer from Jesus' day, Pliny, reported that one way to treat an old sore is to dip unwashed wool into honey and apply it to the wound.

RX CENTURY ONE

Bizarre medical treatment that didn't work helped drive the sick to Jesus.

Science writer Pliny (AD 23–79) recorded hundreds of the treatments in a collection of books called *Natural History*. Among several that Jesus is said to have cured with a touch of his hand:

AFFLICTION: Poor eyesight

Mix fish fat with honey. Apply to eyes.

AFFLICTION: Heavy menstrual periods

Smash a jellyfish. Apply topically.

AFFLICTION: Swelling

Mix dirt with sweat of wrestler. Apply.

GOSPEL.

The four New Testament books about Jesus—Matthew, Mark, Luke, and John—are known as Gospels. *Gospel* is an Old English word that means "good news." Bible students often use it to talk about the story and teachings of Jesus.

WHY KEEP THE HEALING SECRET?

Jesus once healed a man of leprosy and then told him, "Don't tell anyone about this" (Matthew 8:4). The Bible doesn't say why Jesus wanted this kept secret. Guesses include that he didn't want the crowds flocking to him yet. Or perhaps he didn't want them to come just for physical healing, when he intended to offer spiritual healing that lasts forever.

WHAT'S WRONG WITH HEALING ON THE SABBATH?

Jewish law forbids working on the day of rest, from sunset Friday to sunset Saturday. Though the Bible doesn't define work, a group of tradition-minded Jews did: the Pharisees. They created a long list of activities to avoid on the Sabbath, including the practice of medicine—unless a person's life was at risk (see "Jesus breaks Sabbath rules," page 344).

Back from the dead

BEFORE JESUS RISES FROM THE DEAD after his crucifixion, he raises several others from the dead.

// The son of a widow from Nain; he had probably died that day (see Luke 7:11–15).

// Lazarus, who had been dead four days (see John 11).

// The daughter of synagogue leader Jairus (JI-rus) in Capernaum, who had "just died" (see Matthew 9:18–19, 23–26; Mark 5:22–24, 35–43).

Jairus is apparently so impressed with the healings he has seen Jesus do in his village that he believes Jesus can take it to the next level. "You can bring her back to life again if you just come and lay your hand on her" (Matthew 9:18).

The girl's mourners, however, aren't convinced. When Jesus tells them the girl is just sleeping, they reverse gears—they stop crying and start laughing.

At least until the girl stands up.

Then they start spreading the word. "The report of this miracle swept through the entire countryside" (Matthew 9:26).

RISE AND SHINE / "She's only asleep," Jesus tells a group of people mourning the death of their synagogue leader's daughter. Then Jesus "took the girl by the hand, and she stood up!" (Matthew 9:24–25).

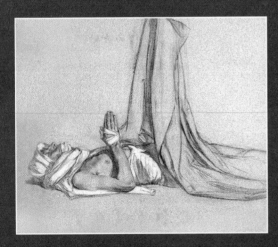

▲ **SAME-DAY BURIAL.** When Jesus interrupted the funeral of the Nain widow's son, he probably did so on the very day the boy died. In this hot part of the world where corpses began to smell of decay within hours, people commonly buried their dead the same day or the next morning.

WHY BOTHER RAISING ANYONE? THEY ALL DIED LATER. But in the meantime, they lived again, enjoying a second wind—literally. These resurrections, like the many healings Jesus performed, also provided convincing evidence that Jesus got his life-giving power from God, the Life Giver. Many followers believed in him because of these unprecedented miracles. Jesus once urged his disciples: "At least believe what the miracles show about me" (John 14:11 NIrV).

CAPERNAUM. Fishing village and home of at least five of Jesus' disciples. Jesus used this as his home base of ministry (see map page 315).

NAIN. A village about six miles (10 km) southeast of Jesus' hometown of Nazareth—about a two-hour walk. But Nain was a day's walk from Capernaum, roughly 25 miles (40 km).

The unforgivable sin

CUSSING GOD is not the unforgivable sin that Jesus warned about, Bible experts say. Nor is telling the Holy Spirit to go to hell. Or calling Jesus an SOB conceived out of wedlock.

None of these is polite. But each one is forgivable, scholars and New Testament writers agree: "If we confess our sins to God, he can always be trusted to forgive us and take our sins away" (1 John 1:9 CEV).

Yet Jesus warns a group of Pharisees, "Every sin and blasphemy can be forgiven—except blasphemy against the Holy Spirit, which will never be forgiven" (Matthew 12:31).

Bible experts say the way to understand what Jesus meant is to look at what provoked him to say that. He had just healed a man triple-dipped in trouble: demon-possessed, blind, and unable to speak. And instead of attributing this miracle to the power of God, the Pharisees said, "No wonder he can cast out demons. He gets his power from Satan, the prince of demons" (Matthew 12:24).

Scholars interpret Jesus' warning a variety of ways. Among the theories about what the unforgivable sin is:

// giving the devil credit for God's work
// rejecting the work of the Holy Spirit, who is the one who calls us to God, and
// talking ourselves out of believing in Jesus.

Pharisees saw the proof of God's power with their own eyes but refused to believe it. God won't forgive people who refuse to admit their sin and repent.

For people worried that they've committed the unforgivable sin, scholars say, their worry itself is evidence they haven't committed it. God forgives everyone who asks for forgiveness.

▶ **BAD-MOUTHING JESUS.** Jewish scholars accuse Jesus of getting his power to exorcise demons from the "prince of demons" (Matthew 12:24). Jesus says it makes no sense for the devil to evict his own. Worse, it's a sin to credit the devil with God's work—and it's unforgivable if they persist.

Orthodox Jew at turn of 1900s

◀ **PHARISEES.** One of several branches of the ancient Jewish religion. Their leaders included scholars in the Jewish laws. Pharisees were obsessed with keeping not only the laws written in the Jewish Bible (the Old Testament), but also the unwritten laws passed down by word of mouth from one generation to the next. These unwritten laws were a bit like a church manual with rules of behavior intended to apply Bible principles to current times. For example, the Bible says not to work on the Sabbath. But Pharisees defined *work* so people would know what they could and couldn't do. Jesus wasn't a fan of their new rules.

Tale of a farmer

JESUS TELLS STORIES. Not just to entertain. But to get his point across in an interesting way—without boring his audience into the head-bobbing brink of unconsciousness. These stories are called *parables*, each with a spiritual message woven into the story line.

In one story, Jesus tells about a farmer planting what sounds like wheat—a popular crop in the fertile fields of Galilee. The farmer throws his seed in a sweeping motion, left to right, as he walks the plowed field.

This seed falls on four kinds of soil—some fertile, some not. The farmland, seed, and four kinds of soil are all symbols. Jesus explains these symbols to his disciples.

FARMLAND. It represents the world.

SEED. It's the message Jesus is delivering, the good news about what God's spiritual kingdom is like and how people can become citizens of God's kingdom.

PACKED DIRT. Hard-hearted people who hear the message but don't even bother trying to understand it.

ROCKY DIRT. People who accept the message but don't let it sink roots deep in their life. Their shallow faith dies.

THORNY DIRT. People who accept the message but let the worries of life and the lure of wealth crowd it out of their life.

FERTILE GROUND. People who take the message to heart and spread the word to others, producing a bumper crop for God's kingdom.

STORYTELLER. Jesus packages some of his most profound teachings in stories and word pictures that even children can follow. "Not a single sparrow can fall to the ground without your Father knowing it. . . . So don't be afraid; you are more valuable to God than a whole flock of sparrows" (Matthew 10:29, 31).

FARMING IN GALILEE. Galilee was known for its fertile fields. That's why many of Jesus' parables deal with farming: workers in a vineyard, fig trees without figs, a farmer worrying over what to do about weeds. A Jewish history writer in Jesus' century, Josephus, said there were only two large cities in Galilee. The rest was farmland and countryside.

PARABLES OF JESUS

Gospel writers report 40–65 parables of Jesus. Numbers vary because scholars can't agree on which stories and sayings qualify as a parable. Below is a short list of 43 parables that most agree are parables. John's Gospel is a no-show. It skips parables, though some scholars argue that John includes at least two: the Good Shepherd (see 10:1–18) and the True Vine (see 15:1–8).

PARABLE	MATTHEW	MARK	LUKE
Lamp hidden under bowl	5:14–16	4:21–22	8:16; 11:33–36
Praying for fish, getting a snake	7:9–11		11:11–13
Wise, foolish builders	7:24–27		6:46–49
No fasting at wedding banquet	9:15	2:19–20	5:33–39
New cloth sewn on old cloth	9:16	2:21	5:36
New wine in old wineskins	9:17	2:22	5:37–38
Farmer planting in four soils	13:3–8, 18–23	4:3–8, 14–20	8:5–8, 11–15
Separating weeds from wheat	13:24–30, 36–43		
Mustard seed becomes big plant	13:31–32	4:30–32	13:18–19
Yeast in bread	13:33		13:20–21
Hidden treasure found in field	13:44		
Selling everything for a valuable pearl	13:45–46		
Fishing net in water	13:47–50		
Homeowner with gems	13:52		
Searching for lost sheep	18:12–14		15:4–7
Ungrateful creditor	18:23–34		
Vineyard workers getting a day's pay	20:1–16		
Two sons who won't work	21:28–32		
Tenant farmers who murder	21:33–44	12:1–11	20:9–18
Invitation to a banquet	22:2–14		14:15–24
Blooming fig tree	24:32–35	13:28–31	21:29–33
As unexpected as a thief at night	24:42–44		12:39–40
Good servant, bad servant	24:45–51		12:42–48
Ten bridesmaids waiting for wedding	25:1–13		
Three servants with investment money	25:14–30		19:12–27
Separating sheep from goats	25:31–46		
How seed grows secretly		4:26–29	
Servants watching for master's return		13:34–37	12:35–38
Lender who writes off two loans			7:41–43
Good Samaritan			10:30–37
Friend in need at midnight			11:5–8
Fool who dies rich			12:16–21
Fig tree without figs			13:6–9
Taking a humble seat at a banquet			14:7–14
Cost of constructing a building			14:28–30
Cost of war			14:31–33
Lost coin			15:8–10
Lost (prodigal) son			15:11–32
Shrewd business manager			16:1–8
Rich man and Lazarus in afterlife			16:19–31
Servant treating master with respect			17:7–10
Persistent widow and unfair judge			18:2–8
Prayers of Pharisee and tax collector			18:9–14

Two fish for 5,000 hungry men

JOHN THE BAPTIST IS DEAD, executed by Galilee's ruler, Herod Antipas. When Jesus gets the news, he climbs into a fishing boat and sails to a remote area to be alone.

Crowds from several villages have been following him—some for healing, some to hear more of his teaching, and some because they think he may be the promised Messiah. By the thousands, they manage to keep his boat in view and follow him along the shoreline.

By the time Jesus arrives at the isolated place where he may have intended to pray alone and mourn, it's not isolated anymore. Five thousand men are waiting for him—in addition to women and children traveling with them. Perhaps 10,000–20,000 souls.

Moved by their devotion, he heals the sick among them.

As evening approaches, Jesus' disciples urge him to send them home so they can eat.

"You feed them," Jesus replies (Matthew 14:16).

All they can round up is a sack lunch from a little boy: five small loaves of bread and two cooked fish. Jesus prays a blessing over the food, breaks the food into pieces, and has the disciples distribute it. The food is not only enough, there are leftovers: 12 baskets, one carried by each disciple.

FOOD FOR THOUSANDS / A Holy Land tourist at a Sea of Galilee café holds up a plate of St. Peter's Fish, a mild-tasting tilapia common to the lake. All four Gospel writers report the miracle of Jesus feeding the crowd.

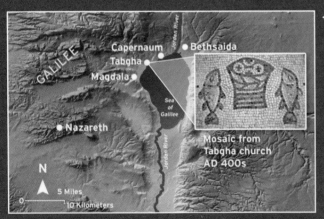

Mosaic from Tabgha church AD 400s

◄ON LOCATION. Matthew doesn't say where the remote site was. Luke says only that Jesus was headed "toward the town of Bethsaida" (Luke 9:10). But a tradition that dates back to at least the AD 300s says the miracle took place at Tabgha, about two and a half miles (four km) west of Capernaum.

JESUS, THE NEW MOSES. Matthew continues comparing Jesus to Moses, to show the Jews that a radically new day has dawned. When Jews following Moses were hungry, Moses prayed and God sent manna-bread and quail. When Jews following Jesus were hungry, Jesus prayed and fed them bread and fish.

Calling Jesus a lousy rabbi

JESUS' REPUTATION reaches Jerusalem. Pharisee experts in the law decide to take the weeklong hike north to Galilee to check out the stories.

They're not pleased.

Jesus may be healing people left and right, but he's breaking some of their rules while he's doing it.

These aren't rules in the Jewish Bible. These are rules of rabbis. Jews call them "tradition."

The Pharisees ask Jesus why he lets his disciples ignore the tradition of ceremonial hand washing before they eat. Priests have to wash before offering a sacrifice (see Exodus 30:21). But Pharisees say it's a good rule for all Jews to follow before eating—and that not obeying it is a sin.

In a blunt response, Jesus says these traditions are as kosher as hogwash. Worse, Jesus says, some actually "violate the direct commandments of God" (Matthew 15:3).

He cites one. God says we're to honor our father and mother. But the scholars created a loophole for Jews who didn't want to spend money helping elderly parents. The adult kids could devote their money to God. That doesn't mean they have to give it to God. It just means it's on reserve.

Jesus calls the scholars hypocrites who teach flawed, manmade laws as though they come directly from God himself.

Gold coin of Caesar Augustus (27 BC–AD 14)

TAXING JESUS.
Scholars try to trick Jesus into a lose-lose scenario by asking if Jews should pay taxes to the Romans. If Jesus says yes, it will erode his popularity, especially among Jews who think he's the Messiah who will free them from Roman occupation. If Jesus says no, he could be arrested for insurrection. Jesus answers with a question: Whose picture is on the coin used to pay the tax? Caesar, they answer. "Give to Caesar what belongs to Caesar, and give to God what belongs to God" (Matthew 22:21).

MEALTIME CLEANSING RITUAL.
Pharisees taught that the body becomes ritually unclean and unfit to enter the Temple area for worship if a person eats food without washing their hands. Jesus said what we put in our mouth doesn't defile us; it just passes through the body. It's what comes out of the mouth that defiles us—hateful words, lies, and warped teachings.

◀ **RITUAL BATH.**
A Sikh pilgrim in India cleanses himself in a ritual bath so he's pure enough to worship. Jews in Jesus' day took ritual baths to wash off spiritual contamination such as from touching a corpse.

Peter says Jesus is God's Son

ON A WALK to Caesarea Philippi, a scenic city at the base of Mount Hermon, Jesus asks his disciples who people say he is.

"Some say John the Baptist," they reply, "some say Elijah, and others say Jeremiah or one of the other prophets" (Matthew 16:14).

Those guesses aren't surprising. Jews of the day have been expecting God to send a messiah—a leader from King David's descendants to free them from their century-long Roman occupation. Many expected this leader to be a prophet, perhaps one coming back from the dead.

Moses said, "The LORD your God will raise up for you a prophet like me" (Deuteronomy 18:15). This may help explain why Matthew works so hard to compare Jesus to Moses.

Malachi wraps up the Old Testament by promising that the Lord will "send you the prophet Elijah. He will come before the day of the LORD arrives" (Malachi 4:5 NIrV).

Jesus turns to Peter and asks his opinion.

"You are the Messiah," Peter answers, "the Son of the living God" (Matthew 16:16).

HOME OF THE GODS / Caesarea Philippi was a worship center for Greek and Roman gods. (1) Temple of Caesar Augustus, (2) Cave of Pan, (3) Court of Pan and the Nymphs, (4) Temple of Zeus, (5) Temple of Sacred Goats, (6) Temple of Pan. Near here is where Peter declares Jesus the Son of the "living God" (Matthew 16:16), as opposed to dead and imaginary gods.

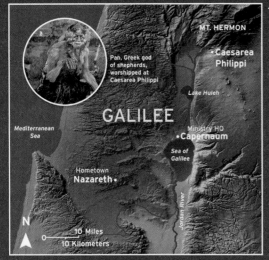

◀ **CAESAREA PHILIPPI.** Today it's an archaeological site called Banias. In Jesus' day it was mostly a non-Jewish city about a day's walk north of the Sea of Galilee, some 25 miles (40 km). In Old Testament times it was a center of worship, first for Baal and later for Pan, the Greek god of shepherds and their flocks. It eventually became a worship center for Caesar—emperors worshipped as gods. The city used to be called Paneas, after Pan. But the regional ruler in Jesus' day—Herod Philip—renamed it after himself and the Roman emperor.

SON OF GOD. "Son of God" is a phrase Jews used in many ways. It could refer to the coming Messiah and even to devout Jews—"children of. . .God" (Deuteronomy 14:1 NRSV). Peter may not have realized Jesus was God's unique Son until after the Resurrection, many Bible experts say.

Jesus shines on the mountain

CRUCIFIXION IS COMING, perhaps just months or weeks away. Jesus tells his disciples he has to go to Jerusalem and die. He adds that "on the third he would be raised from the dead" (Matthew 16:21). The disciples don't get it. Perhaps they think he's talking about his soul going to heaven.

Jesus takes his three closest disciples—Peter, James, and John—with him to pray on an unidentified mountain. The Gospel of Luke (see 9:32) says all three fall asleep, just as they'll do later when Jesus takes them with him to pray in the Garden of Gethsemane on the night of his arrest.

When the three wake up, they see that Jesus "was transformed so that his face shone like the sun, and his clothes became as white as light" (Matthew 17:2). Moses and Elijah appear with him.

Peter offers to build a shrine for each of the three, but a bright cloud lowers and from it a voice speaks: "This is my dearly love Son, who brings me great joy. Listen to him" (Matthew 17:5).

Jesus tells the men not to say anything about this until after the Resurrection.

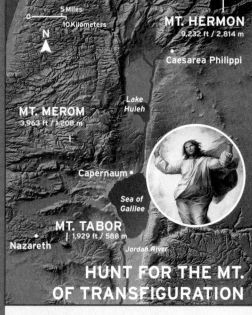

HUNT FOR THE MT. OF TRANSFIGURATION

MOUNT OF TRANSFIGURATION. The oldest tradition puts this miracle on Mount Tabor, near Jesus' hometown of Nazareth. Other contenders: Mount Merom and Mount Hermon, the latter of which is near Caesarea Philippi, Jesus' last reported location before the Transfiguration.

JESUS MORPHED. The Greek word describing Jesus' transformation into what sounds like a being of light is *metamorphoo*, from which we get "metamorphosis."

SHINERS OF THE BIBLE. The Bible tells of several people or celestial beings glowing.

Moses. Coming down from Mount Sinai, "his face had become radiant" (Exodus 34:29).

A celestial man. Seen by the prophet Daniel in a vision. "His face flashed like lightning" (Daniel 10:6).

An angel. At Jesus' resurrection. "His face shone like lightning, and his clothing was as white as snow" (Matthew 28:3).

TABOR, LONELY MOUNTAIN / The Transfiguration of Jesus into a being of light may have taken place here on Mount Tabor, an isolated mountain rising from the Galilean plains.

Jesus' advice for a rich man

"SELL ALL YOUR POSSESSIONS and give the money to the poor," Jesus tells a rich, young Jew. "Then come, follow me" (Matthew 19:21).

All the rich man wanted to know was how to get saved: "What good deed must I do to have eternal life?" (Matthew 19:16). That's his question.

When Jesus tells him to obey the 10 Commandments, the man says he does, but he'd like to know what else he has to do—as if 11 is the magic number.

That's when Jesus says if the man wants perfection, he can buy it. But the price is everything he owns.

Deal breaker. The man walks away.

Jesus turns to his disciples and says, "It is easier for a camel to go through the eye of a needle than for a rich person to enter the Kingdom of God!" (Matthew 19:24).

. . . .

LAP OF LUXURY / Elegantly appointed, a merchant's house in Sepphoris, a village near Nazareth, may represent the kind of lifestyle Jesus told a rich young Jew to give up.

WHO WAS THE RICH MAN?

Some Bible experts guess he was a Pharisee because he seemed obsessed with earning salvation by keeping all the rules.

. . . .

WHAT'S WRONG WITH BEING RICH?

Nothing. Rich people helped fund Jesus' ministry (see Luke 8:3). But scholars guess that for this particular rich man, money was his god.

. . . .

CAN A CAMEL GO THROUGH THE EYE OF A NEEDLE?

Not until someone builds a bigger needle. Jesus didn't mean rich people won't make it into heaven, most scholars agree. He was using a metaphor—an exaggerated word picture of the region's largest animal trying to squeeze through the smallest opening. Jesus' point was that it's tough for rich people to live like citizens of God's kingdom when they're focused on building their own.

Jesus rides a donkey

JESUS COULD HAVE WALKED into Jerusalem on the Sunday before his crucifixion. There's only one reason he didn't.

Some 500 years earlier a prophet predicted the Messiah's arrival—at least that's how many Jews in Jesus' day understand the prophecy.

"City of Zion, be full of joy!
People of Jerusalem, shout!
See, your king comes to you.
He always does what is right.
He has the power to save.
He is gentle and riding on a donkey.
He is sitting on a donkey's colt."

ZECHARIAH **9:9** NIrV

(continued next page)

◄ **RENT A DONKEY.** A Jordanian girl sells donkey rides to tourists at Petra. Jesus had arranged to borrow someone's donkey for his ride into Jerusalem.

TWO DONKEYS? Only Matthew reports two critters: "the donkey and the colt" (Matthew 21:7). Some scholars say Matthew was trying overly hard to prove that Jesus fulfilled a prophecy about the Messiah riding into Jerusalem "on a donkey—riding on a donkey's colt" (Zechariah 9:9), and that Matthew didn't realize this prediction was written as a poetic reference to one donkey. Hebrew poetry, instead of rhyming, repeated ideas—saying one thing two different ways. Other scholars say there were two donkeys: a young colt that Jesus rode on, along with the mother to calm the colt during the noisy ride into Jerusalem.

WHY A DONKEY? Jews associated it with royalty and with peace. *Royalty:* When David wanted to introduce his son Solomon as Israel's next king, "Solomon rode on David's mule" (1 Kings 1:38 CEV). *Peace:* A predicted savior of Israel removes the "warhorses from Jerusalem" and rides in on a donkey to "bring peace to the nations" (Zechariah 9:10).

Jesus wants the people to make the connection. They do, as they show in their response. Not only do they welcome Jesus as royalty, paving his path with palm branches and cloaks, they cheer him with Bible quotes they associate with the Messiah. "Praise God for the Son of David! Blessings on the one who comes in the name of the LORD! Praise God in highest heaven!" (Matthew 21:9).

A Christian pilgrim carries a palm leaf during Jerusalem's annual Palm Sunday procession.

JESUS' LAST WEEK.

The four Gospels allow scholars to piece together Jesus' final week, from Palm Sunday to Easter Sunday.

- **//** **Sunday:** rode into Jerusalem on what becomes the first Palm Sunday
- **//** **Monday:** chased merchants from the Temple
- **//** **Tuesday**: taught crowds at the Temple
- **//** **Wednesday**: Judas arranged to betray him
- **//** **Thursday**: Last Supper, arrest in Garden of Gethsemane
- **//** **Friday:** overnight trial and morning crucifixion
- **//** **Saturday**: Roman guards posted at his tomb
- **//** **Sunday**: Resurrection

▼ MOUNT OF OLIVES.

Before Jerusalem's urban sprawl, this is what the Mount of Olives looked like from Jerusalem's western slopes in about 1900. Jesus rode over the distant ridge, down into the Kidron Valley, and up Mount Zion's hill into Jerusalem.

Jesus rips up religious leaders

THEY DON'T WALK THE TALK. In a sentence, that's Jesus' complaint about religious leaders of his day—top Bible scholars, rabbis, and priests.

"Obey whatever they tell you," Jesus says to Jerusalem crowds, "but don't follow their example" (Matthew 23:3).

They say they're into God but fail to mention that ego is their god. "Everything they do is for show," Jesus says (Matthew 23:5). To let everyone know how religious they are, they:

// wear wide prayer boxes on their forehead and arms

// wear prayer robes with extra long tassels

// sit at the head of a table

// refer to themselves with honored titles, like "Rabbi."

These aren't God's children, Jesus says. These are children of hell.

As far as God is concerned, Jesus adds, "The greatest among you must be a servant" (Matthew 23:11).

WORSE THAN A TAX COLLECTOR. "Thank God I'm not a sinner like this tax collector," a Pharisee prays, in a parable Jesus tells. Then Jesus said, "It was the tax collector and not the Pharisee who was pleasing to God. If you put yourself above others, you will be put down. But if you humble yourself, you will be honored" (Luke 18:14 CEV).

REJECTING HONORED TITLES. Don't let anyone call you "Rabbi," "Teacher," or "Father," Jesus tells his disciples. That's an exaggeration, many doctors of biblical studies say. Jesus wasn't opposed to titles such as "Doctor," "Professor," or "Reverend." But he didn't want his disciples craving honored titles and insisting that others address them that way. He wanted them to serve—not to expect to be served.

PRAYER BOXES / Phylacteries (Hebrew: *Tefillin*) are small, cube-shaped leather cases strapped to the forehead and left arm. Inside are key Bible passages written on tiny scrolls, such as "Love the LORD your God will all your heart" (Deuteronomy 6:5). The idea comes from a literal read of Deuteronomy 6:8, which tells Jews to tie God's commands to their hands and forehead.

JERUSALEM WILL FALL. Before a generation is over, Jesus warned his disciples, Jerusalem and the Temple "will be completely demolished. Not one stone will be left on top of another!" (Matthew 24:2). About 40 years later, in AD 70, Roman soldiers crushed a Jewish revolt. In the process, they destroyed Jerusalem, burning the city and dismantling the walls.

Parable of the investment brokers

ONE LAZY WORKER and two go-getters help Jesus make a point about what it's like to serve God. At least that's what many Bible experts say is the point of the story.

Jesus says a man leaving on a trip entrusts three employees with money. One man gets five bags of silver. Another gets two. The last man—who turns out to be the lazy one—gets just one.

The two go-getters invest the money for their boss. Each man doubles his investment. Five bags of silver become 10. Two bags become four. When the boss gets back, he praises both men and promises to give them more responsibilities—promotions, we could call them.

The one-bag fellow, however, still has just one bag.

"I was afraid I might disappoint you," he explains. "So I found a good hiding place and secured your money. Here it is, safe and sound down to the last cent" (Matthew 25:25 MSG).

The boss is furious. His employee could have at least deposited the money in a bank to earn some interest. The boss takes back the bag of silver and gives it to the go-getter with 10 bags. Then he fires the lazy bum.

AND THE POINT IS?

Jesus didn't spell out what he meant by this parable. But many Bible experts say it means God expects us to use the talents he gave us—whatever they are—to build his kingdom.

HOW MUCH MONEY?

Each bag of silver weighed about 75 pounds (34 kilograms). In Bible times, each bag was worth about 15 years of salary for the average working man.

REWARD OFFERED Coins from Roman times. Jesus tells a tale of what three men did with investment money their boss gave them. Two get promoted. One gets the boot.

Jesus' last meal

THE NIGHT BEFORE his early-morning crucifixion in Jerusalem, Jesus eats one last meal with his disciples.

He knows he'll be arrested in a few hours and then executed. "The Son of Man must die," he says, "as the Scriptures declared long ago" (Matthew 26:24).

The men are eating the Passover meal, a meal already rich in symbolism. Each item on the menu represents something that tracks with the story of God freeing Jews from slavery in Egypt more than 1,000 years earlier. But Jesus adds a new layer of symbolism to the menu—one that tracks with the unfolding story of his sacrifice, which is intended to free everyone from slavery to sin.

He takes a loaf of bread, blesses it, and breaks it to pieces, instructing each disciple, "Take this and eat it, for this is my body." Then he passes around a cup of wine and says, "Each of you drink from it, for this is my blood. . . . It is poured out as a sacrifice to forgive the sins of many" (Matthew 26:26–28).

(continued next page)

. . . .

THE LAST SUPPER, AT NAPOLEON'S REQUEST /
Jesus shares a final meal with his disciples in this life-sized mosaic copy of Leonardo da Vinci's painting. Napoleon commissioned Italian artist Giocomo Raffaelli to produce the art in 1809. Weighing about 20 tons, the tile image covers the wall of a church in Vienna.

CHRISTIAN CANNIBALS.
Romans persecuted Christians partly because they thought Jesus' followers practiced cannibalism. Christian author Minucius Felix, a Roman writing the book *Octavius* perhaps between AD 150–250, reports a debate between a pagan and a Christian. The pagan charges that Christians initiate new members by having them drink the blood and eat the flesh of a sacrificed child. "With great thirst— oh the horror—they lick up its blood. Eagerly, they rip apart its limbs."

. . . .

NAME THAT RITUAL.
Ministers and priests call the ritual by various names, each name related to a Bible passage or a tradition. Three of the most common:

> **Communion**. "The cup of blessing which we bless, is it not the communion of the blood of Christ? The bread which we break, is it not the communion of the body of Christ?" (1 Corinthians 10:16 NKJV).
> **Eucharist** (Greek for "thanks"). "He took a cup of wine and gave thanks to God for it" (Mark 14:23).
> **Mass** (Latin *missa*, for "dismissed"). Early Christians used this word from Rome's preferred language to conclude the ritual: *Ite, missa est.* "Go, you are dismissed."

ARE COMMUNION BREAD AND WINE THE REAL BODY AND BLOOD OF JESUS? / No way, say most Protestants; they are just symbolic reminders of Jesus' sacrifice. Most Catholics and Eastern Orthodox Christians beg to differ. They argue that Jesus said the bread and wine "is my body...is my blood" (Matthew 26:26, 28). Not "is a metaphor." The first known Church manual, the *Teaching*, perhaps written in the early AD 100s, makes no mention of the bread and wine changing into the body and blood of Jesus.

A Catholic priest raises "the host," a wafer that Catholics teach becomes the actual body of Jesus.

Jesus prays before his arrest

AFTER HIS LAST MEAL, Jesus decides to spend his final hours of freedom in prayer.

He retreats with his disciples to a nearby olive grove called Gethsemane. Since olives aren't harvested until fall, the grove would have been a quiet place in the spring.

Jesus tells his disciples to wait while he prays nearby. He takes his three best friends with him, Peter and the brothers James and John. He confides in them: "I am so sad that I feel as if I am dying" (Matthew 26:38 CEV).

Slipping off to be alone, Jesus prays: "My Father, if there is any way, get me out of this. But please, not what I want. . . . If there is no other way than this. . .I'm ready. Do it your way" (Matthew 26:39, 42 MSG).

Security guards from the Temple arrive. They arrest Jesus and take him to into the city for an overnight trial.

A PLACE TO PRAY / An olive grove in Israel shows what Gethsemane may have looked like in Jesus' day. Under a canopy of olive trees is where Jesus chose to pray, as he waited for arresting officers to arrive and take him into custody.

WAS JESUS DEPRESSED?

Perhaps. Jesus was so upset, according to Luke, that his sweat fell "like great drops of blood" and an angel appeared "and strengthened him" (Luke 22:43–44). Some ancient copies of the Bible drop these verses. Scholars speculate it's because early Church leaders thought it made Jesus look too human. Many Christians in the first several centuries were Gnostics (NAH-sticks), part of an influential movement later dubbed a heresy. Gnostics taught that Jesus wasn't really human—that he only appeared to look human.

GETHSEMANE.

This is probably a composite word, Bible experts say: *gat semanim* is Hebrew for "oil press." There's evidence that a cave on the Mount of Olives once contained an olive press. It had a notch like those used for weighed beams that pressed baskets of olives. The first Holy Land pilgrim on record, a woman named Egeria writing in the AD 300s, said pilgrims went "into Gethsemane" with candles "so they can see." Jesus' disciples may have waited inside the cave while he prayed outside.

A savior dead and buried

JESUS IS FOUND GUILTY of disrespecting God by calling himself God's Son. The verdict comes within hours of his arrest—after a secret, overnight trial before the Jewish council, which functions a bit like a Supreme Court for Jews.

The Jews take him to Pilate, the Roman governor—the only person who can legally condemn someone to death. Pilate refuses to execute Jesus for a religious crime. But he gives in when the Jews say Jesus is an insurrectionist who claims he's King of the Jews.

By 9 o'clock that Friday morning, according to Mark's report, Jesus is nailed to a cross—the method of execution reserved for the worst offenders. About six hours later, around 3 p.m., Jesus is dead.

Sabbath, the Jewish day of rest, begins at sundown on Friday. By law, Jews can't work on the Sabbath. And preparing a body for burial is work.

In a shocker of a revelation, Matthew reports that Jesus had the support of at least one member of the Jewish council: a rich man named Joseph, from the village of Arimathea. If Joseph hadn't done it earlier, he boldly outs himself. He asks Pilate for permission to bury Jesus in his own family tomb.

There's just enough time to quickly wrap Jesus in a shroud and lay him in the tomb. John's report adds that Joseph included 75 pounds (about 33 kilograms) of scented ointment with the shroud—to mask the smell of decay. After the Sabbath, Jesus' close friends could come back to wash his body and give him a decent burial.

That's the plan.

TRIAL.
See page 375.
(*Five trials of Jesus*)

CRUCIFIXION.
See page 393.
(*Killing Jesus*)

JEWISH BURIALS
See page 388.

▲ **SON DOWN.** Jesus dies shortly before dusk on Friday. Sunset marks the beginning of the Sabbath—a day of rest from all work, including burial. Family and followers rush his body to a grave. They'll have to wait until Sunday morning to finish preparing him for burial.

Garden Tomb. British General Charles Gordon (1833–1885) speculated that this might be where Jesus was buried. Most scholars say it doesn't fit the Bible description of a "new tomb" (Matthew 27:60).

WHERE WAS JESUS BURIED? Holy Land tourists often visit two burial sites in Jerusalem: the Garden Tomb and the Church of the Holy Sepulchre. The Garden Tomb offers a better idea of what Jesus' cemetery may have looked like. But most scholars agree that the Church of the Holy Sepulchre is probably built over Christ's ancient tomb. Christians built the first church there in the AD 300s, after Rome legalized Christianity in AD 313. Jesus was buried in a "new tomb" (Matthew 27:60). But archaeologists say the Garden Tomb was chiseled from rock hundreds of years before Jesus.

Church of the Holy Sepulchre. Roman Emperor Hadrian (AD 76–138) unintentionally preserved this site by erecting a Roman temple, hoping to replace a Christian memorial.

Jesus, back from the dead

ROMAN SOLDIERS SHAKE, rattle, and roll to the ground in a dead faint. Or perhaps they were just paralyzed with fear. In either case, they froze.

The soldiers were guarding the tomb of Jesus when an earthquake shook them and a glowing angel rolled aside the disk-shaped rock blocking the tomb. Perhaps they saw Jesus walk out, too.

Jewish leaders had asked Pilate to post the guards because they heard about Jesus' promise to return from the dead in three days. The Jews said they thought Jesus' disciples would try to steal the body and then tell everyone he's alive again.

That's the story the Jews stick with. When the fainting soldiers wake up, they report directly to the Jewish leaders who bribe them into telling everyone they fell asleep on duty and that the disciples stole the corpse.

Mary Magdalene comes to the tomb at daybreak, apparently with several other women according to Luke's version of the story. The angel tells the ladies, "He isn't here! He is risen from the dead, just as he said would happen" (Matthew 28:6).

Sure enough, Jesus shows up. He tells the women to have the disciples meet him on a hill in Galilee, perhaps a favorite spot of his. There, he gives them a mission:

"Go to the people of all nations and make them my disciples. . . . Teach them to do everything I have told you. I will be with you always, even until the end of the world."

MATTHEW 28:19–20 CEV

HE'S ALIVE. In the emerging daylight of Sunday, an angel opens the tomb where Jesus is buried. Roman soldiers guard the tomb to make sure no one carries off the corpse and later claims Jesus rose from the dead. But the soldiers seem uncertain about what to do when Jesus steps out of the tomb. Killing him may have seemed redundant.

JESUS' RESURRECTION, IN A ROMAN HISTORY BOOK. A Jewish citizen of the Roman Empire, Josephus (about AD 37–100), wrote the following account of the resurrection story.

There was a wise man who was called Jesus, and his conduct was good. . . . Pilate condemned him to be crucified. . . . His disciples didn't abandon their loyalty to him. They reported that he appeared to them three days after his crucifixion, and that he was alive.

ANTIQUITIES OF THE JEWS

HOW MANY WOMEN WERE AT THE TOMB? Matthew reported only two women: Mary Magdalene and another Mary. Mark said there were three: Mary Magdalene, Salome, and Mary the mother of James. Luke said there were several women including Mary Magdalene, Joanna, and Mary the mother of James. John reported only one woman: Mary Magdalene. Most Bible experts say there was a group of women.

WOMEN AS UNRELIABLE WITNESSES / ▶

Many Bible experts say that a Christian writer inventing the resurrection story wouldn't have rested his case on the word of women. Jews and Romans both treated the testimony of women like courts today treat minors—with caution.

First-century historian Josephus offered this advice: "Don't accept evidence from women. Rash and frivolous by nature, they shouldn't be taken seriously."

Another first-century historian, Philo (about 15 BC–AD 45), called women "irrational" and untrustworthy.

. . . .

ROLLING STONES / Many cavelike tombs in Jesus' day were cut from solid rock and sealed by a huge, rolling stone placed inside a trench in front of the opening. At some tombs, like this one, the trench was sloped to make it hard to open the tomb—requiring several people to push the stone uphill. But it was easier to close, with a downhill push. Matthew says an angel "rolled aside the stone, and sat on it" (Matthew 28:2) ▼

MARK 1

Jesus ignites his ministry by healing the sick. Almost overnight, everyone in Galilee knows his name.

BIG SCENE
HEALER

BIBLE HISTORY

ALL DATES APPROXIMATE

AD 30
*John baptizes Jesus
(AD 28 alternate date)*

AD 33
*Death, resurrection of Jesus
(AD 30 alternate date)*

WORLD HISTORY

*Pontius Pilate begins 10
years as Judean govenor*
AD 26

MARK

JESUS' STORY FOR THE EASILY BORED

STORY LINE

SKIP THE BIRTH OF JESUS. Mark does.

Pay no attention to Bethlehem shepherds visiting him at the manger, or wise men bringing him gold, frankincense, and myrrh. And forget Jesus' family tree. Mark takes no time for any of this.

Instead, he jumps feetfirst into the Jordan River. That's where Jesus begins his public ministry, with John the Baptist baptizing him.

Mark, presumed to be the author of this shortest and most action-packed of the four Gospels about Jesus, rushes through Jesus' baptism, temptation in the desert, and selection of a dozen disciples. Mark seems in a hurry to get to the miracles and the unconventional teachings of Jesus—and the controversy it whips up among Jewish leaders.

Crowds welcome Jesus as the long-awaited Messiah whom they hope will deliver them from a century of Roman occupation. But the Jewish leaders, who keep their positions of power by collaborating with the Romans, worry that Jesus might stir up a doomed rebellion that would threaten them and the Jewish nation.

They set him up for a fatal fall by convincing the Roman governor, Pilate, to execute him as a threat to Roman control over the Jews. But to everyone's surprise—including the disciples—Jesus returns from the dead.

// TIME: Lifetime of Jesus, from about 6 BC–AD 33, give or take a few years.

// AUTHOR: Unknown. Church leaders in the early AD 100s said the author was John Mark. Nicknamed Mark, he was a minister who traveled with Paul but had apparently never met Jesus. Church leaders said John Mark's source of information was Peter, leader of the disciples.

// LOCATION: Israel. Most of Jesus' ministry takes place in Galilee, in what is now northern Israel.

AD 65
*Mark's Gospel
is written*

*Nero blames Christians
for burning Rome*
AD 64

*Jews revolt, drive
out Romans*
AD 66

*Romans crush revolt,
destroy Jerusalem*
AD 70

Jesus' advance man

JOHN THE BAPTIST fulfills two ancient prophecies, according to Mark. Both prophecies throw the spotlight on what many Jews say is an advance man for the Messiah.

> *"I am sending my messenger to get the way ready for you."*
>
> MARK 1:2 CEV, REFERENCING MALACHI 3:1

> *"In the desert someone is shouting, 'Get the road ready for the Lord! Make a straight path for him.'"*
>
> MARK 1:2 CEV, REFERENCING ISAIAH 40:3

"This messenger," Mark says, "was John the Baptist" (Mark 1:4). He fit the qualifications in at least three ways:

// He taught in the desert—the Judean Desert.

// He urged people to repent of their sins, and he baptized them in the Jordan River when they did. Jews associated forgiveness and ritual bathing with holiness—spiritual purification that made them fit to worship.

// He announced the coming of someone greater than him—"so much greater that I'm not even worthy to stoop down like a slave and untie the straps of his sandals" (Mark 1:7).

....

BAPTISM / See page 313. (John baptizes Jesus)

◄ **FASHION SENSE OF A PROPHET.** John wore clothes woven from coarse camel hair. Jews associated this with the uniform of a prophet, much like people today recognize monks by their robes. Spartan in his diet as well, John ate wild honey and locusts which, oddly enough, are kosher grasshopper insects Jews are allowed to eat (see locust image page 258).

MESSIAH. It's a Hebrew word meaning "Anointed One," a title Jews used to describe some of their special leaders—especially the king. The Greek translation is *Christ*. In Jesus' day, many Jews were expecting the arrival of a unique king predicted by the prophets. Reading into those prophecies, they expected this king to free them from the Romans and restore peace and prosperity to the Jewish homeland.

BAPTISM WITH THE HOLY SPIRIT. John said that though he baptized people with water, the Messiah would baptize people with the Holy Spirit. The Old Testament reports that God poured out his Spirit on people only rarely. But centuries before John, a prophet named Joel quoted God as promising that someday "I will pour out my Spirit upon all people" (Joel 2:28). Many Bible experts say that day came when the disciples followed Jesus' advice and, after Jesus returned to heaven, gathered in a room and waited for the Holy Spirit. "Everyone present was filled with the Holy Spirit" (Acts 2:4). Then those followers began teaching that God's Spirit was available to everyone.

Jesus launches his ministry

JESUS HAS A BUSINESS PLAN for launching his start-up ministry. Or so it seems.

It's a three-part strategy—every part a shocker.

1. SELECT A DOZEN STUDENTS. Many rabbis have disciples—students who learn from them and help them in their ministry. The disciples usually choose the rabbi, much like doctoral students today choose their school based on the profs. Jesus, however, handpicks his own disciples. A dozen of them—for two reasons, scholars say:

// to symbolize the original 12 tribes of Israel
// to mark a new beginning for God's people, with the new covenant the prophets had said was coming (see Jeremiah 31:33).

2. TEACH LIKE AN EXPERT WHO DOESN'T NEED TO QUOTE OTHERS. Many rabbis in Jesus' day flaunt their education by quoting revered rabbis from ages past. Jesus doesn't do that. He speaks as though he knows what he's talking about, from personal experience. "The people were amazed at his teaching" (Mark 1:22).

3. HEAL THE SICK. Jesus' first healing on record is an exorcism, which leaves the people believing that he walks the talk. "What sort of new teaching is this?" the people ask. "It has such authority! Even evil spirits obey his orders!" (Mark 1:27). Jesus goes on to heal many others in the village, and then throughout Galilee.

FISHING FOR FISHERMEN / The first men Jesus invites to join him as disciples are fishermen: brothers Peter and Andrew, followed by brothers James and John.

RUINS OF CAPERNAUM. Jesus began his ministry here, in what are now ruins visited by tourists. An octagon-shaped chapel sits over what some say was likely the home of Peter. The white-walled ruin, right, is all that remains of an ancient synagogue. It was built a century or more after Jesus, but probably on the foundation of the one in which Jesus taught and healed.

Jesus breaks Sabbath rules

IT'S THE LAW. Jews are supposed to rest on the Sabbath—24 hours from sundown Friday to sundown Saturday.

> *"Work and get everything done during six days each week, but the seventh day is a day of rest to honor the LORD your God."*
> EXODUS 20:9–10 NCV

This single law generates more than a thousand laws—most of which define *work*. Respected rabbis come up with these laws so Jews will know what they can and can't do on Saturdays. These laws get passed down by word of mouth from one generation to the next.

Many Jews, including a group of Bible scholars known as Pharisees, treat these traditional laws as though they came from God himself.

Jesus disagrees. He proves it by breaking some rules and defending himself when the scholars criticize him.

PICKING GRAIN. Jesus' disciples walk through a grain field on Saturday, pausing long enough to pick a few heads of grain for a snack. Pharisees call that "harvesting," which is work. Jesus calls it eating when you're hungry. And he adds that King David once took the holy bread from Israel's worship center to feed his hungry men.

HEALING THE SICK. Jesus heals a man who has a crippled hand. He does it not only on the Sabbath, but in the synagogue. Practicing medicine isn't allowed on the Sabbath, Pharisees teach. Not unless the person's life is at risk. But Jesus insists that the Sabbath is the perfect day to do something good for someone.

"The Sabbath was made for people," Jesus says, "not people for the Sabbath" (Mark 2:27 TNIV).

FORBIDDEN ON THE SABBATH. Observant Jews today avoid hundreds of Sabbath activities—many of which are restrictions that sound more inconvenient than helpful. A sampling:

- // Don't cook (prepare Sabbath food ahead of time).
- // Don't drive (you can walk beyond the city limits only about half a mile, almost a kilometer).
- // Don't carry a key, not even to your house.
- // Don't talk on the phone.
- // Don't turn anything on or off, including the house lights, computer, or air conditioner.

◄ **SABBATH BREAD.** There's no cooking on the Sabbath—not for observant Jews. Sabbath meals are prepared ahead of time. By tradition, the three meals—Friday night along with Saturday morning and afternoon—begin with bread that commemorates the manna God sent to feed the Jews during their exodus out of slavery in Egypt.

Take a lesson from mustard seed

TALKING TO FARMERS and shepherds in Galilee—Israel's most fertile farmland even today—Jesus teaches them about God by telling stories they can relate to. Stories about a shepherd looking for a lost sheep, or about a farmer planting seeds.

These aren't just entertaining stories. They're parables—stories with a spiritual message, usually about God or how to live as children of God.

In one short parable, Jesus compares God's kingdom to one of the tiniest seeds in Galilee: a mustard seed. It's a ball about two millimeters thick—about as thick as a quarter or a one euro coin.

"When you plant the seed," Jesus says, "it becomes the largest of all garden plants. Its branches are so big that birds can rest in its shade" (Mark 4:31–32 NIrV).

Many Bible experts say Jesus is talking about his own ministry of pointing people to God. His ministry starts small, with just himself preaching out in the boonies of Israel. But the movement he starts soon sweeps through the country. And in time, throughout the world.

Black mustard seed

HOW PEOPLE USED MUSTARD SEEDS.
Black mustard (*Brassica nigra*) grew on the shoreline of the Sea of Galilee. Today, we use the seeds to make mustard seasoning. But in Bible times, people crushed the seeds to produce cooking oil. They also used it to make strong-smelling mustard poultices—medicine bags placed over aching or injured parts of the body.

HOW MANY PEOPLE TODAY CALL THEMSELVES CHRISTIAN?
About 2.1 billion. That's almost a third of the world's population of 6.8 billion souls. Muslims rank second, with about 1.5 billion. Hindus rank third, with about 1 billion. As for Jews, there are around 14 million. Almost half that many died in the Holocaust, 6 million Jews.

MUSTARD FIELD / Toting his wooden plow, a Middle Eastern farmer walks through a mustard field. In Israel, the shrub generally grows two to five feet high (less than two meters).

Jesus the exorcist

LIVING IN A CEMETERY is a man possessed by an army of demons. In fact, when Jesus asks the demon its name, it uses Roman army lingo to describe itself. "My name is Legion, because there are many of us inside this man" (Mark 5:9). A legion is the Roman army's largest unit of soldiers: 6,000 at full strength.

The man has incredible strength. The Bible's description of it sounds like a person today juiced up on a stimulant, like crack cocaine or methamphetamine. "No one was strong enough to subdue him" (Mark 5:4). He even broke through ropes and chains securing him.

Legion addresses Jesus by name, also calling him "Son of the Most High God" (Mark 5:7). Legion pleads with Jesus to let them possess a nearby herd of 2,000 pigs. Apparently, they consider that better than being sent out to wander aimlessly.

Jesus grants the request, but the herd immediately plunges into the lake, leaving readers today wondering why, and what happened to the demons.

BOTTLED DEMON / A Sri Lankan *kattadiya*—demon expert—holds a bottle that he said contains a demon he exorcized from a person. He said he planned to throw the bottle in the ocean. When Jesus exorcized a man possessed by many demons, Jesus sent the demons into a herd of pigs that stampeded into the Sea of Galilee and drowned.

Though the man is healed, the villagers are terrified. At their request, Jesus leaves. The man asks if he can go with Jesus. "Go home to your family," Jesus says. "Tell them everything the Lord has done for you" (Mark 5:19).

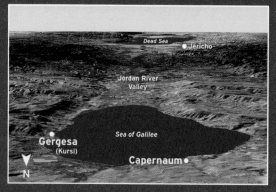

EAST SIDE STORY. Jesus exorcises a demon in the region of the Gerasenes. Ancient tradition places the miracle near the village of Gergesa, now called Kursi, along the Sea of Galilee's east bank. That's about six miles (10 km) of sailing from Jesus' ministry headquarters in Capernaum.

EXORCISM IN A ROMAN HISTORY BOOK. Writing in Jesus' century, Jewish historian Josephus said he saw an exorcism. He said a priest tied a ring to the root of a plant and then put the ring up to the man's nose to pull the demon out through the nose. The man passed out, and the priest started reciting incantations, ordering the demon out. To prove the demon had come out, the priest ordered it to knock over a cup of water. (Source: *Antiquities of the Jews 8:2, 5*).

John the Baptist beheaded

CALLING HEROD'S WIFE A SEX PERVERT lands John in big trouble—and he soon gets his head handed to her on a platter.

Herod Antipas, ruler of Galilee, apparently has a thicker skin than his wife. He has no intention of executing John for calling his marriage incestuous and illegal.

John publically condemns the marriage because Herod's wife, Herodias, used to be Herod's sister-in-law. But she divorced Herod's brother, Philip, to marry Herod. It's a husband upgrade. Both men, sons of Herod the Great, rule part of the former Jewish nation. But Herod's realm is more prosperous; it includes the fertile farmland of Galilee.

Herod respects John and enjoys listening to him, though sometimes he's troubled by what John says.

Herodias is more than troubled. She's crazy furious. An opportunist on a vendetta, she starts looking for a chance to silence John. It comes on Herod's birthday. Herodias's daughter, Salome, dances for her stepdad. He's so taken by the dance that he promises her anything she wants. After consulting her mother, she asks for John's head.

Herod is saddened by the request, but not saddened enough to set his ego aside. He made the promise in front of his guests. And he keeps it in front of them, too.

. . . .

JOHN'S DEATH IN A ROMAN HISTORY BOOK / Josephus, a first-century Jewish historian, wrote about the death of John, "who was called the Baptist." Josephus reported: "Herod killed John, a good man who commanded the Jews to exercise virtue, both in righteousness to one another and in faithfulness to God" (Source: *Antiquities of the Jews*).

John condemns marriage of Herodias and Herod Antipas.

HIS HEAD ON A PLATTER. A woman scorned, the wife of Galilee's ruler Herod Antipas demands the head of John the Baptist. The prophet had accused her of incest for marrying her brother-in-law.

HEROD ANTIPAS, NOT QUITE A KING. When King Herod the Great died in 4 BC, Rome agreed to his wish that the nation be divided among his three sons. Rome divided the territory four ways. Herod Antipas (ruled 4 BC–AD 39) got two sections: Galilee and Perea, in what are now northern Israel and part of Jordan. Herod Philip (ruled 4 BC–AD 34) got several small provinces in what is now Syria. Herod Archelaus (ruled 4 BC–AD 6) got what is now central Israel and the West Bank. Only Herod Archelaus was called "king," but Rome fired him and appointed their own governors (Pilate was one of several). Herod Antipas and Herod Philip were both called by a less prestigious title: *tetrarch*, meaning "ruler of a fourth."

Jesus walks on water

JESUS NEEDS A BREAK. After teaching crowds and then miraculously feeding 5,000 men and their families with two fish and five loaves of bread, Jesus retreats to a hillside to pray. He sends his disciples by boat to Bethsaida.

Around 3 a.m. or later, Jesus sees they're in trouble. A windstorm has stirred up huge waves, apparently threatening to sink the boat.

Three Gospels—Matthew, Mark, and John—report that Jesus walks to the boat. When the disciples see a figure approaching them, walking on the water, "they cried out in terror, thinking he was a ghost" (Mark 6:49). Maybe they figured it was the Angel of Death coming to escort them to the next life.

"Don't be afraid," Jesus says. "I am here!" (Mark 6:50).

Only Matthew reports Peter getting out of the boat and trying to walk to Jesus (see Matthew 14:29–30). When Peter starts to sink, Jesus grabs him. They climb into the boat. And the windstorm dies.

OVERBOARD / Peter sees Jesus walking on water and steps out of the boat to meet him. When he starts to sink, Jesus grabs him and says, "You have so little faith" (Matthew 14:31).

▶ **A WALK ON THE WET SIDE.** Jesus probably walked on the water somewhere along the Sea of Galilee's north shore, scholars say. After feeding 5,000 people—near Tabgha if ancient tradition is right—Jesus stayed in the nearby hills to pray while his disciples sailed ahead to Bethsaida. High waves put them at risk somewhere along the way.

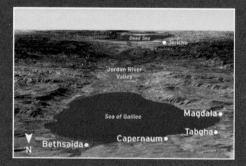

Greek water clock with small drain hole at bottom

◀ **ROMAN CLOCKS.** Mark said Jesus walked on water during the fourth watch of the night. That's Roman time for the three-hour guard-duty shift starting at 3 a.m. Romans used a water clock called a *clepsydra* ("water thief"). Some worked a little like an hourglass that drained water instead of sand.

Jesus insults a lady

JESUS SOUNDS LIKE A RACIST when he answers a non-Jewish woman begging him to heal her demon-possessed daughter.

Jesus says, "First I should feed the children—my own family, the Jews. It isn't right to take food from the children and throw it to the dogs" (Mark 7:27).

Okay, that's harsh. It sounds like Jesus—in a vicious, anti-Gentile slur—is calling the lady a bitch, a female dog.

Yet given the big picture, many Bible experts insist, the words of Jesus read more like a riddle—a setup for the Gentile ministry that Jesus will eventually commission his disciples to start.

For one thing, he's on Gentile turf, in what is now the vicinity of Tyre, Lebanon. As Mark's story unfolds, it's clear he's not there to bad-mouth the people. He's there to do what he has been doing in Israel: teach and heal.

The woman, a quick wit, replies to the apparent insult: "Even the dogs under the table are allowed to eat the scraps from the children's plates" (Mark 7:28).

"Good answer!" Jesus says. "Now go home, for the demon has left your daughter" (Mark 7:29). The woman finds her daughter resting in bed, and the demon gone.

TWO DAYS TO TYRE

ON A ROLL TO TYRE.
Jesus makes the two-day walk from Galilee, perhaps from his headquarters in Capernaum, to the vicinity of Tyre, in what is now Lebanon—about 35 miles (56 km). From there, he moved north to Sidon, another day's walk along the coast: 20 miles (36 km).

WHY CALL THE WOMAN A DOG?
Ancient Jewish writings report rabbis sometimes referring to non-Jews as dogs, just as some Muslims today call non-Muslims "infidels" and as some Christians call atheists "pagans." It's an insult the woman may have heard from Jews many times, which could explain why she seemed prepared with a comeback.

◄ **LADY OF LEBANON.**
It's a tough life in Lebanon's village of Bint Jbeil, near Israel's northern border. Locals, such as this woman, have in recent decades suffered through many battles between Muslim militants and Israelis. Jesus once took a walk to Lebanon. What he said about the people there seems shockingly out of character—and downright rude.

Jesus predicts his death

JESUS RETREATS FROM THE CROWDS.
With his disciples, he heads north to Caesarea Philippi, a long day's walk from the Sea of Galilee, about 25 miles (40 km).

There, he shocks them with news that must seem unbelievable. Jewish leaders will turn on him, and he'll be killed.

This is unbelievable because they think he's the Messiah sent from God. They expect the Messiah to save Israel from Roman occupiers, not to die trying.

What they don't understand, scholars say, is that the salvation the Messiah is bringing isn't political and temporary. It's spiritual and eternal.

Jesus promises that three days later he will rise from the dead. But the disciples probably misunderstand that, too. Many Jews of the time say the soul lingers by the body for up to three days before moving on. That's what the disciples may have understood Jesus to be saying.

Peter pulls Jesus aside and pleads with him to stop all this negative talk. But Jesus assures him there's more to life than flesh and blood. Perhaps looking toward the martyrdom that Church writers say most of the disciples would face, Jesus says, "If you give up your life for my sake and for the sake of the Good News, you will save it" (Mark 8:35).

....

MESSIAH, WHAT JEWS EXPECTED / Jews at the time expected the Messiah would be a warrior king, like David, who would lead Israel to victory over her enemies. In Jesus' day, her enemy was the Roman Empire, which had already occupied Israel for a century. Jews expected the Messiah to drive out the Romans and restore Israel's sovereignty as an independent nation. They drew this conclusion by linking promises from several prophets, including that God would send a descendant of David to save the nation (see Jeremiah 23:5–6). "His government and its peace will never end" (Isaiah 9:7).

GOOD PLACE FOR BAD NEWS / On its way to the Sea of Galilee, water from melting snow on Mount Hermon flows through Caesarea Philippi (today called Banias) at the base of the mountain. Here in this peaceful oasis, Jesus breaks the news to his disciples. He's going to be killed.

Messiah, suited for battle

Jesus, not a fan of divorce

WHEN IT COMES TO DIVORCE, Jesus sounds like his Father's Son.

"I hate divorce!" God says, through one of his prophets. "To divorce your wife is to overwhelm her with cruelty" (Malachi 2:16).

Jesus says much the same thing when a group of Bible scholars known as Pharisees ask him if it's okay for a man to divorce his wife. Jesus admits that Moses allowed it—even on the vaguest of grounds: "He finds something objectionable about her" (Deuteronomy 24:1 NRSV). But Jesus said Moses allowed divorce because some people are more callous than caring. The intent of the law, some scholars say, is to work like a pressure valve—to give an out for a man who might grow hateful and abusive toward his wife.

But divorce wasn't God's plan for a husband and wife, Jesus says. " 'The two will become one flesh.' . . . What God has joined together, let no one separate" (Mark 10:8–9 TNIV).

That seems to surprise Jesus' disciples. When they ask him about it privately, he adds that if a man or woman get a divorce and then remarry, he or she is committing adultery.

(continued next page)

. . . .

HUNTING DOWN VINDICTIVE EX-HUSBANDS / Jerusalem rabbi Yehuda Gordon builds cases against divorced Jewish men who refuse to give their ex-wives a letter of divorce, called a *get*—as in "Get gone." Without the letter, which functions a bit like a license to remarry, a divorced Jewish woman would be hard-pressed to find a rabbi to conduct her next marriage ceremony.

WAS JESUS AGAINST DIVORCE ON ANY GROUNDS?

He allowed it for adultery (see Matthew 5:32), without requiring it. After all, he forgave a woman caught committing adultery, perhaps as an example of what her husband could do (see John 8:4–11). Many Bible experts say Jesus, like Moses, would allow for divorce on other grounds, too—rather than forcing someone to remain in an abusive marriage. They argue that Jesus was simply giving the counterpoint—exaggerated for effect—to the prevailing, male-friendly view of divorce.

. . . .

ANCIENT JEWISH GROUNDS FOR DIVORCE.

One famous rabbi, Shammai (about 50 BC–AD 30), taught that adultery was the only grounds for divorce. Another rabbi, Hillel (about 70 BC–AD 10), said a man could divorce his wife for any displeasure she caused. Including: not looking pretty, not healing quickly from a dog bite, or talking to a stranger in public. There was no procedure for a woman to divorce her husband. It was a man's world.

. . . .

GETTING A DIVORCE, THE EASY WAY.

Jews who agreed with Rabbi Hillel that a man could divorce his wife for any displeasure she caused followed a three-step procedure. It's based on the words of Moses in Deuteronomy 24:1.

> Write a certificate of divorce.
> Give her the document.
> Show her the door.

SMOOCHING IN THE PARK / Enjoying his golden years, a Jewish man plants a wet one on his lady. When scholars asked Jesus if it was okay for a man to divorce his wife, Jesus said God intended for marriage to last a lifetime. But Jesus admitted that the Bible allows some accommodation because of "hard-hearted" souls.

Jesus gives children clout

JESUS GETS DISTRACTED while teaching the crowds one day. At least that's how the disciples see it.

"Some parents brought their children to Jesus so he could touch and bless them. But the disciples scolded the parents for bothering him" (Mark 10:13).

Perhaps the disciples thought of it like we would if a politician got interrupted at the podium by a parent holding a baby that needed kissing.

But Jesus doesn't think of it as an intrusion at all. He gets angry at the disciples for shooing away the children.

"Let the children come to me," he says. Then he seizes the opportunity to teach his disciples what it means to be a citizen of God's kingdom: "The Kingdom of God belongs to those who are like these children" (Mark 10:14).

....

IN WHAT WAY DOES GOD'S KINGDOM BELONG TO CHILDLIKE PEOPLE? / Some scholars say Jesus was making the point that instead of being bossy, like the disciples were when they drove away the children, God's people should be submissive—with the attitude of a servant. Jesus said much the same thing a few verses later: "If you want to be great, you must be the servant of all the others" (Mark 10:43 CEV).

KIDS GET A FRONT-ROW SEAT / When the disciples try to stop children from bothering Jesus while he's teaching, Jesus overrules his handlers. He welcomes the children and blesses them. Then he uses them as an object lesson— to teach the adults a thing or two about the value of childlike devotion.

Small offering, big heart

DURING HIS LAST WEEK before the Crucifixion, Jesus spends much of his time teaching in Jerusalem's Temple courtyards. One day, he takes a seat near a collection box in one of the outer courtyards. It's the courtyard where only Jews are allowed, men and women.

He and his disciples watch as rich men—the cream of society's crop—drop in their large offerings.

Then along comes a widow who drops in two small coins, the lowest-valued coins in circulation.

"I tell you the truth," Jesus says to his disciples, "this poor widow has given more than all the others who are making contributions. For they gave a tiny part of their surplus, but she, poor as she is, has given everything she had to live on" (Mark 12:43–44).

CHUMP CHANGE / A widow's two coins—the smallest in circulation—seems like a poor excuse of a donation to the Temple, compared to hefty offerings of the well-to-do. Jesus tells his disciples it's the other way around.

Lepton

WAS JESUS ENCOURAGING POOR PEOPLE TO GIVE AWAY ALL THEIR MONEY? / Not likely, scholars say. Instead, he may have been saying that rich people don't get special treatment in God's kingdom for being rich—as they often do on earth. Jesus had just criticized rich Bible scholars who "shamelessly cheat widows out of their property and then pretend to be pious" (Mark 12:40). By commending the poor widow's radical faith in God, Jesus was showing that the faith of the rich men wasn't anywhere close. The widow's coin, *lepton* (above), was the salary for four minutes of an eight-hour day.

Ram horn

TEMPLE OFFERING HORNS / The Temple had 13 receptacles in which people would drop their offering. The containers were said to be shaped like ram horns, called *shofars*.

Jesus and the mystery lady

IT WAS SUPPOSED TO BE A QUIET MEAL. A Jewish Bible scholar and former leper named Simon was entertaining Jesus and others at Simon's home in Bethany, on the outskirts of Jerusalem.

Suddenly, a woman shows up while the men are eating. She's carrying an alabaster stone jar full of expensive, imported nard perfume. She breaks it open and pours some of it on Jesus.

Some at the table are appalled. They scold the woman for wasting such a treasure that "could have been sold for a year's wages and the money given to the poor!" (Mark 14:5).

"Leave her alone," Jesus says. "You will always have the poor among you, and you can help them whenever you want to. But you will not always have me. She has done what she could and has anointed my body for burial ahead of time" (Mark 14:6–8).

Jesus will be dead within a few days. This anointing is the closest he will get to the customary anointing of his body for burial. He will die too late in the day, with Sabbath quickly approaching. Followers will rush him to a tomb, planning to give him a decent burial after the Sabbath, on Sunday morning.

But he won't be there.

PERFUME FOR JESUS / A mystery woman shows up at a dinner party and pours imported perfume on Jesus.

WHO WAS THE MYSTERY WOMAN? The woman is Mary, sister of Martha and Lazarus, according to the story in John 12:1–8. Luke 7:36–50 tells a similar story, calling the lady an "immoral woman" (verse 37). Some Bible experts say this is a different version of the same story, while others say it's a separate story. If it's a different story, the same man seems hosting Jesus again: a Jewish scholar named Simon.

WHY PERFUME? Hosts would sometimes welcome guests by offering them olive oil or perfumed oil for their hair, to cool the head from the hot sun. Hosts would also greet them with a kiss and wash their feet, soiled from the dust of the dirt trails. Simon did none of these. But the mystery lady did, according to details pieced together from the various Gospel reports.

◄ **BETHANY.** This was the hometown of sisters Mary and Martha, along with their brother Lazarus, whom Jesus raised from the dead. Called Al 'Ayzarïyah today, Arabic for "place of Lazarus," it's just over the hill beside Jerusalem's ridge, on the eastern slopes of the Mount of Olives.

Bethany, about 1900. Jerusalem is over the hill behind the camera.

Jesus, under arrest

DURING THE LAST SUPPER Jesus has with his disciples, Judas Iscariot leaves early (see John 13:28–30). The others probably think he's taking to the Temple the customary Passover offering for the poor, since he's the group's treasurer. Jesus knows different.

Jesus takes the rest of the disciples with him to a nearby olive grove called Gethsemane. There, he'll spend his final hours of freedom in prayer. (See "Jesus prays before his arrest," page 335.)

Jewish leaders want to arrest Jesus and execute him for teaching what they consider heresy. But they don't want to risk causing a riot during peak season, when Jerusalem is crammed with pilgrims celebrating Passover—some of whom think Jesus is the Messiah.

Judas makes the Jewish leaders an offer they can't refuse. For a price, he agrees to lead a detachment of Temple guards and Roman soldiers to arrest Jesus while he's alone at night with his disciples.

Arresting officers take Jesus to the high priest, where he is rushed through a secret trial and hanging from a cross by 9 the next morning (see Mark 15:25).

. . . .

KISS OF DEATH / Judas gives the prearranged signal, tagging Jesus as the target for an armed escort of Temple police and Roman soldiers.

Silver shekels from Tyre

HOW MUCH BLOOD MONEY DID JUDAS GET?
Probably about four months of salary for the average working man. The reward was 30 silver coins (see Matthew 14:15), likely shekels stamped in what is now Tyre, Lebanon. This is the currency Jews used to pay their Temple taxes.

. . . .

PASSOVER CROWDS.
Greater Jerusalem was home to an estimated 100,000 souls. During Passover week, the population exploded to anywhere from double that, to 10 times that many: a million. Ancient estimates vary wildly.

. . . .

WHY DID JUDAS TURN JESUS IN?
Mark doesn't say. Luke and John both say Satan entered into him (see Luke 22:3; John 13:27). Beyond demon possession, two popular theories are that he wanted the money or he wanted to force Jesus' hand as Israel's Messiah and provoke a Jewish rebellion to drive out the Romans. In either case, he seemed shocked that the Jews decided to execute Jesus. When he realized that this is where the case was going, he returned the reward and then hanged himself.

Jesus, back from the dead

BY FIRST LIGHT after the Saturday Sabbath, Mary Magdalene and some other women are walking to Jesus' tomb to finish what was started on Friday: preparing his body for burial.

Along the way, someone asks, "Who will roll away the stone for us from the entrance to the tomb?" (Mark 16:3). Mark adds that it's a whopper of a stone. Most were disk-shaped, like a stone Frisbee (see picture page 339).

They need not have worried.

The stone is already rolled away. A young man is sitting beside the entrance—an angel according to other Gospel reports.

"Don't be alarmed," the angel says. "You are looking for Jesus of Nazareth, who was crucified. He isn't here! He is risen from the dead! Look, this is where they laid his body. Now go and tell his disciples, including Peter, that Jesus is going ahead of you to Galilee. You will see him there, just as he told you before he died" (Mark 16:6–7).

Mark says the bewildered women left and said nothing to anyone. This is where the oldest copies of Mark's account ends. Other writers say that the women do eventually find the courage to report what seems impossible to believe—that Jesus is alive and headed home to Galilee.

THE END / Mark's Gospel ends after verse eight in the Codex Sinaiticus, the oldest complete copy of the New Testament—handwritten more than 1,600 years ago.

◀ **OUT OF THE TOMB.** Mary Magdalene sees the risen Jesus. But in the oldest copies of Mark's Gospel, she's too shocked to tell anyone. At least at first, as Mark reports it.

WHAT ABOUT VERSES 9–20? They aren't in the oldest copies of Mark's Gospel. Church leaders in the first couple of centuries seemed unaware of them. And Bible experts say they're written in a different style, and using words Mark didn't use earlier. For reasons such as these, most scholars say verses 9–20 are an add-on perhaps by some editor troubled by Mark's odd ending. As the theory goes, the editor simply pulled facts from the other Gospel stories and tacked them onto Mark's version to end the story with the Ascension of Jesus into heaven and the disciples beginning their job of spreading the teachings of Jesus.

LUKE 2:1-20

Joseph and Mary travel to Bethlehem for a census. Finding no place to stay, they camp in a shelter for livestock, possibly a cave.

BIG SCENE
JESUS, BORN IN A BARN

BIBLE HISTORY

ALL DATES APPROXIMATE

6 BC
Birth of Jesus (estimates range from 7–4 BC)

WORLD HISTORY

Herod begins expanding the Temple
20 BC

Herod the Great dies, three sons take over
4 BC

LUKE

JESUS, THROUGH THE EYES OF A DOC

STORY LINE

A DOCTOR'S VIEW OF JESUS. That's the Gospel of Luke, according to early Church leaders. They said it was written by a physician named Luke who traveled with the apostle Paul.

If that tradition is right, it helps explain why Luke gives us:

// the most detailed version of Jesus' birth

// the only account of Jesus' parable of the Good Samaritan who helped an injured traveler

// emphasis on Jesus' concern for the needy.

Luke begins his story with Gabriel announcing the births of John the Baptist and Jesus. Unlike other Gospels, Luke adds the story of 12-year-old Jesus talking theological shop with Jerusalem scholars. Then, like the other Gospels, Luke fast-forwards to the baptism of Jesus, which marks the beginning of Jesus' public ministry.

Then the Gospel is off and running, with Luke reporting on the teachings of Jesus, along with his miraculous healings, the Crucifixion, and the Resurrection. But Luke tells Jesus' story in a way that, more than the other Gospels, emphasizes Jesus' concern for society's hurting people.

Dr. Luke wasn't a Jew. Scholars say that, too, comes through in his writing. He alone traces Jesus' family tree all the way back to Adam, though Matthew traces him back to only Abraham. While Matthew portrays Jesus as the promised Messiah the Jews are expecting, Luke paints a portrait of him as the Savior of everyone—Jews and non-Jews.

// **TIME:** Lifetime of Jesus, from about 6 BC– AD 33, give or take a few years.

// **AUTHOR:** Unknown. Early Church leaders said the man who wrote this Gospel along with the book of Acts was Paul's colleague: "Luke, the beloved doctor" (Colossians 4:14).

// **LOCATION:** Israel. Most of Jesus' ministry takes place in Galilee, in north Israel.

AD 30
*Jesus begins his ministry
(AD 28 alternate date)*

AD 33 *Death and resurrection of Jesus
(AD 30 alternate date)*

*Pontius Pilate, a Roman,
appointed Judean governor*
AD 26

*Rome fires
Pontius Pilate*
AD 36

Birth announcements from heaven

JESUS AND JOHN THE BAPTIST each get a celestial introduction.

Gabriel, an angel who explained visions to Daniel 600 years earlier, provides the birth announcements for both of them.

First, Gabriel appears to an old priest, Zechariah, who's serving his twice-annual one-week rotation of Temple duty in Jerusalem.

"Your wife, Elizabeth, will give you a son, and you are to name him John. . . . He will be a man with the spirit and power of Elijah. He will prepare the people for the coming of the Lord" (Luke 1:13, 17).

Six months later Gabriel appears to Mary, a young woman engaged to a Nazareth carpenter, Joseph.

"You will conceive and give birth to a son, and you will name him Jesus. He will be very great and will be called the Son of the Most High. . . . His Kingdom will never end!" (Luke 1:31–33).

BEYOND A HALLMARK BIRTH ANNOUNCEMENT / Gabriel tells Mary, an unmarried virgin, that she will soon have a son she's to name Jesus.

WHO'S THEOPHILUS? He's the mysterious person for whom the books of Luke and Acts were written. Some scholars guess he was a Roman official in charge of Paul's trial, and that Luke was giving him background about the Christian movement to show that Christians were more of an asset to the Roman Empire than a threat.

WERE JESUS AND JOHN THE BAPTIST COUSINS? The Bible doesn't say. It says only that their mothers were related. Gabriel tells Mary "your relative Elizabeth [John's mother] has become pregnant in her old age!" (Luke 1:36).

VIRGIN BIRTH. When Mary asks Gabriel how she will become pregnant since she's a virgin and her marriage with Joseph is still apparently many months away, Gabriel simply says, "The Holy Spirit will come down to you, and God's power will come over you" (Luke 1:35 CEV). Exactly how God's Spirit produces the child is unknown. But the description is similar to other instances of God's Spirit changing people—as the Spirit did later by enabling the disciples to speak in languages they hadn't learned (see Acts 2:4)

Born in a Bethlehem barn

ROMAN EMPEROR AUGUSTUS orders a census. In the Jewish homeland, it's decided—perhaps by the Jews themselves—that the best way to get an accurate record is for every man to take his family to his ancestral hometown.

For Joseph, that's Bethlehem—hometown of his ancestor King David.

There, his fiancée, Mary, delivers her son, Jesus. The inn was full, so they stayed in a shelter for animals—perhaps a cave that served as a barn.

That night, in a nearby field where shepherds are guarding their flock, a crowd of angels lights up the darkness. One speaks: "I bring you good news that will bring great joy to all people. The Savior—yes, the Messiah, the Lord—has been born today in Bethlehem, the city of David! And you will recognize him by this sign: You will find a baby wrapped snugly in strips of cloth, lying in a manger" (Luke 2:10–12).

The shepherds rush to Bethlehem, where they find Jesus and then spread the word about what has just happened.

. . . .

UNDERGROUND PRAYER / A nun pauses for prayer in the remains of a cave below Bethlehem's Church of the Nativity. Christianity's oldest church was built above the cave in the AD 300s, shortly after the Roman Empire legalized the religion.

MANGER.

It's a feeding trough for animals. Soranus, a Roman physician a century later who wrote a book about delivering babies, recommended feeding troughs as cribs. He said they were tilted just enough to properly elevate the baby's head.

. . . .

WHEN DID THE CENSUS TAKE PLACE?

Unknown. "This was the first census taken when Quirinius was governor of Syria" (Luke 2:2). A Jewish historian of that century, Josephus, says Quirinius wasn't appointed governor until AD 6. But that's 10 years after the death of King Herod, whom the Bible says ordered the slaughter of Bethlehem boys in an attempt to kill Baby Jesus. Some scholars theorize that Quirinius served an earlier term, too. A partial inscription suggests he may have served from 10–7 BC.

. . . .

BETHLEHEM, THE PROPHECY.
See page 275.

The dedication of Baby Jesus

JESUS IS BORN INTO A POOR FAMILY. The evidence shows up at his infant dedication 40 days later. His parents bring the offering that Jewish law allows for poor people: a pair of doves or pigeons (see Leviticus 12:8). Families that can afford it bring the birds along with a year-old lamb.

Like other Jewish boys, Jesus is circumcised and given his name eight days after his birth. But as Mary's first child, he must also be taken to the Jerusalem Temple and dedicated to God. By Jewish law, Mary has to wait another 33 days after the circumcision before she can go to the Temple. This waiting period is part of the ritual purification after the bleeding associated with childbirth.

Dedicating Jesus is an old priest named Simeon. God's Spirit had promised Simeon he would see the Messiah before he died. Simeon somehow recognizes Jesus as the Messiah, calling him "a light to reveal God to the nations" (Luke 2:32).

Listening in is Anna, an 84-year-old prophetess. She joins in praising God, too, and spreads the word that the Messiah has finally been born.

DEDICATING JESUS. An elderly priest dedicates Baby Jesus, about six weeks old, while a prophetess praises God for finally sending the Messiah.

CIRCUMCISION. See page 20.

JESUS, THE NAME. It's the Greek-friendly version of the Hebrew name *Joshua*, much like *Jacque* is the French version of *James*. The name of Jesus means "the Lord saves," which seems a fitting name for someone Luke calls "a mighty Savior" (Luke 1:69).

PURIFICATION FROM BLEEDING OF CHILDBIRTH. Women were considered ritually unclean when bleeding from their menstrual cycle or after childbirth, which produces bleeding that can last 4–6 weeks. They were not permitted to worship at the Temple during this time.

Jesus, the 12-year-old

JOSEPH AND MARY are faithful Jews, if their frequent trips to the Jerusalem Temple are any measure of faith. Luke says they traveled there every spring, to celebrate Passover. That's about a four-day trip each way from Nazareth, some 90 miles (145 km), depending on the route taken.

When Jesus is 12 years old, it seems they travel with a group—a good idea for protection from highway robbers. The clue is that when it's time to come home, they travel a full day before realizing he isn't with them. They must have figured he was traveling with friends or relatives.

He's missing for three days. Perhaps the travel day, followed by his parents' one-day trip back to Jerusalem, and then another day scouring Jerusalem for their son.

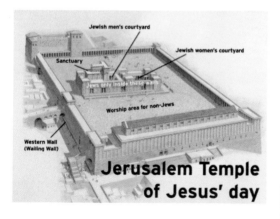

Jerusalem Temple of Jesus' day

HEROD'S MASSIVE TEMPLE / Twelve-year-old Jesus may have been in any one of three Temple courtyards talking with the scholars: the sprawling courtyard of the non-Jews, the courtyard for Jews only (including women), or perhaps the inner courtyard for Jewish men only. The entire hilltop complex would have held about 27 football fields (see larger picture of Temple, pages 292–293).

They find him at the Temple, wowing scholars with his questions and answers. Mary, not impressed, scolds him: "Why have you done this to us? Your father and I have been frantic, searching for you everywhere" (Luke 2:48).

Jesus says he doesn't understand why they needed to search. "Didn't you know that I had to be here, dealing with the things of my Father?" (Luke 2:49 MSG).

ROAD TO JERUSALEM

PASSOVER / See page 38.

WHAT DID JESUS AND THE SCHOLARS TALK ABOUT? / Probably the Jewish laws and religion. The *Infancy Gospel of Thomas*, possibly written a century later, says Jesus asked well-informed questions about Jewish law and he offered his own take on some of those laws.

Nazareth turns on native Son

WITH HIS FAME ON THE RISE, Jesus returns home to Nazareth. But he gets the religious folks so upset that they try to throw him off a cliff.

It happens on the Sabbath. He stands up and reads a Bible passage that many Jews say refers to the Messiah.

> *"The Lord's Spirit has come to me, because he has chosen me to tell the good news to the poor. The Lord has sent me to announce freedom for prisoners, to give sight to the blind, to free everyone who suffers."*
>
> LUKE **4:18**, QUOTING ISAIAH **61:1** CEV

Reading this isn't the problem.

The problem is what Jesus says next: "The Scripture you've just heard has been fulfilled this very day!" (Luke 4:21). In other words, "I'm the Messiah."

Jesus doesn't expect them to believe it. He does, however, expect them to demand Messiah-style miracles as proof—which he refuses to perform.

A riot erupts inside the worship center. The crowd takes Jesus to the edge of town to pitch him over a cliff, but he slips away.

*Israel, no shortage of stones—
the preferred method of execution*

READING THE SYNAGOGUE SCROLL.

Holding a pointer (Hebrew: *yad*) allows a synagogue worship leader to read scripture without touching the scroll, which would soil it with body oil. As a respected rabbi returning home, Jesus was invited to read the day's passage and talk about it. The hometown crowd was in for a surprise.

. . . .

WHY DIDN'T THE NAZARETH JEWS BELIEVE JESUS WAS THE MESSIAH?

Most Jews didn't expect God's promised Savior to come from the family of a poor carpenter. Nor did they expect a pacifist rabbi. They were looking for a fighter fit to become a king.

. . . .

WHY DID JESUS REFUSE TO DO MIRACLES IN NAZARETH?

He typically did miracles not to convince skeptics but to help those who believed in him. Matthew's version of the story says, "He did only a few miracles there because of their unbelief" (Matthew 13:58).

. . . .

◄ WHY DID JESUS' FORMER NEIGHBORS TRY TO KILL HIM?

They assumed he was a liar, which made him a false prophet. Jewish law ordered false prophets "put to death" (Deuteronomy 13:5). The manner of execution was either pelting the offender with stones or throwing the person at the stones by tossing the individual off a cliff like a sack of bone garbage.

Jesus heals a paralyzed man

JESUS DOES A GOD THING—telling a man his sins are forgiven.

Religious scholars are watching: Pharisees and teachers of the law. Mumbling among themselves, they call Jesus a blasphemer for claiming he has the authority to do what only God can do.

This happens in the fishing village of Capernaum, Jesus' ministry headquarters and the hometown of several of his disciples. Jesus is inside a house, teaching a tight-packed crowd of people. Luke says they came from all over what is now Israel. The scholars likely come from Jerusalem, the Oxford of ancient Jewish scholarship.

Some men carrying a paralyzed man on a mat try unsuccessfully to push through the crowd and reach Jesus. Instead, they resort to carrying the man to the roof. There, they remove some tile and lower him to Jesus—who's so impressed with their faith that he tells the paralytic: "Young man, your sins are forgiven" (Luke 5:20).

When Jesus somehow senses the objection of the scholars, he asks what's harder: to forgive the man or to heal him. Jesus does both. The healed man jumps up and runs off praising God—now carrying the mat that once carried him.

. . . .

PHARISEE / One of four main Jewish groups, along with Sadducees, Zealots, and Essenes. See page 321.

. . . .

TEACHERS OF THE LAW / Sometimes called "scribes," they were the Bible scholars of their day—with a dash of politician. They advised Jewish leaders, such as the top priests who told the Jews what they should and shouldn't do if they hoped to stay in a good relationship with God.

CAPERNAUM FLATTOPS / Roofs of Capernaum homes, like most roofs throughout ancient Israel, were flat. Outside stairs or ladders allowed people to climb up, using the roof as a place to work or relax. Most roofs were probably built of mud, sticks, and thatch. Some were covered with tiles of baked mud. Several men once dug through a roof to reach Jesus.

Pacifist Jesus helps a man of war

A ROMAN OFFICER is worried.

He's a centurion, commander of a unit of 100 soldiers. And he's concerned about one of his servants who is "sick and near death" (Luke 7:2). Matthew's version of the story says the servant is a boy "paralyzed and in terrible pain" (Matthew 8:6).

Piecing the two stories together, it looks like the soldier, who's stationed in Capernaum, sends some respected Jewish elders to Jesus. They ask Jesus to come and heal the boy, commending the soldier: "If anyone deserves your help, he does. . . for he loves the Jewish people and even built a synagogue for us" (Luke 7:4–5).

Jesus heads toward the soldier's home. Along the way the soldier meets him. He tells Jesus he's not worthy of having him in his home.

"Just say the word from where you are, and my servant will be healed," the soldier says.

"I know this because I am under the authority of my superior officers, and I have authority over my soldiers. I only need to say, 'Go,' and they go" (Luke 7:7–8).

Astonished, Jesus replies: "I tell you, I haven't seen faith like this in all Israel!" (Luke 7:9).

When the officer and his friends return home, they find the boy healed.

CENTURION'S RABBI / When the servant of a Roman commander falls deathly ill, the soldier calls on Jesus for help.

Ruins of Capernaum synagogue

◄ **HOW COULD A SOLDIER AFFORD TO BUILD A SYN-AGOGUE?** An average worker's pay was a denarius a day—about 300 a year. Centurions made more than 10 to 50 times that. Their salaries ranged from 3,750 to 15,000 denarii.

WHY WOULD HE BUILD A SYNAGOGUE? He may have become a "God-fearer," at least a partial convert to Judaism. Some non-Jews worshipped God but stopped short of the two most extreme Jewish requirements: circumcision and eating only kosher food.

WHY THE SOLDIER DIDN'T WANT JESUS IN HIS HOME. The soldier probably knew that stepping into the home of a non-Jew would have rendered Jesus ritually unclean—at least in the eyes of some Jews. This would have left Jesus unfit to worship at the Temple until he went through a series of cleansing rituals, including a bath. Though this attitude toward Gentiles isn't mentioned in the Bible, some rabbis from Roman times taught it: "The homes of Gentiles are unclean" (Mishnah, *Ohalot* 18.7).

Jesus, the storm soother

BEYOND STORM CHASING, Jesus talks to the wind—and the wind listens. It's a miracle reported in three Gospels: Matthew, Mark, and Luke.

Piecing together the three accounts of this story, Jesus has finished teaching a crowd of people somewhere near Capernaum. Exhausted, he gets in a boat with his disciples and tells them to sail across the lake to the village of Gergesa.

Jesus falls into a deep sleep. He's still sleeping when a sudden windstorm churns up waves big enough to flip the boat. Even the seafaring fishermen among the disciples are afraid.

They wake Jesus screaming, "We're going to drown!" (Luke 8:24).

"Where is your faith?" Jesus answers the men. Turning to the wind he says, "Silence!" (Mark 4:39).

Suddenly, the wind hushes and the waves collapse, placid.

In astonishment mingled with terror, the disciples whisper to each other: "Who is this? He can give orders to the wind and the waves, and they obey him!" (Luke 8:25 CEV).

TAKING ON WATER / Jesus and some of his disciples sail into a windstorm on the Sea of Galilee. Afternoon windstorms spawned by cool sea breezes clashing with hot air rising from the shallow lake can churn up waves topping out at seven feet (two meters), more than enough to swamp a small boat.

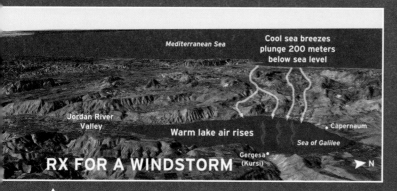

Mediterranean Sea

Cool sea breezes plunge 200 meters below sea level

Jordan River Valley

Warm lake air rises

Capernaum

Sea of Galilee

Gergesa (Kursi)

N

RX FOR A WINDSTORM

▲ **SUDDEN WINDSTORMS.** Cool sea breezes pour in from the Mediterranean Sea, 26 miles (42 km) west. When they crash into the hot afternoon air rising off the shallow lake that sits near the edge of the Syrian Desert, violent windstorms can erupt without notice.

SEA OF GALILEE, THE SPECS.

It's a freshwater lake shaped like a harp and known by locals as the Sea of Kinnereth, Hebrew for "harp."

> About 700 feet (213 meters) below sea level

> 13 miles long, 7 miles at its widest (21 x 11 km)

> Shallow: only about 50 yards (46 meters) deep at its deepest

> Surrounded by hills, some soaring above the lake's surface by up to half a mile (almost 1 km)

The bleeding stops

IN A CROWD BRUSHING AGAINST HIM, Jesus feels the touch of someone who has been healed.

He has just returned from the Gentile side of the Galilee lake, on the east. Back in his home region on the west, he's welcomed by a rush of Jews.

"Someone deliberately touched me," he says, "for I felt healing power go out from me" (Luke 8:46). A woman admits her sin, falling to her knees and trembling.

And it is a sin by Jewish standards if she's suffering from menstrual bleeding, as many Bible experts guess.

Jewish law says women are ritually unclean for a week after the start of their menstrual cycle (see Leviticus 15:19). Only afterward—and after taking a ritual bath—are they permitted to have contact with others. Until then, anyone they touch becomes ritually unclean, too, which leaves them unfit to worship God for the rest of the day. They, too, must purify themselves with a ritual bath.

With his first word, however, Jesus puts the woman at ease. "Daughter," he says, "your faith has made you well. Go in peace" (Luke 8:48).

HEALED / After a dozen years of incessant bleeding, a woman is healed when she touches Jesus' robe. Jesus tells her it was her faith that made her well.

◄ WHAT CAUSED THE WOMAN'S BLEEDING. She may have suffered from menorrhagia, a disease that produces excessive or prolonged menstrual bleeding.

ROMAN PRESCRIPTIONS FOR EX-CESSIVE MENSTRUAL BLEEDING. Mark's version of the story said she "suffered a great deal from many doctors" and "spent everything she had" looking for a cure (Mark 5:26). Scores of treatments for this particular ailment are preserved in a Roman science book from the first century: *Natural History*. One painful prescription: crush a jellyfish and apply it topically.

RITUAL BATH. See page 325.

How to be a good Samaritan

PICKING THE BRAIN OF JESUS, perhaps looking for flaws in his teachings, an expert in Jewish religion asks him a question.

Jesus had just told the man to "love the LORD your God" and "love your neighbor as yourself"— both of which are quotes from the Jewish Bible (Deuteronomy 6:5; Leviticus 19:18).

That's when the man asks, "Who is my neighbor?" (Luke 10:29). He probably expects Jesus to say "your fellow Jews," since that was a common interpretation of the ancient law. But Jesus takes the law in a new direction.

He does it with one of his most famous parables. It's about a good Samaritan, a mixed race of people that many Jews hated.

A Jewish man traveling the daylong walk between Jericho and Jerusalem gets mugged and left for dead. Two Jews walk past him, first a priest and later a Temple assistant. It's a Samaritan who bothers to stop and help the man, treating his wounds and taking him to an inn—even paying for his room and meals during his recovery.

When Jesus asks the scholar which of the three travelers was a neighbor to the injured man, the scholar admits, "The one who showed him mercy."

"Go and do the same," Jesus replies (Luke 10:37).

◄ **ON THE JERICHO ROAD.** Hikers trudge uphill from Jericho toward Jerusalem. It's a daylong, 17-mile (27 km) walk through Judean badlands. A bandit's delight in Bible times, and today, this isolated path is ideal for ambushing a lone hiker.

WHY JEWS HATED SAMARITANS. Racially and spiritually, Samaritans were considered Jewish half-breeds. They descended from Jews who intermarried with Assyrians (from what is now Iraq) who settled in the area about 700 years earlier. Samaritans revered only the first five books of the Bible—Genesis, Exodus, Leviticus, Numbers, and Deuteronomy. But Jews said Samaritans edited the original books. One alleged edit: Mount Gerizim, in Samaria, replaced Jerusalem as the sacred place for worshipping God.

DISSING SAMARITANS. One rabbi said the following about Samaritans, in a teaching that Jews passed on by word of mouth until it was written down in about AD 200: "Those who eat the food of Samaritans are like those who eat pig" (*Shev'it* 8:10). Jewish law prohibits eating pork.

How Jesus prayed

LONG-WINDED, SELF-PROMOTING PRAYERS are apparently all too common in ancient Jewish circles—if the advice Jesus gives his followers is any clue.

"When you pray," he tells the crowd during his famous Sermon on the Mount, "don't be like the hypocrites who love to pray publicly on street corners and in the synagogues where everyone can see them. I tell you the truth, that is all the reward they will ever get" (Matthew 6:5).

Luke's version of this sermon says the disciples ask Jesus to teach them how to pray.

Off the cuff, it seems, Jesus speaks a short, simple prayer—the most famous in the Bible: The Lord's Prayer.

> *"Father, may your name be kept holy. May your Kingdom come soon. Give us each day the food we need, and forgive us our sins, as we forgive those who sin against us. And don't let us yield to temptation."*
>
> LUKE 11:2–4

PRAY IN PRIVATE / That's what Jesus recommended, to a generation used to hearing pious Jews pray in public three times a day. Jesus took his own advice, often retreating from the crowds "to pray alone" (Luke 9:18).

A VERY JEWISH PRAYER. The start of Jesus' prayer sounds much like the start of an ancient Jewish prayer called the *Kaddish*, Hebrew for "holy."

LORD'S PRAYER	KADDISH
May your name be kept holy.	Holy and honored is his great name. . . .
May your kingdom come soon.	May he set up his kingdom in your lifetime.

THREE PRAYERS A DAY. Many observant Jews in Jesus' century prayed three times a day: 9 a.m., noon, and 3 p.m. Some apparently arranged their schedule so they'd be with others during those times, so people could see how religious they were.

A rabbi for lowlifes

JESUS KEEPS BAD COMPANY.

Not a good idea for a rabbi, insist Jewish scholars. Birds of a feather flock together, and good rabbis should hang out with godly souls, not with prostitutes, the demon-possessed, and tax collectors collaborating with the Roman occupiers.

Rabbi Jesus says the scholars have it backward.

Rabbis are spiritual guides, and they should surround themselves with lost souls searching for God.

Jesus makes his point with three parables, all featuring the same theme: lost.

LOST SHEEP. A shepherd of 100 sheep leaves his 99 to go find one sheep that has turned up missing. When he finds it, he tells all his neighbors so they can share his happiness.

LOST COIN. A woman with 10 silver coins loses one and hunts frantically for it. When she finds it, she rejoices like she has inherited a wagonload of silver.

LOST SON. In perhaps Jesus' most famous parable, of the prodigal son, a young man takes his share of the family inheritance and wastes it on wild living. But when he comes home, his father is so happy that he throws a party.

This is the kind of joy that erupts in heaven, Jesus says, when even one sinner repents.

▼**DAPPER RABBIS.** Rabbi Arie Zeev Raskin (left), chief rabbi of Cyprus, meets with Israel's chief rabbi, Rabbi Yona Metzger at the inauguration of a synagogue. Rabbi Jesus bucked conventional wisdom of his day by avoiding the religious elite in favor of society's down-and-out. He said that's where he was most needed.

WAS IT OKAY FOR A SON TO TAKE HIS SHARE OF INHERITANCE BEFORE HIS FATHER DIED? No more than it is today. Rabbis advised men to distribute their inheritance only when "you know that death is near" (Wisdom of Jesus Son of Sirach 33:24 NRSV, about 200 BC).

WHAT DID JEWS THINK ABOUT PEOPLE DOWN ON THEIR LUCK? Conventional wisdom said there was no such thing as luck. God was in charge. So people in tough situations were there because God put them there, to punish them. Jesus didn't agree (see John 9:3).

Parable of a rich man in blazes

RICH PEOPLE HAVE TROUBLE warming up to a story that suggests they're headed to hell.

But that's the story Jesus tells, in an apparent attempt to urge rich people to spread their wealth—sharing it with people in need.

The story stars a beggar named Lazarus, sick and covered in open sores. He sits at the front gate of a rich man's house, hoping in vain for leftover food. He dies, and angels carry him to his reward, to the eternal home of Abraham, father of the Jews. Sounds like heaven, many scholars say.

The rich man dies, too. He goes to a place of torment but can see Abraham across a huge chasm. He asks Abraham to send Lazarus with some water to "cool my tongue. I am in anguish in these flames" (Luke 16:24). But the chasm is impassible.

So the rich man asks Abraham to send someone from the dead to warn his rich brothers, so they don't end up in blazes.

But Abraham replies, "If they won't listen to Moses and the prophets, they won't listen even if someone rises from the dead" (Luke 16:31). This is a jab, some scholars say, at the prevailing Jewish response to Jesus after his death and resurrection.

BEGGAR AT WORK / An elderly man walks down the Mount of Olives where he begs for donations from tourists. The ridge top behind him is a favorite photo spot—the best view of Jerusalem. As in Bible times, beggars follow the money hoping for mercy.

BEGGARS. People unable to earn a living and without family to help them often resorted to begging. They usually begged in places where people with money had to walk by them: busy entrance gates into a city, the marketplace, and outside the homes of the rich and famous.

CAN PEOPLE IN HELL SEE PEOPLE IN HEAVEN? Most Bible experts today advise against taking this parable that literally. Jesus was simply using a story that people could visualize to help them understand that the way we behave in this lifetime has consequences for the next.

Jesus heals 10 lepers

ON HIS WAY TO JERUSALEM, where he will be crucified, Jesus comes to a village on the border of Galilee and Samaria.

Ten lepers see him but by Jewish law aren't allowed to approach. So they cry out, "Jesus, Master, have mercy on us!" (Luke 17:13).

He does. He tells them to go the village priest so he can examine them and confirm they've been healed. As they rush to the priest, they are healed.

One man, apparently the only Samaritan among the 10, runs back to thank Jesus when he realizes his skin lesions are gone.

"Where are the other nine?" Jesus asks, apparently talking to his disciples. "Why was this foreigner the only one who came back to thank God?" Jesus then tells the man to go. "Your faith has made you well" (Luke 17:17–19 CEV).

LEPER / Fingertips lost to leprosy, a woman pauses for a portrait in the Mutemwa Leprosy Settlement in Zimbabwe. The disease destroys nerves in the skin. Without the sense of touch, patients sometimes leave injuries untreated, which can cause infection that requires amputation.

SAMARITAN.
See page 369.

LEPROSY.
Docs today call it Hansen's Disease. It's an infection caused by the bacterium *Mycobacterium leprae*, treated today with antibiotics. It produces lesions on the skin, including patches that numb the nerves. Without the sense of feeling, lepers can ignore injuries until life-threatening infections set in, requiring amputation.

THE BIBLE VERSION OF LEPROSY.
Not every leper in the Bible fit the modern definition of leprosy. Some just had comparatively minor skin problems: eczema, psoriasis, or a rash. That's why some Bible translations replace "leprosy" with "a skin disease."

WHY LEPERS KEPT THEIR DISTANCE FROM HEALTHY PEOPLE.
Jewish law required it (see Numbers 5:2).

PRIESTS AS PHYSICIANS.
People healed of skin diseases had to get the priest's okay to return to society—but only after undergoing an eight-day cleansing ritual described in Leviticus 14. An ancient Jewish collection of traditions, called the Mishnah, tells priests to search for any one of four shades of white patches on the skin—considered telltale signs of leprosy: bright like snow, soft white like limestone, eggshell white, and wool white.

Jesus gets Jericho a tax refund

ARRIVING IN JERICHO, a busy oasis town, Jesus draws a crowd. He's still a day's walk from his destination: Jerusalem.

He's famous now, near the end of his ministry. Everyone wants to see him. Including a tax collector named Zacchaeus. The tax man is too short to see over the crowd, so he scrambles up a sycamore fig tree just as Jesus is passing by.

Jesus sees him. To the horror of the crowd—who hate tax men—Jesus tosses Zacchaeus one sweet apple of an honor: "Zacchaeus, hurry down! I want to stay with you today" (Luke 19:5 CEV).

By the time Jesus leaves town the next morning, Zacchaeus is a changed man. He vows to give half his money to the poor. And he offers a quadruple tax refund to anyone he overtaxed—four shekels for every shekel he extorted.

For Jesus, it's a mission accomplished: "The Son of Man came to find lost people and save them" (Luke 19:10 NCV). Jesus declares Zacchaeus saved.

TREE-CLIMBER'S DELIGHT / To catch a glimpse of the crowd-swarmed Jesus, Zacchaeus climbed a sycamore tree—perhaps like this one in Ramat Gan, near Tel Aviv.

BEAN COUNTER WITH MUSCLE. Chiseled in marble, a 2,000-year-old scene shows a Roman official taking a census, backed up by an armed soldier. Romans used the tally to estimate how much income they could expect in taxes. Locals then bid for the right to collect taxes from their neighbors—a popularity killer.

TAXES. Jewish farmers reportedly paid a land tax of up to 20–25 percent of their harvest and new livestock, collected by fellow Jews who bid for the right to collect taxes for Rome. Jews also paid a personal tax equal to a day's labor, along with toll taxes of 2–5 percent of the products they were transporting to market. Tax men like Zacchaeus, backed up by Roman soldiers, were notorious for overcharging and pocketing the extra.

RABBIS UNITED AGAINST TAX MEN. Rabbis went on the record in ancient writings—such as the revered Talmud and Mishnah—telling Jews not to take anything from tax collectors. Not change back. Not donations for the poor. The rabbis add that it's okay to lie to tax men. "It's perfectly acceptable to tell. . .tax collectors. . .that you're a member of the king's family and exempt from taxes" (Mishnah, *Nedarium* 3:4).

Five trials of Jesus

JESUS ARRIVES IN JERUSALEM on what will become known as Palm Sunday. The city is crowded with Jewish pilgrims. They've come to celebrate the Jewish festival of Passover.

Many welcome Jesus as the Messiah, paving his path with palm branches and cloaks. Through Thursday, they listen to his teachings in the Temple courtyards (see Luke 21:37–38). But on Thursday evening, while he's praying on the Mount of Olives, Temple guards arrest him.

This begins what some say are five overnight and early morning trials, none fair. The judges:

// **ANNAS.** He's the retired high priest and father-in-law of the current high priest. This is Jesus' first stop, possibly for an interrogation if not a preliminary trial.

// **CAIAPHAS.** He's the current high priest. By daybreak, the Jewish high court known as the Sanhedrin, led by Caiaphas, convicts Jesus of blasphemy for claiming to be God's Son.

// **PONTIUS PILATE.** Roman governor of Judea, Pilate is the only local official who can sentence Jesus to death. Pilate finds no cause for that. When he learns that Jesus comes from Galilee, he gladly sends him to the Galilean ruler, who's in town for the Passover.

// **HEROD ANTIPAS.** Ruler of Galilee and executioner of John the Baptist, Herod toys with Jesus. Then he sends him back to Pilate dressed in a royal robe—a joke. Pilate and Herod become friends over this.

// **PONTIUS PILATE.** After resisting Jewish pressure to crucify Jesus, Pilate caves. Jesus is hanging on the cross by about 9 a.m. on Friday, as Mark reports it. He's dead sometime between 3 p.m. and sunset (see Luke 23:44).

◄ **PROGRESSIVE TRIAL.** Within hours of his nighttime arrest, Jesus is rushed through four sets of inquisitors—one inquisitor twice: Roman governor Pontius Pilate.

CHARGES AGAINST JESUS. Pilate refused to convict Jesus for the religious offense of claiming to be God's Son. So the Jews accused Jesus of stirring up a revolt against the Roman Empire and claiming to be king of the Jews.

WHY PILATE CAVED. Scholars who say Jesus died in about AD 33 speculate that Pilate was already on shaky ground with Caesar Tiberius. The Roman official who had recommended Pilate for the job of governing Judea, Sejanus, was executed during an attempted coup in AD 31, along with many of his allies. Jews told Pilate, "If you release this man, you are no 'friend of Caesar' " (John 19:12).

A walk with resurrected Jesus

JESUS RISES FROM THE DEAD on Sunday morning. He first shows up outside the tomb, appearing to women who have come to finish preparing his body for burial.

Luke reports that later in the day Jesus takes a walk. Two of Jesus' followers, including a man named Cleopas, have left Jerusalem and are apparently walking home to the village of Emmaus. Jesus suddenly shows up on the trail and begins walking with them, asking what they're talking about so intently.

For some reason, they don't recognize him. They say they're talking about Jesus, and they're disappointed that he wasn't the Messiah.

Jesus then starts telling them about Bible prophecies that said the Messiah would have to go through exactly the kind of suffering Jesus endured.

Still, the men don't recognize Jesus until he sits down with them for a meal in Emmaus and blesses the food. He breaks bread, hands it to them, and disappears.

Within the hour the men are on back on the road to Jerusalem, to report the news.

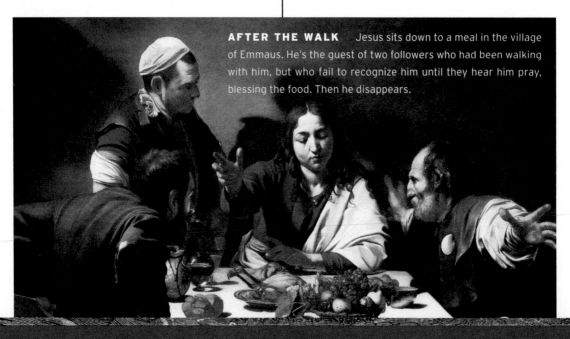

AFTER THE WALK   Jesus sits down to a meal in the village of Emmaus. He's the guest of two followers who had been walking with him, but who fail to recognize him until they hear him pray, blessing the food. Then he disappears.

WHAT PROPHECIES DID JESUS SAY HIS SUFFERING FULFILLED? Luke doesn't report this. But some of Isaiah's predictions, many scholars say, sound dead-on. See pages 216–217.

◀ **LOOKING FOR EMMAUS.** Luke says the village was 60 *stadia* from Jerusalem. That's about seven miles (11 km). Scholars don't agree on the location. Crusaders favored the Arab village of El-Qubeibeh, which means "little dome," a possible reference to a church. The village is about seven miles northeast of Jerusalem. Crusaders found an old Roman fort there, called Castle Emmaus. In 1852, Franciscans found ruins of a church there, and in 1902 built a church that sits there today.

Jesus, back from the dead

DISCIPLES ARE TERRIFIED when the resurrected Jesus shows up at the very moment two men from Emmaus are trying to convince them that they saw Jesus a few hours ago.

"Peace be with you," Jesus says (Luke 24:36).

But apparently it's tough to look at a walking corpse and relax. The disciples think he's a ghost.

"Touch me," Jesus says (Luke 24:39). And to further prove that he's not a spirit vapor of some sort, he eats some of their broiled fish.

Then Jesus reminds his disciples of what he had taught them before his death and what he had apparently told the pair from Emmaus earlier in the day. Moses, the prophets, and even the song writers of Psalms had said "the Messiah would suffer and die and rise from the dead on the third day" (Luke 24:46).

The next step is up to them, Jesus says. He promises to send them the Holy Spirit to fill them with the power they will need to spread the story of Jesus and the good news: "There is forgiveness of sins for all who repent" (Luke 24:47).

Then Jesus leads them to Bethany, where he blesses them and then ascends into the heavens.

ALIVE AGAIN / The resurrected body of Jesus seems physical and beyond. He can eat. People can touch him. But he can suddenly appear out of nowhere, and disappear as quickly. Some students of the Bible wonder if that's what's in store for believers in the afterlife.

WHAT JESUS COULD DO WITH HIS RESURRECTED BODY.

- Suddenly appear and disappear (see Luke 24:13, 15, 31)
- Pass through walls of a locked house (see John 20:19)
- Eat (see Luke 24:42)
- Levitate (see Acts 1:8–9)

BETHANY. See page 355.

JOHN 19:30

Jesus bows his head and dies—crucified on charges of inciting rebellion against Rome by calling himself the king of Israel.

BIG SCENE
THE SON OF GOD DIES

BIBLE HISTORY

ALL DATES APPROXIMATE

6 BC
Jesus is born (estimates range from 7–4 BC)

WORLD HISTORY

Herod Antipas rules Galilee most of Jesus' life
4 BC

J O H N

JESUS' STORY FOR DEEP THINKERS

STORY LINE

IN THE BEGINNING Jesus is there. At Creation. Long before his birth in Bethlehem.

That's how John begins his unique take on the life and ministry of Jesus. And it is unique. Unlike the first three Gospels: Matthew, Mark, and Luke. Bible experts call those three the Synoptic Gospels, after the Greek word that means "viewing together." They're so much alike that it's easy to compare the stories side by side.

Not so with John. This writer skips the parables. He skips most of Jesus' miracles, too. He mentions only seven of them, which he calls signs. These signs, along with most everything else John reports, point to the one purpose driving his book—the reason he wrote it: "so that you may believe that Jesus is the Christ, the Son of God" (John 20:31 NCV).

After placing Jesus at Creation, John jumps to the launch of Jesus' earthly ministry. Jesus' relative, John the Baptist, baptizes him and presents him to the crowd as the Lamb of God who has come to take away the sins of the world.

John spends the first half of his book reporting the teachings of Jesus. The second half he devotes mainly to Jesus' final week—from what is now called Palm Sunday, when he arrives in Jerusalem to cheering crowds, to Easter Sunday when he rises from the dead.

// TIME: Lifetime of Jesus, from about 6 BC–AD 33, give or take a few years.

// AUTHOR: He identifies himself only as one of the 12 disciples (see John 21:24). At least as early as the AD 100s, church leaders said he was John—one of Jesus' three closest friends, along with Peter and John's brother, James.

// LOCATION: Israel. Most of Jesus' ministry takes place in Galilee, in what is now northern Israel.

AD 30
John baptizes Jesus
(AD 28 alternate date)

AD 33
Death, resurrection of Jesus
(AD 30 alternate date)

Rome fires
Pontius Pilate
AD 36

Rome exiles
Herod Antipas
AD 39

Jesus, the Creator

IT SOUNDS LIKE A CODE NAME—maybe to protect the writer from Jews with stones.

The mysterious person John introduces is the "Word."

John says the Word "was God" and "existed in the beginning with God" (John 1:1–2). As though this Word is somehow separate from God, and yet the same as God.

As if that's not confusing enough, John adds that "God created everything through him, and nothing was created except through him" (John 1:3).

The Word is Jesus. John doesn't say it outright, but the clues are there:

// "[He] became human, and made his home among us."

// "He came into the very world he created, but the world didn't recognize him."

// "He came to his own people, and even they rejected him" John 1:10–11, 14.

WHY CALL JESUS THE "WORD"?
It's *Logos*, in Greek. That's the term Greek philosophers used to talk about the mysterious principle behind the universe. *Logos* was the eternal force that drives everything. Jews understood *Word* differently. God created the universe by speaking the word. "God said, 'Let there be light,' and there was light" (Genesis 1:3). So with this single word—*Word*—John is telling the people of two cultures, Greek and Jew, that Jesus is the divine force behind all of Creation. It's a remarkable thesis. John spends the rest of his book trying to prove it.

....

THE "WORD" OF HERACLITUS (ABOUT 535–475 BC).
A Greek philosopher in Ephesus, he said "all things come to be in accordance with this Word."

LET THERE BE LIGHT /
A rainbow paints the Kenyan sky. John seems to acknowledge that God created everything that exists, as Genesis reports. But John adds a little something: "God created everything through him. . . . The Word" (John 1:3–4). The "Word" is Jesus.

Jesus, the Lamb of God

JOHN THE BAPTIST is the prophet Jews have been waiting for. He says so, though indirectly.

"I am a voice shouting in the wilderness, 'Clear the way for the LORD's coming!'" (John 1:23).

The Baptist is quoting Isaiah's prophecy from 700 years earlier—one that many Jews of the day connect to the Messiah. They teach that a prophet the caliber of Elijah is coming as an advance man for the Messiah, preparing his way and announcing his arrival.

That's exactly what John the Baptist does. He introduces Jesus to the world. In his own words:

> *"Look! The Lamb of God! He takes away the sin of the world! This is the One I was talking about. I said, 'A man who comes after me is more important than I am. That's because he existed before I was born.' I did not know him. But God wants to make it clear to Israel who this person is. That's the reason I came baptizing with water."*
>
> JOHN 1:29–31 NIrV

At this point, John's ministry begins to wane. Some of his followers leave him and start following Jesus. One of them is Andrew, brother of the man who will become Jesus' lead disciple: Peter.

SACRIFICE / Since ancient times, Jews sacrificed animals to atone for their sins. As far as they were concerned, there was no forgiveness without the shedding of blood. New Testament writers present Jesus as the last sacrifice anyone would need.

WAS JESUS BORN BEFORE JOHN THE BAPTIST? No. When Gabriel told Mary she would become pregnant with Jesus, Gabriel also said Mary's relative Elizabeth was already six months pregnant with John the Baptist (see Luke 1:36). So when John the Baptist said Jesus "existed before I was born" (John 1:30 NIrV), scholars say he was probably talking about Jesus being present with God the Father before Creation.

LAMB OF GOD. Jews sacrificed lambs and other animals to atone for their sins. "Christ died once for all time as a sacrifice to take away the sins of many people" (Hebrews 9:28). New Testament writers describe this moment as the end of God's ancient agreement with the Jews. Forgiveness has become freely available without the need for blood sacrifices. The Jewish sacrificial system would end about 40 years later when Roman soldiers leveled the Temple in AD 70.

Wine, the first miracle

A WEDDING PARTY in the village of Cana runs out of wine, late into the festivities. Jesus is one of the guests, along with his mother, Mary, and the first of his disciples; Jesus apparently hasn't finished picking the full dozen.

Mary tells Jesus the problem. But he says it's not their worry, adding: "My time has not yet come" (John 2:4).

Seeming to ignore his reply, Mary simply tells the servants to do whatever her son says. It's easy for some to imagine Jesus shaking his head and smiling. He tells the servants to fill the nearby stone water jars with water. There are six jars, each holding 20–30 gallons (75–113 liters).

"Dip some out," he says, "and take it to the master of ceremonies" (John 2:8).

The emcee is impressed. He tells the groom—who's responsible for providing the wine—"You have kept the best until now!" (John 2:10).

John calls this miracle the first "sign. . .the first time Jesus revealed his glory" (John 2:11).

DOING WHAT MOM SAYS / When a wedding party runs out of wine, Jesus performs his first miracle on record: turning water into wine. He didn't seem to want to do it. But his mother asked, and he honored her request.

"MY TIME HAS NOT YET COME" (JOHN 2:4). In John, this is a phrase that refers to Jesus' coming crucifixion. Perhaps Jesus was concerned that this miracle, revealing his power, would start the clock ticking toward the countdown to crucifixion. When the time arrives and Judas leaves the Last Supper to betray him, Jesus says, "The time has come" (John 13:31).

SEVEN MIRACLES, SIGNS OF DEITY. John reports just seven miracles of Jesus. Many scholars say that each intended to reveal some aspect of Jesus' deity.

1. **Turns water into wine** (see John 2:1–12). He has creation power.
2. **Heals a boy by long-distance** (see John 4:46–54). He's not limited by geography.
3. **Heals lame man on the Sabbath day of rest** (see John 5:1–17). He's not limited by time.
4. **Feeds 5,000** (see John 6:1–15). He's the bread of life, physical as well as spiritual.
5. **Walks on water** (see John 6:16–22). He's the master of his creation.
6. **Heals the blind** (see John 9:1–41). He's the light of the world, physical as well as spiritual.
7. **Raises Lazarus from the dead** (see John 11:1–44). He's more powerful than death.

Archaeologists sift through the ruins of Khirbet Cana.

CANA
(Khirbet Cana)

Capernaum

Sea of Galilee

Nazareth

N

5 Miles

0   10 Kilometers

Jordan River

CANA. No one knows for certain where this village was. The name *Cana* means "place of reeds." And one guess is an ancient ruin near a marshy plain filled with reeds. It's called Khirbet Cana (*Khirbet* is Arabic for "ruins"). It's about a half-day walk north of Jesus' hometown of Nazareth, about nine miles (14 km).

"You must be born again"

THE BIBLE'S MOST FAMOUS one-liner is spoken at night. It's Jesus talking to a Jewish leader who apparently doesn't want to be seen with him.

The one-liner:

> *"God loved the world so much that he gave his one and only Son, so that everyone who believes in him will not perish but have eternal life."*
>
> JOHN **3:16**

The conversation begins with the Jewish leader, Nicodemus, telling Jesus he knows God sent him; the miracles prove it. Jesus says that's not enough.

"I tell you the truth, unless you are born again," Jesus says, "you cannot see the Kingdom of God" (John 3:3). Nicodemus is a Pharisee, a branch of the Jewish faith famous for trying to obey all the Bible teachings—sometimes going to extremes.

Nicodemus objects to Jesus' teaching, saying it's impossible. "I can't go back inside my mother! I can't be born a second time!" (John 3:4 NIrV).

Jesus says he's talking about a spiritual rebirth, not a physical one: "People give birth to people. But the Spirit gives birth to spirit" (John 3:6 NIrV).

Nicodemus helps bury Jesus.

NICODEMUS, AN ENCORE. He shows up two more times in John's story of Jesus. Nicodemus defends Jesus, asking, "Is it legal to convict a man before he is given a hearing?" (John 7:51). And after Jesus is crucified, Nicodemus teams up with another Jewish leader, Joseph of Arimathea, to help with the burial. Nicodemus buys 75 pounds (about 33 kilograms) of burial spices (see John 19:39).

JOHN 3:16, A PROTESTANT'S VIEW. Martin Luther (1483–1546) called this verse the "Gospel in a sentence." Luther was the Catholic priest who launched the religious revolt against abuses in the Church, starting the Protestant movement.

JESUS AND THE CAUTIOUS SCHOLAR / Nicodemus, a top Jewish scholar, comes to Jesus under the cover of darkness. The scholar is intrigued by this young rabbi's teachings and miracles—and wants to learn more. But not at the risk of his reputation, it seems.

Jesus and the divorcee

A SHADY LADY bumps into Jesus at a village well.

Jesus and his disciples are on their way home to Galilee from Jerusalem. They've stopped to rest at about the halfway point, near the village of Sychar in Samaritan territory—a region many Jews avoid.

The disciples have gone into the village to buy food while Jesus waits by a well. When the woman arrives, Jesus asks her for a drink of water. She's shocked that he would say anything to her. For one thing, Jews and Samaritans avoid each other. And for another, she has been divorced five times and is living with a man who isn't her husband—facts that Jesus knows; and he tells her so, which makes her think he might be a prophet.

Jesus says, "If you only knew the free gift of God and who it is that is asking you for water, you would have asked him, and he would have given you living water. . . . Whoever drinks the water I give will never be thirsty" (John 4:10, 14 NCV).

The woman seems to think he's talking about magical water that forever quenches thirst. He explains that he's talking about the spiritual source of eternal life. He also admits to her that he's the Messiah.

She runs back to get the villagers. They welcome Jesus and host him for two days—"long enough for many more to hear his message and believe" (John 4:41).

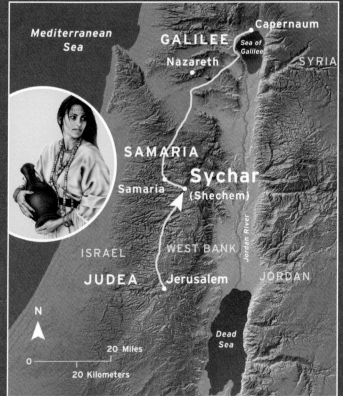

◀ SYCHAR. In Old Testament times, this village was called Shechem. Today it's Nablus, one of the largest Palestinian cities in the West Bank, with a population of about 135,000. (See picture of Nablus on page 82.)

WHY COULDN'T JESUS GET HIS OWN DRINK? Many wells weren't equipped with ropes and buckets. Villagers brought their own.

LIVING WATER. It's water from a moving source, such as a river, stream, or a well fed by an underground spring. Later in Jerusalem, Jesus said: "Let anyone who is thirsty come to me and drink. If anyone believes in me, rivers of living water will flow out from that person's heart, as the Scripture says" (John 7:37-38 NCV). Jesus may have been referring to Isaiah 58:11: "You will be like a garden that has plenty of water or like a stream that never runs dry" (CEV).

Jesus, bread of eternal life

AFTER FEEDING THOUSANDS of hungry men and their families with a measly pair of fish and five loaves of bread, Jesus has everyone's attention. When he leaves, the crowd follows.

The next day, when he shows up at the Capernaum synagogue, the crowds are there.

"You want to be with me because I fed you," Jesus said, "not because you understood the miraculous signs" (John 6:26).

Then he explains the miracle.

"Don't be so concerned about perishable things like food. . . . I am the bread of life. Whoever comes to me will never be hungry again" (John 6:27, 35).

In a flashback, he compares himself to the manna of the Exodus, saying he's the true bread who comes down from heaven.

And in a flash-forward, to the Communion ritual he will inaugurate at the Last Supper, he says anyone who eats the flesh of his broken body will live forever.

The crowds still don't get it. They know him as Joseph's son, not as a God who came down from heaven. And they have no idea how they're supposed to eat his flesh. Even his disciples don't understand.

MATZO BREAD: TASTE OF FREEDOM /
Jews celebrating Passover each spring eat cracker-like bread made without yeast. It's a reminder of the hurried meal-for-the-road that their ancestors ate the night God freed them from Egyptian slavery. When Jesus called himself the "bread of life," some Jewish Christians reading the story likely saw the Passover connection: Jesus delivers people from slavery to sin.

Jesus: "I am the light of the world."

I AM. That's God's name. Moses once asked him what his name was. God answered: "I AM" (Exodus 3:14). Jesus latched on to this by describing himself with seven "I Am" phrases—as though he, too, is the Great I Am. Jesus said, "I Am the:

// "Bread of life" (John 6:35). *Source of spiritual nourishment.*
// "Light of the world" (John 8:12). *Source of insight, direction.*
// "Gate for the sheep" (John 10:7). *Doorway to heaven.*
// "Good shepherd" (John 10:14). *Protector.*
// "Resurrection and the life" (John 11:25). *Source of eternal life.*
// "Way, the truth, and the life" (John 14:6). *The bridge from earth to heaven.*
// "True grapevine" (John 15:1). *Like bread, source of spiritual nourishment.*

Blindness Rx: spitball

A MAN BORN BLIND is probably begging on a Jerusalem street when Jesus and his disciples walk by. The disciples ask Jesus a question about that.

"Why was this man born blind? Was it because of his own sins or his parents' sins?" (John 9:2)

"This happened so the power of God could be seen in him," Jesus answers. "I am the light of the world" (John 9:3, 5).

Jesus spits on the ground, picks up the mud, and smears it onto the man's eyes. Then he tells the man to wash his eyes in the pool of Siloam.

The man is healed. On the Sabbath. Pharisees consider it sinful to practice medicine on the God-ordained day of rest and worship. So when they get word of the healing, they interrogate the man and his parents.

Their conclusions:

// They "refused to believe the man had been blind" (verse 18; see also 32).

// Accused him of being a disciple of Jesus (see verse 28).

// "Threw him out of the synagogue" (verse 34).

// Declared Jesus a sinner for practicing medicine on the Sabbath (see verses 16, 24).

WHY DID JESUS USE SPIT TO HEAL THE MAN?

Perhaps to help build the man's faith by drawing from a familiar treatment. First-century Roman author, Pliny (AD 23–79), included these two treatments in his 37-volume work called *Natural History*:

"To cure inflammation of the eyes, wash the eyes each morning with spit from your overnight fast" (Source: *Remedies from Living Creatures*, chapter 10).

"To protect your eyes from developing eye diseases including inflammation of the eyes, do this and you will never ever again develop an eye disease. Each time you wash the dust off your feet, touch your eyes three times with the muddy water" (Source: *Remedies from Living Creatures*, chapter 10).

WHY DID THE DISCIPLES ASSUME THE BLIND MAN DESERVED HIS BLINDNESS?

Many Jews believed that God blessed faithful people with health and prosperity, and punished the unfaithful with sickness and poverty. The book of Job seemed to teach otherwise, since Job suffered in spite of his faithfulness. But many Jews didn't make that connection.

POOL OF SILOAM / Jesus tells a blind man to wash his eyes in this rock-cut pool at the low end of Jerusalem. The pool was fed by water from nearby Gihon Spring, traveling through a tunnel cut from solid rock about 700 years before Christ (see "Hezekiah's secret water tunnel," page 137).

Lazarus, four days dead and walking

JESUS IS CELEBRATING HANUKKAH in Jerusalem when Jewish leaders try to arrest him. He escapes to a village where John the Baptist had baptized some people, east of the Jordan River: Bethany beyond the Jordan.

There, perhaps a two-day walk from Jerusalem, he gets word that a friend is dying: Lazarus, the brother of Mary and Martha—two women who had invited Jesus into their home and fed him. Lazarus lives with his sisters in a Jerusalem suburb that's also called Bethany.

Instead of rushing to Lazarus, or healing him from a distance—as he has done for others—Jesus does nothing. For two days.

By then, Lazarus is dead. Jesus then tells his disciples much the same as he had said earlier, about the man born blind—that this tragedy would reveal God's power.

Lazarus is four days dead and smelling like it by the time Jesus arrives. Jesus orders the tomb opened, over the objection of Martha. Then he raises Lazarus with a single sentence: "Lazarus, come out!" (John 11:43).

Ironically, the response of the Jewish leaders to this man who can raise the dead is to kill him. They begin plotting his arrest, trial, and execution.

CHURCH OF ST. LAZARUS / This Franciscan church in Bethany commemorates the miracle of Jesus raising Lazarus from the dead. It's located near an ancient, rock-cut tomb said to be the tomb of Lazarus.

BETHANY BEYOND THE JORDAN. The Bible doesn't say where this village was. One common guess is across the river from Jericho, in what is now Jordan.

HANUKKAH. It's the Hebrew word for "dedication." This eight-day Jewish holiday in December celebrates the rededication of the Jerusalem Temple in 164 BC, and the restart of worship there after invaders had desecrated the Temple by sacrificing pigs on the altar. For the Temple rededication, Jews needed the Temple menorah lamp to burn eight days, long enough to prepare more consecrated oil. But they had only enough for one day. Miraculously, according to Jewish tradition, the one-day supply lasted eight days. That's why Hanukkah is also known as the Festival of Lights.

JEWISH BURIALS. Jews in this hot region of the world usually gave their dead same-day burials. The typical process in Jesus' day:

> wash the body
> dress the body
> wrap the body in cloth strips
> scent the body with spices such as myrrh, aloe, and spikenard
> cover the face with a separate cloth
> wrap the entire body in a shroud—a long roll of cloth stretching from head to toe, front and back
> seal tomb after a week of mourning
> put the bones into a bone box once the corpse had decomposed, after a year or two.

Jesus washes feet of disciples

JOHN SKIPS THE LAST SUPPER—at least the meal part of the event, which gave the Christian Church the ritual of communion. He doesn't mention it.

Instead, he tells the story of Jesus washing the feet of the disciples sometime during the meal. This is just a few hours before Jesus' arrest, which leads to his execution the next morning.

Jesus takes off his robe, wraps a towel around his waist, pours water in a basin, and starts washing the feet of his disciples.

Peter, the lead disciple, objects to the very idea of a renowned rabbi—let alone the Messiah—acting like a slave and washing the feet of his students. "You will never wash my feet!" (John 13:8).

Jesus convinces him otherwise, explaining that this foot washing is an object lesson. It's a clue about the job description of these men who will launch the Christian movement—"an example to follow" (John 13:15).

Instead of thinking of themselves as high and mighty leaders—like CEOs who deserve huge bonuses—they're to think of themselves as servants.

"If I can wash the feet of others," Jesus says, essentially, "you can, too."

FOOT PATROL / Priests wash the feet of worshippers at a Maundy Thursday mass in Rome. Many churches throughout the world observe this ritual on the Thursday before Easter, to commemorate Jesus' washing the feet of his disciples.

COMMUNION, LAST SUPPER. See pages 333–334.

FOOT WASHING, A SLAVE'S JOB. Travelers walked in sandals on dusty trails, so their feet got dirty fast. Middle Easterners in Bible times showed hospitality by welcoming guests with a basin of water so they could wash their own feet. Some hosts provided non-Jewish servants to do the washing. But rabbis taught that washing the feet of guests was too undignified for Jewish servants.

Jesus, the way to God

JESUS MAKES NO SENSE when he offers up a couple of statements that sound like exact opposites. At least the disciples seem confused, as do many Bible experts today.

The confusion begins when Jesus tells his disciples he'll be leaving soon, but that they will join him because they know the way. Thomas—better known as Doubting Thomas—says he has no idea where Jesus is going, or how to get there from here.

That's when Jesus answers with a one-two combo mystery:

I AM THE WAY TO GOD. "I am the way, the truth, and the life. No one can come to the Father except through me" (John 14:6).

I AM GOD. "Anyone who has seen me has seen the Father!" (John 14:9).

Adding to the confusion, Jesus promises that when he leaves he will send what many Bible experts describe as yet another entity from within the godhead: the Holy Spirit.

"I will ask the Father to send you the Holy Spirit who will help you and always be with you. The Spirit will show you what is true" (John 14:16–17 CEV).

Jesus doesn't try to explain this Trinity of Gods, which seems separate and yet one—as though it's beyond the ability of physics-bound humans to understand it. Instead, he simply asks his disciples to believe him: "At least believe what the miracles show about me" (John 14:11 NIrV).

DIVINE FAMILY PORTRAIT / The Holy Trinity: God the Father, Son, and Holy Spirit—with the Spirit depicted as a dove because Gospel writers describe the Spirit descending at the baptism of Jesus as gently as a dove. The Bible presents the three as distinct persons, scholars say, yet mysteriously united: three in one.

ONE GOD, THREE PERSONS. After three centuries of dead-end debate, most Bible scholars decided to accept by faith what they couldn't explain. Augustine (AD 354–430), a North African scholar, summed up the consensus: "The Father is God, the Son is God, the Holy Spirit is God. . .yet we do not say that there are three gods, but one God, the most exalted Trinity." Ambrose (about AD 340–397), bishop of Milan, Italy added: "We don't understand the mystery of how this can be, or what causes it. But we trust the evidence of this truth."

Ambrose, bishop of Milan

Jesus prays for all believers

AFTER THE LAST SUPPER, Jesus offers a tender prayer for himself, his disciples, and for everyone who will believe in him as a result of their future ministry. "Father, the hour has come," Jesus says (John 17:1). He's talking about his crucifixion, which will follow in the morning.

A PRAYER FOR HIMSELF. "Now, Father, bring me into the glory we shared before the world began" (John 17:5).

A PRAYER FOR HIS DISCIPLES. "Keep them safe from the evil one. They do not belong to this world any more than I do. . . . Just as you sent me into the world, I am sending them into the world" (John 17:15–16, 18).

A PRAYER FOR ALL BELIEVERS. "I am praying not only for these disciples but also for all who will ever believe in me through their message. I pray that they will all be one, just as you and I are one—as you are in me, Father, and I am in you. And may they be in us so that the world will believe you sent me" (John 17:20–21).

HOLINESS.
Jesus asked God the Father to make the disciples "holy." Some "holiness" Christian denominations (Salvation Army, Nazarenes, Wesleyans) teach that people can be "sanctified" in what they describe as a second, definite work of God's grace—a work as distinctive as getting saved by asking for forgiveness. But in this work, Christians ask to be entirely sanctified. In doing so, they're asking God, in a spiritual sense, to rewire them so they're better connected to him—and more inclined to do right than to do wrong.

CHRISTIANS IN RUSSIA
Christians gather for a Christmas service in Novosibirsk, third-largest city in Russia, after Moscow and Saint Petersburg. Hours before Jesus died, he prayed for himself, his disciples, and all believers yet to come.

Peter chickens out, rooster crows

"DIE FOR ME?" Jesus says when Peter boasts that he'd give his life for Jesus. "Peter—before the rooster crows tomorrow morning, you will deny three times that you even know me" (John 13:38).

That conversation had taken place earlier in the evening, during the Last Supper. Since then, Temple police reinforced by Roman soldiers had arrested Jesus while he prayed in an olive grove, and had taken him to the home of Caiaphas, the high priest.

Giving some credit to Peter on the most humiliating night of his life, he at least has the courage to follow along with another unidentified disciple, perhaps John—traditionally considered the writer of this Gospel. Peter waits in the high priest's courtyard, standing by the fire with others.

// A woman asks him if he's one of the disciples. Peter denies it.

// Others ask if he's a disciple. Peter denies it.

// A household servant related to a man whose ear Peter had cut off during the arrest asked if Peter was there in the olive grove with Jesus. Peter denies it.

"Immediately a rooster crowed" (John 18:27).

STRIKE THREE ON PETER / Jesus holds up three fingers, predicting that Peter will deny knowing him three times before the morning rooster crows. This artwork decorates the front door of the Jerusalem church commemorating Peter's denial: the Church of the Gallicantu (Latin: "Rooster Crowing").

◀ROOSTER CROWING OR ROMAN TRUMPET? Some scholars say the "cock crow" that Peter heard was a Roman trumpet signaling the end of the third three-hour watch of the night, at about 3 a.m. Romans called that signal the "cock crow." But most scholars say that what Peter likely heard was a rooster crowing. Perhaps the critter crowed at the approach of dawn, the cackling of a hen, or to announce his territory to a trespasser. Roosters, like dogs, sound off for lots of reasons.

PETER'S NORTHERN ACCENT. In Matthew's version of Peter's denial, some recognize Peter by his northern accent (Matthew 26:73). Galileans dropped their *h* sounds, according to an ancient story in the Talmud, a collection of Jewish traditions, laws, and commentary. "Hammer" would become "ammer." The Bible also says Jews from the tribe of Ephraim, north of Jerusalem, pronounced "Shibboleth" as "Sibboleth" (Judges 12:6). One warrior hated the tribe, and when he suspected a man came from there he had the fellow pronounce Shibboleth. If the man dropped the *h*, the warrior dropped him. Phonetics became fatal.

Killing Jesus

AFTER A SECRET ALL-NIGHT TRIAL, Jewish leaders convict Jesus of blasphemy for claiming to be God's Son. Then they convince Pilate, Roman governor of what is now southern Israel, to sentence Jesus to death.

WHIPPING. Pilate orders Jesus beaten. Romans often used whips with half a dozen leather lashes or more, each embedded with chunks of metal or bone—to tear skin and muscle.

WALKING. Jesus carries his cross toward Golgotha, the place of execution—until he collapses. All three other Gospels report that Romans order a passerby to finish carrying the cross for Jesus: "Simon. . .from Cyrene" (Matthew 27:32), in what is now Libya.

(continued next page)

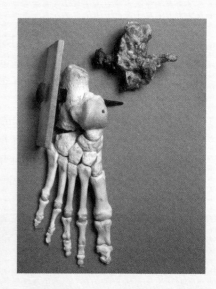

SECURED.
A wooden slab locks the nail in place, so the victim can't wiggle the nail through the bone and escape. Top right: A nailed heel bone from Jesus' time.

. . . .

CRUCIFIXION HORROR: ROMANS ON RECORD

"Each criminal who goes to execution must carry his own cross on his back."
Plutarch (AD 46–about 120), *Sera*, 554

"He was whipped until his bones showed."
Josephus (about AD 37–101),
Wars of the Jews, 6.5.3

"Is there such a thing as a person who would actually prefer wasting away in pain on a cross. . .rather than dying quickly. . .especially after the beating that left him deathly weak, deformed, swelling with vicious welts on shoulders and chest, and struggling to draw every last, agonizing breath? Anyone facing such a death would plead to die rather than mount the cross."
Seneca, (about 4 BC–65 AD), *Epistulae morales* (Moral Letters), 101.14

CRUCIFIED / Jesus hangs on a cross between two criminals. The execution site outside Jerusalem's city walls is called Place of the Skulls—perhaps because of a nearby rock quarry turned into a garden cemetery.

ACTS 2:1–13

The Holy Spirit arrives, roaring into a meeting room with the sound of a windstorm. An aura that looks like glowing tongues of fire settles on each person.

BIG SCENE

IN A BLAZE OF GLORY

BIBLE HISTORY

ALL DATES APPROXIMATE

AD 33 *Death, resurrection, ascension of Jesus; Holy Spirit arrives (AD 30 alternate date)*

AD 46 *Paul's first missionary trip*

WORLD HISTORY

Romans fire Pilate as governor of Judea
AD 36

ACTS

AFTER JESUS: BIRTH OF THE CHURCH

STORY LINE

IN A SEQUEL to the story of Jesus, started in the Gospel of Luke, Acts tells how the Christian movement caught fire and spread throughout the Roman Empire in a single generation.

The story begins with the disciples watching Jesus ascend into the sky from the Mount of Olives. Then, on Jesus' instructions, they go back to Jerusalem and wait for the arrival of the Holy Spirit—who is supposed to empower and guide them in their ministry.

When the Spirit arrives, they're suddenly able to speak foreign languages, at least for the day. They start telling the story of Jesus to pilgrims in town for the Jewish holiday of Pentecost. In one sermon by Peter, 3,000 Jews join the movement.

Jewish leaders retaliate, launching a wave of arrests and some executions that send many Jewish Christians running for their lives, scattering abroad. But they take their new faith with them.

One Jewish persecutor, a scholar named Saul (Roman name: Paul), sees a vision of Jesus. As a result he converts, taking his story on the road as the first missionary, expanding the movement to include non-Jews.

Romans eventually arrest him in Jerusalem and ship him off for trial in Rome. That's where the story ends as a cliff-hanger—without reporting the trial's outcome.

// TIME: The story covers more than 30 years, from the early AD 30s to the AD 60s. Bible experts estimate the story was written in the 70s or 80s.

// AUTHOR: Unknown. Church leaders in the AD 100s said Luke wrote both Acts and the Gospel of Luke.

// LOCATION: The story plays out in what are now many countries, including Israel, Egypt, Syria, Lebanon, Turkey, Greece, Italy, Cyprus, and Crete.

AD 57
Paul arrested

AD 64
Peter and Paul executed in Rome

Rome burns, Emperor Nero blames Christians
AD 64

Jews revolt, drive out Romans
AD 66

Romans retaliate, destroy Jerusalem
AD 70

Good-bye Jesus

TELLING HIS STORY to a mystery man called Theophilus, the writer says Jesus stays on earth about six weeks after the Resurrection—appearing to the disciples from time to time.

In his last visit with them, Jesus takes his disciples to the ridge of hills called the Mount of Olives, across a valley from Jerusalem. There he tells them not to leave Jerusalem until the Holy Spirit arrives to give them power and guidance for their ministry ahead:

> *"You will be my witnesses, telling people about me everywhere—in Jerusalem, throughout Judea, in Samaria, and to the ends of the earth."*
>
> ACTS 1:8

Suddenly, from the hilltop, Jesus ascends into the sky.

The disciples return to Jerusalem. There, they use lots to select a man named Matthias to replace Judas.

ASCENSION OF CHRIST / Impressionist artist Salvador Dali said his painting of the Ascension was inspired by a vividly colorful dream in which he saw the nucleus of an atom. In Acts, the disciples of Jesus were so mesmerized by his gravity-defying departure that angelic beings had to snap them out of it. Appearing suddenly, two white-robed men told them that when the time is right, Jesus "will return from heaven in the same way you saw him go!" (Acts 1:11).

LOTS. It's uncertain what these were. They could have been stones put in a bag or a jug—with one stone marked. Whoever picks the marked stone wins, or loses. It's a bit like drawing the short straw. Jews used this practice because they believed God was in control of everything. By using this technique, they figured they were letting God make the decision about who should replace Judas (see also page 271).

WHY REPLACE JUDAS? Some Bible experts say the 12 disciples represented the 12 tribes of Israel. Peter told the group that the need for a replacement was predicted in an ancient song about an evil man who turns against his master, accusing him of a crime: "Give his job to somebody else" (Psalm 109:8 MSG).

MATTHIAS. The Bible doesn't say anything more about him. One church leader—Hippolytus of Rome (about 170-235)—says Matthias died of old age in Jerusalem. Another legend says he took the story of Jesus to what is now the country of Georgia, northeast of Turkey—where he was crucified.

The Church is born

SOME 120 SOULS gather in a Jerusalem building. They are the disciples and other believers, waiting for the Holy Spirit to come.

Jesus had left the planet about 10 days earlier. Now, at about 9 a.m. on the day of Pentecost, the Spirit arrives.

// **GLOW.** Glowing auras, like tongues of fire, hover over each believer.

// **BLOW.** The sound of a windstorm fills the building; Jews from all over the city come running.

When the believers open their mouths to speak, they find themselves talking in languages they had never learned—languages spoken by Jewish pilgrims from abroad who have crowded into Jerusalem for the religious holiday.

Suddenly, everyone seems to be hearing the story of Jesus in their own language.

Peter steps forward and preaches a sermon about the death and resurrection of Jesus. He quotes Old Testament prophets to prove that what the Jews are seeing and hearing was predicted long ago.

Some 3,000 believe him and join the Christian movement.

THE FIRE FELL / When the Holy Spirit arrives, as Jesus promised, believers are meeting for prayer and worship. "What looked like flames or tongues of fire appeared and settled on each of them" (Acts 2:3).

MAGICIAN OFFERS TO BUY HOLY SPIRIT POWER. A magician named Simon offered the disciples Peter and John money for the power they had: "so that when I lay my hands on people, they will receive the Holy Spirit!" (Acts 8:19). Peter said God's gift can't be bought.

EVIDENCE OF RECEIVING THE HOLY SPIRIT. Initially, there was a sound of wind, a glow, and the ability to speak in unlearned human languages. Later, some spoke unintelligible sounds ("the language. . .of angels" [1 Corinthians 13:1]). Others prophesied. These may be what Simon the magician saw later, hoping to buy the power to produce these effects. Paul later taught that people shouldn't speak in celestial "tongues" during worship services unless someone else "is present who can interpret" (1 Corinthians 14:28).

Peter: healer and preacher

JESUS HAD PREDICTED Peter would become a support pillar of the Church: "You are Peter (which means 'rock'), and upon this rock I will build my church" (Matthew 16:18). Peter starts to see the Church rise up around him after his first sermon, which produces 3,000 converts. Now comes an encore.

Peter and John go to the Temple for the regular Jewish afternoon prayer time, at three o'clock. A man crippled for 40 years sits begging by one of the entrance gates, called the Beautiful Gate. When the man asks Peter and John for money, Peter replies, "I don't have any silver or gold for you. But I'll give you what I have. In the name of Jesus Christ the Nazarene, get up and walk!" (Acts 3:6).

The man does just that, jumping around and praising God. He goes with Peter and John to Solomon's Colonnade, a meeting area for Christians in the Temple courtyard. Many recognize him as the former cripple, and it causes such a stir that a crowd forms.

Peter knows an audience when he sees one. So he preaches his second sermon. He tells the Jews that prophets had predicted that through their race, "all the families on earth will be blessed" (Acts 3:25). Peter says that Jesus—a Jew— fulfilled this promise by offering forgiveness to everyone.

Another 2,000 souls join the movement, for a total of 5,000 men, not counting women and children (Acts 4:4).

TEMPLE PRAYER TIMES.
First-century Jewish historian Josephus said that twice a day, "in the morning and about 3 p.m.," priests led a worship service that began with a sacrifice, followed by singing and prayer.

BEAUTIFUL GATE.
It's unclear which gate this was. Many scholars guess it was the Nicanor Gate, which leads into the Temple's innermost courtyard where priests burned animal sacrifices on the altar. First-century Jewish historian Josephus said this gate was made of shimmering bronze (see *The Jewish War*, 5:3).

"IN THE NAME OF JESUS" (ACTS 3:6).
Peter healed the man by invoking the power of Jesus. It's not a phrase with magical power like an incantation, scholars say. It's Peter saying that he's not the power behind the healing. Jesus is.

Solomon's Colonnade

Jerusalem Temple

◄ **FIRST CHURCH.**
Jewish Christians met for worship at a colonnade similar to this one in a monastery (see Acts 5:12). Called Solomon's Colonnade, it was an open-air walkway along the eastern wall of the Temple courtyard. It stretched about 300 yards (275 meters), with pillars supporting a cedar roof.

Jewish court order: Stop it

TEMPLE SECURITY GUARDS supported by priests and Jewish scholars interrupt Peter's sermon. They arrest Peter and John, jail them overnight, and the next day take them before the Sanhedrin, the same Jewish court that had sentenced Jesus to death a few weeks earlier.

"By what power, or in whose name, have you done this?" the court asks Peter and John (Acts 4:7).

Peter boldly replies, "Rulers and elders of our people, are we being questioned today because we've done a good deed for a crippled man? . . . He was healed by the powerful name of Jesus. . . the man you crucified but whom God raised from the dead" (Acts 4:8–10).

Suddenly, the Jewish leaders are facing the Jesus problem all over again. They thought they laid it to rest when they killed Jesus. But neither Jesus nor the problem stayed dead.

They want to punish Peter and John for teaching what they consider a heresy, but they can't deny the miracle. They see that thousands are praising God for it.

Rather than spark a riot, the court simply orders Peter and John to never again speak in the name of Jesus.

"Do you think God wants us to obey you rather than him?" the disciples reply. "We cannot stop telling about everything we have seen and heard" (Acts 4:19–20).

DÉJÀ VU FOR JUDGES / Members of the Jewish high court orchestrate the execution of Jesus, thinking they've silenced a heretical movement. Several weeks later, two of Jesus' disciples appear before the same court, charged with doing miracles in Jesus' name.

ANNAS, THE HIGH PRIEST? The writer of Acts calls Annas the high priest. But Annas was more like a high priest emeritus: retired and respected. He served from AD 6–15. His son-in-law Caiaphas served from about AD 18–36.

SANHEDRIN. Jewish supreme court, made up of about 70 scholars, rabbis, and other religious leaders. They rule on matters of faith and on how Jews should behave.

JESUS, THE REJECTED CORNERSTONE. Peter quotes the Bible to the Bible scholars. "The stone that you builders rejected has now become the cornerstone" (Acts 4:11, quoting Psalm 118:22). Peter's point: God predicted Jewish leaders would reject Jesus, the single most important building block of faith in God. "Jesus is the only One who can save people" (Acts 4:12 NCV).

MIRACLES. Jesus' disciples continue to draw crowds as Jesus did, mainly through miracles of healing. Without this evidence to back up their seemingly absurd teaching—that Jesus rose from the dead—it's a fair bet that few Jews would have paid any attention to them.

You lie, you die

ALL THEY WANTED, it seems, was a little recognition for their charitable giving. They were a husband and wife named Ananias and Sapphira.

They apparently saw the attention the apostles lavished on a Jew named Joseph, from the island of Cyprus. He sold some property and gave the money to the apostles to distribute among the poor. Grateful for the gift, the apostles gave Joseph a nickname of endearment: Barnabas, which means "Son of Encouragement."

Ananias and Sapphira do the same thing Joseph did, with one exception. They keep some of the cash for themselves but tell the apostles they donated the full amount.

Peter somehow sees through the lie when Ananias brings the donation, and he says so. "You weren't lying to us but to God!" Peter tells him (Acts 5:4).

Instantly, Ananias drops dead.

Three hours later, his wife comes and repeats the lie. Peter tells her that the men who had just buried her husband would bury her, too. She collapses, dead. Fear grips all the Christians.

DID GOD KILL ANANIAS AND SAPPHIRA?

Most likely, many Bible experts say. That's how they interpret the writer's original language. If they're right, some Christians today would argue, God's behavior seems like ironic overkill—*Ananias* means "God is merciful." But apparently not always. Some students of the Bible defend God's action by saying the deaths produced a snap-to effect. Members of the emerging Christian movement saw they'd better not mess with God or his ministers.

CHRISTIAN COMMUNISTS?

Many of the first Christians seemed to treat their assets as community property. "They felt that what they owned was not their own, so they shared everything they had. . . . There were no needy people among them, because those who owned land or houses would sell them and bring the money to the apostles to give to those in need" (Acts 4:32, 34–35). Many Christians, however, argue that this story isn't about communism, which is a political system, but that it's about compassion and generosity.

TIME TO SAY GOOD-BYE / Death comes calling when Sapphira exaggerates the amount of a charitable contribution that she and her husband gave to the disciples.

Stephen, the first martyr

RUNNING A SOUP KITCHEN doesn't sound like a job that would get a person brought up on charges of blasphemy and stoned to death by an angry mob. But the job seemed to give a man named Stephen an opportunity to run his mouth, too. That's what gets him killed.

As the Church's compassionate ministry program grows, Jesus' disciples decide to delegate the job of distributing food each day to widows and other poverty-stricken believers. They appoint seven men of faith, Stephen among them.

One day some Jews start debating him, most likely about Jesus and his teachings. These Jews are from one of the synagogues in Jerusalem, the Synagogue of Freed Slaves. They apparently lose the debate and are terribly sore losers. They convince some men to lie, charging Stephen with speaking disrespectfully about the Jewish laws and Temple.

Stephen is brought before the same Jewish high court that had arranged the execution of Jesus and had ordered Peter and John to stop preaching about Jesus. Instead of denying the charges against him, Stephen levels charges against the Jewish leaders.

"Your ancestors killed anyone who dared talk about the coming of the Just One. And you've kept up the family tradition—traitors and murderers, all of you" (Acts 7:52 MSG).

The Jews prove Stephen right. They kill him, too.

STONING OF STEPHEN / Jews stone Stephen for insulting the high court, calling them murderers. It probably didn't help that at the end of his closing statement, Stephen saw a vision of Jesus standing beside God in heaven, and he told the court about it—the same court that had orchestrated the crucifixion of Jesus.

◀**STONING ANOTHER STEPHEN.** Author Stephen M. Miller, in his rental car that was stoned in East Jerusalem. Rented from an Israeli vendor, the car had a color-coded license plate distinguishing it from Palestinian-owned cars. When Miller and several colleagues drove to see Hezekiah's Tunnel, in a Palestinian part of town, someone rushed the car and heaved a cantaloupe-sized rock. No one was injured. As in Bible times, there are still plenty of rocks in Jerusalem.

EXECUTION BY STONING. Jewish law prescribes execution by several methods, depending on the crime. Jews pummeled fellow Jews with stones for committing crimes such as rejecting the Jewish faith, talking disrespectfully about God, dabbling in sorcery, committing adultery, or working on the Sabbath.

Saul, the most famous convert

JEWS CATCH THE SCENT OF HERETICS after executing Stephen. His death unleashes a wave of persecution throughout Jerusalem.

The target: Jews who follow the teachings of Jesus. To avoid arrest and possible execution, many Jewish Christians scatter to distant cities.

One Jew tracks them down—like a bounty hunter hoping for a divine reward. His Hebrew name is Saul, but he's better known today by his Roman name: Paul.

He heads off to Damascus, north about 150 miles (240 km). He's armed with letters from the high priest, demanding that distant synagogue leaders cooperate in the hunt for heretics.

Somewhere along the way, a beam of light hits him, shocking him to the ground and blinding him. A voice, identifying itself as Jesus, asks why Saul is persecuting him. "Get up," Jesus says, "Go into the city, and you will be told what you must do" (Acts 9:6).

Colleagues traveling with Paul lead him to Damascus. There, God orders a man named Ananias to heal Paul's blindness.

Paul's encounter with Jesus, followed by the healing, convinces him that he has been on the wrong side of the religious debate. He says so publicly, declaring in the synagogues of Damascus that Jesus "is indeed the Son of God!" (Acts 9:20).

PAUL—HEADLINES ON A TIMELINE

Dates Approximate

Gamaliel, top Jewish scholar of his day

Escape from Damascus

AD

6	20	33	36
Paul born in Tarsus	Trained as Pharisee by Gamaliel	Becomes a Christian	Meets Peter in Jerusalem

Co-minister in Antioch	Jerusalem Meeting; mission trip #2	Third missionary trip	Sails to Rome for trial	Executed in Rome

44	46	48	49	52	57	60	64
	First missionary trip	Starts church in Corinth			Arrested in Jerusalem		

WHY DID JESUS TAKE SUCH EXTREME MEASURES TO CONVERT PAUL? / The closest Jesus comes to explaining that is to tell Ananias, "Saul is my chosen instrument to take my message to the Gentiles and to kings, as well as to the people of Israel" (Acts 9:15). Perhaps Jesus knew that the best way to battle intolerant Jewish traditionalists was with the insight of a former intolerant Jewish traditionalist.

Peter's non-kosher vision

PETER HAS A VISION that leaves him scratching his head. It happens while he's waiting for lunch in the home of a tanner in the seaside town of Joppa. In this vision, Peter sees a huge tarp descend from the sky. The tarp is loaded with all kinds of animals Jews aren't supposed to eat, including scavenger birds, snakes, and other reptiles.

"Get up, Peter," a voice says. "Kill and eat them."

Peter refuses: "I have never eaten anything that our Jewish laws have declared impure and unclean."

"Do not call something unclean if God has made it clean" the voice replies (Acts 10:13–15). The vision repeats three times.

Just then, three messengers arrive at the house. They tell him that an angel told their master, Cornelius, a God-loving Roman officer in Caesarea, to invite Peter to his home. Peter leaves with them the next day. By the time he steps into Cornelius's house, he has figured out the meaning of the vision.

Peter tells Cornelius, "You know it is against our laws for a Jewish man to enter a Gentile home like this or to associate with you. But God has shown me that I should no longer think of anyone as impure or unclean" (Acts 10:28).

Cornelius receives the Holy Spirit, convincing Peter and Jews traveling with him that God wants the Christian movement opened to everyone, Jews and Gentiles.

Caesarea aqueduct

CAESAREA MARITIMA / A long day's walk north of Joppa, about 30 miles (50 kilometers), this coastal city was Rome's headquarters in the Jewish homeland—the Roman capital of what is now Israel. Herod the Great rebuilt this once-tiny town, turning it into a thoroughly Roman-style city with a harbor, theaters, a hippodrome for horse-racing, palaces, and an aqueduct, channeling water from a spring about 10 miles (16 kilometers) away in the foothills of the Mount Carmel range.

Co-pastors: Barnabas and Paul

JEWISH CHRISTIANS flee the persecution in Jerusalem. Some end up in Antioch of Syria, about 300 miles (482 km) north. There, they tell the story of Jesus to non-Jews. Many of these Gentiles embrace the teaching, and start meeting regularly to hear more.

Jesus' disciples and other Church leaders still in Jerusalem hear about the congregation. They decide to send Barnabas as their representative to check it out. He's apparently impressed with them, and they with him. He stays on as pastor.

Barnabas travels some 150 miles (240 km) north to Paul's hometown of Tarsus and recruits Paul to come down and help out. Paul has been a believer for perhaps a decade. Though the Bible says little about him during those years, scholars say it's a fair guess he had been preaching about Jesus in his hometown—just as he had done in Damascus within days of his conversion.

Antioch is where believers are first called Christians—a hint, scholars say, that Gentile believers are starting to develop their own identity (see Acts 11:26). Jewish Christians call their movement "the Way" (Acts 9:2).

CHRISTIANITY STARTS HERE / Women wait for a bus in Antakya, Turkey—known as Antioch in Paul's day. It was in this city with its predominately non-Jewish congregation that followers of Jesus first got the nickname Christians. It stuck.

ANTIOCH, TURKEY. In Paul's day it was one of the largest cities in the Roman Empire. Many scholars say that with a population of half a million or more, it ranked third, after Rome and Alexandria, Egypt. Romans made it capital of their Syrian province. A quake devastated the city in AD 37, a few years before Paul arrived in about 44. But Rome quickly rebuilt it. Today it's called Antakya, located on Turkey's side of the border with Syria.

APOSTLE JAMES, MARTYRED. About this time Herod Agrippa I (reigned AD 37–44) joined in the persecution of Jewish Christians by executing one of Jesus' closest disciples: James, the brother of John (see Acts 12:1-2). James is the only disciple whose martyrdom is reported in the Bible. But early Church leaders wrote that most of the other disciples died because of their teachings, too.

The first missionaries

UNTIL NOW, spreading the story of Jesus seemed haphazard. Wherever believers happened to go, they took their faith and shared it. But during what sounds like a spiritual retreat for five church leaders at Antioch, a mission trip gets organized.

Barnabas and Paul are worshipping and fasting with three other leaders when the Holy Spirit somehow sends the group a message: "Dedicate Barnabas and Saul for the special work to which I have called them" (Acts 13:2).

There seems to have been more to the message than that because the two leave for the port city of Seleucia and sail for the island of Cyprus, Barnabas's homeland. There, they travel from one end of the island to the other, teaching in the synagogues about Jesus. They even manage to convert the Roman governor, Sergius Paulus.

From Cyprus, they catch a ship sailing north to what is now Turkey, preaching in several towns before heading home. The entire expedition seems to have taken about two years, covering some 1,400 miles (2,250 km), round trip. Afterward, they return to their home base in Antioch.

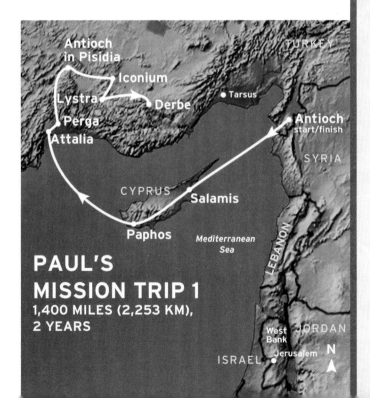

PAUL'S MISSION TRIP 1
1,400 MILES (2,253 KM), 2 YEARS

Antioch in Pisidia
Iconium
Lystra
Derbe
Tarsus
Perga
Attalia
Antioch start/finish
SYRIA
CYPRUS
Salamis
Paphos
Mediterranean Sea
LEBANON
West Bank
JORDAN
ISRAEL
Jerusalem
TURKEY
N

Messenger god Mercury, with wings from head to foot: helmet and heels

MISTAKEN FOR GODS.
In the city of Lystra, Paul and Barnabas heal a man who had been crippled since birth. Witnesses mistake the two for gods: Barnabas becomes the top god, Zeus; Paul—who apparently did most of the talking—becomes Zeus's son, the messenger god Hermes, also known as Mercury. When priests from the temple of Zeus come to them with sacrifices, Barnabas and Paul tell them, "We are merely human beings—just like you! We have come to bring you the Good News that you should turn from these worthless things and turn to the living God" (Acts 14:15).

TARGETING NON-JEWS.
During this trip, Jews became so hostile toward Paul that he decides to concentrate in the future on ministering to non-Jews. For support, he quotes a famous Jewish prophet: "I have made you a light for those who aren't Jews. You will bring salvation to the whole earth" (Acts 13:47, quoting Isaiah 49:6 NIrV).

JEWS ON THE TRAIL.
Jews (from previous cities the two apostles visited) arrived in Lystra on a mission of their own: to silence the heretics. They stir up a mob that stones Paul and leaves him for dead. He recovers and goes back to preaching.

Church split

YOU CAN'T BE A GOOD CHRISTIAN if you're not a good Jew. That's what some Jewish Christians are telling non-Jewish converts. In other words, Christians should eat only kosher food, honor the Saturday Sabbath, and follow all the other laws of Moses—including the painful ritual of circumcision for the gents.

Peter, Paul, and Barnabas all beg to differ.

So Church leaders convene a summit meeting in Jerusalem, led by James, a brother of Jesus.

There, Peter tells the council that he saw the Gentile family of Cornelius filled with the Holy Spirit. Paul and Barnabas tell of God blessing the non-Jews in Antioch as well as in the many cities they visited on their missionary trip.

James settles on a compromise. Non-Jewish Christians have to observe only these rules:

// Don't eat food offered to idols.

// Don't eat meat with blood in it.

// Don't commit sex sins.

COMPROMISE IN THE WORKS / Peter makes his case at a summit meeting of Church leaders in Jerusalem. He argues that non-Jewish Christians shouldn't be expected to follow Jewish laws. Many Jewish Christians disagree strongly enough that the dispute threatens to split the Church.

DID THE COMPROMISE WORK?

No. Jewish Christians known as Judaizers (JEW-day-EYES-urs) continued to press hard against Paul, following him and telling his converts that they needed to obey Jewish laws, too. Paul eventually abandoned the compromise, as well, telling his converts that it doesn't matter what they eat as long as they try not to offend those eating with them (Romans 14:2–3; 1 Corinthians 8).

STRANGLED ANIMALS.

James prohibited eating animals strangled to death, probably because the strangling was intended to keep the blood in the animal—which to some made the meat more tasty: rare meat versus well done.

Animal sacrifice

WHAT'S WRONG WITH EATING BLOODY MEAT?

Jews considered animal blood sacred. They offered it in sacrifices to God as a substitute for their own blood—because sin is a capital offense. As Jewish law puts it, quoting God: "Life is in the blood, and I have given you the blood of animals to sacrifice in place of your own. That's also why I have forbidden you to eat blood" (Leviticus 17:11–12 CEV).

Paul's second missionary trip

KNOWING HE HAS THE SUPPORT of the Church leaders in Jerusalem for his work among non-Jews, Paul hits the road again. He wants Barnabas to return with him to the cities they visited in Cyprus and Turkey on their first missionary expedition. But the two argue over one detail—and end up going their separate ways.

The detail is John Mark, Barnabas's cousin. Barnabas wants to take him. Paul doesn't. John Mark went with them on the first expedition, but he turned tail once they hit the swamps of southern Turkey, abandoning the two and sailing for home.

Barnabas and Paul split up. Barnabas takes John Mark and revisits Cyprus. Paul picks a new partner, Silas, and heads northwest to revisit cities in Turkey. Along the way, he picks up some other traveling associates and rich supporters. A vision prompts him to cross into Europe, where he plants several churches in Greece—the most famous of which is in Corinth.

In several cities, Jews react violently to his message and stir the crowds to mob action—sometimes getting him arrested or driving him out of town.

Paul returns to his home church in Antioch, by way of Jerusalem, where he visits Christianity's mother church and probably reports to the apostles and other Church leaders.

PAUL'S MISSION TRIP 2
2,700 MILES (4,345 KM), 3 YEARS

Outbound route
Return route

JOHN MARK. This is a combo name, merging his Hebrew name (John) with his Greek name (Mark). Early Church writers said he wrote the Gospel of Mark. Paul later reconciled with him.

◄ **TRIP HIGHLIGHTS:**

> Timothy of Lystra joins Paul as an associate minister.

> Lydia, a rich merchant in Philippi, lets them start a church in her home.

> Paul is beaten and jailed in Philippi with Silas, another associate minister. But city officials later apologize and release them.

> Paul preaches in Athens, a college town. But most of the scholars laugh at his story of Jesus rising from the dead.

> Paul spends a year and a half in Corinth, planting a church there.

Paul's last missionary trip

A RIOT MAKER—not by choice—Paul isn't good for the status quo. Wherever he goes, he's trying to change things. And that tends to stir up trouble. This pattern continues on this third and final missionary expedition.

Sometimes the trouble comes from Jewish Christians trailing him, trying to undo the "damage" he causes when he teaches non-Jewish Christians they can ignore Jewish laws, such as the laws about circumcision and kosher food. Not true, they insist, ignoring the compromise that Christian leaders agreed on at the Jerusalem summit meeting (see page 408).

Sometimes the trouble comes from other Jews who consider it blasphemy when Paul—or any other Christian—says God has a Son.

TEMPLE OF ARTEMIS. The greatest of the Seven Wonders of the World was this Ephesus temple, according to Greek architect Philon (200s BC), who said he had seen them all. Four times larger than the Parthenon of Athens, the Temple of Artemis rose six stories high and stretched 130 yards (119 meters) long and 70 yards (64 meters) wide. Framing it were 127 pillars, each 60 feet (18 meters) high and 6 feet (2 meters) thick.

And sometimes, as in Ephesus, the problem is money. Paul spends about three years there, starting the church. He's so successful that the idol-making industry feels the pinch. Ephesus is home to one of the Seven Wonders of the World: the Temple of Artemis. Yet sales of Artemis figurines plummet.

Demetrius, owner of a large business that manufactures the figurines, calls a guild meeting about how to stop Paul from further damaging "this magnificent goddess" (Acts 19:27). A riot erupts. The mayor manages to calm the people, but Paul leaves town. He revisits church groups in Greece and then stops in Miletus to greet leaders from neighboring Ephesus.

Sadly, he tells the people that they'll never see him again. The Holy Spirit, he says, has let him know that prison and suffering lie ahead.

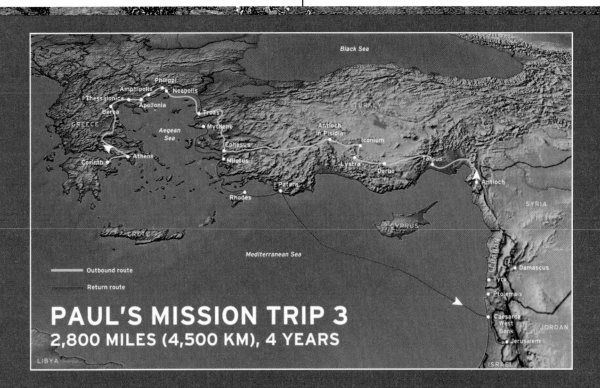

PAUL'S MISSION TRIP 3
2,800 MILES (4,500 KM), 4 YEARS

EPHESUS. One of the five largest cities in the Roman Empire. See also pages 441–442.

ARTEMIS. Goddess of forests, hunting, and concerns of women: virginity, fertility, and childbirth. Considered the daughter of Zeus, she was one of the most widely worshipped Greek goddesses. Romans called her Diana.

DEMETRIUS. Archaeologists found his name on a list of men honored as protectors of the Temple of Artemis. They also found an inscription about a silversmith guild in the city: "May the guild of the silversmiths prosper!"

Paul, out of circulation

THE HOLY SPIRIT IS RIGHT. Prison and suffering greet Paul in Jerusalem—just as Paul said the Spirit had predicted. But first, a riot.

Jews who had seen Paul in Ephesus spot him in the Temple. They get the local Jews worked up about two false charges against Paul:

// Paul tells people to disobey Jewish laws (actually, he tells only non-Jews they don't have to obey these laws).

// He brought a non-Jew into the Temple area reserved for only Jews.

A riot erupts. Roman soldiers break it up, arrest Paul, and escort him to Caesarea for trial.

Rome's governor in Caesarea is a politician on the take. His name is Felix. And he keeps Paul in jail for two years, hoping "Paul would bribe him" (Acts 24:26).

When Rome replaces Felix with Festus, Jews ask the new governor to transfer Paul back to Jerusalem. The Jews intend to assassinate Paul along the way. Paul refuses to go. As a Roman citizen, he can and does appeal to the empire's supreme court, headed by Caesar.

"Very well!" Festus replies. "You have appealed to Caesar, and to Caesar you will go!" (Acts 25:12).

....

FELIX AND FESTUS / Felix: former slave of Roman emperor Claudius, served about AD 52–60. Festus: ruled about AD 60–62. Married to granddaughter of Antony and Cleopatra.

ROMAN ESCORT OUT OF TOWN. Roman history enthusiasts reenact military maneuvers. When the Roman commander in Jerusalem found out that 40 Jews planned to ambush his men and kill Paul while they escorted him across town to stand trial before the Jewish high court, he beefed up his patrol. Two hundred soldiers and 70 cavalrymen would escort Paul. But not across town. Under cover of night they whisked him some 60 miles (96 km) west to Caesarea, Rome's headquarters in the Jewish homeland.

Boat-busting trip to Rome

IN A SHIPWRECK OF A DECISION, Roman soldiers assigned to escort Paul to Rome sail out of Caesarea in late summer or early fall.

That's near the end of safe sailing. Yet they have at least a month of sailing ahead of them: 2,000 miles (3200 km) against the seasonal headwinds blowing toward the southeast. Sea voyages get risky in mid-September and dangerous in mid-December through spring.

It's late September or early October by the time they reach Myra, yet they press on. There, Paul and his escort transfer to an Egyptian grain ship headed to Rome, carrying 276 passengers and crew. A savvy traveler, Paul advises wintering in Fair Havens, Crete. But the ship's captain sails on for the better-protected harbor at Phoenix.

Along the way, a typhoon engulfs the ship and pummels it for two weeks, driving it first toward the dangerous shallows of Syrtis Major along Africa's coast before running it aground near the island of Malta.

The boat splinters under the battering waves, but no one dies. Paul and his military escort spend three months there before sailing on to Italy.

In Rome, Paul lives under house arrest for two years—preaching while waiting for his trial. With that cliff-hanger, the story ends.

ROUGH SAILING
PAUL'S VOYAGE TO ROME

FRANCE

Black Sea

ITALY
Rome   Adriatic Sea

• Puteoli

GREECE   Aegean Sea   TURKEY

• Rheghium   Corinth •   • Athens   • Ephesus

SICILY
• Syracuse

Malta   SHIP RUNS AGROUND   • Myra
BREAKS UP

CYPRUS   SYRIA

STORM DRIVES SHIP   Phoenix •   CRETE
OFF COURSE   • Fair Havens   LEBANON

Mediterranean Sea   Sidon •

Syrtis Major   Caesarea •
JORDAN
Jerusalem •
ISRAEL

LIBYA   EGYPT

SCENIC ROUTE TO ROME. Paul sails out of the Jewish harbor of Caesarea during a risky season for sailing: the end of summer or early fall. He has no choice. Under armed guard, he's headed for a trial at Caesar's court in Rome. He makes it. But the ship doesn't. A typhoon runs it aground in Malta, where the storm surge hammers it into toothpicks.

ROMANS 3:23–25

Everyone has sinned, Paul writes. Though sin is a capital offense in God's eyes, no one needs to be punished. Jesus died so we don't have to. God forgives the sins of those who believe that.

BIG SCENE

WE'RE FORGIVEN

BIBLE HISTORY

ALL DATES APPROXIMATE

AD 33
Paul becomes a Christian

AD 46
Paul begins first missionary trip

WORLD HISTORY

ROMANS

WHAT REAL CHRISTIANS BELIEVE

STORY LINE

ABOUT 20 YEARS into Paul's ministry—which includes three missionary trips and at least 20 church start-ups in the eastern half of the Roman Empire—he decides to head west.

He wants to take the story of Jesus to Spain, on the empire's western frontier. Along the way, he plans to stop off in Rome. Though it's the capital of the empire, he has never been there before.

But he does have a lot of friends there. More than two dozen, whom he mentions by name.

This isn't just a friendly visit he's paying them. It's a whistle stop for money. He's launching a missionary expedition into Spain. And he wants the Roman Christians to help fund the trip: "You can provide for my journey" (Romans 15:24).

Paul apparently wants them to know exactly what they're getting for their money. So he introduces himself by summing up his beliefs.

That summary becomes the letter of Romans—Christianity's first known theology book: Christianity 101.

Many Bible experts say it's still the most concise, eloquent description of the Christian faith ever written.

// TIME: Paul wrote Romans in about AD 57, near the end of his last missionary trip but before his arrest in Jerusalem, which eventually takes him to Rome for trial.

// AUTHOR: Paul apparently dictates this letter to an associate named Tertius (see Romans 16:22). Of all the letters attributed to Paul, Bible experts consider this the most reliable—and the gauge in style and teaching to measure the authenticity of his other letters.

// LOCATION: Somewhere on the road to Jerusalem—perhaps in Turkey or Greece—Paul writes this letter to fellow Christians in Rome, a city he hopes to visit.

AD 57
Paul writes letter to Christians in Rome

AD 60
Paul arrives in Rome

Romans learn to use soap, from the French (Gauls)
AD 50

Nero becomes Roman Emperor (dies AD 68)
AD 54

Rome burns, Paul executed in Rome
AD 64

Paul's question for atheists

PAUL SEEMS TO WONDER how any human beings in their right mind can work up the faith it takes to become an atheist.

He admits that it takes faith to become a Christian, too. After all, he says, we have to trust in the teachings of Jesus—"This Good News tells us how God makes us right in his sight. This is accomplished from start to finish by faith. As the Scriptures say, 'It is through faith that a righteous person has life' " (Romans 1:17).

But Paul implies that it takes even more faith to ignore God as the artist responsible for the masterpiece on creation's canvas.

"They know the truth about God because he has made it obvious to them. For ever since the world was created, people have seen the earth and sky. Through everything God made, they can clearly see his invisible qualities—his eternal power and divine nature. So they have no excuse for not knowing God" (Romans 1:19–20).

To be an atheist, Paul implies, people have to amp up their faith big-time. They have to convince themselves that in this universe, playing by the rules of physics, it's possible for nothing to become something.

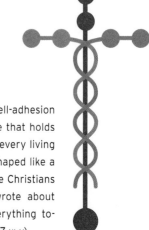

LAMININ / A cell-adhesion molecule, it's the glue that holds together the body of every living organism on earth. Shaped like a cross, it reminds some Christians of something Paul wrote about Jesus: "He holds everything together" (Colossians 1:17 NIrV).

ROMAN EMPIRE

◄ROAMING THE ROMAN EMPIRE. By the time Paul writes the letter of Romans to non-Jewish Christians in Rome, he has started churches throughout what is now Turkey and Greece. Now, he's hoping to visit Rome before moving on to start churches in Spain.

HAS GOD ABANDONED ATHEISTS? No. Paul says that since atheists "thought it foolish to acknowledge God, he abandoned them to their foolish thinking" (Romans 1:28). But not forever. Paul says God lets people make their own decisions. If they decide later to acknowledge him, he welcomes them.

Why Jesus died

SIN IS A CAPITAL OFFENSE, in the eyes of a holy God. Any sin. It's as incompatible with God's spiritual kingdom as matter is with antimatter in our physical world.

Jesus died, Paul says, to make sinful people compatible with God and his kingdom.

During the 1,400 years or so between the time of Moses and Jesus, Jews found forgiveness by sacrificing animals as substitutes for themselves. "The life of an animal is in the blood. I have provided the blood for you to make atonement for your lives on the Altar; it is the blood, the life, that makes atonement" (Leviticus 17:11 MSG).

But Paul says God had promised a new and better system that would work for everyone, Jew and non-Jew. And he delivered:

> *God presented Jesus as the sacrifice for sin. People are made right with God when they believe that Jesus sacrificed his life, shedding his blood.*
> **ROMANS 3:25**

The death of Jesus, Paul says, changes everything.

People no longer have to follow the old Jewish system of obeying laws about circumcision, kosher food, and animal sacrifices. "There is only one God, and he accepts Gentiles as well as Jews, simply because of their faith" (Romans 3:30 CEV).

· ·

CRUCIFIXION, FRONT AND CENTER / Framed by 700-year-old stained-glass windows, the crucifixion of Jesus takes center stage in St. Dionysius Church in Esslingen, Germany—as it does in Paul's teaching about salvation. Paul says sin warrants the death penalty, but that the blood of Jesus took care of that penalty for everyone—much like the blood of sacrificed animals once atoned for sins of the Jews.

SALVATION ROAD.
Calling it the "Roman road to salvation," Bible experts say Paul's letter to the Romans works like a spiritual map. Paul points readers in the direction he says they should go.

> "Everyone has sinned" (Romans 3:23).
> "The wages of sin is death" (Romans 6:23).
> "God showed his great love for us by sending Christ to die for us while we were still sinners" (Romans 5:8).
> "If you confess with your mouth that Jesus is Lord and believe in your heart that God raised him from the dead, you will be saved" (Romans 10:9).

· ·

THE JEWISH BIBLE PREDICTED SALVATION THROUGH JESUS.
That's what Paul said (see Romans 3:21). Paul was talking about the many prophecies scattered throughout the Old Testament, according to Bible experts. For examples, see pages 210, 217.

Being good doesn't save us

AS AN ULTRA-CONSERVATIVE JEW, Paul grew up believing that what God wanted most was for people to obey the Jewish laws. To name a few of the hundreds: Sacrifice animals to atone for sins. Rest on the Sabbath. Eat only kosher food.

Paul doesn't believe that anymore. Not since his encounter with the resurrected Jesus while he was on his way to arrest Jewish Christians in Damascus (page 404).

To make his case against the Jewish religion, Paul calls on an unlikely witness: Abraham, father of the Jewish religion. Paul says God approved of Abraham not because Abraham obeyed the Jewish laws; those laws wouldn't exist for another 600 years or so, when Moses shows up.

"God accepted Abraham because Abraham had faith in him," Paul says, quoting Genesis 15:6 (Romans 4:3 CEV).

What God did for Abraham, Paul argues, he does for everyone. "We have been made right with God because of our faith. . . . Through faith in Jesus we have received God's grace. In that grace we stand" (Romans 5:1–2 NIrV).

BY FAITH, ABRAHAM HITS THE ROAD /
Abraham packs up his family and moves away from his home in what is now Iraq. He moves first to Turkey, but finally settles in what is now Israel. He does this because God asked him to. About 2,000 years later, Paul uses Abraham's confidence in God to prove a point: Trusting God is all it takes to win the Lord's approval.

GRACE. It's love that isn't earned, but given anyway. Some Bible experts describe God's grace this way: He accepts us where we are, but he's not willing to leave us there.

MARTIN LUTHER, TRYING TO EARN SALVATION. Luther, founder of the Protestant movement, said when he was a Catholic monk, he tried everything he could to earn his place in heaven. He fasted so much that he permanently damaged his digestive system. "If ever a monk could get into heaven by his monkery," Luther wrote, "it was me." Still he felt no assurance—until he studied Romans. There, in Romans 1:17, he discovered that we're saved by faith, through God's grace and sheer mercy. "This passage of Paul," he said, "became my gateway into heaven."

DON'T YOU HAVE TO DO GOOD DEEDS TO MAKE IT TO HEAVEN? No. Not according to Paul. We're saved by putting our trust in Jesus. Period. James seems to argue otherwise: "I will show you my faith by my good deeds" (James 2:18). But most scholars say James is simply correcting an abuse of Paul's teaching. Faith is more than intellectual. It rolls up its sleeves and gets to work. People of faith tend to serve others, just as Jesus instructed his disciples (see page 389).

Breaking free of sin's death grip

Augustine (AD 354–430)

CHRISTIANS AREN'T SLAVES TO SIN, Paul says. Jesus is our master. So Paul says Christians shouldn't do what they know is wrong, as though they don't have any choice.

He gives three reasons not to sin—each a metaphor to help people see a mental picture of the reason.

BAPTISM. Paul says when we go under the water, we're symbolically dying as Jesus died. And when we rise, we're rising to "new lives" (Romans 6:4).

CRUCIFIXION. "What we used to be was nailed to the cross with him [Jesus]" (Romans 6:6 NIrV).

SLAVERY. "You can be slaves of sin. Then you will die. Or you can be slaves who obey God. Then you will live a godly life" (Romans 6:16 NIrV).

Paul admits that even an apostle like himself doesn't have the strength to manhandle sin: "I want to do what is right, but I can't" (Romans 7:18).

Yet Paul says there's good news: "Who will free me from this life that is dominated by sin and death? Thank God! The answer is in Jesus Christ our Lord" (Romans 7:24–25).

HOW PAUL'S LETTER TO ROME CHANGED A SEX ADDICT.

Before Augustine became the most respected theologian since Paul, in the early centuries of the Church, he was a party guy who struggled with a sex addiction. That changed at age 32. Troubled by his addiction, he was crying in a garden when he heard a voice that told him to read. He said he rushed to the bench where he'd placed his Bible and read the first words his eyes fell on: "Don't go to wild parties or get drunk.... Let the Lord Jesus Christ be as near to you as the clothes you wear. Then you won't try to satisfy your selfish desires" (Romans 13:13–14 CEV).

◄ **ADDICTED.**
Powerfully addictive, cocaine has been abused for more than a century—and eaten as coca leaves for thousands of years. That makes it one of the oldest known drugs. Paul's description of how sin latches on to people sounds strangely similar to an addiction: "I don't want to do what is wrong, but I do it anyway.... This power makes me a slave" (Romans 7:19, 23).

Jews aren't the only ones chosen

GOD'S PLAN STARTED WITH THE JEWS. But it doesn't end there, Paul assures his non-Jewish readers.

In fact, Paul is worried about the Jews. He says they've tried hard to get right with God but they've gone about it the wrong way—"by keeping the law instead of by trusting in him" (Romans 9:32).

Jews were God's Chosen People—chosen to become a blessing to the nations of the world (see Genesis 12:3). Paul says Jesus, a Jew, fulfilled that promise. And now the blessing of salvation is available to everyone.

Paul adds that the prophets predicted it: "Just as the Lord says in the book of Hosea, 'Although they are not my people, I will make them my people. I will treat with love those nations that have never been loved'" (Romans 9:25 CEV).

This doesn't mean God has rejected the Jews, Paul adds. If it did, Paul's in trouble since he's a Jew. Instead, it means "Jew and Gentile are the same in this respect. . . . For 'Everyone who calls on the name of the LORD will be saved'" (Romans 10:12–13).

THE LAW.
This refers to the Jewish laws of behavior, preserved in the first five books of the Bible. The most basic laws are the 10 Commandments. But there are hundreds of others that grow out of those 10.

WHY WASN'T IT ENOUGH FOR THE JEWS TO OBEY THE LAW?
Paul says they tried to keep the letter of the law, but missed the spirit of it. The law was intended to draw them closer to God and to mature their trust in God. Instead, it became a bunch of rules. So when they sinned, they just offered the designated sacrifice. Instead, they should have taken the advice of a Jewish song writer: "Offerings and sacrifices are not what you want. The way to please you is to feel sorrow deep in our hearts. This is the kind of sacrifice you won't refuse" (Psalm 51:16–17 CEV).

▼ **GOD'S NEW CHOSEN PEOPLE.**
A Jew himself, Paul says God chose the Jewish people to launch his plan of salvation. But Paul says that Jesus takes that plan to the next level, offering salvation to everyone. Sadly, Paul adds, many Jews couldn't make the climb. For them, Jesus became "a huge rock in the middle of the road. And so they stumbled into him and went sprawling" (Romans 9:32 MSG).

What a real Christian looks like

CHRISTIANS ARE ODDBALLS compared to non-Christians—at least in the way they think and act.

That's Paul's hope, anyway. He tells Christians in Rome, "Don't become so well-adjusted to your culture that you fit into it without even thinking" (Romans 12:2 MSG).

Paul says that instead of trying to look and act like everyone else, they should set their sights higher. "Fix your attention on God. You'll be changed from the inside out. . . . Unlike the culture around you, always dragging you down to its level of immaturity, God brings the best out of you" (Romans 12:2 MSG).

Paul's to-do list of "the best" includes:

// Love each other with genuine affection.
// Work hard, and don't be lazy.
// Be patient when you're in trouble, and keep praying.
// Help others in need.
// Don't take revenge; leave that for God.
// Submit to governing authorities. They'll answer to God.
// Don't argue with new Christians; accept them as they are, as Christ accepted you.

CHILLING, AMISH STYLE / An Amish man dresses in black. It's the preferred color of a Christian group known for its simple lifestyle, which includes stern limits on modern technology and on colorful clothing. Just as today's Amish stand out in looks, Paul says should all Christians should stand out in behavior.

WHEN PAUL WROTE HIS LETTERS

DATE, AD	BOOK	PAUL'S SITUATION
50	1, 2 Thessalonians	Ministering in Corinth
53	Galatians	Ministering in Ephesus
55	1, 2 Corinthians	Ministering in Ephesus
57	Romans	At the end of his third missionary trip, on his way back to Jerusalem
60-62	Colossians, Philemon, Ephesians, Philippians	Under house arrest in Rome, awaiting trial
63	1 Timothy, Titus	After release from prison in Rome
64 OR 67	2 Timothy	In prison at Rome again, awaiting execution

Dates approximate, debated by scholars

1 CORINTHIANS 5

A man in the church is living in sin with his stepmother. Paul orders the church to remove him from the fellowship in the hopes it will convict him and convince him to repent.

BIG SCENE

JUST SAY NO TO INCEST

BIBLE HISTORY

ALL DATES APPROXIMATE

AD 48 *Paul supports himself as tentmaker during one and a half years in Corinth*

WORLD HISTORY

AD 48 *Emperor Claudius executes third wife for plotting coup, marries niece Agrippina later*

AD 54 *Claudius's wife allegedly kills him with poison mushrooms; her son Nero rules (AD 54–68)*

1,2 CORINTHIANS

CHURCH OF THE PAIN IN THE NECK

STORY LINE

PAUL IS LONG GONE from the church he started in Corinth on his second mission trip—perhaps by several years. He's now on mission trip three, starting a church in the megacity of Ephesus some 250 miles (400 km) across the Aegean Sea.

A courier brings him a letter from Corinth. The congregation has a bunch of questions, and they want Paul's advice. The courier apparently tells Paul about other problems the church seems afraid to put in writing, including arguments over who's in charge.

Paul addresses every concern in a letter: 1 Corinthians. Then he revisits the church. It's a tense reunion. At least one church member mouths off to him. After Paul leaves, intruders he calls false apostles arrive in Corinth and stir up even more trouble.

Paul writes the follow-up letter of 2 Corinthians. To some extent, it's a letter of self-defense. Paul shoots holes into the charges made against him by the false apostles—including that he's in the ministry for money.

Oddly—maybe even stubbornly—Paul adds to this letter a fund-raising appeal. He's collecting an offering for the poor in Jerusalem, and he wants Corinth to contribute. The Jewish word for that is *chutzpah* (KHOOTS-pah), as in, "Where does he get the nerve?"

// **TIME:** Paul probably wrote 1 Corinthians in about AD 55 and 2 Corinthians a few months later.

// **AUTHOR:** Paul wrote these letters, possibly dictating the first to Sosthenes and the second to Timothy (see 1 Corinthians 1:1; 2 Corinthians 1:1), as he had dictated Romans to Tertius.

// **LOCATION:** Paul wrote from Ephesus, where he was starting a church along the coast of what is now Turkey. He addressed members of the church he started in Corinth, Greece.

AD 55
Paul writes letters to Corinth

AD 57
Paul arrested in Jerusalem

AD 64
Rome burns, Paul executed in Rome

Who's the church boss?

A CHURCH SPLIT IS BREWING. With Paul, their founder, gone, the church of Corinth can't seem to agree on who's in charge. At least four factions develop—perhaps representing different worship styles or different slants on controversial ideas.

// **PAUL.** Some may have favored a worship leader who, like Paul, emphasizes that we're saved by faith, not by following Jewish laws.

// **APOLLOS.** Famed as an "eloquent speaker" (Acts 18:24), he visited Corinth as a guest minister. Some may have wanted to appoint him as pastor.

// **PETER.** Some may have favored Peter's balanced approach to the heated debate about Jewish Christians and non-Jewish Christians: Jews obey Jewish laws, non-Jews honor the compromise worked out at the Jerusalem summit (see page 408).

// **JESUS.** Some may have appealed to Jesus, who observed Jewish traditions, to justify their hard-line stance that all Christians obey Jewish laws.

Paul pleads for unity. He says it doesn't matter who builds the church from this point on, as long as they build on the foundation he laid: the teachings of Jesus.

"After all," Paul writes, "who is Apollos? Who is Paul? We are only God's servants. . . . Each of us did the work the Lord gave us" (1 Corinthians 3:5).

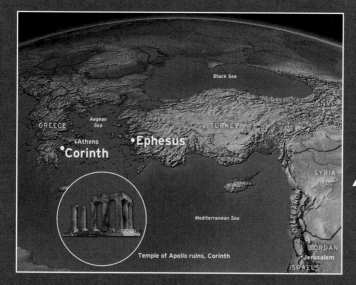

▲ **FOLLOW THE LEADER.** Christians at the church in Corinth can't seem to agree which leader to follow. They seem split at least four ways—perhaps based on different ideas about how to worship, or on what teachings are most important.

APOLLOS. A Jewish Christian from Alexandria, Egypt. A gifted preacher, he spoke in Corinth and later met with Paul in Ephesus. Church leader Jerome (about AD 345–420) said Apollos became bishop of Corinth.

Sex sins in the church

PAUL CAN'T BELIEVE HIS EARS. He just heard that a churchman in Corinth is sleeping with his own stepmother. That's illegal. For Jews as well as for pagan Romans.

Yet the church is acting like it's no big deal.

It's a big deal to Paul.

He tells the church leaders to show this man the door. For two reasons.

// This man's sin is like bad yeast that works its way into dough; it would sour the entire church.

// Excommunication might shock the man back to his spiritual senses.

Aside from this specific case, Paul has just one piece of advice for any Christian facing the invitation to commit a sex sin:

"Run away" (1 Corinthians 6:18 NCV).

"Your body is the temple of the Holy Spirit, who lives in you and was given to you by God," Paul explains. "You do not belong to yourself, for God bought you with a high price. So you must honor God with your body" (1 Corinthians 6:19–20).

· ·

MOTHER DEAR / A man at the young church in Corinth is sleeping with his stepmother, while church leaders ignore the sin. Paul has a suggestion: Ignore the man instead. Shun him by removing him from the fellowship.

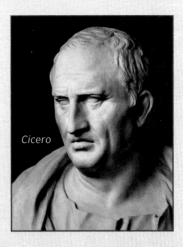

Cicero

CICERO, ON INCESTUOUS MARRIAGE. A Roman lawyer, Cicero (106–43 BC) wrote of his disgust about women who married their son-in-laws: "Oh, to think of the woman's sin, unbelievable, unheard of."

· ·

STEPMOTHER OR NATURAL MOTHER? Paul describes the woman's relationship to the man: She's "his father's wife" (1 Corinthians 5:1 NRSV). Bible experts speculate Paul phrased it this way because it tracks best with the Jewish law that forbids a man from having sex with "your father's wife."

· ·

CORINTH'S BAD REPUTATION. Corinth had a reputation as the go-to town for sex. There was probably some truth to that, scholars say, because it was a heavily traveled crossroads town for sailors and home to Aphrodite, goddess of love. But much of the bad PR came from writers in the competing town of Athens. Aristophanes, a playwright there, turned the city's name into a verb: *corinthianize*. It's a crass way of saying "fornicate." Plato, also in Athens, invented the phrase *Corinthian girl* as a euphemism for "hooker."

Christians suing Christians

CORINTH CHURCH MEMBERS are suing each other, Paul learns.

"How dare you file a lawsuit," Paul writes, "and ask a secular court to decide the matter instead of taking it to other believers!" (1 Corinthians 6:1).

Paul considers it a damaging embarrassment to the local church and a setback to the Christian mission, which is to spread Jesus' teachings of love and forgiveness throughout the world. What kind of message does it send to the community when a group of people who preach brotherly love can't settle their own disputes? Instead, they verbally shred each other in front of a godless soul.

"Why not just accept the injustice and leave it at that?" Paul asks. "Why not let yourselves be cheated?" (1 Corinthians 6:7). As far as he's concerned, that's better than waging war—Christian on Christian—and then asking pagans to be the peacemakers.

SHOULD CHRISTIANS NEVER SUE CHRISTIANS?

Paul was talking about Christians in the same local church, scholars say. Also, the lawsuits probably involved money—not violent crimes, which fall under the jurisdiction of the government. Paul told the Corinth locals that as Christians within the same congregation, they should be able to call on fellow church members to help them settle the dispute.

ALTERNATIVES TO CHRISTIANS SUING CHRISTIANS.

Some national Christian organizations offer neutral mediation and arbitration services to help settle a wide range of disputes between Christians. Their Web sites show up in an Internet search for "Christian legal services."

JESUS, ON PEACEMAKING.

"God blesses those people who make peace. They will be called his children!" (Matthew 5:9 CEV).

◄ NOTHING BUT THE TRUTH.

A courtroom artist captures the scene of a witness taking questions from a lawyer. Paul tells Christians at Corinth that the truth is this: Christians shouldn't sue Christians in a court run by nonbelievers. Many Bible experts, however, say there are exceptions to that rule.

To marry, or not to marry

UNTIL NOW, Paul has been dealing with Corinth church problems he has only heard about. But at this point, he starts answering questions the church asked him in a letter.

Based on Paul's answer, some Bible experts say it sounds like the question was a two-parter that went something like this:

"Is it better to stay single than get married? And if we're already married, should we abstain from sex?"

Paul gives them a two-part answer.

// CELIBACY BEATS MARRIAGE:

"I say to those who aren't married and to widows—it's better to stay unmarried, just as I am" (1 Corinthians 7:8). On the other hand, he says it's better to get married than to live as single people constantly thinking about the sex they're not getting.

// IF YOU'RE MARRIED, ENJOY SEX:

"The husband should fulfill his wife's sexual needs, and the wife should fulfill her husband's needs" (1 Corinthians 7:3).

WHAT'S PAUL'S ARGUMENT FOR PREFERRING THE SINGLE LIFESTYLE?

Time management. "An unmarried man can spend his time doing the Lord's work and thinking how to please him. But a married man has to think about his earthly responsibilities and how to please his wife. . . . I want you to do whatever will help you serve the Lord best, with as few distractions as possible" (1 Corinthians 7:32–33, 35).

▼ BRIDE OF CHRIST.
Roman Catholic nuns take a vow of chastity, considering themselves the brides of Christ. Some priests take the same vow, which they say frees them from family duties and gives them more time to devote to ministry. Paul would have approved, if what he wrote to Christians in Corinth is any clue.

On the menu: holy cow

IS IT WRONG to eat the meat of animals sacrificed to pagan gods, such as Jupiter and Aphrodite?

Cows, sheep, goats, pigs, and other critters are offered as sacrifices on pagan altars. But priests usually burn only part of the animal. The rest goes on sale at local butcher shops. Or it gets eaten onsite in temple banquet halls—in a holy party hosted by the worshipper for family and friends.

Paul advises against eating in a pagan temple. He says some weaker Christians might get the wrong idea and conclude it's okay to worship God like he's just one of many gods.

As for eating the meat offsite, Paul says he sees nothing wrong with it: "We can't win God's approval by what we eat" (1 Corinthians 8:8).

On the other hand, he says, if this might cause weaker Christians to stumble back into their old habit of worshipping pagan gods, then he advises against eating it in front of them.

That would be a bit like taking a recovering alcoholic out to dinner and ordering a bottle of Chardonnay.

. . . .

FOOD FIT FOR A GOD / A Roman worshipper leads a parade of animals headed for sacrifice at a temple altar, in art created about the same time Paul wrote 1 and 2 Corinthians. Christians in Corinth asked Paul if it was okay to eat meat left over from these pagan rituals.

WAS PAUL AN APOSTLE?

Some in Corinth seemed to argue he wasn't.

"Apostle" was the top job in the first-generation Church. Jesus' 11 surviving disciples and the one replacement for Judas (Matthias) were all called apostles.

There were two qualifications for becoming one of the 12 apostles.

First, each man had to have known Jesus and traveled with him throughout his ministry (see Acts 1:21–22).

Second, each man had to have been among the people Jesus personally sent on the mission to spread his teachings to all nations. *Apostle* means "send."

Paul considered himself an apostle for three reasons:

> **He saw Jesus.** "Haven't I seen Jesus our Lord with my own eyes?" (1 Corinthians 9:1). He was referring to his miraculous encounter with Jesus on the road to Damascus (see page 404).

> **He was commissioned by Jesus.** "Take my message to the Gentiles and to kings, as well as to the people of Israel" (Acts 9:15).

> **He did miracles.** "I certainly gave you proof that I am an apostle. For I patiently did many signs and wonders and miracles among you" (2 Corinthians 12:12).

Worship etiquette

WORSHIP SERVICES have spiraled out of control. Problems range from folks getting drunk on communion wine to worshippers competing for attention by speaking in tongues—a language that makes no earthly sense. Not without an interpreter.

Paul offers advice in several problem areas.

HATS IN CHURCH. Men should take off their head coverings during worship. Women should wear theirs. Scholars today can only guess why (see right).

COMMUNION. The Lord's Supper isn't a potluck, Paul says. But Corinthians are treating it that way—and not sharing. Rich people bring lots of food and wine—and drink too much. Poor people go hungry. Paul tells the Corinthians to eat at home. He says he'll teach them how to celebrate Communion when he visits.

SPEAKING IN TONGUES. To combat chaos in a worship service, Paul says, "No more than two or three should speak in tongues. They must speak one at a time, and someone must interpret what they say" (1 Corinthians 14:27).

WHY SHOULD MEN TAKE OFF THEIR HATS DURING WORSHIP?
One guess: Romans sometimes pulled the hood of their robe up over their head during worship. So Paul may have been saying Christians should distance themselves from pagan worship practices.

WHY SHOULD WOMEN WEAR HEAD COVERINGS DURING WORSHIP?
A guess: It was customary at the time for women to cover their heads while out in public, much like it's still a custom in some world areas for women to wear veils in public.

WHY DOES PAUL SAY WOMEN SHOULD ZIP THEIR LIPS DURING WORSHIP SERVICES?
Again, Bible experts are left guessing. Paul allows women to pray and prophesy in church (see 1 Corinthians 11:5). But he later tells them to "be silent" in church (1 Corinthians 14:34). They can't do both. Scholars look to the context for clues. In the "be silent" section, Paul might be telling the ladies not to publicly question the prophecies of their husbands, potentially embarrassing the gents. If the women have questions, "they should ask their husbands at home" (1 Corinthians 14:35).

◄ **CHURCH LADY.**
Head covered, she's ready to worship. Paul told women in Corinth to wear a head covering during worship. Men, on the other hand, had to go bareheaded. Scholars are still puzzling over why. See a couple of their guesses above.

Re-ranking spiritual talents

THE PREACHER'S NOT THE TOP DOG in the Church. Nor is the priest. Not by Paul's standard.

Christians in Corinth seem to have a ranking system of spiritual gifts. Based on what Paul tells them, it sounds like they give a five-star rating to the spiritual gift of speaking in tongues.

But Paul puts that gift in the basement—bottom-dweller of godly gifts.

Paul's ranking:

// apostles
// prophets
// teachers
// miracle-workers
// healers
// helpers of others
// leaders
// speaking in unknown languages

SOURCE: 1 CORINTHIANS 12:28

Paul inserts a couple of caveats.

First, spiritual gifts are like body parts. The Church—a spiritual body—needs every part doing its job if the Church is going to function.

Second, none of the gifts matter a bit without the greatest gift in all of heaven and earth: "If I don't have love, I am nothing at all" (1 Corinthians 13:2 NIrV).

PRAYER FOR HEALING / During a healing service in a California church, Christians place their hands on a fellow believer and pray. Paul said God gave some people the gift of healing. James agreed: "Are any of you sick? You should call for the elders of the church to come and pray over you, anointing you with oil in the name of the Lord" (James 5:14).

SPEAKING IN TONGUES. It's a language most people don't understand, including the speaker. Paul says someone in the worship group should be able to interpret it. Christians who speak in tongues say the Holy Spirit is speaking through them, praising God, praying, or delivering a message. Christians who practice this are often described as charismatic, worshipping in Pentecostal churches.

WHY RANK SPEAKING IN TONGUES SO LOW? It's a gift easy to abuse, to draw attention to the showboating speaker. It can also be disruptive and distract from other gifts—as when a person giving a speech gets interrupted by a heckler who stands up and starts babbling nonsense. At least that's what speaking in tongues sounds like to many people.

WHY DOES PAUL RANK HIS JOB OF APOSTLE AT THE TOP? Apostles were the top Church officials at the time. But some Bible experts wonder if Paul's list is more about chronology. Christianity started with the apostles. Their work produced prophets, teachers, and other gifted leaders.

No Resurrection, no Christianity

LIVING FOREVER IN A PHYSICAL BODY is a little too sci-fi for some Christians in Corinth.

They have no trouble believing Jesus rose from the dead; he's God. They just can't believe humans will do the same.

Paul tries to convince them otherwise.

First, he establishes the fact that Jesus rose from the dead—his physical body intact. Jesus appeared not only to the disciples and Paul, but "to more than 500 believers at the same time" (1 Corinthians 15:6 NIrV).

Next, Paul appeals to logic: How can anyone who believes Jesus rose from the dead say there's no such thing as resurrection?

"If there is no resurrection of the dead," Paul adds, "then Christ has not been raised either" (1 Corinthians 15:13).

If Jesus stayed dead, then Christianity is a fraudulent religion—and Christians are a sorry lot of losers, "more to be pitied than anyone in the world" (1 Corinthians 15:19).

RISING TO THE OCCASION / When the last trumpet sounds, Paul promises, the dead will rise to live forever. As for Christians still alive at the time, "our mortal bodies must be transformed into immortal bodies" (1 Corinthians 15:53).

WHAT DID MOST PEOPLE OF PAUL'S DAY THINK ABOUT LIFE AFTER DEATH? Jews debated it. Pharisees taught that there's life after death. Sadducees said there's no such thing as a resurrection. Greek philosophy, widespread in Paul's day, taught that the soul is immortal—but in a mysteriously disembodied form. When Paul tried to convince Greek philosophers in Athens that our physical bodies will rise from the dead, they laughed him out of town (see Acts 17:32).

WILL WE HAVE PHYSICAL BODIES IN THE AFTERLIFE? Christians debate this with vigor, some wondering why we should expect anything close to a physical body in a spiritual dimension. Others argue that Jesus ate fish after his resurrection. Paul simply says our physical body will be changed into an immortal spiritual body (see 1 Corinthians 15:50, 53).

JESUS' RESURRECTION BODY. (See page 377).

Paul: I'm not a crook

HE'S A CRACKED POT, but not a crook. Essentially, that's what Paul tells the Corinthians in his follow-up letter.

By "cracked pot," he means a mere human: "We ourselves are like fragile clay jars" (2 Corinthians 4:7). But Paul quickly adds that he holds a "great treasure," the good news of forgiveness and salvation.

Paul is on the defensive. After writing 1 Corinthians, he visited the city. It was a painful visit. Someone in the congregation trash-talked him to his face. To make matters worse, after Paul left, some intruders came to Corinth and started bad-mouthing him, too. Based on Paul's defense in 2 Corinthians, they accused him of being a fraud apostle on the take for cash.

Paul tells the church to forgive the church member who spoke out against him; apparently, most of the church had responded by giving this gent the cold shoulder.

As for the other charges, Paul fires back. He reminds the Corinthians that they saw for themselves the miracles he did. And they know that during the year and a half he stayed with them, he paid his own way. He made tents as a bi-vocational pastor (see Acts 18:3). That's why he doesn't have to say anything more than "Unlike many people, we aren't selling God's word" (2 Corinthians 2:17 NIrV).

. . . .

TENTS, NEW AND USED / Paul made and repaired tents for a living. Many rabbis did the same—supporting themselves with jobs so they could teach for free. But many non-Jewish teachers, like the philosophers Paul met in Athens, expected to get paid for teaching.

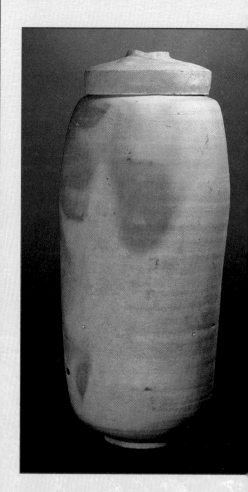

TREASURE IN CLAY JARS.
A community of Jewish scribes stored their most cherished possessions—the Dead Sea Scrolls—in this clay jar and others like it. The oldest copies of the Bible discovered so far, these scrolls are 1,000 years older than the manuscripts used to translate the revered King James Version of the Bible. Other people in Bible times also trusted simple clay jars with their greatest treasures: gold, silver, and jewels (see photo page 332). Paul compared himself to a simple clay jar, filled with the treasure of eternal life.

This world is not our home

IT'S A HARD-KNOCK LIFE for Paul. Literally.

"We are knocked down," he says. "But we are not knocked out" (2 Corinthians 4:9 NIrV).

"We live under constant danger of death because we serve Jesus. . . . But this has resulted in eternal life for you" (2 Corinthians 4:11–12).

For Paul, that's an acceptable trade-off because he expects to live forever, too.

A tentmaker, it's natural for him to compare life to a tent. "When this earthly tent we live in is taken down (that is, when we die and leave this earthly body), we will have a house in heaven" (2 Corinthians 5:1).

But he's in no hurry to get there. Even though he wants desperately to be with the Lord, he says he has a job to do—as do all Christians.

"We are Christ's ambassadors; God is making his appeal through us. We speak for Christ when we plead, 'Come back to God!' " (2 Corinthians 5:20).

. . . .

PAUL'S PAIN / His preaching sparked riots, getting him jailed and chased out of town many times. See his tally of beatings, stoning, and shipwrecks, page 435. Yet to come: two more years in a jail in Caesarea, a shipwreck on the way to his trial in Rome, followed by execution there.

TEA TIME / A Bedouin herder pours tea in a tent at Wadi Rum, Jordan. Paul, a tentmaker by trade, compared the human body to a tent. He said it's just a temporary place for us to live until God gives us an everlasting body when we die.

Send money

PAUL HAS NERVE, if nothing else.

In this very letter, defending himself in part against allegations that he's in the ministry for money—a teacher on the take—he asks the Christians at Corinth to take an offering and send it to him.

He says it's for poor Christians in Jerusalem. A line that, among his critics, would probably have flipped the switch on the eye rolls.

This isn't a light-touch fund-raising appeal. Paul goes hard sell.

> *I am not commanding you to do it. But I want to put you to the test. I want to find out if you really love God. I want to compare your love with that of others.*
>
> 2 CORINTHIANS 8:8 NIrV

Who are the "others"? The "very poor" people of their neighbor province to the north: Macedonia. "They gave even more than they could. . .more than we expected" (2 Corinthians 8:3, 5 NIrV).

The implication, if the believers of Corinth refuse to give or if they give only a dinky donation: They are tightwads whose love for God can be measured in small change.

Clearly, this offering for Jerusalem is important to Paul.

CHEERFUL GIVER / A passerby decides not to pass by a street person and his dog. Paul said "God loves a cheerful giver" (2 Corinthians 9:7 TNIV). Whether the gift is cold cash or a warm gesture, cheerful givers are welcome folks.

WHY WAS THE OFFERING SO IMPORTANT? Two big reasons. **(1)** Jerusalem church leaders asked Paul to "keep on helping the poor" (Galatians 2:10). **(2)** Paul hoped that the offering would help heal the rift between Jewish Christians and non-Jewish Christians, arguing over whether all Christians needed to obey Jewish laws. The offering was intended mainly for Jewish Christians, from non-Jews who didn't observe Jewish laws.

WHY WERE THE JERUSALEM CHRISTIANS POOR? A famine had struck the region a few years earlier. In addition, Jews targeted Jewish Christians for persecution. Perhaps part of the persecution was to isolate them economically by boycotting their services and products.

TITHING. Paul was asking for an offering, not a 10 percent tithe. The New Testament never speaks of Christians observing the Jewish tradition of tithing. Historians say Christians didn't start tithing until the 1800s, after governments began withdrawing their tax support for churches (see page 302).

Paul puts his life on the line

PAUL HAS CRITICS. Some arrive in Corinth after he's gone—so he's not there to defend himself when they start pummeling him with sharp words.

He's a liar, they say. He's a preacher for profit. He's a self-promoting egomaniac. And he's more blow than go, writing stern letters that he doesn't back up in person.

Paul's response?

He'll be there in person soon enough, and he hopes "we won't need to demonstrate our authority when we arrive" (2 Corinthians 13:7). In the meantime, Paul reminds the Corinthian Christians that he's putting his life on the line every time he preaches:

// *"Five times the Jews gave me thirty-nine lashes with a whip."*

// *"Three times the Romans beat me with a big stick."*

// *"Once my enemies stoned me." (They stopped because they thought he was dead [see Acts 14:19].)*

// *"I have been shipwrecked three times, and I even had to spend a night and a day in the sea."*

// *"I have gone hungry and thirsty."*

// *"I have been cold from not having enough clothes to keep me warm."*

2 CORINTHIANS 11:24–25, 27 CEV

Paul says he's not suffering all this for money or fame. He's doing it because Jesus asked him to, and because the rewards are much greater. "I suffer for Christ" (2 Corinthians 12:10).

◄ **POISON.** Poisonous snakes are no longer native to Malta, where Paul says he was bitten by one. But the neighboring island of Sicily along with Italy are home to a sometimes lethal viper (*vipera aspis*). In most cases the bite, though painful, isn't fatal even left untreated. About one in 25 bite victims die.

◄ **RX FOR MALARIA**
What was Paul's "thorn in [the] flesh" (2 Corinthians 12:7)? He didn't say. He said only that he asked God three times to take it away.

A few theories:

// **Corinthian Christians.** They're a pain in the neck. The Hebrew version of the Greek word Paul used for "thorn" describes the Canaanites that way: "thorns in your sides" (Numbers 33:55).

// **Physical problem.** Perhaps poor eyesight, epilepsy, or malaria picked up while traveling through coastal swamps in Turkey.

// **Emotional problem.** Depression or anger, for example.

GALATIANS 2

Paul bluntly criticizes Peter for refusing to eat with non-Jewish Christians. Peter had sided with Jewish Christians who considered non-Jews ritually unclean—even if they were Christian.

BIG SCENE

PAUL SCOLDS PETER

BIBLE HISTORY

ALL DATES APPROXIMATE

AD 46
Paul's first mission trip

AD 48
Paul writes Galatians (mid-50s alternate date)

WORLD HISTORY

Emperor Claudius confirms Jewish right to worship
AD 41

GALATIANS

CLASH OF THE CHURCH TITANS: PETER VS. PAUL

STORY LINE

PAUL CALLS PETER A HYPOCRITE. It's old news, but Paul reports it to make a point.

His point: Jewish Christians are dead wrong to insist that non-Jewish Christians have to convert to the Jewish faith before they can become Christians—as in Jew first, Christian second.

That's what some Jewish Christians are telling the Galatians, insisting they obey Jewish laws—especially laws about circumcision and kosher food.

Some Galatians are buying the Jewish take on Christianity.

To put a stop to it, Paul tells them a story.

Once upon a time the apostle Peter came to visit the non-Jewish church in Antioch. Peter treated those Gentiles like family—until some friends joined him from Jerusalem. Those friends, Jewish Christians, followed Jewish tradition. They refused to eat with the Gentile Christians because Jews considered Gentiles ritually unclean. Peter followed their lead.

Paul says, "I told him to his face that I was against what he was doing. He was clearly wrong" (Galatians 2:11 NIrV).

Christians aren't saved by trusting in Jewish laws, Paul insists. They're saved by trusting in Jesus.

// TIME: Some Bible experts say he wrote it in about AD 48, making it his first surviving letter. Others push the date to the early to mid-50s.

// AUTHOR: Paul apparently dictates this letter, signing it "in my own handwriting" (Galatians 6:11).

// LOCATION: Paul writes to "the churches of Galatia" (Galatians 1:2), a Roman province in what is now central Turkey.

AD 57
Paul finishes final mission trip

AD 64
Paul executed in Rome

Claudius expels Jew from Rome over trouble related to "Chrestus" (possibly Christ)
AD 52

Nero blames Christians for burning Rome
AD 64

Paul gives Peter what for

PETER SHOULD HAVE KNOWN BETTER, Paul says.

Peter shouldn't have refused to eat with the non-Jewish Christians in Antioch—treating them like they were second-class souls.

For several reasons.

// **THE VISION.** Years earlier, Peter had a vision that taught him Gentiles were no longer ritually unclean. After that vision, he brought the Holy Spirit to a Roman soldier (see Acts 10:44–45).

// **THE SUMMIT MEETING.** Peter had joined Paul and Barnabas in lobbying for the rights of non-Jewish Christians (see Acts 15:7–11). They did this at a Jerusalem summit meeting of Church leaders, trying to iron out a compromise with Jewish Christians who said all Christians need to obey Jewish laws.

// **THE LIFESTYLE.** "Peter," Paul says in front of everyone at Antioch, "you are a Jew, but you live like a Gentile. So how can you force Gentiles to live like Jews?" (Galatians 2:14 CEV).

WHAT HAPPENED NEXT?

Paul never reports what Peter had to say for himself. But Paul won the debate. Christians eventually abandoned Jewish traditions. By the end of the first century, Jewish leaders gave Jewish Christians a choice. Worship in the synagogue as Jews or worship in church groups with Christians. You can't do both. Many returned to the Jewish religion, which is why scholars say the book of Hebrews was written—to argue that Jesus made the Jewish religion obsolete.

WHY DID PETER ACT AGAINST HIS PRINCIPLES?

Peer pressure: "Peter was afraid of the Jews" (Galatians 2:12 CEV). He had been getting along fine with the Gentiles until tradition-minded Jewish Christians arrived from Jerusalem. They came apparently on a scouting mission from James, brother of Jesus and leader of the mother church in Jerusalem.

APOSTLES AT ODDS / Peter and Paul show up as partners in ministry, in this image inscribed onto a tomb in the AD 300s. But for one tense moment, in what is now a Turkish town, they find themselves in a duel of words.

Paul goes ballistic

GO CUT YOUR TESTICLES OFF! That's Paul's advice to fellow Christians.

Not to Christians in Galatia, in churches he started. But to a traveling group of tradition-loving Jewish Christians. They're talking non-Jewish Christian men into getting circumcised—the most extreme ritual for a convert to Judaism.

Paul doesn't get any angrier than this—at least not in the Bible:

> *"Why don't these agitators, obsessive as they are about circumcision, go all the way and castrate themselves!"*
>
> GALATIANS 5:12 MSG

Or as another translation puts it, "cut off everything that marks them as men!" (NIrV).

Paul's not talking about whiskers.

"Christ has set us free," Paul says, referring to the hundreds of laws Jews follow. "He wants us to enjoy freedom. So stand firm. Don't let the chains of slavery hold you. . . . Don't let yourselves be circumcised" (Galatians 5:1–2 NIrV).

DANCING FOR THEIR GOD / A mosaic from Pompeii shows worshippers playing instruments often associated with Cybele, mother goddess of earth and nature. Cybele priests in Galatia had themselves castrated in devotion to Cybele. Some Bible experts wonder if Paul was comparing his critics to these pagan priests since Paul said his critics should castrate themselves, too.

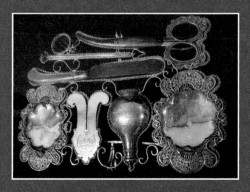

◄ **CIRCUMCISION TOOLS.** Extra skin from the end of a penis is wedged into the slot of a guide (bottom row, second object to left) and clipped off. The guide protects from clipping more than just the skin.

CIRCUMCISION. Cutting off the excess skin at the end of a penis. It's a ritual that marks a male's entry into the Jewish faith. Jewish boys are circumcised at eight days old. Adult male converts are circumcised at whatever age they are when they convert (see page 20).

WHY WAS PAUL SO ANGRY? Bible experts say Paul knew that if Christians bought in to the idea that they had to convert to the Jewish faith, the Christian movement would have gotten assimilated into the Jewish religion. It would have become just one of several branches, as were the Pharisees and Sadducees.

But Paul insisted that Jesus ended that old agreement (covenant) between God and the Jewish people, replacing it with a new agreement between God and everyone.

"The law was our guardian leading us to Christ so that we could be made right with God through faith. Now the way of faith has come, and we no longer live under a guardian" (Galatians 3:24–25 NCV).

BIG SCENE

SUIT UP

EPHESIANS 6:10–20

Paul tells the Ephesians there's a spiritual battle coming and they should put on every piece of God's armor, from the helmet of salvation to the shoes of peace.

**BIBLE
HISTORY**

ALL DATES APPROXIMATE

AD 53
*Paul starts church
in Ephesus*

**WORLD
HISTORY**

*Romans invade
England*
AD 43

EPHESIANS
DEAR ABBY ADVICE FOR CHRISTIANS

STORY LINE

ODDLY, this is Paul's most upbeat letter in the Bible. It's more encouraging than any of the other dozen letters he wrote.

That's odd for two reasons.

He's in chains, probably under house arrest in Rome—a perfect place to complain.

And his letter follows three fiery letters in which he defended himself against critics: 1, 2 Corinthians and Galatians. For readers today, that makes Ephesians a welcome change of pace.

The letter reads like the text of a warm sermon spoken to a deeply loved congregation. In it, Paul offers practical advice about how to live as children of God. A sampling:

// "Patiently put up with each other" (Ephesians 4:2 CEV).

// "Let love be your guide. Christ loved us and offered his life for us" (Ephesians 5:2 CEV).

// "We are fighting against. . .powers in the spiritual world. So put on all the armor that God gives. . .truth. . .justice. . .peace. . . faith. . .God's saving power" (Ephesians 6:12–17 CEV).

// **TIME:** Paul probably wrote this sometime between AD 60–62, near the end of his life.

// **AUTHOR:** "This letter is from Paul" (Ephesians 1:1).

// **LOCATION:** Paul is writing "to God's holy people in Ephesus" (Ephesians 1:1), in what is now Turkey. Some old manuscripts say "to God's holy people," as though to Christians everywhere. He's writing "in chains" (Ephesians 6:20), probably under house arrest in Rome.

AD 62
Paul writes Ephesians

AD 64
Romans execute Paul and Peter

Nero executes his wife, Octavia, and marries Poppaea Sabina
AD 62

Nero blames Christians for burning Rome
AD 64

Romans begin building Rome's Coliseum
AD 70

God's Chosen People 2.0

JEWS ARE NO LONGER GOD'S CHOSEN PEOPLE.
At least not the only Chosen People.

Not according to Paul, a Jew himself.

"This is God's plan," Paul tells Christians at Ephesus. "Both Gentiles and Jews who believe the Good News share equally in the riches inherited by God's children" (Ephesians 3:6).

That was God's plan all along, say most Christian Bible experts.

God started with one man of faith: Abraham. From Abraham, God grew a nation of faithful people: the Jews.

Out of this nation, came a servant of God—whom Christians identify as Jesus. He became "a light for all nations to show people all over the world the way to be saved" (Isaiah 49:6 NCV).

▲ **EPHESUS /** It was a busy riverside port town on Turkey's west coast and one of the five largest cities in the Roman Empire. Some scholars rank it number three, after Rome and Alexandria, Egypt. It's a ruin today. That's because the river leading to the Mediterranean Sea silted up. Ships stopped arriving and businesses moved away.

◄ **JEWISH, AND THEN SOME /** An Orthodox Jew, in a branch of the Jewish faith known for strictly obeying Jewish laws. Paul tells the mainly non-Jewish Christians of Ephesus that Jews are no longer God's only Chosen People. Thanks to Jesus, Paul says, God has laid out the welcome mat for everyone else, too.

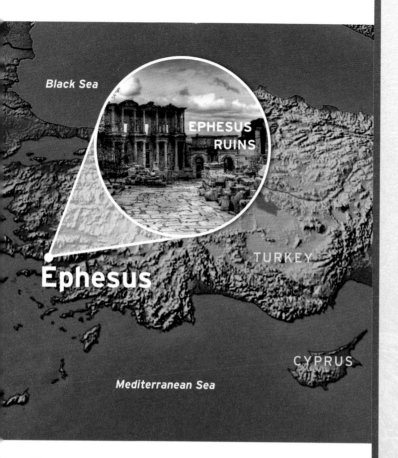

Black Sea

EPHESUS
RUINS

Ephesus

TURKEY

CYPRUS

Mediterranean Sea

THE JEWISH MISSION.

It was never God's intent for Jews to keep their religion to themselves, many scholars argue. The Jews weren't the only Chosen People of God. They were the first Chosen People of God. And they were chosen with a purpose: "Let your light shine for all to see. . . . All nations will come to your light" (Isaiah 60:1, 3).

"UNCIRCUMCISED HEATHENS."

That's what Jews used to call non-Jews. Paul said Jews did this to brag about their circumcision, "even though it affected only their bodies and not their hearts" (Ephesians 2:11). Paul mentioned this as a warning so Gentile Christians wouldn't get too full of themselves and think of everyone else as an outsider. "Don't forget that you Gentiles used to be outsiders" (Ephesians 2:11).

◄ WHY DO CHRISTIANS SAY JESUS IS GOD'S JEWISH SERVANT THAT PROPHETS PREDICTED WOULD COME TO SAVE THE WORLD?

Jesus fulfilled many prophecies about this mysterious servant (see page 210). Even Simeon, the priest who dedicated Baby Jesus, somehow saw the connection and declared: "He is a light to reveal God to the nations" (Luke 2:32). See also page 361.

Priest Simeon and prophetess Anna admire Baby Jesus (left).

A Christian's to-do list

GROW UP. That's what Paul wants to see newbie Christians in Ephesus do—mature in the faith.

Their target: perfection.

"We become like Christ and have his perfection" (Ephesians 4:13 NCV).

The path to perfection, as Paul maps it out, reads a bit like Paul's 10 Commandments:

// Be humble.

// Be patient with each other.

// Don't get angry.

// Don't lie.

// Don't steal.

// Don't talk dirty.

// Instead of tearing people down with slander, build them up with compliments.

// Don't commit sex sins.

// Don't be greedy.

// Don't get drunk.

DOES PAUL REALLY EXPECT SPIRITUAL PERFECTION?

Probably not in this lifetime. He confesses in another letter, "I have not yet been made perfect" (Philippians 3:12 NIrV). But perfection is his goal. And he says he's pushing on toward it.

"DON'T LET THE SUN GO DOWN WHILE YOU ARE STILL ANGRY"?

That's a quote from Paul (Ephesians 4:26). Like "perfection," scholars say, Paul's suggested goal might be elusive. Especially since some anger seems justifiable. Even Jesus got angry—once at religious leaders who showed no compassion for a sick man (see Mark 3:5). But in many cases, Paul's suggestion is a worthy, can-do goal.

CHRISTIANS IN A MUSLIM LAND / Christians gather for worship at a church in Tur Abdin, Turkey—a nation 99 percent Muslim. Paul advised Christians in ancient Turkey to follow Christ's example: "Live a life filled with love" (Ephesians 5:2).

Harmony in the home

SOUNDING LIKE A MALE CHAUVINIST— and some might argue that's the reason he's still single—Paul serves up his recipe for peace on the home front.

WIVES. "Submit to your husbands as to the Lord. For a husband is the head of his wife as Christ is the head of the church" (Ephesians 5:22–23).

Fortunately for the ladies, Paul doesn't start there—or end there.

HUSBANDS. Paul starts one sentence earlier, advising wives and husbands to "submit to one another" (Ephesians 5:21). Then he goes on to tell husbands to "love your wives, just as Christ loved the church. He gave up his life for her" (Ephesians 5:25).

Paul offers pretty much the same advice about other potential head-butting relationships under one roof: parent to child, and employer to household worker.

CHILDREN. "Obey your parents. . .that you may enjoy long life on the earth" (Ephesians 6:1, 3 TNIV).

PARENTS. "Don't be hard on your children" (Ephesians 6:4 CEV).

(continued next page)

◄ SLAVERY. The "household workers" Paul spoke about were, in fact, slaves. Slaves included prisoners of war along with sailors and passengers captured by pirates. Some poverty-stricken people sold themselves into slavery to a rich person for housing and meals—and some learned a trade in the process. Many Romans rewarded their slaves for hard work by freeing them. Most were freed by age 30. Still, it was an abusive and degrading way of life for most slaves.

▲ WOMEN'S WORK. Women collect water for household cooking and cleaning—chores most men in Paul's day wouldn't think of doing. Paul lived in a man-run culture, where men were men and everyone else was pitifully less. Remarkably, Paul sounds countercultural when he urges husbands to "go all out in love for your wives, exactly as Christ did for the church" (Ephesians 5:25 MSG).

HOUSEHOLD WORKERS. "Don't just do what you have to do to get by, but work heartily, as Christ's servants doing what God wants you to do. And work with a smile on your face, always keeping in mind that no matter who happens to be giving the orders, you're really serving God" (Ephesians 6:6–7 MSG).

HOUSEHOLD OWNERS. "No abuse, please, and no threats. You and your servants are both under the same Master in heaven. He makes no distinction between you and them" (Ephesians 6:9 MSG).

SENECA ON SLAVERY. Some Romans, such as philosopher Seneca (4 BC–AD 65) argued that slaves should be treated humanely.

Seneca

....

PULL DADDY'S BEARD / The lady of the house gives her baby an up-close look at the *pater familias*—"head of the family." With large families considered a blessing in Bible times, homes were often a tight pack of relatives. Though Paul was a single man, it didn't stop him from offering some family counseling.

BAD-MOUTHING WOMEN
Paul's plea for husbands to put their wives first, above themselves, was a giant leap past what other Jews and Romans were saying about women.

They're inferior
A woman is inferior to her husband in everything. For that reason, she should obey him. . . . God has put the husband in charge.

JOSEPHUS (ABOUT AD 37–101)
JEWISH HISTORIAN

They're weak
Our ancestors, in their wisdom, considered that all women, because of their innate weakness, should be under the control of guardians.

CICERO (106–43 BC)
ROMAN PHILOSOPHER

They rub us the wrong way
A Roman general who divorced his beautiful wife and married another was asked why. He held up one of his shoes. "This is attractive, isn't it? And it's new, isn't it? But you can't see where it pinches my foot."

LUCIUS AEMILIUS PAULLUS MACEDONICUS
(ABOUT 229 BC–160 BC)
ROMAN GENERAL

Suit up for battle

IT'S WAR.

Paul warns Christians they're in a battle that's waging from another dimension.

"We are not fighting against flesh-and-blood enemies, but against evil rulers and authorities of the unseen world, against mighty powers in this dark world, and against evil spirits in the heavenly places" (Ephesians 6:12).

Paul advises Christians to put on God's armor.

And he does it in a creative way, using military metaphors that make sense to non-Jewish Christians who are all too familiar with Roman armor. Yet these metaphors produce even deeper connections for Jewish Christians who know their Bible.

PAUL'S MILITARY METAPHOR	JEWISH BIBLE BACKGROUND
Belt of truth	"He will wear righteousness like a belt and truth like an undergarment" (Isaiah 11:5).
Body armor of righteousness	"He put on righteousness as his body armor" (Isaiah 59:17).
Shoes of peace	"How beautiful. . .are the feet of the messenger who brings. . .good news of peace" (Isaiah 52:7).
Shield of faith	God is my. . .shield and my saving strength" (2 Samuel 22:3 NCV).
Helmet of salvation	"He. . .placed the helmet of salvation on his head" (Isaiah 59:17).
Sword of God's Word	"[The LORD] made my words like a sharp sword" (Isaiah 49:2 NIrV).

ARE DEMONS AND SATAN REAL ENTITIES?
Paul seemed to think so. Jesus did, too. He exorcised demons from people. He talked to the demons, ordering them out. He asked one demon, "What is your name?" (Mark 5:9).

. . . .

EXORCISM. See page 346.

. . . .

SHOULD CHRISTIANS BE AFRAID OF DEMONIC POWERS?
Paul warned Christians to take seriously the powers of evil. But he implied that demonic power is nothing we can't handle when we're suited up with the spiritual armor God gives us.

There is no fear factor, according to one of the most famous songs in the Bible: "Even when I walk through the darkest valley, I will not be afraid, for you are close beside me" (Psalm 23:4).

Another Bible writer seems to explain why we shouldn't be afraid: "The Spirit who lives in you is greater than the spirit who lives in the world" (1 John 4:4).

PHILIPPIANS 3:12–21

Comparing himself perhaps to an Olympic runner, Paul says, *"I press on to reach the end of the race and receive the heavenly prize for which God, through Christ Jesus, is calling us"* (verse 14).

BIG SCENE

LIFE IS A RACE

BIBLE HISTORY			**AD 46** Paul's first mission trip	**AD 49** Paul starts church at Philippi on second mission trip

ALL DATES APPROXIMATE

WORLD HISTORY

AD 41 *Emperor Caligula murdered, succeeded by Claudius, lame and with speech impediment*

PHILIPPIANS

A PREACHER'S THANK-YOU LETTER

STORY LINE

JAIL IS A GOOD PLACE FOR PAUL.

He does some of his best work there, writing fatherly letters of advice to churches he started. Philippians is one such letter.

Paul says he's "in chains." Where, no one knows. Rome is the best guess, most scholars say. That's because he hints that he might be executed, and he says the palace guards know why he's there: "because of Christ" (Philippians 1:13).

Christians of Philippi, in what is now Greece, send him a care package—maybe warm clothes, food, and money.

For this, Paul writes the letter of Philippians; it's a thank-you letter.

But it's also a pastor's letter of warning and encouragement.

Paul warns the Philippians that they, too, may one day face the threat of death because of their faith. But he encourages them to focus their thoughts on what is "true, and honorable, and right. . . . Then the God of peace will be with you" (Philippians 4:8–9).

// TIME: Uncertain. Many guess it was during Paul's two-year arrest in Rome as he waited for his trial from AD 60–62.

// AUTHOR: "This letter is from Paul and Timothy" (Philippians 1:1). Paul seems to be the main contributor, though. He uses the *I* word a lot.

// LOCATION: Paul is "in chains" (Philippians 1:13). Guesses include cities where he was arrested: Caesarea, Ephesus, and Rome—with Rome the top contender since he mentions the threat of execution (see Philippians 1:20). He's writing to Christians in Philippi.

AD 62 *Under arrest, Paul gets Philippi gift, writes thank-you letter: Philippians*

AD 64 *Romans execute Paul*

AD 64 *Rome burns, Nero blames Christians for the fire*

AD 65 *Roman philosopher Seneca commits suicide, at Nero's order*

The good side of prison

IT'S BAD NEWS that Paul's in prison. Yet he seems downright cheery because he says being in prison "has helped to spread the Good News" (Philippians 1:12).

It helps in several ways.

// GUARDS MEET JESUS. The palace guard is getting acquainted with Jesus.

// PAUL'S BOLDNESS INSPIRES LOCAL CHRISTIANS. Believers in town see Paul taking a stand for Jesus, and they start doing the same—boldly sharing their faith.

// JERKS GET IN ON THE ACT. Some preach about Jesus for selfish reasons, perhaps to draw attention to themselves. But whatever their motives, Paul says, "Christ is being preached. . .so I rejoice" (Philippians 1:18).

UNCHAINED MINISTRY / Paul writes the letter to Philippi "in chains" (Philippians 1:13). But he insists his ministry continues—influencing his Roman guards, emboldening free Christians in the city, and inspiring local preachers.

Church ruins
Philippi AD 400s

Black Sea

•Philippi

Thessalonica•

GREECE

Aegean
Sea

TURKEY

•Athens
Corinth

•Ephesus

SYRIA

CYPRUS

CRETE

Mediterranean Sea

LEBANON

▲ **PHILIPPI.** Greek settlers started this city in about 360 BC, lured into the area by gold and silver in the nearby hills along with springs nourishing the plain. Philippi is about 10 miles (16 km) inland. Alexander the Great's father, King Philip II of Macedon, captured the settlement a couple of years later, expanded it, and named it after himself. Rome captured it a couple of centuries later, populated it with retired soldiers, and connected it to other cities with a main road: the Via Egnatia. Today, it's a ruins visited by tourists.

PAUL'S WARNING. "You saw me suffer, and you still hear about my troubles. Now you must suffer in the same way," Paul writes. "Be brave when you face your enemies. Your courage will show them that they are going to be destroyed, and it will show you that you will be saved. God will make all of this happen" (Philippians 1:28, 30 CEV). If Paul wrote this letter in about AD 62, as many scholars guess, Roman persecution of Christians began two years later, when Nero blamed Christians for setting fire to Rome.

◄ **X-RATED ENTERTAINMENT.** Romans executed Christians—sometimes as entertainment in packed arenas. Gladiators slaughtered them. Wild animals tore them to pieces. Soldiers torched them. The slaughter continued off and on for three centuries, with some emperors pursuing Christians more aggressively than others. Trajan (ruled AD 98–117) advised one governor, Pliny—who said he executed Christians—to free them if they recant their religion and promise to worship Roman gods. Otherwise, Trajan said, Pliny should continue punishing them.

Stay humble, keep it real

GET ALONG WITH EACH OTHER. That's Paul's advice, whether he's writing to a church in trouble—like Corinth—or to churches doing just dandy, like Philippi and Ephesus.

> *Make me completely happy! Live in harmony by showing love for each other. Be united in what you think, as if you were only one person.*
>
> PHILIPPIANS 2:2 CEV

That's pretty much what parents want for their kids. And it's what ministers want for their congregations.

Easier said than done.

So Paul gives the Philippians a crash course on the how-to.

// "Don't be selfish."

// "Don't try to impress others."

// "Be humble; thinking of others as better than yourself."

PHILIPPIANS 2:3

In other words, "You must have the same attitude that Christ Jesus had" (Philippians 2:5). Jesus left heaven, became human, and died like a criminal on a cross. That's the flip side of putting himself first. Jesus put us first, Paul implies.

We should do the same, putting others first "readily and cheerfully—no bickering, no second-guessing allowed! Go out into the world uncorrupted, a breath of fresh air in this squalid and polluted society" (Philippians 2:14–15 MSG).

CHURCH CHAT. No arguing going on here. That's the way Paul likes it. He tells Christians in the church at Philippi—as in other cities—to work hard at unity. "Be united in what you think, as if you were only one person" (Philippians 2:2 CEV).

TIMOTHY. Paul's most trusted associate minister. Paul seemed to love him like a son. Timothy was the son of a Jewish Christian mother and a non-Jewish father. Hometown: Lystra, a city Paul visited on all three of his mission trips. Timothy joined Paul on trip two. Paul began using Timothy as a troubleshooter who carried messages to problem churches and stayed to help work out solutions. Paul eventually appointed him pastor of the large congregation at Ephesus and wrote him letters of advice about how to be a good pastor: 1, 2 Timothy. When Paul was sentenced to die, he asked Timothy to come and be with him. Church leaders said Timothy, too, later died a martyr—during a wave of Roman persecution in AD 97.

▶ **EYES ON THE FINISH.** Runners decorate an ancient Greek storage jar. Paul may have attended some of the Olympic-style games near Corinth, because after spending a year and a half in Corinth his letters began to include examples from athletic competitions (see next page).

Life: It's a marathon race

A HERESY STARTS POPPING UP in churches Paul started. Or so it seems, given what he writes in this letter.

The warped teaching goes something like this: You can reach a state of spiritual perfection. "A complete mind," as some Greek philosophers called it—enlightenment.

Paul teaches no such thing. For him, the Christian faith isn't a destination. It's a journey.

He wants spiritual perfection, but he admits: "I have not achieved it" (Philippians 3:13). He chases it, though. He plans to chase it all the way to heaven—like an Olympic runner racing to the finish line:

> *I've got my eye on the goal, where God is beckoning us onward—to Jesus. I'm off and running, and I'm not turning back.*
>
> PHILIPPIANS 3:13–14 MSG

Paul urges the Philippians to do the same. "Stick with me, friends," he says. "There are many out there taking other paths." Easier paths that promise wealth and fame. "But easy street is a dead-end street. Those who live there make their bellies their gods; belches are their praise" (Philippians 3:17–19 MSG).

Italy's Stefano Baldini crosses the finish line, winning the men's marathon at the 2004 Athens Olympic Games.

TRACK AND FIELD METAPHORS?
Paul started writing word pictures from athletic competitions after spending a year and a half in Corinth. While there, he may have seen the Olympic-style games held on the outskirts of town every two years: Isthmian Games. Or perhaps he saw the actual Olympics hosted every four years at Olympia, west about 75 miles (120 km).

Laurel wreath

▲ **PAUL'S GOAL IN THE RACE?**
Eternal life: "the heavenly prize for which God, through Christ Jesus, is calling us" (Philippians 3:14). That's a much better prize than the athletes got: Before Paul's time, it was bragging rights and a wreath made of wilted celery. But perhaps by Paul's time, laurel leaves from a broadleaf evergreen replaced the celery.

COLOSSIANS 2:18
Fraud preachers are hawking their bizarre ideas about Christianity—everything from promoting angel worship, to astrology and circumcision.

BIG SCENE
WORSHIPPING ANGELS

BIBLE HISTORY

ALL DATES APPROXIMATE

Colosse, mound of buried city

AD 53
Paul begins three-year stay in Ephesus

WORLD HISTORY

London founded by Romans
AD 43

COLOSSIANS

FIBBERS AND FRAUDS IN THE CHURCH

STORY LINE

WITH HIS CHURCH IN TROUBLE, the founding pastor asks Paul for advice.

It's hard to tell exactly what the troubles were, because we're getting only Paul's side of the conversation—suggestions he offers the church in a letter. But based on his advice, it looks like intruders have weaseled their way into the church and are pitching weird religious ideas as though they're the gospel truth.

Which weird ideas? Scholars can only guess. A few popular guesses:

// **MIND-OVER-MATTER RELIGION.** The heresy teaches that our minds have incredible power, even over sickness. We just need the secret knowledge to unlock the power. When we get it, we've got the key to salvation. This idea grew into a movement a century later: Gnosticism (NAHS-tah-ciz-um). A modern variation: Unity School of Christianity.

// **JEWISH CHRISTIANITY.** Every Christian has to obey Jewish laws—even non-Jews.

// **A LITTLE OF THIS, A LITTLE OF THAT.** Christian teachings get mixed in with ideas from other religions: Jewish, local Roman gods, and astrology.

Whatever heresy is going on, there's enough truth to make it sound inviting, but there's more than enough fraud to make it dangerous.

Paul's advice: "Plant your roots in Christ. . . . Don't let anyone fool you by using senseless arguments. These arguments may sound wise, but they are only human teachings" (Colossians 2:7–8 CEV).

// **TIME:** Uncertain. He was in chains, perhaps about AD 60–62.

// **AUTHOR:** Paul.

// **LOCATION:** Possibly writing from Rome, Paul addresses Christians in Colosse—a small town east of Ephesus, some 120 miles (193 km).

AD 62
Paul writes letter of Colossians

AD 64
Romans execute Paul

Mark's Gospel is written
AD 65

Jews hide Dead Sea Scrolls from Roman invaders
AD 70

Don't demote Jesus

JESUS CONFUSED CHRISTIANS in the early centuries, which may be one reason Paul had to write this letter.

In the several centuries after Paul, Christian scholars will go toe-to-toe in shouting matches debating the nature of Jesus. Was he God in human flesh, or did he just pretend to be human? Is he a separate entity, or simply God on earth?

Questions like these seem to pop up early. Paul begins to answer them, quoting what many scholars say sounds like the lyrics of an ancient song.

A few notable excerpts:

// *"Christ is exactly like God."*

// *"Everything was created by him."*

// *"By him everything is held together."*

// *"He is the head of his body. . .the church."*

// *"He is. . .the first to be raised from death."*

// *"By sacrificing his blood. . .all beings in heaven and on earth would be brought back to God."*

COLOSSIANS 1:15–18, 20 CEV

"You must continue to believe this truth and stand firmly in it," Paul says. "Don't drift away" (Colossians 1:23).

COLOSSE / A week's walk inland from the Aegean Sea, Colosse was once a busy trade-route city famous for producing dyed purple wool called *colossinus*. But in Paul's day, it was a city past its prime and off the beaten trail. Romans had built a shortcut that ran through Laodicea, bypassing Colosse. An earthquake nearly destroyed Colosse sometime between AD 60–64, perhaps shortly after Paul wrote the letter of Colossians. Citizens rebuilt the town but later abandoned it, perhaps because of more earthquakes or repeated raids. All that's left today is a mound that archaeologists haven't started excavating.

HERE COMES THE SON / Laced in clouds and framed in light, a statue of Jesus crowns the mountain overlooking Rio de Janeiro. Some 30 years after Jesus returned to heaven, Christians apparently were confused enough about the nature of Jesus that Paul felt compelled to give them a refresher course.

Follow Jesus, not manmade rules

FRAUD CHRISTIANS are spreading nonsense at the church of Colosse, and perhaps in neighboring Laodicea, too.

Instead of preaching the gospel of faith in Jesus, they're preaching from their own private rule books.

Some of their rules:

// **EAT AND DRINK APPROVED FOOD.** Perhaps a reference to the kosher Jewish diet.

// **HONOR THE SABBATH.** And the New Moon, along with other holy days—presumably Jewish holidays such as Passover in the spring.

// **PRACTICE SELF-DENIAL.** Perhaps the beginning of the ascetic movement, and its obsession with fasting, beating oneself, and suffering through other hardships such as sleeping in the cold without a blanket.

// **WORSHIP ANGELS.** Possibly a reference to calling on angels for help.

Paul says the Jewish rules were "only shadows of the reality yet to come. And Christ himself is that reality" (Colossians 2:17).

As for the other rules, such as self-denial and angel worship, Paul says they're "empty philosophies and high-sounding nonsense that. . .seem wise because they require strong devotion. . . . But they provide no help in conquering a person's evil desires" (Colossians 2:8, 23).

The way to conquer evil desire is by replacing it with holy desire.

"You have accepted Christ Jesus as your Lord. Now keep on following him. Plant your roots in Christ and let him be the foundation for your life" (Colossians 2:6–7 CEV).

SPIRITS IN THE SKY / Stars circle above the church of Saint John the Baptist in Stanton, England—captured in a time-lapse composite of 80 photos, each exposed for 45 seconds. Many Romans and some Christians in Paul's day seemed to believe that celestial spirits, constellations, and planets (named after Roman gods) affected their day-to-day life. But Paul said Jesus created everything, rules over it all, and "has set you free from the spiritual powers of this world" (Colossians 2:20).

(continued next page)

◄ **PRAYING TO ANGELS.** A jasper amulet, worn for protection, pleads for help by invoking the power of four angels: Michael, Raphael, Gabriel, and Ouriel (names at top right). A rooster-headed, snake-legged spirit cracks a whip to chase away evil spirits.

KOSHER FOOD. See page 51.

NEW MOON SACRIFICES. Jewish priests offered sacrifices at the beginning of every new month, when the new moon rose (see Numbers 28:11–15).

PENANCE IN RED / Draped in his own blood, a Roman Catholic in San Pedro Cutud, Pampanga, in the Philippines observes Good Friday by beating himself with bamboo rods laced to a whip—to express sorrow for his sins. Paul took a stand against Church leaders who prodded Christians toward painful practices he called "self-denial" (Colossians 2:23).

What a Christian looks like

THINKERS AND DO-GOODERS, that's what Paul says real Christians look like.

"Think about the things of heaven, not the things of earth," he writes. Then "whatever you do or say, do it as a representative of the Lord Jesus" (Colossians 3:2, 17).

So what kind of good-doing do do-gooders do?

Paul offers up a starter list:

CHRISTIANS PURSUE:
- // tenderhearted mercy
- // kindness
- // humility
- // gentleness
- // patience
- // forgiveness for offenders

CHRISTIANS AVOID:
- // anger
- // slander
- // dirty language
- // lies
- // sexual immorality
- // greed

ROMAN PORTRAIT / The likeness of an Egyptian woman from Roman times, painted on a board and attached to her mummy. Paul painted word pictures of Christians from his day, portraying them as kind souls who treat non-Christians with courtesy.

PAUL'S ADVICE FOR DEALING WITH NON-CHRISTIANS. "When you are with unbelievers, always make good use of the time. Be pleasant and hold their interest when you speak the message. Choose your words carefully and be ready to give answers to anyone who asks questions" (Colossians 4:5–6 CEV).

TYCHICUS AND ONESIMUS. Associates of Paul, they deliver his letter to Colosse. Tychicus (TICK-ee-cuss) also delivered the letter of Ephesians (Ephesians 6:21) and perhaps of Philemon. Onesimus (oh-NESS-uh-muhs) was a slave of Philemon.

BIG SCENE
LOOKING FOR THE SECOND COMING

1 THESSALONIANS 4:16–17

"The Lord himself will come down from heaven." Dead Christians will rise. Then living Christians. They're all headed to heaven, where they'll live forever.

BIBLE HISTORY			

ALL DATES APPROXIMATE

BIBLE HISTORY

AD 33 *Jesus crucified for claiming to be Messiah, God's Son (AD 30 alternate date)*

AD 44 *Paul co-pastors church in Antioch, with Barnabas*

WORLD HISTORY

Caligula becomes emperor, says he's a god
AD 37

Theudas beheaded for claiming he's the Messiah
AD 46

1,2 THESSALONIANS

DON'T WAIT FOR JESUS, WORK FOR JESUS

STORY LINE

RIOTING JEWS run Paul out of Thessalonica three weeks after his arrival. That's all the time he gets to start a church there. But start it, he does.

Paul is traveling on his second church-planting expedition. But it's his first time venturing into Europe, in what is now Greece. Paul moves on to Berea and then to Athens before arriving in Corinth, where he'll stay for a year and a half.

Bible experts guess that while he's there in Corinth, he gets word that the Christians he left behind in Thessalonica are facing persecution—perhaps by the same Jews who drove Paul out of town. The new Christians want to know when Jesus is coming back.

Paul writes them two letters, one after the other. He tells them no one knows when Jesus will return. And he encourages them to spend their meantime living like God's people: loving each other, working hard, and trying to live in peace with everyone.

That's apparently easier said than done, which is why there's a second letter perhaps just a few weeks or months later.

// TIME: Most Bible experts say Paul probably wrote these two letters during his second missionary trip, and his year-and-a-half stay in Corinth—sometime between AD 49–51.

// AUTHOR: Paul says the letter comes from him, Timothy, and Silas. But it's written in one person's voice, probably because it represents Paul's thoughts.

// LOCATION: Paul is likely writing from Corinth, addressing the congregation in Thessalonica, about a 300-mile (480 km) walk to the north.

AD 49 *Paul starts church in Corinth*

AD 50 *Paul writes 1, 2 Thessalonians*

AD 64 *Romans execute Paul*

Jews revolt against Rome, Christians flee Jerusalem **AD 66**

Romans level Jerusalem **AD 70**

SECOND COMING. Jesus told his disciples he had to leave, adding, "When everything is ready, I will come and get you, so that you will always be with me where I am" (John 14:3).

Christians don't agree when Jesus will return or what his comeback will look like.

Some say it already happened—in the resurrection or in the arrival of the Holy Spirit at Pentecost (see page 399).

Others say it will be a two-part event. First a secret Rapture—a snatching away of Christians—followed years later by Jesus' public and glorious return with all the godly people who ever lived. Others say both events will happen at the same time.

RAPTURE. When Jesus returns, Paul says all godly people—the living and the resurrected dead—will be snatched away to be with Jesus. Many Christians call this event the Rapture. It means "caught up." It's from the Greek word, *harpazo*, which seems to have given us the English word for "harpoon."

Titus

◄ **WHO IS THE MAN OF LAWLESSNESS?** Whoever he is, he loses: "He will be completely destroyed by the Lord's glorious return" (2 Thessalonians 2:8 CEV).

Some Bible students say he's an evil end-time leader. Many link him to the "Antichrist" briefly mentioned 1 John 2:18, and to one of two beasts described in Revelation 13.

Many others link him to first-century rulers in the doomed Roman Empire. Contenders:

▸ **Emperor Nero** *(ruled AD 54–68). He started persecuting Christians in AD 64. Also, his name tracks with the Mark of the Beast (see pages 531, 533).*

▸ **Emperor Caligula** *(ruled AD 37–41). He tried unsuccessfully to erect a statue of himself in the Jerusalem Temple.*

▸ **Roman general Titus** *(ruled as emperor AD 79–81). He demolished Jerusalem and the Temple in AD 70, crushing a Jewish revolt.*

ENTIRE SANCTIFICATION. Paul ends his first letter by praying that God will "sanctify you through and through. . . . He will do it" (1 Thessalonians 5:23–24 TNIV). Some holiness and Pentecostal denominations teach that mature believers can become "entirely sanctified" as a second definite spiritual work after conversion, and that it makes people less likely to sin. Most churches, however, teach that maturing toward holiness is a lifelong process, with ups and downs.

Don't be lazy busybodies

IF YOU DON'T WORK, YOU DON'T EAT. That's Paul's message to some Christians in Thessalonica who for some reason have stopped working.

Bible experts can only guess why some of the believers "just loaf around and won't do any work, except the work of a busybody" (2 Thessalonians 3:11 CEV).

Whatever the reason they're not working—and it's not because they can't—Paul hates it. He attacks the problem three times:

// When he visited the city: "Even while we were with you, we gave you this command: 'Those unwilling to work will not get to eat' " (2 Thessalonians 3:10).

// In his first letter: "We urge you to warn those who are lazy" (1 Thessalonians 5:14).

// In his second letter: "Start working for a living" (2 Thessalonians 3:12 CEV).

THEORIES ABOUT WHY SOME CHRISTIANS STOPPED WORKING.

Bible scholars offer several guesses. Two popular guesses:

> **Second Coming.** They think Jesus is coming back any minute. They don't see any point in working, since they'll be leaving the planet soon.

> **Saintly Sugar Daddies.** Others are covering their expenses. Rich Christians may have taken them under their fiscal wing, much like some rich people today take care of an entourage in exchange for little more than gratitude, emotional support, and occasional chores.

WAS PAUL AGAINST A WELFARE SYSTEM?

No. He worked as a welfare leader. He took up offerings for "the believers in Jerusalem" (2 Corinthians 9:1). The Jerusalem folks were apparently struggling against a drought and perhaps against ongoing persecution from the Jews.

◄ CARPENTER ON THE JOB.

A carpenter totes a hand-tooled board into his shop—which apparently is more work than some Christians in Thessalonica were willing to do. They quit working and lived off the charity of others, perhaps because they thought Jesus was coming back soon. Paul bluntly told them if he can pay his own way, so can they.

THESSALONICA.

This bustling trade town of perhaps more than 100,000 souls had the best naturally protected port in what is now Greece. Today, with a population of about 364,000, Thessaloniki is the second-largest city in Greece, after Athens.

BIG SCENE
DEAD MAN WRITING

2 TIMOTHY 4
On the brink of execution, Paul says he has finished his race and is ready for his reward. But he wants Timothy nearby: "Please come as soon as you can" (2 Timothy 4:9).

BIBLE HISTORY

ALL DATES APPROXIMATE

AD 33
Paul sees the light, converts to Christianity

WORLD HISTORY

1,2 TIMOTHY

A MINISTER'S SURVIVAL GUIDE

STORY LINE

THERE'S TROUBLE IN EPHESUS, at the church—false teachers pitching warped ideas. The Ephesus church is perhaps the largest Paul has started, certainly in the largest city where he planted a church. But it's time to move on to Macedonia in what is now northern Greece. So he leaves Timothy behind to keep the church on track.

Later, Paul writes Timothy two letters.

First Timothy is a bit like a pastor's manual, full of advice about how to lead a church. Paul offers suggestions about prayer, helping the poor, a woman's role in the church, what to look for in church leaders Timothy will need to appoint, and how to deal with would-be leaders spreading distorted ideas about Christianity.

Second Timothy is a tear-jerker. At times, it feels intrusive to read. It's that personal. Most Bible experts say these are probably the last surviving words of Paul. He's in a Roman prison, facing imminent execution. A single man, he writes as though Timothy is his beloved son. Paul offers not only the kind of advice a senior minister might give to a younger pastor, but he adds the kind of advice a Christian father might give to his son.

Then, from a thousand miles away (1,600 km), Paul asks for Timothy to come quickly. Like most others on the brink of death, Paul doesn't want to die alone.

// TIME: Perhaps about AD 63. Bible experts debate when Paul wrote these letters. Most say it was after the events in Acts.

// AUTHOR: Paul gets the credit, though many Bible experts today have their doubts.

// LOCATION: Paul was in a jail in Rome when he wrote the second letter to Timothy, who was pastoring in Ephesus. Paul was apparently still free when he wrote the first letter.

AD 52
Paul starts church in Ephesus, on third mission trip

AD 57
Paul arrested in Jerusalem

AD 63
Paul writes 1 Timothy

AD 64
Paul writes 2 Timothy

Paul freed in Rome after four-year arrest that began in Jerusalem
AD 62

Nero blames Christians for burning Rome; Romans arrest and behead Paul **AD 64**

Put a lid on warped ideas

JOB ONE FOR TIMOTHY is to "stop those whose teaching is contrary to the truth" (1 Timothy 1:3). That's the reason Paul said he left him behind in Ephesus.

Paul gives us only hints about what those distorted teachings might be.

Here are a few guesses Bible experts offer, along with supporting evidence from the Bible.

JEWS MAKE THE BEST CHRISTIANS. Paul says some false teachers are convincing Ephesus Christians to "waste their time in endless discussion of myths and spiritual pedigrees" (1 Timothy 1:4). These teachers may be Jews bragging about their family ties to ancient heroes of the faith, and about being God's first Chosen People. As though first is best. They may also be the same brand of Jewish Christians who, for years, have been arguing that all Christians need to obey the Jewish laws. "They want to be known as teachers of the law of Moses," Paul says, "but they don't know what they are talking about" (1 Timothy 1:7).

MONKLIKE SELF-DEPRIVATION HELPS US EARN OUR SALVATION. "They will say it is wrong to be married and wrong to eat certain foods" (1 Timothy 4:3). Jewish Christians may be lobbying for the traditional kosher Jewish diet, alongside an emerging Christian idea that celibacy ratchets up our faith a notch.

GETTING IT RIGHT IN THE HEAD IS BETTER THAN GETTING IT RIGHT IN LIFE. Some teachers have "an unhealthy desire to quibble over the meaning of words" (1 Timothy 6:4). Paul says that those philosophizing brainiacs see Christianity only as a way to get rich. Paul's advice: "Don't pay any attention to that godless and stupid talk that sounds smart but really isn't" (1 Timothy 6:20 CEV).

Burial portrait of man from Roman times

TIMOTHY, AT A GLANCE

Born: Lystra, in what is now Turkey

Mother: Eunice, a Jew

Father: Non-Jew

Early ministry: Joined Paul as associate on second mission trip, about AD 48, serving as troubleshooter and courier who delivered Paul's letters and handled church problems in Thessalonica and Corinth

Late ministry: Pastor of the church in Ephesus

Death: Early Church leaders say he became the bishop at Ephesus and died a martyr in AD 97

DID PAUL WRITE THE LETTERS TO TIMOTHY AND TITUS? Many Bible experts today say they doubt it. They say the writing style and word choices don't match his other letters, and that some key teachings are missing—such as the idea that Jewish laws are obsolete. They say students of his wrote them, in his honor.

Early Church leaders, however, included these letters in the Bible because they said Paul wrote them. The differing styles could suggest only that Paul dictated his letters to professional scribes who polished his words; he hints that he dictated some, including Romans. Also, Paul may have omitted key teachings because he was writing to a couple of associates who already knew them.

▲ **JUST THINKING.** Paul warns Timothy away from philosophizing heretics who sound smart but are nothing more than "ignorant windbags who infect the air with germs of envy, controversy, bad-mouthing, suspicious rumors" (1 Timothy 6:4 MSG).

How ladies should behave in church

PAUL'S ADVICE TO WOMEN might explain why he's a bachelor. At least as far as some Bible students are concerned. For them, it's hard to read Paul's words as anything but male chauvinism to the bone and beyond—all the way to his soul.

Paul tells Timothy, newly appointed pastor in Ephesus, that when women come to church they should:

// wear modest clothes

// skip fancy hairdos

// leave the jewelry home

// keep quiet, and learn about Jesus by listening to the men talk

// never publicly teach a man or assume authority over men

Why would Paul say such things? Bible experts don't agree about how to interpret Paul's advice. Scholars tend to scatter in one of three directions.

PAUL'S ADVICE APPLIES JUST TO THIS LOCAL CHURCH. He gives similar advice to women in Corinth. But these two churches were exceptions, perhaps because women were causing problems. Closing his letter to Roman Christians, Paul compliments women leaders in the church.

One is Junias. Depending on which Bible translation gets it right, she is either one of the "leaders among the apostles"(Romans 16:7 NIrV)—serving in the highest church office at the time—or "highly respected by the apostles" (CEV).

Another lady leader is Phoebe, "a deacon in the church" (Romans 16:1). Yet another is Paul's coworker, Priscilla (see Romans 16:3). She and her husband taught a preacher named Apollos: "They took him aside and explained the way of God even more accurately" (Acts 18:26).

"THEY SHOULDN'T BRAID THEIR HAIR" (1 Timothy 2:9 NIrV). At the time, respectable women wore veils over their heads when out in public. This covered any fancy hairdos they might have. But some women apparently were starting to take their fashion cues from Rome, and they began wearing elaborately braided hair like Emperor Nero's three wives—who weren't what Paul would have called godly role models.

PAUL'S ADVICE APPLIES JUST TO THIS MAN-RUN CULTURE. Scholars supporting this theory say Paul wants Christians to work with the culture in which they live. In this case, it's a man's world. And Paul doesn't want the ladies publicly humiliating their husbands, which could throw cold dishwater on the Christian movement.

PAUL'S ADVICE APPLIES TO WOMEN EVERYWHERE. Some scholars call this the complementarian view, though many women don't see the compliment. As the theory goes, men and women are equal partners, but they have different roles to fill. For example, men take the lead in church while women take the lead in childcare.

▼ **WORSHIP MODE /** Modestly dressed. Hair covered. Mouth closed. Eyes and ears alert—to listen and learn from the men. That's how the apostle Paul said he liked his ladies in worship services. Bible experts don't agree on what he'd say about women at worship today. But some guess he'd be no less politically incorrect.

"WOMEN WILL BE SAVED THROUGH CHILDBEARING" (1 Timothy 2:15). It's a puzzler why Paul would say something like this. Reading between the lines, some scholars speculate that women became so involved in church leadership roles that their families suffered. So Paul was saying the women didn't need to do anything more than live out their faith by accepting their God-given role as wife and mother.

WHAT KIND OF TROUBLE MIGHT THE WOMEN HAVE BEEN CAUSING? Ephesus was a feminist-leaning town, some Bible experts say, famous for its worship of Artemis—daughter of Zeus and Mother Goddess of childbirth and nature. With Artemis as the city's patron god, some local women felt a sense of superiority that women elsewhere never experienced. Other scholars say that's just speculation, and there's no solid evidence that Ephesus was any less of a man's town than other cities in the Roman Empire.

Do's and don'ts of a church leader

TIMOTHY NEEDS MINISTERS and other workers to help him—in Ephesus as well as in neighboring towns, starting new church groups.

Paul gives Pastor Timothy a checklist of what to look for in candidates for ministry.

Paul zeroes in on two kinds of leaders. They sound a bit like the ancient version of today's (1) local pastor or parish priest and (2) church volunteer, such as a Bible teacher or an elected board member.

Depending on the Bible translation we read, Paul calls the pastor an "elder," "overseer," or "bishop." And he calls the volunteer a "deacon" or a "church officer."

The list of character traits doesn't read like it's exhaustive—or even carefully organized (see next page). For example, some of the traits he wants to see in volunteers would be important for ministers, too, such as integrity and honesty in finances. So Paul may be simply writing or dictating some of the characteristics that quickly come to mind. By the time he writes this letter, he probably has a couple decades of experience in starting churches.

. . . .

MARRY A GOOD WOMAN / Two young women take a stroll through the streets of Istanbul, the largest city in Turkey. Paul tells Timothy—a pastor in Turkey—what kind of men to appoint as church leaders. If they're married, Paul says, they'd better be married to respected women who don't run off at the mouth, running people down.

A little attitude in Turkey

WHY DID PAUL EXPECT PASTORS TO HAVE OBEDIENT CHILDREN?

He was single and didn't know any better, some Bible students would say. He didn't know kids have minds of their own. But Bible experts say that in Paul's day, when men ruled and family members spent more time together than families do today, the children were considered more a reflection of the father than they are now.

. . . .

WHY A HIGHER STANDARD FOR SENIOR CHURCH LEADERS THAN FOR OTHERS?

The bigger the job, the more it takes to get the job done. Not all church workers need to be able to teach, for example. But pastors do. Not all church volunteers need to be a people person. But pastors do.

Paul's Character Trait List

REQUIRED TRAITS	PASTOR, STAFF	VOLUNTEERS
Good reputation	X	X
Integrity		X
Admired by non-Christians	X	
Faithful to wife	X	X
Good family manager	X	X
Obedient, respectful children	X	
Respected wives who don't slander others		X
Dependable		X
Self-controlled	X	X
Sensible	X	
Gentle	X	
Enjoys having houseguests	X	
Able to teach	X	
Committed to the faith		X
Clear conscience		X
Passes evaluation by church leaders		X
Not a heavy drinker	X	X
Not violent	X	
Not quarrelsome	X	
Not money-hungry	X	
Not dishonest with money		X
Not a new believer	X	

How to treat the congregation

MEDDLING WIDOWS, grumpy old men, and good pastors gone bad—Paul assumes Timothy will come across all of these, and then some. So he gives young Timothy advice about how to minister to them.

MEDDLING WIDOWS. Stop it before it happens by encouraging younger widows to marry again and to devote themselves to their families.

GRUMPY OLD MEN. Never speak harshly to them. Address them respectfully, as you would your father.

PASTORS GONE BAD. Don't even listen to charges against an elder unless it is confirmed by at least two witnesses.

HARDWORKING PASTORS. "Elders who do their work well should be respected and paid well, especially those who work hard at both preaching and teaching" (1 Timothy 5:17).

DESTITUTE WIDOWS. Take care of them if they have no family who will do it. "But if she has children or grandchildren, their first responsibility is to show godliness at home and repay their parents by taking care of them. This is something that pleases God" (1 Timothy 5:4).

SLAVES. Tell them to show respect for their masters. And if their masters are believers, they should work all the harder.

. . . .

NEAR THE END / On end-of-life hospice care, 83-year-old Ginny Lothrop sleeps while her daughter, Susan Myrland, catches some rest, too. Ginny moved from her home in Florida to be near Susan in California. The apostle Paul urged adult children to take care of their widowed mothers. But if the children don't, he said, the Church needs to step up and do it.

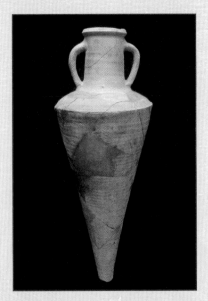

Wine amphora, pointed for burial in ground to cool wine

A LITTLE WINE FOR THE STOMACH.

That's Paul's medical advice to Timothy, "for the sake of your stomach because you are sick so often" (1 Timothy 5:23). A small amount of wine can aid digestion by helping break down food and eliminate bad bacteria. Some Bible experts wonder if Paul was afraid that if Timothy didn't drink some wine, people might mistake him for one of the self-denial heretics who taught that people earn their salvation through hardship, like fasting.

. . . .

WHY NOT TELL CHRISTIANS TO FREE THEIR SLAVES?

Perhaps Paul realized that the best way to make social change in his culture was from the inside out. Spiritual change tends to work itself out into attitudes and behavior. But until then, he didn't want to make Christianity look like a threat. So he advised each Christian slave to give "respect to his master so that outsiders don't blame God and our teaching for his behavior" (1 Timothy 6:1 MSG).

Christian, no matter what

ON THE BRINK OF EXECUTION, writing from a Rome prison Paul preaches the Gospel of No Fear.

He knows he's about to die. And he knows these words might be his last to Timothy.

What to say?

"My dear son. . . .I thank God for you. . . . I long to see you again" (2 Timothy 1:2–4). Tender words from a single man to the closest thing he would ever know to a son of his own.

Then come Paul's words of warning—and encouragement. Paul knows that like himself, Timothy may someday face death because of his faith in Jesus.

Paul's advice:

// **DON'T BE ASHAMED TO TELL OTH-ERS ABOUT JESUS.** But "be ready to suffer with me for the sake of the Good News" (2 Timothy 1:8).

// **DON'T FEAR DEATH.** Jesus defeated death. And he lights "the way to life and immortality" (2 Timothy 1:10).

// **KEEP THE FAITH, PLAYING BY GOD'S RULES.** "Anyone who takes part in a sport doesn't receive the winner's crown unless he plays by the rules" (2 Timothy 2:5 NIrV).

// **EXPECT ETERNAL LIFE.** "If we die with him, we'll live with him; if we stick it out with him, we'll rule with him" (2 Timothy 2:11–12 MSG).

HOW DID TIMOTHY DIE? Some early Church writings such as *Acts of Saint Timothy* say he was stoned and clubbed to death in Ephesus in AD 97. The report says it happened while he was speaking out against a festival honoring a god. Perhaps the city's patron goddess Artemis (also called Diana). Or perhaps Dionysus, god of wine who was celebrated in ritual orgies.

▲ **HAZARDOUS FAITH.** Saint Sebastian lies dying, said to have been martyred during Emperor Diocletian's persecution of Christians in about AD 288. Paul warned Timothy that tough times were coming. Romans persecuted Christians off and on for about three centuries, until Emperor Constantine legalized Christianity.

Countdown to good-bye

LIKE A FATHER ABOUT TO DIE, giving his son a few final, heartfelt words to live by, Paul scribbles out the best advice he has to offer to "Timothy, my dear son" (2 Timothy 1:2).

Paul's words pour out, not in thoughtful, rhythmic poetic verse. But in a jumble of jewels. Sometimes randomly mixed and matched. But keepers every one.

// "Do your best to win God's approval."

// "Run from temptations that capture young people."

// "Be. . .easy to get along with."

// "Worship with people whose hearts are pure."

// "Stay away from stupid and senseless arguments. These only lead to trouble."

// "Be kind to everyone. . .and very patient."

// "Keep on being faithful to what you were taught and to what you believed."

// "Stay calm and be willing to suffer."

// "Work hard to tell the good news and to do your job well."

> 2 TIMOTHY **2:15, 22–24; 3:14; 4:5** CEV

PAUL'S BIBLE / Paul tells Timothy, "All Scripture is inspired by God and is useful to teach us what is true and to make us realize what is wrong in our lives. It corrects us when we are wrong and teaches us to do what is right. God uses it to prepare and equip his people to do every good work" (2 Timothy 3:16–17). Paul wasn't talking about the Christian Bible, with the New Testament. He was talking about the Jewish Bible, which Christians call the Old Testament. Paul probably had no idea that his words would become just as revered. His byline shows up on almost half of the books in the New Testament: 13 of 27.

SADDLE UP / Circuit-riding preacher and Methodist church founder John Wesley (1703–1791) rode over 250,000 miles on horseback—a distance that would circle the globe at the equator 10 times. He preached over 40,000 sermons. If Paul's advice to Timothy is any clue—"work hard to tell the good news" (2 Timothy 4:5 CEV)—Paul would have approved of Wesley's devotion to ministry.

Paul's last request

"MY DEATH IS NEAR," Paul writes Timothy from a prison in Rome. "I have fought the good fight, I have finished the race, and I have remained faithful" (2 Timothy 4:7).

Like most people headed into the valley of the shadow of death, he wants company. He knows God is with him, but there are times when even people of great faith need someone wearing skin.

"Please come as soon as you can," Paul pleads (2 Timothy 4:9).

"Do your best to get here before winter. . . . When you come, be sure to bring the coat I left with Carpus at Troas. Also bring my books, and especially my papers" (2 Timothy 4:13, 21).

Most of Paul's associates had left him, either on assignments by him or for self-preservation. Only one remains, the physician Luke, said to have written the Gospel of Luke and Acts. But Paul wants his dearest friend, Timothy. And he asks Timothy to bring John Mark, another associate who's credited with writing what many scholars say was the first of the four Gospels: Mark.

The Bible doesn't report the end of this story. We don't know if Timothy made the trip at all, let alone if he arrived in time.

HOW DID PAUL DIE?

Beheaded by a sword—the quick death permitted for Roman citizens, as opposed to the lingering death of crucifixion. That's how early Church writers said he died, adding that the execution took place at mile marker three on the Ostian Way, on the outskirts of Rome. Marking the spot today is a fitting memorial to a church planter: a church. It's called Saint Paul of the Three Fountains. Romans built it in the AD 400s, after they legalized Christianity.

WHY ASK TIMOTHY TO COME BEFORE WINTER?

Winter weather made long-distance travel dangerous, by land or by sea. Rome is about as far north as Chicago, Detroit, and Beijing.

▶ **BY LAND OR BY SEA.** Traveling from Ephesus by land, it could have taken Timothy a month or two to reach Paul about 1,000 miles (1,600 km) away, imprisoned and waiting on death row in Rome. By sea, with favorable winds, Timothy could have made the trip in just a couple of weeks.

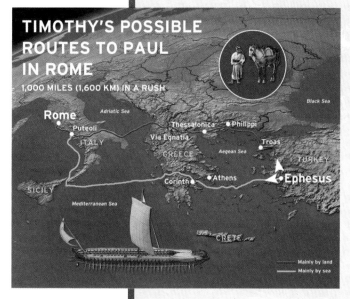

TIMOTHY'S POSSIBLE ROUTES TO PAUL IN ROME
1,000 MILES (1,600 KM) IN A RUSH

Rome · Puteoli · ITALY · Adriatic Sea · Thessalonica · Phillppi · Via Egnatia · GREECE · Aegean Sea · Troas · TURKEY · Corinth · Athens · Ephesus · SICILY · Mediterranean Sea · Black Sea · CRETE

Mainly by land
Mainly by sea

Wanted: pastors for scumbags

DIAMONDS IN A COAL MINE is Titus's quest. He's looking for something shiny in a grimy hole.

The hole is Crete. The grime is the Cretan people. And the diamonds are undiscovered pastors.

Paul's assignment for Titus reads like a Mission Impossible—the comedy. For from the island's inventory of "lazy evil liars"—paraphrasing Paul's description of the locals—Titus is supposed to find a few good men who live "a blameless life" (Titus 1:6). Once Titus finds them, he's to appoint them as church leaders in cities throughout the island.

Paul lists some of the specific character traits Titus should look for—traits much like those on the list he sent to Timothy in Ephesus.

QUALIFICATIONS:

// have a good reputation
// be sensible and fair
// be faithful to his wife
// have well-behaved children
// be friendly and enjoy having strangers in their home
// stick to the true message about Jesus
// correct anyone who teaches otherwise
// not be bossy
// not be quick-tempered
// not be heavy drinkers
// not be bullies
// not be dishonest in business

Minoan art from Crete

CULTURED HISTORY, PIRATE HISTORY.
Once home to the culturally advanced Minoans, who were named after their legendary king, Minos, this civilization mysteriously collapsed by about 1200 BC. That's around the time the Exodus Jews were settling in the Promised Land. Mercenaries and pirates began using it as a home base for attacks on ships, until Romans conquered them and restored peace in 67 BC.

WHERE DID PAUL COME UP WITH SUCH AN ANTI-CRETAN QUOTE?
From the Cretans. Writing about 600 years before Paul, Cretan prophet Epimenides said his fellow Cretans are "always liars, evil animals, and lazy people who do nothing but eat" (Titus 1:12 NCV). Another Cretan, poet Callimachus writing 200 years before Paul, repeated the slam. In time, the ancient word for *Cretan* became a Greek verb: *Kretizo*. It means "to lie." As in, "You lie!"

◄ **BEGGING PAUL'S PARDON.**
A Cretan woman is photographed while crocheting fabric for sale in one of the village shops at Kritza. Like most hardworking Cretans today, she probably wouldn't take kindly to the apostle Paul calling her ancestors lazy liars. But he did.

How to spot a Christian Cretan

IN HIS SPARE TIME, when Titus isn't looking for blameless souls to pastor Crete churches, he's supposed to teach the Cretan believers how to behave.

Paul offers situation-tailored guidelines.

OLDER MEN. Be sensible and serious. Focus on self-control. Don't forget love and patience.

OLDER WOMEN. Don't gossip. And don't get drunk. Let the younger women learn from your example what loving wives and mothers are supposed to look like.

YOUNG MEN. One word: *self-control.*

YOUNG WOMEN. Look to "older women" as an example of how you should live.

SLAVES. Obey your masters. Don't talk back to them. And don't steal from them. Show them what a Christian looks like.

ALL THE ABOVE AND EVERYONE ELSE. Be kind. Earn the respect of others. And obey your rulers.

IS A CRETAN A CRETIN?
Only to the ear. Same sound. Different meanings. A *Cretan* is a native of Crete. A *cretin* is a person who is dumber than a bag of lug nuts, which they'd prefer honey-roasted.

WHY OBEY GODLESS RULERS?
Paul told Titus to "Remind the believers to submit to the government and its officers" (Titus 3:1). Paul may have done this so Christianity would get a stamp of approval—as a religion that didn't pose a political threat.

WHO WAS THE TOP ROMAN RULER?
Nero (reign AD 54–68). Roman historians of the day didn't paint him with happy colors. He executed his own mother. Historian Tacitus (AD 56–117) said Nero sent three assassins to stab her so he could divorce his wife and marry a woman his mother didn't like.

◀ PRIEST AT PEACE.
It hasn't always been peaceful for Crete religious leaders like this priest. In 1866, the abbot at Arkadi Monastery ordered the fortresslike facility blown up rather than surrender to 15,000 Muslim Turks charging over the walls. Cretans later won their independence and rebuilt the monastery, now a national treasure. Yet Paul gave a different order for dealing with occupiers such as the Romans in his day: Submit. He targeted the spiritual, not the political.

BIG SCENE

GOING BACK TO SLAVERY

PHILEMON 21

Paul orders a runaway slave back to his Christian slave master, but in not-so-subtle hints, lobbies for the slave's release.

BIBLE HISTORY	ALL DATES APPROXIMATE	**AD 57** Paul arrested in Jerusalem	**AD 60** Paul sails to Rome for trial	**AD 62** Paul writes Ephesians, Colossians, Philemon, Philippians
WORLD HISTORY			Romans execute Paul **AD 64**	Jews revolt, drive Romans out **AD 66**

PHILEMON

RUNAWAY SLAVE TURNS HIMSELF IN

STORY LINE

A RUNAWAY SLAVE meets Paul and gets converted to the Christian faith.

Paul is a prisoner at the time, perhaps under house arrest in Rome, awaiting a trial that most Bible experts say found him not guilty.

The slave is a man named Onesimus (oh-NESS-uh-muhs).

In a shocker, Paul orders Onesimus to go back to his slave master, Philemon (fi-LEE-mon), leader of the church at Colosse. Christians meet in Philemon's home.

But Paul doesn't send Onesimus home empty-handed. He writes a letter of recommendation, which he asks the runaway slave to hand-deliver.

This is one humdinger of a letter. Paul appeals to Philemon not only to forgive Onesimus, but to treat him like a brother instead of a slave. Paul even hints that he'd like Philemon to free Onesimus and send him back to help Paul.

In what could read like an implied threat, Paul adds that he hopes to pay Philemon a visit soon: "Please prepare a guest room for me" (Philemon 1:22).

// LOCATION: Paul is a prisoner, probably in Rome. He's writing to Philemon, who lives in Colosse, more than 1,000 miles (1,600 km) away. Paul probably writes this at the same time he writes Ephesians and Colossians. Onesimus delivered the Colossians letter to Colosse, with help from Tychicus (see Colossians 4:9). The two may have delivered all three letters in the same trip. Colosse was about a week's walk past Ephesus, 120 miles (193 km) (see map on page 485).

// TIME: Paul probably writes this while under house arrest in Rome, from AD 60–62.

// AUTHOR: Paul.

Romans return to crush revolt
AD 67

Romans destroy Jerusalem
AD 70

Pompeii slave sells for 625 denarii (working-class salary for one and a half years)
AD 79

Paul twists a slave owner's arm

TWO LETTERS IN ONE is what Paul writes to Christian slave owner Philemon.

There are the actual words, politely asking Philemon to show mercy to returning runaway slave Onesimus. And there's the stronger message, written between the lines.

PAUL'S WORDS	BETWEEN THE LINES
"I am boldly asking a favor of you. I could demand it. . . . But because of our love, I prefer simply to ask you" (8–9).	"I'm an apostle—your boss. I could order you to do what I'm about to ask. And if you don't, I just might."
"I became his father in the faith while here in prison" (10).	"Treat Onesimus like he's my own son."
"I wanted to keep him here with me. . .and he would have helped me on your behalf. But I didn't want to do anything without your consent" (13–14).	"Give your consent. Send him back to me."
"He is no longer like a slave to you. He is more than a slave, for he is a beloved brother" (16).	"He's not just my son. He's your brother. Since you're my son as well, call me Dad and do what I say."
"If he. . .owes you anything, charge it to me. . . . I won't mention that you owe me your very soul!" (18–19).	"Okay, I mentioned it. So how could you possibly charge me anything when you owe me everything?"
"I am confident as I write this letter that you will do what I ask and even more!" (21).	"And if you don't, you'll be sorry."
"Prepare a guest room for me, for I am hoping that God will answer your prayers and let me return to you soon" (22).	"If you don't do as I ask, you'll have some explaining to do when I come to town."

DID PHILEMON FREE ONESIMUS?

Probably. Paul addressed the letter to the entire church at Colosse. So Philemon would have been under intense peer pressure to obey the father of the Christian movement in what is now Turkey. About 50 years later, Church leader Ignatius (died between AD 98–117) wrote a letter to the Church leader in Colosse's neighbor city of Ephesus: Bishop Onesimus. Perhaps the former slave.

A BAD IDEA: COLOR-CODING SLAVES.

The Roman Senate once considered ordering slaves to wear special clothes such as color-coded robes. The bill died because the Senate feared that if the slaves saw how many of them were working in Rome, they could unite and rebel. Some historians estimate that a third to a fourth of the people living in the Roman Empire were slaves.

ROMAN SLAVERY.

Many Romans treated their slaves well, as valued property. Others didn't. Roman historian Dio Cassius (about AD 150–235) reported that one cruel slave master, Vedius Pollio, punished slaves by throwing them into a pool of man-eating moray eels. Well fed, a giant moray can grow to nearly 13 feet (4 meters). For more on slavery, see pages 445–446.

Toothy moray eel

FREED SLAVE. A freed slave made good is what this funeral relief from the first century suggests. An inscription identifies the man as a freed slave and a silversmith. His toga and ring hint of wealth. Paul's letter to Christian slave owner Philemon seems to request freedom for a runaway slave—so the slave can help Paul.

GOOD-BYE COLOSSE. Runaway slave Onesimus flees the Colosse home of his master, Philemon. Possibly passing through Ephesus, a week's walk away, he seems to end up in Rome with Paul, more than 1,000 miles (1,600 km) west.

RUNAWAY SLAVE
ONESIMUS: GOOD-BYE COLOSSE

Jew from Yemen, early 1900s

HEBREWS 8:13
The new covenant Jesus activated leaves the old covenant agreement God made with the Jews obsolete. As prophets predicted, God's new agreement is open to everyone.

BIG SCENE
SAY GOOD-BYE TO JUDAISM

BIBLE HISTORY

ALL DATES APPROXIMATE

AD 62
Paul probably released after Rome trial

AD 64
Mystery man writes Hebrews between AD 64–70

WORLD HISTORY

Nero blames Christians for Rome fire, begins persecution, kills Paul and Peter
AD 64

HEBREWS

OBSOLETE: JEWISH RELIGION

STORY LINE

A SYNAGOGUE IS NO PLACE FOR JEWS. They belong in church.

That's the main point of Hebrews, a letter that seems to target Christian Jews quitting Christianity and going back to Judaism—the safer religion.

By AD 64, Christianity is taking heat not only from tradition-minded Jews, but from Romans as well. Nero blames Christians for starting the fire that burned down much of Rome in the summer of 64.

But the Christian Jews can't go back to Judaism, the Hebrews writer argues, because the Jewish religion is obsolete. It has been for three decades— ever since Jesus activated the new covenant that prophets had predicted God would set up. The old covenant agreement between God and the Jews has been upgraded to Covenant 2.0.

So the writer of Hebrews says there's no longer any need to observe the hundreds of Jewish laws about things like circumcision, kosher food, and sacrifices.

Not only does Covenant 2.0 trump Covenant 1.0, Jesus is a wild card trump of everything Jewish.

> He's a better leader than anyone in Jewish history, including Abraham, the founder, and Moses the lawgiver.
> He's a better advocate for sinful people than any Jewish priest because he never sinned.
> He's a better sacrifice for humanity's sins because he's perfect.

There's nothing for Jews to go back to. Christianity is God's new deal.

// LOCATION: Possibly an open letter to Jewish Christians scattered throughout the Roman Empire.

// TIME: Most scholars guess it was written between AD 64–70—after Nero started persecuting Christians, but before Romans destroyed Jerusalem and the Temple.

// AUTHOR: Contenders: Paul, Barnabas, Apollos, Luke, Silas.

Battle at Temple altar

Jews revolt, drive out Romans
AD 66

Roman army returns to crush revolt
AD 67

Last stand of Jews at Temple altar
Romans destroy Jerusalem, Temple
AD 70

Jesus is no angel

ANGELS ARE CURIOUS CREATURES, objects of speculation as far as first-century Jews are concerned. Educated Jews make educated guesses about what angels are really like and what they do.

Because of the stories in the Jewish Bible, which Christians call the Old Testament, Jews know that angels appear in human form on earth, serve God in heaven, deliver God's messages to prophets and others, and protect humans. For this, Jews and Christians alike revere angels—some even worship them, praying to them for protection from evil forces.

As wonderful as angels are, the Hebrews writer says, Jesus is better.

For evidence, the writer quotes Old Testament Bible passages that many Jews associate with the promised Messiah.

"God never said to any angel what he said to Jesus:
'You are my Son.'
'Let all of God's angels worship him.'
'Your throne, O God, endures forever.' "

HEBREWS 1:5, 6, 8

Seal stamp, clay impression

"THE SON. . .EXPRESSES THE VERY CHARACTER OF GOD" (Hebrews 1:3). The Greek word for *character* described an engraver's tool, such as a stamp to make coins or to press a signature image into globs of soft clay used to seal private letters. The point of the Hebrews writer, as *The Message* translates it: "This Son perfectly mirrors God, and is stamped with God's nature." What God is, Jesus is. Or as Jesus put it, "Anyone who has seen me has seen the Father!" (John 14:9).

ANGELS AMONG US / Some Jews and Christians in the first century not only revered angels, they invoked their power in prayers and inscribed their names on amulets to ward off evil spirits. As wonderful as these celestial beings are, the Hebrews writer says they're no match for Jesus—a perfect reflection of God's glory.

Jesus: Moses and then some

JEWS LOVE MOSES. In the first century, many Jews consider him God's top-of-the-line hero—the greatest human who ever lived.

"The LORD would speak to Moses face to face, just like a friend" (Exodus 33:11 CEV).

Moses gave the Jews the laws that guide their lives every day of the week. The Hebrews writer doesn't try to diminish the respect Jews have for Moses. But he says Jesus deserves even more respect.

Moses was "faithful in God's house as a servant," the writer explains, but Jesus "is in charge of God's entire house. And we are God's house, if we keep our courage and remain confident in our hope in Christ" (Hebrews 3:5–6).

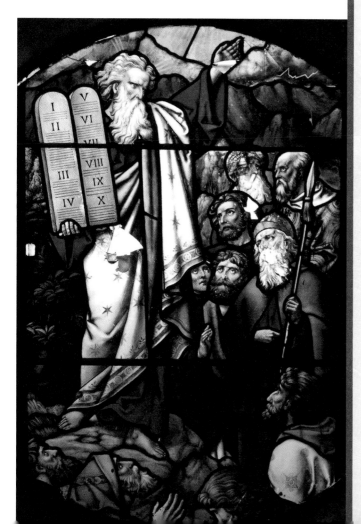

WHY JEWS PERSECUTED JEWISH CHRISTIANS. Jews considered them heretics for two main reasons.

> Christians taught that Jesus was God's divine Son, though Jews believed in just one God: "The LORD is our God, the LORD alone" (Deuteronomy 6:4).

> Christians taught that we're saved by believing in Jesus, while Jews taught that people need to obey the laws God gave Moses.

WHY ROMANS PERSECUTED CHRISTIANS. Besides getting blamed for setting Rome on fire, rumors portrayed Christians as deviants.

> **Cannibals.** In the Communion ritual, Christians eat bread and drink wine representing the body and blood of Jesus. See also page 333.

> **Incest.** Christians call each other brother and sister, and greet one another with a kiss on the cheek.

> **Traitors.** Christians worship Jesus as the King of kings and refuse to worship the Roman emperor as a god.

◀ **LAWGIVER.** The greatest man who ever lived, according to many Jews, Moses carries the 10 Commandments down Mount Sinai. He organizes the descendants of Abraham into a nation and delivers hundreds of other laws from God, which will guide the Jews in their worship as well as their daily lives. Though Moses set up God's first covenant agreement with Israel, the Hebrews writer says it's now obsolete because Jesus brought us a new and better covenant. Instead of keeping the law, God's people keep the faith: trusting in the salvation that Jesus offers.

Jesus: the best high priest

IN THE RELIGIOUS PECKING ORDER, there's no one on earth higher than the high priest. Not among the Jews.

The high priest is the spiritual leader of not only the nation, but of Jews scattered all over the world.

Yet the Hebrews writer says Jesus is higher than the highest high priest who ever lived. And that includes the mysterious Melchizedek (mel-KIZ-uh-deck)—portrayed in the Jewish Bible as the spiritual superior of Abraham, father of the Jews.

The writer makes his case:

HIGH PRIEST	JESUS
Ministers in a manmade facility (tent or Temple)	Ministers in God's presence
Ministry is temporary because he dies	Ministry is forever because he rose from the dead
Is a sinner who sacrifices for himself before sacrificing for others	Is sinless
Sacrifices animals	Sacrifices himself
Offers sacrifices every day	Only one sacrifice needed, "once for all"

STUCK IN THE BADLANDS

◄**WHAT IS GOD'S "PLACE OF REST"** (HEBREWS 4:3)? Bible experts debate what the writer meant. He mentioned God resting on the seventh day of Creation. And he mentioned that the Jews of the Exodus failed to enter their "rest," which meant their destination: the Promised Land, now called Israel. They had disobeyed God and were sentenced to die in the badlands; only the next generation got to enter. One theory is that the "place of rest" has a double meaning. Like God who no longer has to work at creating, we don't have to work at our salvation. Jesus finished the work for us. But like the Jews in the badlands, we're still looking forward to our destination—our Promised Land in heaven.

MELCHIZEDEK. He was both "the king of Salem [possibly short for "Jerusalem"] and a priest of God Most High" (Genesis 14:18). After Abraham won a battle, he gave Melchizedek a tithe offering—a tenth of all he had captured. Jews came to revere this mysterious priest. One song that many Jews said pointed to the coming Messiah, predicted that Israel's savior would be "a priest forever in the order of Melchizedek" (Psalm 110:4).

Jesus: the best sacrifice of all

ANIMAL SACRIFICES were God's temporary fix for sin—just the first step toward a permanent solution, according to the Hebrews writer.

In the eyes of a holy God, sin is a capital offense.

GOD'S TEMPORARY FIX: "I have given you the blood of animals to pay for your sin on the altar. Blood is life. That is why blood pays for your sin" (Leviticus 17:11 NIrV).

THE PROBLEM: "The blood of bulls and goats cannot take away sins. It only reminds people of their sins from one year to the next" (Hebrews 10:4 CEV).

GOD'S PERMANENT FIX: "We have been made holy because Jesus Christ offered his body once and for all time" (Hebrews 10:10 NIrV).

HOW DOES THE SACRIFICE OF JESUS MAKE US HOLY?

Many Bible experts say it's not that we're already holy, but that Jesus paid the price for us to become holy—the entrance fee into holiness. We live our life walking on the tollway to holiness, constantly seeking it, and following the road to where it leads: eternity with Jesus.

WHY DIDN'T GOD SKIP THE TEMPORARY FIX AND JUMP RIGHT TO THE PERMANENT SOLUTION, SENDING JESUS IN MOSES' DAY?

The writer doesn't say. But in Moses' day, the Jews were just getting organized into a nation. After that, they had a learning curve to master. They had to discover how serious sin is. They hit bottom in 586 BC when, as the prophets tell it, centuries of sin led God to allow invaders from Babylon (now Iraq) to dismantle the Jewish nation and deport many Jews. Only after discovering the seriousness of sin could they appreciate the sacrifice Jesus made.

◀ SACRIFICIAL LAMB.

Roman governor Pontius Pilate washes his hands at the trial of Jesus—a dramatic display of his refusal to take responsibility for the execution Jewish leaders demand. Many Christians say Isaiah predicted this execution 700 years earlier: "The servant was pierced because we had sinned. He was crushed because we had done what was evil. He was punished to make us whole again. . . . He was led away like a sheep to be killed" (Isaiah 53:5, 7 NIrV).

It's faith that matters, not rituals

JEWISH RELIGION in Bible times is loaded with ritual. Animal sacrifices to atone for sin. Baths to wash away spiritual defilement such as touching a corpse. Religious holidays to observe, such as Passover and Yom Kippur.

But the Hebrews writer says Jewish religion was never about the rituals. It was about what the rituals were intended to produce: faith in God, expressed in repentance and obedience.

A Jewish song writer put it this way: "The sacrifice you desire is a broken spirit. You will not reject a broken and repentant heart, O God" (Psalm 51:17).

Prophet Samuel added: "Obedience is better than sacrifice" (1 Samuel 15:22).

The Hebrews writer then presents his case with the help of a gallery of witnesses—godly heroes who lived before the Law of Moses with all its ritual.

// **NOAH** obeyed God by building a boat, escaping the Flood.

// **ABRAHAM** obeyed God by moving to what is now Israel.

// **MOSES** obeyed God and went back to Egypt to free Abraham's descendants from slavery.

Faith, the writer says, is what these men had in common. "Faith is being sure of what we hope for. It is being certain of what we do not see. That is what the people of long ago were praised for" (Hebrews 11:1–2 NIrV).

◄ **FREE AT LAST.** Jews leave Egyptian slavery and head home to the Promised Land of Canaan, in what is now Israel. They owe their freedom to the faith of one man, Moses.

FOLLOWING IN THE FOOTSTEPS OF FAITH HEROES. "Do you see what this means—all these pioneers who blazed the way, all these veterans cheering us on? It means we'd better get on with it. Strip down, start running—and never quit! No extra spiritual fat, no parasitic sins. Keep your eyes on *Jesus*, who both began and finished this race we're in" (Hebrews 12:1–2 MSG).

STRANGE HEROES OF FAITH

Not all of the 16 "heroes of faith" cited in chapter 11 come across as spiritual heroes in the Old Testament:

> **Rahab** was a Jericho hooker (see Joshua 2:1)
> **Barak** was a cowardly general (see Judges 4:8–9)
> **Samson** seemed driven only by lust and revenge (see Judges 13–16)
> **Jephthah** was a military leader who honored a stupid vow he made by sacrificing his daughter (see Judges 11–12)

Yet even these people—who were anything but role models—believed in God's power. They backed up their

VIRGIN DEATH / Doomed to die, the daughter of Jephthah becomes the victim of her father's careless vow. Stoked from a battlefield victory, Jephthah promises to sacrifice the first thing that greets him when he gets home. His daughter welcomes him, playing her tambourine. And Jephthah blames her: "You've brought disaster on me!" (Judges 11:35). Oddly, as far as some are concerned, Hebrews lists Jephthah among 16 heroes of the faith. See "Strange Heroes of the Faith," facing page.

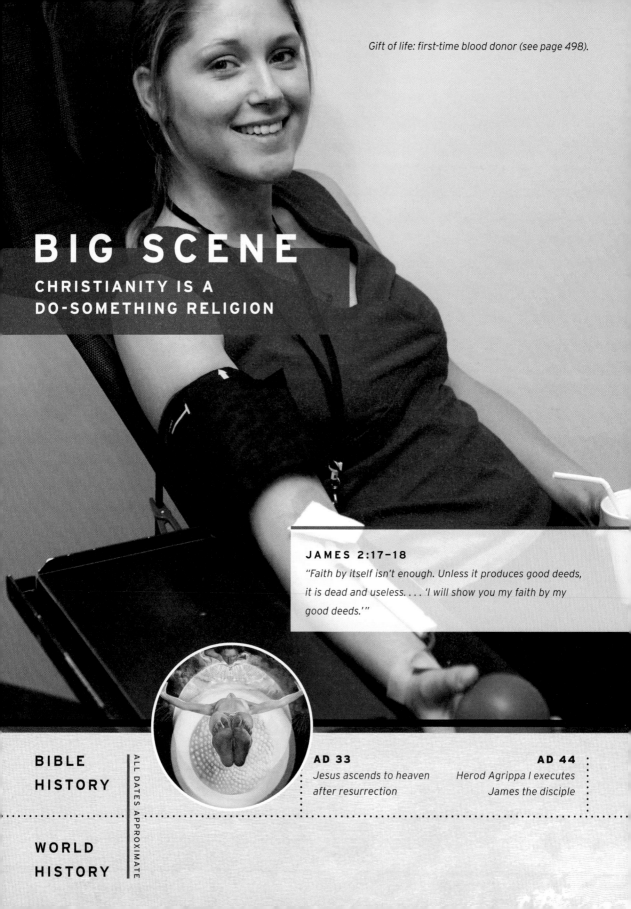

Gift of life: first-time blood donor (see page 498).

BIG SCENE

CHRISTIANITY IS A
DO-SOMETHING RELIGION

JAMES 2:17–18

"Faith by itself isn't enough. Unless it produces good deeds, it is dead and useless. . . . 'I will show you my faith by my good deeds.'"

BIBLE HISTORY

ALL DATES APPROXIMATE

AD 33
Jesus ascends to heaven
after resurrection

AD 44
Herod Agrippa I executes
James the disciple

WORLD HISTORY

JAMES

GOSPEL OF WATCH YOUR MOUTH AND GET BUSY

STORY LINE

ONE-LINERS of wise advice, accessorized with mini-sermons.

That's the letter of James, addressed to Christian Jews scattered all over the Roman Empire.

There is no story line. There's not even a main idea. Like the Old Testament book of Proverbs, this letter is a collection of wise sayings—which is why some Bible experts slap a brand on it: wisdom literature.

In this letter, James offers his best advice about what Christians should and shouldn't do.

Some of his most famous one-liners:

> **LEND AN EAR.** "Be quick to listen, slow to speak, and slow to get angry" (James 1:19).

> **LEND A HAND.** "You come upon an old friend dressed in rags and half-starved and say, 'Good morning, friend! Be clothed in Christ! Be filled with the Holy Spirit!' and walk off. . . .

Isn't it obvious that God-talk without God-acts is outrageous nonsense?" (James 2:15–17 MSG).

> **WATCH YOUR MOUTH.** "If you claim to be religious but don't control your tongue, you are fooling yourself, and your religion is worthless" (James 1:26).

// **TIME:** James the brother of Jesus was executed in about AD 66. James the disciple was beheaded in about AD 44.

// **AUTHOR:** "This letter is from James, a slave of God and of the Lord Jesus Christ" (James 1:1). Most scholars seem to favor the brother of Jesus. The other was the disciple of Jesus: James the brother of John (see page 496).

// **LOCATION:** James addresses the book to "Jewish believers scattered abroad" (James 1:1).

AD 50
Paul writes 1 Thessalonians, which many consider the oldest book in New Testament

Stoning of James

Romans execute Peter and Paul in Rome
AD 64

Jerusalem Jews stone James the brother of Jesus
AD 66

Romans destroy Jerusalem, exile Jews from the city
AD 70

Suffering: faith's muscle builder

A POSITIVE THINKER, James tells his readers to look on the bright side of suffering.

"When troubles come your way, consider it an opportunity for great joy. For you know that when your faith is tested, your endurance has a chance to grow" (James 1:2–3).

It's probably a timely message. His Jewish Christian readers are taking heat from tradition-minded Jews who consider them members of a breakaway Jewish cult that degrades God by calling Jesus his Son. If James is writing after the summer of AD 64, these Jewish Christians are under fire from Romans, too, following Nero's accusation that they torched Rome.

James advises his readers to patiently endure the suffering, and to resist the temptation to give up. James points them to role models: the prophets and Job. "We praise the ones who endured the most" (James 5:11 CEV).

. . . .

HUMBLING THE RICH / A host entertains a guest, while a servant waits nearby. Poverty and wealth are two different kinds of suffering, James seems to say. The rich suffer when they lose everything, or when all the money in the world can't fix their problem. When that time comes, James says, they should look for the value in their poverty—which may include the strengthening of their faith.

Funeral portrait of man from Roman times

JAMES, BROTHER OF JESUS?

James is first on the Bible's list of Jesus' brothers, perhaps because he's the oldest: "James, Joseph, Simon, and Judas" (Matthew 13:55). Jesus' brothers weren't convinced that he was the Messiah and God's Son, at least not in the beginning of his ministry. That changed somewhere along the way, perhaps after the resurrected Jesus appeared to James (see 1 Corinthians 15:7).

James the Just, as Church historians later called him, became leader of the Jerusalem church. There, he negotiated a compromise between (1) leaders who wanted Christians to observe Jewish laws and (2) leaders like Paul who opposed that (see Acts 15:13–21).

Jewish leaders in Jerusalem eventually charged James with breaking Jewish law and had him stoned to death. The execution is reported by Jewish-Roman historian Josephus (AD 37–100) and by church writer Eusebius (about AD 263–339).

Respect the poor

A FIGHTER FOR THE LITTLE GUY, James warns Christians not to give rich people the VIP treatment while ignoring the poor.

"Treat everyone the same," he says, implying that they all deserve the VIP treatment.

"Suppose a rich person wearing fancy clothes and a gold ring comes to one of your meetings. And suppose a poor person dressed in worn-out clothes also comes. You must not give the best seat to the one in fancy clothes and tell the one who is poor to stand at the side or sit on the floor. That is the same as saying that some people are better than others" (James 2:2–4 CEV).

James offers two solid reasons why Christians should respect the poor.

// **THE POOR DON'T PERSECUTE CHRISTIANS.** And they don't bad-mouth Christianity, either. "Isn't it the rich who oppress you and drag you into court? Aren't they the ones who slander Jesus Christ, whose noble name you bear?" (James 2:6–7).

// **GOD BLESSES THE POOR.** James quotes an excerpt from his brother's famous Sermon on the Mount: "God blesses those who are poor and realize their need for him, for the Kingdom of Heaven is theirs" (Matthew 5:3).

TENT CITY. Unemployed trucker, Tina Garland, 50, living in a tent during 2009 alongside other homeless people in what became known as "Tent City" in Sacramento. She moved to California from Indiana two years earlier, looking for work. If James got it right, she deserves the same respect given to the richest soul in town.

SERMON ON THE MOUNT, A RERUN

A lot of the advice James offers sounds like it's coming right out of Jesus' Sermon on the Mount. There are about 20 links to the Sermon, perhaps more. Three samples:

	JAMES	JESUS, SERMON ON THE MOUNT
HAPPY IN TOUGH TIMES	"When troubles come your way, consider it an opportunity for great joy" (James 1:2).	"God blesses you when people mock you and persecute you. . . . Be happy about it! Be very glad! For a great reward awaits you in heaven. And remember, the ancient prophets were persecuted in the same way" (Matthew 5:11–12).
FAITH IN ACTION	"Don't just listen to God's word. You must do what it says. Otherwise, you are only fooling yourselves" (James 1:22).	"Anyone who listens to my teaching and follows it is wise. . . . But anyone who hears my teaching and doesn't obey it is foolish" (Matthew 7:24, 26).
MONEY-HUNGRY	"Your wealth is rotting away, and your fine clothes are moth-eaten rags" (James 5:2).	"Don't store up treasures here on earth, where moths eat them and rust destroys them. . . . Store your treasures in heaven, where moths and rust cannot destroy" (Matthew 6:19–20).

Christians do more than yap, yap, yap

BEING A DO-GOODER isn't a spiritual gift. Not for a Christian—not according to James.

It's not as though some people have the gift of faith, which they politely keep to themselves, and others are more hands-on.

James says he can almost hear someone saying, "You take care of the faith department, I'll handle the works department" (James 2:18 MSG).

Real Christians multitask. They believe. And they act like they believe.

Even demons believe in Jesus, James argues. But they act like the devil. So they don't qualify as Christians.

"What good is it, dear brothers and sisters, if you say you have faith but don't show it by your actions? Can that kind of faith save anyone?" James asks. "Can't you see that faith without good deeds is useless?" (James 2:14, 20).

Martin Luther (AD 1483–1546)

WHY MARTIN LUTHER WANTED TO RIP JAMES OUT OF THE BIBLE.
The founder of the Protestant movement once called James a "letter of straw," meaning it had no substance. A former monk who had tried unsuccessfully to find spiritual fulfillment by earning his salvation through good works and self-deprivation, he hated James's emphasis on good works. Later in life, Luther retracted his criticism. For like James, he, too, was a man of action. Which is how the Protestant movement got started.

◀ FIRST-TIME BLOOD DONOR.
A young woman gives blood, squeezing a ball to help keep the blood flowing. She's a minority: 3 out of 100 people donate blood, according to the American Red Cross. Some churches invite community blood banks into the church to collect blood from worshippers. James—big on Christians doing good things for others—may well have approved.

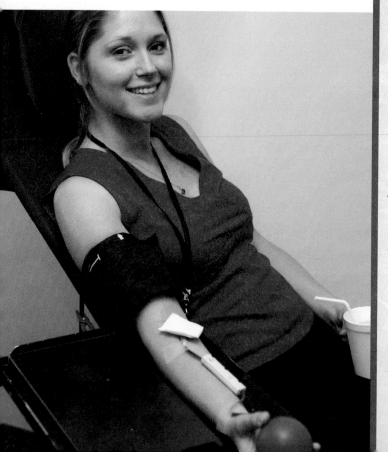

Danger: mouth ahead

"THE TONGUE IS A FLAME," James warns. "It can set your whole life on fire" (James 3:6).

It's just a tiny part of the body, little more than a tenth of a pound—70 grams for gents, 60 for the little ladies. Only about three slices of uncooked bacon.

Tiny, however, sometimes packs a wallop.

// A spark ignites a forest fire.

// A rudder steers a ship.

// A steel bit no bigger than an ink pen turns a horse.

So James says it should come as no surprise that the miniature muscle inside our mouth can make big and bad things happen with the speed of a syllable.

And once that syllable is spoken, there's no rewind. A syllable can live as long as a memory. We can speak other syllables as antidotes. But we shouldn't have to live that way, James argues. "A spring doesn't gush fresh water one day and brackish the next, does it?" (James 3:10–11 MSG).

We can't be perfect, James admits. But we can be careful.

◄ **WILD THING.** "You can tame a tiger," James says, "but you can't tame a tongue" (James 3:7 MSG). Still, James urges Christians to try—or to at least cage the wild thing when necessary.

CRITICISM. "Don't bad-mouth each other" (James 4:11 MSG). When Christians do that, James says, God takes a beating. It makes him look bad because his children are behaving badly. Scholars say James would have agreed with Paul that there are times to discipline fellow Christians—as when Paul suggested excommunicating the church member who was sleeping with his stepmother (1 Corinthians 5:1–5). Some things are worth criticizing, though in a spirit of love and with the hope of helping.

Don't play by the world's rules

IF YOU WANT IT, GET IT. It doesn't matter how many people you have to scream at, fight with, or kill. Whatever it takes. That's the way the world operates, James says.

But it's not the way Christians operate.

If Christians want something, James says, "You should pray for it" (James 4:2 CEV). But not with selfish motives.

James warns Christians not to fall in love with this world.

"If all you want is your own way, flirting with the world every chance you get, you end up enemies of God and his way" (James 4:4 MSG).

The two worlds run on different rules, written by different masters. The devil runs the world, and he promotes pride. God runs the kingdom of heaven, and he promotes humility.

James's advice: "Obey God. Stand up to the devil. He will run away from you" (James 4:7 NIrV).

DON'T GET COCKY.

James warns Christians not to get so overconfident that they assume their will is God's will. "You don't even know what will happen tomorrow," he says (James 4:14 NIrV). So Christians shouldn't brag about how much money they'll make or what they'll do with it. "You should say, 'If it pleases the Lord, we will live and do this or that' " (James 4:15 NIrV). Keep God on the program.

▼ **MORNING MIST.**

"What is your life? It is a mist that appears for a little while. Then it disappears" (James 4:14 NIrV). Our life is in God's hands, James writes. We shouldn't presume it's in ours.

Pray for each other: It works wonders

WANT HEALED? "A prayer offered in faith will heal the sick, and the Lord will make you well" (James 5:15).

Period.

Pray in faith and you'll get well.

Bold words for a dead man.

Jews later stone him to death, according to early Church writers. They say James died praying—apparently not fast enough, some might add.

The prayer advice James gives in his letter sounds like he thinks if we have enough faith in God, we can get anything we want.

His brother said something similar: "If you had faith even as small as a mustard seed, you could say to this mountain, 'Move from here to there,' and it would move. Nothing would be impossible" (Matthew 17:20).

Most scholars say James and Jesus both assume the person is praying in the same selfless spirit Jesus did on the night of his arrest—deferring to God's will:

> *"My Father, if it is possible, take this cup of suffering away from me. But let what you want be done, not what I want."*
>
> MATTHEW 26:39 NIrV

John Calvin (AD 1509–1564): "Eternal life is foreordained for some, eternal damnation for other" (Institutes of the Christian Religion).

ONCE SAVED, ALWAYS SAVED? Christians don't agree.

Pro. Some teach that once a person is saved, they can't get unsaved; they're headed to heaven on a non-stop flight. A support text: Jesus says his sheep "will never perish. No one can snatch them away from me" (John 10:28). Churches that follow this theological tradition popularized by John Calvin include many Baptist churches along with Presbyterians.

Con. Other Christians teach that we can decide to bail out of the flight to heaven. Backsliding, some call it. James offers one of the support texts: "If someone among you wanders away from the truth and is brought back, you can be sure that whoever brings the sinner back will save that person from death and bring about the forgiveness of many sins" (James 5:19–20). Churches that follow this theological tradition popularized by John Wesley (AD 1703–1791) include United Methodists, the Salvation Army, and Nazarenes.

◄ **MOMENT IN PRAYER.**
A lone soul sits in a Rome church that holds the remains of Christian leaders from centuries past. James said the prayer of a faithful person will heal the sick. But not always. Everyone dies.

BIG SCENE
JESUS SUFFERED, YOU'LL SUFFER

1 PETER 4:12–13

"Don't be surprised at the fiery trials you are going through....
Instead, be very glad—for these trials make you partners
with Christ in his suffering."

BIBLE
HISTORY

ALL DATES APPROXIMATE

AD 30
Peter becomes
disciple of Jesus

AD 33
Peter preaches first
sermon after Jesus' Ascension

WORLD
HISTORY

Roman emperor Caligula
declares himself a god
AD 37

1,2 PETER

ADVICE FOR CHRISTIANS IN HOT WATER

STORY LINE

THERE'S TROUBLE IN TURKEY for Christians.

Peter gets word of the persecution they're facing. He doesn't say what's going on. Maybe the Jews are after them for dissing God by saying he has a Son. Or it could be the locals, angry that their neighbors have stopped worshipping the village gods. It might be Romans, enraged by Nero's claim that Christians set fire to Rome.

Whatever the source of the persecution, Peter feels compelled to write—even though there's no hint he ever visited this area where Paul started so many churches. Peter doesn't mention any readers by name.

He tells the Christians that Jesus suffered all the way to the grave, and that they may have to do the same. But he reminds them that there's life after the grave.

By the time Peter writes his second letter, he knows he's headed to the grave himself. Once more he encourages the Christians to hang on to their faith—and to not be fooled by fake ministers or discouraged by Jesus' delayed return: 30-plus years and still on hold. Peter says Jesus will come back when the time is right.

// LOCATION: Though there's no location mentioned in Peter's second letter, his first letter says he's writing to Christians in what is now Turkey: then called the Roman provinces of "Pontus, Galatia, Cappadocia, Asia, and Bithynia" (1 Peter 1:1). Second Peter may address the same readers since Peter describes it as "my second letter to you" (2 Peter 3:1).

// TIME: Perhaps shortly before Romans executed him, between AD 64, when Emperor Nero began persecuting Christians, and AD 68, when Nero committed suicide.

// AUTHOR: Both letters open by introducing Peter as the writer who admits to using "the help of Silas" (1 Peter 5:12).

AD 63	AD 64
Peter writes 1 Peter	Peter writes 2 Peter

Paul freed in Rome after four-year arrest that began in Jerusalem
AD 62

Rome burns, Nero blames Christians, executes Peter, Paul
AD 64

Suffering: small price for eternal life

CHRISTIANS ARE IN BIG TROUBLE. They're facing orchestrated, violent persecution.

"Don't jump to the conclusion that God isn't on the job," Peter writes, to encourage believers. "Instead, be glad that you are in the very thick of what Christ experienced. This is a spiritual refining process, with glory just around the corner" (1 Peter 4:12–13 MSG).

Just as fire refines gold, Peter explains, persecution does the same to faith—which is "worth more than gold." And just as gold brings praise to its owner, the tested faith of a believer brings "praise, honor and glory to God" (1 Peter 1:7 NIrV).

Jesus suffered and died, Peter writes. Christians will, too. But Jesus rose from the dead. And so will Christians. "We've been given a brand-new life and have everything to live for, including a future in heaven—and the future starts now!" (1 Peter 1:3–4 MSG).

GOLD STANDARD / Gold melts at temperatures around 2000 degrees Fahrenheit (1093 C). These high temps also burn off impurities and separate residue into a top layer of slag that's easily removed. What's poured into the mold is refined gold, about 99 percent pure. Peter says fiery tests do the same to a person's faith, purifying it.

Jesus in hell

▲ **DID JESUS PREACH TO DEAD SPIRITS IN HELL?** (see 1 Peter 3:19). Scholars debate what this verse means. One theory, based on Peter's mention of Noah in the same verse: Noah delivered Christ's message to the unbelieving people of his day. Less popular theories: While Jesus was in the grave on Saturday, he preached to fallen angels awaiting judgment in the place of the dead, or perhaps to sinners there.

PERSECUTIONS EARLY CHRISTIANS FACED BEFORE ROMANS KILLED THEM IN ARENAS.

The book of Acts, other New Testament books, and early Church writings reveal some of the kinds of persecution Christians faced in the first few decades of the movement:

> insults
> threats
> economic boycotts
> arrest
> beatings
> lawsuits
> fines
> confiscation of property
> jail time
> mob attacks
> execution by stoning

Grow up to look like your Father

CHRISTIANS ARE GOD'S CHILDREN and they should act like it, Peter says.

"Be holy in everything you do, just as God who chose you is holy" (1 Peter 1:15).

By that, Peter says he means Christians shouldn't live to satisfy their own selfish desires, or slip back into their old, sinful habits.

"Clean house! Make a clean sweep of malice and pretense, envy and hurtful talk. You've had a taste of God. Now, like infants at the breast, drink deep of God's pure kindness. Then you'll grow up mature and whole in God" (1 Peter 2:1–2 MSG).

Think of this life as temporary, Peter adds.

"This world is not your home, so don't make yourselves cozy in it. . . . Live an exemplary life among the natives so that your actions will refute their prejudices. Then they'll be won over to God's side and be there to join in the celebration when he arrives" (1 Peter 2:11–12 MSG).

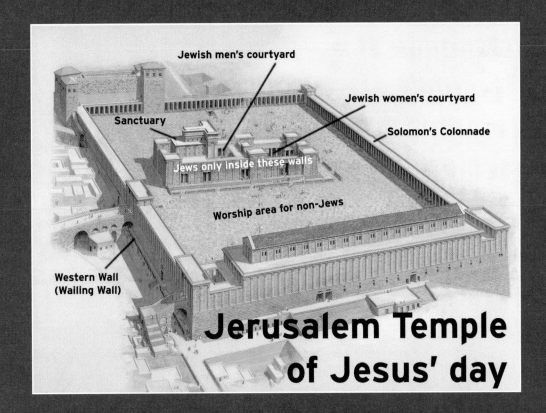

Jewish men's courtyard

Jewish women's courtyard

Sanctuary

Solomon's Colonnade

Jews only inside these walls

Worship area for non-Jews

Western Wall (Wailing Wall)

Jerusalem Temple of Jesus' day

"YOU ARE LIVING STONES THAT GOD IS BUILDING INTO HIS SPIRITUAL TEMPLE" (1 Peter 2:5). One interpretation Bible experts offer: Like Jesus—who called himself "living water" (John 4:10) and "living bread" (John 6:51), metaphors describing him as the source of eternal life—Christians (1) enjoy eternal life and (2) can become a source of eternal life for others by pointing them to Jesus. In a sense, Christians are each a living, breathing part of God's spiritual temple, a place where people can come to find Jesus.

Respect your boss

IN ADVICE THAT MAKES NO SENSE to many people today, Peter tells his readers to respect anyone in authority over them—including self-serving politicians and cruel slave masters.

That advice would have been especially hard to swallow for Christians living anywhere in the Mediterranean world, since Romans from Italy conquered, occupied, and controlled most of that territory.

Peter gives two reasons why Christians should do as he says.

WHY OBEY POLITICIANS? "It is God's will that by doing good, you might cure the ignorance of the fools who think you're a danger to society" (1 Peter 2:15 MSG).

WHY OBEY CRUEL SLAVE MASTERS? "God is pleased with you when you do what you know is right and patiently endure unfair treatment" (1 Peter 2:19).

Jesus is the perfect example to follow, Peter says. "He did not retaliate when he was insulted, nor threaten revenge when he suffered. He left his case in the hands of God, who always judges fairly" (1 Peter 2:23).

IS IT WRONG TO CRITICIZE POLITICIANS TODAY?

Perhaps it depends on which government we're talking about. In a free society, Peter might have seen nothing wrong with expressing the Christian perspective on a political topic. But in a strictly controlled society, like the one in which he lived, both he and Paul advised against bucking the system. Instead, they seemed more interested in convincing leaders that Christianity was a religion of loving service to others, and no political threat.

▼ THE BOSS.

A stern-looking bust of Emperor Caracalla (AD 188–217), described by one historian as "the common enemy of mankind." He arranged the murder of his brother and ordered thousands of others killed. In Peter's day, the Roman Senate had little authority. Emperors ruled as dictator for as long as they could survive. Caracalla, reportedly, was assassinated by one of his bodyguards while Caracalla was relieving himself at the side of a road.

Recipe for a happy family

CHRISTIAN MEN AGREE. Women need to submit to the authority of their husbands.

Peter says so: "You wives must accept the authority of your husbands" (1 Peter 3:1).

Paul says so: "Wives. . .submit your husbands as to the Lord" (Ephesians 5:22).

Yet even in this man-run world—when the Christian movement is still young and more focused on changing individuals than changing society—both of these top leaders urge husbands to do no less for their wives.

Peter: "You husbands must give honor to your wives. . . . She may be weaker than you are, but she is your equal partner in God's gift of new life. Treat her as you should so your prayers will not be hindered" (1 Peter 3:7).

Paul: "Submit to one another. . . . For husbands, this means love your wives, just as Christ loved the church. He gave up his life for her" (Ephesians 5:21, 25).

DID PETER HAVE A FAMILY?
Yes. Peter lived with his family in the fishing village of Capernaum, where much of Jesus' ministry took place. It was there that Jesus healed Peter's mother-in-law, who was "sick in bed with a high fever" (Matthew 8:14). Church leader Clement of Alexandria, Egypt, said Peter and his wife had children, and that Peter and his wife both died as martyrs.

PAUL'S ADVICE FOR HARMONY IN THE HOME.
See page 445.

PETER'S FASHION TIPS FOR THE LADIES.
"Don't be concerned about the outward beauty of fancy hairstyles, expensive jewelry, or beautiful clothes. You should clothe yourselves instead with the beauty that comes from within, the unfading beauty of a gentle and quiet spirit, which is so precious to God" (1 Peter 3:3–4).

◀ **WHEN IN ROME.**
In a reenactment of Roman times, a woman wears an intricate hairstyle similar to some that survive on statues of woman from the first century. Peter, like Paul, advised Christian women to forgo the fancy hairdo and focus instead on inner beauty.

How to be a great pastor

IT ALL STARTS WITH ATTITUDE, Peter says. When it comes to leading a congregation, pastors should accept the responsibility willingly: "Not because you have to, but because you want to" (1 Peter 5:2 MSG).

Beyond that, Peter advises:

DON'T BE ON THE TAKE; BE ON THE GIVE. "Don't do it because you want to get more and more money. Do it because you really want to serve" (1 Peter 5:2 NIrV).

DON'T BE BOSSY. "Don't act as if you were a ruler over those who are under your care. Instead, be examples to the flock" (1 Peter 5:3 NIrV).

KEEP IT REAL. "Be content with who you are, and don't put on airs. God's strong hand is on you; he'll promote you at the right time" (1 Peter 5:6 MSG).

DON'T WORRY. "Give all your worries and cares to God, for he cares about you" (1 Peter 5:7).

HOMECHURCHING.

Like homeschooling today, Christian education and worship in Bible times often took place in a home. One of the believers served as the host—sometimes wealthy Christians because they often had larger houses. Sometimes, however, Christians would gather at another meeting spot, such as Solomon's Colonnade at the Jerusalem Temple (see Acts 5:12) or alongside a stream in Philippi (see Acts 16:13). Church buildings didn't show up until AD 313, when Rome legalized Christianity and later adopted it as the empire's official religion.

▼ **FIRST-CENTURY CAVE CHURCH.**

Jordanian archaeologists work in a cave in what some are calling the oldest church yet discovered—dating to the time of Peter's ministry and beyond, roughly AD 33–70. It's under the Saint Georgeous Church in Rehab, 40 miles (65 km) north of the Jordanian capital of Amman. Dr. Abdel-Qader Hussein, leading the team of archaeologists, said the meeting place was likely used by Christian Jews who fled the persecution in Jerusalem.

How a Christian grows

PETER WILL DIE SOON, he writes in his second letter. "Our Lord Jesus Christ has shown me that I must soon leave this earthly life" (2 Peter 1:14).

But before Peter leaves the planet, he has a few last words.

For one, he says he wants Christians to keep growing spiritually. So he tells them how, saying "God has given us everything we need for living a godly life" (2 Peter 1:3).

Faith. It starts here. We trust in God's promises to save us through Jesus. Then, one by one, Christians add the following:

// moral excellence
// knowledge
// self-control
// patient endurance
// godliness
// brotherly affection
// love for everyone

"The more you grow like this, the more productive and useful you will be," Peter writes. "Do these things, and you will never fall away" (2 Peter 1:8, 10).

▲ HOW DID PETER DIE?

The Bible doesn't say. Early Church writers said he was executed in Rome after Nero blamed Christians for starting the AD 64 fire that raged for six days, burning much of Rome. According to church leader Origen (about AD 185–254), "Peter was crucified at Rome with his head downward, as he himself had desired to suffer." As the story goes, Peter didn't feel worthy to be crucified head up, as Jesus had died.

HOW DID PETER KNOW HE WAS GOING TO DIE?

He didn't say. Perhaps he had a vision or a vivid dream about it, which is how God often communicated to prophets. Peter did have at least one vision reported in the Bible. See page 405.

◀ FEEDING GRANDMA.

A little girl in an Istanbul café serves her grandmother a taste of Turkish cuisine. Peter offers his readers spiritual food, which he assures will help them grow up strong in the Christian faith.

Lying preachers ahead

NOT EVERY PREACHER is the genuine article, Peter warns. Some only say they're Christian. But their warped ideas and their shameful behavior give them away.

Peter tells Christians that if they see the following in a preacher, they'll know they're eyeballing a fraud.

// REJECTING JESUS. "They. . .deny the Master who bought them," perhaps by teaching ideas Jesus never would have approved (2 Peter 2:1).

// BRAGGING. "They brag about themselves with empty, foolish boasting" (2 Peter 2:18).

// MONEY-HUNGRY. "They will make up clever lies to get hold of your money" (2 Peter 2:3).

// SCOFFING AT EVIL FORCES. "Angels, who are far greater in power" wouldn't dare say such things "against those supernatural beings" (2 Peter 2:11).

// INDULGING IN EVIL PLEASURES. "With an appeal to twisted sexual desires, they lure back into sin those who have barely escaped" (2 Peter 2:18).

// NO RULES, NO FEAR. "They promise freedom, but they themselves are slaves of sin" (2 Peter 2:19).

Peter says to avoid these frauds because when Christians "get tangled up and enslaved by sin again, they are worse off than before. . . . They prove the truth of this proverb: 'A dog returns to its vomit'" (2 Peter 2:20, 22).

ANGELS IN HELL?

"God did not spare angels when they sinned. Instead, he sent them to hell. He put them in dark prisons. He will keep them there until he judges them" (2 Peter 2:4 NIrv). Some scholars say Peter is talking about the destiny of angels—that they're as good as dead, eternally. Others say Peter is talking about the common Jewish view that in the early years after Creation, the "sons of God" (Genesis 6:2) were angels who had sex with human women.

WHO WERE THE FRAUD PREACHERS?

Bible experts can only guess. One guess: an early version of Gnostics (NOSS-ticks). They taught that we're saved not by faith or good behavior, but by secret knowledge that leads to divinity. Others guess Epicureans (EP-ah-CURE-ee-ans). They said people are happiest when they overcome their fear of supernatural beings, death, and punishment in the afterlife.

◀ **WARPED WORDS, INC.**

Peter warns Christians to watch out for preachers on the take—for money, sex, and power. "These people are nothing but brute beasts. . .predators on the prowl. In the very act of bringing down others with their ignorant blasphemies, they themselves will be brought down" (2 Peter 2:12 MSG).

What's taking Jesus so long?

FOR 30 YEARS or more, Christians have been listening to preachers like Paul say, "The Lord is coming soon" (Philippians 4:5).

Peter anticipates that critics of the faith will jump on that phrase as a mocking point—as in "What part of 'soon' doesn't Jesus get?"

Peter quotes a Jewish song to remind his readers that with God, "a thousand years are as a passing day" (Psalm 90:4).

Sadly for the curious, Peter doesn't explain why "soon" didn't get that qualifier to begin with—that "soon" referred to time as understood by the timeless, eternal God. But quoting Psalms is apparently the best explanation Peter can offer—along with the point that the longer God waits, the more time people have to get saved (or to sin, critics would add).

Yet offering an explanation isn't Peter's point. His point is that Christians should trust in God's timing and be ready when Jesus comes.

"And so, dear friends, while you are waiting for these things to happen, make every effort to be found living peaceful lives that are pure and blameless in his sight" (2 Peter 3:14).

Relative size of sun and earth, not relative location. Earth is farther away.

THE END OF THE WORLD. Judgment Day: "The sky will collapse with a thunderous bang, everything disintegrating in a huge conflagration.... The galaxies will burn up and the elements melt down that day" (2 Peter 3:10, 12 MSG). Though Peter may have been speaking poetically, his words track with some modern theories. As one theory goes, Earth will get swallowed up in fire when the sun swells into a red giant in five billion years. The universe will eventually stop expanding, reverse direction, and then collapse into its pre-Big Bang compressed state—a coming cataclysm nicknamed the Big Crunch.

◄ **FLIGHTS DELAYED.** An artist's interpretation of Christ's return, 2,000 years after first-generation Christians said he was coming soon. Peter offers his thoughts on the delay.

BIG SCENE
SHOWDOWN AT CHURCH

3 JOHN 10

John vows to come to town and deal with a maverick minister who excommunicates anyone in his church who disobeys him by welcoming traveling Christians.

BIBLE HISTORY				

BIBLE HISTORY

AD 64 *Paul and Peter write final letters (2 Timothy, 2 Peter, respectively) before execution*

WORLD HISTORY

Jews revolt, drive out Romans
AD 66

Romans arrive in Galilee, John and disciples flee Jerusalem
AD 67

Romans destroy Jerusalem
AD 70

ALL DATES APPROXIMATE

1,2,3 JOHN

NOT OKAY: REINVENTING JESUS

STORY LINE

THERE'S BIG TROUBLE IN THE CHURCH, perhaps 60 years after Jesus left the planet. Trouble like nothing reported anywhere else in the New Testament: Splinter churches with bizarre beliefs are leaving the Christian movement.

With most eyewitnesses to Jesus dead and gone, some Christians are beginning to make wild guesses about what Jesus was really like.

Based on what John writes, their speculation sounds like the beginning of what grows into a Church-wide debate over the nature of Jesus— a debate that will dominate the Church for several centuries. Key points in the most widely accepted heresy:

> Jesus wasn't human. He was either a spirit all along who only pretended to be human, or he was a human who morphed into a spirit being.
> With the right knowledge, we can do what Jesus did: ascend from physical existence to the spiritual dimension.

> As spirit beings, it doesn't matter how we behave.

John says this isn't just hogwash. It's poisonous hogwash. And it's sucking the eternal life right out of the Church.

Second John is a reminder to love each other and avoid false teachers. Third John is a personal note to Gaius, urging him to continue showing hospitality to traveling Christians.

// LOCATION: John probably writes from Ephesus to churches in the area.

// TIME: Written as late as the AD 90s. Early Church leaders said John and other disciples left Jerusalem in AD 67.

// AUTHOR: The writer doesn't identify himself by name. But he says he saw and touched Jesus (see 1 John 1:1). Since the early AD 100s, Church leaders have credited the apostle John. The writing style matches the Gospel of John.

AD 90
Elderly John writes letters of 1, 2, 3 John

Domitian becomes Roman emperor
AD 81

Heretics in the Church

SPLINTER GROUPS have left the Church, taking with them a warped idea of Jesus—and spreading it around like it's the real deal.

Based on John's letter confronting the problem, many scholars say this sounds like the beginning of a heresy that nearly took over the Christian movement in the AD 100s and 200s: Gnosticism (NAHS-tah-ciz-um).

Key teachings:

// Everything physical is evil. Only the spiritual is good.

// Jesus was not physical. He didn't really die or rise from the dead. It was just an act for our benefit.

// Since we're physical, we can't live good lives no matter how hard we try. But we can achieve holiness of spirit, even while we're sinning like the devil.

John begs to differ. His arguments:

JESUS WAS PHYSICAL. "We saw him with our own eyes and touched him with our own hands" (1 John 1:1).

GOD'S PEOPLE DON'T LIVE LIKE THE DEVIL. "Anyone who says, 'I know God,' but does not obey God's commands is a liar" (1 John 2:4 NCV).

WE'RE ALL SINNERS. "If we claim that we're free of sin, we're only fooling ourselves. A claim like that is errant nonsense" (1 John 1:8 MSG).

Man from Roman times

GNOSTICISM / A Christian-based movement that teaches people aren't saved by faith in Jesus but by secret spiritual knowledge. Key leader: Marcion (about AD 144). See also page 455.

SON OF GOD. Superhero Hercules overpowers the hounds of hell, a three-headed beast said to keep doomed souls from escaping Hades. Greek legend says Hercules is the lust child of the top Greek god, Zeus, and a beautiful human woman. Zeus disguised himself as the woman's husband and had sex with her. Greek philosophers insisted it's impossible for spirit beings to actually become human; they only looked human. Some Christians apparently picked up on that idea and argued that Jesus only appeared human.

Antichrists unlimited

THERE'S NO ANTICHRIST waiting to make life miserable for Christians at the end of the world. Not according to John, the only Bible writer to briefly mention the word *antichrist.*

Every time John uses this word, he's talking about heretics—especially splinter groups that broke away from the Church and are building a new Christian-like movement based on lies about Jesus (see 1 John 2:19). Some groups seem to be saying Jesus wasn't human. Others say he wasn't divine. But genuine Christianity, John argues, teaches that Jesus was both.

Here's every verse in the Bible that uses the word *antichrist.* Surprisingly, Revelation never mentions it.

THEY'RE EVERYWHERE. "You heard that Antichrist is coming. Well, they're all over the place, antichrists everywhere you look."

1 JOHN 2:18 MSG

THEY DENY THE DEITY OF JESUS. "This is what makes an antichrist: denying the Father, denying the Son. . . . It's the person who denies that Jesus is the Divine Christ."

1 JOHN 2:22 MSG

THEY DENY JESUS CAME IN A REAL BODY. "Many deceivers have gone out into the world. They deny that Jesus Christ came in a real body. Such a person is a deceiver and an antichrist."

2 JOHN 1:7

THEY LIVE IN JOHN'S DAY. "But if someone claims to be a prophet and does not acknowledge

(continued next page)

HOW DID CHRISTIANS GET THE IDEA THAT AN END-TIME ANTICHRIST DICTATOR WAS COMING?

John says, "You have heard that the Antichrist is coming" (1 John 2:18). That leads some to suspect John was talking about one person.

Bible historians say that during the early Middle Ages, between AD 600 and 1000, preachers started connecting some disconnected sections of the Bible to form a combo profile of the Antichrist—like piecing together a jigsaw puzzle until you can see the full picture.

For example, they linked to the Antichrist:

Man of Sin

That day [of Christ's return] will not come until people rise up against God. It will not come until the man of sin appears. He is a marked man. He is sentenced to be destroyed. He will oppose everything that is called God. He will oppose everything that is worshiped. He will give himself power over everything. He will set himself up in God's temple. He will announce that he himself is God.

APOSTLE PAUL,
2 THESSALONIANS 2:3-4 NIrV

The Beast

The beast was allowed to wage war against God's holy people and to conquer them. And he was given authority to rule over every tribe and people and language and nation. And all the people who belong to this world worshiped the beast.

JOHN, REVELATION 13:7-8

Many Bible experts today, however, say the Roman Empire is a good match for both the "man of sin" and the "beast." Others argue we should be looking to the future, not the past.

the truth about Jesus, that person is not from God. Such a person has the spirit of the Antichrist, which you heard is coming into the world and indeed is already here."

1 JOHN **4:3**

John isn't writing about antichrists to warn future Christians of the misery that awaits them in some distant end time. He's writing to warn about false teachers in his own time, the first century—though many Bible experts insist that his word of caution also applies to the generations that will follow.

Don't be misled by heretics, John says. Then he gives his readers an acid test for telling the difference between a genuine Christian teacher and a fraud.

GENUINE CHRISTIAN: "Everyone who confesses openly his faith in Jesus Christ—the Son of God, who came as an actual flesh-and-blood person—comes from God and belongs to God" (1 John 4:2 MSG).

FAKE CHRISTIAN: "Everyone who refuses to confess faith in Jesus has nothing in common with God" (1 John 4:3 MSG).

◀ **JESUS' DEMONIC TWIN.** Italian artist Luca Signorelli (about AD 1450–1523) paints the Antichrist as a Jesus lookalike. But when the Bible talks about the "antichrist," it's usually referring to a lot of people—anyone who denies that Jesus is the Son of God who lived on earth in a human body.

"THE LAST HOUR IS HERE" (1 John 2:18). John wrote this about 17 million hours ago. Most Bible experts say he wasn't talking about the imminent end of the world. Instead, they say he was talking about the last step in God's plan to save humans from sin. Jesus took that last step when he walked into human history as the Messiah. As the theory goes, the "last hour" begins and ends with Jesus: his first coming and his Second Coming. The minutes of life in between make up the last hour.

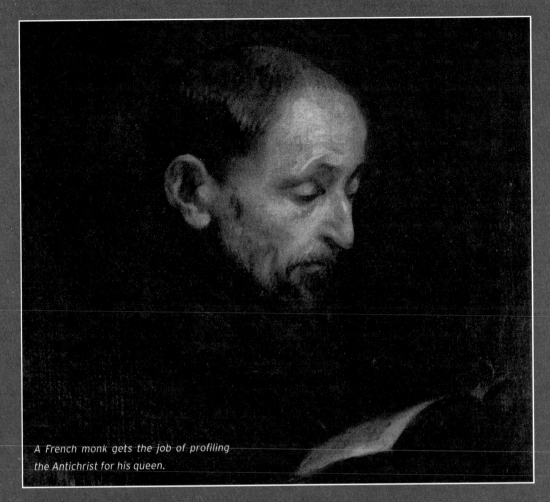

A French monk gets the job of profiling the Antichrist for his queen.

PROFILE: ANTICHRIST AD 950

End-time fever struck parts of the Christian world as the calendar rushed toward AD 1000.

Worried that the Antichrist might come during her reign, in the last generation of the first millennium, French Queen Gerbera asked a respected French monk to brief her on what to expect.

The monk's name was Adso of Montier-en-Der. He sent his report in a letter written about AD 950.

Excerpts describing the Antichrist:

> **Jewish.** "The Antichrist will be born from the Jewish people.... At the very beginning of his conception the devil will enter his mother's womb. . .just as the Holy Spirit came into the mother of Our Lord Jesus Christ."

> **Born in Iraq.** "Antichrist will be born in that city [Babylon], which once was a celebrated and glorious pagan center and the capital of the Persian Empire."

> **Killer of Christians.** "He will come to Jerusalem and. . .will kill all the Christians he cannot convert."

> **Claims to be the Messiah.** "He. . .will circumcise himself and say to the Jews, 'I am the Christ [Messiah] promised to you.'"

> **Dies in Israel.** "That Antichrist will be killed on the Mount of Olives."

> **God forgives his followers.** "The Lord will grant former believers forty days to do penance because they were led astray by the Antichrist."

Where did Adso get all this?

"I find it all written down in books," he told the queen.

The Bible wasn't one of them, modern Bible scholars would add.

God is love; so are his people

REAL CHRISTIANS don't act like Cain, who murdered his own brother. Instead of killing their brothers, John says, real Christians will die for them if necessary.

> *Christ sacrificed his life for us. This is why we ought to live sacrificially for our fellow believers, and not just be out for ourselves. If you see some brother or sister in need and have the means to do something about it but turn a cold shoulder and do nothing, what happens to God's love? It disappears. . . . Let's not just talk about love; let's practice real love.*
>
> 1 JOHN 3:16–18 MSG

God is love, John says, and so are God's people.

> *If anyone boasts, "I love God," and goes right on hating his brother or sister, thinking nothing of it, he is a liar. If he won't love the person he can see, how can he love the God he can't see? The command we have from Christ is blunt: Loving God includes loving people. You've got to love both.*
>
> 1 JOHN 4:20–21 MSG

NO GREATER LOVE. Followers of Jesus grieve at the foot of his cross. Jesus had predicted his fate: "Love one another the way I loved you. This is the very best way to love. Put your life on the line for your friends" (John 15:12–13 MSG).

"ALL WICKED ACTIONS ARE SIN, BUT NOT EVERY SIN LEADS TO DEATH" (1 John 5:17). Most Catholics teach that there are two kinds of sins: mortal and venial. Mortal sins are more serious, such as murder and adultery. Unconfessed, they would send a Christian to hell. Venial sins are less serious, such as failure to pray every day. Unconfessed, they would send a Christian to purgatory for a time of punishment and purification.

Many Protestants, who say they see no biblical evidence for a purgatory, wonder if John was talking about sins that can kill us physically: such as execution for murder. Still others wonder if he was talking about people who reject God by refusing to confess any sin at all.

Welcome Christians, shun heretics

READING LIKE CLIFFSNOTES on 1 John, the single-chapter letter of 2 John says much the same thing as 1 John, but condensed.

// "Love one another" (2 John 1:5).

// Stay away from antichrists who say Jesus didn't come in a real body. "Don't invite that person into your home or give any kind of encouragement" (2 John 1:10).

Third John is a private letter to someone named Gaius.

John commends Gaius for showing hospitality to traveling Christian ministers. But in the next breath John criticizes a man who might be Gaius's pastor: Diotrephes, who slams the door of hospitality on the faces of those same traveling ministers. To make matters worse, he excommunicates church members who don't follow his example.

"Diotrephes likes to be the number-one leader," John complains, "and he won't pay any attention to us" (3 John 1:9 CEV). John says if he's able to come to town, he'll confront the control freak.

Meanwhile, John says, Gaius shouldn't follow this pastor's bad example. Instead, "Follow the example of people who do kind deeds" (3 John 1:11 CEV).

Roman mailman driving two-wheeled cart (cisium).

◄ **YOU'VE GOT MAIL.** John sends his letter by private courier, a man named Demetrius. Roman officials had access to a public postal service set up by Emperor Augustus (63 BC–AD 14). They called it the Public Course (*cursus publicus*). It featured relay stations that allowed couriers to rush messages more than 150 miles (240 km) in a 24-hour day. Most messages traveled by cart or carriage. More urgent messages traveled by horseback, Pony Express-style. Citizens, however, depended on private individuals traveling to the place where the letter needed to go.

WHAT TO DO WITH STRANGERS. Hospitality in Bible times was treated as a matter of life or death—as it still is in many parts of the Middle East. That's because in a land that's hot, arid, and sparsely populated, the offer of shelter and food can mean the difference between life and death.

BIG SCENE

BAD-BOY PREACHERS ON THE PROWL

JUDE 4

Preaching warped ideas, frauds infiltrate the Church and argue that it's okay to commit sex sins because God forgives us.

BIBLE HISTORY

ALL DATES APPROXIMATE

AD 33
Jesus crucified, resurrected, ascends to heaven

WORLD HISTORY

JUDE

SIN ISN'T SEXY

IT'S OKAY TO SIN because God forgives us—sex sins included. So says a group of heretics who worm their way into leadership roles in the Church.

Worse, they practice what they preach.

They:

> "live immoral lives"
> "defy authority"
> "scoff at supernatural beings"
> "are. . .living only to satisfy their desires"
> "brag loudly about themselves"
> "flatter others to get what they want."

JUDE 1:8, 16

Jude doesn't argue about God's forgiveness. Instead, he reminds Christians that God punishes sin. Then he cites a few examples: God exiled Cain from his homeland for murdering his brother; he seared off the planet the twin cities of Sodom and Gomorrah; he executed Jews who revolted against Moses; he let Babylon conquer and exile the Jewish nation for worshipping idols.

Jude's point: Though God forgives the repentant, he punishes those who keep on sinning as though it's no big deal.

// LOCATION: This is an open letter to Christians everywhere. Jude may have written from Jerusalem, his Nazareth hometown, or Jesus' Capernaum ministry headquarters.

// TIME: Possibly written in the AD 60s, about the same time as 2 Peter. Both letters deal with the same problems: heretical teachers and fallen angels.

// AUTHOR: "This letter is from Jude, a slave of Jesus Christ and a brother of James" (Jude 1:1). Most Bible experts say this Jude and James were two of Jesus' four brothers: "James, Joseph, Simon, and Judas" (Matthew 13:55). Jude is a nickname for Judas. James led the Jerusalem church.

AD 46
Paul's first missionary trip spreads the gospel

AD 64
Jude writes letter

Romans execute Peter, Paul
AD 64

Jerusalem Jews stone James the brother of Jesus
AD 66

REVELATION 21

John sees heaven as a city—New Jerusalem—bathed in divine light, decorated in jewels, and populated with God's people who live with him forever.

BIG SCENE

HEAVEN

BIBLE HISTORY		**AD 64** *Paul and Peter write their final letters (2 Timothy, 2 Peter)*		
WORLD HISTORY	ALL DATES APPROXIMATE	*Jews revolt, drive out Romans* **AD 66**	*Romans arrive in Galilee, John and disciples flee Jerusalem* **AD 67**	*Nero commits suicide* **AD 68**

REVELATION

HEAVEN AHEAD, THE SCENIC ROUTE

STORY LINE

TRANSPORTED TO HEAVEN in a vision, a mysterious writer named John catches a glimpse of what looks like a terrifying future for Earth.

Standing in God's throne room, John—perhaps the disciple of Jesus—watches as Jesus breaks seven seals so he can open a scroll. Each snapping seal unleashes tragedy on earth: war, famine, disease, earthquakes, falling stars, raging fire, massive human death—half the world population.

Many scholars read these as symbols of hardship that Christians faced in John's century. Others point to an age yet to come.

Beyond the terror, though, John sees a wonderful future for God's people.

Jesus returns to earth. He gathers faithful souls from all time, living and dead. And he takes them into God's presence, to a glorious celestial city called New Jerusalem. It's God's home. But it becomes the eternal home of God's people as well.

John describes it as a place of everlasting happiness. "There will be no more death or sorrow or crying or pain. All these things are gone forever" (Revelation 21:4).

After seeing it all—the good and the bad—John closes his journal of visions with one request.

"Come, Lord Jesus!" (Revelation 22:20).

// LOCATION: John writes from the tiny prison island of Patmos, off Turkey's west coast. He addresses seven churches along the coast.

// TIME: Perhaps around AD 95.

// AUTHOR: "This letter is from John" (Revelation 1:4). But which John? Most early Church leaders said the apostle John. Other early Church leaders along with many scholars today said the writer was an otherwise unknown John—partly because of the different writing style and a reference to the apostles as though he's not one of them.

AD 95
*John writes
Revelation*

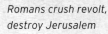

*Romans crush revolt,
destroy Jerusalem*
AD 70

*Domitian becomes
Roman emperor*
AD 81

Seven letters from Jesus

PUNISHED FOR BEING A CHRISTIAN, John is exiled to a penal colony on Patmos Island. There, worshipping on a Sunday, he experiences a vision.

The "Son of Man"—Jesus' favorite way of describing himself—speaks in a booming voice (Revelation 1:13). He tells John to take a letter—seven, actually. Jesus then begins to dictate the letters—one to each church along Turkey's west coast.

For most churches, Jesus offers compliments and complaints (see chart below).

Nuke test, Moruroa atoll, French Polynesia, 1970

JESUS CRITIQUES SEVEN CHURCHES

	EPHESUS	**SMYRNA**	**PERGAMUM**
	 Tourists at library ruins	 Fisherman mending net	 City ruins
CLAIM TO FAME:	Temple of Artemis, one of Seven Wonders of the World	Medicine, science	Library, second largest in the world after Alexandria, Egypt
COMPLIMENT:	They don't tolerate fake Christians teaching weird ideas.	They're spiritually rich, though financially poor.	They've stayed true to the faith.
COMPLAINT:	Their love for God and each other has faded. They're in danger of dying.	None	They tolerate two heretical groups that commit sex sins.
STATUS TODAY:	A ghost town, visited by tourists	Izmir, population 2.6 million	Bergama, population 55,000

◄ APOCALYPTIC LIT 101

When John wrote Revelation he used a style of writing that's as unique as poetry or parables. It's called apocalyptic (up-POC-uh-LIP-tick). And it's famous for coded messages wrapped in symbolic lingo.

Apocalyptic comes from Greek. It means "revelation." That's how John's book got its name. John says what he's writing is a "revelation [*apokalypsis*] from Jesus Christ" (Revelation 1:1).

Writers often used this literary style in times of persecution or enemy occupation. Symbols that show up—like the 666 Mark of the Beast or the invasion of human-headed locusts—were understood by insiders but not by the enemy, scholars say. If the enemy intercepted the letter, it would sound like nonsense. So they wouldn't bother arresting the writer or the recipient.

Scholars today disagree about how to interpret the symbolism in Revelation.

Many say John's visions of disaster point to the past—to Rome's destruction of Jerusalem in AD 70. They add that John's visions about the fall of evil forces are a prediction of the Roman Empire's collapse several centuries later.

Many other scholars, however, say John is talking about worldwide disasters yet to come.

THYATIRA	SARDIS	PHILADELPHIA	LAODICEA
Ruins in public park	Gymnasium-bathhouse	Roman columns	Hot springs nearby
Purple dye	River gold	Earthquakes leveled the city in AD 17	Eye ointment, and expensive clothing of black wool
They're growing in faith, love, service.	There are still a few Christians left.	Though small, the church is strong and persevering.	None
"Jezebel," a false prophet, is teaching idolatry and immorality.	The church is nearly dead.	None	They are wishy-washy.
Akhisar, population 82,000	Ruins. Mongols destroyed the city in 1402.	Alasehir, population 41,000	Ruins

Breaking open the seals of doom

IN ALL OF HEAVEN, teeming with millions, only one person is worthy of opening a scroll that contains God's plan for the world.

It's Jesus, most scholars agree.

John doesn't call him by name. But the description fits:

// "Lion of the tribe of Judah" and "heir to David's throne," both titles referring to the Messiah (Revelation 5:5).

// "Lamb. . .slaughtered," a reference to Jesus' sacrificial death (Revelation 5:6).

Seven plugs of hardened clay or wax seal the scroll closed. Jesus has to break them to open the scroll. The snapping of each seal cues a disaster, starting with seals 1–4, which cue the deadly four horsemen of the apocalypse.

Bible experts debate whether the symbols point to Roman history in John's century or to future horrors yet to come (see chart below).

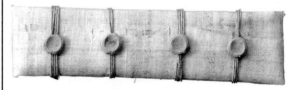

SEALED FOR PRIVACY / To read this letter, you have to break the clay seals pressed into strings tied around the parchment. John says Jesus has to break seven seals to open the scroll that contains God's plan for the future.

SEVEN SEALS OF DOOM _____

SEAL	1. Rider on white horse brings war	2. Rider on red horse brings slaughter	3. Rider on black horse brings famine
IT'S ABOUT HISTORY	Rome's bloody victory over Jerusalem defenders in AD 70	Rome's bloody victory over Jerusalem defenders in AD 70	Starvation inside Jerusalem caused by Rome's five-month siege
IT'S ABOUT FUTURE	The Antichrist, riding out to conquer the world	The Battle of Armageddon, with nukes as the "mighty sword" (Revelation 6:4)	Famine and economic disaster caused by wars during the Tribulation

◄ REMEMBERING / Wearing a haunting look and a badge that IDs her as a Holocaust Jew, a high school cast member plays the part of a World War II Holocaust victim in the play "We Had Names." John doesn't say who the 144,000 souls are that God marks for protection. But one theory suggests that as the "Jude" badge once marked Jews for annihilation, a divine seal will one day mark the Jews for protection.

144,000 MARKED WITH GOD'S SEAL

Before Jesus opens the scroll that will cue a fresh wave of disasters, John sees 144,000 people marked on their forehead with a protective seal—12,000 from each of the 12 tribes of Israel. A few of the many theories about the meaning:

It's a reference to the Holy Spirit marking all God's people for eternal life. "Do not make God's Holy Spirit sad. He marked you with a seal for the day when God will set you completely free" (Ephesians 4:30 NIrV).

It's Jewish Christians fleeing Jerusalem. Many Christians fled Jerusalem before Rome attacked in AD 70. They acted on Jesus' advice: "When you see Jerusalem surrounded by armies. . .those in Jerusalem must get out" (Luke 21:20–21).

It's Jewish Christians in the future Tribulation. Some Bible students say that Jesus will come to take the Christians away, but that some Jews left behind will convert during a horrifying era called the Tribulation.

4. Rider on pale horse brings death	5. Christians are martyred	6. Earthquake, falling stars, dark sky	7. Heaven falls silent
Death by diseases inside Jerusalem during the siege	Christians killed by Jews and Romans	Symbols of God's judgment marking the end of the Jewish nation	Calm before the storm: God unleashing judgment on Jerusalem in AD 70
A fourth of the world's people dying of disease and starvation	Christians killed during the Tribulation	Literal earthquake and possibly nuclear winter caused by nuke war	Calm before the storm: God unleashing judgment on the world in end times

Seven trumpets of doom

THE WORST IS YET TO COME. God's scroll is finally unsealed and open—with all seven seals broken. Just when John's reader might expect good news, seven angels appear—each blowing a mean horn.

Each horn cues a new disaster, just as the snapping of each seal had done earlier.

TRUMPET/DISASTER

1—Hail and fire destroy a third of the earth's plant life.

2—A mountain of fire crashes into the sea, killing a third of ocean life.

3—A falling star pollutes a third of all fresh water.

4—Darkness blocks a third of light from sun, moon, stars.

5—A falling star drills a shaft, releasing underground locusts.

6—Four angels of death kill a third of the world's people.

7—A victory blast signals that the world is now God's kingdom.

WHERE'S THE LINK TO THE FALL OF JERUSALEM IN AD 70?
Many scholars read Roman history into these seven horns: Trumpets 1–4 and 6 describe disasters Rome inflicted to crush the Jewish revolt of AD 66–70, trumpet 5 describes the siege of Jerusalem, and trumpet 7 describes the fall of the Jewish nation and the emergence of Christianity. Examples of links:

> **Hail and fire:** flaming projectiles from Roman catapults.

> **Destroyed plants:** Roman general Titus ordered all the Jerusalem-area trees cut down to make siege towers and other weapons.

> **Mountain thrown into the sea:** Romans destroyed the hilltop city of Jerusalem.

> **Polluted water:** Romans slaughtered many Jews in the Sea of Galilee, a freshwater lake that's a main source of drinking water.

> **Five-month terror of locusts:** Romans lay siege to Jerusalem for five months, March–August AD 70.

SEVEN, THE NUMBER.
It symbolizes completion, because after God created the universe in six days, he rested on the seventh day.

A THIRD, THE PERCENTAGE.
It's not a literal percentage, many scholars say. It's just a symbol for partial destruction.

◄ **THE BLUES.**
One by one, seven angels sound the blast of a trumpet, cuing cataclysmic disasters that will destroy a third of all life on Earth—if we're to take John's prophecy literally. Many Bible experts say we shouldn't.

Battle of the angels

IN A VISION UNUSUALLY STRANGE, even by Revelation's extreme standard, John witnesses three odd events:

- // A red dragon waits for a woman to give birth so it can gobble up her newborn baby boy. Fresh meat.
- // War breaks out in heaven—with angels fighting angels in fairly nonangelic behavior.

// Flashing back to the dragon, it's now after the baby boy's family. The baby himself has been airlifted into God's protective custody in heaven.

Go figure.

Trying to make sense of this fractured vision by piecing it into a flowing plot, Bible experts offer differing theories—based on whether they read Revelation as mostly about history or mostly about the future. A sampling of the many theories:

(continued next page)

ANGELS ARMED AND DANGEROUS / John sees a vision of a battle in paradise—angels on the warpath. Michael leads the angelic warriors of God in driving out of heaven the rogue forces of Satan and his devilish angels.

THE SCENE	IT'S ABOUT HISTORY	IT'S ABOUT FUTURE
Woman delivers a son (12:1)	The son is the Messiah and the woman is Israel—the Jewish people suffering "birth pangs" under centuries of oppression before the Messiah is born.	This is a flashback to Mary delivering Jesus and suffering the birth pains that women typically experience during a delivery.
Red dragon tries to eat the son (12:4)	The dragon is Satan who tempts Jesus and opposes him in other ways, in an effort to derail his ministry.	Satan plots to kill Baby Jesus by convincing King Herod to kill Bethlehem's baby boys.
Son taken to heaven (12:5)	Jesus, in the Ascension, is carried back to heaven when his ministry is over.	The Ascension.
Woman escapes to desert (12:6)	Jewish Christians in Jerusalem flee before the Roman army surrounds the city and destroys it in AD 70.	Jewish or Christian refugees find a safe haven from the Antichrist during last half of seven-year Tribulation.
Satan falls from heaven after losing war (12:8)	Satan is no longer allowed to accuse people before God now that Jesus' death provides forgiveness.	Satan, now allowed in heaven, will lose a celestial war and get exiled to Earth during the Tribulation.
Dragon attacks woman's other children (12:17)	Satan, failing to stop Jesus, tries to destroy the Christian movement.	Empowered by Satan, the Antichrist martyrs the faithful.

Tag team of bad-boy beasts

JOHN SEES TWO BEASTS. One comes by sea. The other by land. They're both nasty.

SEA BEAST

Whoever or whatever the sea beast is, it's no friend of God. It crushes God's people in a war, and it rules the entire world. Everyone worships this beast.

Many Bible experts see the Roman Empire in this critter. Even many of those who read the future into most of Revelation see the similarities, though they suggest the sea beast might be a revived Roman Empire or a similar empire that runs the world during the end times.

Links to Rome:

// **SEVEN HEADS, SEVEN HILLS.** The beast has seven heads. An angel says, "The seven heads of the beast represent the seven hills of the city where this woman [the Great Prostitute of Babylon] rules" (Revelation 17:9). Rome was famous as the city of seven hills; it was built on seven hills.

// **BABYLON, ROME'S NICKNAME.** Jews nicknamed the Roman Empire "Babylon" because both empires leveled Jerusalem: Babylon in 586 BC and Rome in AD 70.

(continued next page)

EMPEROR 666. Stamped onto Roman coins, the letters "Nero Caesar" had numerical value. Translated into Hebrew from Greek, the letters add up to 666 (see chart page 533). Translated from Rome's language of Latin into Hebrew, they add up to 616. Early copies of the Bible reported both. The Revelation fragment (above), written in the AD 200s or 300s, reads 616: *XIC* in Greek.

// CALL TO WORSHIP. Many Roman emperors ordered people to worship them as a god, including the emperor in John's time: Domitian.

// WORLD DOMINATION. Rome ruled the entire Mediterranean world, considered the civilized world of John's time.

LAND BEAST

This beast is a miracle-worker who convinces people to do what he says. He orders everyone to wear a mark on their right hand or forehead—the Mark of the Beast.

Without this mark, no one can buy or sell anything.

John gives a clue for identifying the beast: "It is the number of a man. His number is 666" (Revelation 13:18).

2 QUIRINAL 3 VIMINAL 4 ESQUILIN
1 CAPITOLINE
5 PALATINE
TIBER RIVER
6 CAELIAM

Emperor Domitian

ROME: CITY OF 7 HILLS

7 AVENTINE

ROMAN BEAST / Rome began as individual hamlets on seven hills. John said the beast from the sea had seven heads that represent the seven hills of a city. Domitian, Roman emperor when John is believed to have written Revelation, ordered the people to worship him—as did the sea beast in John's vision.

MARK OF THE BEAST

IT'S A NUMBER: 666—though some of the oldest copies of the Bible say it's 616.

Makes no difference, according to many scholars.

Both numbers link to Nero (AD 37–68), the first Roman emperor to persecute Christians.

The link is money. Coins in Nero's day were stamped with his name and title: "Nero Caesar" (see photo page 531). Letters had numerical values.

666. "Nero Caesar" adds up to 666 when we translate the letters from Greek, the international language of the day, into Hebrew, the language of the Jews.

616. "Nero Caesar" adds up to 616 when we translate the letters from Latin, the language of the Romans, into Hebrew.

Though most Bible experts say they see the link to Nero, they don't agree on what to do about it. Some say John's vision points back to that era, some 20 years before his vision. Others say it points to a future Nero-like tyrant, possibly the Antichrist.

Mark of the Beast

N E R O N	C A E S A R	Greek
נ ו ר ו נ	ק	ס ר	Hebrew
50 200 6 50	100 60 200 = 666	

N E R O	C A E S A R	Latin
נ ו ר ו	ק	ס ר	Hebrew
50 200 6	100 60 200 = 616	

Jews skipped writing most vowels, as shorthand.

Seven final disasters

IT'S ALMOST THE END OF BAD NEWS—only seven more horrors to go.

John watches as seven angels dump seven bowls of God's punishment onto the planet.

Bible experts disagree over what to make of it all. Scholars who read Roman history into the prophecy offer one set of theories. Those who read the future into it offer another.

The chart below is just a sampling of the theories.

(feature continues through page 536)

SEVEN BOWLS OF PUNISHMENT

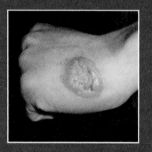  

DISASTER	1. Deadly skin sores	2. Bloody sea	3. Bloody rivers
IT'S ABOUT HISTORY	Perhaps skin lesions and disease suffered during the fall of Jerusalem in AD 70 or the fall of Rome around AD 400	Symbol of carnage during the fall of Jerusalem or Rome	Streams of blood flowing down the streets of Jerusalem or down the streets of Rome
IT'S ABOUT FUTURE	Possibly skin damage caused by exposure to radiation during an end-time nuclear war	Symbol of carnage throughout the non-Jewish world during the Tribulation	Blood of the slaughtered during the Tribulation, or symbol of the joy of life, polluted by sin

OPERATION SKY FIRE   A nuke takes out a city, in a photo illustration that uses a picture of an actual nuclear test. With speculation running wild—as many scholars put it—some Bible students mix and match various descriptions of end-time battles, concluding that a massive bloodbath erupts at Armageddon—perhaps a nuclear holocaust: "Fire will pour out of Heaven and burn them up" (Revelation 20:9 MSG). John, however, never reports what happens at Armageddon.

4. Solar blast scorches earth	5. Darkness	6. Drought at Euphrates River lets army cross to Armageddon	7. Earthquakes
"Sun" refers to tyrannical leaders who made life miserable for the Jews or perhaps for the Romans	Chaos in the Roman Empire after Nero's suicide or before the fall of Rome centuries later	The battle describes either the slaughter of Jews in the fall of Jerusalem or the slaughter of Romans in the fall of Rome	The final collapse of Jerusalem in AD 70 or of Rome centuries later
Satanic government ruling the people during the Tribulation; or solar flares; or result of nuke-thinned atmosphere	. Trouble erupting in the beast's empire during the Tribulation; or a blackout from smoke	End-time battle by army of the beast, leader of a worldwide empire, perhaps in a civil war or a fight against Christ	Society crumbles, perhaps because of lingering war that only Jesus can stop

BATTLE OF ARMAGEDDON

A DROUGHT evaporates the Euphrates River that courses through Syria and Iraq. "Kings from the east" seize the moment, marching their armies across the dry riverbed, which points them in the general direction of Israel (Revelation 16:12).

Among today's well-known nations to the river's east: Iran, China, Japan, Russia.

Led by demonic spirits, the coalition gathers for battle at a place called "Armageddon" (Revelation 16:16).

Over the past 3,000 years, more than 30 major battles have already been fought in this valley that Napoleon once called the perfect battlefield.

Many say another battle is coming—an apocalyptic battle. Pulling from Revelation's other end-time battle descriptions, some Bible students link the carnage John describes with the battle of Armageddon:

> **200 million-man army.** "I heard the size of their army, which was 200 million mounted troops" (Revelation 9:16).

> **They attack God's people.** "They will surround the camp of God's people and the city that his people love" (Revelation 20:9 CEV).

> **There's a bloodbath.** "Blood flowed. . .in a stream about 180 miles [296 km] long and as high as a horse's bridle" (Revelation 14:20).

> **A fireball destroys the invaders.** "Fire from heaven came down on the attacking armies and consumed them" (Revelation 20:9).

Two problems with this, many scholars add.

First, those scattered details pieced together may have nothing to do with what happens at Armageddon— John never reports that a battle is fought there.

Second, many Bible experts say the battle details scattered throughout Revelation are only symbols of God's inevitable judgment. Yet many others take the specs literally.

ARMAGEDDON, ISRAEL? There's no such place on the world map. But many Bible students speculate that the word *Armageddon* refers to *Har Megiddo* (hill of Megiddo). Megiddo was an ancient hilltop fortress guarding an important pass out of Israel's largest valley—the Valley of Jezreel—and through the Carmel Mountains. As the theory goes, forces of good and evil will fight an end-time battle in this valley that some Bible students have taken to calling the Valley of Armageddon.

Good-bye Babylon

"BABYLON IS FALLEN," an angel shouts. "Babylon the Great, Mother of All Prostitutes and Obscenities in the World" (Revelation 18:2; 17:5).

Which Babylon? It couldn't be the Babylonian Empire, most Bible experts agree. Persians conquered and assimilated it into their empire in 539 BC.

Popular theories:

// **BABYLON IS A CODE NAME FOR ROME.** Jews gave Rome that name because the Roman Empire did to them what the Babylonians had done more than 600 years earlier: invade, conquer, and occupy their homeland, and eventually turn their capital city of Jerusalem into a ruin.

// **BABYLON IS JERUSALEM.** This Jewish city—the first to persecute Christians—gets leveled by the Romans in AD 70.

// **BABYLON IS AN EVIL EMPIRE YET TO COME.** The Antichrist will run the show during a time of great terror for people of faith, a period many call the Tribulation.

SEVEN KINGS, PLUS ONE. The prostitute of Babylon rides a beast with seven heads. An angel tells John the heads represent seven kings as well as the seven hills of the city where the beast comes from (see "Rome: city of seven hills," page 532). The angel adds that the seventh king will be a short-termer, followed by an eighth king. Many Bible experts link these eight to the Roman emperors from the time of Jesus to the time John wrote Revelation.

AUGUSTUS
(ruled 27 BC–AD 14)

TIBERIUS
(AD 14–37)

CALIGULA
(AD 37–41)

CLAUDIUS
(AD 41–54)

NERO
(AD 54–68)

VESPASIAN
(AD 69–79)

TITUS
(AD 79–81)

DOMITIAN
(AD 81–96)

Jesus to the rescue

RIDING A WHITE HORSE, Jesus leads a cavalry of angels charging to earth where they crush an international coalition of armies allied with "the beast and his false prophet" (Revelation 19:20).

Actually, John never calls Jesus by name. Romans have outlawed Christianity, so paying homage to Jesus in a letter could be dangerous. Yet John clearly identifies him in ways that Christian insiders would know, most Bible experts say. Perhaps the most obvious is by calling him "the Word of God" (Revelation 19:13), a title attributed to Jesus in the opening chapter of the Gospel of John.

The big questions are: What's going on, and when's it going on?

Many scholars say this vision is a symbol of Christianity's ongoing battle against evil—a spiritual battle that Jesus is leading, and will win.

Others say it's a literal battle yet to come. One theory is that Jesus is coming back to defeat the Antichrist, toss him into the lake of fire, and then

set up a thousand-year reign on earth—a reign called the Millennium.

HEAVEN'S CAVALRY. Out of the sky Jesus appears riding a white horse and leading an army of white-robed angels. With nothing but a word, it seems, he defeats the evil forces of earth allied against him: "From his mouth came a sharp sword to strike down the nations" (Revelation 19:15). Some Christians say the fight is physical—perhaps the battle of Armageddon. Others say the battle is waging now, as Christians use God's Word—the teachings in the Bible—to bring peace on earth.

Millennium
1,000 years of peace on earth

Crucifixion   **Second Coming**   **Last judgment**

TRIBULATION   MILLENNIUM

MILLENNIUM TIMELINE, ONE OF MANY THEORIES. Either figuratively or literally, Satan is locked up for a thousand years, while Jesus rules the world in peace. But first, some Christians say, the world will suffer through seven years of hell on earth led by the Antichrist—a period many call the Tribulation. Others say there will be no literal Tribulation or Millennium, but that the era of peace started 2,000 years ago when Jesus defeated Satan by rising from the dead and launching the Church, with its message of forgiveness and love.

Judgment Day for Satan

WITH THE BEAST DEFEATED and pitched into the lake of fire, heaven turns its attention to another beast: "the dragon—that old serpent, who is the devil, Satan" (Revelation 20:2).

An angel arrests him and tosses him into "the bottomless pit" (Revelation 20:3) for what could sound like a thousand-year free fall.

Meanwhile, life on earth takes a turn for the better. Some Christians call this period the Millennium, Jesus' thousand-year reign on earth.

Afterward, Satan is released. He rallies the nations to his evil cause—nations John calls "Gog and Magog" (Revelation 20:8). Some Christians wonder if this is the battle of Armageddon, or perhaps a later fight—Satan's one last stab at God.

Either way, "fire from heaven" (Revelation 20:9) burns up Satan's army. Then he, too, like the beast and the false prophet earlier, gets himself tossed into the lake of fire to be "tormented day and night forever and ever" (Revelation 20:10).

Judgment Day follows.

Everyone who ever lived appears before God's throne to be judged based on what they did with their lives. Everything they ever did is recorded in books that sound like they distinguish between naughty and nice. "Anyone whose name was not found recorded in the Book of Life was thrown into the lake of fire" (Revelation 20:15).

FIRED. Losing his job as humanity's accuser, Satan lands in a lake of fire—another term for "hell," according to many Bible experts. Scholars debate whether Satan and his followers will suffer torture forever, or if they'll be destroyed, suffering the consequences forever.

HELL. Another term for "the lake of fire," some scholars say—a place of eternal punishment for Satan and his followers, demons and humans alike.

The Greek word is *Gehenna*, a valley just outside Jerusalem's city walls. Jews associated this valley with God's punishment. That's because they once sacrificed to idols there, and in 586 BC lost their homeland to Babylonian invaders because of sins like these.

Theories about hell:

> Hell is a literal place of eternal torture.

> It's just separation from God, where people who wanted nothing to do with him in life get their wish in the afterlife.

> It's annihilation. Sinners won't suffer forever, but their destruction will last forever.

> There's a second chance. Even in the afterlife, God will welcome sinners (see Colossians 1:20).

Tourist in heaven

IN THE BIBLE'S CLIMAX, John sees his last vision. It's wonderful.

But as with most of John's visions, Bible experts don't agree on what it means.

> *I saw a new heaven and a new earth. The first heaven and the first earth were completely gone. . . . I saw the Holy City, the new Jerusalem. It was coming down out of heaven. . . . I heard a loud voice from the throne. It said, "Now God makes his home with people. . . . He will wipe away every tear from their eyes. There will be no more death or sadness."*
>
> REVELATION 21:1–4 NIrV

Scholars offer different kinds of advice about how to read this.

TAKE IT LITERALLY—IT'S A NEW UNIVERSE. Some Bible experts say God will destroy the universe and create a new one, with a new earth where people will live with God in glorified bodies, perhaps like the one Jesus had after his resurrection.

TAKE IT SYMBOLICALLY—IT'S HEAVEN. Other scholars say John's vision has nothing to do with physics. John is talking about heaven.

TAKE IT SPIRITUALLY—IT'S ABOUT CHRISTIANS' LIVING IN THE HERE AND NOW. Some scholars say John is talking about people, each of whom becomes a "new creation" through Jesus. "Anyone who belongs to Christ has become a new person. The old life is gone" (2 Corinthians 5:17). Christians don't fear death "like people who don't have any hope. We believe that Jesus died and was raised to life" (1 Thessalonians 4:13–14 CEV).

RIVER OF LIFE / John sees a river in New Jerusalem, a city many scholars say refers to heaven. John says the river flows from God's throne, carrying the "water of life" that nourishes the "trees of life." The scene conjures up images of both humanity's beginning and its final destiny. Beginning: Eden still perfect before the fall, with its river and tree of life. Destiny, as promised by Jesus: "Those who drink the water I give will never be thirsty again. It becomes a fresh, bubbling spring within them, giving them eternal life" (John 4:14).

ΑΩ

ALPHA AND OMEGA / First and last letters in the Greek alphabet. Jesus described himself as "the Alpha and the Omega, the First and the Last, the Beginning and the End" (Revelation 22:13). Some scholars interpret Jesus as saying he's the source of the universe's beginning and end. He existed before it. And he'll exist when it's gone.

· ·

▼ **CELESTIAL UPGRADE** / Precious gemstones on earth are nothing but foundation blocks in New Jerusalem. Some Christians take John's description literally. Others say his vision is just a symbol—an attempt to deliver a message about a spiritual dimension to folks who need a physical frame of reference. John's message: Heaven is so wonderful that earth's greatest treasures seem mundane by comparison.

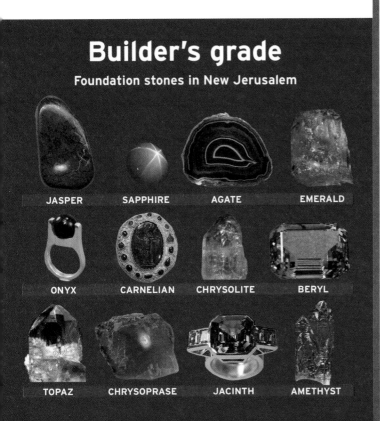

Builder's grade
Foundation stones in New Jerusalem

JASPER · SAPPHIRE · AGATE · EMERALD

ONYX · CARNELIAN · CHRYSOLITE · BERYL

TOPAZ · CHRYSOPRASE · JACINTH · AMETHYST

HEAVEN'S SPECS

John describes New Jerusalem with intriguing detail.

> **Cube-shaped city**: 1,400 miles (2,200 km) in all directions
> **Jewel foundation stones**: jasper, sapphire, emerald, and more
> **Golden streets**: so pure it's see-through
> **Pearl gates**: a dozen gates, each made of a giant pearl

EDEN 2.0

Still touring New Jerusalem, John sees what sounds like a return to paradise lost: Eden, with the sin mess cleaned up. No more toxic spiritual pollution.

As in Eden in the Genesis story, there's a river feeding life throughout New Jerusalem. But in what many Bible experts interpret as heaven, John says the river he sees comes from the throne of God. "The water of life" nourishes the "tree of life," which grows leaves "used for medicine to heal the nations" (Revelation 22:1–2).

In Eden 1.0, Adam and Eve sinned—and were cursed with punishment for it. But in Eden 2.0, "No longer will there be a curse upon anything" (Revelation 22:3).

Having seen the future, John closes the book on the Bible with a benediction:

"Lord Jesus, please come soon! I pray that the Lord Jesus will be kind to all of you" (Revelation 22:20–21 CEV).

ART CREDITS

Abbreviations: AR=Art Resource, NY; BAL=Bridgeman Art Library; BB=Balage Balogh; BMM=Bradley M. Miller; DA=DeviantArt.com; FL=Flickr; GS=GoodSalt; II=Israelimages; IS=iStockphoto; KR=Kevin Rolly; LC=Library of Congress; PD=public domain; RC/GSI= Rani Calvo/Geological Survey of Israel; SMM=Stephen M. Miller; TBM=Trustees of the British Museum; TF=TopFoto; THP=Tyndale House Publishers; TP=Tom Patterson; WM=WikiMedia; ZR=Zev Radovan.

Old Testament Introduction
8, sand: Getty; Moses with tablet: Royalty Free Christian Art; **9,** scroll: Chris AKA Shrek/FL; Cain and Abel: BMM; crying woman: Ricardo Frantz/WM/artist: Pedro Américo

Genesis
10, solar system: NASA/JPL-Caltech/R.Hurt (SSC); Noah's ark: Edward Hicks/WM; **11,** Abraham: Gerhard Wilhelm von Reutern/WM; Egyptian plowing: Jeff Dahl/WM; **12,** nebula: NASA/JPL-Caltech/R. Gutermuth (Harvard-Smithsonian Center for Astrophysics); rib cage: Stephen Thomas; **13,** God creates light: William Blake/WM; sea and sky: Gilad Benari; land teeming with plants: Cain Pascoe; sun and moon: NASA; sea life and birds: Miguel Lasa; man: David Martin Anton; **14,** TP/rendered by SMM; **15,** Fernand Corman/WM; **16,** Creation Museum, Petersburg, Kentucky, www.creationmuseum.org; **17,** Adam: Sailko/WM; Methuselah: Andreas Praefcke/WM/artist: Tilman Riemenschneider; Noah: Marie-Lan Nguyen/WM/artist: Donatello; lightning: Ian Boggs/WM; Shem: Anual/WM/artist: Juan de Mesa; Abraham: AlMare/WM; Moses: Marie-Lan Nguyen/WM/artist: Camillo Rusconi; David: Marie-Lan Nguyen/WM/artist: Nicolas Cordier; Sumerian prism: Ashmolean Museum; Noah's Flood map: RC/GSI/rendered by SMM; map art of Mt. Ararat (top): Andrew Behesnilian/WM; map art of Mt. Ararat (bottom): NASA/JPL/NIMA; map art of people entering ark: Wolfgang Sauber/WM; map art of dove: IS; map art of rainbow: Laurent Deschodt/WM; **18,** mud bricks: Soare/WM; ziggurat: BMM; **19,** RC/GSI/rendered by SMM; map art of caravan: G. Eric and Edith Matson Photograph Collection/LC; **20,** © Jonathan Blair/Corbis; **21,** destruction of Sodom: © The Art Archive/Corbis; map: NASA/rendered by SMM; **22,** Ivan Petrovich Keler-Viliandi; **23,** PD; **24,** mandrake: Robert Svensson/msitua.net; Jacob's dream: artist: Jusepe de Ribera; **25,** map: RC/GSI/rendered by SMM; Jacob wrestling angel: Erik Möller/WM/artist: Rembrandt; **26,** dreamer: Arkadiusz Walerczuk; sheaves: Masaki Ikeda/WM; **27,** Egyptians: crayonmaniac; chalice: Scala/AR; **28,** Akhenaton in color: Gian-boy/FL; Akhenaton statue: E. Michael Smith/WM; **29,** map: NASA/rendered by SMM; map art of shepherd and sheep: IS.

Exodus
30, parting of Red Sea: Gustave Doré; baby Moses: Juanpdp/WM/artist: Lawrence Alma-Tadema; **31,** Moses with tablets: WM/artist: Rembrandt; Pharaoh Thutmose: Hay Kranen/WM; Pharaoh Rameses II: Tiny Packages/FL; **32,** map: NASA/rendered by SMM; map art of cow: L. Miguel Bugallo Sánchez/WM; map art of sheep: Bärbel Schwarzer/WM; map art of globe: WorldSat; **33,** Jochebed: Ricardo Frantz/WM/artist: Pedro Américo; papyrus harvesting: Reza/Webistan/Corbis; Moses and burning bush: William Blake/The Art Archive; **34,** Mount Sinai: Jose Fuste Raga/Corbis; map: NASA/rendered by SMM; map art of pharaoh: shd-stock/DA; map art of walking man: Jeff Dahl/WM; **35,** mud brick: TBM; Moses before Pharaoh: THP © Joseph Mirales; **36,** Jeff Dahl/WM/artist: Charles Sprague Pearce; **37,** all illustrations: Jeff Dahl/WM; **38,** Michael Jacobs; **39,** reeds: Claudio Marcio Lopes/FL; map: NASA/rendered by SMM; **40,** Napoleon: PD/artist: Jacques-Louis David **41,** barberry: Kurt Stueber/WM/botanist: Otto Wilhelm Thome; oasis: Luca Galuzzi/WM; **42,** BMM; **43,** God on Mount Sinai: Jean-Leon Gerome; ark of the covenant: Ben Schumin/WM; map: NASA/Rendered by SMM; map art of charioteer: King & Country HK Ltd.; **44,** Derek and Chantal Chen/FL; **45,** Florian Prischl/WM.

Leviticus
46, lamb: The Yorck Project/WM/artist: Francisco de Zurbarán; Moses with tablets: WM/artist: Rembrandt; Chinese priest: WM; **47,** Trojan horse: Deror avi/WM; Jewish temple: BB; ship: Phoenicia.org.uk; **48,** Sailko/WM; **49,** pigeon: Luc Viatour/WM; grain: Scott Bauer/USDA; sheep: Daniel Camargo; goat: Emmanuel Keller/FL; ram: Charles G. Summers, Jr.; **50,** Roy Fokker/WM; **51,** Miguel Lasa; **52,** trout: Stephen Ausmus/USDA; crab: WM; deer: Ianaré Sévi/WM; pigs: Keith Weller/USDA; duck: Branko Kannenberg/WM; eagle: AngMoKio/WM; grasshopper: Siga/WM; ladybug: Scott Bauer/USDA; **53,** scapegoat: William Holman Hunt; Jesus on cross: José Manuel/WM/artist: Diego Velázquez; **54,** man blowing ram's horn: Kristin Lindell; girl with Hanukkah candles: Tamelyn Feinstein; booth: Ori229/WM; Queen Esther: Louis Garden/WM/artist: Andrea del Castagn; unleavened bread: Daniel Schwen/WM; grain: Craig Nagy/WM; **55,** carrots: Stephen Ausmus/USDA; grape harvest: Karl Briullov.

Numbers
56, spies in Canaan: Photographersdirect.com; Exodus from Egypt: Juanpdp/WM/artist: Edward Pointer; children in school: Tom Lovell/National Geographic; sun worship: Erich Lessing/AR; **57,** Merneptah stele: PD; **58,** travelers: HIP/AR; soldier icon: WM; **59,** woman statue: Camden/FL; drowning woman: CountVisigoth/DA; **60,** Stewart Butterfield/WM; **61,** manna bug: Q. Holdman/USDA; quail: Perry Kuo/FL; **62,** spies in Canaan: Photographersdirect.com; map: NASA/rendered by SMM; map art of crowd: Cesare Biseo; map art of three men: PD; map art of palm tree: SMM; **63,** frankincense: Snotch/WM; incense burner: Calapito/WM; Moses watching earth punish rebels: THP © Joseph Mirales; **64,** ST/WM; **65,** map: NASA/rendered by SMM; map art of cobra: Anil Walia/FL; map art of palm tree: SMM; map art of bronze snake: Anthony van Dyck; horned viper: Böhringer Friedrich; **66,** Ilco Trajkovski/FL; **67,** women: Sergio Andreu Atance; map: RC/GSI/rendered by SMM.

Deuteronomy
68, Moses on Mount Nebo: BAL; Pharaoh Thutmose: Hay Kranen/WM; Moses with hands upraised: Ivan Kramskoi; **69,** golden idol: Pascal Radigue/WM; iron pick: Vassil/WM; **70,** both images: Bill Aron; **71,** golden idol: The Oriental Institute Museum/University of Chicago; temple prostitute: John William Godward; **72,** Karl Pavlovich Briullov; **73,** family: William-Adolphe Bouguereau; Jehu relief: Erich Lessing/AR; **74,** map: NASA/rendered by SMM; map art of crowd: Cesare Biseo; **75,** Moses on Mount Nebo: Frederic Edwin Church; view from Mount Nebo: John Thomas/FL.

Joshua
76, battle of Jericho: THP © Don Gabriel; slinger: WM/artist: Johnny Shumate; Nefertiti: WM; **77,** Rameses II, Dominik Knippel/WM; Merneptah stele: PD; **78,** map: NASA/rendered by SMM; map art of men on donkeys: SMM; map art of campers: David Roberts/LC; Rahab: William Whitaker; flax: Zita Bartasyte; **79,** map: NASA/rendered by SMM; map art of priests carrying ark: Art Resource: Jordan River cliffs: Frank and Frances Carpenter Collection/LC; **80,** battle of Jericho: THP © Don Gabriel; **81,** jars: Courtesy of the Michael C. Carolos Museum of Emory University; Jericho ruins: Photo by Francesco Fullone/WM; **82,** Matthew Lazor; **83,** THP © Don Gabriel; **84,** map: NASA; map art of hailstones: Samuel Zinn; art of water shaft: Bill Latta; photo of water shaft: ZR; **85,** battle scene: Tom Lovell, National Geographic; charioteers: Jon P. Davis Jr.; **86,** RC/GSI/rendered by SMM; **87,** RC/GSI/rendered by SMM.

Judges
88, Delilah cutting Samson's hair: Corbis; burial scene: LC; **89,** panda: CPacker/WM; Chinese woman: Robert Frederick Blum; **90,** idol: SMM; Arab raiders: John Singer Sargant; **91,** Jael: KR; map: NASA/rendered by SMM; map art of sword: Pitert/WM; map art of chariot: Niall Corbett/FL; **92,** Kamran Safdar; **93,** drink from spring: SMM; map: NASA/rendered by SMM; map art of torch: Simon L./DA; map art of camp: Makovsky Nikolay; **94,** Carl Bloch/Statens Museum for Kunst; **95,** map: RC/GSI/rendered by SMM; harvesting olives: Yves L Coupez/FL; **96,** The Oriental Institute Museum/University of Chicago; **97,** map: RC/GSI/rendered by SMM; woman screaming: KR.

Ruth
98, Ruth and Naomi: Aidan McRae Thomson/FL; mummy: G. Elliot Smith/WM; Merneptah stele: PD; **99,** Bedouin woman: Claudia/FL; ship: Phoenicia.org.uk; **100,** map: NASA/rendered by SMM; map art of three women: William Blake/WM; **101,** Bedouin woman: Claudia/FL; hills of Moab: Nir Ben-Yosef; widow: SMM; **102,** Jewish wedding: Owen Franken/Corbis; grain harvest: LC; **103,** mother and child: The Yorck Project/WM/artist:Pierre-Auguste Renoir; sandals: Luis García/WM.

1, 2 Samuel
104, David and Goliath: THP © Blas Gallego; Samuel, Eli: Lawrence Lew/FL; Saul profile: Kimberly Katiti/DA; Damascus: Abanima/WM; **105,** King David: Lars Justinen/GS; Hebrew letters: WM; **106,** weeping woman: Ozgur Cakir; map: RC/GSI/rendered by SMM; map art of boy: Jean-Leon Gerome; **107,** Samuel and Eli: John Singleton Copley; cows: Shane Young/FL; **108,** map: RC/GSI/rendered by SMM; map art of Philistine: Remih/WM; map art of swords: Pitert/WM; map art of priests and ark: Vassil/WM; rat: Stefano Bolognini/WM; **109,** Meirion Matthias/FL; **110,** Samuel anointing David: Felix-Joseph Barrias/Getty Images; oil: Lemone/WM; **111,** map: NASA/rendered by SMM; map art of Philistine: Remih/WM; map art of slinger: Johnny Shumate/WM; **112,** David and Goliath: THP © Blas Gallego; slingshot: Robert Kyllo/IS; Philistine coffin: ZR; pottery shard: Machaerus/WM; **113,** David playing harp: Nikolai Petrovich Zagorsky; woman with tambourine: artist John Hoppner, SMM; **114,** map: NASA/rendered by SMM; map art of En-Gedi: Todd Anderson; waterfall: Jon Arnold/JAI/Corbis; **115,** Saul and witch of Endor: PD; map: NASA/rendered by SMM; map art of Philistine: Remih/WM; map art of witch of Endor: PD; map art of Saul: Kimberly Katiti/DA; **116,** David: Frederick Arthur Bridgman; harem woman: Frederick Arthur Bridgman; **117,** David's Jerusalem: Doron Bar; water shaft to Jerusalem: Bill Latta; **118,** Dome of the Rock: Francisco Martins/http://www.flickr.com/photos/betta_design/; rock inside dome: II/Roy Brody; David dancing with ark: THP © Blas Gallego; **119,** map: NASA/rendered by SMM; map art of king: Marie-Lan Nguyen/WM; bearded man: Jamal Alayoubi www.jamalphoto.com; **120,** William Whitaker; **121,** BB; **122,** KR; **123,** Absalom caught in tree: Look and Learn/BAL; two men: © Abir Sultan/epa/Corbis.

1, 2 Kings
124, Solomon's temple: BB; Pharaoh with prisoners: Erich Lessing/AR; **125,** both images: SMM; **126,** man with crown: Lars Justinen/Goodsalt; Bathsheba: William Whitaker; **127,** Nicolas Poussin/Louvre, Paris, France/Lauros/Giraudon/BAL; **128,** map: RC/GSI/rendered by SMM; **129,** cedar: Charles Fred/FL; men in quarry: G. Eric and Edith Matson Photograph Collection/LC; Solomon's temple: BB; **130,** map: TP/rendered by SMM; map art of horses: Richard Bartz/WM; map art of ivory: PD; map art of chariot: PD; map art of ape: Malene Thyssen/WM; map art of gold: PD; map art of emerald: Géry Parent/WM; **131,** man and wives: LC; Molech: Jeff Preston/GS; **132,** map: NASA/rendered by SMM; map art of bull: The Oriental Institute of The University of Chicago; map art of temple: BB; golden calf: Ted Olson; **133,** RC/GSI/rendered by SMM; **134,** Elijah and chariot of fire: Guisepee Angeli, 2007 Board of Trustees, National Gallery of Art, Washington; tornado: Nizar Moussa; **135,** map: Christoph Hormann; map art of chariot: Noel Taylor; map art of dog: Jim Clark/WM; map art of palace: WM; Jehu bowing: John Whitmarsh; Jezebel: BAL; **136,** Assyrian torture: TBM; map: TP/rendered by SMM; map art of statue: WM; **137,** Sennacherib: BB; tourist in tunnel: Wendy L. Scott; rat: Katrin Solmdorff/WM; **138,** Hezekiah: Lars Justinen/GS Inc.; shadow clock: WM; Taylor Prism: David Castor/WM; **139,** eyes of boy: Othman Al zanki/FL; Manasseh: Lars Justinen/GS Inc.; **140,** battle of Jerusalem: THP © Blas Gallego; map: TP/rendered by SMM; map art of ziggurat: BMM; **141,** Ishtar Gate: BB; Masada ramp: Derek and Chantal Chen/FL; Assyrian ram and tower: Capillon/WM; catapult: Karel Jakubec/WM.

1, 2 Chronicles
142, caravan: BAL; Egyptian soldier: Hans Ollermann/FL; **143,** Assyrian archers: Iglonghurst/WM; camel and rider: WM/artist: Théophile Lybaert; Persian soldiers: BMM; **144,** king: Marie-Lan Nguyen/WM; blacksmith: Lars Justinen/GS; **145,** Faraz Shanyar; **146,** Jonathan Blair/Corbis; **147,** ZR; **148,** map: NASA/rendered by SMM; map art of chariot: King & Country HK Ltd.; Egyptian warrior: Erich Lessing/AR; **149,** BB; **150,** map: TP/rendered by SMM; map art of Egyptian: Marcus Cyron/WM; map art of swords: Pitert/WM; map art of soldiers: Poppy/WM; **151,** Lars Justinen/GS.

Ezra
152, Jerusalem ruins: Lars Justinen/GS; camel caravan: LC; **153,** Marie-Lan Nguyen/WM; **154,** TBM; **155,** map: TP/rendered by SMM; map art of caravan: Norman MacDonald/Saudi Aramco World/SAWDIA; map art of dead camel: Carl Haag; **156,** people reading scroll: BB; Jerusalem ruins: Lars Justinen/GS; **157,** Léon Bonnat.

Nehemiah
158, builders: THP © Don Gabriel; ruins of Jerusalem: Lars Justinen/GS; Ishtar Gate: BB; **159,** Lluís Sala/FL; **160,** profile of king: BMM; wine steward: Erich Lessing/AR; **161,** Jerusalem model: Leen Ritmeyer; city wall with donkey: Bill Aron.

Esther
162, Esther: Minerva Teichert; ruins of Jerusalem: Lars Justinen/GS; Persian king: Gianni Dagli Orti/Corbis; **163,** Vaggelis Vlahos/WM; **164,** harem: Staszek99/WM/Artist: Fernand Cormon; Iranian woman: Hamed Saber/FL; **165,** Francois Leon Benouville; **166,** Susa: Faraz Shanyar; knucklebone: ancientouch.com; **167,** Bill Aron.

Job
168, God: Michelangelo/WM; caravan: Norman MacDonald/Saudi Aramco World; battle scene: Tom Lovell, National Geographic; **169,** Job and wife: Erik Möller/WM/artist: Albrecht Dürer; cuneiform tablet: The Oriental Institute of The University of Chicago; **170,** Emerald D.E. de Leeuw/DA; **171,** Painting by Tamara Lindahl/DA/based on photo by Marco C. Stoppato; **172,** man writing: Norman MacDonald/Saudi Aramco World/SAWDIA; map: TP/rendered by SMM; **173,** Ilya Repin; **174,** William Blake; **175,** light ray: NASA/JPL-Caltech; Pleiades: NASA, ESA, and AURA/Caltech.

Psalms
176, weeping woman: Ozgur Cakir; singing women: Simeon Solomon/Bridgeman; **177,** flutist: WM; Plato: Ricardo André Frantz/WM; **178,** lyre player: Albert Joseph Moore; street musicians: Lalupa/WM; **179,** shepherd and son: Greg Schneider; shepherd painting: GS; **180,** Greg Schneider; **181,** Vasily Polenov; **182,** Bryullov Pavel; **183,** Lars Justinen/GS.

Proverbs
184, boy: Corbis; Solomon: Jean-Pol Grandmont/WM; **185,** Ulysses on boat: Bibi Saint-Pol/WM/artist: John William Waterhouse; scribe: Bill Aron: Sappho: Wolfgang Rieger/WM; **186,** boys: Sonny Saguil; old man and great-granddaughter: Bill Aron; **187,** SMM; **188,** Nasib Bitar; **189,** farmer: David Silverman, Getty Images; ant: Noodle snacks/WM; **190,** scales: Poussin jean/WM; grocer: Bill Aron; **191,** mouth: Miklós SZABÓ, Miki3d/deviantart.com; honey: Tohma/WM; **192,** sleeping student: Bill Aron; crying child: Jill Greenberg/Corbis; **193,** beggar woman: Tomas Castelazo/WM; elderly couple: Bill Aron.

Ecclesiastes
194, soldier helping girl: Technical Sergeant Mike Buytas of the United States Air Force; King David: Marie-Lan Nguyen/WM/artist: Nicolas Cordier; **195,** burial mound: Oliver Abels/WM; Mexican statue: Luidger/WM; **196,** monks: Gaetano Bellei; Monument Valley: Luca Galuzzi/WM; **197,** soldier helping girl: Technical Sergeant Mike Buytas of the United States Air Force; birth: Tom Adriaenssen/WM; crying: David Shankbone/WM; finding: Andreas Praefcke/WM; love: Ferdinand Reus/WM; killing: U.S. Army/WM; hugging: Chad Miller/WM; tearing: Albert Anker; **198,** BB; **199,** Bacchus: Yorck Project/WM/artist: Michelangelo; Solomon: Jean-Pol Grandmont/WM.

Song of Songs
200, Arab couple: Étienne Dinet; Solomon: Nicolas Poussin/Louvre, Paris, France/Lauros/Giraudon/BAL; dancing woman: The Yorck Project/WM/artist: Christian Bernhard Rode; **201,** Robot H3ro; **202,** Wolfgang Sauber/WM; **203,** Arik Ninio; **204,** myrrh: Gaius Cornelius/WM; mandrake root: Robert Svensson/msitua.net; banquet: Used with permission from *Illustrated Dictionary of Bible Life and Times,* copyright © 1997 The Reader's Digest Association, Inc., Pleasantville, New York, www.rd.com. Illustration by H. Tom Hall; **205,** bride and groom: Bill Aron; seal and clay: The Oriental Institute of The University of Chicago.

Isaiah
206, Jesus: EliasAlucard/WM/artist: Domenico Fetti; Isaiah: Duccio di Buoninsegna; Romulus and Remus: Marie-Lan Nguyen/WM; **207,** Assyrian archer: Iglonghurst/WM; statue in museum: Shaun Che/WM; **208,** RC/GSI/rendered by SMM; **209,** Alex Bakharev/WM/artist: Mikhail Vrubel; **210,** the Annunciation: Mikhail Nesterov; Mary and baby Jesus: The Yorck Project/WM/artist: Antonio da Correggio; **211,** deported Jews: Erich Lessing/AR; map: NASA/rendered by SMM; **212,** Assyrian entrance: Shaun Che/WM; map: TP/rendered by SMM; **213,** Arabia: Nasib Bitar/WM; Damascus: Seier/FL; Edom: Marcelo Ruiz/FL; Egypt: Karl Richard Lepsius/WM; Ethiopia: Marie-Lan Nguyen/WM; Moab: BMM; Philistia: Rémih/WM; Tyre: BB; **214,** Duby Tal/Albatross; **215,** Lachish note: TBM; Assyrians: David Castor/WM; **216,** Ivan Glazunov; **217,** despised: Matthias Stom; led to slaughter: Vicky Baze/FL; silent: WM/artist: Feodor Bruni; sinless: Jan Mehlich/WM/artist: Jacek Malczewski; whipped: Thebrid/WM/artist: William Adolphe Bouguereau; sin offering: José Manuel/WM/artist: Diego Velázquez; criminal: BB; rich burial: Marina Vostrikova; sin offering: Shakko/WM/artist: Francisco de Zurbarán.

Jeremiah
218, Jerusalem falls: Henry J. Soulen/National Geographic; Assyrians dismantling walls: Zereshk/WM; scribe: BMM; **219,** exiles: Erich Lessing/AR; Persian soldiers: BMM; **220,** bar mitzvah: Philippe Lissac/Godong/Corbis; Jonah: WM/Michelangelo; **221,** temple priestess: Jan Mehlich/WM/artist: Jacek Malczewski; idol: Erich Lessing/AR; **222,** Jeremiah in cistern: GoodSalt; **223,** cistern: Mark Reese/FL; shepherds: George Steinmetz/Corbis; **224,** clay jar: Guillaume Blanchard/WM; man wearing yoke: Jeff Preston/GS; harvesting: Danel W. Bachman; **225,** seal: ZR; Nebuchadnezzar: Alexander Jubran/DA; **226,** Henry J. Soulen/National Geographic; **227,** map: NASA/Rendered by SMM; map art of horses and riders: Victor Vasnetsov; map art of chariot: Noel Taylor.

Lamentations
228, starving mother and children: Yorck Project/WM/artist: Egon Schiele; Assyrians dismantling walls: Zereshk/WM; Babylonian soldiers: Poppy/WM; **229,** Persian soldiers: BMM; **230,** pile of skulls: Vasily Vereshchagin; Jerusalem: Mario Lapid/FL; Ur: Michael Lubinski/FL; Nippur: PacziWiraku/FL; **231,** PD.

Ezekiel
232, dry bones relief: Andreas Praefcke/WM; archers: ChrisO/WM; Ezekiel and angel: Mattes/WM/artist: Michelangelo; **233,** THP © Blas Gallego; **234,** four-faced angel: Jonathan Edward Guthmann/DA; Mark with eagle: Thorskegga Thorn/FL; **235,** map: TP/rendered by SMM; map art of ziggurat: BMM; **236,** Ezekiel and angel: Mattes/WM/artist: Michelangelo; baking bread: Matteo Cavallino/FL; **237,** cloud: Anuhealani444/deviantart; Yom Kippur crowd: Gilad Benari/FL; **238,** Bill Aron; **239,** Tyre: BB; map: NASA/rendered by SMM; map art of Egyptian soldiers: Hans Ollermann/FL; map art of horseman: Gustave Boulanger; **240,** dry bones relief: Andreas Praefcke/WM; Tel Aviv: Niv Singer/FL; **241,** Dead Sea: Vadim Levinzon; Solomon planning temple: Andreas Praefcke/WM/artist: Andreas Brugger.

Daniel
242, Daniel in lion's den: Darrel Tank/GS; ship: Phoenicia.org.uk; deportation of Jews: Art Resource; **243,** Xerxes: WM; **244,** kosher restaurant: Bill Aron; grapes: USDA/Peggy Greb; **245,** dream: Nesster/FL; **246,** golden idol: The Oriental Institute Museum, University of Chicago; lion mosaic: FL; Median helmet: Stewart Miller/http://flickr.com/photos/z0Op/; Persian soldier: BMM; Greek helmet: Matthias Kabel/WM; Roman soldier: Laith Majali/DA; **247,** kiln: ZaaArt Studios/FL; fiery furnace: THP © Joan Pelaez; **248,** powerful Nebuchadnezzar portrait: Alexander Jubran/DA; crazy Nebuchadnezzar: William Blake; sequoia: Flavio Spugna/FL; **249,** map: TP/rendered by SMM; map art of soldier: BMM; handwriting on wall: THP © Joan Pelaez; **250,** Stephen Gjertson; **251,** roaring lion, Mats Carnmarker/FL; lion mosaic: BMM; bear: IS; Persian soldier: BMM; leopard: Edgar Thissen/FL; Greek helmet: Matthias Kabel/WM; beast: Mewot/FL; Roman soldier: Laith Majali; **252,** map: TP/rendered by SMM; map art of Alexander: Janek/FL; elephant: Tigg-stock/DA.

Hosea
254, woman: KR; Jonah: Lars Justinen/GS; eclipse: NASA; **255,** map: TP/rendered by SMM; Hosea: PD; Rome's forum: Maurice/FL; **256,** map: RC/GSI/rendered by SMM; woman and baby: Richard Messenger; **257,** woman: KR; slave sale: Olpl/WM/artist: Jean-Leon Gerome.

Joel
258, locust: Scott Thompson/FL; boxing: Tatoute/WM; **259,** Parthenon: Lluís Sala/FL; Jerusalem ruins: Lars Justinen/GS; **260,** Luis Garcia/WM; **261,** map: TP/rendered by SMM; locust egg pod: G. Eric and Edith Matson Photograph Collection/LC; locust: Asadbabil/FL.

Amos
262, woman: Amer S Raja, Pakistan–www.aiaphotography.co.uk; prophet: Lars Justinen/GS; **263,** coin: PHGCOM/WM; Jerusalem battle: THP © Blas Gallego; athletic woman: Marie-Lan Nguyen/WM; **264,** map: NASA/rendered by SMM; map art of cow: Kim Hansen/WM; map art of sheep: Bärbel Schwarzer/WM; map art of tree: IS; figs: IS; Martin Luther King, Jr.: S. G. Vietnam/Fresno Discovery Museum; **265,** plumbline: IS; cattle: PhotoStock-Israel.com; nose hook: Photo Credit : Erich Lessing/AR.

Obadiah
266, refugees: Art Resource; camel caravan: LC; globe: WM; **267,** SMM.

Jonah
268, Jonah stained glass: Brother Lawrence Lew/FL; prophet portrait: Jeff Preston/GS; Ulysses resisting the sirens: Bibi Saint-Pol/WM/artist: John William Waterhouse; **269,** exiled Jew relief: Ian Anthony Smith: opium_den/FL; market scene: Filippo Bartolini; **270,** TBM; **271,** Jonah: Lars Justinen/Good Salt; knucklebone: ancientouch.com; **272,** eclipse: NASA; map: TP/rendered by SMM; map art of whale: SMM; map art of Assyrian genie: WM; **273,** aerial photo of Nineveh ruins: United States Geological Society/rendered by SMM; Jonah and vine: Jeff Preston/GS.

Micah
274, Nativity scene: Erich Lessing/AR; Micah portrait: Duccio di Buoninsegna; exiled Jews: Ian Anthony Smith: opium_den/FL; **275,** cuneiform tablet: Ian Anthony Smith: opium_den/FL; Confucius: Helanhuaren/WM; **276,** SMM/Berlin Holocaust Museum; **277,** Dome of the Rock: SMM; Bethlehem: G. Eric and Edith Matson Photograph Collection/LC.

Nahum
278, soldier: KR; Jonah: Lars Justinen/Good Salt; prism: David Castor/WM; **279,** ruins near Thebes: David Roberts/LC; Nineveh: TF; **280,** TF; **281,** map: TP/rendered by SMM; map art of statue: WM.

Habakkuk
282, warriors: Victor Vasnetsov; Habakkuk: Duccio di Buoninsegna; **283,** soldiers: Capillon/WM; Pythagoras: Deborah Lynn Guber/artist: Raphael; **284,** warriors: Victor Vasnetsov; Luther statue: Robert Wirrmann/FL; idols: The Oriental Institute Museum/University of Chicago; **285,** Hans Reinhard/Corbis.

Zephaniah
286, nuclear blast: Pierre J./FL; Zephaniah: LC; **287,** volcanic eruption: Taro Taylor/WM; Ishtar gate: BB; **288,** TP/rendered by SMM; **289,** tower of Babel: Ziv Qual/DA, tank: Bukvoed/WM.

Haggai
290, Israeli farmland: Duby Tal/Albatross; Darius: Dynamosquito/FL; **291,** Jewish temple: BB; plow: Roger Griffith/WM; **292,** temple: BB; map inset: NASA/rendered by SMM.

Zechariah
294, Triumphal Entry: BAL; Jerusalem ruins: Lars Justinen/GS; Darius: Dynamosquito/FL; **295,** Zechariah: Jeff Preston/WM; cockfighting: Nasim Fekrat; **296,** Corbis; **297,** both images: Vicky Baze/FL; **298,** money: Melissa Goodman/FL; Palestinians: Tommy Tonkins/FL/Mark Pearson; **299,** baptism: Reuters/Corbis; Jesus riding donkey: Eugene/WM/artist: Duccio di Buoninsegna.

Malachi
300, sheep: Meirion Matthias; Xerxes: Wendy B. Harns; **301,** Malachi: Duccio di Buoninsegna; Socrates and Plato: Justin Norris/FL; **302,** James Neeley/FL; **303,** Transfiguration: WM/artist: Raphael; Assyrian art: The Metropolitan Museum of Art/AR; cup: ©Joshua Bousel.

New Testament Intro
304, montage: Royalty Free Christian Art; sand: Getty; **305,** prophet: IS; coin: Portable Antiquities Scheme/FL; wise men: Nina-no/WM.

Matthew
306, resurrected Jesus: Tate, London/AR/artist: Edward Burne-Jones; baby Jesus: The Yorck Project/WM/artist: Georges de La Tour; Pontius Pilate: Csanády/WM/artist: Munkácsi Mihály; **307,** José Manuel/WM/artist: Diego Velázquez; **309,** Horace Vernet; **310,** angel with Joseph: The Yorck Project/WM/artist: Georges de La Tour; bride with dowry: American Colony/LC; **311,** wise men: Bashar Amin Sheglila; map: TP/rendered by SMM; map art of nativity: WM; map art of wise men: Nina-no/WM; **312,** photo illustration: sky by Hans-Peter Scholz/WM, Jerusalem by Hynek Moravec/WM; **313,** John baptizing Jesus: Alex Bakharev/WM/artist: Grigory Gagarin; John the Baptist: El Greco; **314,** tour guide: Ben Shiff/FL; temptation of Jesus: Ivan Nikolayevich Kramskoi; **315,** map: RC/GSI/rendered by SMM; map art of Jesus: © Patrick Devonas; Jesus and disciples: Pavel Popov; **316,** II/Hanan Isachar; **317,** both images: Berthold Werner/WM; **318,** Lars Justinen/GS; **319,** fish: Jón Helgi Jónsson/WM; jellyfish: Mike Johnston/WM; wrestlers: Mike Johnston/WM; **320,** daughter of Jairus: Lars Justinen/GS; burial: LC; **321,** faces: Miklós Szabó, Miki3d/deviantart.com; Jew with scroll: G. Eric and Edith Matson Photograph Collection/LC; **322,** Lars Justinen/GS; **324,** girl with fish: Deborah Duke; map: RC/GSI/rendered by SMM; map art of mosaic: SMM; **325,** coin: Portable Antiquities Scheme/FL; Sikh pilgrim: Paul Rudd/WM; **326,** Caesarea Philippi: Berthold Werner/WM; map: RC/GSI/rendered by SMM; map art of Pan: Alex Bakharev/WM/artist: Mikhail Vrubel; **327,** map: RC/GSI/rendered by SMM; map art of Jesus: WM/artist: Raphael; Mount Tabor: Carol/FL; **328,** BB; **329,** Ryan Whisner; **330,** girl with palm: Gil Cohen Magen/Reuters/Corbis; Mount of Olives: LC; **331,** Jewish boy: Yoram Biberman; Pharisee and tax collector: Johannes Böckh/WM; **332,** ZR; **333,** WM/artist: Giacomo Raffaelli; **334,** Lawrence Lew/FL; **335,** olive grove: II/Itsik Marom; Jesus and angel: Carl Heinrich Bloch; olive press: Used by permission from *Illustrated Dictionary of Bible Life and Times,* copyright 1997, The Reader's Digest Association, Inc., Pleasantville, New York, www.rd.com. Illustration by Christopher Magadini; **336,** Marina Vostrikova; **337,** Charles Gordon: PD; garden tomb: SMM; Church of the Holy Sepulchre: Mike Murrill; Hadrian: Glenn Gulley/FL; **338,** Jeff Preston/GS; **339,** women at tomb: A. M. McRae Thomson/FL/artist: Sir Edward Burne Jones; cave tomb: Brian Morley.

Mark
340, Jesus healing man with crippled hand: Patrick Devonas; Jesus with crown of thorns: Domenico Fetti; Pontius Pilate: Jan Mehlich/WM/artist: Jacek Malczewski; **341,** Roman soldier: Dave Nash/FL; **342,** El Greco; **343,** Jesus calling disciples: Museums Sheffield/BAL; ruins of Capernaum: Duby Tal/Albatross; **344,** WM; **345,** mustard seed: Anita Cadonau-Huseby; mustard field: Amit Gupta/Reuters/Corbis; **346,** man with bottle: Fortean/Topham/

The Image Works; map: NASA/rendered by SMM; **347,** head of John the Baptist: Oscar Gustav Rejlander; map: RC/GSI/rendered by SMM; map art of Herod: PD; John preaching: Lars Justinin/GS; **348,** Jesus walking on water: Peter Ivan Aivazovskiy; map: NASA/rendered by SMM; water clock: Marsyas/WM; **349,** map: NASA/rendered by SMM; map art of Jesus: Nikolai Pavlovich Shakhovskoy; woman: Martin Asser/FL; **350,** Caesarea Philippi: II/Duby Tal/Albatross; Jesus in armor: Digital illustration by SMM/artists: Frederic Edwin Church, Victor Matorin, Jacek Malczewski; **351,** Stuart Freedman/Corbis; **352,** Bill Aron; **353,** Lars Justinen/GS; **354,** widow with coins: James C. Christensen, christcenteredmall.com; coin: Eric S. Weiss; ram's horn: Travis Kraft, model; **355,** woman anointing Jesus: James Tissot; Bethany: LC; **356,** shekels: ZR; Judas kissing Jesus: Đorđe MarkoviĐ/DA; **357,** Codex Sinaiticus: British Library; Mary Magdalene and Jesus: Lalupa/WM/artist: Gian Lorenzo Bernini.

Luke
358, nativity: Gerard van Honthorst; baby Jesus: The Yorck Project/WM/artist: Georges de La Tour; Herod's temple: BB; Herod the Great: PD; **359,** Pontius Pilate: Jan Mehlich/WM/artist: Jacek Malczewski; Jesus: Alexander Andrejewitsch Iwanow; **360,** Arthur Hughes; **361,** nativity: Erich Lessing/AR; nun praying: Abed Al Hashlamoun/epa/Corbis; **362,** Darrel Tank/GS; **363,** temple: akg-images/Peter Connolly; map: RC/GSI/rendered by SMM; map art of travelers: Rembrandt; **364,** scroll: Bill Aron; stones: Meir Ben Ari; **365,** BB; **366,** centurion: David Bracher; Capernaum ruins: II; **367,** Jesus in boat: Estormiz/WM/artist: Eero Järnefelt; map: NASA/rendered by SMM; **368,** Lars Justinen/GS; **369,** SMM; **370,** Lars Justinen/GS; **371,** WM; **372,** Charles Shawr; **373,** Simon Roberts/Getty; **374,** sycamore: Avishai Teicher/WM; Roman census: Marie-Lan Nguyen/WM; **375,** KR; **376,** Jesus at meal: Caravaggio; map: RC/GSI/rendered by SMM; **377,** Lars Justinen/GS.

John
378, Jesus on cross: Photos.com; baby Jesus: Royalty Free Christian Art; John the Baptist and Herod Antipas: Vassil/WM/artist: Pieter Fransz de Grebber; **379,** baptism of Jesus: El Greco; Jesus with crown of thorns: IS; **380,** Ben Heine © benheine.com; **381,** sacrifice: Lars Justinen/GS; holy family: Royalty Free Christian Art; **382,** Vladimir Makovsky; **383,** archaeologists: Justin Garland/FL; map: RC/GSI/rendered by SMM; **384,** burial of Jesus: Marina Vostrikova; Jesus and Nicodemus: Jeff Preston/GS; **385,** map: RC/GSI/rendered by SMM; map art of woman: Darrel Tank/GS; **386,** Passover bread: Musicpb/WM; woman with lamp: Erik Stenbakken/GS; **387,** Jeff Preston/GS; **388,** RC/GSI/rendered by SMM; Church of St. Lazarus: II/Garo Nalbandian; **389,** P Deliss/Godong/Corbis; **390,** Trinity: PD; Ambrose: Réunion des Musées Nationaux/AR; **391,** Valery Titievsky; **392,** Jesus: Anthony Cerminaro; rooster: Aske Holst/FL; **393,** crucifixion: Marcus Mashburn/GS; nail in heel bone: ZR; **394,** BB; **395,** Bildarchiv Preussischer Kulturbesitz/AR/artist: Caravaggio.

Acts
396, Pentecost stained glass: Dave Webster; Rome ruins: Maurice/FL; **397,** both images: Lars Justinen/GS; **398,** Salvador Dali; **399,** Dave Webster; **400,** colonnade: Reinante El Pintor de Fuego/FL; temple: akg-images/Peter Connolly; **401,** Lars Justinen/GS; **402,** Ondra Havalah/FL; **403,** stoning of Stephen: BAL; author in auto: SMM; **404,** map: RC/GSI/rendered by SMM; Gamaliel: Lars Justinen/GS; escape from Damascus: Jeff Preston/GS; Paul and Peter: El Greco; Paul in chains: Lars Justinen/GS; **405,** Chaim Jaskoll/FL; **406,** women in Antioch: Luca Gargano; map: RC/GSI/rendered by SMM; **407,** Ricardo Frantz/WM; map: TP/rendered by SMM; **408,** Jerusalem council: Lars Justinen/GS; sacrifice: BMM; **409,** TP/rendered by SMM; **410,** BB; **411,** TP/rendered by SMM; **412,** Dave Nash/FL; **413,** map: TP/rendered by SMM; map art of ship: Eric Gaba/WM.

Romans
414, close-up of man: Trey Ratcliff/FL; man on shore: Alex Bakharev/WM/artist: Vasily Polenov; soap: Malene Thyssen/WM; **415,** Paul: Lars Justinen/GS; Nero: Johan Wilbrink; **416,** laminin model: Faceout Studios; map: TP/rendered by SMM; map of soldier: Luc Viatour/WM; **417,** BMM; **418,** Csanády/WM/artist: József Molnár; **419,** Augustine: Lawrence Lew/FL; cocaine user: Maria Lawton/FL; **420,** Lars Justinen/GS; **421,** Jay P. Morgan/Getty.

Corinthians
422, faces: BAL; tent: Martin Allen; Claudius: Luis García/WM; **423,** writing letter: Lars Justinen/GS; mushroom: Will Bryson/FL; Rome ruins: Maurice/FL; **426,** map: TP/rendered by SMM; map art of temple ruins: Tim Barton; four people: Lars Justinen/GS; **425,** Cicero: William Storage/FL; man and woman: John Collier; **426,** Franklin McMahon/Corbis; **427,** digital artist: Angela Marie Quakernack; photographer: Jesus Arregi; texture artist: Angela Wolf; **428,** John Pollini; **429,** Yorck Project/WM/artist: Antonello de Messina; **430,** Jerry Berndt/Getty; **431,** photo illustration: Sandra Hopp, artistical-insanity.com/woman photo: Tania and Diana Carvalho, stock-lunar.deviantart.com/sky photo: gromitsend.

deviantart.com/sea photo: stock.xchng/brush 1: miss69-stock.deviantart.com/brush 2: scully7491.deviantart.com/; **432,** tent: Martin Allen; clay jar: Israel Antiquities Authority; **433,** Robert Harding Picture Library/SuperStock; **434,** Matt Wilson/FL; **435,** snake: Sergio Battaglia; swamp: Thomas, Dianne Jones/FL.

Galatians
436, eyes of Paul: Juan E. de Francisco/FL; artist: El Greco; Paul portrait: Diego Valazquez; Jewish man with scroll: G. Eric and Edith Matson Photograph Collection/LC; **437,** Paul statue: WM; Nero: Johan Wilbrink; **438,** Erich Lessing/AR; **439,** dancers: Lalupa/WM; circumcision tools: Marco Repola.

Ephesians
440, soldier: Luc Viatour/WM; map: TP/rendered by SMM; **441,** Poppaea Sabina: Cristoph Houbrechts; execution of Peter: Caravaggio; **442,** Robert Huberman; map: TP/rendered by SMM; map art of Ephesus ruins: Nejdet Düzen/FL; Simeon and Anna with baby Jesus: Darrel Tank/GS; **443,** Zeynep Erdim/FL; **445,** slave market: Olpl/WM/artist: Jean-Leon Gerome; women: BMM; **446,** Seneca: Massimo Finizio/WM; family: BMM/artist: Charles Sprague Pearce; **447,** photo illustration by SMM/model photo: Luther Thomas,lrtphoto.50webs.com/fire photo: lucy-eth-stock. deviantart.com.

Philippians
448, vase: Tim Paul; Caligula: Ed Uthman/WM; **449,** Nero: Johan Wilbrink; Seneca: Massimo Finizio/WM; man with sword: Steven Miscandlon/FL; **450,** Lars Justinen/GS; **451,** map: TP/rendered by SMM; map art of Philippi ruins: Robert Elzey; martyrs in arena: Jean-Leon Gerome; **452,** Erik Stenbakken/GS; **453,** vase: Tim Paul; laurel wreath: WM/artist: Jules Joseph Lefebvre; runner: Damir Sagolj/Reuters/Corbis.

Colossians
454, angel: Carlo Natale, flickr.com/photos/cienne/artist: Giulio Monteverde; Colosse mound: Gbs055/FL; **455,/**FL; man with sword: Steven Miscandlon/FL; scroll fragment: Israel Antiquities Authority; **456,** map: RC/GSI/rendered by SMM; map inset of globe: WorldSat; Jesus statue: Olivier Petit, flickr.com/photos/iko; **457,** star trails: Andrew Stawarz; amulet: Kelsey Museum of Archaeology, University of Michigan; **458,** Adrian Tecson; **459,** Keytone16/WM.

Thessalonians
460, people looking up: is Faraz Shanyar/DA; Caligula: Ed Uthman/WM; **461,** Theudas: Marshall Astor/FL; Paul writing: Lars Justinen/GS; Roman soldiers: Dave Nash/FL; **462,** street musicians: Zeynep Arkök/FL; Thessaloniki church: John Sie Yuen Lee; **463,** Nastassia A. Davis/FL; **464,** Second Coming: Lars Justinen/GS; Titus: EllenM1/FL; **465,** Lars Justinen/GS.

Timothy
466, both images: Lars Justinen/GS; **467,** Paul arrested: Darrel Tank/GS; man with sword: Steven Miscandlon/FL; **468,** Dimitri Korobov/FL; **469,** Magdalena Dadela/mdadela. com; **470,** BMM; **471,** woman with head covering: Zinaida Serebriakova; mother and baby: Tom Adriaenssen/WM; **472,** Turkish women: Charles Roffey/FL; girl: Dietmar/FL; **474,** wine amphora: ZR; mother and daughter: Susan Myrland/FL; **475,** Lawrence Lew/FL; **476,** Chris Bertram/FL; **477,** man with sword: Steven Miscandlon/FL, map: TP/rendered by SMM; map art of ship: Eric Gaba/WM; map art of man and horse: LC.

Titus
478, bearded man: National Geographic; Paul statue: Alberto Fernandez Fernandez/WM; **479,** Paul arrested: Darrel Tank/GS; letter writing: Lars Justinen/GS; **480,** woman of Crete: Magda Indigo; Minoan art: Oboulko/FL; **481,** © Joel W. Rogers/Corbis.

Philemon
482, man looking up: David Martin Anton; ship: Eric Gaba/WM; letter writing: Lars Justinen/GS; **483,** soldiers: Dave Nash/FL; Pompeii mosaic: Arianna Gallo/FL; **484,** Philippe Guillaume/FL; **485,** statue: Penny Green; map: TP/rendered by SMM; map art of Onesimus: William Bouguereau.

Hebrews
486, Yemeni Jew: LC; Paul in jail: Erik Stenbakken/Goodsalt; Christians in arena: Pacific Press Publishing/GS; **487,** Francesco Hayez; **488,** seal and clay: Rama/WM; angel: digital artist: www.barncrouchphotography.com; building photographer: Claus Rebler; angel photographer: Ruby L, xAngelx-stock, deviantart; **489,** DMY/WM; **490,** map: NASA/rendered by SMM; map art of crowd: Cesare Biseo; map art of palm tree: SMM; **491,** KR; **492,** Lars Justinen/GS; **493,** KR.

James
494, blood donor: IS; Ascension: Salvador Dali; **495,** stoning of James: Jeff Preston/GS; Roman soldiers: Dave Nash/FL; **496,** funeral portrait: Jenni Scott/FL; wealthy household:

Stepan Bakalovich/WM; **497,** Amy Sussman/Corbis; **498,** blood donor: IS: Martin Luther: PD; **499,** Lars Justinen/GS; **500,** photo by Rebecca Parker, digital enhancement by SMM; **501,** John Calvin: LC; Rome church: Trey Ratcliff.

Peter
502, Jesus fallen with cross: KR; Jesus calling disciples: Museums Sheffield/BAL; Caligula: Ed Uthman/WM; **503,** Peter writing: Lars Justinen/GS; Peter crucified: Caravaggio; **504,** molten gold: Gaila Hiebert-Martin; Jesus in hell: WM; **505,** akg-images/Peter Connolly; **506,** Richard T. Nowitz/Corbis; **507,** Paolopenna/FL; **508,** Jamal Nasrallah/epa/Corbis; **509,** Peter crucified: FL/artist: Guido Reni; grandmother and child: Collin Key/www.flickr.com/photos/collin_key; **510,** man with money bag: Lars Justinen/GS; fallen angel: PD; **511,** Second Coming: Rolf Jansson/GS; sun and earth: NASA.

1, 2, 3 John
512, bust of Roman man: William Storage/FL; Roman solider: Paolopenna/FL; **513,** Domitian: photographed at The Musée du Louvre in Paris, France by Mary Harrsch; John writing: Frank Gampel/GS; **514,** man from Roman times: William Storage/FL; Hercules: Ivan Petrovich Koehler; **516,** Luca Signorelli; **517,** Thomas Gainsborough; **518,** Lars Justinen/GS; **519,** Erich Lessing/AR.

Jude
520, man kissing woman's hand: BAL; Ascension: Salvador Dali; map: TP/rendered by SMM; **521,** man writing: Frank Gampel/GS; stoning of James: Jeff Preston/GS.

Revelation
522, vision of heaven: BAL; death of Nero: J. Svjagintsev/artist: Vasily Smirnov; **523,** Domitian: Mary Harrsch/FL; John's vision: Lars Justinen/GS; **524,** nuclear explosion: Pierre J./FL; Ephesus ruins: Veyis Polat/FL; Smyrna fisherman: Veyis Polat/FL; Pergamum ruins: Özgür MülazımoĐlu, Turkey; **525,** Thyatira ruins: Metin Canbalaban/WM; Sardis gymnasium: Burcu Akin/FL; Philadelphia ruins: Rsproje Hasan Yilmaz; Laodicea hot springs: Joan Bellver; **526,** seals on letter: ZR; riders on white, red, and black horses: Viktor Mikhailovich Vasnetsov; **527,** Holocaust actress: Kenny Mathieson/FL; rider on pale horse: Viktor Mikhailovich Vasnetsov; martyrs in coliseum: Jean-Leon Gerome; earthquake damage: United Nations Development Programme; angel with red sky: Grassi Stefano, GrassiStefano.com; **528,** Vicenç Feliú, Sabreur76/FL.com; **529,** photo illustration: Rick Blackwell, Rickbw1.deviantart. com/photo of model: Rineil Mandre, ahrum-stock.deviantart. com/wings: Alana Seibert, yana-stock.deviantart.com; **530,** Mary and baby Jesus: MM; dragon: Nick Deligaris, deligaris. com; ascension of Jesus: Ricardo André Frantz/WM; woman in desert: Elihu Vedder; martyr with arrows: Lawrence Lew/FL; Satan's fall: Sandara/DA; **531,** Nero coin: Natalia Bauer/TBM; Revelation fragment: Ian W. Carter/WM; **532,** model of Rome: André Caron; inset of Domitian: Mary Harrsch/FL; **534,** skin sores: Walter Reed Army Institute of Research; bloody sea: Josh Sommers/FL; bloody river: Jerry Hazard; **535,** nuclear explosion: photo illustration by Tobias Roetsch, www.gt-graphics.de; burning city: Petteri Sulonen/WM; moon and clouds: Wing-Chi Poon/WM; dry riverbed: Mark A. Wilson; earthquake damage: United Nations Development Programme; **536,** Armageddon map: TP/rendered by SMM; Jezreel Valley map inset: RC/GSI/rendered by SMM; Megiddo ruins photo inset: Duby Tal/Albatross; **537,** Augustus: Giovanni Dall'Orto/WM; Tiberius: Shakko/WM; Caligula: William Storage/FL; Claudius: Luis García/WM; Nero: Yair Haklai/WM; Vespasian: Shakko/WM; Titus: William Storage/FL; Domitian: Mary Harrsch/FL; **538,** Jesus on white horse: Lars Justinen/GS; Jesus crucified: Escarlati/WM/artist: Diego Velázquez; rider on pale horse: Viktor Mikhailovich Vasnetsov; Jesus ascending: Ricardo André Frantz/WM; lion and lamb: © DLILLC/Corbis; man representing God: Igor Kamenev; **539,** man burning: Shane Gorski/FL; lake of fire: photo illustration: SMM/photo of man: Ari and Rachel Ailin, AilinStock/DA /background: LadyDeath666/DA; **540,** colinjcampbell.co.uk; **541,** Greek letters: Grifomaniacs/WM; jasper: Saperaud/WM; sapphire: Daniel Torres, Jr./WM; agate: Hannes Grobe/WM; emerald: Géry Parent/WM; onyx: Bence FördĐs/FL; carnelian: Marie-Lan Nguyen/WM; chrysolite: Géry Parent/WM; beryl: Orbital Joe Kienle/FL; topaz: Orbital Joe Kienle/FL; chrysoprase: WM; jacinth: Vienna gems/FL; amethyst: Orbital Joe Kienle/FL.

Barbour Publishing would like to thank these art suppliers and copyright owners for permission to reproduce their images. We have attempted to obtain permission to publish every image. If we have inadvertently overlooked any, we would be happy to hear from the copyright owners.